THE OXFORD HANDBOOK OF

SWEDISH POLITICS

THE OXFORD HANDBOOK OF

SWEDISH

POLITICS

Edited by

JON PIERRE

OXFORD

UNIVERSITY PRESS

OXFORD
UNIVERSITY PRESS

Great Clarendon Street, Oxford, OX2 6DP,
United Kingdom

Oxford University Press is a department of the University of Oxford.
It furthers the University's objective of excellence in research, scholarship,
and education by publishing worldwide. Oxford is a registered trade mark of
Oxford University Press in the UK and in certain other countries

Published in the United States of America by Oxford University Press
198 Madison Avenue, New York, NY 10016, United States of America

British Library Cataloguing in Publication Data
Data available

Library of Congress Control Number: 2015958065

ISBN 978–0–19–966567–9

Printed and bound in Great Britain by
Clays Ltd, St Ives plc

Acknowledgments

Coordinating academics is often said to be like herding cats. As a student of public administration, my first question as I began organizing this project was "how would Weber have done this?" I was lucky enough to persuade ten colleagues to be editors of the ten sections. Their commitment to the project has been a definite condition for its success. I simply could not have done it without them.

A project of the magnitude of a Handbook involves a very large number of people, each of whom is integral to its success. The list of contributors includes fifty individuals. Although they are all busy people, none declined the invitation to join the project. I was impressed by the collegiality and professionalism with which the contributors and Section Editors went about preparing their contributions, with Section workshops over weekends or other meetings to get everything right.

At Oxford University Press, Dominic Byatt's contagious enthusiasm and support have been a major source of inspiration. Olivia Wells has sorted out numerous tricky issues related to texts, tables, and figures; Saipriya Kannan has skillfully managed the project; and Jess Smith has done an excellent job copyediting the entire text. My sincere thanks to you all.

Gothenburg, June 2015
Jon Pierre

Contents

SECTION 3   THE PARTY SYSTEM
SECTION EDITORS: HANNA BÄCK AND GISSUR Ó. ERLINGSSON

SECTION 4   ELECTORAL BEHAVIOR
SECTION EDITORS: SÖREN HOLMBERG AND HENRIK OSCARSSON

SECTION 5 PUBLIC ADMINISTRATION
SECTION EDITOR: GÖRAN SUNDSTRÖM

SECTION 6 SUBNATIONAL GOVERNMENT
SECTION EDITOR: ANDERS LIDSTRÖM

SECTION 7 SWEDEN'S INTERNATIONAL RELATIONS
Section Editor: Ole Elgström

SECTION 8 SWEDEN AND THE EU
Section Editor: Ulrika Mörth

SECTION 9 THE POLITICAL ECONOMY OF SWEDISH GOVERNANCE
SECTION EDITOR: JOHANNES LINDVALL

SECTION 10 POLICY-MAKING IN SWEDEN
SECTION EDITOR: CARL DAHLSTRÖM

LIST OF FIGURES

List of Tables

LIST OF CONTRIBUTORS

Lisbeth Aggestam is Associate Professor of Political Science at Gothenburg University.

Shirin Ahlbäck Öberg is Associate Professor of Political Science at Uppsala University.

Jenny Andersson is a Senior CNRS Research Fellow at Centre d'études européennes, Sciences Po, Paris.

Nicholas Aylott is Associate Professor of Political Science at the School of Social Sciences at Södertörn University.

Hanna Bäck is Professor of Political Science at Lund University.

Rikard Bengtsson is Associate Professor of Political Science at Lund University.

Annika Bergman Rosamond is Assistant Professor of Political Science at Lund University.

Torbjörn Bergman is Professor of Political Science at Umeå University.

Christina Bergqvist is Professor of Political Science at Uppsala University.

Ulf Bjereld is Professor of Political Science at Gothenburg University.

Douglas Brommesson is Associate Professor of Political Science at Lund University.

Lars Calmfors is Professor of International Economics at the Institute for International Economic Studies, Stockholm University.

Carl Dahlström is Professor of Political Science at Gothenburg University.

Peter Ehn holds a PhD in Political Science and is an investigator at the Swedish Agency for Public Management.

Ole Elgström is Professor of Political Science at Lund University.

Gissur Ó. Erlingsson is Associate Professor of Political Science at the Center for Municipal Studies, Linköping University.

Peter Esaiasson is Professor of Political Science at Gothenburg University.

David Feltenius is Associate Professor of Political Science at Umeå University.

Patrik Hall is Associate Professor of Political Science at Malmö University.

Jörgen Hermansson is Professor of Political Science at Uppsala University.

Sören Holmberg is Professor of Political Science at Gothenburg University.

Adrian Hyde-Price is Professor of Political Science at Gothenburg University.

Bengt Jacobsson is Professor of Management and Organization Theory at Södertörn University.

Ann-Kristin Kölln is a postdoctoral researcher and COFAS Marie Curie Fellow at the Department of Political Science, Gothenburg University.

Leif Lewin is Skytteansk Professor Emeritus in Rhetoric and Political Science, Uppsala University.

Anders Lidström is Professor of Political Science at Umeå University.

Anders Lindbom is Professor of Political Science at Uppsala University.

Johannes Lindvall is Professor of Political Science at Lund University.

Ingvar Mattson holds a PhD in Political Science and is the Director General of the Swedish Agency for Public Management.

Stig Montin is Professor of Public Administration, School of Public Administration, Gothenburg University.

Tommy Möller is Professor of Political Science at Stockholm University.

Ulrika Möller is Assistant Professor of Political Science at Gothenburg University.

Ulrika Mörth is Professor of Political Science at Stockholm University.

Lars Niklasson is Deputy Professor of Political Science at Linköping University.

PerOla Öberg is Professor of Political Science at Uppsala University.

Patrik Öhberg is an International Postdoc of the Swedish Research Council at the Department of Political Science, Gothenburg University and a Research Fellow at the Canada Research Chair in Electoral Studies at the Department of Political Science, Université de Montréal.

Richard Öhrvall is a PhD candidate in Political Science at Linköping University and researcher at Statistics Sweden and the Research Institute of Industrial Economics.

Henrik Oscarsson is Professor of Political Science at Gothenburg University.

Maria Oskarson is Associate Professor of Political Science at Gothenburg University.

Thomas Persson is Associate Professor of Political Science at Uppsala University.

Olof Petersson is former Professor of Political Science at Uppsala University.

Jon Pierre is Professor of Political Science, Gothenburg University, and Professor of Public Governance, Melbourne School of Government, University of Melbourne.

Malena Rosén Sundström is Assistant Professor of Political Science at Lund University.

Bo Rothstein holds the August Röhss Chair in Political Science at Gothenburg University where he is head of the Quality of Government Institute.

Jesper Strömbäck is Professor of Journalism and Media and Communication at Mid Sweden University.

Stefan Svallfors is Professor of Sociology, Umeå University and affiliated with the Swedish Institute for Future Studies in Stockholm.

Göran Sundström is Associate Professor of Political Science at Stockholm University and Research Fellow at Stockholm Center for Organizational Research.

Torsten Svensson is Professor of Political Science, Uppsala University.

Lena Wängnerud is Professor of Political Science at Gothenburg University.

Helena Wockelberg is Associate Professor of Political Science at Uppsala University.

INTRODUCTION

The Decline of Swedish Exceptionalism?

JON PIERRE

THIS *Handbook* represents the outcome of an extensive research effort across the Swedish political science community.[1] Early drafts of the chapters have been discussed at numerous meetings and seminars. The assignment struck many of us as daunting. We were trained to select cases for study based on theoretical analysis and to strive for comparison whenever possible. This project urged us to do exactly the opposite; to take case selection as "a given"—a case we are extremely familiar with—and to write chapters that helped make sense of that case to an international audience.

An initial step in that process has been to gauge the images of Sweden that the international audience of the book will have to engage. If asked to identify the features of Swedish politics and society that stand out in an international comparison, most casual observers of Swedish politics over the past several decades would probably mention the dominance of social democracy; full employment achieved in part through a "historical compromise" between capital and labor; a universal and generous welfare state redistributing income and creating an exceptionally high level of equality while maintaining international competitiveness; an active foreign policy defined by non-alliance and international solidarity; exceptional levels of institutional and social trust; and a high level of political mobilization defined primarily by social class. Some would also probably add consensualism, rationality, high taxes, and a big public sector to the list. This portrait has been painted many times, sometimes with admiration and sometimes with a cautionary finger raised (see, for instance, Childs 1936; Elder, Thomas, and Arter 1983; Heclo 1974; Huntford 1971; Rustow 1957). To be sure, it is an intriguing image of a small, industrialized country harnessing resources across its society to provide equal opportunity and well-being for all—and doing so in a consensual, rational, and deliberated fashion.

This is a logical, coherent, and almost a tad romantic storyline of a country building its wealth on industry and dispersing the fruits of its capitalism among all constituencies in society. There is only one problem with this account of Swedish politics: it reflects, at best, times past when Sweden, according to some observers, stood out as an economic, political, and social success story in any international comparison. As Bo Rothstein, one of the contributors to this *Handbook*, recently argued, "the days of Swedish exceptionalism are over" (Rothstein 2014). Social democracy is weakened, inequality is increasing, and taxes and public spending are more or less at par with most comparable countries. Furthermore, Sweden as a member of the European Union has surrendered significant parts of its sovereignty to a transnational institution; electoral behavior is decreasingly explained by social class; and although difficult to measure, consensualism appears less distinctive today compared to a few decades ago.

These profound changes in Swedish politics raise a series of questions with relevance far beyond the Swedish case. To what extent are these developments outcomes of global forces, structural changes in the Swedish economy, or of domestic policy choice (for Sweden, see Pierre 2013; Steinmo 2012)? How can we understand political change and political mobilization against the backdrop of society's evolving into a postindustrial economy? To what degree has the growing international embeddedness, de jure or de facto, rendered policy objectives such as non-alliance and neutrality moot?

This *Handbook* is intended to serve a multitude of purposes. It presents state-of-the-art accounts of all significant aspects of Swedish politics, institutional changes, political decision-making, foreign affairs, and political behavior. The contributors also share an ambition to review the Swedish case in a conceptual and theoretical context and to provide not a case-based but a theoretical account of the trajectory of change we observe in Swedish politics, broadly defined. Not least important, perhaps, the *Handbook* aims to introduce the Swedish political case to an international audience of scholars and practitioners to be considered either in its own right or as a case among others in a comparative perspective.

Finally, these developments raise the question of what remains distinctive about Swedish politics. As the chapters in this *Handbook* will argue, although Sweden stands out less today than it did a few decades ago, the case it presents still attracts large numbers of social scientists who are interested in a variety of issues, such as the transformation of the Swedish welfare state, its changing political economy, or developments in regional or local governments. While it is true that Sweden is less exceptional today compared to a few decades ago, there are still core features of Swedish politics and administration that make it a case well worthy of study. Given the deep institutionalization of welfare state politics, social justice, impartiality and legal security of public administration, and other fundamental societal values, changes in public policy and institutional arrangements must be understood against the backdrop of those normative structures. Obviously, these issues will be discussed in detail throughout the *Handbook*.

The Historical Backdrop

Once the texts in this *Handbook* have dispelled the common myths and stereotypes about Swedish politics and society, pervasive and often politically charged as they may be, the reader will discover that Swedish politics is situated in a society undergoing rapid and profound transformation. A small country (the population in early 2015 is just below ten million; population density is about 22 people per square kilometer) situated in northern Europe, Sweden developed into an industrial economy in the nineteenth century. Along with industrial products, Sweden has long been an exporter of iron ore, paper and pulp, and wood.

Industry soon became the economic backbone of the country. With the coming of industry, urbanization followed, along with the emergence of the labor movement. Democratization in Sweden was, comparatively speaking, late but swift once it got underway, facilitated by liberalism, national unity, and legality. Perhaps most importantly, democratization was propelled by the growth and mobilization of the working and lower middle classes opting for a reformist rather than a revolutionary strategy and the Conservatives' belief that accommodation rather than confrontation was the better strategy as it would facilitate a smooth transition toward democracy. This is not to suggest that democratization, i.e. extending the suffrage, was an altogether consensual process. There was deep, potential conflict between the disenfranchised working class and lower middle class on the one hand and the landowning aristocracy, the senior civil servants, and the economic elite on the other. What is consensual is rather the absence of manifest conflict (Rustow 1971).

With universal male (1909) and female (1921) suffrage in place and a parliamentary model of government de facto established in 1918, Sweden had built a framework for democratic governance. The King was increasingly detached from the exercise of political leadership; he remained head of state and led the process of government formation after general elections but other than that played mainly ceremonial roles. It is noteworthy that all these developments—extending the franchise, introducing parliamentary government, and removing the monarch from all offices of any political consequence—were undertaken without any significant constitutional reform. It was not until 1974 that a new constitution came into force—a reform which in large parts corroborated institutional and political developments that had taken place since the previous reform (see Section 2).

The first half of the twentieth century saw a dramatic expansion of Sweden's industry (see Lewin and Lindvall and also Calmfors, this volume). Given the small domestic market, bigger industries had to explore international markets in order to generate an economy of scale and competitive prices. As what Katzenstein (1985) calls a "price taker" rather than a "price maker," the Swedish economy and its key corporate players had little choice but to implement a wage development that ensured international competitiveness while compensating the domestic labor force for its exposure to overseas competition.

More broadly, the combination of high trade dependency, a growing public sector, and strong unions created a rather peculiar model of political economy where the state, unions, and employers all had a stake in the accommodation of interests while at the same time thinking creatively about how to balance their interests against the more long-term development of the economy (Milner and Wadensjö 2001; see Sections 9 and 10). With growing public sector employment that was set on a different wage trajectory than that of private industry, economic policy and wage bargaining had to accommodate significant differences in wage levels and development between these two segments of the labor force (Krantz 2008).

Politically, the first two decades of the twentieth century were characterized by relatively short-lived and unstable minority governments (see Möller 2011). Following the 1932 general elections, however, the Social Democrats ascended to power—a position they would not surrender until 1976 (except for a three-month Agrarian Party government in the summer of 1936). Although this government was yet another minority government, the Social Democrats successfully embarked on a radical new political agenda to attack soaring unemployment, modernize economic policy, and address the need for social reform. The Social Democrats governed in coalition with the Agrarians from 1936–9 and again in 1951–7 and led a war cabinet from 1939–45. Amazingly, during the party's 44 years in power it controlled a majority of its own in the Riksdag only between 1968 and 1970. The remainder of its long tenure in office was secured either by coalition partners or by some other form of collaborative arrangement with one or two parties. Table I.1 presents the composition of governments in Sweden from 1945 onwards (see also Bäck and Bergman, this volume).

Thus, Sweden from the 1880s or so onwards witnessed two parallel trajectories which reshaped and modernized the country. One was industrialization and urbanization and

Table I.1 Governments in Sweden, 1945–2014

Year	Prime Minister	Party (parties) in government
1945–6	Per Albin Hansson	Social Democrats
1946–51	Tage Erlander	Social Democrats
1951–7	Tage Erlander	Social Democrats and Agrarian Party
1957–69	Tage Erlander	Social Democrats
1969–76	Olof Palme	Social Democrats
1976–8	Thorbjörn Fälldin	Moderates, Center Party, and Liberals
1978–9	Ola Ullsten	Liberal
1979–81	Thorbjörn Fälldin	Moderates, Center Party, and Liberals
1981–2	Thorbjörn Fälldin	Center Party and Liberals
1982–6	Olof Palme	Social Democrats
1986–91	Ingvar Carlsson	Social Democrats
1991–4	Carl Bildt	Moderates, Christian Democrats, Center Party, and Liberals
1994–6	Ingvar Carlsson	Social Democrats
1996–2006	Göran Persson	Social Democrats
2006–14	Fredrik Reinfeldt	Moderates, Center Party, Christian Democrats, and Liberals
2014–	Stefan Löfven	Social Democrats and Greens

the consolidation of a capitalist economy; the other was the consolidation of democratic government and the mobilization of social class. These two processes soon became closely linked. In the politically radical early post-Second World War years, nationalization of industry was part of the labor movement's "postwar program" but never made its way onto the government's agenda. Instead, what appears to have evolved was a "historical compromise" between capital and labor. In this compromise, the Social Democrats recognized private industry's need to make a profit and agreed not to seek to change the structure of ownership in Swedish industry. Industrialists, in return, acknowledged that there would be a transfer of wealth from corporations and high-income earners to a universal welfare state (Magnusson 2000).[2]

The compromise was more a way of accommodating differences than resolving them. The conflict between left and right—that is to say between labor and capital—has been a defining feature of Swedish politics for the past century. It was not until fairly recently that other dimensions, such as the "green vs growth" dimension, have become salient in shaping electoral behavior (see Section 4).

This very brief account of the historical trajectory of democratization and economic modernization brings us into the present history. In addition, many of the chapters in this *Handbook*, with obvious variation, provide brief historical accounts in their respective fields of study.

Swedish Exceptionalism?

We will now briefly further discuss the decline of exceptionalism thesis by way of introducing issues which will be addressed in detail in the subsequent sections in order to see to what extent and in which specific areas Swedish politics still stands out as exceptional. Is there still a distinct Swedish policy "style" (see Richardson 1982)? Does the welfare state, despite cutbacks and marketization, still provide more comprehensive and generous social security than other comparable countries? Are there any distinctive features of the party systems and political involvement?

Welfare State Politics

In the welfare state sector—perhaps the most obvious defining feature of Sweden from an international perspective—it is not difficult to see that there has been a decline in Sweden's exceptionalism. Sweden's performance on several key welfare measures is down; among comparable countries Sweden now ranks twelfth in terms of poverty rate (Eurostat Online Database 2013); tenth in NEET rate (Neither in Education nor Employed; Eurostat Online Database 2013); sixth in Gini coefficient (Eurostat Online Database 2013); ninth in life expectancy (World Bank 2012), and fifth in preventing infant mortality (World Bank 2012). So, overall Sweden's performance in these areas could be regarded as good but not great, or perhaps great but not exceptional. Much obviously depends on which benchmark you use. If we use the Scandinavian countries and the Netherlands as a benchmark, it is clear that Sweden today has a less generous and successful welfare state. That said, Sweden comes top in terms of gender equality in parliament. Also, since the 2014 elections, the Social Democrat and Green coalition has comprised 50 percent female cabinet members—to our best knowledge an unprecedented achievement.

Constitutional Design

In constitutional design, as Shirin Ahlbäck Öberg points out in her Introduction to Section 2, Sweden presents an intriguing case of extensive reform of the modus operandi of its democratic system, including introducing universal suffrage and parliamentary government without any formal changes in the constitutional framework. Dankwart Rustow (1971: 15) suggests that Swedes have a "deepseated devotion to legal rules." While that may or may not be the case, Swedes apparently also master the art of taking advantage of the elasticity in constitutional rules (see Ahlbäck Öberg, Introduction to Section 2).

If there are any exceptional features related to Sweden's constitutional design, it should probably be the early (eighteenth-century) formalization of freedom of information and the idea that all government documents are public. When Sweden joined the EU in 1995, there were concerns voiced that Sweden would have to surrender some of that freedom in order to harmonize with the Union. The Swedish response was to argue that one of its missions in the EU should be to increase transparency and open government—a mission that is yet to be fulfilled. In fact, Sweden in 2014 had to accept the EU's liberalization of the rules exempting documents from public scrutiny (for a critical account, see Funcke 2014).

The Party System

Turning now to the party system, the longevity of the Social Democrats in government has clearly been a defining feature of Swedish politics (see Table I.1; Aylott, this volume). Sweden is sometimes included in the small group of "one-party-dominant democracies," together with Japan, Israel, and Mexico. In these countries, the early postwar period (or earlier) saw one of the parties securing a position of being more or less continuously in power (Pempel 1990). Interestingly, in all four cases that dominance is now broken and the previously dominant party is now more or less at the same level of electoral support as its competitors. Again, while there are some historical exceptional features to the Swedish case, Sweden now stands out less in international comparison.

In terms of changes to the party system, we should consider Seymour Lipset and Stein Rokkan's classic "freezing" hypothesis. Their argument was that "the party systems of the

1960s reflect, with few but significant exceptions, the cleavage structures of the 1920s ... the party alternatives, and in remarkably many ways the party organizations, are older than the national electorates" (Lipset and Rokkan 1967: 50). As an ex post facto observation this argument is obviously difficult to dispute (see Mair 1997). What is more pertinent to the present discussion is the rapid "thawing" of the Swedish party system which began in the 1980s. In the unicameral parliament that was set in place from 1970, the electoral system has a 4 percent threshold for parties to enter parliament. This arrangement probably helped keep the number of parties with parliamentary representation steady at five for almost two decades. In 1988, however, the Greens gained parliamentary representation (at first only for one election period but they returned to the Riksdag after the 1994 elections).

Furthermore, in 1991 the "New Democracy" and the Christian Democrats made their way into parliament, and in 2010 the Sweden Democrats also secured representation in the Riksdag. "New Democracy," a right-wing party with a diffuse agenda albeit with an anti-immigration orientation, remained in the Riksdag for only three years while the Greens and the Christian Democrats have successfully defended their parliamentary representation. Thus, the Swedish parliamentary party system in 2015 comprises eight parties: the Moderates, the Liberals, the Center Party, and the Christian Democrats on the center-right side of the political spectrum, and the Social Democrats, the Left Party, and the Greens on the center-left side, and the Sweden Democrats, which although pivotal in the 2014–18 parliament have not been invited to any collaboration by either bloc.

The Sweden Democrats' entry in Swedish politics is perhaps the most dramatic development in the party system in recent years. In the 2010 parliamentary election they received 5.7 percent of the votes and thus passed the 4 percent threshold with good margin. In the 2014 election they more than doubled their support, receiving 12.9 percent of the votes cast. The Sweden Democrats pursue a distinct anti-immigration and EU-skeptic agenda. The bulk of their electoral support seems to come from former Social Democrats and Moderates voters, primarily younger male voters. Seen as a racist party by the other parties, the Sweden Democrats are left outside all discussions among the other parties in parliament.

The emergence of the Sweden Democrats could be seen as one of the developments that support the "decline of exceptionalism" argument mentioned earlier (Rothstein 2014). Right-wing, anti-immigration parties have existed for some time in all the other Nordic countries and indeed across Europe. In Sweden, immigration as a topic of political debate was kept off the political agenda for a long time, almost as a tacit agreement among the established parties.

Thus, in comparison with the other Scandinavian countries, the only exceptional aspect of the increasing fragmentation of the Swedish party system and the emergence of anti-immigration parties is that it did not happen sooner. In Denmark the party system changed dramatically in the 1973 "landslide election" when no less than ten parties gained parliamentary representation. In Norway, too, the number of parties in parliament has grown albeit in a less eruptive way than in Denmark. Furthermore, both Denmark and Norway witnessed right-wing populist parties entering parliament in the early 1970s but it was not until 2010 that Sweden experienced the same development with the Sweden Democrats passing the threshold to the Riksdag. Thus, today all three Scandinavian countries have significant anti-immigration parties in their national parliaments: the Danish People's Party in Denmark, the Progress Party in Norway, and the Sweden Democrats in Sweden. Again, notwithstanding institutional differences, the main difference between Sweden and her neighbors is the timeline.

Electoral Behavior

Needless to say, changes in the party system are ultimately driven by changes in electoral behavior. The "frozen" party system, according to Lipset and Rokkan (1967) rested on entrenched societal cleavage structures and the mobilization of social class. Voters were for the most part strongly identified with a particular party—or at least committed to either the socialist or non-socialist bloc of parties—and therefore not likely to change preferences from one election to the next.

As the editors of Section 4 point out in their Introduction, the four chapters in their section present "four studies of Swedish exceptionalism." As the chapters also substantiate, voting behavior is changing dramatically, and has been changing continuously and consistently over the past several decades. Voting according to social class, although still high in international comparison, is declining (see Oskarson, this volume), while issue-based voting is increasing. As a result, electoral volatility increases and with that the importance of the election campaigns (see Strömbäck, this volume). If previously elections campaigns served primarily to mobilize the party's core constituencies, contemporary campaigns are essential to mobilizing marginal voters. There has been a steady decline in party identification and today's voters are much more likely to switch party preference from one election to the next.

Again, it would appear as if Sweden's political system is moving in a direction fairly much in tune with the rest of Europe. The patterns we observe in Sweden are not unique in any sense; if anything they may only be more marked and dramatic.

Public Administration

The structure and modus operandi of the Swedish public administration is another example of Sweden's development from previously displaying some unique features to moving closer toward the international mainstream. Agencies were first introduced during the era when Sweden was one of the leading powers in Europe. Indeed, some agencies, like the National Board of Trade, date as far back as the seventeenth century. Later, agencies became the preferred institutional arrangement to curtail the executive powers of the pre-democratic monarchy. Constitutional arrangements ensured that the king could not use agencies to harass individual citizens. This executive autonomy in relationship to other branches of government is the epitome of the "dualism" between policy-making and administration which continues to shape public administration in Sweden (see Bäck and Larsson 2006; Jacobsson, Pierre, and Sundström 2015; Premfors and Sundström 2007).

Such executive, autonomous agencies have been a defining feature of administrative reform across the world for the past couple of decades (Pollitt et al. 2004). While there are several important differences between the century-old agencies and the much more recent public-management-style executive agencies, there are also important similarities. However, in the early days of reform, Sweden was perceived as somewhat of a role model in its organization of the executive branch of government.

The Swedish public sector has undergone major reform over the past couple of decades. Much of that reform has been cast in the New Public Management (NPM) format although reform has been much less extensive than in countries like Britain, Australia, or New Zealand. The objectives and pace of reform have been more similar to those seen in Norway (see, e.g., Christensen and Laegreid 1998): gradual, piecemeal reform rather than rapid, across-the-board changes.

As a result of this trajectory of reform in Sweden and overseas there is today a growing resemblance between the Swedish model of public administration and those found in most other developed countries. That having been said, Sweden still stands out to some extent as a country with a history in a legalistic administrative tradition but now introducing more managerial objectives to its public sector.

Subnational Government

Local autonomy is exceptionally strong in Sweden. It is written into the Constitution to safeguard local institutions from impositions by central government. Except for a few stipulated types of actions, municipalities are essentially free to pursue their interests in whatever way they choose. At the same time, however, local authorities are essential to the implementation and delivery of central government services in a wide array of sectors. Balancing these assignments against local autonomy has always been a problem for local authorities.

The local and regional system of government has been reformed several times during the past decades. Perhaps most importantly, from the 1950s into the early 1970s central government implemented a comprehensive reform of merging municipalities into fewer but bigger units. This reform was believed to be necessary to enable local authorities to shoulder the responsibilities associated with delivering the growing number of welfare-state-related services. Interestingly, the new, bigger local authorities had the financial and organizational capabilities to take a tougher negotiating position vis-à-vis central government. And the widespread concerns that the mergers would be detrimental to local democracy largely proved wrong; the new municipalities had a more vibrant political and democratic life and were more attractive to media coverage compared to the former, smaller municipalities (Strömberg and Westerståhl 1983).

International Relations

As a small country pursuing a policy of nonalignment, Sweden is not a major player in international affairs in modern times. The intriguing question here is if there is anything that would suggest that Sweden has, or has had, an influence on international politics which is disproportionate to its size or geopolitical location. Swedish foreign policy emphasizes international law and national sovereignty. This stance has led the country to criticize violations of small states' sovereignty as happened for instance during the Vietnam War, when Sweden was a leading international critic of the United States' war effort in Southeast Asia (Jerneck 1983).

Sweden furthermore has a distinctly internationalist profile in its foreign policy, supporting the UN as an arena of international affairs and emphasizing global collaboration, foreign aid, and international solidarity. In that spirit, former Prime Minister, Fredrik Reinfeldt (Moderate) once described Sweden as a "humanitarian superpower" (*Dagens Nyheter* 2014; see also Nilsson 1991).

As Ole Elgström argues in the Introduction to Section 7, Sweden's strategy of combining nonalignment with an internationalist policy orientation "seems to be one example of 'Swedish exceptionalism.'" This policy remains in place. At the same time, it is easy to note that Sweden today is less of an international critic—a role that largely disappeared with Olof Palme's removal from the political scene in 1986 (Ekengren 2005). Instead, foreign policy has been conducted more *sotto voce*, still underscoring international solidarity but also emphasizing common interests, a commitment to Europe and to international organizations. Thus, while there was exceptionalism in Sweden's basic foreign policy stance, that exceptionalism might be less conspicuous today compared to previous decades.

Sweden and the EU

Given her long history of nonalignment, some might see an inconsistency with Sweden's joining the European Union (EU) in 1995. But the EU was not a military union; indeed, it was seen as a part of the postwar European peace project. Over time, the EU has become increasingly vertically integrated and added portfolios to the original areas of collaboration. While Sweden's EU membership has provided the country with access to an arena where it can promote global issues like increasing foreign aid and human rights, the project of harmonizing the Swedish legislative and regulatory framework with the EU rules has been an extensive process affecting essentially all aspects of policy-making and administration (see Section 8; Jacobsson and Sundström 2006). Indeed, Sweden has made an effort in being a "good European" by harmonizing its legislation and regulatory frameworks to EU norms swiftly and carefully.

Thus, the EU membership has meant a de facto concession on several aspects of Sweden's sovereignty. To some extent that development is indigenous to the idea of integration; as Vivien Schmidt (1999) points out, the more leverage you want to give to transnational institutions and the more successful you want a transnational structure to be, the more individual countries must be willing to surrender their sovereignty to the collective project.

Sweden has conducted two referenda concerning EU membership. In 1994, a majority supported the proposal to join while another majority in 2003 rejected the proposal that Sweden should join the Eurozone (see Mörth's Introduction to Section 8). It is difficult to find anything "exceptional" about Sweden's relationship with the EU, other than perhaps the relatively smooth process in which a country professing neutrality and nonalignment joined a transnational organization with extensive plans for its vertical integration.

Political Economy of Swedish Governance

In Andrew Shonfield's seminal book *Modern Capitalism* (Shonfield 1965) there is an account of a British union representative asking a Swedish colleague how disagreements with employers are settled in Sweden. The answer is "we has (*sic*) a meeting" (Shonfield 1965: 199; see also Introduction to Section 9). As several contributors to this *Handbook* point out, Sweden is what Johan P. Olsen (1983) calls an "organized democracy" with numerous organizations in all sectors of society. Decisions, as the Swedish union man pointed out, are typically negotiated among collectivities.

This applies particularly to the labor market. We have already mentioned the evolution of the Swedish political economy with regard to the relationships among labor market organizations. Indeed, the autonomy of these organizations was significant; although wage bargaining outcomes had a distinct impact on the economy, there was a strong belief that the state should not interfere in the process in other respects than providing mediation, if necessary. This was the essence of the *Saltsjöbaden* agreement in 1938 which is still in effect. That said, government has on some occasions tried to make for a smooth bargaining process, for instance by adjusting income taxes or using macroeconomic policy instruments to facilitate increased purchasing power without significantly increasing nominal wages.

Policy-Making

The search for accommodation of conflicting interests has been said to characterize not only labor market decision-making but is also thought to be emblematic of how decisions are made in the political sphere. Dankwart Rustow (1957) once saw Sweden as the epitome of the "politics of compromise." Similarly, Olof Petersson (1994: 33) notes that "an emphasis on compromise and pragmatic solutions has led to the development of a political culture based on consensus." Elder et al. (1983) make a distinction between consensus with regard to the rules of the political game on the one hand and consensus within the political process on the other, and find that while consensus remains in the first regard it is less so in the second dimension.

While there is very little evidence indeed of a declining consensus in terms of the rules of the political game, as demonstrated by the papers in Section 10, it would appear that consensus-seeking behavior in the policy-making process is declining. With the consolidation of a non-socialist and a socialist/green bloc in the party system, the political discourse has become increasingly divided. The two blocs stand for rather different ideas in terms of economic governance and the balance between "state" and "market" in more general terms. Parliamentary behavior today follows party lines to an overwhelming extent.

Furthermore, as the papers in Section 10 show, policy-making in Sweden has tended to adopt a rational approach to societal problems and the role and capacity of public policy to address those problems. Sweden is probably not exceptional in this respect but it is nonetheless a rather defining feature of how policy is made there. There is strong belief, at least within the political system, in social engineering and the problem-solving capacity of the state and therefore a lingering expectation on the state to solve all sorts of societal problems (see Hirdman 2000).

Why the Loss of Exceptionalism?

As this very brief discussion on the degree of Swedish exceptionalism in the sectors covered in the *Handbook* suggests, Sweden today presents itself less as an "exceptional" country and more as one country among others on the European continent. Each set of issues that has been discussed here will obviously be scrutinized in detail in the ten sections of the *Handbook*.

For the present context, it is intriguing to speculate about what has caused the decreasing exceptionalism of Swedish politics. We can see three potential explanations to this pattern. In order of increasing agency, the three factors accounting for decreasing Swedish exceptionalism would be the increasing affluence of the Swedish working class, globalization, and policy choice. Let us inspect these three in turn.

The first potential explanation is related to changes in political and electoral behavior and Karl Marx's notion of *embourgeoisment*, i.e. the process through which the working class acquires middle-class ideas and values. The chapters in Section 4 show declining Social Democratic support among working-class voters who increasingly cast their votes for parties on the center-right side of the political spectrum. The decline in class voting (see Oskarson, this volume) has led the parties to alter their electoral strategies. For instance, the previous focus on "workers" in Social Democratic rhetoric has gradually been replaced by references to "wage earners" or "the Swedish people."

The *embourgeoisment* hypothesis does not in any way suggest that poverty has been eradicated in Sweden; in fact, as discussed earlier, there is today evidence of a growing poverty problem. Poverty remains closely related to work; the difference between today's situation and the situation at the time when the labor movement emerged is that today's unemployed do not seem to have the same political efficacy or class awareness as those who formed unions and the Social Democratic Party more than a century ago. Today, those who are well established in the workforce, including conventional working-class occupations in the public or private sector, are relatively well off in material terms whereas those who are outside the workforce tend to constitute a new social underclass; long-term unemployed people with limited prospects of returning to the workforce, immigrants, people living on social welfare support, young people struggling to find a way into the labor market, etc. This new underclass is not very politically involved. This potential explanation for decreasing exceptionalism would thus state that the growing middle class is less dependent on, and therefore reluctant to contribute to, the welfare state. This would also explain the decline of the Social Democratic hegemony in the postwar period.

The second hypothesis states that the decreasing exceptionalism can be attributed to globalization which is sometimes said to drive a convergence among different countries (for a review of this argument, see Pierre 2013). Convergence in terms of policy agendas, policy procedures, and policy choice can be the outcome of numerous factors of which globalization is but one. For instance, a growing number of countries today are experiencing vexing problems coping with the demographic situation of a growing senior population and therefore tend to apply similar approaches to that issue.

Convergence can also be the result of cognitive and anticipatory processes; for instance, the political elite's conviction that economic policy which deviates from that of most other similar countries can be a dangerous strategy. After three decades of a continuous increase in public spending in Sweden, the 1990s saw increases in public spending significantly slowing down (see Tanzi and Schuknecht 2000). The country at that time was in the midst of a deep financial crisis and public expenditure had to be fundamentally reassessed. A firm financial regulatory framework was put in place and new ideas of governance and public management were explored. The country's bad experience with overseas speculation against its currency in the wake of financial deregulation helped put measures on the agenda which previously had been likely to be rejected.

In this perspective, the pertinent question is not so much why Swedish exceptionalism is decreasing but more why that decrease did not happen sooner. Sweden has in many ways experienced globalization long before the deregulation of financial markets created the kind of globalization we see today. As a small trade-dependent country building much of its wealth on export revenues, Sweden has lived with the problem of adjusting to international markets for almost a century. The welfare state expansion took place against the backdrop of these contingencies.

A third explanation, finally, is policy choice. This hypothesis suggests that Sweden's becoming increasingly similar to the OECD average in political, social, and economic respects is not so much the outcome of structural changes in the economy as it is a result of policy choices. The cutbacks in welfare state support and the rearticulation of work as the founding principle for public support which have been implemented during the early 2000s are all, in fact, policy choices. These choices were articulated in policies and programs to induce the long-term unemployed to actively seek work, thus reducing the number of people living on seemingly permanent public support, and thus facilitating tax cuts for people with employment. This policy model thus combined carrots and sticks to reduce unemployment and the number of people living more or less entirely on welfare state support. This is essentially a neoliberal approach to unemployment and welfare spending not terribly different from the projects pursued by neoliberal governments in other countries. It is, however, different from the policy model which built the welfare state and thereby also contributed to much of the "Swedish exceptionalism." Perhaps a more correct way of describing the development would be to say that if Sweden today is more similar to countries with a long experience of neoliberal policies, it could be argued that Sweden previously was not very exceptional but in fact rather similar to another family of countries (Esping-Andersen 1990).

The Organization and Themes of the *Handbook*

The *Handbook* is divided into ten sections centered round a specific aspect of Swedish politics, each with an Introduction and four substantive chapters. By organizing the *Handbook* into sections, the reader will find a coherent discussion among different aspects of a particular area of Swedish politics with chapters that speak to and complement each other. We also believe that the ten sections capture all the key aspects of Swedish politics. One could argue that the *Handbook* should have been more focused on a number of substantive policy areas but that would by necessity have meant less attention to presentations and analyses of the framework of Swedish politics and typical political and electoral behavior within that framework or Sweden's behavior in international arenas. For those readers who wish to acquaint themselves with Swedish politics, the *Handbook* will serve as a gateway into exciting research areas; it will not, and cannot, provide answers to all questions about Swedish politics.

Notes

1. I am grateful for comments on previous drafts from the Section Editors and Guy Peters.
2. Conventional corporate taxes have always been comparatively low in Sweden; instead, employers have been charged a tax ("arbetsgivaravgift," employer's fee) related to wages.

References

Bäck, H. and Larsson, T. (2006). *Den svenska politiken*. Malmö: Liber.
Childs, M. W. (1936). *Sweden: The Middle Way*. London: Faber & Faber.

Christensen, T. and Laegreid, P. (1998). "Administrative Reform Policy: The Case of Norway," *International Review of Administrative Sciences* 64: 457–75.

Dagens Nyheter (2014). "En öppenhjärtlig Reinfeldt," August 17.

Ekengren, A.-M. (2005). *Olof Palme och utrikespolitiken: Europa och Tredje världen* [Olof Palme and Foreign Policy: Europe and the Third World]. Umeå: Boréa.

Elder, N., Thomas, A. H., and Arter, D. (1983). *The Consensual Democracies: The Government and Politics of the Scandinavian Countries*. Oxford: Basil Blackwell.

Esping-Andersen, G. (1990). *The Three Worlds of Welfare Capitalism*. Princeton, NJ: Princeton University Press.

Eurostat Online Database (2013). Brussels: European Commission.

Funcke, N. (2014). "Offentlighetsprincipen är väg att vittra sönder" [The principle of public access is disintegrating], *DN Debatt*, March 10.

Heclo, H. (1974). *Modern Social Politics in Britain and Sweden*. New Haven, CT: Yale University Press.

Hirdman, Y. (2000). *Att lägga livet tillrätta* [freely translated: Organizing the Good Life]. Stockholm: Carlssons.

Huntford, R. (1971). *The New Totalitarians*. London: Allen Lane.

Jacobsson, B., Pierre, J., and Sundström, G. (2015). *Governing the Embedded State: The Organizational Dimension of Governance*. Oxford: Oxford University Press.

Jacobsson, B. and Sundström, G. (2006). *Från Hemvävd till invävd: Europeiseringen av svensk förvaltning och politik* [From Homegrown to Embedded: The Europeanization of Swedish Administration and Politics]. Malmö: Liber.

Jerneck, M. (1983). *Kritik som utrikespolitiskt medel* [Critique as a Foreign Policy Instrument]. Stockholm: Dialogos.

Katzenstein, P. J. (1985). *Small States in World Markets: Industrial Policy in Europe*. Ithaca: Cornell University Press.

Krantz, O. (2008). "Economic Growth and Economic Policy in Sweden in the 20th Century: A Comparative Perspective," in M. Müller and T. Myllyntaus (eds), *Pathbreakers: Small European Countries Responding to Globalisation and Deglobalisation*. Bern: Peter Lang, 39–64.

Lipset, S. M. and Rokkan, S. (1967). "Cleavage Structures, Party Systems, and Voter Alignments: An Introduction," in S. M. Lipset and S. Rokkan (eds), *Party Systems and Voter Alignments: Cross-National Perspectives*. New York: Free Press, 1–64.

Magnusson, L. (2000). *An Economic History of Sweden*. London: Routledge.

Mair, P. (1997). *Party System Change: Approaches and Interpretations*. Oxford: Clarendon Press.

Milner, H. and Wadensjö, E. (eds) (2001). *Gösta Rehn, the Swedish Model and Labour Market Policies: International and National Perspectives*. Aldershot: Ashgate.

Möller, T. (2011). *Svensk politisk historia: Strid och samverkan under 200 år*. Lund: Studentlitteratur.

Nilsson, A. (1991). *Den moraliska stormakten: En studie av socialdemokraternas internationella aktivism*. Stockholm: Timbro.

Olsen, J. P. (1983). *Organized Democracy: Political Institutions in the Welfare State*. Bergen: Universitetsforlaget.

Pempel, T. J. (ed.) (1990). *Uncommon Democracies: The One-Party Dominant Regimes*. Ithaca: Cornell University Press.

Petersson, O. (1994). *The Government and Politics of the Nordic Countries*. Stockholm: Fritzes.

Pierre, J. (2013). *Globalization and Governance*. Cheltenham: Edward Elgar.

Pollitt, C., Talbot, C., Caulfield, J., and Smullen, A. (2004). *Agencies: How Governments Do Things through Semi-Autonomous Organizations*. Basingstoke: Palgrave.

Premfors, R. and Sundström, G. (2007). *Regeringskansliet*. Malmö: Liber.

Richardson, J. J. (ed.) (1982). *Policy Styles in Western Europe*. London: Allen and Unwin.

Rothstein, B. (2014). "The End of Swedish Exceptionalism," *Foreign Affairs*, September 18.

Rustow, D. A. (1957). *The Politics of Compromise*, 2nd edn. Princeton: Princeton University Press.

Rustow, D. A. (1971). "Sweden's Transition to Democracy: Some Notes toward a Generic Theory," *Scandinavian Political Studies* 6: 9–26.

Schmidt, V. (1999). "Convergent Pressures, Divergent Responses: France, Great Britain and Germany between Globalization and Europeanization," in D. A. Smith, D. J. Solinger, and S. C. Topik (eds), *States and Sovereignty in the Global Economy*. London: Routledge, 172–92.

Shonfield, A. (1965). *Modern Capitalism*. Oxford: Oxford University Press.

Steinmo, S. (2012). *The Evolution of States: Sweden, Japan and the United States*. Cambridge: Cambridge University Press.

Strömberg, L. and Westerståhl, J. (eds) (1983). *De nya kommunerna*. Stockholm: Liber.

Tanzi, V. and Schuknecht, L. (2000). *Public Spending in the 20th Century: A Global Perspective*. Cambridge: Cambridge University Press.

World Bank (2012). *World Development Indicators*. Washington, DC: World Bank.

SECTION 1

THE POLITICS OF THE WELFARE STATE

SECTION EDITOR
BO ROTHSTEIN

CHAPTER 1

....

INTRODUCTION

The Politics of the Welfare State

....

BO ROTHSTEIN

THE Swedish type of welfare state has been seen as a central part of what used to be known as "the Swedish model." Although this "model" during its heyday contained many other central features, such as the consensual model in industrial relations, centralized wage-bargaining, a culture of compromises in central political issues, and a strong reliance on experts in policy-making, the specific characteristics of the system for social protection and social services have been a central part. Generally, the Swedish welfare state has been seen as the most typical of the social democratic welfare states. In a comparative perspective, this means that it has generally been seen as more encompassing, more universalistic, and more redistributive than other welfare state systems. Whether or not this is still the case is currently a matter of intense debate. The number of studies of the origin, characteristics, and political effects of this welfare state is huge, and in this section only a small part of this literature can be presented. Since this is a volume about Swedish politics, many aspects from other disciplines such as economics, history, and psychology have had to be left out. The chapters in this section try to answer four larger questions. First, Stefan Svallfors analyzes the shifts and particularities of support among the population for this system as a whole and also for its various specific policies. Based on extensive and detailed survey research, Svallfors shows that the system has strong, stable, and lately also increasing support among the Swedish population. Some of the results from this research are quite surprising, for example the findings that support from the middle class has increased and that people's suspicions about overuse or abuse have diminished. This is a remarkable result, especially in light of the fact that during this period, immigration to Sweden from outside the Nordic countries has increased substantially and that Sweden now has quite a large anti-immigration party in Parliament which has put this issue high on the agenda.

Since the Swedish welfare state has been singled out as the most typical social democratic welfare state, it is of course interesting to analyze what type of changes have taken place during the center-conservative government that came to power in 2006. Many international observers expected extensive cuts, maybe to a degree that one could speak about a systemic shift. In his chapter, Anders Lindbom analyzes this specific issue. Using the theory about "feedback" mechanisms in which existent policies determine what is politically feasible, Lindbom argues that while there have been incremental cutbacks in some policies, the basic universal and encompassing features of the Swedish welfare state are still in place. A surprising finding is that the cuts in the social insurance system implemented by the Social Democratic government that ruled from 1994 to 2006 were more pronounced in some important areas that what has taken place after 2006 under the conservative-center coalition government. His conclusion is that the dominant party in the center-right coalition has to a considerable extent changed its ideology, moving away from neoliberalism as it has come to embrace the basic characteristics of the universal welfare state.

A central feature of Swedish society is the importance of gender equality. In achieving its world-leading role in gender equality, Christina Bergqvist shows that many welfare state policies have played an important part. She shows that when the foundations of the Swedish welfare state were laid during the 1930s, issues about gender equality were already important for the reformers. The shift away from the "male breadwinner" model to the "dual-income-earner model" has been dramatic and came about with a surprisingly high level of political agreement between the left and the center-right political parties. However, Bergqvist also shows that despite the many policies that have been put in place in this area, there is quite some disappointment about the results. Women still work more part-time and carry more responsibility for domestic duties than men, the labor market is still quite segregated, and despite doing very well in the educational system, few women reach the highest levels in the occupational sphere. Bergqvist also provides a detailed analysis of the politics of one of the currently most discussed issues in Sweden in this area, namely what measures to use for increasing the time fathers take from the internationally quite generous (16 months) parental leave insurance.

The final chapter by Rothstein analyzes three issues. The first is the normative foundations of the Swedish welfare state. Should it be characterized as a liberal rights-based operation or is it to be understood as foremost a communitarian project? He defines two lines in this debate—one inspired by Jürgen Habermas's view of the welfare state as a state-led "colonization" of the private sphere and the other inspired by Amartya Sen's idea about "basic capabilities." Coupled to this question is the issue whether the Swedish welfare state should be seen as a result of a specific Swedish (or Nordic) historically inherited culture or if it should be understood as "designed" from above by the creation of specific political and administrative institutions. Lastly, he presents an analysis of why, contrary to what seems intuitive, a universal welfare state where "everyone" pays taxes and receives benefits turns out to be more redistributive than a residual one in which you tax the rich to give to the poor.

In sum, these four chapters analyze the Swedish welfare state through different theoretical lenses using a variety of methods. They answer important yet different questions about how this project should be understood; how political support for the system works and has changed; what effects it has on redistribution between social groups as well as between men and women; and what changes in the political landscape have meant for its viability.

CHAPTER 2

....

WHO LOVES THE SWEDISH WELFARE STATE? ATTITUDE TRENDS 1980–2010

....

STEFAN SVALLFORS

INTRODUCTION

....

ANALYSES of attitudes to the Swedish welfare state were slow to get off the ground.[1] Although election studies and other general surveys had occasionally surveyed welfare attitudes from the 1950s onwards, more extensive and systematic research did not take hold until the 1980s. When the doyen of Swedish welfare state research Walter Korpi surveyed the state of the art in the late 1970s, in his classic study *The Democratic Class Struggle,* he found that "social scientists have made few attempts to describe public opinion concerning different aspects of the welfare state" (Korpi 1983: 200).

Why was this the case? There were both internal scientific and external political reasons. In social science, both Marxists and reformist social researchers came in the late 1960s to share a skepticism about the value of surveying attitudes. In the former case, because such surveys were argued to be profoundly unable to capture the true beliefs of people in their everyday lives, and hence would register only the "false consciousness" implanted in the masses (Christiansson 1969; Fredriksson 1970). In the latter case, because it was argued that an enlightened social reformism should rely on objective facts rather than people's perceptions and evaluations of their situation. As put by Robert Erikson, one of the chief architects behind the celebrated Swedish level-of-living surveys:

> The individual's perception of his situation depends not only on his objective circumstances but also on his aspiration level, i.e. his assessment of what is his rightful

due. The aspiration level may vary sharply between individuals and is contingent upon their earlier experiences, so that persons who have lived under modest circumstances tend to have a lower aspiration level than those who have been better off. From a subjective definition of welfare could follow that an individual who lives in relative misery may well be regarded as enjoying more welfare than one who lives in good circumstances, an inference that I find absurd. (Erikson 1974: 274; see also Johansson 1973)

Neither the Marxist critique of attitude research nor the social reformist misgivings about subjective data explicitly targeted welfare state attitudes. However, the result was nevertheless a general and widespread feeling in the Swedish social science community that attitude research was of little value. In such an intellectual atmosphere it took a long time for Swedish social scientists to realize the need for surveying the legitimacy of public institutions.

Politically, many achievements of the welfare state, and the continuing expansion of welfare policies, were more or less taken for granted by a broad political spectrum (Svallfors 1989: chs. 8–9). The attitudes and opinions about the welfare state among the electorate were therefore seen as of less political interest. As long as the continuous gradual extension of welfare policies was largely unquestioned in Swedish politics, political interest in public opinion about the welfare state remained lukewarm. It took the political questioning of the welfare state, as articulated by neoliberals in the 1980s, to make this public opinion a salient political issue. Now, the electorate was suddenly seen by political pundits as increasingly skeptical about the further expansion of the welfare state, with younger generations seen as the harbingers of what was to come in terms of increased resistance against an overbearing welfare state. But still little was known about the actual state of affairs when it came to citizens' attitudes.

THE SWEDISH WELFARE STATE SURVEYS

This was the background to the fielding in 1986 of the first survey in what was to become the *Swedish Welfare State Survey* (*SWS*) series. This survey laid the first broad ground for analyses of patterns of welfare attitudes, as well as for subsequent replications (Svallfors 1989). To some extent it also built on previous surveys and publications by Hadenius and by Laurin, probing attitudes to taxes and social spending (Hadenius 1986; Laurin 1986).

In SWS, nationally representative samples of the Swedish population were asked their opinions about spending levels in the welfare state, collective vs private financing, and public organization of welfare policies, but also about their perceptions of abuse of welfare policies (such as cheating with benefits). In later surveys, trust in the task performance of the welfare state was added as an important factor.

A set of key findings from the first welfare state surveys, and compilations of the few then-existing single-indicator time series may be summarized as follows (the summary builds mainly on Svallfors 1989, 1991):

(1) Swedish attitudes were on the whole strongly supportive of an encompassing welfare state. In contrast to the sweeping statements in the public debate about generational processes leading younger generations away from support for welfare policies, or about rising resistance against bureaucratic-administrative intrusions, the early research in general showed the welfare state to be quite popular. Encompassing welfare policies, which are collectively financed and publicly organized, proved to have overall support from the Swedish citizens.

(2) However, early research also found a clear difference in support for comprehensive and selective or targeted programs. Programs such as pensions and health care received strong support, while more targeted or selective programs such as housing allowances and social assistance received much lower support.

(3) This research also found a clear difference between general and specific support for the welfare state. General support, taking the form of attitudes toward objects such as "the public sector" or "social reforms," was shown to be more dependent on changes in the public discourse and general ideological dispositions. Public support was therefore more volatile at this level. Specific support for concrete welfare policy programs, on the other hand, was shown to be more stable because it was rooted in everyday life experiences.

(4) The clear support for welfare policies coexisted with considerable ambivalence regarding several aspects of welfare policies. Quite widespread suspicions about welfare abuse and cheating, for example, and concerns about bureaucracy and inefficiencies in the public sector were important qualifications of the overall support for the redistributive and risk-reducing aspects of welfare policies.

(5) The early research also confirmed the continuing importance of class and "class-related" factors (such as income and education) as the most important determinants behind welfare attitudes—in contrast to widespread arguments about sector-related cleavages as the new main factors behind welfare attitudes (Dunleavy 1980; Saunders 1986: ch. 8; Zetterberg 1985).

Although these first-generation analyses of attitudes to the Swedish welfare state were severely restrained by the shortage of comparable time series, they form an important backdrop to later developments. Simply by making welfare attitudes a topic for systematic social scientific research, instead of the object of political and speculative projections, they laid the ground for subsequent extensions and improvements (for a selection of later analyses of the Swedish Welfare State Surveys, see Edlund 1999a, 2000, 2006; Edlund and Johansson Sevä 2013; Johansson Sevä 2009, 2010; Svallfors, 1995, 1996, 2004, 2011a).

DIMENSIONS OF SUPPORT

What is the current situation when it comes to public support for the welfare state? To begin, one could ask how an "optimal" public support for public welfare policies should look. What conditions should be met in order for us to speak of a strong public support for the welfare state? First, there should be trust that the welfare state can actually solve its tasks (Meuleman and van Oorschot 2012). This trust could be expressed both as a belief about the general task performance of the welfare state, and as a subjective feeling of being protected against the vicissitudes of market exposure and life-course risks.

Second, because extensive welfare policies are expensive, there should be support for high social spending and for taxes used for welfare policies. And since the welfare state is a collective financial commitment, there should also be support for collective forms of financing over private insurance and user fees for services. Third, there should be trust in and support for public authorities as providers of care and services. If there are widespread feelings that other service providers than public authorities are best suited, there is a problem of support. Lastly, there should not be widespread suspicions about cheating and "free riding" in the welfare state. If large groups of people believe there are many others who abuse welfare policies, the legitimacy of the welfare state is threatened.

It should be emphasized that this support is "optimal" only in the sense of offering as strong and underpinning support for extensive welfare policies as possible. In other respects and from other perspectives such attitudes could well be regarded as completely dysfunctional. For example, when ingrained attitudes hinder necessary or desirable reforms of existing policies, or when they clash with other values and perceptions (such as various forms of free-market ideologies).

This exposé of the optimal support for the welfare state also suggests that attitudes toward welfare policies are best seen as multidimensional. People may well support the welfare state in some respects but have less positive attitudes toward other aspects. As already pointed out, early Swedish research on welfare attitudes indeed showed that attitudes toward welfare policies were multidimensional. Other research, using both simple interpretations and descriptive/exploratory methods (Svallfors 1991, 1995; Taylor-Gooby 1982, 1983, 1985) and more advanced confirmatory analyses (van Oorschot and Meuleman 2012) point in the same direction. So there are strong reasons to tap attitudes to the welfare state with a broad spectrum of questions. Trends are not necessarily the same across different dimensions and aspects of the welfare state.

ATTITUDE TRENDS IN THE 1990S AND 2000S

What do the Swedish attitudinal trends look like in these different dimensions of support? To describe this, we rely here on the replications of the SWS in 1992, 1997, 2002, and 2010. The survey questions cover (by length of the time series) (1) attitudes toward welfare spending, (2) financing and (3) service delivery, (4) perceptions of abuse of welfare policies, (5) welfare risk perceptions, (6) individual willingness to pay taxes for welfare policies, and (7) perceptions about the task performance of the welfare state. The actual figures that substantiate the summaries provided below can be found in Svallfors (2011a: Tables 1–8).

Starting with the issue for which the longest time series is found, there is a large degree of stability in *attitudes toward spending*. Support for increased spending grew substantially in the crisis of the 1990s—probably as a reaction to substantial cutbacks in the public sector at that time. The current crisis has not prompted similar reactions. Now a more mixed pattern is found, in which somewhat fewer people ask for increased spending on health care and schools, while more people want to increase spending on social assistance and employment policies. The dividing line between support for more comprehensive programs and for those aimed at ameliorating weak market positions has become somewhat less accentuated in the last survey round. The weakening support for employment policies from 1981–2002 was reversed in 2010, although support for higher spending is still far from what used to be the case in (the far better labor market situation) of the 1980s. In all, there are no signs of any large shifts in attitudes toward spending for different policy purposes.

But does this general support for high welfare state spending combine with a stated *willingness to pay higher taxes* oneself for these purposes? It is easily conceivable that many people would like to increase spending but at the same time see themselves as unable to pay more taxes (Edlund and Johansson Sevä 2013).

There are two remarkable findings in this regard. One is the sharply increased willingness to pay more taxes between 2002 and 2010. While attitudes were very stable from 1997–2002, the share that is willing to pay more taxes for welfare policies jumps dramatically between 2002 and 2010. The second is that for all listed policies, the share that is willing to pay more taxes in 2010 is actually *larger* than the share that wants to increase overall spending for that policy. This was clearly not the case in earlier surveys and is indeed a surprising finding.

What about attitudes toward *collective or privatized financing* of care, services, and social insurance? There is a large degree of stability in attitudes toward the financing of care and services, in the share that chooses collective forms of financing before increased user fees. The one important trend that may be detected is the gradually increasing support for collective financing of child care.

Stability and increasing support is also found when it comes to the collective financing of social insurance, even when respondents are presented with the prospects of lower taxes. In fact, support for collective financing increased in 2010 for all three major social insurances (pensions, sickness benefits, and unemployment benefits). The deteriorating support for unemployment insurance from 1992–2006 reverses, and the support for collective financing of sickness insurance and pensions increases substantially from 2006 to 2010.

What about *delivery of care and services*? Here we find the largest policy changes in recent times in the Swedish welfare state (Bergh 2008a, 2008b; Bergh and Erlingsson 2009). While virtually all education, care, and welfare service provision is still publicly *funded* in Sweden, the actual *delivery* of these services has changed quite dramatically since the 1990s. By now, a substantial proportion of such care and services are provided by non-public actors. In the early phases of private sector growth in these areas a substantial share of the non-public service delivery came from cooperatives and other non-profit actors. Nowadays most of it comes from for-profit companies, in many cases large shareholding companies that are sometimes not even based in Sweden.

Does the increased privatization of care delivery lead to increased support for other instances than public authorities as best suited service deliverers? The findings show that this is hardly the case. The share that chooses "state or local authorities" when faced with a number of alternative service providers remains very stable. The single clear trend is that support for public authorities as best suited to deliver child care increases over time (at the expense of "family and relatives").

Yet another issue for which there are a long-term time series concerns *suspicions of welfare abuse*. One should emphasize that this issue does not cover only outright cheating, but also more general perceptions of dysfunctional adaptations of behavior and "overconsumption."

The interesting finding here is a clear decline in welfare suspicions, first in the crisis of the 1990s, and then again in the last survey. Especially large changes are registered for the question if the unemployed really want a job, and whether those who report themselves sick are really sick. Suspicions about welfare abuse are now at their lowest level ever, and substantially different from what was the case in the mid-1980s. Fears that increased ethnic heterogeneity would undermine welfare state support by increasing suspicions that "the others" would act as free riders seem to receive little support from these findings (Alesina and Glaeser 2004; Finseraas 2008).

These attitudinal trends are all the more striking since they coincide with a more extensive political and media debate about welfare cheating and abuse (Johnson 2010; Lundström 2011). Debate and reporting on welfare abuse increase, and yet suspicions among the public go down. The worsening labor market situation and more stringent conditions in the sickness insurance seem rather to drive perceptions in this regard.

Finally, how have *risk perceptions and evaluations of task performance* of the welfare state changed? This question is of course prior to all the others, but is nevertheless the one for which there are the shortest time series (1997–2010). We find a large degree of stability in welfare-related risks from 2002–10. The most striking thing about this is that figures are substantially lower in 2010 than in the last economic crisis (the 1997 survey). It is clearly not the case that the current economic crisis has made Swedes feel much more insecure in relation to their own sustenance problems.

But we also find an interesting mixture of increasingly positive evaluations of public care and services, and decreasing trust in the task performance of social insurance. Since the government after 2006 made spending on care and services a priority, and made conditions harsher in the social insurances (stricter eligibility and qualifying rules, and increased individual costs for the unemployment insurance), figures show that this shift is clearly recognized by the public. Trust in the task performance is especially low for policies related to the elderly, something that is also reflected in the high level of perceived risk in relation to one's own pensions.

The trends of weakening trust in the task performance of the welfare state are especially pronounced among workers and marginal groups, such as those with severe problems related to unemployment and sustenance (Svallfors 2011b). Furthermore, satisfaction with social insurance has decreased most among supporters of the political left (Oskarson 2013). It seems that those who are most dependent on the welfare state, and among the traditional supporters of the welfare state, that dissatisfaction with the task performance of social insurances is now particularly widespread.

IS SWEDEN DIFFERENT?

Comparative research on the question of whether inhabitants in different countries display different attitudes to the welfare state often take their starting point in the "worlds of welfare" categorization famously introduced by Esping-Andersen (1990). A number of studies have analyzed whether attitude patterns and group differences correspond to the typology he suggested, and what might explain instances of non-correspondence. Pioneering studies in this regard were Svallfors (1993) and Svallfors (1997), which compared attitudes to redistribution in different Western countries, using Esping-Andersen's worlds of welfare as a frame for country selection and analysis. These studies were followed by many others (Andress and Heien 2001; Arts and Gelissen 2001; Bean and Papadakis 1998; Bonoli 2000; Edlund 1999b, 1999c; Evans 1998; Gelissen 2000; Jæger 2006; Larsen 2006, 2008; Matheson and Wearing 1999; Svallfors 2003).

The main findings of this "comparing-attitudes-in-regimes" industry are not completely clear-cut, since both conceptual and empirical problems abound. But there seems to be agreement on the following set of findings: we do find substantial differences among countries in overall public support for the welfare state, corresponding roughly to welfare policy commitment. Support for equality, redistribution, and state intervention is strongest in the social democratic regime, weaker in the conservative regime, and weakest in the liberal regime. However, we do not find any clear regime-clustering of countries. Differences and similarities between countries show interpretable patterns, but they are too complex to be summarized as "worlds of welfare attitudes." An important and still somewhat neglected institutional factor behind varying welfare state support is the "quality of government" in terms of the efficiency and fairness of implementing agencies (Svallfors 2013).

Furthermore, there are general similarities across countries in the impact of different social cleavages: categorical differences along class, gender, or labor market status lines show similar *patterns* across welfare regimes. Where interesting differences between countries in the *magnitude* of categorical attitude differences were found, they did not at all follow the model suggested in the closing chapter of Esping-Andersen's treatise. Instead, they seem to follow the historical articulation of particular social cleavages in different contexts. For example, class differences were especially pronounced in Sweden and some other northwestern countries, reflecting the comparatively high salience of distributive and class-related issues in the political programs and practices of these countries.

Later research confirms that support for extensive welfare policies is stronger in the Nordic countries than in continental Europe and liberal Britain. But it also shows that support for a wide-ranging public responsibility is even stronger in southern and eastern Europe (Svallfors 2012). These analyses have also confirmed the continuing, although varying, impact of "class" and "class-related" factors (such as income and education and various risk-related factors) on the structuring of welfare attitudes (see Cusack, Iversen, and Rehm 2006; Edlund and Svallfors 2011; Kumlin and Svallfors 2007; Svallfors 2004, 2006). Class differences in attitudes toward the welfare state are substantial in many countries, and patterns are fairly consistent across countries. Still, the magnitude of these differences varies substantially among countries, although in a more complex pattern than previous research suggested (Svallfors, Kulin, and Schnabel 2012).

One should be clear that commonalities in attitudes to the welfare state across Europe are just as important as are differences. Strong support for an extensive welfare state, the similarities in cleavage structures, and the similar value bases for the welfare state across Europe are strong common elements and quite clearly contrast with attitudes in the US (Brooks 2012; Svallfors 2012).

It should be emphasized, however, that comparative research on welfare attitudes is restricted to fairly general survey questions from the *European Social Survey* and the *International Social Survey Program*, and never posed at the level of detail provided by the Swedish Welfare State Surveys. So little is known even now about the finer details of whether and how Swedish attitudes to the organization and financing of the welfare state differ from those found in other countries.

SUMMING UP

In summary, what may be said about the trends in Swedish attitudes toward the welfare state? First, there are virtually no signs of any decreasing public support for welfare policies. Overall, there is a large degree of stability in attitudes, and where change is registered, it tends to go in the direction of increasing support. More people state their willingness to pay higher taxes for welfare policy purposes, more people want collective financing of welfare policies, and fewer people perceive extensive welfare abuse in 2010 than was the case in previous surveys. Furthermore, class patterns change so that the salariat and the self-employed become more similar to workers in their attitudes.

Hence it seems well founded to argue that the unprecedented loss of the Swedish Social Democrats in two subsequent elections in the 2000s, and the rise of the Moderate

(Conservative) party as a dominant party on par with the Social Democrats cannot be explained by changing attitudes toward the welfare state. It is rather the Moderate shift toward the political middle ground, and their embracing of the key aspects of the Swedish welfare state, that have made their political fortune (see Lindbom's chapter, this volume).

Explaining the recent electoral misfortunes of the Swedish (and European) social democratic parties lies beyond the focus of the present chapter. But a key aspect seems to be the failure to address rising and persistent unemployment in any convincing manner. This is reflected in declining confidence in the competence of the Swedish Social Democrats in the field of (un)employment, starting already in the 1990s (Davidsson and Marx 2013; Martinsson 2009: ch. 5). Swedish voters care deeply about the welfare state, but they care even more about employment, and when seemingly facing a trade-off between social protection and employment growth, voters often opt for the latter.

In a more long-term perspective, what is indicated by the surveys is the gradual integration of the middle class in the welfare state. The postwar Swedish welfare state was always predicated on integrating large sections of the salaried groups in the core of the welfare systems. But still this was always combined with substantial resistance from the higher echelons of the class structure against higher taxes and the socialization of care and services. What seems to have taken place in the last few years is that since their main party—the Moderates—have embraced the core aspects of the welfare state, even the higher salariat and the self-employed have increasingly become supporters of a collective welfare state. The Social Democratic *Party* may be in dire straits electorally, but the social democratic welfare state is more popular than ever. However, support for the welfare state was no longer automatically translated into support for the Social Democrats, once the Moderates shed their market-liberal leanings.

A few final conclusions regarding the broader aspect of welfare state development and attitudinal change are also in order. One important observation is that the current crisis has not made Swedes feel more insecure. Perceived risks and judgments about the task performance of the welfare state show little change from 2002 to 2010, and Swedes feel less exposed to risks themselves than was the case in the economic crisis of the 1990s. This is in itself a powerful testimony to the cushioning effects of the welfare state. At the same time, it may explain why the current crisis has not been translated into any decreasing support for the government in power. Swedes feel on average no more insecure in the midst of the crisis than they did previously; hence there is little reason to blame the government.

At the same time, we should not forget that for some welfare state areas—especially those related to old age—trust is not impressive. Swedes clearly feel that the task performance of the welfare state leaves a lot to be desired in these respects. Whether this is indicative of any long-term trends is impossible to judge since we have no such data; the only thing we know is that this lack of trust has become neither worse nor better in recent years.

Taking into account the institutional changes in the Swedish welfare state over the last decade, where privatization of the service delivery of welfare policies has been substantial, we can observe that this does not seem to have any clear-cut effects on attitudes to private vs public service delivery. At least not in the sense that we observe any shifts in the aggregate views about who is the best service and care provider. Whether this is the result of different people changing in different directions, so that overall changes cancel out, or a true non-effect of the increased privatization is hard to judge. Nor do we find any tendencies for increased support for private financing, so any ideas about "spillover" effects to other aspects of the welfare state are unfounded. Neither the hopes of the market-liberal right nor the fears of the political left get much support from these findings.

Hence, no corrosive feedback effects from changing welfare policies may be detected in the Swedish public. It seems rather that the changes in institutional practices and political rhetoric that have taken place in the 1990s and 2000s have further strengthened middle-class support for the welfare state. In an ironic twist of fate, market-emulating reforms of the welfare state and the changed political rhetoric of the political right-of-center completed the full ideological integration of the middle class into the welfare state. The electoral base for any resistance against a high-tax, high-spending, collective welfare state now looks more or less eroded. At the same time, the working class and other groups with weaker market positions display weaker trust in the social insurance system, combined with their traditional support for the basic tenets of the model. Hence, we may perhaps see the current Swedish welfare state as even more of a middle-class welfare state than used to be the case.

FUTURE ANALYSES AND EXTENSIONS

Current research on attitudes to the Swedish welfare state has a relatively descriptive bent. Although it relies on theoretical notions such as feedback effects and tries to explain categorical patterns and changes in attitudes, it is to a large degree descriptive rather than explanatory. In order to become more explanatory, there are a number of points that should be addressed.

One point where more work is clearly needed concerns explanatory mechanisms. Rather little is actually known about the mechanisms that tie specific locations in the social structure with attitudes, or exactly what explains change and stability in such attitudes. In the absence of clear-cut empirically based arguments, much research in the field has been based on an explicit or implicit assumption that self-interest is the mechanism that links social location and change with attitudes. However, this assumption runs counter to much of what is now argued in widely different fields, namely that self-interest has a rather limited role in the formation of attitudes, beliefs, values, and actions. Hence, a broader conception of explanatory mechanisms and also new empirical indicators of such mechanisms are clearly needed, including values, beliefs, and norms of reciprocity.

However, here we encounter a difficult problem. We run the risk of entering endogeneity problems; that is, the risk that some of the things we are trying to explain—such as variations among social categories in attitudes—are so closely and almost by definition linked to some of the proposed explanatory mechanisms that explanations risk becoming empty and self-evident. This seems to be an important unresolved issue for this whole field of research, but one that should be tackled head-on.

What is needed in order to better analyze explanatory mechanisms? Better indicators in survey research, but also innovative method combinations. Although most would agree that combining methods is a good strategy for this field, very little actual cooperation is taking place. This may have different explanations, but it truly hampers our understanding of processes in the field. There is clearly a need to complement wide but thin survey data with more intensive experimental and/or ethnographic data, in order to study processes and mechanisms in more detail.

A second point where we also need more work is to get a better handle on the dynamics of attitudes. In this respect, it seems researchers in the field have often been unduly constrained by a mechanical application of "independent" and "dependent" variables. Research would perhaps be better served by moving toward evolutionary stories, in which the dynamics of attitudes are seen as coevolving with institutional and political change, subject to mutual and recurring feedback loops. The challenge is to do this without becoming speculative and empirically unfounded.

But dynamics are also relevant to take into account at an individual level. Currently, there are no longitudinal datasets that allow us to analyze the development of welfare attitudes along the life cycle, or even across an extended stretch of time. Comparative longitudinal datasets do simply not exist, and even existing national panels that to any extent include welfare attitudes tend to be either too short term or too sparse to be of much use. Any move to address this shortage would be most useful for the field.

Consequently and furthermore, we know little about the relative importance of the past (that is, biography), the present (that is, the current position) and the future (that is, anticipation) in forming attitudes. In particular, we know very little about how anticipated futures affect present-day attitudes. We all live in the shadow of the future, and the attitudes we hold are to some extent a function of what we believe about alternative futures and their implications for our personal lives and society at large. But very few surveys even include any questions about respondents' views about the future. The latest Swedish Welfare State Survey (2010) has incorporated items related to conceptions of the future, but so far they have not been put to analytical use.

So even if there is clearly scientific and sociopolitical value in replicating surveys of attitudes to the welfare state and keeping up the descriptive time series, a more analytical and explanatory approach would add even more value. By doing a better job at explaining patterns and dynamics, by moving to more combinatory method strategies, and by incorporating the future in explaining current attitudes, researchers of welfare attitudes would move the field substantially forward.

NOTE

1. Sections of the current chapter have previously been published in Stefan Svallfors, "A Bedrock of Support? Trends in Welfare State Attitudes in Sweden, 1981–2010," *Social Policy & Administration* 45 (2011): 806–25. They are reproduced here by permission of John Wiley & Sons, Inc.

REFERENCES

Alesina, A. and Glaeser, E. L. (2004). *Fighting Poverty in the US and Europe: A World of Difference*. Oxford: Oxford University Press.

Andress, H. J. and Heien, T. (2001). "Four Worlds of Welfare State Attitudes? A Comparison of Germany, Norway, and the United States," *European Sociological Review* 17: 337–56.

Arts, W. and Gelissen, J. (2001). "Welfare States, Solidarity and Justice Principles: Does the Type Really Matter?" *Acta Sociologica* 44: 283–99.

Bean, C. and Papadakis, E. (1998). "A Comparison of Mass Attitudes towards the Welfare State in Different Institutional Regimes, 1985–1990," *International Journal of Public Opinion Research* 10: 211–36.

Bergh, A. (2008a). *Den kapitalistiska välfärdsstaten: Om den svenska modellens historia och framtid* [*The Capitalist Welfare State: On the History and Future of the Swedish Model*], 2. uppl. Stockholm: Norstedts.

Bergh, A. (2008b). "Explaining the Survival of the Swedish Welfare State: Maintaining Political Support through Incremental Change," *Financial Theory and Practice* 32: 233–54.

Bergh, A. and Erlingsson, G. O. (2009). "Liberalization without Retrenchment: Understanding the Consensus on Swedish Welfare State Reforms," *Scandinavian Political Studies* 32: 71–93.

Bonoli, G. (2000). "Public Attitudes to Social Protection and Political Economy Traditions in Western Europe," *European Societies* 2: 431–52.

Brooks, C. (2012). "Framing Theory, Welfare Attitudes, and the United States Case," in S. Svallfors (ed.), *Contested Welfare States: Welfare Attitudes in Europe and Beyond*. Stanford, CA: Stanford University Press, 193–221.

Christiansson, L. (1969). *Konsten att dressera människor: Mentalhälsa—arbete—ideologi* [*The Art of Drilling People: Mental Health—Work—Ideology*]. Stockholm: Prisma.

Cusack, T., Iversen, T., and Rehm, P. (2006). "Risks at Work: The Demand and Supply Sides of Government Redistribution," *Oxford Review of Economic Policy* 22: 365–89.

Davidsson, J. B. and Marx, P. (2013). "Losing the Issue, Losing the Vote: Issue Competition and the Reform of Unemployment Insurance in Germany and Sweden," *Political Studies* 61: 505–22.

Dunleavy, P. (1980). "The Political Implications of Sectional Cleavages and the Growth of State Employment," *Political Studies* 28: 364–83.

Edlund, J. (1999a). *Citizens and Taxation: Sweden in Comparative Perspective*. Umeå: Umeå University.

Edlund, J. (1999b). "Progressive Taxation Farewell? Attitudes to Income Redistribution and Taxation in Sweden, Great Britain and the United States," in S. Svallfors and P. Taylor-Gooby (eds), *The End of the Welfare State? Responses to State Retrenchment*. London: Routledge, 106–34.

Edlund, J. (1999c). "Trust in Government and Welfare Regimes: Attitudes to Redistribution and Financial Cheating in the USA and Norway," *European Journal of Political Research* 35: 341–70.

Edlund, J. (2000). "Public Attitudes towards Taxation: Sweden 1981–1997," *Scandinavian Political Studies* 23: 37–65.

Edlund, J. (2006). "Trust in the Capability of the Welfare State and General Welfare State Support: Sweden 1997–2002," *Acta Sociologica* 49: 395–417.

Edlund, J. and Johansson Sevä, I. (2013). "Exploring the 'Something for Nothing' Syndrome: Confused Citizens or Free Riders? Evidence from Sweden," *Scandinavian Political Studies* 36/4: 293–319.

Edlund, J. and Svallfors, S. (2011). "Cohort, Class and Attitudes to Redistribution in Two Liberal Welfare States: Britain and the United States, 1996–2006," in A. Goerres and V. Pieter (eds), *Generational Politics and Policies: Comparative Studies of Ageing Post-Industrial Democracies*. London: Routledge, 206–24.

Erikson, R. (1974). "Welfare as a Planning Goal," *Acta Sociologica* 17: 273–88.

Esping-Andersen, G. (1990). *The Three Worlds of Welfare Capitalism*. Cambridge: Polity Press.

Evans, G. (1998). "Britain and Europe: Separate Worlds of Welfare?" *Government and Opposition* 33: 183–98.

Finseraas, H. (2008). "Immigration and Preferences for Redistribution: An Empirical Analysis of European Survey Data," *Comparative European Politics* 6: 407–31.

Fredriksson, G. (1970). "Om arbetskraftsforskning" [On Labor Force Research], *Häften för kritiska studier* 3: 30–41.

Gelissen, J. (2000). "Popular Support for Institutionalised Solidarity: A Comparison between European Welfare States," *International Journal of Social Welfare* 9: 285–300.

Hadenius, A. (1986). *A Crisis of the Welfare State? Opinions about Taxes and Public Expenditure in Sweden*. Stockholm: Almqvist & Wiksell International.

Jæger, M. M. (2006). "Welfare Regimes and Attitudes towards Redistribution: The Regime Hypothesis Revisited," *European Sociological Review* 22: 157–70.

Johansson, S. (1973). "The Level of Living Survey: A Presentation," *Acta Sociologica* 16: 211–19.

Johansson Sevä, I. (2009). "Local Contexts, Social Risks and Social Spending Preferences: A Multi-level Approach," *Acta Sociologica* 52: 249–62.

Johansson Sevä, I. (2010). "Suspicious Minds: Local Context and Attitude Variation across Swedish Municipalities," *International Journal of Social Welfare* 19: 225–35.

Johnson, B. (2010). *Kampen om sjukfrånvaron* [*The Struggle about Sick Leave*]. Lund: Arkiv.

Korpi, W. (1983). *The Democratic Class Struggle*. London: Routledge & Kegan Paul.

Kumlin, S. and Svallfors, S. (2007). "Social Stratification and Political Articulation: Why Attitudinal Class Differences Vary across Countries," in S. Mau and B. Veghte (eds), *Social Justice, Legitimacy and the Welfare State*. Aldershot: Ashgate, 19–46.

Larsen, C. A. (2006). *The Institutional Logic of Welfare Attitudes: How Welfare Regimes Influence Public Support*. Aldershot: Ashgate.

Larsen, C. A. (2008). "The Institutional Logic of Welfare Attitudes: How Welfare Regimes Influence Public Support," *Comparative Political Studies* 41: 145–68.

Laurin, U. (1986). *På heder och samvete: Skattefuskets orsaker och utbredning*. Stockholm: Norstedts.

Lundström, R. (2011). *Den kalkylerande medborgaren* [*The Calculating Citizen*]. Umeå: Umeå University.

Martinsson, J. (2009). *Economic Voting and Issue Ownership: An Integrative Approach*. Gothenburg: Department of Political Science, University of Gothenburg.

Matheson, G. and Wearing, M. (1999). "Within and Without: Labour Force Status and Political Views in Four Welfare States," in S. Svallfors and P. Taylor-Gooby (eds), *The End of the Welfare State? Responses to State Retrenchment*. London: Routledge, 135–60.

Meuleman, B. and van Oorschot, W. (2012). "Welfare Performance and Welfare Support," in S. Svallfors (ed.), *Contested Welfare States: Welfare Attitudes in Europe and Beyond*. Stanford, CA: Stanford University Press, 25–57.

Oorschot, W. van and Meuleman, B. (2012). "Welfarism and the Multidimensionality of Welfare State Legitimacy: Evidence from the Netherlands, 2006," *International Journal of Social Welfare* 21/1: 79–93.

Oskarson, M. (2013). "Stödet för socialförsäkringarna," published online in L. Wängnerud et al. (eds), *Ökat missnöje med socialförsäkringarna*. Göteborg: SOM-insitutet, Göteborg University.

Saunders, P. (1986). *Social Theory and the Urban Question*, 2nd edn. London: Hutchinson Education.

Svallfors, S. (1989). *Vem älskar välfärdsstaten? Attityder, organiserade intressen och svensk välfärdspolitik* [*Who Loves the Welfare State? Attitudes, Organized Interests and Swedish Welfare Policies*]. Lund: Arkiv.

Svallfors, S. (1991). "The Politics of Welfare Policy in Sweden: Structural Determinants and Attitudinal Cleavages," *British Journal of Sociology* 42: 609–34.

Svallfors, S. (1993). "Policy Regimes and Attitudes to Inequality: A Comparison of Three European Nations," in T. P. Boje and S. E. Olsson Hort (eds), *Scandinavia in a New Europe*. Oslo: Scandinavian University Press, 87–133.

Svallfors, S. (1995). "The End of Class Politics? Structural Cleavages and Attitudes to Swedish Welfare Policies," *Acta Sociologica* 38: 53–74.

Svallfors, S. (1996). *Välfärdsstatens moraliska ekonomi: Välfärdsopinionen i 90-talets Sverige* [*The Moral Economy of the Welfare State: Welfare Opinions in 1990s Sweden*]. Umeå: Boréa.

Svallfors, S. (1997). "Worlds of Welfare and Attitudes to Redistribution: A Comparison of Eight Western Nations," *European Sociological Review* 13: 283–304.

Svallfors, S. (2003). "Welfare Regimes and Welfare Opinions: A Comparison of Eight Western Countries," *Social Indicators Research* 64: 495–520.

Svallfors, S. (2004). "Class, Attitudes and the Welfare State: Sweden in Comparative Perspective," *Social Policy & Administration* 38: 119–38.

Svallfors, S. (2006). *The Moral Economy of Class: Class and Attitudes in Comparative Perspective*. Stanford, CA: Stanford University Press.

Svallfors, S. (2011a). "A Bedrock of Support? Trends in Welfare State Attitudes in Sweden, 1981–2010," *Social Policy & Administration* 45: 806–25.

Svallfors, S. (2011b). "Trygg, stöttande, tillitsfull? Svenskarnas syn på socialförsäkringarna" [Safe, Supportive, Trustful? Swedes' Views about Social Insurance], Underlagsrapport nr 4 till den parlamentariska socialförsäkringsutredningen. Stockholm: Statens Offentliga Utredningar.

Svallfors, S. (ed.) (2012). *Contested Welfare States: Welfare Attitudes in Europe and Beyond*. Stanford, CA: Stanford University Press.

Svallfors, S. (2013). "Government Quality, Egalitarianism, and Attitudes to Taxes and Social Spending: A European Comparison," *European Political Science Review* 5: 363–80.

Svallfors, S., Kulin, J., and Schnabel, A. (2012). "Age, Class, and Attitudes towards Government Responsibilities," in S. Svallfors (ed.), *Contested Welfare States: Welfare Attitudes in Europe and Beyond*. Stanford, CA: Stanford University Press, 158–92.

Taylor-Gooby, P. (1982). "Two Cheers for the Welfare State: Public Opinion and Private Welfare," *Journal of Public Policy* 2: 319–46.

Taylor-Gooby, P. (1983). "Legitimation Deficit, Public Opinion and the Welfare State," *Sociology* 17: 165–82.

Taylor-Gooby, P. (1985). *Public Opinion, Ideology, and State Welfare*. London: Routledge & Kegan Paul.

Zetterberg, H. (1985). *An Electorate in the Grips of the Welfare State*. Stockholm: Swedish Institute for Opinion Polls.

CHAPTER 3

POLITICAL PARTISANSHIP AND POLICY FEEDBACK

The Swedish Welfare State after Eight Years of Center-Right Government

ANDERS LINDBOM

POLITICAL PARTISANSHIP AND WELFARE STATE EXPANSION

HISTORICALLY, the Social Democratic Party has been the dominant party in Swedish politics. During the period 1932 to 2006, the party dominated the governments that were formed for 66 out of a total of 75 years. But in 2006, a center-right coalition government came to power in Sweden and ruled until 2014. How has this affected the iconic Swedish welfare state?

Before presenting data that shed light on that question, the chapter describes the evolution of comparative research on welfare state development and the most important theories on the importance of political partisanship. This is followed by a review of the empirical research on parties and welfare retrenchment. The bulk of the chapter consists of an empirical study of the dominant party in the center-right government, the Moderate Party. First, the changes it underwent in opposition are outlined, and then the welfare reforms the center-right government implemented from 2006–14 are scrutinized. These changes are largely *decremental*, i.e. small but often yearly changes, that however add up over time and hence are important, particularly in the case of unemployment benefit. The importance of decrementalism (cf. Lindblom 1959) is then illustrated by the recent proposals regarding taxation from the Social Democratic opposition which clearly has adapted to the policy legacy of the center-right parties. Last but not least, the chapter presents data on how citizens' attitudes to the public sector have

developed in Sweden over the last 20 years of more or less permanent welfare austerity: has the welfare state's legitimacy been undermined?

The first wave of comparative (large-N) research of welfare expansion explained rising welfare state expenditures in the industrialized countries in a largely functionalistic
way. Public policy was seen as the product of large structural societal forces, whereas
politics was of secondary importance at the most. As agrarian societies eroded, support
based on kinship eroded with it and the unfortunates who could not sell their labor for
a wage became largely unprotected. As a consequence, new forms of social protection
were developed. Economic growth in combination with demographic change were seen
as the root causes of welfare expansion (Wilensky 1975), not politics.

The power resource approach (PRA) sees the efforts of the labor movement as the
cause of welfare state expansion. This approach was developed in opposition to the
functionalistic argument presented above, primarily by Scandinavian scholars, and
the Swedish case is the ideal typical example of the arguments (Korpi 1981; Esping-
Andersen 1985, 1990). Contrary to the functionalistic studies above, Esping-Andersen
(1990) contends that welfare effort should not be measured in terms of expenditure
if we want to study the importance of political partisanship for welfare expansion.
Rising expenditure has not been the goal of political welfare reform, but often an
effect. The political struggles have been fought over the welfare state's effects on the
relative power between capital and labor in the labor market (*decommodification*), or
more concretely over policies like unemployment benefit, pensions, and the sickness
cash benefit that affect reservation wages. It is worthwhile pointing out that scholars
within the PRA approach—in spite of not seldom making reference to the "welfare
state"—focus heavily on social insurance schemes and rarely analyze welfare services
like health care, education, child care, or elder care. This separates it from the other
approaches presented here.

But the welfare state is also a key factor that affects which societal interests organize
and how they perceive their self-interest (*stratification*). Intuitively, we often think of
the opposite causal direction: interest groups are the driving force in the political process. But where do their interests come from? Esping-Andersen (1990) is particularly
interested in the middle class, which is often the group that determines the results of the
political elections. What determines whether the middle class will see welfare expansion
as something positive?

Swedish political history, specifically the introduction of the supplementary pension (ATP) in the 1950s, is often used to illustrate the argument. Already at this point in
time, the Swedish Social Democratic Party was concerned that the working class, their
core voters, was decreasing due to the economic transformation Sweden was undergoing into what we would today call postindustrial society. Their solution was to appeal
to white-collar employees by giving them income security at retirement by introducing an income-related pension scheme. After the introduction of the ATP, the Social
Democrats gained new supporters among middle-class voters and this helped them to
keep their political dominance (cf. Svensson 1994; Korpi and Palme 1998).[1]

Despite their belief in the welfare state's effects on interest formation, Esping-Andersen and Korpi and other researchers in the power resource approach believe that the forces that drove the expansion of the welfare state also are necessary to maintain it. But exactly on this point, the dominance of the PRA is challenged by the theory of *The New Politics of the Welfare State* (*NP*) (Pierson 1994, 1996, 2001). Pierson argues that the political situation today is fundamentally different from the situation during welfare state expansion. The welfare state has created its own political support that makes it quite resilient to retrenchment and hence, according to Pierson, a strong labor movement is not necessary to preserve it. Pierson thus takes the analysis of stratification a step further than Esping-Andersen himself did.

The basic logic of Pierson's argument is that before generous public social insurance such as pensions was introduced, many different policy solutions were possible. Today the situation is different. During their working life, current seniors have based their behavior on the expectation that the public pension system will take care of them when they became old. If the welfare state had been organized differently, they would have acted differently and saved up for their old age, but they cannot now change their historical behavior. Unless a party is willing to make these citizens "penniless" and meet the reactions that this action would entail, it is impossible to dismantle existing pension systems. Today the political reform agenda is therefore comparatively restricted. This phenomenon is known as path dependence and is particularly apparent in the area of pensions, but Pierson's explanation of welfare state resilience is based on the same basic idea.

To sum up, there is a general agreement in the current welfare literature regarding the importance of the existing organization of the welfare state for the electoral support of the welfare state. But there is nevertheless a theoretical disagreement on whether this means that the importance of political partisanship for welfare reform has declined. One central issue in this debate concerns the character of party preferences.

Exogenous or Endogenous Party Interests?

The power resource approach essentially conceptualizes parties as class-based organizations. However, confessional parties, such as the Christian Democratic parties on the European continent, use the religious dimension to appeal to all classes including the working class. While their welfare policies are designed to generate cooperation between employers and employees, in Korpi's (2006: 176) words: "to be credible the confessional strategy for attracting workers' votes had to place some limits on employers' choices, limitations tending to give confessional parties a middling position along the left-right continuum." In Korpi's conceptualization, the behavior of the Christian

Democratic parties seems to be primarily strategic whereas in the more empirical and detailed account of van Kersbergen (1995), Catholic ideology, e.g. subsidiarity and the non-primacy of the market, seems to be important for policy.

Similarly, in order to win elections, secular center-right parties are expected to try to attract the support of the median voter, i.e. to adapt to welfare state popularity (Korpi 1981). This adaptation is however only strategic; their real preferences remain unchanged. Korpi (2006) makes it clear that the PRA is deductive when it comes to assigning preferences and interests to actors. Once center-right parties have won an election, we should therefore expect them to implement radical cutbacks (cf. Korpi and Palme 2003). But unless the center-right parties' only aim to win occasional elections or middle-class voters can be cheated time and again, this does not seem to be a reasonable proposition.

Lindbom (2008) argues, on the other hand, that we cannot rule out the possibility that the change of preferences is "real." He takes inspiration from Rothstein's argument (1998) that what citizens view as rational as well as appropriate depends on their context, and generalizes this proposition to political parties. Over longer time periods, generational change may lead to changing views of what is "natural." For example, the Moderates were generally hostile to public child care during the 1960s, but the current leadership put their own children in such institutions. Whereas it was considered unnatural to do so in the 1960s (a woman's place was in the home), in the twenty-first century it is not (Hinnfors 1992). That is, certain parts of the ideology remain (largely) intact: the family is a central societal institution and the state should not intervene in how the husband and wife organize family life. Other parts of the ideology change, however: the belief that child care institutions are bad for children. The example illustrates that ideology probably often changes in one respect but not in others. It is reasonable to make a distinction between the core values on the one hand and views regarding reality on the other (Tingsten 1941). Whereas the first largely tend to be highly stable, the latter are probably much more volatile.

The supplementary pension (ATP) provides another example of changing preferences. The center-right parties' proposals in the 1950s argued that the state should only be responsible for providing basic security for pensioners. However, the Social Democratic proposal that public pensions should also provide earnings-related benefits prevailed. In the 1990s the pension scheme faced a crisis: it would go bankrupt if changes were not implemented. However, the existing pension system had matured and the center-right parties concluded that the path dependence of the pension scheme meant that it could not be reformed to fit their preferences from the 1950s (Lindbom 2001). The point of the example is that the distinction between a real change of preferences and strategic change largely disappears in a highly path-dependent context. Once a publicly financed earnings-related scheme has been institutionalized and crowded out private alternatives, a significant proportion of risk-aversive center-right parties' core voters will be particularly affected if it is taken away (Baldwin 1990; Rothstein 1998; Lindbom 2009).

Empirical Analyses of Welfare State Retrenchment

Korpi and Palme's analysis of welfare retrenchment (2003) suggests that political partisanship remains important for welfare state generosity, even in a statistically controlled welfare regime, but also that the cutbacks are larger in liberal welfare states than in universal welfare states. Others use similar data to confirm the result (Allan and Scruggs 2004). These analyses calculate the generosity of benefits for certain types of households with average incomes, but only include certain aspects of the sickness cash and the unemployment benefit. Hence large parts of the welfare state are left out of the analyses. On the other hand, effects of tax cuts are included in the analyses. Other studies focus on expenditures. Swank (2003) does not find a partisan effect on welfare expenditure (controlled for unemployment etc.), but remarks that several significant independent variables, e.g. corporatism, correlate with the variable political partisanship.

But quantitative studies of the importance of party policy have certain weaknesses. While it is possible to refine the analysis by making separate analyses of different geographical contexts, the number of countries studied then becomes so small that much of the benefit of the statistical method is lost. Hence Lindbom (2008) suggests that in-depth case studies provide a more fruitful approach to the question of the importance of partisan politics for welfare retrenchment than a more superficial analysis of many, or at least more, countries.

Balslev's case study (2002) of cuts in twelve Swedish social policies is based on budget forecasts on the size of the cutbacks. The total cutbacks undertaken by the Social Democrats (1994–8) are then found to be greater than the cutbacks of the center-right government (1991–4). A study of Denmark and the Netherlands shows similar results (Green-Pedersen 2002). Lindbom (2008) shows that the political conflict regarding the Swedish welfare state since the 1980s has focused on compensation levels and on whether to allow private alternatives in the welfare services, not on issues of dismantling the welfare state. In fact, the Social Democratic government (1994–2006) implemented lower replacement rates than the "neoliberal" Moderate Party proposed during the 1980s. Thus the hypothesis that a "universal" welfare state makes a "neoliberal" party fairly moderate gains support even when tested under very unfavorable conditions, i.e. in the most liberal Swedish party during its most neoliberal period. Hence Lindbom (2008) cannot confirm the stereotype that all right-wing parties are more or less disguised versions of Thatcher and Reagan's neoliberal parties. A comparison between the Moderates' policy proposals and the legislative changes implemented by the Conservative Party in the UK during the 1980s provides further evidence for this.

These conclusions receive some support from some statistical studies. Brooks and Manza (2006) show that the varying policy preferences of the electorate tend to explain much of the variation in social spending levels between countries—no matter which parties are in government. Jensen (2010) even shows that the right-wing governments in the period 1980–2000 in the Nordic countries spent *more* on social policy than the left parties during their time in government. In contrast, right-wing governments in countries that have traditionally right dominance tend to cut expenditure the most.

To sum up, there is mixed evidence regarding partisan effects on welfare retrenchment. How retrenchment is measured seems to matter a great deal for the empirical results. Party politics seems to be better at explaining changes of net replacement rates of important cash transfers than more general changes of welfare expenditures (including expenditures for welfare services). But even if parties of the right tend to be less generous than parties to the left in the same country, this does not mean that all parties in the same ideological tradition—e.g. conservative parties—but acting in different countries strive to achieve the same replacement rates (cf. Swenson 2002).

In what follows, the ideological changes of the dominant party of the center-right government—*Moderaterna*—are presented, and then the measures of welfare reform taken by the government (2006–14) are scrutinized. This analysis sheds light on the restricted room for maneuver for a center-right government in a "universal" welfare state (Lindbom and Rothstein 2004).

The "New" and More Moderate Party

Reformulating the Party Platform in Political Opposition (2003–6)

After the debacle of the 2002 election when the Moderates received only 15.2 per cent of the votes, compared to 22.9 percent in 1998, the new leadership re-evaluated its proposals. They came to the conclusion that "the doubts of many voters that the Moderates' proposals for tax cuts were compatible with a sound state of the public finances was one reason that the party lost voters in the election in 2002" (Reinfeldt, Odenberg, and Borg 2004). As a consequence of this analysis, the party reformulated its core policy: promises of future tax cuts were reduced significantly, but tax cuts have also been retargeted toward people with low or average wages.

Moreover, the party no longer proposes to cut state subsidies to local government, since that might affect the quality of education, health care, and so on which are the responsibility of the local governments. The quality of these services has been at the forefront of recent elections in Sweden. It is clear that most voters want public spending to increase—not decrease—in these areas (Svallfors 2011 and in this volume).

In a speech to the party congress in the autumn 2005, Reinfeldt (the party leader) put a strong emphasis on the need to make policies trustworthy. Policy reform has to be possible to implement, trustworthy, and appear to be "safe" to the electorate. Or as he memorably put it: "I didn't become a conservative because I believed in the idea of the revolution" (Reinfeldt 2005). The new party leader wanted to be seen as pragmatic and in favor of gradual change.

In many ways, incremental reform seems to be one of the major differences between the "new" Moderates and the party during the 1990s. The party used to take a very theoretical starting point: what type of (welfare) arrangements would economic theory suggest? This way of thinking starts from a *tabula rasa* and constructs an "ideal" system (irrespective of empirical context). Since 2003, the party has started rather from what it conceives to be problematic with the actual situation in Sweden and tried to "patch" one problem after the other (piecemeal engineering). Faith in theoretical models is much lower than it was around 1990 when the party expected dynamic effects from tax cuts and productivity gains from private competition in the production of welfare services in its budget proposals to finance tax cuts (Lindbom 2008).

Apart from that, there are some indications that the party does not want to change the existing welfare state in a fundamental way (i.e. toward a more liberal welfare state with more means-testing and private insurance schemes). The tendency of means-tested benefits to create poverty traps goes against the party's ambition to increase the incentives to work (Lindbom 2008).

The political conflict with the Social Democrats regarding social insurance is not really about the fundamentals such as "universalism," but is rather on how big the self-risk should be for the insured. The Moderates wanted to increase the—or as they see it rather create a—difference between income from working and living on a benefit, particularly for low-income workers. Both their tax cuts and their cutbacks fit this profile.

But the proof is in the pudding. What changes has the welfare state gone through during the eight years of center-right government?

The Center-Right Government 2006–14

Welfare policies in Sweden come in two kinds: welfare services (e.g. health care, education, child and elder care) and cash transfers. The resources for welfare services have continued to expand since 2006 (*Dagens Samhälle* 2014: 6) and hence this analysis will focus on the cash transfers. Pensions are the dominating cash transfer, but no major changes have occurred in this policy area.[2] Since 1998 there has been an agreement between the Social Democratic Party and the four center-right parties that a consensus among the five is necessary in order to make any changes to the existing pension system.

Instead this essay will focus on unemployment benefit and sickness benefit (cf. Korpi and Palme 2003). The legislated replacement rate of *unemployment benefit* used to be 80 percent throughout, but the new government—just like it promised in the 2006 election campaign—has lowered it for the long-term unemployed. After 200 days of unemployment, the replacement rate decreases to 75 percent and after 300 days it is further lowered to 65 percent.

But in comparison, in the US the replacement rate is around 50 percent for the benefit's entire duration whereas the contributory benefit in the UK is a very low standardized amount (£71/week if the client is aged 25 or more). Hence it is obvious that the center-right government has not even been close to making the legislated replacement rate of the unemployment benefit as low as it is in the so-called "liberal" welfare states (Esping-Andersen 1990; US Social Security Administration 2014).

However, the maximum benefit is also important for medium- and high-income earners. In October 2006, the newly elected government nullified the raised maximum benefit that the Social Democrats had implemented from July 1, 2006. On the one hand, this is an important change since the maximum benefit had been increased by 7 percent. But on the other hand, the fact that the increase had hardly been established before it was taken away means that it had not yet become perceived as an established social right. If the lower maximum benefit was politically correct Social Democratic policy in June, it was difficult to argue that it was impossible to live on in October the same year.

The main change to the *sickness cash benefit* was not related to the replacement rates, but to the duration of the scheme. The duration used to be unlimited, but the new government introduced a time cap of 2½ years. If we compare this to the situation in other countries, however, this change does not seem to be particularly neoliberal. A report from LO (the blue-collar union) states that "(i)t is unclear whether any other country than Sweden and Ireland lacks a limit in the duration of the sickness cash benefit" (LO 2007). In all the other Nordic countries, which are usually argued to have welfare states that are very similar to the Swedish one, there are time limits that restrict the benefit to a maximum of about a year (LO 2007).

To sum up, the legislative changes to unemployment benefit and sickness cash benefit have been gradual or, as I prefer to call them, decremental. But by 2014 the basic character of the unemployment benefit had been undermined. The two arguments are not contradictory. The most important changes to the benefit have not come through parliamentary decisions but through the lack of them. The maximum benefit for unemployment has not been raised as much as the wage levels have increased for a very long time. The consequence is that the income security of average wage earners has decreased substantially. The following paragraphs will focus on this critical case: unemployment benefit.

The Hollowing Out of the Earnings-Related Character of the Public Benefit

For unemployment benefit, the net replacement rate for an average worker has fallen rather dramatically (13 percentage points) between 2005 and 2010, i.e. during the time of the center-right government. The consequence is that the replacement rate is no longer higher than the average level among seventeen comparable countries (Ferrarini et al. 2012). A large part of the decline registered by the PRA scholars is however the effect of the EITC. Since the unemployed did not enjoy the tax cut but the employed did, the unemployed relatively speaking became worse off, but in absolute terms their benefit did not decrease.

Since the maximum benefit has not been adjusted to follow increasing wages, in 2013 today only 11 percent of full-time employees have incomes low enough to receive the legislated 80 percent replacement rate. The rest will receive the maximum benefit (680 kronor per day) (Arbetslöshetskassornas samorganisation 2013) so the system has almost entirely stopped being earnings-related. During the 1990s, the Social

Democratic governments had already allowed the maximum benefit of unemployment benefit to be hollowed out. According to some estimations, this benefit was one of those most targeted for cutbacks (Lindbom 2007). After the crisis, the maximum benefit was raised in 2001 and then again in 2006. But in hindsight, the impact of the center-right government's nondecisions suggests that the Social Democratic Party made a considerable strategic mistake when it implemented the last raise of the maximum benefit as late as in the last months of the election campaign. It seems fairly obvious that the idea was that this would mobilize the core troops of the party in order to win the election, but once it did not, it made the unemployment benefit very vulnerable.

As a consequence of the hollowing out of the earnings-related benefit, a new development in the welfare mix has taken place. It is not so much a development in the direction of a liberal welfare state with individual insurance as toward a corporatist one. Many unions have institutionalized mandatory group insurance schemes for all members of the union and the associated unemployment fund. The first group insurance for unemployment was created in 2001 and by 2007 they had spread over large parts of the labor market. Hence this implicit privatization of the earnings-related unemployment benefit started before the center-right government came to power in 2006, but the more recent developments have of course made it increasingly important.

Interestingly, the regulations of the group insurance are very similar to those of the public scheme. The duration is however shorter (100–200 days), but most importantly, the maximum benefit is higher and therefore many will actually receive 80 percent replacement of their earlier income. Whereas the monthly maximum of the public scheme is less than 15.000 kronor, the maximum monthly benefit in the white-collar groups insurances varies between 50.000 kr and 100.000 kr whereas it is 35.000 kr for the blue-collar workers unions (Rasmussen 2013).

Compared to a public scheme, the individual schemes redistribute about as much. The varying risks of unemployment and wage levels *between* unions, however, affect costs and/or benefits. Most importantly, whereas all white-collar unions are able to offer group insurances, several blue-collar unions that have higher and more fluctuating unemployment risks cannot, e.g. the industrial workers union (Metall), the unions for construction workers (Byggnads), and the union for employees in hotels and restaurants (Davidsson 2014). Whereas the first two represent relatively high-income blue-collar workers, the members of the last have low incomes.

Universalism

In 2006, the center-right government decreased the public subsidy of the unemployment benefit scheme. The consequence was that membership fees had to be increased and that around half a million people left the unemployment insurance. The proportion of the labor force that are members of the insurance scheme fell from 81 to 72 percent (Lindgren 2013). Sometimes it is argued that this shows that the center-right government wants to change the universal character of the Swedish welfare state.

But as Bergqvist's article "The Myth of the Universal Welfare State" (1990) makes clear, Swedish unemployment benefit has never been universal, and the reason for this is a strong resistance from the labor movement.[3] This is contrary to the common perception that in Sweden, strong social democratic governments have created a universal welfare state. She therefore argues that Esping-Andersen and Korpi (1987) confuse the description of Scandinavian real welfare states with the theoretical universal model. Ever since 1934, the Swedish unemployment insurance has had eligibility criteria: to qualify for the unemployment benefit, an unemployed person must have been a member of an unemployment insurance scheme and have satisfied certain work requirements.

In fact, during the 1970s and the early 1980s, the percentage of the workforce that were members of an unemployment fund was comparable to now, i.e. around 70 percent. Coverage gradually increased and peaked during the Swedish economic crisis (87 percent in 1998). Once the crisis was over, membership declined. At the time of the center-right government's induced increase in the fees for membership, the ratio had declined and was back at about the same level as before the crisis (81 percent) (Lindgren 2013). Since 2008 the number of members has been increasing somewhat (AEA 2012).

But which groups stopped paying membership: those with a low risk of becoming unemployed or those who earn so little that they could not take the cost increase? If it was the latter group, it would register in increasing costs of the social assistance scheme. While social assistance spending (in constant prices) was almost 25 percent higher in the middle of the financial crisis in 2010 than in 2006 when the center-right parties formed the new government, spending was still 17 percent lower than in 1997 when the Social Democrats were in power. The costs have remained fairly stable thereafter (National Board of Health 2013).

Summing up, decremental change has occurred within the sickness cash benefit and unemployment benefit. The center-right government has not tried to legislate on radical changes that would change the Swedish welfare state into a liberal one. By non-decisions they have, however, allowed the long-term hollowing out of the maximum benefit of public unemployment insurance to continue, and the power resource approach suggests that this may produce large feedback effects in the future (Korpi and Palme 1998).

Moderate Room for Maneuver?

Were the changes of the Moderate Party's political rhetoric from 2003–6 real or were they deceiving the voters? My answer is that: (1) in the short term the party can only hope to achieve incremental change and it realizes this; but also (2) in the long term, the party does (eventually) change society. The goal does not seem to be a residual welfare state, but they still want to reduce taxes (cf. Lindbom 2008).

However, the argument stressing path dependence should not be taken too far. As Pierson (1994) stressed, there are the possibilities of decremental (and blame-avoiding) reforms and of systemic reform that weaken political support for the welfare state and hence open future opportunities to reform it. One interpretation of the center-right government's changes to unemployment benefit is that they had a systemic character: (1) the reduction of public subsidies led to higher membership fees and thus reduced the incentive to be a member of unemployment benefits, and/or member of the union; and (2) reducing the maximum benefit may make unemployment benefit less interesting to the middle class and hence make it more vulnerable in the future. Another interpretation is however also possible: the center-right parties had to finance their tax cuts and they used the same methods to reduce spending as the previous Social Democratic government had successfully used (Lindbom 2007, 2011). The two explanations are moreover not mutually exclusive.

A counter-argument to the "systemic retrenchment" interpretation is that the center-right government also could have changed the legislation regarding job security (LAS) if it wanted to weaken the unions, but it chose not to do so. The difference between the LAS and the change in unemployment benefits is that only the latter results in decreased public spending. Furthermore, the subsidy for the unemployment benefit scheme has been increased again and reforms to health insurance increase the incentive to join the unemployment insurance (Parliamentary proposal 2008/9: 1). The criticized differentiated fees for unemployment funds were abolished which entailed a cost of almost 3 billion kronor (*Dagens Arbete* 2014), and this will obviously increase the incentives to join the schemes.

How Decremental Policy Changes Still Matter: The Social Democratic Opposition in 2013–14

The argument that policy changes tend to be incremental is sometimes misunderstood as implying that the changes are not important. But in order for the incrementalist argument to be consistent, the next government will tend to make only incremental policy changes as well. That means that if a government has had eight years to make benefits less generous and to lower taxes, it is likely that it will take the next government many years to raise them back to where they were to start with.

The situation of the current Social Democratic Party leadership in Sweden can illustrate this argument. The center-right government has implemented income tax cuts (EITC) five times over. In the view of the Social Democrats, these changes add up to a considerable drainage of public finance and they have opposed all five waves of tax cuts. However, they are not promising to nullify the tax cuts. Instead they only propose to diminish the tax cuts just for people with a very high income, i.e. on the margin. The reduced tax income for the state after the first four tax cuts has been estimated at 70 billion kronor and the Social Democratic clawback has been estimated to take only 2.5 billion of those back (cf. Lindbom 2011).

In a television interview the party's leader, Stefan Löfven, has argued that "Every new government has to accept the situation at hand. Reinfeldt's government has not dismantled all the policies that they disfavored while they were in opposition." Löfven also argued that households have adapted their consumption to their new level of income and that for this reason a new government cannot restore the earlier tax levels (*Agenda* 2013).

To sum up, the leadership of the Social Democratic Party argues that the center-right government's tax cuts have decreased its freedom of maneuver. The argument has been illustrated with the EITC, but the same is true for tax deductions for household services (RUT), the abolished real estate tax, and the increased market share of independent schools etc. At least some of the party activists do not want to acknowledge these restrictions, but the party leadership is relatively autonomous when it comes to deciding on policy proposals (cf. Katz and Mair 1995 and 2009).

The Future of the Swedish Welfare State

In theory, the Swedish welfare state is largely designed to provide income security, i.e. even people with relatively high incomes should not have to drastically change their way of living in case they are between jobs or are sick and unable to work for a couple of months. But as we saw above, the reality of Swedish unemployment benefit has become very different from the theory. The trend in sickness benefit is the same, but it still provides most clients with an 80 percent replacement rate (Lindgren 2013).

Both the theoretical approaches that this chapter has focused on place significant importance on feedback mechanisms. With the changes to the Swedish welfare state that have been described above in mind, they give different forecasts, however. The power resource approach expects the legitimacy of the welfare state to be undermined by the declining replacement rates over the last 20 to 25 years (Korpi and Palme 1998) whereas the New Politics approach would not expect citizens' attitudes to change, at least not in the short term.

SOM-data provides a long yearly time series (1986–2013) for the question "Would you like to diminish the Swedish public sector?". If we combine that data with yearly data on the replacement rate of the unemployment benefit for an average worker's wages (CWED data), then we get the graph presented in Figure 3.1.

In the year 1990 negative opinion regarding the public sector reached its maximum and a majority (56 percent) agreed with the statement that the public sector should be diminished. The replacement rate of the unemployment benefit also reached its maximum that year. After 1990, the share of the population that wanted to diminish the public sector decreased, and from 1995–2009 it was relatively stable at around 30 percent. There seems to be no effect produced by the center-right government's decision to make the unemployment benefit less generous (c.5 percentage points) in 1993, nor by the raising of maximum benefit in 2001/2002 (increasing the benefit around 10 percentage points). And when a center-right government again decreased the replacement rate in 2007 (by 5–6 percentage points) it does not register either. Since 2010 however, the share of people that agree that the public sector should be diminished has been decreasing and in 2012 the share that agreed was only 21 percent. In short, the pattern in Figure 3.1

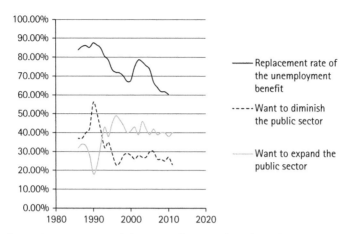

FIGURE 3.1 The replacement rate of the unemployment benefit and citizens' attitudes toward the public sector.

Sources: Top line: Scruggs et al. (2014). Lower two lines: Nilsson (2014).

suggests that the higher the replacement rate of the unemployment benefit, the more negative the public opinion regarding the public sector (r=0,77***).[4]

As mentioned before, the development of sickness benefit follows the same general direction as unemployment benefit, but the changes are not as accentuated. The results also remain the same if we use other indicators of welfare state legitimacy. Svallfors (2011) concludes that support for a collective financing of social insurances is strong and increasing. Moreover, the perception that social insurance schemes work well and that they should be publicly financed is much more common among white-collar workers than blue-collar workers.

While at first it seems like the PRA has gotten the effect all wrong, a revised version which allows for a lagged and weaker effect may perform better. Maybe the effect is mediated by citizens' knowledge of the situation, and it takes considerable time for this knowledge to establish itself.

But it is quite clear that the data is more in line with the New Politics approach. Pierson's argument was however rather unclear regarding the exact nature of the long-term feedback mechanism. In the thermostatic public response model (Soroka and Wlezien 2010), people's preferences are assumed to be shaped by policy in such a way that they for example react to a decrease in policy by increasing preferences for more of that policy (cf. Bendz 2013 and 2015). But while the immediate reaction may be that citizens want to spend more, in the long run it would seem to be irrational to stay willing to contribute to a system that is considered inefficient (Kumlin 2007).

If we switch focus from understanding change over time to understanding the level of legitimacy of the Swedish public sector, it appears to be likely that legitimacy is rather connected to the universal welfare services, e.g. education and health care, than it is to social insurance like the unemployment benefit. The explanation of positive welfare attitudes then is less the self-interest of the middle class and more citizens' perceptions of procedural justice (Kumlin and Rothstein 2005). Larsen (2008) points out that unemployment benefit raises questions about deservedness which makes the policy less popular among citizens, and this may partly explain why this benefit is relatively easy to target for retrenchment (Vis 2009).

This would also provide a partial answer to why the center-right government managed to win the election in 2006 and be re-elected in 2010 in spite of having implemented cutbacks in unemployment benefit and sickness benefit. The center-right government has argued that the reforms were implemented to strengthen the incentives of proper behavior of the clients of these programs and that they would lead to an increase in employment which will help to provide the "core of the welfare state," the welfare services, with enough resources in the future.

Conclusion: Reinfeldt Is Not Thatcher

This chapter presents the debate within welfare research regarding the importance of partisanship for welfare state reform in times of permanent austerity. In contrast to the power resource approach, a version of the New Politics approach is developed that argues that the importance of political partisanship has declined in Sweden because of the specific context of the "universal" welfare state specific context. There are strong theoretical reasons to believe that the center-right parties' preferences have changed over time and in line with the changed preferences of a significant portion of the electorate.[5]

The Moderate Party's primary concern is that the (potential) income from work should be higher than the (potential) income from social insurance schemes. It believes that this is both fair and that it has desirable effects (provides incentives to work). The exact level of compensation is not determined by that point, but the varying proposals at varying times are influenced both by what is politically possible and how reality is perceived (e.g. the unemployment level and its trend).

This theory suggests that parties primarily propose gradual (incremental) changes in the existing political institutions to address perceived problems (cf. Lindblom 1959). But incrementalism does not mean that politics is unimportant. Although the Moderate leader Reinfeldt is not Thatcher, he is not a Social Democrat either. The political right and left perceive various things as social problems and their ideologies tend to give rise to various proposals on marginal changes. For this reason there will probably always be conflict about marginal issues regarding the welfare state.

In the long run, more dramatic changes to the welfare state can be made. But just as it took decades to build the current welfare state, it will probably take decades to fundamentally restructure it. The political implication of the analysis is that the "universal" welfare state's general political resilience is far stronger than the power resource approach claims. This mechanism where the popularity of the universal welfare state creates a pressure on right parties to promise that the welfare state is safe in their hands should be expected to be important in all the Scandinavian countries and probably in many other European countries as well. A neoliberal party has restricted room for maneuver.

However, the political context in the 2010s has partly changed due to the incremental changes that the Swedish welfare state has gone through during the period of center-right rule. The Social Democratic party leadership does not think it can attack the implemented tax cuts head-on. Hence this party is now experiencing the feedback effects of the center-right policies, just like the center-right parties were forced to do during the long period of Social Democratic reign.

NOTES

1. This explanation differs from the cultural explanations, which argue that Sweden is a Social Democratic welfare state because the Swedes—unlike, for example, Americans—are predisposed to love equality and hence the welfare state. Instead, Esping-Andersen sees the welfare state as the result of a long historical process in which the outcome could have been different.
2. The earned-income tax does not benefit the retired, which has clearly upset many of them, but this reform is nonetheless not an example of welfare retrenchment.
3. The unions see voluntarism as necessary to keep administrative powers over unemployment benefit, which in turn provides a selective incentive for the employed to be union members (Rothstein 1992).
4. Recently, certain researchers have started to question whether the empirical relationships found by Korpi and Palme hold over time (Kenworthy 2011; Marx et al. 2013).
5. It is also quite possible that they have come to see large parts of the welfare state as conducive to economic growth. In an interview with the Minister of Finance, he repeatedly made such remarks (see Lindbom 2008). According to the Varieties of Capitalism argument, different types of capitalism can be effective and enjoy broad political support, which again questions the assumption often made by the PRA that all conservative parties are the same irrespective of the context (Hall and Soskice 2001; Korpi and Palme 2003).

REFERENCES

AEA (2012). *Arbetslöshetsrapport 2012*. Stockholm: Akademikernas a-kassa.

Agenda (2013). "Löfven: Ni får behålla pengarna," August 25, <www.svt.se/agenda/lofven-ni-far-behalla-pengarna>.

Allan, J. P. and Scruggs, L. (2004). "Political Partisanship and Welfare State Reform in Advanced Industrial Societies," *American Journal of Political Science* 48/3: 496–512.

Arbetslöshetskassornas samorganisation (2013). "Rapport över kompensationsgrad vecka 35/2013," December 20.

Baldwin, P. (1990). *The Politics of Social Solidarity*. Cambridge: Cambridge University Press.

Balslev, A. (2002). "Gensyn med blame avoidance-hypotesen: En empirisk analyse af nedskäringer i 12 svenske overførselsindkomster," Master's thesis, Institut for Statskundskab, Århus.

Bendz, A. (2015). "Paying Attention to Politics," *Policy Studies Journal*, forthcoming.

Bendz, A. (2014). "Slimming down the Giant." Presentation at the ECPR Joint Sessions, Salamanca, April 10–15.

Bergqvist, C. (1990). "Myten om den universella svenska välfärdsstaten," *Statsvetenskaplig tidskrift* 3: 223–33.

Brooks, C. and Manza, J. (2006). "Social Policy Responsiveness in Developed Democracies," *American Sociological Review* 71/3: 474–94.

Dagens Arbete (2014). "A-kassan: från medlemsras till socialbidragsnivå," July 4.

Dagens Samhälle (2014). "Rekordstora skatteintäkter räcker inte till," no. 6.

Davidsson, J. B. (2014). "The Limits of Solidarity: Unions and the Rise of Private Unemployment Insurance in Sweden." Paper presented at NOPSA 2014, Göteborg.

Esping-Andersen, G. (1985). *Politics Against Markets: The Social Democratic Road to Power.* Princeton: Princeton University Press.

Esping-Andersen, G. (1990). *The Three Worlds of Welfare Capitalism.* Cambridge: Polity Press.

Esping-Andersen, G. and Korpi, W. (1987). "From Poor Relief to Institutional Welfare States: The Development of Scandinavian Social Policy," in R. Erikson, E. J. Hansen, S. Ringen, and H. Uusitalo (eds), *The Scandinavian Model: Welfare States and Welfare Research.* Armonk, NY: M. E. Sharpe, 39–74.

Ferrarini, T., Nelson, K., Sjöberg, O., and Palme, J. (2012). "Sveriges Socialförsäkringar i ett jämförande perspektiv." Background paper for Den parlamentariska Socialförsäkringsutredningen.

Green-Pedersen, C. (2002). *The Politics of Justification.* Amsterdam: Amsterdam University Press.

Hall, P. A. and Soskice, D. (2001). *Varieties of Capitalism: The Institutional Origins of Comparative Advantage.* Oxford: Oxford University Press.

Hinnfors, J. (1992). *Familjepolitik: Samhällsförändringar och partistrategier 1960–1990.* Stockholm: Almqvist & Wiksell International.

Jensen, C. (2010). "Issue Compensation and Right-Wing Government Spending," *European Journal of Political Research* 49/2: 282–99.

Katz, R. S. and Mair, P. (1995). "Changing Models of Party Organization and Party Democracy: The Emergence of the Cartel Party," *Party Politics* 1/1: 5–28.

Katz, R. S. and Mair, P. (2009). "The Cartel Party Thesis: A Restatement," *Perspectives on Politics* 7/4: 753–66.

Kenworthy, L. (2011). *Progress for the Poor.* Oxford: Oxford University Press.

Kersbergen, K. van (1995). *Social Capitalism: A Study on Christian Democracy and the Welfare State.* London: Routledge.

Korpi, W. (1981). *Den demokratiska klasskampen: Svensk politik i jämförande perspektiv.* Stockholm: Tiden.

Korpi, W. (2006). "Power-Resources and Employer-Centered Approaches in Explanations of Welfare States and Varieties of Capitalism," *World Politics* 58/2: 167–206.

Korpi, W. and Palme, J. (1998). "The Paradox of Redistribution and Strategies of Equality," *American Sociological Review* 63/5: 661–87.

Korpi, W. and Palme, J. (2003). "New Politics and Class Politics in the Context of Austerity and Globalization," *American Political Science Review* 97/3: 425–46.

Kumlin, S. (2007). "Overloaded or Undermined? European Welfare States in the Face of Performance Dissatisfaction," in S. Svallfors (ed.), *The Political Sociology of the Welfare State: Institution, Social Cleavages, and Orientations.* Stanford: Stanford University Press, 80–116.

Kumlin, S. and Rothstein, B. (2005). "Making and Breaking Social Capital," *Comparative Political Studies* 38/4: 339–65.

Larsen, C. A. (2008). "The Institutional Logic of Welfare Attitudes," *Comparative Political Studies* 41/2: 145–68.

Lindblom, C. E. (1959). "The Science of 'Muddling Through,'" *Public Administration Review* 19/2: 79–88.

Lindbom, A. (2001). "De borgerliga partierna och pensionsreformen," in J. Palme (ed.), *Hur blev den stora kompromissen möjlig?* Stockholm: Pensionsforum, 52–87.

Lindbom, A. (2007). "Obfuscating Retrenchment," *Journal of Public Policy* 27/2: 127–50.

Lindbom, A. (2008). "The Swedish Conservative Party and the Welfare State," *Government & Opposition* 43/4: 539–60.

Lindbom, A. (2009). "Den reformerade bostadspolitiken," in P. Santesson-Wilson and G. Ó. Erlingsson (eds), *Reform*. Stockholm: Norstedts, 138–50.

Lindbom, A. (2011). *Systemskifte?* Lund: Studentlitteratur.

Lindbom, A. and Rothstein, B. (2004). "The Mysterious Survival of the Swedish Welfare State." Paper presented at the American Political Science Association (APSA), Chicago, September 2–5.

Lindgren, K.-O. (2013). "Nya villkor för socialförsäkringarna?" *Ekonomisk debatt* 4: 18–31.

LO (2007). "Sjukas rätt till stöd: En idéskrift om morgondagens sjukförsäkring." Stockholm: LO.

Marx, I., Salanauskaite, L., and Verbist, G. (2013). "The Paradox of Redistribution Revisited," IZA Discussion Paper, No. 7414.

National Board of Health (2013). "Ekonomiskt bistånd: Årsstatistik 2012." Stockholm: Socialstyrelsen.

Nilsson, Lennart (2014). "Starkt stöd för välfärdsstaten," in Annika Bergström and Henrik Oscarsson (eds), *Mittfåra och marginal*. Göteborg: SOM-institutet, Göteborgs Universitet, 281–93.

Parliamentary proposal (2008/9). Budgetpropositionen för 2009: 1.

Pierson P. (1994). *Dismantling the Welfare State? Reagan, Thatcher and the Politics of Retrenchment*. Cambridge: Cambridge University Press.

Pierson P. (1996). "The New Politics of the Welfare State," *World Politics* 48/2: 143–79.

Pierson, P. (ed.) (2001). *The New Politics of the Welfare State*. Oxford: Oxford University Press.

Rasmussen, P. (2013). "Privatizing Unemployment Protection: The Rise of Private Unemployment Insurance in Denmark and Sweden," CCWS Working Paper no. 2014-83, Aalborg University.

Reinfeldt, F. (2005). "Anförande på den moderata partistämman" [Speech at the Moderate Party meeting].

Reinfeldt, F., Odenberg, M., and Borg, A. (2004). "Vi lägger om vår ekonomiska politik," *DN-debatt*, March 4.

Rothstein, B. (1992). "Labour Market Institutions and Working-Class Strength," in S. Steinmo, K. Thelen, and F. Longstreth (eds), *Structuring Politics: Historical Institutionalism in Comparative Analysis*. Cambridge: Cambridge University Press, 33–56.

Rothstein, B. (1998). *Just Institutions Matter*. Cambridge: Cambridge University Press.

Scruggs, L., Jahn, D., and Kuitto, K. (2014). "Comparative Welfare Entitlements Dataset 2. Version 2014-03." University of Connecticut and University of Greifswald.

Soroka, S. and Wlezien, C. (2010). *Degrees of Democracy*. New York: Cambridge University Press.

Svallfors, S. (2011). "Trygg, stöttande, tillitsfull." Background paper for Den parlamentariska Socialförsäkringsutredningen.

Svensson, T. (1994). *Socialdemokratins dominans*. Stockholm: Almqvist & Wiksell International.

Swank, D. (2003). *Diminished Democracy?* Cambridge: Cambridge University Press.

Swenson, P. (2002). *Capitalists Against Markets*. Oxford: Oxford University Press.

Tingsten, H. (1941). *Idékritik*. Stockholm: Bonniers.

US Social Security Administration (2014). "Social Security Programs throughout the World," <http://www.ssa.gov/policy/docs/progdesc/ssptw/>>.

Vis, B. (2009). *Politics of Risk-Taking*. Amsterdam: Amsterdam University Press.

Wilensky, H. L. (1975). *The Welfare State and Equality*. Los Angeles: University of California.

CHAPTER 4

THE WELFARE STATE AND GENDER EQUALITY

CHRISTINA BERGQVIST

INTRODUCTION

> Men with prams have become such a familiar sight since shared paren-
> tal leave was first introduced in 1974 (a full 41 years before parents are
> scheduled to get it in the UK under the government's proposals) that
> there's even a name—"latte pappas"—for the tribe ... At the free-of-
> charge, drop-in play group in Malmö that is my morning refuge, the pap-
> pas often outnumber the mammas. I'll find myself sitting cross-legged
> next to a taciturn Swedish engineer, a heavily tattooed biker, or another
> migrant—there's a computer programmer from Chennai—as our chil-
> dren play with the wooden blocks, rattles and drums.
>
> (*The Guardian* on Facebook, November 18, 2012)

VISITORS in Sweden are often fascinated by sight of many fathers with kids in strollers, groups of fathers and kids playing in the park, or the "latte pappas" in the cafés, while the mothers are at work. Parental leave is an illustration of how the Swedish welfare state promotes gender equality. The possibility of being able to combine paid work and having children has become a fundamental goal in the Swedish welfare state in recent decades. Sweden has introduced policies such as an income-related parental leave benefit and publicly funded child care services available for all children. The parental leave lasts for more than a year and can be shared by the parents as they like, but at least two of the months have to be taken by the father and two by the mother otherwise they are lost. These policies have thus been explicitly designed with the goal of increasing gender equality. In this individual earner-carer model, women as well as men are encouraged and expected to be breadwinners as well as caregivers. Thus, the welfare state has taken on a leading part in gradually abolishing the traditional roles of women as the main caregivers and men as the main breadwinners in the family. In international comparisons the Swedish welfare state is often pictured as a paradise for gender equality, but there are also critical voices claiming that there still is a long way to go (Ahlberg, Roman, and Duncan 2008).

Women are still doing the major part of unpaid care work, take up most of the parental leave, and have fewer opportunities to pursue a career. In addition, the labor market is gender-segregated, and women, especially mothers of small children, work part-time to ease the burden they have of taking care of the family. An example of gender segregation in the labor market is that hardly any men work in the child care and elderly care sectors. Men also dominate in leadership positions in business, in universities, and in society in general (Statistics Sweden 2012). However, politics is an exception to the "rule" that the higher up the hierarchy one looks the fewer women are to be found. In the Riksdag (the parliament) and in the government we find roughly the same number of women and men. Hard work from, among others, the political parties' women's sections as well as recommendations from the parties to nominate more women explain the comparatively high share of women in politics (Sainsbury 2005; Bergqvist, Olsson Blandy, and Sainsbury 2007).

Some critics of the persisting inequalities, however, claim that they are the result of the expansion of a generous welfare state of the Swedish type, as women will mainly work in public sector jobs that pay less than jobs in the private sector. The long parental leaves encourage mothers to abstain from the labor market for a long time and thereby hurt women's career opportunities. This has been referred to as the "welfare state paradox" (Mandel and Semyonov 2006). Others claim that this critique ignores the gender-equalizing effects of having most women participate in the labor market and point out that the women-dominated public sector employment in general offers very good working conditions and that the gender wage gap is lower than in other welfare state regimes. According to this claim, the persisting gender inequalities cannot be explained by the policies as such; on the contrary, the Swedish welfare state has increased class as well as gender equality (Korpi 2000; Korpi, Ferrarini, and Englund 2013). Thus, the picture of the Swedish welfare state and gender equality is complex and sometimes contradictory. This chapter aims to give the reader a deeper understanding of historical and recent developments in the Swedish welfare state and gender equality.

The chapter proceeds in the following way. First, it gives an introduction to how research has understood and conceptualized the Scandinavian/social democratic welfare model when gender is included in the analysis. Second, it gives an account of the historical background to and the development of parental leave, child care, and other policies of significance for the possibility for women and men to combine work and family. In the 1970s, when introduced, these policies were seen as very innovative and gender-progressive, thus aimed at changing historically institutionalized gender patterns by making men into caring fathers and mothers into breadwinners—in other words, by abolishing stereotyped gender roles. This chapter focuses on how these policies were designed and relates them to changing gender patterns in the labor market and in the family. In what ways has gender equality been improved? What are the short-comings? This will be followed by a discussion of the political actors and ideas that can explain the establishment of this progressive gender equality model as early as the 1970s. The analysis shows that the involvement of women in politics and women's political agency have been of importance for the formulation of the policies in focus here. Today there is, as already mentioned, a disturbing gap between the visions and ideas about gender equality that were formulated in the discourse around the reforms introduced in the 1970s and the outcomes we see today. A critic of the failure to even out inequalities between women and men has pointed to the institutional design of the parental leave legislation as a contributing factor. Lastly, the difficulties of promoting gender equal-ity will be illustrated by the case of political resistance to individualizing parental leave legislation, which in practice would mean earmarking more than two months of the 16-month-long parental leave for the father.

Gender and Welfare State Regimes

A fundamental question for gender analysts of welfare states is whether welfare states can promote gender equality. In 1987 Helga Maria Hernes coined the concept of the woman-friendly welfare state and claimed that the Scandinavian social democratic welfare state has come further than other welfare states in making equality between the sexes possible. Her vision was that:

> A woman-friendly state would not force harder choices on women than on men, or permit unjust treatment on the basis of sex. In a woman-friendly state women will continue to have children, yet there will also be other roads to self-realization open to them. In such a state women will not have to choose futures that demand greater sacrifices from them than are expected of men. It would be, in short, a state where injustice on the basis of gender would be largely eliminated without an increase in other forms of inequality, such as among groups of women. (Hernes 1987: 15)

Hernes did not claim that gender equality had been fully achieved, only that the Scandinavian welfare states were potentially women-friendly. Her conclusion was that "Sweden and Norway embody a state form that may open the way for their transforma-tion into women-friendly societies and polities, which are reasonably just in terms of gender" (Hernes 1987: 135). Thus, Hernes stresses that how welfare state arrangements are organized—the institutional design—is important for the possibility to achieve gen-der equality.

Since then, research about gender and the welfare state has exploded and there have been many attempts to develop typologies of different types of welfare states. This has to some extent been a reaction to mainstream welfare state research for ignoring gender.

Much of the recent feminist literature on the welfare state employs a framework in which social and labor market policies are considered in terms of their support for the male breadwinner model versus the individual model (also referred to as the individual earner-carer model) (Sainsbury 1994, 1996). These models are premised on the idea that gender relations are embedded in tax, social, labor, and family policies. Analyses focus on examining the institutional design of these policies and the different effects and influences they may have on gender equality.

Fundamental to gendered analysis of the welfare state is the need to understand how care is organized and what women's and men's different relations to the labor market look like. Women's lives and their role in the family and society at large are linked with the organization of social care for dependent children and elderly relatives (Sipilä, Anttonen, and Baldock 2003). In all welfare states, as we know them today, there is a general pattern where women have more substantial care obligations than men. Women do unpaid work in the household and take care of children and the elderly to a higher degree than men. However, the pattern takes different shapes in different welfare states according to how social arrangements and policies are constructed. For example the design of social policies, especially family policies, has an impact on the material situation of families with children, and family policies also influence women and men's decisions about how to reconcile work and family. To exemplify, public support for good, affordable, and generally available child care for small children enables mothers to participate in the labor market, while a care allowance paid to stay-at-home mothers encourages mothers to abstain from the labor market.

Today most welfare states are moving away from the male breadwinner model (Lewis 2001; Daly 2011). Women prefer being able to combine having a family with gainful employment and this is also encouraged by, for example, the EU employment strategy. Also the role of men/fathers is changing, although not at the same pace as for women/ mothers. Few countries are moving toward a fully individual earner-carer regime. However, the Swedish and the other Scandinavian welfare states are seen as coming close. According to welfare state researchers, Sweden is among those few countries that support an egalitarian vision where social policies enable men as well as women to combine care and employment (Mahon 2002).

It is also important to point out that a family today does not have to consist of mom, dad, and kids. Single-parent families, where the child lives with one parent or alternates between the parents, and same-sex parents have become more common. Since the late 1980s same-sex couples in Sweden have by and by gained the same rights as heterosexual couples to registered partnership, marriage, and adoption. The development of social policies in Sweden fits in with theories about postmodern values and individualization processes showing that traditional social structures of class, gender, religion, and family are changing and even withering away (Beck and Beck-Gernsheim 2001; Inglehart and Norris 2003). These theories predict that gender equality and the relationship between fathers and their children will become more important in the postindustrial world (Giddens 1998; Ahlberg, Roman, and Duncan 2008).

THE HISTORICAL LEGACY

Feminist welfare state research has shown that issues about gender were central to the development of the welfare state very early on. Around the time of the transition from an agrarian to an industrial society, there were intensive debates about women as workers and women as mothers. The question of women's place in the family, in society, and in the labor force was the object of continual discussion and reconsideration. In the early twentieth century many feminists, for example in the US, pursued a "maternalist" agenda where claims to citizenship rights were based on women's "difference" in their capacity to become a mother (Skocpol 1992; Koven and Michel 1993). The "maternalists" also had proponents in Sweden, but were on the whole not very influential. Here a feminism promoting women's dual roles as mothers *and* workers characterized the main part of the women's movement from early on. Equal rights between women and men rather than women's and men's difference were emphasized.

The issue of working mothers/married women is an illustrative case of how different ideologies about gender shaped legislation in the early phase of welfare state development. During the 1920s and 1930s, many countries simply imposed bans, prohibiting married women from working (Frangeur 1999). The reason for the ban was that married women should be financially provided for by their husbands. If they participated in the labor market they were seen as bad wives/mothers who took jobs from male breadwinners. In contrast to Sweden's neighbor country Norway, Sweden did not take that path. When Sweden in 1925 introduced a law that granted women (almost) the same rights as men to employment in the civil service, Norway introduced a curtail decision on married women's employment opportunities. The effect of the curtail decision on married women's employment opportunities, in terms of dismissal rate, or not being hired, does not appear to have been great overall, but it was of great symbolic and ideological significance in terms of supporting and maintaining a male breadwinner ideology in Norway (Leira 1992). During the unemployment and population crisis in the 1930s the question of married women's employment again became an issue in Sweden. Proponents of a male breadwinner ideology claimed that married women should be supported by their husbands and not take jobs from men. However, all women's organizations in Sweden "including the National Housewives Association, defended women's right to work on the basis that it was a citizenship right" (Hobson and Lindholm 1997: 486).

The Swedish Riksdag decided to embark on a path which differed from most countries at the time and passed anti-discrimination legislation in 1938 that prohibited the firing of married and/or pregnant women, or single mothers. The work most crucial in influencing the parliamentarians and the leadership in the Social Democratic government was done by the Committee on Women's Employment (Kvinnoarbetskommittén). The Social Democratic ministers, Ernst Wigforss, Minister of Finance, and Gustav Möller, Minister of Social Affairs, stood behind the appointment of the committee consisting of five women and two men. It was unusual that women had such prominent roles in policy-making and it was noticed both in the national and international context. Furthermore, all five women were well known for their strong political and social engagement in women's rights and they were highly in favor of married women's right to work. The first female Member of Parliament, Kerstin Hesselgren, was appointed as the leader of the committee. The important position of secretary was given to Alva Myrdal, a well-known young academic who was already highly engaged in the political debate about social issues. She and her husband, Gunnar Myrdal, were the authors of the very influential book *Crisis in the Population Question* (1934) where they had put forward several radical recommendations for social reforms.[1] At about the same time as the Committee on Women's Employment was formed, the Minister of Social Affairs also appointed the members to the better-known Population Committee, amongst them Gunnar Myrdal. The placing of the Committee on Women's Employment under the Ministry of Finance signalled that married women's rights in the labor market were seen as separate from social issues and thus given a certain legitimacy which would not have been the case had it been part of the population issue placed under the Ministry of Social Affairs (Frangeur 1999: 247).

At the outset, one of the two men on the Committee on Women's Employment had been in favor of a curtail decision (Frangeur 1999). When the committee presented its report in 1938, the female majority on the committee had managed to rephrase the problem from an issue of conflict between employment and marriage to an issue about how society could support employed women's right to marriage and motherhood (Frangeur 1999). Taken together, the two committees suggested policies that strengthened women both as workers and as mothers. Apart from the anti-discrimination legislation of 1938, a maternity benefit covering about 90 percent of all mothers, free maternity and childbirth services, and a housing program for families with several children were also introduced in the 1930s (Olson 1986). In sum, during the 1930s the state took a prominent role in supporting mothers' right to work and care, but still not on a universal basis.

In mainstream welfare literature, the period after World War II is seen as very important for the formation of the welfare state. Several measures were taken in terms of supporting families with children, but less was done to support working mothers. A universal family cash benefit (*barnbidrag*) was introduced, which went directly to the mother. A universal maternity benefit, covering all mothers, was introduced in 1954, which also included an income replacement for working mothers.

THE TRANSITION TO AN INDIVIDUAL EARNER-CARER MODEL

Ideas in line with an individual earner-carer model started to influence the development of the Swedish welfare state from the end of the 1960s. Policies like parental leave, public child care, and individual taxation of married couples that were meant to facilitate a more gender-equal division of paid and unpaid work were then introduced in the 1970s. The policy shift took place in a context where there was a labor shortage and an increase in the number of working mothers entering the labor market. For sure, no welfare state has ever relied on a pure male breadwinner model; women have always been engaged in the labor market (Lewis 2001). For Swedish women with children under the age of seven, participation increased from 35 percent in 1964 to 50 percent in 1970 and to 60 percent in 1975 (Hinnfors 1992: 42). Since then the expansion of women's share in the labor market has increased continually and today 82 percent of women and 89 percent of men belong to the workforce (Statistics Sweden 2012).

Many mothers with young children entered the labor market before public child care became available. Only a few percent of preschool children (ages 0–6) were enrolled in public child care institutions in the 1960s (Bergqvist and Nyberg 2002). An important step toward institutionalizing the new ideas about gender equality was the introduction of an individual tax reform in 1970/1. An individual taxation instead of joint taxation for married couples works as a very strong encouragement for both adults to engage in paid work, and as women's labor market participation continued to increase the demand for child care also increased. Several political initiatives then resulted in a strong expansion of child care for small children during the mid-1970s and 1980s. Before this expansion the first public provisions of child care had been developed as a means mainly to aid working single mothers who needed to engage in paid employment. Later the child care institutions came to include more and more middle-class children and children of the married women who in increasing numbers had joined the labor market (Leira 1992; Ellingsaeter 1998; Bergqvist, Kuusipalo, and Styrkarsdóttir 1999).

To further support gender equality a new parental leave system was introduced in 1974. Sweden then became the first country in the world to transform the maternal leave legislation into parental leave, thereby giving fathers the right to paid leave when a child was born. The introduction of this parental insurance reform is a sign of the new attitude to gender relations being developed. The reform was an expression of, and institutionalized, two radically new attitudes to gender relations. First, it is not only mothers but also fathers who can and should take responsibility for the care of small children. Second, the idea of the male breadwinner was abandoned in favor of the idea of the dual earner-carer family. The question of shared parental leave intervenes in the private sphere in a more explicit way than is the case with public child care. Child care and maternal leave can be seen as policies to make it possible for women to combine motherhood and gainful employment without interfering in the private relationship between the sexes or laying down the role of the father. The basic idea behind shared parental leave is to abolish the effects that an unequal gender relationship would have for women's and men's chances of advancing at work. If fathers were to take an equal part of the paid parental leave this would probably have consequences for the organization of work and the general attitude to gender in the workplace.

A strong labor movement and presence of Social Democratic governments have been seen as major factors behind the Swedish type of universal and egalitarian welfare state regime (Esping-Andersen 1990; Korpi 2006). This combined with advantageous economic conditions, labor market shortages, and public sector expansion has often been highlighted in research that tries to understand the promotion of the individual earner-carer model described above (Ruggie 1984; Haas 1991). However, more recent research also stresses the importance of the mobilization of women's movements and women's political participation, a strong consensus among the political parties from left to right, and important alliances between women and men.

Toward the end of the 1960s when the Social Democratic government began to take gender equality into consideration, women were actually highly influential in the political documents and debates that formed the basis of parliamentary decisions that led to the introduction of parental leave insurance and investment in public child care. Women were in general relatively well represented in politics compared to other non-Nordic countries at the time, with approximately 15 percent of seats held by women Members of Parliament toward the end of the 1960s. In the Social Democratic parliamentary group the proportion of seats held by female members of the second chamber was about 20 percent. The government of 1970 contained Alva Myrdal, who we already know from the 1930s, and Camilla Odhnoff, both of whom were responsible for family policy. Both were strong campaigners for equal rights and conditions for women and men (Bergqvist, Kuusipalo, and Styrkarsdóttir 1999; Bergqvist 2011).

Despite certain initial political differences concerning whether to support the male breadwinner by introducing a child care allowance for mothers staying at home to care or to support a dual breadwinner principle, there was, on the whole, a remarkable level of political agreement concerning the state's economic undertaking relating to child care. Even if the Liberal/Conservative bloc parties have frequently questioned different aspects of, for example, Social Democratic child care policy, as a rule they have not opposed the increasing public costs. It was really only during the latter part of the 1980s that the Liberal/Conservative bloc questioned public expansion in this area (Uddhammar 1993: 250). In 1976, after 44 years of Social Democratic rule, the parties from the Liberal/Conservative bloc formed the new government. Despite the change of government, there were no major changes to family policy, and in fact, the policy program started by the Social Democrats was actually strengthened (Hinnfors 1992: 166). Thus, policies promoting women's integration into the labor market by expanding the length of the parental leave and child care facilities have been rather uncontroversial. It has though been much harder to introduce policies that more forcefully make men take parental leave.

The issue of which direction family policy should take and, more generally, which welfare and gender equality model was preferable became a controversial political issue again toward the end of the 1980s and the 1990s. Following the period of relative consensus that had existed since the 1970s when the individual earner-carer model was developed, a child care allowance was introduced for the first time in 1994. The concept of the child care allowance conforms to the idea of a male breadwinner model where a stay-at-home mother is encouraged. After the election of 1991, a Liberal/Conservative government had come to power. In contrast to the previous non-Social Democratic coalition governments of the 1970s and 1980s, the new government included the Christian Democrats for the first time. This meant that the Center Party had gained an ally to support the introduction of child care allowances. The Liberal Party, as previously, supported a continuation of the gender equality and family policies according to the model established during the 1970s, which to a large extent coincided with Social Democratic policy. The Moderate Party (*Conservatives*) had developed into a more free-market, neoliberal party than a traditional conservative party. The Moderates did not regard family policy as a central issue during the 1980s and were prepared to make deals and coalitions with both right and left.

The most common argument put forward in favor of child care allowances was that they increased the freedom of choice for parents to decide for themselves how their children should be cared for. Despite advocates of child care allowances attempting to "dress up" their arguments using a gender-neutral language, we can derive the origins of the allowances from the debate of the 1960s concerning the separate spheres of the sexes. The Social Democrats and the Left Party argued in strong terms against the notion of a child care allowance. However, the history of the child care allowance was short-lived as the Social Democrats were once again returned to government in the autumn of 1994 and abolished it (Bergqvist 2007).

Bringing Men In

Parallel to the discussion about the child care allowance ran another debate more in line with "the vision of gender equality." This discussion concerned the low utilization of parental leave by fathers. Despite campaigns aimed at giving information and changing public opinion, the proportion of parental leave days taken by fathers continued, as we have seen, to be low, even at the start of the 1990s. As early as the 1970s demands had been made by women's movement actors and several women parliamentarians that part of the parental leave should be earmarked for fathers, but such demands were never accepted by the predominantly male political leadership. Interestingly, in the 1990s, the issue was pursued more by men who were themselves fathers, than by women in parliament or the women's associations of the political parties. Of central importance was the so-called "fathers' group" within the parliamentary gender equality unit. They recommended a minimum period of three months for compulsory paternity leave (Bergqvist, Kuusipalo, and Styrkarsdóttir 1999).

In February 1994 the same government that introduced the child care allowance also proposed that a month of the total parental leave payments should be earmarked for each parent.[2] Within the Liberal/Conservative government it was the Liberal Party, and in particular the Social Affairs and Gender Equality Minister (*social- och jämställd-hetsministern*) Bengt Westerberg, who became the driving force behind this policy.[3] The Social Democratic government has in this case kept the "daddy month." With the support of the Left Party and the Green Party, the Social Democratic minority government in 2002 also introduced two more earmarked months, one for the father and one for the mother. The earmarking was linked to an extension of the parental leave period by 30 days to 390 days (Bergqvist 2007).

The above shows that men had been brought into the debate regarding gender equality and parenthood in a new way. In the 1970s it had been women and women's groups that had been the driving force, even if they had the support of many men. During the 1990s men took a more active role in the discussion and formulated their own demands and visions of an equal parenthood. One possible interpretation of this is that the issue of child care and parental leave had become an issue for both of the sexes, in accordance with the 1970s vision of gender equality. Combining working and family life in a modern dual-income family is no longer merely a "women's" problem but also an issue for men. However, the issue of making men take more parental leave is politically more sensitive than the expansion of child care/preschool policies, as we will see in the next section.

So Far But No Further?

The institutionalization of policies strengthening an individual earner-carer model has continued over the years. Parental leave has been expanded stepwise from six months in 1974 to 16 months in 2013. The basic design of parental leave is that the parents can share the time as they like until the child is eight years old. The reimbursement rate today is 80 percent of the income up to a ceiling for 13 months and three months with a low flat-rate benefit. The increase of fathers' share of parental leave has been rather slow and in 1990 only 7 percent of the days were taken by men.[4] After the introduction of earmarked months, fathers' leave has increased from 12 percent in 2000 to 24 percent in 2011 (Statistics Sweden 2012). Thus, there is still a large gap between mothers' and fathers' take up of the leave. However, it is worth pointing out that almost all fathers take *some* leave. Sweden's position is rather unique: outside the Nordic countries it is still somewhat unusual to find such a high proportion of children being looked after by fathers on parental leave.

Also the area of publicly financed child care facilities outside the home has seen a significant expansion. The provision of child care/pre-school has now become a universal right. The provision of pre-school places is implemented at the local level, but there is central regulation and a national curriculum that has to be followed. Given the length of parental leave, most children start preschool at the age of 15–18 months. Today around 85 percent of children between one and five participate in preschool activities. The development in the child care sector has to a large extent facilitated the possibility for mothers to reconcile care and work obligations. It has also evened out class differences between children from different socioeconomic groups. According to international comparisons, the standard of early childhood care and education is very high in Sweden with university-trained staff and rather small groups of children.

Even if the individual carer-earner policies have been strengthened, a persistent gender pattern prevails, which is obvious in how parental leave is shared, and this also spills over into the labor market. In 1970 the Prime Minister and leader of the Social Democratic Party, Olof Palme, made a speech at the Women's National Democratic Club in Washington. He talked about his vision of gender equality and said: "(p)ublic opinion nowadays is so well informed that if a politician today should declare that the woman ought to have a different role than the man and that it is natural that she devotes more time to the children, he would be regarded to be of the Stone Age" (cited from Klinth 2002: 14). In 2006 the Prime Minister and leader of the Social Democratic Party, Göran Persson, told media that there would be no more "father quotas." The Social Democratic Party Congress was approaching and the issue of an individualization of parental leave had again become a hot topic.

The struggle for policy measures to make men take more parental leave has, as we have seen, been going on for more than 40 years, but with limited success. The gap between the radical rhetoric with its vision of the caring father and an actual willingness to introduce more effective policies is wide. Many feminists (women as well as men) see individualized parental leave policies as very important in promoting gender equality. In contrast to most other gender equality policies this kind of policy put the pressure on men to change. Sweden has taken a step toward individualization by earmarking two months for the father and two for the mother, while the remaining eleven months can be shared as the couple like.

However, there is a gap between what the major party in Sweden, the Social Democrats, say and what they do. In contrast to the principle of the individual as the basis for social entitlements, parental leave legislation is not fully individualized. The sharing of parental leave has been *voluntary*, and as such, the tendency has been for women to be the primary takers of the leave.

For many Swedish gender equality proponents the individualization of the parental leave system has become a very important issue and is seen as a key for the improvement of equality between women and men, in the home and in the labor market. Women's agency and role in policy-making have been of vital importance for a feminist impact on a wide array of policies improving gender equality in Sweden. However, certain feminist claims have been met with stronger resistance than others. According to Barbara Hobson, "(t)he Swedish universalistic frame allowed feminists to make gendered claims based on equal treatment of citizens as well as solidarity with weaker parties, in which women were included in the class of vulnerable persons. But this frame has inhibited claims-making that articulates gender differences in power and agency between men and women" (Hobson 2003: 66). Anyway, it is clear that an introduction of earmarking/individualization is different from, for example, child care because it does in a more explicit way challenge traditional gender roles and put pressure on men to change.

To conclude, there is a discrepancy between the radical rhetoric and policy goals of gender equality on the one hand and the actual political will to introduce policies that directly affect men's behavior. By legislating on the issue of parental leave in the 1970s, the Swedish Social Democratic government took a huge step away from the idea of the male breadwinner family. The most important principle of the reform was that it opened up the *possibility* of more equal parenting, something that was previously made difficult by women-specific legislation in this area. Men got the same rights as women, and women's and men's opportunities to combine parenthood and paid employment increased. The basic idea underlying shared *parental* leave can be viewed as that of evening out the consequences that unequal gender relationships have for women's and men's opportunities, e.g. advancing at work. If an employer, for example, had to assume there was an equal probability that a father of young children would take as much leave as a mother, it would likely have consequences for workplace organization and perceptions of gender.

Sweden probably has the world's most generous parental leave legislation when it comes to length and income-related benefits. Parental insurance as a whole is also very flexible and includes several benefits other than those discussed here, such as the right to additional days of paid leave if the child is sick and cannot attend daycare or school. There are also possibilities to reduce working hours. Women are in the majority among those who use these possibilities. On the whole, job security is strong in Sweden, but even so the long periods of absence affect women's careers, wages, pensions, etc. It is therefore something of a paradox that the Social Democrats, known for their egalitarian ideals and women-friendly welfare state, have been so reluctant to individualize parental leave. Each time the parental leave time has been extended there have been demands for earmarking. Even though the Social Democrats have been in power for long periods of time during the last 30 years it was a center-right government that first introduced a "daddy month" in 1994. It was implemented in 1995, and in 2002 the Social Democrats followed suit with another month. After that, a debate started about further individualization, but there have not yet been any more changes.

NOTES

1. Later Alva Myrdal would become a Social Democratic minister, diplomat, and co-winner of the Nobel Peace Prize in 1982 for her efforts to promote world disarmament.
2. There are certain special rules applicable to single parents.
3. Westerberg is himself one of a growing band of well-known men who have taken parental leave.
4. The parental leave insurance also includes several other benefits such as paid pregnancy leave, the right of the father to ten days' paid leave with the mother in case of birth, and occasionally paid leave to care for a sick child.

BIBLIOGRAPHY

Ahlberg, J., Roman, C., and Duncan, S. (2008). "Actualizing the 'Democratic Family'? Swedish Policy Rhetoric versus Family Practices," *Social Politics* 26: 79–100.
Beck, U. and Beck-Gernsheim, E. (2001). *Individualization: Institutionalized Individualism and its Social and Political Consequences*. London: Sage.
Bergqvist, C. (2007). "The Debate about Childcare Allowances in the Light of Welfare State Reconfiguration: The Swedish Case," in M. Hausmann and B. Sauer (eds), *Gendering the*

State in the Age of Globalization: Women's Movements and State Feminism in Post-Industrial Democracies. Lanham: Rowman and Littlefield, 245–62.

Bergqvist, C. (2011). "The Nordic Countries," in G. Bauer and M. Tremblay (eds), *Women in Executive Power: A Global Overview.* New York: Routledge, 157–70.

Bergqvist, C., Kuusipalo, J., and Styrkarsdóttir, A. (1999). "The Debate on Childcare Policies," in C. Bergqvist et al. (eds), *Equal Democracies? Gender and Politics in the Nordic Countries.* Oslo: Scandinavian University Press, 137–56.

Bergqvist, C. and Nyberg, A. (2002). "Welfare State Restructuring and Child Care in Sweden," in S. Michel and R. Mahon (eds), *Child Care at the Crossroads: Gender and Welfare State Restructuring.* New York: Routledge, 287–307.

Bergqvist, C., Olsson Blandy, T., and Sainsbury, D. (2007). "Swedish State Feminism: Continuity and Change," in J. Outshoorn and J. Kantola (eds), *Changing State Feminism.* Basingstoke and New York: Palgrave Macmillan, 224–45.

Daly, M. (2011). "What Adult Worker Model? A Critical Look at Recent Social Policy Reform in Europe from a Gender and Family Perspective," *Social Politics* 18: 1–23.

Ellingsaeter, A. L. (1998). "Dual Breadwinner Societies: Provider Models in the Scandinavian Welfare States," *Acta Sociologica* 4: 59–73.

Esping-Andersen, G. (1990). *The Three Worlds of Welfare Capitalism.* Cambridge: Polity Press.

Frangeur, R. (1999). *Yrkeskvinna eller makens tjänarinna? Striden om yrkesrätten för gifta kvinnor.* Lund: Arkiv Förlag.

Giddens, A. (1998). *The Third Way: The Renewal of Social Democracy.* Cambridge: Polity Press.

Haas, L. (1991). "Equal Parenthood and Social Policy: Lessons from a Study of Parental Leave in Sweden," in S. J. Hyde and M. Essex (eds), *Parental Leave and Child Care.* Philadelphia: Temple University Press, 375–405.

Hernes, H. (1987). *Welfare State and Woman Power.* Oslo: Norwegian University Press.

Hinnfors, J. (1992). *Familjepolitik: Samhällsförändringar och partistrategier 1960–1990.* Stockholm: Almqvist & Wiksell.

Hobson, B. (2003). "Recognition Struggles in Universalistic and Gender Distinctive Frames: Sweden and Ireland," in B. Hobson (ed.), *Recognition Struggles and Social Movements: Contested Identities, Agency and Power.* Cambridge: Cambridge University Press, 64–92.

Hobson, B. and Lindholm, M. (1997). "Collective Identities, Women's Power Resources, and the Making of Welfare States," *Theory and Society* 26: 475–508.

Inglehart, R. and Norris, P. (2003). *Rising Tide: Gender Equality and Cultural Change.* Cambridge: Cambridge University Press.

Klinth, R. (2002). *Göra pappa med barn.* Umeå: Boréa Bokförlag.

Korpi, W. (2000). "Faces of Inequality: Gender, Class, and Patterns of Inequalities in Different Types of Welfare States," *Social Politics* 7: 127–91.

Korpi, W. (2006). "Power Resources and Employer-Centered Approaches in Explanations of Welfare States and Varieties of Capitalism: Protagonists, Consenters, and Antagonists," *World Politics* 58: 167–206.

Korpi, W., Ferrarini, T., and Englund, S. (2013). "Women's Opportunities under Different Family Policy Constellations: Gender, Class and Inequality Tradeoffs in Western Countries Re-examined," *Social Politics* 20: 1–40.

Koven, S. and Michel, S. (1993). *Mothers of a New World: Maternalist Politics and the Origins of Welfare States.* New York: Routledge.

Leira, A. (1992). *Welfare States and Working Mothers.* New York: Cambridge University Press.

Lewis, J. (2001). "The Decline of the Male Breadwinner Model: Implications for Work and Care," *Social Politics* 8: 152–69.

Mahon, R. (2002). "Child Care: Toward What Kind of 'Social Europe'?" *Social Politics* 9: 343–79.

Mandel, H. and Semyonov, M. (2006). "A Welfare State Paradox: State Interventions and Women's Employment Opportunities in 22 Countries," *American Journal of Sociology* 111: 1910–49.

Olson, S. (1986). "Sweden," in P. Flora (ed.), *Growth to Limits: The Western European Welfare States Since World War II*, vol. 1: *Sweden, Norway, Finland, Denmark*. New York: Walter de Gruyter, 1–84.

Ruggie, M. (1984). *The State and Working Women: A Comparative Study of Britain and Sweden*. Princeton: Princeton University Press.

Sainsbury, D. (ed.) (1994). *Gendering Welfare States*. London: Sage Publications.

Sainsbury, D. (1996). *Gender, Equality and Welfare States*. Cambridge: Cambridge University Press.

Sainsbury, D. (1999). "Gender and Social-Democratic Welfare States," in D. Sainsbury (ed.), *Gender and Welfare State Regimes*. Oxford: Oxford University Press, 75–117.

Sainsbury, D. (2005). "Party Feminism, State Feminism and Women's Representation in Sweden," in J. Lovenduski et al. (eds), *State Feminism and Political Representation*. Cambridge: Cambridge University Press, 195–215.

Sipilä, J., Anttonen, A., and Baldock, J. (2003). "The Importance of Social Care," in A. Anttonen, J. Baldock, and J. Sipilä (eds), *The Young, the Old and the State: Social Care Systems in Five Industrial Nations*. Cheltenham and London: Edward Elgar, 1–23.

Skocpol, T. (1992). *Protecting Mothers and Soldiers*. Cambridge: Harvard University Press.

Statistics Sweden (2012). *Women and Men in Sweden: Facts and Figures 2012*. Örebro: Statistics Sweden.

Uddhammar, E. (1993). *Partierna och den stora staten: En analys av statsteorier och svensk politik under 1900-talet*. Stockholm: City University Press.

CHAPTER 5

THE MORAL, ECONOMIC, AND POLITICAL LOGIC OF THE SWEDISH WELFARE STATE

BO ROTHSTEIN

INTRODUCTION

IN a comparative perspective, the Swedish welfare state is known for being more universal, comprehensive, and extensive than what is the case for most other OECD countries (Tilton 1990; Olsson 1993; Pontusson 2005; Steinmo 2010; Esping-Andersen 1990). From the 1960s until the 1990s it was common to refer to this welfare state as the central part of an internationally unique and specific "Swedish model" (Milner 1990). Some have even characterized the welfare system as the defining character of the country (Berggren and Trägårdh 2006). Usually, the normative economic and political parts of this enterprise are analyzed separately by scholars in different disciplines. In this chapter I intend to present an argument for how they are integrated and should be understood as a precondition for the system as a whole. The argument is based on the idea that the political (that is, electoral) support for the welfare system cannot be explained without reference to its moral foundations and to the political viability of the system.

THE MORAL FOUNDATIONS OF THE SWEDISH WELFARE STATE

All welfare states have to handle a number of moral issues. One is of course what the welfare system should be about. Or more precisely, which human needs it should cater to.

Since human needs are in principle endless, all welfare systems have to prioritize and set limits and these decisions have to be based on a set of moral considerations that determine what should be the responsibility of the state.[1] Another such issue is to whom such benefits and services should be directed: to "the poor," or should they cover broader categories or even all citizens? A third question is the issue of personal responsibility. For example, what type of demands for efforts to find work should be put on the unemployed and people with disabilities? A fourth issue concerns the matter of citizens' autonomy. If the welfare state is going to provide specific services, for example in child care and elderly care, normative issues about citizens' rights to autonomy and self-determination have to be addressed (Gould 1988).

The purposes animating the moral foundations of the Swedish welfare model have been the object of considerable research. To start with the fourth issue, a large debate has occurred as to whether the Swedish welfare state should be seen as an attempt to increase the autonomy of citizens or as a centrally and expert-led "invasion" of civil society by the state, i.e., as a reduction of citizens to the status of subordinate clients deemed unable to manage their own affairs (Gould 2010; Zetterberg 1992; Rothstein 1998). In the words of two famous political philosophers, does Amartya Sen's (2009) normative ideal that social justice demands that the state furnish all citizens with a set of "basic capabilities" best describe the Swedish welfare model, or is Jürgen Habermas's (1987) apprehension of the welfare state's continuous colonization of the private sphere—and the associated elimination of civil society—the more apposite description?

One of the more widely discussed contributions to this debate was produced by the Swedish Investigation on Power and Democracy—a mega social science research project set up by the government and conducted from 1985 to 1990.[2] In its final report (SOU 1990: 234–5) as well as in a much discussed book from the project (Hirdman 1989), the investigation sought to describe and interpret the ideological ambitions behind Social Democratic social policy—from the time of its founding during the 1930s up to the 1960s—from the perspective of the state's relation to the private sphere. The purpose was to reveal the underlying ideology—in respect to the relation of citizens to the state— that guided some of the most prominent figures involved in the establishment of Social Democratic welfare policy. Most important in this analysis are the two Nobel laureates Alva and Gunnar Myrdal on account of the prominence of their famous book *Crisis in the Population Question* (Sw: *Kris i befolkningsfrågan*), published in 1934, which framed much of the social policy debate in Sweden during this formative period (Myrdal and Myrdal 1934).

The picture that emerges in this analysis largely confirms the thesis of a continuous state invasion of the sphere of the family and totalitarian control of private life (cf. Huntford 1971). This is symbolized by the title of Hirdman's (1989) book about this issue from the project (Sw. *Att lägga livet tillrätta*), which refers to the desire of social policy experts to "put lives in order"—the lives in question being those of ordinary people. The analysis succeeded in depicting the social policy circles in which the Myrdals took a prominent part as being inspired by a view of the relation between citizens and the state that must be termed both paternalistic and utopian (as expressed in the concept of "social engineering"). Through the direction of popular consumption choices, and the lifestyles of "ordinary people" thereby, social policy would help to create a new, more rational kind of citizen—enlightened, well-adjusted, and socially committed (SOU 1990: 234–5; Hirdman 1989). For example, the Myrdals argued that it would be best to raise children in boarding schools; that household work is suitable only for feeble and indolent persons without ambition; that the raising of children should be regulated in detail according to scientific methods; and that the performance of such duties should be assigned in part to publicly appointed experts (Hirdman 1989: 111–24. With the ideologically charged concept of "violation"[3] the Power and Democracy Project called attention to the potential effects of such policies—the price, in other words, that benevolent intentions to "put lives in order" could have for the autonomy of citizens (Hirdman 1989: 17 and 227–31).

This analysis of the normative foundations of the Swedish welfare state produced by the Power and Democracy project undoubtedly performed a valuable service in pointing out the strong paternalism characterizing the political views held by the two Nobel laureates Alva and Gunnar Myrdal.[4] There are, however, two problems with this analysis for understanding the normative foundation of the main parts of the Swedish welfare state. The first is that this analysis did not distinguish between the discussions about social policies and the type of social policies that were actually implemented. Secondly, the claims that there was a "uniform view of man among the Swedish reformers" (Hirdman 1989: 11) and an associated consensus as to the appropriate shape of social policy are not borne out by the historical facts. What happened was that the Myrdal vision of social policy was defeated at the hands of those in the party who were in power, such as the Minister of Social Affairs, Gustav Möller. There was no single or uniform view of the relation between citizens and the state among the leading Social Democrats of the time. On the contrary, two altogether different approaches existed and it was not the Myrdalian vision of the welfare state that got the final say.

GUSTAV MÖLLER AND SOCIAL POLICY AS CITIZENS' RIGHTS

Gustav Möller became the General Secretary of the Swedish Social Democratic Party in 1916, a post that he held until 1940. He was Minster of Social Affairs from 1924–6 and (with a small interruption) from 1932 to 1951. The historical record shows that already in the early 1930s he regarded the Myrdals and their intellectual entourage with great suspicion, as idealists out of contact with political and social realities (Carlson 1990: 56). At the Social Democratic Party Congress in 1936, when the Myrdals' book about the population issue had become central in the political debate, Möller stated that, for his part, he had no interest in the population question, save for the opportunity it presented for "scaring as many conservatives, farmers league representatives and liberals as possible with the threat that our people will die out" if by this he could get their support for his social policy measures (Lindberg 1999; Carlson 1990).

Möller's main goal was to establish a social policy system that would supply citizens with basic capabilities in a manner avoiding the stigmatization and violation of integrity characteristic of the old (and then still in operation) poor relief system. He gave expression to these principles in his directives for one of the major social policy commissions he appointed during the second half of the 1930s:

> A characteristic feature of poor relief is that assistance is rendered after an open-ended means test, in which the authorities' subjective assessment of the individual's need for aid is determinative, both as regards the character of the assistance granted and its extent. Certainly, the first paragraph of the law on poor relief enjoins the municipalities to furnish minors and the disabled with the necessities of life, but in practice the municipal authorities enjoy very much a free hand in implementing this mandatory poor relief ... During recent decades, however, a new type of social assistance has emerged, which in the respects mentioned differs from poor relief altogether. In area after area, arrangements have been undertaken, by means of state measures, which secure to citizens a right to the assistance of society, under certain conditions stated clearly in statute or in law, and comparatively easily ascertained. (cit. in Rothstein 1998: 175)

In these directives is another of Möller's political ambitions, namely to avoid "the dangers of excessive bureaucratization." This was one of his most frequent political themes—how to expand social welfare without increasing the power of bureaucrats over citizens thereby. One of Möller's closest collaborators, Per Nyström (who served as his undersecretary of state from 1945 to 1950, and later became a professor of history), in an article written in 1991, sharply criticized the analysis from the Power and Democracy Project as follows:

> Möller was by no means guided by the theories of the social engineers, but rather by the ideas of K. K. Steinke, and by the Danish social reforms of 1933, which Steinke carried out. The program recommended by the social engineers never came to characterize Swedish welfare policy, in which general security measures dominated altogether. (Nyström 1991: 188)

Wherever possible, Möller tried to organize social policy on the basis of specified rights that were to be distributed as broadly as possible (Thullberg 1989). For those cases in which some form of needs-testing could not be avoided, Möller introduced an interesting innovation in governance. This involved assigning the administration of the needs test to the organizations representing the groups toward whom the policy was directed. Two examples of this approach to problems of governance are the provision of support to help small firms survive and unemployment insurance. In the former case, Möller rejected the idea that the National Board of Commerce should handle this issue. Instead, he entrusted these delicate and difficult decisions about which small firms had a chance of survival, and therefore should be temporarily supported, to the local enterprise associations. In a similar way, unemployment insurance, which entails the complicated question of which type of work an unemployed person should have to accept so as not to lose the benefit, were to be handled by (officially authorized) unemployment funds that were organized by the trade unions. In both cases, Möller justified the chosen arrangement on the grounds that an increase in the power of state officials over citizens could be thereby avoided (Rothstein 1992). What Möller did, in other words, was to make it possible for citizens to solve these intricate problems of implementation by way of their own, partially autonomous institutions. The object of this strategy was double—both to avoid rigid bureaucratization and to solve problems of possible overuse and abuse that can arise in such programs by giving the responsibility for the implementation to the locally appointed representatives of the "policy users" (Thullberg 1989).

If one is looking for a reform that clearly illustrates the difference between what the Myrdals *thought* and what Gustav Möller *carried out*, the program established for assisting low-income families with children is a good candidate. In brief, the approach favored by the Myrdals—which was termed the in-kind line—called for a selective targeting of assistance to families with children suffering from economic deprivation, and urged that such aid be distributed in the form of various goods. The needy mothers would receive clothing, shoes, vitamins, foodstuffs, etc., from municipal retail outlets. The National Board of Social Affairs would see to the standardization of the quality of these goods. The argument for the in-kind line focused on the issues of targeting and quality. Means-testing would ensure that assistance went to the "truly needy," and that maximum efficiency in the use of tax monies was thereby achieved. The in-kind line made it possible, moreover, to guarantee that expenditures on behalf of needy families were converted into goods of the desired quality, for the consumption choices of recipients were directed (Hatje 1974: 204).

The selective, in-kind line lost out, in the end, to the idea of general, in-cash child benefits. Möller argued that the latter method would avoid the stigma associated with means tests. Many other administrative problems arising in connection with means tests would also be avoided thereby, and the need for a large bureaucracy—in order to ascertain who was entitled to support and who was not—would be obviated. Economically deprived families needed neither charity nor paternal instruction, but a cash increase in their household budget. One could, in Möller's view, trust the people themselves to make wise use of these monies. From a gender perspective, it is interesting that the money should go to the mother (Hatje 1974: 202–3). Möller's early involvement in social policy, an involvement which ushered in such reforms—critical to the prospects of women and children—as maternity allowances, advance maintenance payments (i.e., the state acting as a "middleman" guaranteeing maintenance payments to single parents and taking care of securing payment from the parent that does not have custody), free maternity care, widows' pensions, free childbirth services, and a prohibition against discharging female employees on account of pregnancy or marriage (Thullberg 1989). A review of the social policy reforms promulgated by the Ministry of Social Affairs during the years 1933 to 1939 reveals that the greater number concerned children and mothers, and that they strengthened the autonomy of recipients as citizens by granting them clearly specified rights. These reforms did not seek to put the lives of recipients "in order" by means of the discretionary disbursement of resources.

Möller sought by various means to immunize his reforms against both the abuse of power by bureaucrats and overuse or abuse on the part of recipients. Uniform and general cash benefits were of course an important method, as was his attempt to find functioning and reliable organizations to implement the reforms. Another clear example was his opposition to introducing income-graded classes into the system of sickness benefits. What Möller objected to was not the principle of income-related benefits, but rather the invitation to fraud presented by a system in which citizens themselves would state their income class. The temptation to report overly high incomes would undermine the reform's legitimacy, and moreover would require a considerable apparatus of verification and control (Svensson 1994). It should, however, be underlined that this rights-based approach to social policy was thought to cater to people who under ordinary circumstances could support themselves but who either due to personal circumstances or economic downturns had temporarily lost their ability for gainful employment (except in the case of retirement).

It should be underlined that this rights-based and universal (or near-universal) moral "modus operandi" of the Swedish welfare state, while definitively a dominating feature of the system, has also had several important exceptions. Among those one can mention the policy of forced or "semi-forced" sterilization of women who were seen as unfit to be mothers, which was an established social policy up until the early 1970s. The extent and moral implications of this policy have been hotly debated but there should be no question that the rights of a substantial number of Swedish citizens were grossly violated (Lucassen 2010; Hirdman and Lundberg 2002).

Moreover, as in all other modern societies, there exists a category of people who, for various reasons, are permanently or for very long periods unable to support themselves (or live in households where there is a "breadwinner" who can support them). For this category, means-tested social assistance has often been the only option (Salonen 1993). As Sweden has received a considerable number of immigrants during the last two decades who in many cases have encountered difficulties in establishing themselves on the labor market, this has led to an increasing number of people being forced to rely on means-tested social assistance (Gustafsson 2013).

THE POLITICAL LOGIC OF THE UNIVERSAL WELFARE STATE MODEL

One of the most prominent explanations for the political support of the Swedish welfare state is the Power Resource Theory according to which it is largely a function of working-class political mobilization (Huber and Stephens 2001; Korpi 1983). The Power

Resource Theory grew out of an effort by a group of scholars who during the late 1970s tried to find a "middle way" between on the one hand the then popular Marxist–Leninist view that the welfare state should be understood as merely a functional requisite for the reproduction of capitalist exploitation, and on the other hand the idea that welfare states follow from a similar functionalist logic of modernization and industrialization. As a reaction against these functionalist explanations, PRT puts forward two important issues. First, PRT scholars were the first to point out the variation in things like coverage, extension, and generosity among existing welfare states and that this variation needed to be explained. Second, they introduced the importance of political mobilization based on social class as an explanation for this variation (Korpi 1983). Variation in welfare states reflects, according to this theory, "class-related distributive conflicts and partisan politics" (Korpi 2006: 168). The more political resources the working class was able to muster, such as a strong and united union movement that gave electoral support to Labor or Social Democratic parties, the more extensive, comprehensive, universal, and generous the welfare state would become. The logic was, according to the theory, that class-based division of labor led to a situation in which categories with high risks had lower resources to cope with these risks which would result in a collective demand for social insurances. This is a powerful and quite dominant theory but it has been criticized for not being able to answer precisely why that demand for social insurance was to be directed at the state. Unions could, for example, have dealt with this problem by setting up their own social insurance organizations and used their strength at the negotiation table to get employers to contribute financially. In this way, working-class organizations would have had full control over the system for social insurance they demanded. In other words, the PRT approach lacks an explanation for why the working class in some countries more than in others came to entrust the *state* with this important task (Skocpol 1992).

Another central question in this debate has been whether the specific character of the Swedish welfare state should be explained by variables related to historically inherited cultural traits? Or should it be explained by deliberately designed political institutions that have led to more solidaristic norms? The historical–cultural approach argues for the existence of a high level of social trust before the welfare state emerged (Bergh and Bjørnskov 2011), as well as the specific character of the Swedish state during the nineteenth century being less repressive including the relatively high social and political independence granted to the peasants (Knudsen and Rothstein 1993). Others have pointed to the importance of the design of the electoral system at the beginning of the twentieth century, arguing that proportional systems have tended to favour higher levels of public spending than two-party systems (Iversen and Soskice 2006). In addition, there are also arguments for the importance of cultural and ethnic homogeneity as a precondition for the Swedish type of universal welfare state (Alesina and Glaeser 2004), as well as the importance of egalitarian values (Graubard 1986).

One problem for these arguments is that the same broad-based support for the universal type of social policies that Svallfors's chapter in this volume documents for the Swedish case can be found for the same type of social policies in countries with a predominantly targeted and much less encompassing welfare state. One case is the National Health Service in the United Kingdom (Klein 2010) and another is the Social Security programs in the United States (Béland 2005). Moreover, empirical studies show that the huge differences between systems for social protection in countries like Sweden and the United States cannot be explained by different attitudes toward equality and social justice (Larsen 2006). Instead, it is the prevailing institutions for the provision of social policies that are important (Larsen 2008). This implies that it is predominantly the institutional design of the policies and not the specific national culture that determines the broad-based political support for the welfare state in Sweden, as shown by Lindbom and Svallfors in this volume. The issue is how this logic between institutional design and political support can be understood.

If the interests and values of voters/citizens in similar types of societies (in this case the liberal democratic market economies) are to be understood as a unified dimension of human behavior, such self-interested utility maximization or some form of altruism, it becomes very difficult to explain why these societies have established such different systems for social protection. An alternative approach that has recently gained a lot of support in experimental research is to understand human behavior as being based on reciprocity. The central idea here is that people are not so much motivated "from the back" by utility-based calculations or culturally induced norms. Instead, human behavior is to a large extent determined by forward-looking strategic thinking in the sense that *what agents do depends on what they think other agents are going to do* (Fehr and Gintis 2007; Gintis et al. 2005; Bicchieri and Xiao 2009; Fehr and Fischbacher 2005). As stated by Fehr and Fishbacher (2005: 167): "If people believe that cheating on taxes, corruption and abuses of the welfare state are widespread, they themselves are more likely to cheat on taxes, take bribes or abuse welfare state institutions." This implies that the behavior depends on how the existing institutions inform the agents' mutual expectations. Regarding the prospect for solidarity, results from research show that most people are willing to engage in solidaristic cooperation for common goals even if they will not personally benefit from this materially (Levi 1998). However, for this to happen, three specific conditions have to be in place. First, people have to be convinced that the policy is morally justified—what can be called substantive justice. Here, the rights-based universal or near-universal entitlements that dominate the Swedish type of welfare state (and the National Health Service in the UK and Social Security in the US) seem to stand a good chance of getting broad-based support. However, empirical research shows that argument relying only on substantive justice is usually not enough to convince people to cooperate (Levi 1998). Successful cooperation depends on two additional requirements being fulfilled. The second requirement is that people can be convinced that the policy in question will be implemented in a fair and even-handed manner, and the third is that it will not be abused or overused by "free riders." Both these requirements are issues about *procedural justice* (Tyler 1992). On this point, implementation research has shown that means- and need-tested programs are much more difficult to implement in keeping with what is usually seen as procedural justice. One reason is that such programs place great demands on public employees who must actively interpret a general body of regulations and apply them to each individual seeking to qualify for a public service. The difficulty is that the since the regulations have to be general, their application to the individual case requires a huge amount of bureaucratic discretion. The so-called "grassroots bureaucrats" have to handle this problem by developing their own practice in interpreting the regulations which leads them to use "prejudice, stereotype, and ignorance as a basis for determination" (Lipsky 1980: 69). Empirical research has shown that citizens' direct experience of interactions with various social policy programs has a clear influence on their political opinions and, moreover, that such experiences are more important than citizens' personal economic experiences when they form opinions about supporting or not supporting welfare state policies (Kumlin 2004).

As for the problem of "free riding" in means- or needs-testing programs, the person seeking assistance has an incentive and usually also the opportunity to withhold relevant information from the bureaucrat and to try in various ways to convince the latter that she should qualify for the service in question also when this is not the case. This situation easily escalates into a vicious spiral of distrust from the client leading to increasing control from the bureaucrat that in its turn results in still more distrust from the client, and so on. For these reasons, means- and/or needs-testing and bureaucratic discretionary power are often more difficult to reconcile with the principle of procedural justice than are universal public services. Since selective welfare institutions must test each case individually, they are to a greater extent subject to suspicion of cheating, arbitrariness, and discrimination, compared to universal public agencies. To this should be added the well-known problem that targeted programs in the public discourse often lead to a "us and them" political logic that is not conducive for broad-based solidaristic collaboration (Larsen 2007).

The political logic of a welfare state thus depends on the existence of a "feedback mechanism" between people's support for policies that they deem fair and just and their perceptions of the *quality of the institutions* that are set up to implement these principles (Kumlin 2004). Recent empirical research strongly supports this argument. Using survey data from 29 European countries that include questions about the fairness of public authorities (health sector and tax authorities) as well as questions about ideological leanings and policy preferences, Svallfors (2013) has shown the following: citizens that have a preference for more economic equality but that live in a country in which they perceive that the fairness and quality of government institutions are low, will in the same survey indicate that they prefer lower taxes and less social spending. However, the same "ideological type" of respondent, who happens to live in a European country where he or she believes that the authorities that implement policies are basically just and fair, will answer that he or she is willing to pay higher taxes for more social spending. This result is supported in a study using aggregate data about welfare state spending and quality of government for Western liberal democracies (Rothstein et al. 2012)—the higher the quality of government the more countries will spend also when they control for variables that measure political mobilization and electoral success from left parties. To summarize my interpretation of these studies: citizens that live in a country where they perceive that corruption or other forms of unfairness in the public administration are common are likely to be less supportive of the idea that the state should take responsibility for policies for increased social justice, even if they ideologically support the goals such policies have. The most likely reason is that they will believe that their solidarity will not be reciprocated.

The Economic Logic of the Universal Welfare State Model

The economic logic of the Swedish type of welfare state is often misunderstood, even by sympathetic commentators (Judt 2009). The most common error is that this type of welfare state is portrayed as a very costly undertaking that by its high level of taxation becomes a hindrance to economic growth. This reveals a misconception regarding what this welfare state model is about. Its main feature is not benefits to poor people, but universal social insurances and social services that benefit the whole, or very large segments, of the population. These goods are in high demand by almost all citizens, and research shows that having these demands covered by universal systems in many cases becomes more cost-effective. In private health insurance systems, for example, the administrative costs for insurance companies alone (in screening out bad risks and handling legal problems about coverage) can become very high, as seems to be the case in the United States.[5] Universal systems, on the other hand, tend to be more cost-effective for the simple reason that risks are spread over the whole population and the incentives for providers to overbill or use costly but unnecessary treatments are minimal. As the British economist Nicholas Barr has observed, due to what economists call "asymmetric information costs," universalist policies *"provide both a theoretical justification of and an explanation for a welfare state which is much more than a safety net. Such a welfare state is justified not simply by redistributive aims one may (or may not) have, but because it does things which markets for technical reasons would either do inefficiently, or would not do at all"* (Barr 1992: 781; see also Barr 2004). Simply put, if middle-class people in Sweden were deprived of their universal systems for social protection and social services, they would in all likelihood decide that they had to buy these services on the market. This would in most cases be more expensive for them due to the problem of "asymmetric information." A third general misunderstanding about the universal welfare state system is the neoliberal argument that high public expenditures are detrimental to market-based economic growth. As shown by the economic historian Peter Lindert (2004) and also in a recent book by Douglass North, together with John Wallis and Barry Weingast (2009), this is simply not the case. In a global perspective, rich states have a level of taxation that is almost twice as high compared to poor states. And when the rich Western states are compared over time, the evidence that high public spending is negative for economic growth is absent. The reason, according to North et al., is that large parts of public spending go to the provision of public goods that are necessary for economic growth but which markets cannot provide, partly on account of the information problems stated above. Interestingly, among those public goods, North and his colleagues include not only the usual things like infrastructure, research, and the rule of law but also education, social insurances, and social services (North, Wallis, and Weingast 2009).

A fourth common misunderstanding is the notion that targeting welfare benefits on the poor is the best way to achieve economic redistribution. Intuitively, one would assume that redistributive policies that tax the rich and give to the poor would be the most efficient way to reduce poverty, while universal policies that give everyone the same service or benefits would not have a redistributive effect. But the facts are the opposite. The technical reason as to why universal systems are more efficient in reducing economic inequality is that taxes are usually proportional or progressive, but services or benefits are usually nominal; you get a certain sum or a certain type of service. The net effect of proportional taxes and nominal services/benefits results in comparatively high redistribution from the rich to the poor (Moene and Wallerstein 2001; Rothstein 1998; Åberg).

Table 5.1 offers an idealized version of how such a system can work. Here we have five classes of people, in which there is a hypothetical income distribution of 1 to 5. In other words, lowest income earners have a before tax and benefit income of a fifth of the highest income earners.

The redistributive logic of the model of a universal welfare state system is as follows. In the first column, income earners are divided for the sake of simplicity into five groups of equal size, according to average income. We then assume not a progressive but rather a strictly proportional system of income taxes and we set the tax rate at 40 percent. Finally, we assume that all public benefits and services are universal, which means that the individuals in each group receive *on average* the same sum in the form of cash benefits and/or subsidized public services. The result, as seen in the last column, is a dramatic reduction in inequality between group A and group E, from 5/1 down to 2.33/1. The level of inequality has thus been reduced by more than half in this model of how the universal welfare policy works.

Table 5.1 The redistributive effect of the universal welfare state

Group	Average income	Tax (40 percent)	Transfers	Income after taxes and transfers
A (20%)	10000	4000	2400	8400
B (20%)	8000	3200	2400	7200
C (20%)	6000	2400	2400	6000
D (20%)	4000	1600	2400	4800
E (20%)	2000	800	2400	3600
Ratio between groups A & E	5/1	(= 12000)	(12000/5=2400)	2.33/1

No tax system is perfectly flat and no social spending system is perfectly universal. But, as this model implies, a purely flat tax system if combined with universal benefits/ services is likely to be more progressive in its effects than the targeted systems found in many real-world countries. Again, the redistribution is achieved by taxes being paid as a percentage of the income while universal benefits are nominal. Thus, in a universal system where "everyone pays the same" and "everyone receives the same," contrary to what is often thought to be the case, a huge amount of redistribution is taking place.

The political reasons as to why universal policies are more effective in terms of alleviating poverty are that if a state is going to tax the rich and give to the poor, the rich and semi-rich (that is the middle class) will not agree to pay high taxes because they perceive that they do not get enough back from the government (Korpi and Palme 1998). They will perceive social services and benefits programs as policies only for "the poor," and especially the middle class (who, note, are also the "swing voters") will turn away from political parties that argue for an increase in taxes and social policies (Rothstein and Uslaner 2005). One might add that it is often assumed that the social democratic model is the result of highly progressive tax systems. This is incorrect since the social democratic model usually has a relatively flat tax structure but, as explained above, if these taxes are relatively high and are combined with largely universal social spending programs, this creates massive redistribution. It should be noted that this model also can serve to illustrate how the economic and political logic of this system interacts. From a purely self-interest-based idea of political behavior, groups A and B should be against such a model because in strict economic terms they will pay more than they get. Groups D and E should be in favor since they will get more than they pay for. The crucial group then is group C, which we can call "the middle class" since they get what they pay for. Since this group can be seen as the "swing voters," deciding what will be the political majority in elections, they are the crucial group for the system to work. In particular, since according to this hypothetical model they get what they pay for, the system has to deliver what it has set out to deliver. Otherwise, this group will turn against this type of welfare state and then this type of welfare system will cease to exist.

Notes

1. The term "state" covers the whole "public sector" which means that local and regional governments are included. Included also are services that are for the most part politically regulated and financed by public money such as, for example, charter schools, privately operated health clinics, and publicly controlled foundations such as some universities and research foundations.
2. The project was organized and financed by the then Social Democratic government but the researchers operated under established principles of academic freedom.
3. Sw. "kränkning."
4. Alva Myrdal received the Nobel Peace Prize in 1982 and Gunnar Myrdal the Prize in Economic Sciences to the Memory of Alfred Nobel in 1974.

5. For a brilliant journalistic analysis of these problems, see Atul Gawande's article "The Cost Conundrum" in *The New Yorker*, July 1, 2009.

REFERENCES

Åberg, R. (1989). "Distributive Mechanisms of the Welfare State: A Formal Analysis and an Empirical Application," *European Sociological Review* 5/2: 188–214.

Alesina, A. and Glaeser, E. L. (2004). *Fighting Poverty in the US and Europe*. Oxford: Oxford University Press.

Barr, N. (1992). "Economic Theory and the Welfare State: A Survey and Interpretation," *Journal of Economic Literature* 30/2: 741–803.

Barr, N. (2004). *Economics of the Welfare State*. Oxford: Oxford University Press.

Béland, D. (2005). *Social Security: History and Politics from the New Deal to the Privatization Debate*. Lawrence: University Press of Kansas.

Berggren, H. and Trägårdh, L. (2006). *Är svensken människa? Gemenskap och oberoende i det moderna Sverige*. Stockholm: Norstedt.

Bergh, A. and Bjørnskov, C. (2011). "Historical Trust Levels Predict the Current Size of the Welfare State," *Kyklos* 64/1: 1–19.

Bicchieri, C. and Xiao, E. (2009). "Do the Right Thing: But Only if Others Do So," *Journal of Behavioral Decision Making* 22/2: 191–208.

Carlson, A. (1990). *The Swedish Experiment in Family Politics: The Myrdals and the Interwar Population Crisis*. New Brunswick: Transaction Books.

Esping-Andersen, G. (1990). *The Three Worlds of Welfare Capitalism*. Cambridge: Polity Press.

Fehr, E. and Fischbacher, U. (2005). "The Economics of Strong Reciprocity," in H. Gintis, S. Bowles, R. Boyd, and E. Fehr (eds), *Moral Sentiments and Material Interests: The Foundations for Cooperation in Economic Life*. Cambridge, MA: MIT Press, 151–92.

Fehr, E. and Gächter, S. (2000). "Fairness and Retaliation: The Economics of Reciprocity," *Journal of Economic Perspectives* 14/3: 159–81.

Fehr, E. and Gintis, H. (2007). "Human Motivation and Social Cooperation: Experimental and Analytical Foundations," *Annual Review of Sociology* 33: 43–64.

Gintis, H., Bowles, S., Boyd, R., and Fehr, E. (eds) (2005). *Moral Sentiments and Material Interests: The Foundations for Cooperation in Economic Life*. Cambridge, MA: MIT Press.

Gould, A. (1988). *Conflict and Control in Welfare Policy: The Swedish Experience*. London: Longman.

Gould, B. (2010). "Markets in a Democracy," *Political Studies Review* 8/1: 55–66.

Graubard, S. R. (1986). *Norden: The Passion for Equality*. Oslo: Norwegian University Press.

Gustafsson, B. A. (2013). "Social Assistance among Immigrants and Natives in Sweden," *International Journal of Manpower* 34/2: 126–41.

Habermas, J. (1987). *The Philosophical Discourse of Modernity*. Cambridge, MA: MIT Press.

Hatje, A.-K. (1974). *Befolkningsfrågan och välfärden: Debatten om familjepolitik och nativitetsökning under 1930- och 1940-talen*. Stockholm: Allmänna förlaget.

Hirdman, Y. (1989). *Att lägga livet till rätta: Studier i svensk folkhemspolitik*. Stockholm: Carlssons.

Hirdman, Y. and Lundberg, U. (2002). "Fakta fäller faktoiden om steriliseringarna," *Dagens Forskning*, May 24, 16–17.

Huber, E. and Stephens, J. D. (2001). *Development and Crisis of the Welfare State*. Chicago: University of Chicago Press.

Huntford, R. (1971). *The New Totalitarians*. London: Allan Lane.

Iversen, T. and Soskice, D. (2006). "Electoral Institutions and the Politics of Coalitions: Why Some Democracies Redistribute More than Others," *American Political Science Review* 100/2: 165–81.

Judt, T. (2009). "What Is Living and What Is Dead in Social Democracy," *New York Review of Books* 56/20 (December 17): 44–7.

Klein, R. (2010). *The New Politics of the National Health Service*, 6th edn. London: Longman.

Knudsen, T. and Rothstein, B. (1993). "Statebuilding in Scandinavia," *Comparative Politics* 26: 333–53.

Korpi, W. (1983). *The Democratic Class Struggle*. London: Routledge & Kegan Paul.

Korpi, W. (2006). "Power Resources and Employer-Centered Approaches in Explanations of Welfare States and Varieties of Capitalism: Protagonists, Consenters, and Antagonists," *World Politics* 58/2: 167–206.

Korpi, W. and Palme, J. (1998). "The Paradox of Redistribution and Strategies of Equality: Welfare State Institutions, Inequality, and Poverty in the Western Countries," *American Sociological Review* 63/5: 661–87.

Kumlin, S. (2004). *The Personal and the Political: How Personal Welfare State Experiences Affect Political Trust and Ideology*. New York: Palgrave/Macmillan.

Larsen, C. A. (2006). *The Institutional Logic of Welfare Attitudes: How Welfare Regimes Influence Public Support*. Aldershot and Burlington, VT: Ashgate.

Larsen, C. A. (2007). "How Welfare Regimes Generate and Erode Social Capital: The Impact of Underclass Phenomena," *Comparative Politics* 40/1: 83–110.

Larsen, C. A. (2008). "The Institutional Logic of Welfare State Attitudes," *Comparative Political Studies* 41/2: 145–68.

Levi, M. (1998). *Consent, Dissent, and Patriotism*. New York: Cambridge University Press.

Lindberg, I. (1999). *Välfärdens idéer: Globaliseringen, elitismen och välfärdsstatens framtid*, 1. uppl. ed. Stockholm: Atlas.

Lindert, P. H. (2004). *Growing Public: Social Spending and Economic Growth since the Eighteenth Century*. Cambridge: Cambridge University Press.

Lipsky, M. (1980). *Street-level Bureaucracy: Dilemmas of the Individual in Public Services*. New York: Russell Sage Foundation.

Lucassen, L. (2010). "A Brave New World: The Left, Social Engineering, and Eugenics in Twentieth-Century Europe," *International Review of Social History* 55/2: 265–96.

Milner, H. (1990). *Sweden: Social Democracy in Practice*, repr. edn. Oxford: Oxford University Press.

Moene, K. O. and Wallerstein, M. (2001). "Inequality, Social Insurance, and Redistribution," *American Political Science Review* 95/4: 859–74.

Myrdal, A. and Myrdal, G. (1934). *Kris i befolkningsfrågan*, 2. uppl. ed. Stockholm: Bonnier.

North, D. C., Wallis, J. J., and Weingast, B. R. (2009). *Violence and Social Orders: A Conceptual Framework for Interpreting Recorded Human History*. Cambridge: Cambridge University Press.

Nyström, P. (1991). "Hur man löser ett skenproblem: Enligt logikens lagar," *Tiden* 83: 180–9.

Olsson, S. E. (1993). *Social Policy and Welfare State in Sweden*. Lund: Arkiv.

Pontusson, J. (2005). *Inequality and Prosperity: Social Europe vs. Liberal America*. Ithaca, NY: Cornell University Press.

Rothstein, B. (1992). *Den korporativa staten: Intresseorganisationer och statsförvaltning i svensk politik*. Stockholm: Norstedts.

Rothstein, B. (1998). *Just Institutions Matter: The Moral and Political Logic of the Universal Welfare State*. Cambridge: Cambridge University Press.

Rothstein, B., Samanni, M., and Teorell, J. (2012). "Explaining the Welfare State: Power Resources vs. the Quality of Government," *European Political Science Review* 4/1: 1–28.

Rothstein, B. and Uslaner, E. M. (2005). "All for All: Equality, Corruption and Social Trust," *World Politics* 58/3: 41–73.

Salonen, T. (1993). *Margins of Welfare: A Study of Modern Functions of Social Assistance*. Lund: Hällestad Press.

Sen, A. (2009). *The Idea of Justice*. London: Allen Lane.

Skocpol, T. (1992). *Protecting Soldiers and Mothers: The Political Origins of Social Policy in the United States*. Cambridge, MA: Harvard University Press.

SOU, Statens offentliga utredningar (1990). "Demokrati och makt i Sverige (SOU 1990:44)." Stockholm: Allmänna förlaget [Swedish Government Official Report].

Steinmo, S. (2010). *Evolution of the Modern State*. New York: Cambridge University Press.

Svallfors, S. (2013). "Government Quality, Egalitarianism, and Attitudes to Taxes and Social Spending: A European Comparison," *European Political Science Review* 5/3: 363–80.

Svensson, T. (1994). *Socialdemokratins dominans*. Uppsala: Almqvist & Wiksell International.

Thullberg, P. (1989). "Gustav Möller," in *Svenskt Biografiskt lexikon*. Stockholm: Riksarkivet, 231–6.

Tilton, T. (1990). *The Political Theory of Swedish Social Democracy*. Oxford: Clarendon Press.

Tyler, T. R. (1992). *Why People Obey the Law*. New Haven: Yale University Press.

Zetterberg, H. L. (1992). *Den svenska socialstaten: Ett forskningsprogram*. Stockholm: City University Press.

SECTION 2

CONSTITUTIONAL DESIGN

SECTION EDITOR
SHIRIN AHLBÄCK ÖBERG

CHAPTER 6

··

INTRODUCTION
Constitutional Design

··

SHIRIN AHLBÄCK ÖBERG

THE Swedish Constitution consists of four fundamental laws: the 1810 Act of Succession (*Successionsordningen*), the 1949 Freedom of the Press Act (*Tryckfrihetsförordningen*), the 1974 Instrument of Government (*Regeringsformen*), and the 1991 Fundamental Law on Freedom of Expression (*Yttrandefrihetsgrundlagen*). The most important of the fundamental laws is the Instrument of Government (IG), since it sets out the basic principles for political life in Sweden as well as defining rights and freedoms. In terms of government type, Sweden is a parliamentary democracy with a constitutional monarchy. However, by the IG of 1974 essentially all political powers were transferred from the Head of State to the Prime Minister or to the Speaker of the Parliament. Thus, in Sweden, unlike most constitutional monarchies, the monarch is no longer even the nominal chief executive.

Considering the number of fundamental laws as well as, for example, the length of the IG (194 articles), the impression might be that constitutional principles are of great importance in Swedish political life. However, references to such principles are very uncommon in legal rulings or in the public debate. Swedish political culture is best described as pragmatic and consensual, where the government's ability to take action—for example, securing various welfare state policies—has been given deliberate precedence over constitutional ideas that focus on limiting government under higher law. The fact that a section on constitutional design in a handbook on Swedish politics is preceded by a section on the politics of the welfare state is a perfect reflection of this reality.

From a constitutional design perspective, Sweden is an interesting case. During the previous IG of 1809, which was based on the principle of separation of powers, comprehensive changes in the practice of government were made without any corresponding amendments of the IG itself. The most noteworthy of these changes were the introduction of universal suffrage for men and women, parliamentarism, and the abolition of the Parliament of the Four Estates, which was replaced by a bicameral system. All these fundamental changes were made in slightly more than 100 years, without any corresponding amendments or changes to the 1809 IG (which was the second oldest constitution in the world). This certainly raises questions on the elasticity of the Constitution, that is, the significance of constitutional rules for political practice in the Swedish setting. The foregoing changes were in effect by 1921, but the IG was not completely rewritten to reflect the true form of government until 1974—a fact that has led constitutional experts to talk about the period of 1921–74 as "the constitution-less half-century" (Sterzel 2009: 18–19). Despite this radical and needed revision of the IG in the 1970s, the contributions in this section will reveal that a weak constitutional culture still prevails in Sweden. For example, when Sweden joined the European Union in 1995, the constitutional adjustments were kept as small and as technical as possible.

Moreover, when one studies the constitutional debate in the parliamentary commissions of inquiry during the last century, another apparent feature of Swedish constitutional culture is the focus on designing institutions for decision-making but a lack of interest in the output side of the political system. Some aspects of the political system have been the object of explicit constitutional design, while other aspects have not.

This section consists of four contributions that mirror this varying degree of political interest. The first chapter is on constitutional history and provides an important backdrop to the current constitutional setting. Olof Petersson concludes that in Sweden the constitution might be unimportant as a norm, but at the same time it is important as written history. In the major constitutional debates of the last century, the design of the election system was one of the clearest exceptions to the claim of a generally weak constitutional interest by the political parties. In the second chapter of this section Jörgen Hermansson shows how ideology and self-interest have been in conflict, and how, despite various thresholds, there is an ongoing pursuit of perfect proportionality. In the third chapter, Tommy Möller demonstrates that the setup of the parliamentary system has also received a great deal of political attention. However, it is also shown how the parliamentary system was introduced without any change in the constitution, and how the codification of this system—50 years later—has resulted in less stability. In the fourth and final contribution, Shirin Ahlbäck Öberg and Helena Wockelberg show how the public sector and the courts have been closely tied together for centuries, and have also been of less constitutional interest, which has resulted in a series of unresolved issues. For instance, despite the fact that the 1974 IG reflects a unitary model of parliamentary government, forms of vertical separation of powers can be found in the constitutional regulations of the dual Swedish administrative model and local self-government.

REFERENCE

Sterzel, F. (2009). *Författning i utveckling: Tjugo studier kring Sveriges författning.* Uppsala: Iustus.

CHAPTER 7

CONSTITUTIONAL HISTORY

OLOF PETERSSON

EVERY observer of the Swedish Constitution must be struck by a paradox. On the one hand, the Constitution might seem very important. Sweden has one of the longest and most elaborate constitutions in the world, consisting of four separate laws (the Instrument of Government, the Act of Succession, the Freedom of the Press Act, and the Fundamental Law on Freedom of Expression). These constitutional laws are often amended and great care is taken to keep them up to date. On the other hand, the Constitution might seem less important. Swedish political culture is pragmatic and consensual. Even though Sweden is ruled by law, constitutional principles are rarely referred to in legal rulings or in the public debate.

In order to understand the importance of unimportant constitutions one must examine the historic background and keep in mind that the positive analysis of constitutions consists of two separate tasks. One set of questions to be answered concerns the background of constitutions. How should the Constitution be explained? What political and other factors have determined the content of the Constitution? This is the study of the Constitution as *explanans*. Another type of question concerns the legacy of constitutions. What could the Constitution explain? What are the observable effects of the Constitution? This is the study of the Constitution as *explanandum*.

The argument of this chapter is that the list of *explanantia* is longer than the list of *explananda*. Much could be said about the background events that shaped the content of the different constitutions in Swedish history. However, not much can be found when studying the impact of constitutional principles. It is noteworthy that Sweden developed into a modern, democratic welfare state without any significant change to its old Constitution (Herlitz 1964; Metcalf 1987; Stjernquist 1999; Petersson 2009).

MEDIEVAL TIMES:
GOVERNING BY LAW AND CONSENT

The lack of written sources makes it impossible to get an accurate image of the power structure of prehistoric times. However, archeological sources indicate that there might have been some substance to the claims of old myths and sagas of the North. The Forsa rune ring, which has been dated to the ninth century, bears a runic inscription suggesting that this is a sacred ring used when swearing an oath. It was probably used at a *þing* site in the province of Hälsingland (Blomkvist, Brink, and Lindkvist 2007).

There was no distinct, uniform, and lasting social culture in pre-Christian times. On the contrary, the available material shows that customs, beliefs, and governance interacted with other parts of northern and eastern Europe. The Scandinavians formed their own traditions under the influence of Sami, Finnish, Baltic, Slavic, and Celtic culture. There is also evidence of numerous contacts with the European continent and the Mediterranean area. But even if there did not exist one unique form of society in northern Europe there are nevertheless some traces of early manifestations of local government. Obviously the *þing* was important both as a gathering place and as a legal institution whose main task was to interpret and apply legal norms. The *þing* followed certain procedures where disclosure and openness were a basic requirement. Public testimonies were used to make conditions of legal significance generally known. The *þing* (*ting* in modern Swedish) is important as an embryonic model for subsequent types of assemblies, such as the national parliament (*Riksdag*), municipal councils (*sockenstämma* and *kommunfullmäktige*), and district courts of laws (*tingsrätt*).

It is impossible to determine precisely who were eligible to participate in the *þing*. Participation was limited to the circle of free men, but this did not mean that women and slaves were completely excluded. In some cases women had the right to present their case in court and were also entitled to make certain economic agreements. Since slaves were considered the property of their master they had a weaker position than free women. However, slaves were also regarded as individuals and could be held personally accountable for various offenses. It could be questioned whether the *þing* as a court of law really consisted of all free men. Instead, the administration of justice was probably handled by a small number of influential people, where the bystanders could follow the proceedings and might also give their final assent to the verdict (Sanmark 2004).

In older times justice was built on oral tradition. In the thirteenth century the corpus of laws in different regions began to be recorded, sometimes on the initiative of the Church. These regional laws influenced the legislation for many centuries to come, both in terms of their archaic and terse language and their organization of the legal text into separate sections (*balkar*). Some of the expressions in these medieval laws have survived until today. "With law shall the land be built" proclaimed the Swedish Upland Law of 1296. Similar statements expressing the rule of law can also be found in Danish and Norwegian laws as well as in the Icelandic *Njáls saga*, also recorded in the thirteenth century.

With the rise of central power the provincial laws were amalgamated into a national legislation. The first Swedish law covering the whole realm was King Magnus Eriksson's national law code, written down around 1350. It was drawn up on the orders of King Magnus Eriksson and prepared by a royal law commission. This law covered Sweden's country districts and it was followed a few years later by similar legislation for the cities and towns. These laws are evidence of the growing power of the monarchy. The national law code contained one separate section about the monarch (*kungabalk*) that forms a kind of contract between the King and the people with mutual obligations. On the one hand, everyone who lives in the country is to show the King obedience, abide by his commandments, and serve him. On the other hand, the King swears an oath to be faithful to all his folk and to abide by laws and legal judgment. This royal code also contains a special procedure for assuring local consent in that the King was required to make a journey to each province in order to receive homage (*eriksgata*).

These medieval elements of rule by law and local consent justify the contention that Swedish democracy has quite a long history. This is not to say that the history is unique to Sweden. On the contrary, there is evidence of similar institutions in other parts of Europe. Court assemblies corresponding to *þing* existed in the Frankish Empire (*mallus*) and in Anglo-Saxon England. The royal code section regulating the rights and obligations of the King is akin to Magna Carta, enacted more than a century earlier.

THE INSTRUMENT OF GOVERNMENT, 1634: ORGANIZING THE STATE

This legal framework remained unaltered for several centuries, with the royal code section of the national law being the closest equivalent to a written constitution. The late medieval period was marked by the increasing power of the monarchy. Royal power was a crucial prerequisite for the unity of the realm. The election of the King, the coronation, and the provincial assent became more ceremonial. The elective monarchy finally had to yield to the hereditary principle under the reign of Gustav Vasa (1523–60). This period was crucial in the history of state formation in Sweden. Sweden gained sovereignty in relation to its neighbors, joined the Protestant Reformation, and created a centralized state administration.

When Gustavus Adolphus came to the throne in 1611 he had to agree to certain demands from the higher nobility represented in the State Council, the equivalent of the *curia regis* institution found elsewhere in Europe. The King promised to seek the consent of the State Council before levying taxes, enacting new laws, and declaring war.

Nevertheless, the young King soon had Sweden involved in the Thirty Years' War, thus beginning the ascent of Sweden as a Great Power of Europe. The increasing power of the King meant that Sweden developed traits of an absolute form of monarchy, but the King, nevertheless, had to rely on Parliament in order to raise taxes. The Riksdag Act of 1617 stipulated that Parliament was to be more formally regulated. The four estates (nobility, clergy, burghers, and farmers) were recognized as equal in fiscal and legislative decision-making. Parliamentary committees were initiated and became increasingly important in the internal working of the Riksdag.

Princess Christina was only five years old when her father Gustavus Adolphus died in November 1632. Since no rules existed for the regency, a new legal document was drawn up by the young queen's councilors, primarily by Lord High Chancellor Axel Oxenstierna. This *regeringsform*, enacted in 1634, set the model for later constitutions. The title is literally translated as "form of government," but "instrument of government" is the standard translation in use. The term "regeringsform" is indeed accurate, since the new law was basically an organizational chart of the Swedish state. Administrative structures were described in minute detail and the territory was divided into counties, each headed by a governor directly accountable to central government in Stockholm, the capital of Sweden. Formally the 1634 Instrument of Government remained in force during the subsequent period of absolute monarchy. However, in actual practice political power was increasingly centralized to the sovereign head of state. The King controlled the legislative process and was able to neglect the advice of the State Council.

The Age of Liberty, 1719–72: Creating a Public Sphere

The term "collapse" offers the most accurate description of the events in 1718. External as well as domestic relations were fundamentally changed. With the disappearance of King Charles XII the country lost its position as a dominating power on the European scene. The King's death also marked the end of an era of strong royal power. The transition from an exceedingly strong King to a politically insignificant head of state was acknowledged in the new Constitution. The Instrument of Government (1719) elevated Parliament to the central organ of political power. The monarch had to accept that parliamentary consent was a necessary prerequisite for laws and directives. The appointment of members to the State Council also became dependent upon parliamentary approval. Although this fundamental law was proclaimed to last for eternity, it was replaced by a new Instrument of Government after the accession of a new monarch one year later. However, the basic regulations remained intact. For the next few decades Sweden became the testing ground for a constitutional experiment.

The combination of a weak King and a strong Parliament implied that political control of ministries and agencies shifted to the elected representatives of the four estates. Gradually the State Council became an executive body controlled by Parliament. A special procedure (*licentiering*) allowed Parliament to force the resignation of a member of the State Council. Sweden now took its first steps into a parliamentary form of government. Two competing factions in the Parliament (the Hats, adherents of mercantilism and a more aggressive foreign policy, and the Caps, proponents of economic liberty and more peaceful external relations) could be regarded as embryonic forms of political parties. "Parties are the life of free nations," wrote a liberal author in a widely read novel from the time (Wallenberg 1781: 20).

The heated debates in the Parliament also spilled over into other arenas. The printing press became an important tool in the struggle for political power. But according to existing laws all public documents, including parliamentary records, were classified as secret. Neither was public criticism acceptable. The Parliament itself started to question these old rules and finally decided to act. Parliament not only enacted a new law to change the situation but also gave it the status of a fundamental law. The Freedom of the Press Act of 1766 is remarkable in several ways (Hirschfeldt 1998). Inspired by England, the Swedish Parliament abolished censorship of all publications, with the exception of those concerning religious matters. Furthermore, Parliament reversed the previous regulation on the availability of public documents. The new rule implied that all documents held by Parliament and state agencies would be free to consult and to print. This general principle was cautiously supplemented with a set of exceptions which would allow the state to keep military and certain other documents protected from public access. Last, but not least, the new fundamental law stated that any citizen was allowed to print and disseminate publications without the interference of the authorities. Legal responsibility for the content for the publications was to be established after the fact by a court of law. This system of post hoc control of press freedom demanded that printed documents identified the responsible publisher. These general rules formulated in the 1766 Freedom of the Press Act laid the foundation for the legal regulation of Swedish media. The Age of Liberty became an era of Swedish enlightenment. During these years public debate, although mostly confined to literate circles in the capital of Stockholm, was very lively and was stimulated by a multitude of leaflets, journals, and books.

The Age of Liberty ended in 1772. This year Gustav III seized power in a *coup d'état* and in 1789 further strengthened royal supremacy by simply abolishing the old Constitution. After his assassination in 1792 his son Gustav IV Adolf took over the throne. The new King detested the Enlightenment and the French Revolution and tried to preserve the old regime. His efforts were met with criticism and his unpopularity reached a height in 1808 when Russia invaded Finland, which had been an integral part of the Swedish realm since early medieval times. In the early months of 1809 it became clear that Sweden had lost Finland to Russia. Oppositional officers started to conspire against the King and insurgent troops set off toward Stockholm. The King was arrested by a group of officers. Shortly afterwards the King abdicated and the country found itself in a revolutionary situation.

The Instrument of Government, 1809: Separating Powers

Following the dramatic events in the spring of 1809, Parliament convened and immediately decided to exclude the King and his heirs from succession to the throne. A new Constitution was proposed but the draft was rejected. Instead, the majority opted to act according to the principle of "Constitution first, King later." A constitutional committee was elected, and after intense negotiations a compromise was drawn up within a few weeks. The Riksdag unanimously approved the new Constitution in June 1809 (Petersson 2009).

According to its own explanation, the constitutional committee had been driven by a desire to satisfy different demands. The Constitution can be seen as a compromise between the two extreme regimes that preceded the dramatic events in 1809. On the one hand, the founding fathers wanted to avoid the excesses of legislative power which characterized the Age of Liberty. On the other hand, they required that the new Constitution contain safeguards against a return to the extreme form of executive rule that had been the basic feature of absolute monarchy. With the 1809 Constitution, Sweden took a step into that particular hybrid form of regime that characterized several European countries during the nineteenth century: constitutional monarchy.

The rationale behind the 1809 Instrument of Government was strongly influenced by eighteenth-century separation of powers theory. The constitutional committee declared that it had tried to shape an executive power, acting within fixed forms and united in its decision-making and implementing power. It had also created a legislative power, slow to act but strong to resist. Finally, the Constitution had set up a judicial power, independent under the laws but not autocratic over them. These three powers had been deliberately directed to guard against each other, as a mutual containment without mixing them or restraining their basic functions.

As a reaction against the previous periods of royal absolutism the 1809 Instrument of Government and the Riksdag Act of 1810, which was also given the status of a fundamental law, introduced several mechanisms in order to safeguard the freedom and independence of Parliament. First, Members of Parliament were given a more or less unlimited right to introduce private member bills. Second, the parliamentary committees increased in number and influence. The constitutional committee was given a permanent status and became a key institution in the parliamentary control of the Cabinet. The constitutional committee was also granted permission to scrutinize the minutes of the Cabinet. Third, the central bank of Sweden, as well as the national debt office, remained under parliamentary supervision. Fourth, an important innovation in the

1809 Constitution was the establishment of a parliamentary ombudsman. The ombudsman was given the task of supervising the observance of the laws and statutes as applied by the courts and by public officials and employees (Wieslander 1994).

When the 1809 Instrument of Government was finally replaced by a new basic law on January 1, 1975, it had become the second oldest constitution in the world still in force. However, although the general architecture remained the same, the 1809 Constitution went through a number of changes during this long period. The changes consisted of formal amendments of individual articles as well as informal reinterpretations of the legal text. When the Constitution celebrated its 150-year birthday in 1959, a legal scholar calculated that only 13 of the 114 articles remained identical to the 1809 wording, and most of these articles had only peripheral significance (Herlitz 1959: 152).

Just as important as these formal revisions was the constitutional transformation by informal reinterpretations (*Verfassungswandel*). Some articles and concepts were gradually given new meaning. The most notable example is the concept of "the King," which in actual practice came to mean "the Cabinet." Other paragraphs became obsolete. There were also examples of flagrant conflicts between the constitutional text and the actual practice.

The first century of the 1809 Constitution was marked by a gradual shift of power from the King to the Parliament. The ministries were reorganized, and this gave the individual ministers a stronger position. The representation reform in 1866–7 replaced the four-estate Riksdag with a two-chamber Riksdag, though still based upon a very limited suffrage. Toward the end of the nineteenth century, social cleavages had manifested themselves in sharper conflicts along party political lines in the Parliament. The conflict between free-traders and protectionists in the late 1880s included heated political debates across the country and marked the beginning of modern election campaigns in Sweden. Struggles over Cabinet formations lasted several decades. Not until 1917 had the King yielded to Parliament and finally accepted the principle of parliamentary government. The Riksdag also advanced its power over legislation and budget issues.

Despite the large number of amendments to the Constitution, the most important rules remained unchanged. It is true that the Cabinet reorganization in 1840 and the reform replacing the old estates Riksdag with a two-chamber representation in 1866 led to significant alterations of the constitutional texts. However, most of the other amendments concerned details and technical adjustments. The overall conclusion is that formal changes to the Constitution had very limited importance for the constitutional development of Sweden (Sterzel 1998).

The years between 1917 and 1921 were crucial in the history of modern Sweden. The old social structure was replaced by a new system based on general suffrage, a democratically accountable Cabinet, popular movements, a free mass media, and the beginning of a welfare society. The extension of suffrage called for a formal change of the constitutional text, albeit not the Instrument of Government but the Riksdag Act. Otherwise, there were only two constitutional amendments of any significance: the introduction of a consultative referendum and the setting up of an advisory council on foreign affairs.

These changes were the few exceptions to the general rule that formal amendments to the Constitution have only played a secondary role (Sterzel 1998: 13). It is significant that the parliamentary system was introduced without any revision of the Constitution. Although Parliament now had taken control over the Cabinet formation, and royal power had been reduced to mainly ceremonial functions, the Constitution still proclaimed that the King alone ruled the realm. This explains that the first half-century of democracy has been characterized as a "constitution-less" period. The old Constitution became increasingly obsolete and did not play any significant political role. New important principles developed outside the Constitution, without any formal recognition (Sterzel 1998, 2002).

On the occasion of the 150-year celebration of the Instrument of Government in 1959 one scholar looked back and concluded that the question about the impact of the Constitution had to be given a mainly negative answer. The Constitution had not received any recognition, even less been revered, in the public mind. The Parliament and the Cabinet had not treated the Constitution with any great respect but rather mistreated it. In the public debate it had almost become ridiculous to refer to letter and spirit of the Constitution (Heckscher 1959).

It should also be added that Sweden might have moved into a common-law system. This would have meant that the written constitution had been replaced by a jurisprudence based on court rulings and the establishment of constitutional precedents. However, such a development never occurred. Sweden lacks a constitutional court and the ordinary courts have been very reluctant to refer to the Constitution in individual cases. The standard classification in comparative law studies, separating formal systems based on Roman law from common-law systems, should be supplemented with a third category. Sweden has proved that it is possible to install a democratic system of government without either amending the written Constitution or using a legal system based on case law (Smith and Petersson 2004).

THE INSTRUMENT OF GOVERNMENT, 1974: CODIFYING PARLIAMENTARY GOVERNMENT

In the wake of the trauma of World War II and the rise of totalitarian regimes in Europe, Sweden slowly started to realize that it lacked a properly functioning constitution that could safeguard democracy. The Cabinet set up a commission of inquiry, which had both politicians and experts as members. The commission started its work in 1954 and the directives called for a comprehensive review of the problems of democratic governance. This review was to form the basis of a proposal for the modernization of the Constitution.

Almost ten years later, the commission reported that it had found it increasingly difficult to fit all the necessary changes into the 1809 Constitution. Thus, it proposed that a new constitution replace the old one. The main argument against keeping the 1809 Constitution was that it did not meet the requirements of a modern constitution. Whereas the 1809 Constitution was based on the idea of the separation of powers, the new Constitution reflected a unitary model of parliamentary government. Moreover, since the mechanisms of the political system had developed without changing the old Constitution, the legal situation in important areas had become unclear. The commission also stressed that a constitution should be easily accessible, possible to read for the average citizen, and useful as a tool in civics education. Furthermore, it had become obvious that it was impossible from a technical and stylistic point of view to introduce new principles within the frame of the 1809 Constitution. The commission drew the conclusion that now was the time to replace the old Instrument of Government with a new one (SOU 1963:16).

However, it would take another decade before a new constitution was in place. One step in this reform process was the introduction of a unicameral parliament and the formal recognition of the parliamentary system of government. The first election to the new Riksdag took place in 1970. For a few years in the early 1970s Sweden was governed under a partially revised version of the 1809 Constitution. The old article stating that the King alone rules the realm was simply deleted and a new article recognizing the possibility for the Riksdag to remove the Cabinet, or individual ministers, by a vote of no-confidence, was introduced. These articles also became part of the new Constitution, which was formally passed in 1974 and came into force in 1975.

Although the new Instrument of Government was completely rewritten, the material changes were limited. The explicit aim behind the 1974 Constitution was not to install a new form of government but rather to codify constitutional practice. The parliamentary system of government had been established half a century earlier and was now written into the Constitution with some minor additions. The King was no longer formally responsible for the Cabinet formation process since this task was transferred to the Speaker of the Parliament. The 1974 Constitution also stated that the Speaker's proposal for a new Prime Minister had to be put to a vote, giving Parliament the option of rejecting the proposal. Parliament also received full legislative power, which meant that new legislation no longer had to be formally approved by the Cabinet. The formal role of the King was reduced to strictly ceremonial functions.

One major innovation of the 1974 Constitution was the introduction of a separate chapter on rights and freedoms. The 1809 Constitution had been more or less silent about the rights and freedoms of individual citizens. The only relevant article contained the old-fashioned words from the medieval contracts between the King and the people, which set some general limitations on how royal power could be exercised. The articles regulating the rights and freedoms in the initial wording of the 1974 Constitution were, however, very brief and were generally considered to be insufficient. Later, the chapter on rights and freedoms was amended several times and is now the longest chapter of the Constitution.

The entire text of the Instrument of Government was revised in 2011 (SOU 2008: 125). Most changes were of a linguistic and editorial nature. The purpose was also to elucidate the status of certain public institutions. For instance, it was decided that the public administration and the administration of justice should be treated separately instead of being mixed together in one combined chapter. A new chapter on local authorities aimed at clarifying the status of municipal and regional self-government. However, the fundamental principle of local self-government is formulated in vague terms and the interpretation of its meaning and scope is still left to Parliament.

In one basic respect modern Swedish history is characterized by constitutional continuity. The weak constitutional culture which marked the years between 1922 and 1975, the half-century which has been called the "constitution-less" period, has not vanished (Sterzel 2002). Sweden certainly has a constitution, but the Instrument of Government is viewed primarily as a set of administrative rules. Of course, elections are held every four years and Cabinets are formed and resign according to the relevant articles. Constitutional arguments, however, still play a quite marginal role in Swedish political life and public debate. The courts of law are still reluctant to refer to the Constitution. In fact, the European Convention on Human Rights has proved more efficient than the 1974 Constitution when it comes to protecting the civil rights of Swedish citizens (Taube 2004; Åhman 2004).

The constitutional culture of a country can be seen as a part of the country's political culture in general. Swedish political culture has been described as involving a pragmatic approach to decision-making and as stressing utilitarian considerations rather than rights-based principles. The Swedish policy style has been identified as being "deliberative, rationalistic, open and consensual" (Anton 1969). Among other things, this means that negotiations and compromise are preferred rather than overt conflicts and legal battles.

The growth of the Swedish welfare state is intimately tied together with this type of political culture. Major social reforms have been prepared through cooperation between political parties, interest groups, experts, and civil servants. Wage negotiations and labor market relations have been handled through a smooth system of bargaining between employers and trade unions. During later years this corporatist system of governance has been challenged by globalization, individualization, and a more fragmented structure of interest representation. Nevertheless, the fact remains that the Swedish welfare state has been built upon negotiations and practical trade-offs rather than constitutional arguments. Citizens' rights have largely been viewed as social rights granted by the welfare state, rather than inalienable human rights laid down in any abstract constitution or granted by some natural law.

Constitutional arguments and constitutional reform have, therefore, played a very limited role in the establishment of parliamentary democracy and a democratic welfare state in Sweden. The development of a modern, democratic society took place outside the Constitution. Extra-constitutional factors, such as neutrality in wartime and the absence of violent conflicts along ethnic, religious, regional, or social cleavages, help to explain Sweden's progress toward the position of being one of the most democratic and affluent societies in the present world.

SWEDISH CONSTITUTION-MAKING: WRITING HISTORY

The Swedish case follows the general pattern of constitution-making. The major shifts in constitutional history have all occurred in the aftermath of great crises. By designing a new constitution in 1634, the higher nobility secured its influence in the political vacuum following the death of the King. Another period of strong royal power ended in 1718, and the subsequent constitutions marked the ascent of parliamentary power. The constitutional acts of 1772 and 1789 demonstrated that the King again dominated the political scene. Military defeat and domestic strife formed the background of the 1809 Constitution.

Constitutions obviously reflect the prevailing forces of power in society. The medieval system of provincial and national laws set the legal rules for a society dominated by local powerholders and aristocrats. The royal codes of the early modern era reflected the state-building efforts of an increasingly powerful monarchy. During the following centuries, political power shifted from the monarch to Parliament and again back to the monarch. It was not until 1809 that Sweden entered an era of constitutional monarchy and a political system based on a separation of powers. The advent of parliamentary democracy and the declining power of the monarch were acknowledged without changing the Constitution.

This brief overview of the major events in the constitutional history of Sweden indicates that a number of *explanantia* are readily available. Explaining the constitution-making process can rely on rich material. How different is the situation when it comes to the *explananda*! Constitutional arguments are rarely found when explaining the major events of Swedish political history.

Of course, Swedish constitutions are not completely void of meaning and significance. There are a number of constitutional articles regulating elections, Cabinet formation, legislation, and other aspects of the political process. The Constitution is respected to the same degree as any other law. However, the Constitution does not really have a special status in relation to other laws of Sweden. It is noteworthy that the present Instrument of Government proclaims that "Public power is exercised under the law"

(Chapter 1, Article 1, Section 3), not "under the constitution." It has been argued that Sweden should be characterized as a *Gesetzesstaat* but not a *Rechtsstaat*. Thus, Sweden is a country ruled by law but not necessarily a more extensive form of constitutional government (von Beyme 1999: 43).

Among the few constitutional principles that continue to shape public life in Sweden one particularly stands out: the Freedom of the Press Act of 1766. This fundamental law created a legal system that protects the public sphere. It abolished censorship and declared that pamphlets, books, and newspapers could be published relatively freely. Openness and transparency became fundamental for the public administration of Sweden. There are a few more examples of important constitutional factors, such as the parliamentary control mechanisms set up by the 1809 Instrument of Government and the creation of a bicameral Parliament in 1866. However, introducing general suffrage and a parliamentary system of government without changing the Constitution led to what can most accurately be called an "a-constitutional" culture. In the democratic era the Constitution was neither revered nor reviled. Rather, it was simply ignored. Only in the last few decades, largely due to European influence, have rights-based arguments begun to enter the Swedish debate.

Sometimes a distinction is made between *normative* and *descriptive* constitutions. It can be questioned whether Sweden fulfills all the criteria of a normative constitution, which include fundamental and stable principles, a clear hierarchy of norms, a constitution difficult to amend, and a constitution respected and referred to in public life. On the other hand, Sweden obviously has a descriptive constitution. The different constitutions in Swedish history might be read as archeological evidence of past struggles for political influence.

The question remains why so much effort in Sweden is still invested in the exact formulation of the constitutional laws. One answer has been suggested by two political scientists studying the political culture of Sweden. They observed that Swedish politics actually consists of two separate elements. One element is consensus-seeking through pragmatic compromise, the other one is history-writing and justifications in the form of ad hoc rationalizations after the fact (Heclo and Madsen 1987: 314). It has been important for the decision-makers to portray the outcome of the bargaining process as a deliberate part of the grand plan for the rational design of society. A Swedish scholar has argued that the 1809 Constitution should be viewed as the history of Sweden converted into articles of law (Fahlbeck 1910: 29). This observation can be extended to Swedish constitutions in general.

On the one hand, the constitutions of Sweden have been relatively insignificant as norms regulating political and public life. On the other hand, the different constitutions in Swedish history have been important as descriptions and justifications. The Constitution might be unimportant as a norm and at the same time important as history-writing.

ACKNOWLEDGMENT

The author wishes to acknowledge the helpful comments and suggestions made by Shirin Ahlbäck Öberg, Anders Andrén, Jörgen Hermansson, Michele Micheletti, Tommy Möller, Eivind Smith, Fredrik Sterzel, and Helena Wockelberg.

REFERENCES

Åhman, K. (2004). "Rättighetsskyddet i praktiken: Skydd på papperet eller verkligt genom-slag?" in E. Smith and O. Petersson (eds), *Konstitutionell demokrati*. Stockholm: SNS Förlag, 172–204.

Anton, T. J. (1969). "Policy-Making and Political Culture in Sweden," *Scandinavian Political Studies* 4: 89–102.

Beyme, K. von (1999). "Does the Constitution Need Reforming?" in O. Petersson et al. (eds), *Democracy the Swedish Way*. Stockholm: SNS Förlag, 17–46.

Blomkvist, N., Brink, S., and Lindkvist, T. (2007). "The Kingdom of Sweden," in N. Berend (ed.), *Christianisation and the Rise of Christian Monarchy: Scandinavia, Central Europe and Rus' c. 900–1200*. Cambridge: Cambridge University Press, 167–213.

Fahlbeck, P. (1910). *Regeringsformen i historisk belysning*. Stockholm: Norstedts.

Heckscher, G. (1959). "Regeringsformen och författningsutvecklingen," in E. Fahlbeck (ed.), *1809 års regeringsform: Minnesskrift till 150-årsdagen den 6 juni 1959*. Lund: Gleerup, 134–51.

Heclo, H. and Madsen, H. (1987). *Policy and Politics in Sweden: Principled Pragmatism*. Philadelphia: Temple University Press.

Herlitz, N. (1959). "Regeringsformen i nutida författningsliv: Erfarenheter från 1939–1955," in E. Fahlbeck (ed.), *1809 års regeringsform: Minnesskrift till 150-årsdagen den 6 juni 1959*. Lund: Gleerup, 152–69.

Herlitz, N. (1964). *Grunddragen av det svenska statsskickets historia*, 6th edn. Stockholm: Norstedts.

Hirschfeldt, J. (1998). "1766 års tryckfrihetsförordning och offentlighetsprincipens utveckling," *Förvaltningsrättslig Tidskrift* 61/1–2: 1–28.

Metcalf, M. F. (ed.) (1987). *The Riksdag: A History of the Swedish Parliament*. New York: St. Martin's Press.

Petersson, O. (2009). "The Swedish Constitution of 1809," in E. Özdalga and S. Persson (eds), *Contested Sovereignties: Government and Democracy in Middle Eastern and European Perspectives*. Transactions, 19. Istanbul: Swedish Research Institute in Istanbul, 53–66.

Sanmark, A. (2004). *Power and Conversion: A Comparative Study of Christianization in Scandinavia*. Occasional Papers in Archaeology, 34. University of Uppsala.

Smith, E. and Petersson, O. (eds) (2004). *Konstitutionell demokrati*. Stockholm: SNS Förlag.

SOU 1963:16. *Sveriges statsskick. Del 1. Lagförslag*. Författningsutredningen, VI. Statens offent-liga utredningar 1963:16.

SOU 2008:125. *En reformerad grundlag*. Betänkande av Grundlagsutredningen.

Sterzel, F. (1998). *Författning i utveckling: Konstitutionella studier*. Rättsfondens skriftserie, 33. Uppsala: Iustus.

Sterzel, F. (2002). "Ett kvartssekel efter 'det författningslösa halvseklet': Har Sverige nu en författning?" in E. Smith (ed.), *Grundlagens makt*. Stockholm: SNS Förlag, 77–98.

Stjernquist, N. (1999). "Land skall med lag byggas: Sveriges författningshistoria," in O. Petersson and A. Wahlgren (eds), *Sveriges konstitutionella urkunder*. Stockholm: SNS Förlag, 9–45.

Taube, C. (2004). "Regeringsformen: Positiv rätt eller redskap för rättshaverister?" in E. Smith and O. Petersson (eds), *Konstitutionell demokrati*. Stockholm: SNS Förlag, 42–70.

Wallenberg, J. (1781). "Min son på galejan." Reprinted in Jacob Wallenberg, *Samlade skrifter*, 2, ed. T. Stålmarck. Stockholm: Svenska Vitterhetssamfundet.

Wieslander, B. (1994). *The Parliamentary Ombudsman in Sweden*. Stockholm: Bank of Sweden Tercentenary Foundation and Gidlunds Förlag.

CHAPTER 8

THE ELECTION SYSTEM

JÖRGEN HERMANSSON

THE design and development of the election system is one of the few constitutional issues that has attracted consistently high levels of interest amongst Swedish politicians over the last century. At the forefront of the ongoing discussion concerning the appropriate rules of Swedish elections has been the aim of achieving a high turnout and wide inclusion in national, local, and European elections. In this chapter I set out to explore both the underlying principles and the politics behind the debates about the electoral system in the Swedish context.

The basic principles of the Swedish electoral system—i.e. the fundamental rules for national and local elections and for referendums—are found in the 1974 Instrument of Government. The first part of this chapter will describe the characteristics of this system. The ambition is to present the essential components of this system, but sometimes it will also include details found in ordinary law. The main objective, however, is to give evidence for an interpretation where proportional representation is its most fundamental guiding principle. The purpose of the second part of the chapter is to present a historical explanation of how this electoral system came about. This story will give evidence for a picture of Swedish constitutional politics where party interests are always at the surface, but it will also be obvious that the political battles concerning the rules of the game have been constrained and shaped by the norms and values to which Swedish politicians adhere. And it seems as if proportionality has become the specific interpretation of what justice means in this sphere of politics.

THE PRINCIPLES

The gateway article of the Instrument of Government states that "Swedish democracy is founded on the free formation of opinion and on universal and equal suffrage" and that it shall be "realized through a representative and parliamentary form of government and through local self-government" (IG, ch. 1, art. 1). This is maybe seen as a general and vague declaration that Sweden is a democracy, but the article also tells us something important and more specific about how the will of the people is represented in the Swedish system. The specific information is that referendums are not included as an essential part of the Swedish electoral system. There is a possibility for binding referendums on constitutional issues if one third of Parliament calls for it (IG ch. 8, art. 16), but this article rather enforces consensus on constitutional matters. All of the large Swedish political parties have sought to avoid election campaigning on technical details of the Constitution. So all six referendums held in Sweden during the democratic era (1922, 1955, 1957, 1980, 1994, and 2003) have been non-binding and, hence, merely advisory. The same holds true for referendums at the local level (the Municipal Referenda Act (SFS 1994:692)).

The construction of the election system is included in the IG chapter on the Riksdag (i.e. Parliament, ch. 3). The electorate—divided into 28 constituencies, which essentially follows the division into counties—chooses between candidates who appear on various party lists, and the votes are in the end weighted together so that the 349 Members of Parliament are distributed fairly proportionally both in relation to the votes for each party and in relation to the number of eligible voters in the constituencies. Through a partial constitutional reform in 1968 this system had already been applied by 1970, i.e. even before the new Constitution was adopted and entered into force in its entirety in 1974. This system has been relatively stable since then, and with minor modifications it also applies to the elections to local assemblies (i.e. the county councils and municipal assemblies).

The basic principles behind the Swedish electoral system are easy to identify (cf. Hermansson 2010: ch. 5):

- The right to vote is universal and equal, as is the eligibility to stand for election.
- The parties are competing for the voters' favor.
- The party candidates are geographically anchored.
- The representation should be proportional.

But just as with all other rule-based systems, there are exceptions. In practice, these principles are violated. For elections to Parliament universal suffrage means that all citizens of a certain age (18 and over) have the right to vote, while in the local elections it is specified in terms of the adult population; also foreign citizens have the right to vote in the local elections if they are permanent residents. The rules for eligibility follow the franchise.

The Swedish parliamentary election is also essentially a party election, but it leaves some room for "personal voting." Since 1998 it has been possible for the voter to put a mark beside the name of one candidate and under certain circumstances this may change the order on the party list.[1] A candidate needs at least 5 percent of the personal votes for this to take effect (until 2010 it was 8 percent in the parliamentary election but 5 percent in local elections). So when distributing the seats within a party, one starts with those candidates who have passed the threshold. When this has been done and if there are still some empty seats, the distribution follows the order of the party list. In practice this reform has had only minor effects on the distribution of seats in Parliament, since most personal votes have been given to candidates at the top of the party lists (SOU 2007:68: 61). Moreover, the possibility of voting for a specific candidate is used only by a minority of the voters. In the election in 2010 it was only one out of four who cast a personal vote (ibid.: 26; and the Swedish Election Authority's official website <www.val.se>).

From this it has been argued that the introduction of personal voting has been a failure. It has not produced its intended effects. It has, however, been argued that the new system has in fact had an effect on political representation, but indirectly and in a delayed way. It has been shown that the distribution of personal votes has significantly influenced the nomination process within the parties (Folke and Rickne 2012). Furthermore, it is obvious from the official statistics that the new system with personal votes has contributed to a presidentialization of Swedish politics. The new system functions as a competition between the top candidates for the different parties, although none of these needs the personal votes in order to get their seat in Parliament. It also seems as if the political parties have been using the new system as a tool for resolving internal ideological conflicts. This is perhaps most obvious in the case of the Social Democratic Party where you can find both pro-EU candidates and EU-skeptics. The party has candidates of both kind on its lists, thereby letting the voters decide the orientation of the party. You can find similar examples from the Christian Democratic Party in some constituencies where there are ideological tensions between religious and secular voters.[2]

Also the spatial anchoring is in fact just a general principle. The electorate is divided into constituencies based on residence, but a candidate need not be resident in his own constituency. It is far from unusual for a Member of Parliament representing a certain constituency to vote in another constituency.

The proportional representation is also a qualified truth. The idea of proportionality is strictly speaking regularly and deliberately violated in two respects. Most importantly, the small parties are blocked. It requires at least 4 percent of the votes for a political party to enter Parliament. It may also be enough if a party succeeds in conquering 12 percent in a single constituency. The strict proportionality relates only to those parties that pass the 4 percent threshold.

The deviation from the strict geographic proportionality is less striking. The 349 parliamentary seats are divided into 310 fixed constituency seats and 39 adjustment seats. The fixed seats are distributed proportionally among the constituencies in relation to the number of eligible voters. When these seats are distributed between the parties in each constituency the aggregated result for the whole country is that the major parties are overrepresented at the expense of the smaller parties. The remaining 39 adjustment seats aim to correct this anomaly and provide nationwide proportionality between parties. When these adjustment seats are distributed among the constituencies, however, no account of the size of the constituency is taken.

It Is All About Proportionality

With the reservations just mentioned, it is no exaggeration to say that the idea of proportionality is at a premium in Swedish constitutional politics. The very core of the
electoral rules states that they should produce a distribution of seats in Parliament that
reflects strict proportionality to those political parties who gain at least 4 percent of
the national votes. It is difficult to get a proportional distribution of seats in each constituency (especially in the small constituencies where only a few seats are distributed).
When these distributions are aggregated the result may be that some parties are favored
at the expense of others. With a lot of small constituencies it would be a stroke of mere
luck if the aggregated result gave rise to the best possible proportional reflection of the
popular votes.

Due to a special Swedish invention in the formula, the distribution in each constituency tends to favor the big parties. Since the early 1950s Sweden has used the odd number method (Saint-Laguë's method which is named after Webster in the US), but not in
its pure sense. Instead of starting with the number 1 as a denominator, the Swedish rules
stipulate that one has to divide the voting score of each party with the number 1.4. For
the big parties this is of no importance. Once they have received one seat, the formula is
the same as the one proposed by Saint-Laguë, i.e. the voting score is divided by 3, 5, 7, etc.
But the suppression of the voting scores for the small parties postpones their reception
of the first seat, which means that the distribution of seats in each constituency is biased
towards the bigger parties. Moreover, when aggregated you also get a parliament where
the distribution of seats is—in the same way—biased towards the bigger parties. This is
why the electoral rule stipulates that only 310 of 349 seats are included in this first step in
the distribution of seats, and the earlier-mentioned 39 adjustment seats are distributed
to the parties in an attempt to reach a perfect proportional reflection of the votes nationwide. In this second step Sweden as a whole is treated as one constituency.

However, this striving for perfect proportionality suffered an unlikely setback in the
2010 election. The 39 adjustment seats were too few to create proportionality. The election had given rise to two major parties, which were overrepresented in the allocation
of fixed constituency seats, and six smaller parties that would be compensated by means
of the adjustment seats in order to give them their fair number of seats in Parliament.
In previous elections, it had worked, but this time it proved practically impossible.[3] The
biggest parties, the Social Democrats and the Moderates, were still overrepresented. In
order to reach strict proportionality there was need for another 19 adjustment seats. The
fault lies not in the method, the formula, to achieve nationwide proportionality. Saint-
Laguë's method is the unique best formula to achieve proportional representation. But
the problem for Sweden is that we also care about relatively small constituencies in order
to strengthen the MPs' geographical representation. On the margin, the problem is also
reinforced by the first denominator 1.4 in the electoral formula.

The distribution of seats after the 2010 election resulted in the Social Democrats
receiving three more seats than the party deserved according to a strict proportional

distribution. For the Moderates the overrepresentation was two seats. This deviation from strict proportionality did not, however, affect the majority conditions in Parliament. Even with a strict proportional distribution of the seats, the center-right Alliance which formed the new government would have been in the minority. But the outcome of the 2010 election raised concern amongst politicians and commentators, since the deviation from strict proportionality could be of importance for the majority conditions in Parliament. And this would be a clear violation of the ethos of the Swedish Constitution.

As usual in Swedish politics, the government set up a commission of inquiry with representation from all political parties in Parliament. At the end of 2012, this commission presented a proposal on how to change the election system (SOU [Government Official Report] 2012:94). The number of seats in Parliament is proposed to remain at its present level, but instead of 310 fixed constituency seats and 39 adjustment seats, the number of fixed constituency seats may be lower and the adjustment seats may increase if necessary to create proportionality. This technique may be understood as a version of the German system where the seats are distributed until the distribution is proportional. The German elections typically give rise to a certain number of extra seats (*überhang-mandaten*) and the parliament also typically includes more than the stipulated minimum of 598 seats. The Swedish commission also proposed an adjustment of the first divisor from 1.4 to 1.2. Since all political parties have agreed on these two proposals it will most likely take effect.

THE POLITICS

The Swedish electoral system is the result of political compromises, but its development also illustrates the primacy of the idea of proportionality in Swedish constitutional politics during the last century (von Sydow 1989: ch. 1.2). This is the overall picture of the development of the Swedish model of elections. But a more detailed analysis reveals that there is more to be said in an accurate historical explanation.

In the following, the most important steps in this story will be presented. Typically these steps involve other aspects of the Constitution as well. When proportionalism first was introduced, the political context was dominated by the battle between the political left and right about democracy and about a change to a parliamentary model. These two steps were tightly linked, if not simultaneous. At the time of the third step—in the beginning of the 1950s—the principle of political democracy was accepted and embraced by all major parties, but the experience of a grand coalition during the War and the dominance of one single political party gave rise to some new constitutional ideas which did not match with the parliamentary model. The outcome, however, was that the parliamentary model was preserved and protected, and—as a byproduct—that the proportionality was improved. In the fourth and last step, at the end of the 1960s, the revision of the election system was again a byproduct; the main concern was to abolish the bicameral system. But as in the previous steps the byproduct was of great importance for the political parties.

Proportionality Is Introduced, 1911

The basic features of the current Swedish electoral system can be traced back to a decision made in 1911, when the old system from 1866 with a plurality vote (mostly in single-member constituencies) was replaced by a proportional system, according to the d'Hondt method. This variant of the proportional method tends to favor the larger parties. If the constituencies are small, the effect of this will be substantial and produce a powerful barrier against small parties. The system introduced in 1911 did just that. A government commission of inquiry had indeed suggested that the counties (in some cases split in two) and the three largest cities would represent constituencies, but in Parliament a concern was expressed that the contact between voters and candidates would become too weak. The old system with single-member constituencies was instead replaced by a subdivision with 56 constituencies with 3–5 seats in each (SOU [Government Official Report] 1977:94: 42–3).

The reform in 1911 can essentially be seen as a byproduct of the battle between the political right and the parties to the left on the extension of the franchise. The Conservatives were forced to accept equal suffrage for men to the Second Chamber. In return the parties on the left agreed to a change in the method of aggregating the votes. The proportional method was conceived to ensure that the Conservatives would not completely lose their strong position (Lewin 1992: ch. 3).

This is, more or less, the conventional wisdom about Sweden's change to a proportional electoral system. It has been backed up with an interpretation of the political battle as a strategic game with the Conservatives as one of the main actors, and an alliance between the Liberal party and the Social Democrats as the other main actor. The game is quite simple: both actors have dominating strategies and the outcome could be interpreted as the second best for the political left (the best would have been universal suffrage with a plurality vote as in Britain), and as the second worse for the Conservatives (the worst outcome would have been that the left had succeeded). This interpretation also confirms Stein Rokkan's idea from 1970 that the change to proportional representation in Europe hundreds of years ago followed one of two different tracks (Rokkan 1970; cf. Calvo 2009). Sweden is mentioned as one of the prime examples of the first track where proportional representation was introduced in order to mitigate the political impact of the emergence and growth of the labor movement. The second track is represented by, for example, Denmark and Belgium where the intention behind a change to proportional representation was to offer a fair representation for certain cultural minorities.

There are, however, some anomalies in the Swedish case. One can argue that both the Conservatives and the Social Democrats were predictable, and by focusing on these two actors the strategic game becomes foreseeable and easy to solve. But what about the positioning of the Liberal Party? At the time, the Liberal's Party leader, Karl Staaff, was seen as the natural alternative to the Conservative candidate as Prime Minister. When discussing universal suffrage he was a politician to the left, and the liberals were hence seen as part of the political left during the pre-democratic era. Staaff was also a strong supporter, plainly an admirer, of the British parliamentary system. So when the Conservative Prime Minister Arvid Lindman suggested a change to a proportional electoral system, Staaff opposed it in spite of the fact that the proposal included an improvement of the suffrage rules. One may also argue that the Liberal Party was in the same situation as the Conservatives. The party's interest would tell in favor of a proportional system where the new distribution formula would function as an insurance for the party's future presence in Parliament. But that was not how the Liberal Party leader calculated. Staaff saw himself as a "man of principle," and he was never prepared to make compromises (cf. Esaiasson 2010). Instead it was another Member of Parliament who acted in order to protect the party's interest. The idea of shifting to proportional representation came from Alfred Petersson (Påboda) and a few other MPs belonging to a conservative rural party group (*Lantmannapartiet*). Petersson was a politician who shared a strong affinity with the rural group within the Liberal Party (*de frisinnade*) and later also became an MP and a member of Cabinet for the Liberals.

So the political right acted in order to protect the future representation of their parties. The long-term effect of this reform was, however, that the non-socialist camp in Swedish politics long remained fragmented.

Universal and Equal Suffrage, 1918 and 1920

A decade later women's suffrage was introduced. This reform was mainly a byproduct of the parliamentary breakthrough in 1917. King Gustaf V had to accept that a left-wing coalition would form the government, and its main objective was to give Sweden an electoral system based on universal and equal suffrage. The decisions in Parliament were made in 1918, and then in 1920 when the constitutional amendment was confirmed by a similar decision a second time (Olsson 2000). The graded vote, the 40-point scale at local elections which meant that wealthy citizens could have up to 40 votes, was also abolished (this affected the elections to the First Chamber indirectly). Not until this moment did Sweden get a democratic electoral system. But the new system based on democratic principles did not mean that all adult citizens became politically equal. To begin with, the voting age was relatively high: 23 years for the Second Chamber in national elections and 27 years in local elections. In addition, some so-called bars were kept. To be eligible to vote it was required that you had an orderly economy. A few percent of the electorate lost their eligibility to vote due to the fact that they were bankrupt, were in the care of social services, or had failed to pay taxes (Stjernquist 1985: 260).

In the shadow of the battle for an expanded suffrage and the struggle for parliamentarism during the 1910s, there was also a discussion about the lack of proportionality of the system that had been introduced in 1911. It was recognized that a system with many small constituencies was not able to produce a proportional distribution of seats in Parliament. To address this, Parliament in 1921 adopted a system reminiscent of the original proposal ten years earlier. Sweden was then divided into 28 constituencies (SOU [Government Official report] 1977:94: 43–4). Apart from some minor adjustments, the same constituency division still remains today.

Improvement of Proportionality, 1952

The breakthrough of democracy was followed by a long period of constitutional inactivity, the exception being a minor reform in 1945 which abolished the last bars and lowered the voting age to 21 years (Stjernquist 1985: 260). The breakthrough of democracy was also followed by an increasingly clear Social Democratic dominance. The largest party was favored by the electoral system and the construction of the bicameral system. With lagging majorities in the indirectly elected First Chamber, the Social Democrats retained their parliamentary position even when public opinion changed. The non-socialist parties saw their opportunity to seize power by forming political cartels, which had been allowed since the middle of the 1920s. They also proposed a new constitutional strategy in the 1940s: the suggestion was to introduce a stronger referendum institution to counterbalance the parliamentary system dominated by a party in majority. This model was inspired by the constitutional system in Switzerland (cf. Hermansson 1993: ch. 5). The demand from the right-wing parties was also that proportionality should be strengthened.

Naturally, the Social Democrats did not mind that the electoral system favored large parties. There were even groups within the Social Democratic Party who wanted to see a return to the old election system. They wanted a model similar to that in Britain which was able to produce strong governments. For Prime Minister Tage Erlander and other Social Democrats of the same generation, this was the most important lesson from the mid-war period: the democratic political system had to have the capacity to take action in times of crisis. But the constitutional position of the Social Democrats was, of course, not only a matter of principles. The party also cared about its own party interest, and was therefore obviously concerned about the fact that the election system (d'Hondt with cartels) tended to bring together the non-socialist parties. This was a threat to the party's holding of government and therefore required some kind of response. For instance, in the beginning of the 1950s the Social Democrats investigated the possibility of yet again going into coalition with the Agrarian Party (as had been the case in the mid-1930s). The price they had to pay for such a cross-bloc coalition was a reform of the electoral system in which proportionality would be strengthened. In this way they managed, however, to do away with the threat of non-socialist cartels (von Sydow 1989).

The original proportionality method, d'Hondt, was replaced in 1952 by the adjusted odd-number method, i.e. the method of Saint-Laguë with an adjustment of the first divisor: instead of using 1 as the first divisor the adjustment stated that one would use 1.4. As mentioned earlier, the effect of this correction was that it made it difficult for small parties to win their first mandate. In practice, the intention was to decrease the number of seats for the Communist Party. A similar reform of the local government election system, and hence the selection of members of the First Chamber, was conducted in 1954. The non-socialist parties were then provided with a strengthening of proportionality—the remaining gaps were due to the adjustment of the first divisor and the division of constituencies and required some form of additional seats to be addressed. The Social Democrats also got what they wanted: when the method of Saint-Laguë is applied, there is no incentive for small parties to get together (except to show unity to the voters). This reform thus contributed to the consolidation of the split within the non-socialist camp.

Further Strengthening of Proportionality, 1968

Electoral reform in the early 1950s turned out to be the starting point for a broader constitutional discussion that included two subsequent governmental investigations involving constitutional experts and all political parties except the Communists. When the first constitutional commission of inquiry (*Författningsutredningen*) was appointed in the late 1950s it was not primarily problems with the electoral system that required a solution. But when questions such as the chamber system and the government were on the agenda, it was not possible to hold the election procedure outside the discussion. The front line was by now well established. The Social Democrats would have preferred a model that strengthened the government and were therefore not averse to a return to a majority election system. The non-socialist parties desired, however, to see a further strengthening of proportionality. The Liberals especially also wanted to remove the backlog of public opinion which the bicameral model created.

In 1963 this constitutional commission (*Författningsutredningen*) proposed a new electoral system reminiscent of the German system, in the sense that voters would cast two votes. The idea was that the voter would get to vote in two different constituencies, but the transformation of votes into seats was in both cases proportional. In the small constituency there would be a strong element of personal vote. When the second constitutional commission of inquiry (*Grundlagberedningen*) took over in 1966, the political parties instead converged on a system that was built on the old model. This commission proposed a system that included a large number of adjustment seats aimed at further strengthening proportionality. To counteract small political parties and a fragmentation of Parliament the commission also proposed a 4 percent threshold. The new system, however, would achieve a nearly perfect proportionality between the parties that managed to cross this 4 percent barrier. The Social Democrats thus gave in to the demands of the non-socialist parties. In return, they retained a kind of connection between national and local politics: the local elections would be held at the same time as the parliamentary elections (von Sydow 1989; cf Ahlbäck Öberg and Wockelberg in this section).

The modification of the odd number method (1.4 as the first divisor persisted) stands out as a remarkable feature of this electoral system. Its intended effect—to make a barrier for small parties—is handled by the abovementioned component in the system: the 4 percent threshold. On the margin, however, the adjustment of the first denominator still plays a role. It affects to what extent a party is assigned fixed constituency seats, or whether the party is to be compensated with adjustment seats. This also affects how the parties' seats are geographically distributed.

The reform of the chamber system and the electoral system was separated from the rest of the reform of the Constitution, and in 1968 Parliament decided that a new electoral system to a new unicameral parliament would come into force before the 1970 elections. All parties—it was only the Communist Party who stood outside the commission of inquiry—were keen to bring about a rapid reform of the electoral system. They were also anxious that there would be broad agreement on the new system.

Minor Modifications of the System

The partial constitutional reform in 1968 gave Sweden the election system that is still in use. This is, however, a truth that should be provided with some reservations. One of the changes that has taken place should definitely not be considered a marginal adjustment. When the new Constitution finally came into force, the franchise was considerably extended. The voting age was lowered from 20 to 18 years old (reduction to 20 years had been implemented in 1965) and Swedish citizens living abroad got the right to vote in parliamentary elections. Perhaps even more significant is the fact that foreign nationals who had lived in Sweden for more than three years in 1976 were given the right to vote in municipal elections (Stjernquist 1985: 261).

Some other examples of continuous constitutional engineering should also be noted. Before the 1998 election, a system for personal voting was introduced. Voters were given the opportunity to support one of the candidates on the ballot in which the parties already present their own ranking. In addition, the number of seats was adjusted in 1976 from 350 to 349; the constituency division was slightly modified in connection with the formation of the new county Skåne (the province Skåne had been divided into two administrative counties and three different constituencies); and the term was extended from three to four years from the 1994 election (von Sydow 1989). The revision of the Constitution decided after the 2010 election made no significant impact on the electoral system. The only change was that the threshold for votes on individual candidates was reduced to the same level as in the local elections, i.e. from 8 to 5 percent.

All these amendments of the electoral system in the framework of the 1974 IG have been implemented in large political consensus. There have not been any dramatic changes, and this is by no means a coincidence. The IG's rules for constitutional change impose caution and stipulate that broad party agreement should be achieved. A change to the Constitution requires two identical decisions by Parliament with an election in between. For these parliamentary resolutions only a simple majority is required. But the Constitution also provides an opportunity for one third of Parliament to trigger a referendum. Instead of a second parliamentary decision the voters could be given the opportunity in a referendum to vote yes or no to the dormant constitutional proposal.

Such a referendum should, however, be conducted in conjunction with a scheduled general election (see IG 1974: ch. 8, art. 16). It should be added that such a referendum has so far never taken place, since none of the major parties is interested in such a scenario. Each time a change of the electoral system has been on the agenda it has been important to see to it that almost all the political parties in Parliament support the change. From this it also follows that none of these parties has an interest in launching a controversial proposal.

The very careful handling of the components of the election system that characterizes the current political situation is not simply an effect of the constitutional framework, however. There is also a fairly large consensus on the electoral system's fundamental principles.

The Mechanisms and Principles of Constitutional Design

In order to understand the politics of the electoral system, a good starting point is to look for party interests. When confronted with a new proposal about how to construct the electoral system, political parties will always check whether they will gain or lose any seats in Parliament. Hence, constitutional politics is definitely an arena where interests matter. But constitutional politics is also an arena where political parties in the Swedish context stress the need for broad and stable agreements.

These two factors—party interest and stable compromises—might imply that it is hard to change the rules of the political game. Nonetheless, the election system has been changed and revised in several steps during the last century: in 1911, 1920, 1952, 1968, and in several minor amendments under the current Constitution. One important explanation for this is that the politics of election rules has been nested with controversies over other constitutional matters. Not seldom, change to the election system has been the byproduct of a need to settle an agreement among the political parties on another component of the constitutional framework.

The politics of elections, however, is also an arena where principles have a voice. In constitutional politics the democratic principles of universal and equal suffrage are the real trump. This has been the situation since the 1920s when the Conservatives gradually accepted the principles of democracy. In Sweden, the principle of proportionality has today almost gained the same status in the election system. The idea of proportional representation was introduced a hundred years ago by the Conservatives in order to reduce the political impact of the emergence and growth of the labor movement. A more general version of Rokkan's hypothesis also holds true for later revisions of the election system: improvement of proportionality was a technique used to reduce the dominance of the Social Democratic Party. The strength of the idea of proportional representation was that it was easy to frame as a principle of justice for the election system. This fits nicely with socialist rhetoric in most other areas, and it became almost impossible for the Social Democrats to resist it. Today, proportionality seems unquestionable.

ACKNOWLEDGMENT

The author wishes to acknowledge the helpful comments and suggestions made by Edward Page.

NOTES

1. In fact, this had already been introduced in 1995 in the first Swedish election to the EU Parliament.
2. The last two arguments are not based on systematic research, but the evidence can easily be gathered from statistics presented on the Swedish Election Authority's webpage: <www. val.se/tidigare_val/index.html>.
3. In fact, a minor problem of this kind had occurred already in the election in 1979. However, at that time nobody seemed to care about this deviation.

REFERENCES

Calvo, E. (2009). "The Competitive Road to Proportional Representation: Partisan Biases and Electoral Regime Change under Increasing Party Competition," in *World Politics* 61/2: 254–95.

Esaiasson, P. (2010). *Sveriges statsministrar under 100 år: Karl Staaff*. Stockholm: Bonniers.

Folke, O. and Rickne, J. (2012). *Personröster och politiska karriärer*. Stockholm: SNS Förlag.

Hermansson, J. (1993). *Politik som intressekamp*. Stockholm. Norstedts Juridik.

Hermansson, J. (2010). *Valsystem*. Stockholm: SNS Förlag.

Lewin, L. (1992). *Ideologi och strategi: Svensk politik under 100 år*, fjärde upplagan. Stockholm: Norstedts Juridik.

Olsson, S. (2000). *Den svenska högerns anpassning till demokratin*. Acta Universitatis Upsaliensis, Diss. Uppsala: Uppsala University.

Rokkan, S. (1970). *Citizens, Elections, Parties*. New York: David McKay.

SFS 1994:692. The Municipal Referenda Act.

SOU 1977:94. *Personval och valkretsindelning*, betänkande av Personvals- och valkretsutredningen. Stockholm: Justitiedepartementet.

SOU 2007:68. *Ett decennium med personval*. Stockholm: Justitiedepartementet.

SOU 2012:94. *Proportionalitet i val samt förhandsanmälan av partier och kandidater*, delbetänkande av 2011 års vallagskommitté. Stockholm: Justitiedepartementet.

Stjernquist, N. (1985). "Riksdagen i vår tid: Perioden från 1921," in *Riksdagen genom tiderna*. Stockholm: Sveriges Riksdag/Stiftelsen Riksbankens Jubileumsfond, 255–360.

Sydow, B. von (1989). *Vägen till enkammarriksdagen: Demokratisk författningspolitik i Sverige 1944–1968*. Stockholm: Tiden.

CHAPTER 9

....

THE PARLIAMENTARY
SYSTEM

....

TOMMY MÖLLER

LATE CONSTITUTIONAL REGULATION
OF PARLIAMENTARIANISM

ALTHOUGH Sweden has had a parliamentary form of government since 1917, it was not until the 1970s that it was written in the Constitution. With the establishing of the Instrument of Government of 1974 and the partial constitutional reform in 1970, when the bicameral parliament was replaced by a unicameral system, the conditions for Swedish parliamentarianism changed. The idea was that the new Constitution would codify and maintain the stable regime that had existed for so long. However, the stability came quickly to an end.

With the unicameral reform, a 4 percent rule in the election system and a formal procedure for Parliament (the Riksdag) to express its lack of confidence in the Government also followed. The purpose of the former rule was to facilitate the forming of Government and to guarantee a strong governmental power by keeping small parties from being represented in Parliament. With the opportunity to initiate a vote of no confidence (censure), Parliament was provided with a constitutional ability to remove governments that was not previously available. If 10 percent of the members of Parliament (35 members) demanded such a vote against the Prime Minister and at least half of the Members of Parliament in this vote were behind the demand, the Government had to resign. An equivalent motion of no confidence could target a specific Cabinet member, but if it was approved it was only this minister that had to resign and not the entire Government.

It was the principle of negative parliamentarianism that was now consequently implemented, with a weaker concept of confidence than that of positive parliamentarianism. The essential idea was that the Government was accepted by Parliament, not that a majority was openly behind its politics. It was a model that eased the forming of Government and made minority governments possible. As Bäck and Bergman show in their contribution to this *Handbook*, Sweden belongs to a small category of countries where minority governments are the most common form of cabinets.

For a long time this model has functioned well, completely in accordance with the intentions. But in recent years, as more parties have been represented in Parliament, the model has been weakened. There has been a fragmentation of the party system that has made it harder to form strong governments. The difficulties will most likely increase further as a consequence of new regulations imposed by the substantial revisions of the 1974 Instrument of Government in 2011: each election shall be followed by a mandatory vote in Parliament to elect the Prime Minister. On the other hand, it has become easier for minority governments to push through their policy, since Parliament's decision procedures for the budget have changed. I will return to these issues later in this chapter.

Sweden is a constitutional monarchy, and the King is thus head of state. However, the King has lost all formal power in the new Constitution and an important statement for the principle of parliamentarianism is that the Speaker has taken over the King's role in the forming of Government. Sweden is thereby the only parliamentary system where the head of state is not involved in the process of government formation, either by appointing or nominating the Prime Minister (Bergman 2011: 141).

The Speaker's proposal could only be downvoted by an absolute majority (175 members). Another aspect in accordance with the principle of negative parliamentarianism is that the position of the Prime Minister was strengthened. Prior to the Instrument of Government of 1974, a more collegial relation among the ministers was at hand. The Prime Minister was "the foremost amongst equals"—a *primus inter pares*. Now, the role played by the Prime Minister in the forming of Government had been enhanced. The Prime Minister appointed ministers and had the central role when it came to leading and organizing the government's work (see Bäck and Bergman's chapter and Ahlbäck Öberg and Wockelberg's chapter in this volume).

Conceptual and Theoretical Framework

Conceptually, parliamentarianism is characterized by the idea that the formation and policy of the executive power is based on the confidence of the parliament. According to Sartori, the central condition for a parliamentarian form of government is that Parliament appoints and supports the Government, and has the ability to dismiss it (Sartori 1997: 101; Strøm 2000). The constitutional hierarchy is thus clear: Parliament is formally superior to the Government. However, the relative influence over the shaping of politics can vary between Parliament and the Government. Normally, the executive leaves its mark on the parliamentarian form of government when it comes to legislation and financial policy. Only in rare cases do parliaments play the central role (Hermansson and Persson 2010: 16; Tsebelis 2002).

From this conceptual core, two theoretical approaches within parliamentarian research can be perceived. According to the first approach, a delegation of power occurs from Parliament to the Government, which is responsible to Parliament. This delegation of power originally comes from the citizens who choose the members of Parliament. Hence, from a normative point of view parliamentarian democracies can be inserted in a principal-agent perspective: the will of the people is implemented within this process of delegating power. This is one approach.

The British Westminster system has worked as an inherent parliamentarian ideal in previous research, and any deviation from this model has been subjected to close empirical analysis (Verney 1992). Literature talks of "the pure form of parliamentarianism," with a clear separation between the governing and opposition sides (Dahl 1956). In the extensive Swedish parliamentarian research pursued under the lead of Axel Brusewitz this approach was guiding, albeit in an indirect way (Brusewitz 1951). This is also done, more explicitly, by von Sydow (1997) in his analysis of the growth and development of Swedish parliamentarianism up to 1945. The conditions posited by Verney emphasize the differences between parliamentarianism and other political systems, formed according to the separation of powers. An important difference to a presidential system is therefore that the government in such a system is accountable directly to the people, which is not the case in a parliamentarian democracy. An additional difference is that the head of state and the head of government are separate functions in a parliamentarian system.

In constitutional terms, Parliament's ability to dismiss the Government is the core of the concept of the parliamentary system, but in a broader sense it also concerns the Government's formation and composition. There are furthermore additional features, i.e. that ministers ought to be members of Parliament, that the Prime Minister is dominant in the work of Government, and that the Government is collectively responsible for its decisions (von Sydow 1997). This concerns ideal norms, the purpose of which is to determine what degree of compatibility for a particular system there is to the British ideal model.

Whichever of these theoretical perspectives one uses, it is important to point out that parliamentarianism is not about a downright delegation of powers in the simple way that the principal-agent perspective prescribes. In fact, governments act not only on Parliament's command but also have considerable room for maneuver of their own. Within the constitutional frame, the Government can operate relatively independently as long as an incompatible relation with Parliament does not occur. To make sure that such a relation does not occur, the Government usually has significant power instruments: in Sweden for example the opportunity to demand a vote of confidence or to call an election and thereby resolve the Parliament.

As Hermansson and Persson (2010) define a parliamentary system, they consider two aspects. Firstly, it is emphasized that the power balance between the Government and Parliament can fluctuate: to what extent does the executive power dictate? The dominance can be extensive as long as Parliament has the ability to control the executive power. Secondly, it is recalled that the power balance within the Government may vary. The Prime Minister is expected to be the dominant actor, but if the dominance becomes remarkably obvious, collective decision-making tends to be undermined (Hermansson and Persson 2010: 21). The hypothesis that a presidentialization has taken place within the parliamentarian democracies can be interpreted as an indication of the increased power of Prime Ministers (Daléus 2012; Aylott 2005).

This chapter focuses on both these dimensions. The first one, concerning the core of parliamentarianism, is most important. However, it is important to note that a government's ability to dominate the parliamentarian process is not only about the number of seats in Parliament, i.e. whether the government has a majority or not. The Cabinet's internal cohesiveness is a factor that can be at least as important. Hence, size and coherence are the two dimensions explaining the strength of the government.

The other dimension—to what extent the Prime Minister dominates—concerns internal power relations within the Cabinet rather than the relationship between Parliament and the Government. But how these power relations are composed may in some cases have significant implications as to the way parliamentarianism works in practice.

In order to understand the variations of parliamentarianism between different political systems and within these systems over time, a systematic description of two structural dimensions is needed. Firstly, the institutional rules that establish the parliamentarian way of functioning: this concerns the electoral system, rules for Government formation, and Parliament's control power, but also the procedures regulating the legislative process and the means by which the budget is decided. Secondly, the party structure makes up an important piece of the puzzle for the way in which parliamentarianism works. With many parties the premises are often worse when it comes to Government formation, and the ability to govern effectively decreases when minority governments that do not have a pivotal position in the party system are in power. This dimension is to a large part connected to the first: countries with proportional electoral systems are more likely to have a fragmented party system compared to countries that use majoritarian elections (Duverger 1964).

THE GROWTH OF PARLIAMENTARIANISM IN SWEDEN

There are great variations in development, shape, and functioning of parliamentary systems in Europe. In some countries, parliamentarianism has been the result of a revolution and in others it has been part of the process of national independence. Sometimes a parliamentary process occurs due to a weakening of monarchical power. In general, a natural cause has been universal development in a constitutional direction; during the latter part of the nineteenth century the process of democratization was an important factor behind the progress of parliamentarianism in several countries. Although varia-tions concerning the structure of the institutions of parliamentarianism were substan-tial, during the post-World War II period different countries influenced one another. Furthermore, institutional settings such as the role of the head of state and rules of form-ing Government and parliamentary control have become more similar.

First, a distinctive Swedish feature in parliamentary development was the Age of Liberty between 1719 and 1772. During this constitutional period there was a clear par-liamentary tendency. Parliament was in a dominant position over the monarch and his counsel, which was a pre-modern Cabinet (Hallberg 2003).

A second trait differentiating Sweden from the other Nordic countries (although existing also in countries outside Scandinavia) is that parliamentarianism was estab-lished in a bicameral system. The elections to the two chambers differed in several ways, but they were equal in terms of power, which is a potential problem for the function of parliamentarianism. In Sweden, however, this balance of powers worked out quite well, because there were common committees and also common voting on financial issues (von Sydow 1997).

A third distinguishing characteristic of Swedish parliamentarianism is the consen-sual political culture. Swedish governments have been focused on cooperating with the opposition in a way that differs from other parliamentary systems, especially the sys-tem in Great Britain. According to a classic study by Rustow (1955), the pursuit of com-promise has been the characterizing element of Swedish parliamentarianism. The most important institutional cause of this has been the introduction of proportional elections in 1911, although acts of compromise were apparent even earlier.

Parliamentarianism had its definitive breakthrough in 1917 when the coalition of Liberals and Social Democrats was formed. However, when this government resigned three years later, a long period of minority governments began. Not until 1936 was there another majority government, this time a coalition of the Social Democrats and the Farmer's League (agrarians). During the period between these two majority govern-ments, Sweden was governed by a total of thirteen minority governments (including two caretaker governments). In other words, the reality did not follow the ideal pat-tern for the Westminster theory of parliamentarianism. In the years between 1920 and 1936, it proved impossible to form a majority government since the Liberal Party was not willing to govern with other parties (Möller 2011). Instead, the doctrine of parlia-mentary confidence was softened. It was enough for the Government to be accepted by Parliament instead of gaining its confidence in a more absolute sense. Political scien-tists formulated the concept of "negative parliamentarianism" to describe this change of doctrine.

The transition to parliamentary government was not the result of a deliberate consti-tutional reform, but rather was the result of a power struggle. This kind of process is a distinguishing feature of Swedish politics. It has rarely been about constitutional design in the sense of carefully designed and long-planned intentions when constitutional changes have taken place. Rather, those reforms have occurred ad hoc, after intense debate.

Although the final breakthrough was not until 1917, there were clear tendencies toward a parliamentarian path before then. The government successively became more independent of the King, who was head of state; in the late nineteenth century the King's power over governmental policy decreased significantly, even though the King, according to the Instrument of Government of 1809, "had the right to alone rule the kingdom" (§ 4). Instead, governments became more dependent upon the opinion of Parliament. Accordingly, the Swedish form of government was influenced by parliamentarian elements well before the breakthrough of 1917. These parliamentarian tendencies became even clearer with the strengthening of the party system that occurred at the beginning of the twentieth century, when the parties represented in Parliament created strong organizations on a national level and started to pursue more intensive election campaigns (Esaiasson 1990). This led to sharpened ideological disagreements and more disciplined party behavior in the parliamentary work.

The Liberal–Social Democratic coalition government of 1917, led by the Liberal Nils Edén, was formed after a great deal of commotion. 1917 was a year of revolutions in Europe, and radical opinions were apparent in Sweden as well. Demands for the abolition of the monarchy were made. After the left's successes in the election of 1917, it was difficult for the King to oppose the forming of the Liberal–Social Democratic coalition government, despite his obvious reluctance to accept it. However, he did not only give in to public opinion and the left's majority in the Parliament resulting from the election; he also accepted that the opinion in Parliament would be decisive for future Government formation. In addition, the King promised not to make political statements opposing the government's political program. In other words, it was a complete surrender to the principle of parliamentarianism (Möller 2011: 87).

FROM CRISIS TO STABILITY

All governments in Swedish politics after 1917 have had confidence in the sense implied by the concept of negative parliamentarianism. However, parliamentarian work has sometimes been characterized by turbulence, with uncertain and sometimes also unexpected voting outcomes in the chamber. This was especially true of the period up to 1932.

The formation of governments followed a pattern. After the introduction of universal suffrage, every election to the Second Chamber led to a shift in government up until 1940, when Sweden was led by a new coalition government. The party that was successful in elections formed a government. Between 1921 and 1936, five elections took place, and in four of these Social Democratic governments were formed following the party's electoral successes. In 1928, a Conservative government was formed with the same logic. These governments were grounded on the "election wind." The problem was that the governments did not have a majority in Parliament and were not able to get through their most significant policies. Consequently, these governments fell rather quickly and the result was the formation of minority governments with a pivot position.

These governments, in the middle of the political field, did not come about due to election results but rather because of the fall of the previous governments. Although they enjoyed only limited parliamentarian support, these governments were able to influence political decision-making in issues they themselves held most important, because they could rule with the support of shifting majorities. However, in following elections, they failed to get the support of the voters.

Thus, the Swedish parliamentarianism was unstable until the Social Democratic government with Per Albin Hansson as Prime Minister was formed in 1932. Hansson's administration was a minority government, but with 41.7 percent of the votes it was relatively strong. However, this administration did not have support in Parliament for its financial policies, which was at the time a major issue since the economy was in crisis with the rise of mass unemployment. But an agreement with the Farmers' League in 1933 made it possible for the Hansson administration to get its economic program through Parliament. The agreement resulted in a shift to what could be called "partial majority parliamentarianism," and in contrast to other European countries in the 1930s Sweden was characterized by stability. After the 1936 election the Social Democrats and the Farmers' League formed a coalition, which meant that for the first time since Edén's administration Sweden had a majority government. The parliamentarian support for this administration was overwhelming: in the First Chamber both parties had 59 percent of the seats and in the Second Chamber 64 percent. But similar to the Liberal–Social Democratic coalition barely two decades earlier, the government was internally divided, and in the Farmers' League there were critical voices against participating in the government (von Sydow 1997: 215–16).

Following the outbreak of war in 1939, there was a reshuffle: even the Liberal Party and the Conservatives were now to enter the government. Only the Communists were left out. The government was until the end of the war in 1945 based on nearly 99 percent of the Parliament's seats. In terms of size, the coalition government during the war was thus extremely strong. But due to its strong parliamentarian base, and the fact that there was no risk of it losing in any votes, it became possible for individual Members of Parliament, representing one of the four parties in government, to vote against government bills.

The period after World War II was characterized by a remarkable stability. The broad coalition government was replaced in 1945 by a Social Democratic minority government that—not counting six years (1951–7) when a coalition government between the Social Democrats and the Farmers' League ruled once again—was in power until 1976. Between 1968 and 1970, the Social Democrats had their own majority. However, the Social Democrats' dominant position meant they could control policy-making as if they had a majority even during the long period when they had a minority position. The Communists were a reliable supporting party that despite wielding very little influence were conceived as part of the governmental base in Parliament.

During this time, Swedish politics developed the character of a two-party system. The dominant party together with its loyal supporting party mobilized the majority of voters; they were challenged by the three non-socialist parties—the Moderate

Party (Conservatives), the Liberal People's Party, and the Center Party (until 1958 the Farmers' League)—that came to be an increasingly integrated non-socialist bloc. Firstly, a Center–Liberal alliance was established, and after a while the Moderate Party joined them. There were, however, evident disagreements between the three parties and for a long time there was an uncertainty about their ability to govern together. The uniting factor was their common ambition to prevent the, in their perspective, increasingly socialistic politics conducted by the Social Democratic government. Hence, the motive for their collaboration was a strategic decision, motivated by the desire to win power (Möller 2011).

The protracted Social Democratic hold on power can be explained by looking at institutional arrangements. Firstly, up until 1950 an electoral method was used which was beneficial to the largest party when parliamentary seats were distributed. In the election of 1948, the non-socialist parties got more votes than the Social Democrats, who despite this got more seats. Secondly, the two-chamber system that was kept until 1970 did in practice work as a constitutional advantage for the Social Democratic government. The members of the First Chamber were appointed successively—one third of the members were appointed every third year—and this made governmental shifts more difficult. After the election of 1948, for example, the Social Democrats had 56 percent of the seats in the First Chamber even though the party in the prior municipal elections (it was the municipalities that indirectly appointed the members of the First Chamber) had received only 45 percent of the votes.

At the same time as Swedish parliamentarianism copied certain traits from the British Westminster model, there were also clear influences from the consensus-driven parliamentarianism of Switzerland. As mentioned earlier, Swedish political culture has been strongly consensus-oriented. The shape of the political decision-making process facilitated this. Important issues were prepared in committees of inquiry in which frontbenchers, experts, and representatives of relevant interest organizations participated. The work in these committees often resulted in common agreement in identifying the problems that made it easier for the parties to agree on policies (Ruin 1968).

Increased Turbulence

The purpose of the constitutional reform in 1970 was to codify the system that had existed since the parliamentary breakthrough in 1917, but at the same time the reform—through the transition to unicameral parliamentarianism—increased the possibility of a power shift since the opposition no longer needed to win two elections in a row to get a majority. The election in 1973 resulted in an exact balance between the two blocs (175–175) since the total number of seats had been set at 350. A strange period in Swedish political history followed, where the two sides opposed each other on many important decisions, which were decided by lottery. The number of Members of Parliament was consequently reduced to 349 three years later, when a power shift took place. Nearly half a century of uninterrupted governing by one party was thereby broken in the election of 1976.

In 1976, Sweden had for the first time since introducing the unicameral parliament a majority government. However, this government, led by the leader of the Center Party Torbjörn Fälldin, was a weak one due to internal disagreements. The three parties in power were unfamiliar with governing, and inertia as well as lack in coherence came to characterize the government's work. After two years, Fälldin was forced to resign as Prime Minister due to the governing parties' failure to find a compromise on nuclear power. In the following year, Sweden was governed by a Liberal minority government led by Ola Ullsten. This was the weakest government since 1936: Ullsten's Cabinet did, however, fulfill the demand for coherence, although it was unable to get important parts of its policies through Parliament. The government had several significant defeats, and from a formal point of view, Swedish parliamentarianism in the spring of 1979 can hardly be said to have lived up to the parliamentarian requirement of the government having confidence as long as a serious state of opposition does not occur in relation to the Parliament. However, it was tolerated by the majority as a temporary solution while waiting for the election that was to be held within a few months.

During the period of 1976–82 there was a total of four non-socialist governments. After a long period of stability, which could be said to have ended with the equilibrium parliamentarianism of 1973–6, a decade of instability followed. In contrast to the intention of the Instrument of Government of 1974, which was to promote strong governments, there was a weakening of governmental power during this time.

When the Social Democrats returned to power in 1982, Swedish politics returned to the pattern previous in this turbulent decade. Again, the party ruled in minority but acquired around 45 percent of the votes in the three elections of the 1980s. Moreover, as before, the Communists in parliament backed it up. The Social Democratic government thereby had the ability to implement its policies. One exception was, however, when the Communists refused to accept a government bill on a tax policy issued by the Palme administration in the fall of 1982, which, for the first time, forced the government to negotiate with its supporting party.

Until 1990, Sweden had a type of minority parliamentarianism comparable to majority parliamentarianism. This year, however, the Communists refused to endorse the government's financial crisis package with strike prohibitions and wage freezes, and the government was forced to resign. The resignation was the result of Prime Minister Ingvar Carlsson initiating a vote of no confidence on the crisis policies, and actually losing the vote. It proved impossible to form an alternative government, and Carlsson therefore resumed his position within a few days. The period of 1988–91 came to be more unstable than the previous six years. Within the governing party there were disagreements on important issues that undermined the government's authority (Möller 2011: 235).

Furthermore, a new party entered Parliament in 1988, namely the Green Party. It was the first time since the parliamentarian breakthrough that the stable Swedish five-party system had been challenged, and the new party was initially keen on staying neutral to the two political sides that had long opposed each other in a way similar to British parliamentarianism. Moreover, the Green Party's group in Parliament included members with differing views on how parliamentarian work was to be done. When the party's leading representatives made an agreement with the government in 1990, it was not possible to mobilize support among the party's members in Parliament. As a consequence, the Social Democrats regarded the Green Party as unreliable for a long time thereafter. Cooperation between the two parties did not occur until after the election in 1998.

The year following the governmental crisis in 1990, the Social Democrats lost the election and once again a non-socialist government was formed, this time led by the Moderate Party leader Carl Bildt. The Bildt administration included four parties: alongside the three non-socialist parties that had ruled together earlier, the Christian Democrats who entered the Parliament in 1991. Although consisting of four parties, it was a minority government. In this election there was also a new populist protest party, *Ny Demokrati* (New Democracy), which made its way into the Parliament. The new party was formally a supporting party to the Bildt administration as it abstained from voting when Parliament chose the Prime Minister, thereby indirectly making it possible for Bildt to be elected.

During Bildt's years as Prime Minister, it was obvious that Sweden was ruled by a minority government. Several times, the government's bills were downvoted by Parliament. Even so, this minority government ought to be perceived as unexpectedly effective, despite consisting of four parties and consequently as many veto-actors as the broad coalition government during the war. The Bildt administration brought more government bills to Parliament during its first year in power than all previous governments. More clearly than any other government since 1932, the Bildt administration had a reformist agenda (Möller 2011: 76–7). However, as a consequence of the overheated economy from the 1980s, the real estate market fell apart and the banks fell with it, unemployment increased rapidly, and public finances were dramatically weakened. The two crisis agreements that were made in the fall of 1992 between the government and the Social Democrats indicated that the political culture of consensus was still strong.

The Social Democratic minority government that ruled until 2006 sought cooperation with other parties more systematically than previous governments—first with the Left Party (the former Communist Party), and thereafter with the Center Party in a more institutionalized form. After the election in 1998, the Government started cooperating with the Left Party and Green Party instead. Like the Center Party, these parties got to assign political officials in the Cabinet Office. The red–green cooperation was successively increased up to the 2006 election, but did not involve foreign policy and EU issues.

In 2006 Sweden got a majority government for the first time in 25 years with the four-party government under Fredrik Reinfeldt, leader of the Moderate Party. Cooperation with the Social Democrats was now limited almost exclusively to EU issues and foreign policy. After the 2010 election, the Reinfeldt administration lost its majority position. As a result of the entrance of the Sweden Democrats—a right-wing populist party—in

Parliament, the government's situation was considerably weakened, although it lacked only one seat for a majority.

During its first year in Parliament, the Sweden Democrats supported the government's bills to a large extent. But some government bills of central importance for the government were downvoted. To this it should be added that the Reinfeldt government abstained from presenting government bills that could be opposed by potential voting coalitions of the four opposing parties. In some cases, Parliament has pursued so-called "announcements," i.e. assigning the government to work out proposals in certain areas in accordance with the parliamentarian majority's wishes.

FORMALIZED PARLIAMENTARIANISM

With the partial constitutional reform in 1970, parliamentarianism was given a formalized position in the Swedish Constitution. Since then, Parliament has had the ability to remove the Government, which is a central principle for parliamentarianism. But it was with the Instrument of Government of 1974 that parliamentarianism formally became a fundamental principle in the Constitution. There is reason to give a brief recapitulation of the implications and consequences of these constitutional changes.

Firstly, stability decreased. When this new Constitution was formally implemented, stability had been a main trait of Swedish parliamentarianism for a long time. The same five parties had been represented in Parliament since the introduction of universal suffrage, and their relative sizes had remained surprisingly consistent over time. There were no indications that the stability of the party structure was to be decreased as the new Constitution was formed; the parties seemed to have a firm grip on the voters. Besides, the institutional conditions to maintain stability were strengthened: with the 4 percent rule in the election system and state funding beneficial to parties represented in Parliament, the contemporary structure was supposed to be cemented. In the literature, proponents of the cartel party theory argue that the interdependence between political parties and the state, especially when it comes to the financing of the parties, has changed the functions of political parties. In becoming a part of the state instead of civil society, the established parties strive to monopolize their positions and prevent challenging parties from being represented in the parliamentary assemblies (Katz and Mair 1995). However, this was not what happened in Swedish politics: four new parties were elected into the Parliament after 1988.

With the new unicameral Parliament the possibility of power shifts improved, which has also reduced stability. Contrary to how it was previously, the people's will expressed directly in elections has had a direct effect on the forming of governments after 1970. Before, the First Chamber majority worked as a constitutional safety net for the Social Democratic governments.

Secondly, the constitutional codification of parliamentarianism implied a major change: Parliament was now formally the central institution in the political system.

In contrast to the Instrument of Government of 1809 that was based on the principle of the separation of powers, the new Constitution was shaped by a monistic principle emanating from Parliament's superiority. If Parliament lacked confidence in a minister or in the Prime Minister it could make a declaration of no confidence, which meant that parliamentary supremacy was assured by a constitutional mechanism. This possibility has been used only on five occasions. Ironically, the central role of Parliament was most apparent as the new Instrument of Government was put in place in 1975, during the period of parliamentarian stability. But after the 1976 election Parliament was soon downgraded to a form of "Transport Company": during the non-socialist coalition governments in 1976–8 and 1979–81, the Parliament's—or rather its non-socialist majority's—main role was to pass the government bills that the three parties in government were able to agree on. This was hardly unexpected since Parliament tends to play a marginal role in shaping politics when coalition governments with a majority are in power.

Thirdly, in terms of de facto power, the Government's position in relation to Parliament has been strengthened. The extended mandate period from 1994 onwards gives the Government more space to act. The new budget process that was reformed in 1994–6 gives the Government far greater abilities to control financial policy. In the new process of decision-making in Parliament, it is stipulated that the public expenses are to be divided in categories of expense and that each is given a frame of expense determined by Parliament, which is not to be exceeded (Mattson 2011: 258). Moreover, EU membership gives the government more power at the expense of Parliament.

A fourth observation is that minority governments have been the normal type of government in Swedish politics. Before Reinfeldt's first administration, Sweden had had minority governments almost 80 percent of the time since universal suffrage was introduced. It is worth pointing out that these governments have often been strong: with the Social Democratic rule of 1982–91 and 1994–2006, the situation resumed to the way it had been for most of the postwar period, with minority governments which had strong internal coherence and sufficiently strong parliamentary support for them to function practically as majority governments. The cooperation between the three red–green parties in 1998–2006 meant that the government was a hybrid between a majority and minority government and has been described as a form of "contract parliamentarianism." The government had a contract with parties outside the government, in which the contract involved more than a specific question and was not limited to a shorter time (Bergman 2011; Aylott 2005).

The fact that the supporting parties were a part of the parliamentary basis without being part of the government made it difficult to demand accountability. The critics, using the theory that has the Westminster model as an implicit norm, claimed that parliamentarianism in its purity is based on a clear division between the Government and the Opposition. It was claimed that the parliamentarianism that was developed here was something else. The role of the supporting parties was constitutionally unclear, which could, in the end, possibly damage democracy.

The situation after 2010 is reminiscent of the one that existed under the Bildt administration. Then, New Democracy had a role similar to that which the Sweden Democrats have now, even though the Sweden Democrats have been placed more obviously by the other parties in a political quarantine due to the organization's racist past. Since 2010 Sweden has been ruled by a government that has lost important votes. This is a considerable loss for the core idea of parliamentarianism: that the executive has a constitutional legitimacy as long as it is not seriously opposed by Parliament.

It is not sensational for a government without a majority to lose a number of votes as long as they concern issues of lesser political importance. But when they concern more important issues, it is reasonable to speak of a serious conflict between the Government and Parliament. To explain this divergence in more concrete terms: the Government's power has weakened and the parliamentarian doctrine's fundamental concept of confidence has become increasingly hollow. The original principle concerned positive confidence, but this soon eroded and a negative concept of confidence became the new doctrine: it was sufficient if the Government was tolerated, i.e. was not in a serious state of opposition toward Parliament. What we can see now is how the principle of negative parliamentarianism has weakened also: the Government is tolerated by Parliament even if their main policies lack support, at least in some sense.

A change resulting from the 2011 reformation of the Instrument of Government of 1974 is that after every election, an obligatory vote is to be held in Parliament to appoint the Prime Minister. This rule was brought in as the Moderate Party in particular were critical when the Social Democratic party leader Göran Persson chose to stay on as Prime Minister after the significant electoral loss in 1998, and also after the uncertain parliamentarian situation following the 2002 election. The statute aims at determining the Government's parliamentary status and can in some situations, when an obvious majority alternative does not exist, obstruct the forming of governments. Minor parties especially can, if their support is a necessity, be given vast potential power as they can condition their active or passive support for a proposed government (Bergman 2011: 154).

A fifth observation concerns the position of the Prime Minister. When the 1974 Instrument of Government was passed, the office was strengthened. Nowadays, Swedish parliamentarianism clearly revolves around the Prime Minister, who is able to appoint and dismiss Cabinet ministers. The Prime Minister decides what ministries there should be, what assignments these are to have, and how decision-making is to be carried out in the Government. The Prime Minister can even call new elections, and if the Prime Minister resigns, the Government as a whole has to resign. Furthermore, during the 1990s EU membership and the reorganization of the Government Offices have strengthened the Prime Minister's office. These changes involved a transfer of power from the governmental collective to the Prime Minister, who has extensive capacities, especially concerning EU issues (Erlandsson 2007). EU membership in itself also means a substantial power shift from Parliament to the Government since it is the Government that represents Sweden in the European

Council and the Council of the European Union, where most of the important decisions are made.

Is the office of the Prime Minister thus moving towards presidentialization? Research certainly shows that the Prime Minister's position has been strengthened, in Sweden as well as other European democracies, and that an increased media focus is pointed towards the heads of governments. But according to recent studies there is no clear and distinct verification of a presidentialization of the office (Hermansson and Persson 2010; Daléus 2012).

References

Aylott, N. (2005). "President Persson: How Did the Swedes Get Him?" in T. Poguntge and P. Webb (eds), *The Presidentialization of Politics: A Comparative Study of Modern Democracies*. Oxford: Oxford University Press, 176–98.

Bergman, T. (2011). "Parlamentarism," in I. Mattson and O. Petersson (eds), *Svensk författningspolitik*. Stockholm: SNS Förlag, 138–55.

Brusewitz, A. (1951). *Kungamakt, herremakt, folkmakt: Författningskampen i Sverige 1906–1918*. Stockholm: Prisma.

Dahl, R. (1956). *A Preface to Democratic Theory*. Chicago: University of Chicago Press.

Daléus, P. (2012). *Politisk ledarskapsstil: Om interaktionen mellan personlighet och institutioner i utövandet av det svenska statsministerämbetet*. Stockholm Studies in Politics, 146. Stockholm: Stockholm University.

Duverger, M. (1964). *Political Parties: Their Organization and Activity in the Modern State*. London: Methuen and Co.

Erlandsson, M. (2007). *Striderna i Rosenbad: Om trettio års försök att förändra Regeringskansliet*. Stockholm Studies in Politics, 148. Stockholm: Stockholm University.

Esaiasson, P. (1990). *Svenska valkampanjer 1866–1988*. Stockholm: Publica.

Hallberg, P. (2003). *Age of Liberty: Social Upheaval, History Writing and the New Public Sphere in Sweden, 1740–1792*. Stockholm Studies in Politics, 92. Stockholm: Stockholm University.

Hermansson, J. and Persson, T. (2010). "Att regera under parlamentarismen," in J. Hermansson (ed.), *Regeringsmakten i Sverige: Ett experiment i parlamentarism 1917–2009*. Stockholm: SNS Förlag, 9–32.

Katz, R. and Mair, P. (1995). "Changing Models of Party Organization and Party Democracy: The Emergence of the Cartel Party," *Party Politics* 1: 5–28.

Mattson, I. (2011). "Finansmakten," in Mattson, Ingvar and Olof Petersson (eds), *Svensk författningspolitik*. Stockholm: SNS Förlag, 241–61.

Möller, T. (2011). *Svensk politisk historia: Strid och samverkan under 200 år*. Lund: Studentlitteratur.

Ruin, O. (1968). *Mellan samlingsregering och tvåpartisystem: Den svenska regeringsfrågan 1945–1960*. Stockholm: Bonniers Förlag.

Rustow, D. (1955). *The Politics of Compromise*. Princeton: Princeton University Press.

Sartori, G. (1997). *Comparative Constitutional Engineering: An Inquiry into Structures, Incentives and Outcomes*. London: Macmillan.

Strøm, K. (2000). "Delegation and Accountability in Parliamentary Democracies," *Journal of Political Research* 37: 261–89.

Sydow, B. von (1997). *Parlamentarismen i Sverige: Utveckling och utformning till 1945.* Stockholm: Gidlunds Förlag.

Tsebelis, G. (2002). *Veto Players: How Political Institutions Work.* Princeton: Princeton University Press.

Verney, D. (1992). "Parliamentary Government and Presidential Governments," in A. Lijphart (ed.), *Parliamentary versus Presidential Government.* Oxford: Oxford University Press, 31–47.

....

CHAPTER 10

THE PUBLIC SECTOR
AND THE COURTS

....

SHIRIN AHLBÄCK ÖBERG
AND HELENA WOCKELBERG

INTRODUCTION

....

IN the Swedish setting, it makes considerable sense to discuss the set-up of the executive and the judicial branches in the same *Handbook* chapter as we are doing here: the two branches have been closely tied together for centuries (Ställvik 2009). This constitutionally unorthodox perspective was manifested in the fact that for the last four decades (1970–2010) the administration of justice and the administration of the public sector were regulated in the very same chapter in the Swedish fundamental law, Chapter 11 of the 1974 Instrument of Government (IG).

In the present chapter we discuss this constitutional design, claiming that constitutionalism Swedish-style is a story of unresolved issues. The joint chapter of the 1974 IG is a clear example of this: the chapter originates from one of the major parliamentary commissions of inquiry preceding the new Constitution in the 1970s—*Grundlagberedningen* (in operation 1966–72). The commission emphasized that the border between the courts' and the public administration's activities was fluid, since administrative agencies were also to a large extent engaged in the application of law. The commission also pointed out that a major difference between the two bodies was the government agencies' general obligation to follow instructions, an obligation that for obvious reasons was not applicable to the courts. Hence, the commission's proposition was to keep the regulation of the administration of justice and the public administration in separate paragraphs but, nevertheless, within the same article (SOU 1967:26). The minister of justice at the time, however, argued that it was impossible to make a clear distinction between these two things:

According to my opinion it is not meaningful to try to give a detailed characterization of the roles that these different public institutions play in the introductory
chapter of the IG. [. . .] Hence, I propose that the present article only establishes that
for the administration of justice there are courts and for the public administration
there are national and local government agencies. (Government Bill 1973:90: 233, our
translation)

This perspective permeated the Swedish Constitution from the 1970s to the early 2010s,
and this lack of argumentation is also reflected in the lack of discussion of these particular institutions in the preparatory work of the 1974 Instrument of Government
(Wockelberg 2003; Ställvik 2009; Sterzel 2009). Not until 2011, in conjunction with substantial revisions of the IG, were the different branches of government addressed in separate chapters (Government Bill 2009/10:80; IG Chs. 11 and 12).

The strategic elements of Swedish constitutional design in terms of the public sector
and the courts are best understood in relation to the Swedish lawmakers' aim of keeping material principles concerning human and social rights out of the Constitution. By
limiting constitutional content to the basic rules of the democratic game, the lawmakers hope to maximize the incumbent rulers' flexibility and efficiency. In relation to the
role of the courts, the chosen constitutional design can be understood as a result of the
lawmakers being reluctant to appoint courts to be special guardians of the Constitution.
To define the courts as guardians may decrease the efforts to protect the Constitution
made by other actors. The history of Swedish democratic rule, however, also illustrates a
negative argument for limited judicial power, namely the new political elite's distrust or
skepticism toward judges as representatives of the pre-democratic regime.

Regardless of the relationship between politics and law in the Swedish setting,
recurring themes when it comes to central constitutional principles of the public sector and the courts can be summarized as *administrative dualism* (administrative agencies are organized in separate units outside the ministries) and *institutional autonomy*.
The scope of the dual Swedish administrative model, as well as how much institutional
autonomy government agencies and the courts are granted by the Constitution, has
been strongly debated. These debates definitely exemplify what we earlier referred to as
the Swedish Constitution as a story of unresolved issues. Leaving unresolved issues in
the Constitution may be either the result of mistakes, or effects of so-called negotiated
unclarity (Jabko 2006). The latter, strategic, type of lack of clarity stems from political
actors' efforts to reach a stable equilibrium, i.e., an efficient enough institutional version
of important functions in the political system. In this chapter we discuss how unclarity enables the political parties to reinterpret the constitutional role of public authorities and, for example, the dual Swedish model of administration (Wockelberg 2003).
We also discuss how reforms of constitutional relevance are executed in political arenas
other than the constitutional one. We start by unwrapping the constitutional set-up of
central government, the court system, and local government in Sweden (in no order of
importance).

CENTRAL GOVERNMENT

The Executive and the Government Offices

The Instrument of Government is very sparse on the subject of the procedural part of the executive's task of governing the country. This minimalism is far from accidental, the intention rather being to allow a high degree of flexibility to the Prime Minister (PM) in appointing and dismissing Cabinet ministers, and to the Cabinet as a whole in organizing its work (Government Bill 1973:90; Stjernquist 1976).

Chapter 6 of the Instrument of Government declares that the Government consists of the PM and of Cabinet ministers appointed by the PM; that members of the Cabinet must be Swedish citizens; it also provides the procedural rules for forming the government. Chapter 7 in turn states that the Government is assisted by the Government Offices, containing ministries headed by ministers appointed by the PM. A formal requirement regarding the procedures for preparing governmental issues is that the Government must collect "the necessary information and opinions" from public and private stakeholders (IG Ch. 7, Art. 2). Chapter 7 also stipulates that government business is decided upon in Cabinet meetings called by the PM. The Government makes decisions collectively, and any dissenting opinion must be stated in the record of the meeting. It is, however, extremely rare that any minister actually makes use of this option of declaring dissent.

The PM's prerogative to appoint and dismiss ministers and to summon Cabinet meetings sets the PM apart from the rest of the ministers. The latter are formally of equal standing, but this parliamentary ideal of collegiality is in many respects challenged in practice. For example, and as in many similar executive settings, the minister of finance is especially powerful, given the position of that office in the budget-negotiating machinery (Wockelberg 2010). Further, Sweden's EU membership has centralized both decision-making mandates and practical resources to the PM, and to some extent also made some ministers more powerful. One of the main reasons for this development is that the EU policy process is dependent upon government heads (or individual ministers) making decisions in so-called summitries (Johansson and Raunio 2010; Johansson and Tallberg 2010).

In the organization called the Government Offices (*Regeringskansliet*), comprising the Prime Minister's Office, the ministries, and the Office for Administrative Affairs, the political appointees are outnumbered by thousands of merit-based employees. The lion's part of the central state administration is, however, situated outside the Government Offices, in central government agencies.

Central Government Agencies

Depending on how the count is made, there are about 400 central government agencies; needless to say, the size and scope of the agencies vary a great deal (Statskontoret

2010). The organization of the state administration in Sweden differs from that of most other countries since it is characterized by the state administration's independence in relation to Parliament and the Government. For instance, in contrast to countries with ministerial rule, there is an organizational divide between the government ministries and central government agencies. This executive dualism consists of two parts: firstly, since the Swedish Constitution prohibits ministerial control, i.e., when individual ministers influence or instruct administrative agencies, the Cabinet of ministers acts and is accountable collectively. Secondly, the Constitution guarantees the independence of the state administration (IG Ch. 12, Art. 2):

Independence of administration
Art. 2. No public authority, including the Riksdag, or decision-making body of any local authority, may determine how an administrative authority shall decide in a particular case relating to the exercise of public authority vis-à-vis an individual or a local authority, or relating to the application of law.

This means that steering in general, through legislation, ordinances, appropriation letters, etc., is allowed, but not in particular cases when exercising public authority. Thus, the administrative agencies formally enjoy a high degree of discretion that is protected by the Swedish Constitution (see Chapter 22, "The Swedish Administrative Model"). A salient problem when discussing the prescribed independence of the public administration is that the Constitution does not give much guidance on the reach of this independence. The regulation on this is of such brevity that it is open to different interpretations. On the one hand, the IG stipulates that it is the Government that governs "the Realm" (IG Ch. 1, Art. 6) and that the Chancellor of Justice and other state administrative authorities come under the Government (IG Ch. 12, Art. 1). On the other hand, the obligation to follow instructions is restricted in relation to these regulations. Members of the Cabinet cannot—even collectively—decide in particular cases relating to the exercise of public authority vs an individual or a local authority, or relating to the application of law. This latter restriction has for a long time been understood as a far-reaching autonomy for the state administration—one of the "court-like" features of Swedish administrative authorities. The constitutional idea behind this independence is to secure the rule of law and uphold a barrier against the abuse of power, to ensure that the state authorities take responsibility for their judgments.

The term "Swedish model of administration" denotes both the duality of the Swedish executive, that is, central government agencies are located outside governmental ministries, and the idea that central and local government authorities enjoy a constitutionally protected independence of administration in their application of law in individual cases. The principle of executive dualism is literally several centuries old (Pierre 2001; Wockelberg 2003; Andersson 2004). Hence, in the Swedish case, the New Public Management-oriented agentification is to be considered as fine-tuning of an already existing model, rather than as "big news."

Constitutionally speaking, the relationship between demands for loyalty and the right for independence in specific decision-making cases is an example of an unresolved issue that appears to be reproduced throughout history. The constitutional provision of independence of administration has been discussed both as an actual important feature of the balancing of powers (Bull 1999) and as a peculiar but limited deviation from the monocentric parliamentary chain of delegation (Petersson 1998). While it is hard to argue that the government can give direct orders, or in other ways control public authorities' decision-making in individual cases, what actually constitutes an individual case has never been fully defined (see Government Bill 1973:90).

The question of how the Cabinet collective can control its government agencies has been debated. Informal steering between governmental ministries and agencies was discussed in the 1980s as potentially unconstitutional. The risk of intruding on the agencies' legal autonomy was acknowledged, but the government's need for informal contacts was finally deemed to be more relevant than this potential risk. It was suggested, however, that informal contacts should be established *mainly* between ministry and agency officials, and concern *mostly* things other than the area protected by the Constitution. No clear conclusion on actual limits was drawn (Wockelberg 2003), but the political parties reached a stable equilibrium based on a negotiated unclarity of the kind so typical of the Swedish constitutional context.

Issues regarding the Swedish model of administration have not been discussed in any close proximity to constitutional reforms since the 1970s, but rather as parts of public management reforms. In other words, issues concerning the scope, organization, and mandate of the public administration rarely appear in Swedish constitutional debates, or in commissions of inquiry preceding constitutional reform. A striking peculiarity is, thus, that significant reforms—with clear constitutional implications—are implemented outside the constitutional arena. Another example of this is the reformed budget process in the 1990s, which among other things introduced informal budgetary dialogues between the ministries and the government agencies, thereby challenging the executive duality of the Swedish administrative model. Moreover, the budget process, and the management model that went with it, assumes a specified division of labor between politicians and bureaucracy, which in fact has democratic as well as constitutional implications for who has the right to decide what and when. Another salient example of change that has entailed major implications for the "Swedish administrative model" is Sweden's membership in the EU.

Making and Implementing EU Policies

When Sweden joined the EU in 1995, no real amendments of the IG were made, based on the expected consequences of EU membership on the Swedish political system, even though such proposals were presented, for example, by the Constitutional Commission prior to the EC (SOU 1993:14). On the contrary, after intense debate, the Parliament decided to limit constitutional amendments to a minimum, thereby depreciating a constitution that would accurately reflect the actual form of government, and thus giving precedence to sensitivity toward a split electorate (Sweden's membership in the EU was based on the outcome of the 1994 referendum, when 52.3 percent voted in favor and 46.8 percent voted against EU membership).

Lately, a more nuanced and realistic debate concerning executive dualism and EU membership has surfaced. One aspect of dualism is organizational rather than purely constitutional, and concerns the fact that the small governmental ministries lack necessary resources to participate efficiently in EU policy-making processes. Resources (time, expertise, contacts, etc.) are instead located in the organizationally separate central government agencies. To compensate for this asymmetry, ministries have to use and instruct the agencies in ways that may come close to ministerial rule (SOU 2008:118). In practice, Sweden is to a large extent represented by public servants employed by central government agencies, and not by ministerial-level staff, in policy negotiations and "committology" in Brussels (see Section 8, "Sweden and the EU"). The former group's mandate, as well as issues of accountability and responsibility, eventually surfaced as matters of concern, and the idea is now to give these representatives formal, documented mandates to represent the Swedish government as opposed to their actual employer (the central government agency).

The national authorities are important also when EU policies are to be applied. The national legislative process prepares and executes decisions concerning the legal implementation of EU directives (transposition). However, bureaucrats in Swedish government agencies can also be left to make decisions regarding implementation of EU law (e.g. EU regulations) without any substantial input or guidance from formal national lawmakers (Edwardsson and Wockelberg 2013). Also, since the general principle is that EU law has precedence over national law, central government agencies sometimes decide to put national legislation aside with reference to EU law, and this without any explicitly stated support for this action from either the government or the Swedish parliament (Påhlsson 2006; Ståhl 2006). Interpretation and application of EU law can, hence, in effect be law-making based on vague or no formal law-making mandates (Edwardsson and Wockelberg 2013). Finally, it should be noted that EU law is also to be applied by local governments.

In conclusion, membership of the EU has had profound effects on national-level authorities in Sweden. These effects constitute unresolved issues regarding both vertical and horizontal distribution of power. As discussed in the next section, this is also the case when it comes to the role of courts in the Swedish Constitution.

THE COURTS

Swedish courts have historically served as tools in the hands of executive political powers rather than as guardians of individual rights. Another notable feature of the Swedish judiciary is its historical continuity. Reforms have been incremental. The judiciary has been neither an arena for political conflict, nor the object of attention in such conflicts. This peaceful history is in part explained by the fact that Sweden has not been occupied by external hostile powers (occupiers tend to destroy or undermine these systems), and in part by the Swedish political culture, which encourages political and social parties to reach agreements in arenas other than the judicial (Ställvik 2009). An alternative, more dramatic, interpretation of the courts' role concerns modern Swedish political history, when the social engineers of the twentieth century for strategic reasons sought to undermine the courts' opportunity to have a final say concerning welfare policy programs (Rothstein 1985). However, before venturing into the details of the Swedish court system, it should be made perfectly clear that Sweden in all relevant comparisons is a *Rechtsstaat*, where the rule of law is practiced and where corruption is low. Sweden scores very high in international evaluative rankings on rule-of-law indicators as well as on factors measuring the performance of the judiciary system (see, e.g., the World Justice Project 2014).

There are two parallel court systems in Sweden, dealing with civil and criminal law, and conflicts between private parties and the public authorities, respectively (Table 10.1). In addition, special courts exist with the mandate to try cases in specific areas such as the labor market or immigration.

The English translation of some of the Swedish courts' names hides information pertaining to both their geographical location and their historical attachment to the executive powers, i.e., connection to the monarchs or modern democratic governments. It is, however, interesting to note that steps have been taken lately to rid the court system of such symbolic associations to the political executive. When the Supreme Administrative Court was established in 1909, it was called *Regeringsrätten* ("the Cabinet's court"), and this name was changed as late as in 2011.

This history of *Regeringsrätten* illustrates some prominent features of the role of courts in the Swedish political system that will be discussed in this section. First, the name indicates that courts have been regarded as executive tools rather than balancing powers. Second, it illustrates some recent reforms of the judiciary system that can be interpreted either as a normalization aimed at putting Sweden on a par with European and international standards or as an (unwelcome) juridification of politics.

Table 10.1 Swedish court systems (number of specific courts within parentheses)

	General courts	General administrative courts
Hierarchy from first to final ruling		
First ruling	District Courts (48)	Administrative Courts (12)
Second ruling	Courts of Appeal (6)	Administrative Courts of Appeal (4)
Final ruling	Supreme Court (1)	Supreme Administrative Court (1)
Type of cases	Criminal law, civil law	Cases concerning the execution of public authority

The Role of Courts in the Swedish Political System

The judicial system in Sweden is not an independent branch of government as in, for instance, the United States or Germany. The professional career of many judges includes work in the legislative and/or executive branches of government. (Ställvik 2009: 251)

We will discuss here two of the roles that courts can play in a (democratic) political system; these roles tend to vary over constitutional settings. The first role is to protect individual rights against public power, that is, to balance political powers in a society. The other role is to secure effective implementation of public policy: to serve legitimate political governments by providing the kind of stable legal procedures needed in a modern democracy and in a market economy. These roles are in principle very different and have far-reaching effects on fundamental issues such as what law is perceived to be in a society and, in turn, the legitimate roles for both politicians and lawyers.

Swedish courts have historically served as tools for political executive powers and not as balancing powers. This conclusion holds regardless of the type of executive regime, but to varying degrees (Ställvik 2009). The Social Democratic governments of the twentieth century regarded courts and the legal profession as at the same time necessary tools for, and potential obstacles to, the execution of the reform agenda. According to Rothstein, one of the main architects behind the Swedish universal welfare state, Gustav Möller, sought to reduce the power of the traditional legal system. He made sure that the last word in the interpretation of social reform laws was not, as it used to be, in the hands of the high courts. Instead, the last instance of appeal should be the Ministry of Social Affairs, in practice himself (Rothstein 1985). Giving away to the courts the prerogative to interpret welfare policies would be to undermine the political power of the government, and hence of the "new social stratum" that served as its legitimate base. To a social engineer like Möller, the courts represented "the earlier rulers who could no longer secure a majority for their policies" (Rothstein 1985: 159). This skepticism toward judges as political actors appears to have lingered on through the decades of democratic government—it was present also when the courts were discussed in relation to the constitutional reforms in the 1970s (Ställvik 2009). The predominant focus on democratic majoritarian political power has rarely been questioned, even by Swedish judges (Nergelius 1999).

A peculiar feature of the Swedish court system is that the general administrative courts' rulings may concern both formal issues and material content. In addition to judicial review, the administrative courts have the same mandate to hear the case as the administrative authority and may in some cases exchange the appealed decision with its own. In practice, this can mean that judges in these courts alter substantial decisions without having apparent expertise in the matter at hand. This mandate can be regarded as an extensive display of courts exercising power over administrative matters, and it has been discussed whether the administrative courts are too powerful (Petersson 1999; see also Edwardsson 2009). The fact that the courts can exchange an appealed decision with their own in practice means that the courts serve as a "check and balance" to the highly autonomous administrative authorities.

The role of Swedish lawyers and judges is often described as that of a legal/social engineer (Modéer 1999; Ställvik 2009). This role elegantly fits the role of courts as executive tools rather than as guardians of individual rights. It is also a logical conclusion in a political context where the state, and public power, is framed as something essentially good, rather than something intrusive and essentially bad (Ställvik 2009). The social engineers of the young Swedish democracy needed laws, legal methods, lawyers, and courts that supported the reform programs of the welfare state. It is, hence, easy to understand how well the perspective of legal positivism—in essence, that law should be kept separate from moral issues—suited the welfare state, and perhaps also to grasp why Sweden never saw the kind of postwar revival of natural rights other European countries did. Legal positivism supports a constitutional perspective in which all laws, including fundamental laws, can be altered by, in relative terms, simple legislative procedures.

The Swedish legal method rests on detailed, preparatory work on proposed laws which narrows down the space for interpretation once law is made. The essence of this method is interpretation to detect, rather than to create, the meaning of the law. This fact should, however, not be confused with an absence of lawyers in the legislative process as a whole. A glance at the career system for lawyers in the public sphere instead reveals that judges typically serve both in legislative and executive branches of government (Ställvik 2009).

Controlling the Courts and the Judges

We have established that the Swedish executive and the court system historically have been very closely related, in practice as well as constitutionally. Swedish national authorities have for centuries operated at an arm's length from the political executive, and their decision-making processes are "court-like." A relevant follow-up question is whether courts operate or are controlled in ways commonly associated with administrative agencies.

Evidently, there are many signs of historically grounded political skepticism toward the judiciary in the Swedish context. The system of lay judges should be mentioned here. Every district court, court of appeal, administrative court, and administrative court of appeal has a number of lay judges. They are appointed for four years by the municipal councils in the municipalities and by the county council assembly. The lay judges take part in the adjudication both of specific concrete issues and matters of law, and each has an individual vote—in fact, in the lower courts, the lay judges outnumber the professional judges. Lay judges have long historical roots in Sweden and have in modern times been looked upon as a way of balancing the power of the judges—thereby securing public control. However, the lay judges are typically recruited from the political parties (in conjunction with public elections to municipalities and county assemblies), and skeptics have for a long time been warning about the risk of politicization of the courts. Moreover, today the recruitment base has narrowed considerably as membership in political parties has dropped radically over the years. Hence, the representativeness—and "civic competence"—of the lay judges is at the time being heavily questioned.

Since the 1990s, the Swedish public sector as well as the court system have certainly experienced their fair share of management reforms. For instance, court judges are the only group of public officials in Sweden who until recently were exempted from person-based salaries. This was changed in October 2006, almost twenty years after the first steps for person-based salaries were taken in the government sector, a development that is unique in a comparative perspective. The judges' national union has resisted this change (see *Jusektidningen* 05-03-2005), their objection being that it is unethical to differentiate their salaries, since it may cause unwanted incentives which in turn would harm the state governed by law. This position has been supported in a resolution by the European Association of Judges (EAJ Resolution 04-21/22-2005). Obviously, the Swedish government did not respond to the resistance, and the person-based salary system is currently in operation. However, it should be mentioned that it is specified in the collective agreement between the National Court Administration and Swedish Union of University Graduates of Law, Business Administration, and Economics (*Jusek*) that performance-based salaries for judges may not be based on their performance in the courtroom, since that would challenge their independence (Domstolsverket 2008, 2011). Whether that is a distinction that can be upheld still remains to be seen.

The Courts and the EU

EU membership provides national courts with the right, and to some extent obligation, to turn to the European Court of Justice (ECJ) for preliminary rulings on cases involving potential conflict between national and EU law. This is a fairly new constitutional aspect of the role of courts in the Swedish political system, and its practical application tells us important things about national courts as political actors. Swedish courts have so far not activated this opportunity to engage in legal deliberation with the ECJ very often, so they are not in relative terms active. But are they to be perceived as *activist*? Our conclusion is that Swedish courts appear to consider the political aspects of cases. Swedish courts are more prone to argue in favor of national law in cases regarding politically sensitive issues than in cases concerning technical, politically non-salient issues. We should note that Swedish courts do argue in favor of EU law also in politically sensitive issues, and that they often refrain from taking a stand on non-salient issues (Leijon and Karlsson 2013).

The Revised IG in 2011 and Other Reforms

The newly reformed Instrument of Government featured some new content regarding the court system, but less new material with respect to the public sector. Only to a limited extent can these changes be interpreted as clarifications that resolve some of the issues discussed previously. A notable change was the split of the former Chapter 11 on the executive and the courts into two separate chapters. This reform was described as a codification of the actual constitutional role of the courts and was motivated by the need to underline the importance of an independent court system in Swedish political life. The government motivated the reform with explicit reference to other countries' constitutions that commonly contain a separate chapter dealing with courts and judges (Government Bill 2009/10:80).

The most debated reform regarding the courts concerns the increased opportunity to perform judicial review. Before 2011, courts as well as public authorities in general could abstain from implementing laws and regulations with reference to their incompatibility with rules of higher formal status. This judicial review was limited to *apparent* cases of incompatibility. This limitation has been the object of a prolonged debate among Swedish political parties. The constitutional reform lowered the threshold for this type of judicial review; that is, conflicts between laws can now be less than apparent to count as reasons for review (Bull and Sterzel 2013; Government Bill 2009/10:80). The effect of the reform is hard to predict. It is clear that Swedish courts and public authorities historically have been extremely moderate in making use of their opportunity for judicial review, counting a handful or so cases during recent decades. In terms of judicial review, a probably more relevant issue concerns the fact that Swedish courts put Swedish law aside with reference to EU law (Åhman 2011). Further, while judicial review has been conducted mainly with reference to rights regulated in EU law and in the European Convention on Human Rights, Swedish courts today turn also to the Swedish Instrument of Government when trying these cases. Importantly, European law appears to have facilitated an increased acceptance of fundamental law—also national fundamental law—as limiting public decision-making (Bull 2013).

In addition to the new chapter on courts, and the expansion of the judicial review mandate, other changes aimed at underlining the independence of courts were made. An explicit rule prohibiting other authorities than the court itself from distributing cases among the judges was introduced. At the same time, both the Parliamentary Ombudsman and the Chancellor of Justice lost their earlier right to supervise the judges' deliberation concerning a judgment in court trials (Government Bill 2009/10:80)

Stating that "judges shall not only be independent, but also appear to be so" (Government Bill 2009/10:80, p. 132, our translation), the government also introduced constitutional reforms concerning the appointment of judges. The higher positions of chief judges were until recently appointed directly by the government; the positions were not publicly advertised. This system has been criticized since the lack of transparency in the appointment procedure could throw suspicion on the judges' actual independence from the government. Also, the appointed chief judges have to a great extent served within the Government Offices. By international comparison, this is out of the ordinary: the normal practice would be to keep the executive and the judiciary apart. In short, all positions as judges are now to be publicly announced as vacant. A proposals board prepares and ranks a list of candidates, on the basis of which the government makes its appointments (Government Bill 2009/10:181).

Local Government

A cornerstone of Swedish governance is local self-government (*kommunal självstyrelse*) which is distinctly stipulated in the opening article of the IG (Ch. 1, Art. 1, our italics):

> Swedish democracy is founded on the free formation of opinion and on universal and equal suffrage. It shall be realized through a representative and parliamentary polity and through *local self-government*.

Local government in Sweden is organized in two elected tiers comprising county councils (*landsting*) and municipal counties (*kommuner*). This relationship is not hierarchical: the municipalities are not answerable to the counties. Formally speaking, Swedish municipalities (290) and regions (20) have extensive freedom to manage their own affairs. The implementation of welfare policy is carried out by local authorities, and the local authorities account for a very large proportion of the public sector (see Section 6 of this volume, "Subnational Government"). The IG specifically states that administrative functions may be delegated to local authorities. Furthermore, administrative functions may also be delegated to other legal entities or to individuals (Ch. 12, Art. 4). This latter option has made it possible for local authorities to contract out, for example, the production of many of its welfare services to private companies. Ever since the 1990s, this has paved the way for a very diverse landscape of private actors—everything from venture capitalist firms to non-profit organizations—involved in publicly financed activities on the local level. However, the legal consequences, in terms of the reach of administrative and public law, are not keeping up with this development.

Most tasks of municipalities and county councils are regulated by central government in special legislation and are mandatory by law: these include child care and preschools, primary and secondary education, social services, elderly care, support for the physically and intellectually disabled, spatial planning, health and environmental protection, refuse collection and waste disposal, rescue services and emergency preparedness, and water supply and sewerage. The fact that mandatory tasks take up about 80 percent of local government expenditures (SCB 2011) has nurtured a debate on how self-governing local government actually is. This matter is one of the major unresolved issues in the Swedish Constitution. It is clear that this state of negotiated unclarity is sought as a stabilizing equilibrium in an issue that is definitely conflict-laden, thereby giving conflicting interests some flexibility to promote their own ideas on how to interpret the scope of local government. The end result of this issue is that the relationship between central and local government in Sweden is generally speaking very fluid and hard to define. An example of this is that any government ministry seeking to reform welfare policy (which is implemented by local government) has to reach an agreement with the Swedish Association of Local Authorities and Regions (SALAR). This is a member organization for municipalities and regions—and interestingly enough—it is an organization governed by private law. Hence, the legal status of these agreements is quite unclear. Another example of the tension between central and local government is the continuing debate about the frequent occurrence of breaches of municipal law and court decisions. That the legislator has accepted the municipal breach and failed to take any measures despite many proposals shows that the municipality is a difficult arena for central government and the court system to review and to raise questions about liability.

The voluntary tasks that municipalities can decide on lie within policy areas such as leisure and cultural activities, housing, energy, and industrial and commercial services. An interesting feature of the voluntary domain is that whereas, for example, in Britain municipalities are prohibited from activities not specifically allowed by Parliament (according to the *ultra vires* principle), Swedish municipalities have, in contrast, extensive freedoms in areas not prohibited by Parliament (Maycraft Kall 2010).

Another particular aspect that stands out in a comparative perspective is the local governments' financial independence from the state. The municipalities are constitutionally bestowed the right to tax, which means that they set their own income tax rate. On the other hand, in 1996 central government introduced a system of economic equalization—often referred to as the "Robin Hood" tax—between the municipalities. Again, to what extent local authorities, in relation to central government, actually are self-governed will be further discussed in Section 6, "Subnational Government." It should, however, be mentioned here that there is an alternative interpretation, where local government is seen as a state-controlled implementing authority. Hence, despite Sweden being a unitary state, there is a separation of powers between the central and local level which is not fully resolved by the Constitution, but of immediate relevance for the implementation of welfare services—a state of affairs that will be further commented on.

The legal concept of local self-governance was originally expressed in the municipal constitution of 1862 (Bull and Sterzel 2013). This reform has been described as the victory and ascendancy of liberalism over a conservative, state bureaucracy, and as part of a general reform movement for municipal self-governance in European cities in the nineteenth century. Local communities were to be given arrangements for solving joint tasks, and self-governance would thus help to teach the broad masses joint responsibility. By transferring much of the exercise of power to the local level, the liberals also wanted to stem what they saw as the state authorities' wish to intervene in the social and business spheres (Forsell 2005; Petersson 2006).

During the preparatory work of the current Instrument of Government in the 1960s, the subject matter of the municipalities were actually overlooked. However, after the final report from the first parliamentary commission of inquiry (*Författningsutredningen*, in operation 1954–63; SOU 1963:16 and 17), Swedish Prime Minister Tage Erlander (Social Democrat) initiated a debate on the "municipal connection," which, in hindsight, appears to have been one of his main concerns regarding the reformed Constitution.

In this debate he emphasized the intimate connection between, and the intertwining of, national and municipal politics (Ruin 1990). As a result of Erlander's engagement, the issue of the municipalities was upgraded in the constitutional debate, and the stipulation of local self-governance was given a central place in the IG's opening article. This upgrading, however, seems to have little to do with actual management by local authorities, but to be more influenced by considerations concerning how to mobilize the electorate (Bull and Sterzel 2013). Moreover, it was not until the revision that came into effect in 2011 that a separate chapter in the IG was devoted to local authorities (Ch. 14). This new chapter includes six articles that, among other things, lay down that local authorities are responsible for local and regional matters of public interest on the principle of local self-government, and that local authorities may levy tax for the management of their affairs. Substantially, these particular articles do not constitute any change from the IG's earlier provisions. However, a new regulation on proportionality is added to this chapter, which certainly can be seen as an advancement of the protection of local government from central government. Article 3 of Chapter 14 lays down that any restriction in local self-government should not exceed what is necessary with regard to the purpose of the restriction.

In conclusion, the decentralizing tendencies in Sweden have historically been very strong. The historical legacy of local self-government has made it difficult for central agencies to steer and evaluate local government activities. Any hard governance steering ambition by the ministries or central government agencies in terms of health care, school education, etc. is hampered by the independent jurisdiction of the municipalities and regions. In terms of hard governance, only legislation instituted by the Riksdag reaches all the way down to the local authorities, and as a viable alternative the government and its agencies use various methods of soft governance to achieve preferred actions (e.g., general guidelines, benchmarking, recommendations).

CONSTITUTIONALISM IN SWEDEN

In the face of the constitutional development described in this chapter, it is fair to say that substantial constitutional reforms of the public sector and the courts paradoxically rarely come about due to regular constitutional reform-making in Sweden. Instead, major constitutional changes to the public sector and the courts are often the result of formally less demanding, political decision-making. Two examples are the reformed budget process in the 1990s and Sweden's entry into the EU in 1995.

Depending upon the normative perspective applied, recent political events can be regarded as a strengthening of the courts versus political power; or as a quite dramatic New Public Management-oriented attack from political executive powers on the autonomy of the courts.

Placing the courts in a separate chapter was an editorial change with a seriously intended twist: there should be no doubt that Swedish courts were so to speak *real* courts. We must at the same time pay attention to the fact that this new separate presentation of the courts was not accompanied by any reforms of the position of the administrative authorities. These are as court-like as ever, formally speaking. What is, however, new for both courts and administrative agencies is the enhanced mandate for judicial review. However, since constitutional amendments are easy to accomplish, the Parliament has ample opportunities to fight back, should judicial activism start to flourish (Holmström 1999).

Today, factors external to the Swedish political system constitute the most apparent challenges to the Swedish public sector and the courts as we know them. Internationalization, globalization, and in concrete terms Swedish membership of the European Union have brought about fundamental changes—changes of a magnitude far more fundamental than any of the carefully deliberated revisions (or non-revisions) of the Instrument of Government described here.

Finally, the story of unresolved issues in Swedish constitutional politics of the public sector is not complete without mentioning its very clear principle of public access to public documents and to some extent decision-making processes, as well as its protection of whistleblowers in the public sector. The principle of public access means that the general public and the mass media, newspapers, radio, and television are to be guaranteed an unimpeded view of activities pursued by the government and local authorities. While transparency cannot be said to be a perfect substitute for constitutional clarity, our conclusion is that the sometimes pragmatically unclear relationship between Swedish public decision-making institutions (vertically as well as horizontally) would constitute a bigger problem without these far-reaching safeguards of transparency. Moreover, this principle, which is laid down in the Freedom of the Press Act (from 1766) and the Fundamental Law on Freedom of Expression (from 1991), is as close to explicit reference to constitutional principles as politicians and the general public will come in Swedish political culture. Apart from this particular example, strong references to constitutional principles are simply very uncommon.

ACKNOWLEDGMENT

The authors wish to acknowledge the helpful comments and suggestions made by Jörgen Hermansson, Tommy Möller, Olof Petersson, and Thomas Bull.

REFERENCES

Åhman, K. (2011). *Normprövning: Domstolskontroll av svensk lags förenlighet med Regeringsformen och Europarätten 2000–2010*. Stockholm: Norstedts juridik, Institutet för rättsvetenskaplig forskning.

Andersson, C. (2004). "Tudelad trots allt: dualismens överlevnad i den svenska staten 1718–1987," dissertation, Stockholm University, Stockholm.

Bull, T. (1999). "Självständighet och pluralism: Om vertikal maktdelning i Sverige," in Lena Marcusson (ed.), *Festskrift till Fredrik Sterzel*. Uppsala: Iustus Förlag, 107–33.

Bull, T. (2013). "Regeringsformens renässans," in Thomas Bull, Olle Lundin, and Elisabeth Rynning (eds), *Allmänt och enskilt: Festskrift till Lena Marcusson*. Uppsala: Iustus Förlag.

Bull, T. and Sterzel, F. (2013). *Regeringsformen: En kommentar*. Lund: Studentlitteratur.

Domstolsverket (2008). "Lokalt avtal mellan Domstolsverket och Jusek angående lönerevisioner inom ramen för RALS 2007–2010," dnr 807-2008.

Domstolsverket (2011). "Lokalt avtal mellan Domstolsverket och Jusek angående lönerevisionen inom ramen för RALS 2010-T," dnr 51-2011.

EAJ (European Association of Judges) (2005). "Resolution Concerning the New Scheme of Remuneration of Judges in Sweden," Bruges, Belgium, April 21–2, 2005.

Edwardsson, E. (2009). "Domstolsprövning av förvaltningsbesluts lämplighet," in Anna-Karin Lundin (ed.), *Regeringsrätten 100 år*. Uppsala: Iustus Förlag, 97–105.

Edwardsson, E. and Wockelberg, H. (2013). "European Legal Method in Denmark and Sweden: Using Social Science Theory and Methodology to Describe the Implementation of EU Law," *European Law Journal* 19/3: 364–81.

Forsell, H. (2005). *Property, Tenancy and Urban Growth in Stockholm and Berlin, 1860–1920*. Burlington, VT: Ashgate.

Government Bill 1973:90. *Ny regeringsform och ny riksdagsordning, m.m.*

Government Bill 2009/10:80. *En reformed grundlag.*

Government Bill 2009/10:181. *Utnämning av ordinarie domare.*

Holmström, B. (1999). "Demokrati och juridisk kontroll," in Erik Amnå (ed.), *Maktdelning*, Demokratiutredningens forskarvolym, 1, SOU 1999:76. Stockholm: Elanders Gotab, 127–46.

Jabko, N. (2006). *Playing the Market. A Political Strategy for Uniting Europe, 1985–2005*. Ithaca and London: Cornell University Press.

Johansson, K.-M. and Raunio, T. (2010). "Organizing the Core Executive for European Union Affairs: Comparing Finland and Sweden," *Public Administration* 88/3: 649–64.

Johansson, K.-M. and Tallberg, J. (2010). "Explaining Chief Executive Empowerment: EU Summitry and Domestic Institutional Change," *West European Politics* 33/2: 208–36.

Jusektidningen. "Kärva förhandlingar om individuella domarlöner," 05-03-2005.

Leijon, K. and Karlsson, C. (2013). "Nationella domstolar som politiska aktörer: Främjare av rättslig integration eller försvarare av nationella intressen," *Statsvetenskaplig tidskrift* 115/1: 5–34.

Maycraft Kall, W. (2010). "The Governance Gap: Central–Local Steering and Mental Health Reform in Britain and Sweden," dissertation, Uppsala University, Uppsala.

Modéer, K. Å. (1999). "Vem regerar i rättens rike? Maktdelningen i ett historiskt och rättspolitiskt perspektiv," in Erik Amnå (ed.), *Maktdelning*, Demokratiutredningens forskarvolym, 1, SOU 1999:76. Stockholm: Elanders Gotab, 69–85.

Nergelius, J. (1999). "Grundlagsmodeller och maktdelning," in Erik Amnå (ed.), *Maktdelning*, Demokratiutredningens forskarvolym, 1, SOU 1999:76. Stockholm: Elanders Gotab, 113–26.

Påhlsson, R. (2006). "Skatteverkets styrsignaler: En ny blomma i regelrabatten," *Skattenytt* 7–8: 401–18.

Petersson, O. (1998). *Statsbyggnad: Den offentliga maktens organisation*. Stockholm: SNS Förlag.

Petersson, O. (ed.) (1999). *Demokrati på svenskt vis*. Demokratirådets rapport. Stockholm: SNS.

Petersson, O. (2006). *Kommunalpolitik*, 5th edn. Stockholm: Norstedts juridik.

Pierre, J. (2001). "Parallel Paths? Administrative Reform, Public Policy and Politico-Bureaucratic Relationships in Sweden," in B. G. Peters and J. Pierre (eds), *Politicians, Bureaucrats and Administrative Reform*. London: Routledge, 127–6.

Rothstein, B. (1985). "Managing the Welfare State: Lessons from Gustav Möller," *Scandinavian Political Studies* 8/3: 151–70.

Ruin, O. (1990). *Tage Erlander: Serving the Welfare State, 1946–1969*. Pittsburgh: University of Pittsburgh Press.

SCB (2011). *Offentlig ekonomi*. Statistics Sweden, Public Finance Statistics Unit.

SOU 1963:16. *Sveriges statsskick. Del 1, lagförslag*, Författningsutredningen VI (1963). Stockholm.

SOU 1963:17. *Sveriges statsskick. Del 2, Motiv—förslag till regeringsform*, Författningsutredningen VI (1963). Stockholm.

SOU 1967:26. *Partiell författningsreform: Betänkande från Grundlagberedningen*, Grundlagberedningen (1967). Stockholm.

SOU 1993:14. *EG och våra grundlagar: Betänkande*, Grundlagsutredningen inför EG (1993). Stockholm: Allmänna Förlaget.

SOU 2008:118. *Styra och ställa: Förslag till en effektivare statsförvaltning: Slutbetänkande från 2006 års förvaltningskommitté*. Stockholm: Fritzes.

Ståhl, K. (2006). *Skatterna och den fria rörligheten inom EU: Svensk skatterätt i förändring?* Report from the Swedish Institute for European Policy Studies (SIEPS), 2006:8.

Ställvik, O. (2009). "Domarrollen: Rättsregler, yrkeskultur och ideal," dissertation, Uppsala University, Uppsala.

Statskontoret (2010). *Färre men större: Statliga myndigheter åren 2007–2010*. Stockholm: Statskontoret.

Sterzel, F. (2009). *Författning i utveckling: Tjugo studier kring Sveriges författning*, Stiftelsen Rättsfonden nr 41. Uppsala: Iustus Förlag.

Stjernquist, N. (1976). "Statsvetenskaplig forskning kring den nya grundlagen," *Statsvetenskaplig tidskrift* 58/1: 79.

Wockelberg, H. (2003). "Den svenska förvaltningsmodellen: Parlamentarisk debatt om förvaltningens roll i styrelseskicket," dissertation, Uppsala University, Uppsala.

Wockelberg, H. (2010). "Så arbetar svenska regeringar," in Jörgen Hermansson (ed.), *Regeringsmakten i Sverige: Ett experiment i parlamentarism 1917–2009*. Stockholm: SNS, 106–42.

World Justice Project (2014). "The WJP Rule of Law Index 2014 Report," available online at <http://worldjusticeproject.org>.

SECTION 3

....

THE PARTY SYSTEM

....

SECTION EDITORS
HANNA BÄCK AND
GISSUR Ó. ERLINGSSON

CHAPTER 11

....

INTRODUCTION

The Party System

....

HANNA BÄCK AND GISSUR Ó. ERLINGSSON

POLITICAL parties are essential for the proper workings of parliamentary democracies, the form of government which characterizes Sweden. Here, we take as our departure the so-called "parliamentary chain of delegation." This suggests that power relationships in a parliamentary democracy can be described as a chain, where, in a first step, citizens delegate power to representatives. In turn they delegate power to a Cabinet and a Prime Minister, who then further delegates power to line ministers. Hence, this chain consists of several delegation relationships where various problems can occur. As principal-agent theory suggests, such relationships require the principal to employ various control mechanisms to mitigate so called "agency loss" (see e.g. Strøm 2000). Political parties play a critical role in this system. For example, the extensive screening of prospective parliamentarians as well as potential Cabinet members is often assumed to be performed by centralized, cohesive, policy-oriented political parties (see e.g. Müller 2000).

The Swedish political parties have often been described as fulfilling such requirements, being well-organized, cohesive, and policy-oriented (cf. Anckar et al. 2000; Petersson et al. 1999). Furthermore, the Swedish party system has historically been characterized by a high degree of stability, with a moderate number of political parties, following traditional party family lines (cf. Demker and Svåsand 2005). In this section we focus on the Swedish political parties and the Swedish party system, putting these topics in a comparative perspective and analyzing their transformations over time. This section consists of four chapters which cover the role of political parties in the different steps of the parliamentary chain of delegation.

In the first chapter, "The Party System," Nicholas Aylott suggests that the Swedish polity has experienced change at the core of its party system since the establishment of democracy. For many years, the Social Democrats held an exceptionally strong position, from which they could maintain a prolonged grip on government that has no parallel in the democratic world. Aylott suggests that even though this has changed, the Swedish system has long been characterized by simplicity, being dominated by the traditional left-to-right dimension of competition. More recently, however, that assumption has been called into question by the arrival of a new party, the Sweden Democrats, the long-term consequences of whose entry remain unclear.

Gissur Erlingsson, Ann-Kristin Kölln, and Patrik Öhberg turn their focus to the Swedish parties as organizations in their chapter, "The Party Organizations." They ask questions about alleged changes in party organizations, and assess to what extent Swedish parties have followed the transformations of parties suggested in the general party literature. The authors suggest that although parties have become more professionalized, the traditional "mass party" has faded away, and that in Sweden too we see tendencies towards the "cartel party." This does not entail that Swedish parties have become less internally democratic. However, the general movement from mass party to electoral-professional parties forces us to ask questions about new grounds for legitimacy in a democracy where ever fewer citizens find it worthwhile to become party members.

In the chapter "Political Parties and Political Representation," Peter Esaiasson and Lena Wängnerud start by reviewing current debates within political representation research and suggest that we know relatively little about challenges facing political parties that stem from, for example, increased diversity among representatives in terms of social background characteristics. The authors argue that there exists a tension for Swedish political parties—the parties are becoming more professional but at the same time are facing an increasingly complex situation both from within, with more diversity among representatives and more individualism, and from the outside, with less stability among voters and globalization pressures.

In the last chapter of the section, "The Parties in Government Formation," Hanna Bäck and Torbjörn Bergman focus on the role of political parties in the government formation process. They suggest that some features of Swedish cabinets stand out in comparative perspective: for example, many of the postwar governments have been minority cabinets, often single-party governments where the Social Democrats have ruled with the support of the Left Party and the Greens, sometimes even with a written "policy" agreement between the governing Social Democrats and their support parties, forming a "support party coalition," something which has occurred only in a few other systems. When coalitions have formed, they have had a clear-cut "bloc" political character, with the "socialist" parties in one camp and the "non-socialist" parties in the other, making "bloc politics" an important feature of Swedish politics.

REFERENCES

Anckar, D., Karvonen, L., and Isaksson, G.-E. (2000). *Vägar förbi och igenom partier*. Stockholm: SNS Förlag.

Demker, M. and Svåsand, L. (2005). *Partiernas århundrade: Fempartimodellens uppgång och fall i Norge och Sverige*. Stockholm: Santérus.

Müller, W. C. (2000). "Political Parties in Parliamentary Democracies: Making Delegation and Accountability Work," *European Journal of Political Research* 37: 309–33.

Petersson, O., von Beyme, K., Karvonen, L., Nedelmann, B., and Smith, E. (1999). *Demokrati på svenskt vis*. Stockholm: SNS Förlag.

Strøm, K. (2000). "Delegation and Accountability in Parliamentary Democracies," *European Journal of Political Research* 37: 261–89.

CHAPTER 12

....

THE PARTY SYSTEM

....

NICHOLAS AYLOTT

INTRODUCTION

A party system can be defined in a broader or a narrower sense. This chapter uses a narrower definition, which refers to a collection of parties. Sartori described the concept as "the *system of interactions* resulting from inter-party competition" (2005: 39, italics in original). Whatever the precise definition of a party system, few could doubt the significance for political outcomes of having one type rather than another. The party system that prevails at a given election determines the parameters of choice for any elector. It reflects the number of parties that he or she can choose between, the ideological spread between them, and, perhaps most importantly, the likely translation of electoral results into the formation of governments (see Bäck and Bergman in this volume). If we are interested in variation in substantive political outcomes in democracies, the party system must be seen as a powerful intervening variable.

The chapter proceeds as follows. I first present a brief overview of the research on party systems that I subsequently use to analyze the Swedish one. I then describe that system as it has been characterized in the literature.[1] After that, I recount its development, concluding with the situation prior to the 2014 election. This development is punctuated by important turning points, when electoral or institutional change induced a new pattern of interaction between the parties. Finally, I reflect on where that leaves the Swedish party system. The recent emergence of a party on the far right, the Sweden Democrats, may turn out to be particularly disruptive.

STUDYING A PARTY SYSTEM

The study of party systems per se has become less central to political science in recent years. This is, in many ways, a shame. Mair (2006: 64) had a point when he bemoaned "the drift away from case-sensitive and thickly descriptive comparative case studies." Our examination of the Swedish system requires an appreciation of some quite subtle changes and historical sequences that only intensive study can really capture.

Describing the Swedish Party System

We start with what is still arguably the most useful historical perspective on the Swedish party system, Berglund and Lindström's (1978) "five-party model." Three of the five party types were strongly associated with distinct social classes: a *conservative* party represented the economic and social elite; an *agrarian* party the peasantry; and a *social democratic* party the working classes. In addition to these class-based parties, and completing the quintet, a *liberal* party emerged on the center-right, while a *communist* party offered a radical alternative on the left.

This descriptive model was applied to all the Nordic countries bar Iceland, but it fitted Sweden best. This was because the five party types comprised, over fully 71 years from 1917, almost the full set of parties represented in the Swedish parliament (Berglund and Lindström 1978: 16–18).[2]

Sartori, too, was concerned with the number of parties in a party system, which, as he pointed out (2005: 105), was germane to the complexity of the bargaining between them. While other scholars suggested alternative measures of party system "fragmentation" (Rae 1967) or the "effective" number of parties (Laakso and Taagepera 1979), Sartori preferred a simpler focus on "relevant" parties. By this, he meant those that were either in government, at least periodically, or that had "blackmail potential"—that is, sufficient bargaining strength to affect which other parties did end up in government (2005: 107). By that token, Sweden has long had many relevant parties. In fact, it may be arguable that only since 2010 has it had a non-relevant party in its parliament, the Riksdag.

Beyond the numbers of parties, however, Sartori was primarily interested in the "dynamics" of a party system. Political instability was likely, he suggested, if a system had relatively many relevant parties (say, more than five or six); and, in addition, those parties were so dispersed ideologically that opposition to any governing constellation was "bilateral," in that the government would face opposition both to its left and its right. This made the direction of inter-party competition centrifugal, with those "irresponsible oppositions" able to engage in the "politics of outbidding." Such a system was defined as "polarized pluralism" (2005: 116–28).

By the 1970s, Sartori (2005: 156) observed that Swedish pluralism was "moderate" rather than polarized. Scope for bilateral oppositions was constrained, partly by the arrangement of the five parties into two blocs. On the left, there were the social democrats and the communists. On the right, there were the agrarians, liberals, and conservatives—often referred to as *borgerliga*, or bourgeois, parties (without the slightly negative connotations that the word has in English).

There was nothing formal about these blocs. Moreover, the agrarians represented a social class that was essentially removed from the historic social "cleavage" (Lipset and

Rokkan 1990) between workers and owners that gave rise to the left-to-right spectrum. Still, the blocs helped to structure party politics. For instance, the Communists were unthinkable as a party of government. Yet there were no issues on which they might have considered supporting a cabinet that contained center-right parties rather than one in which Social Democrats held all the seats. Their blackmail potential was thus, in practice, limited. With passive Communist support, therefore, minority Social Democratic governments were pretty safe. They had little real opposition from the left.

Another reason for Swedish pluralism being moderate rather than polarized was that the left bloc, due to its containing the Social Democrats, was simply stronger than the right bloc. Sartori described Sweden as veering sometimes towards having a "predominant-party system," due to the Social Democrats' attaining "a winning majority ... of the voters" (2005: 163, 172). In fact, the party twice won a majority of the vote in parliamentary elections, in 1940 and 1968, and won in excess of 45 percent on no fewer than ten other occasions up to 1994. It was by far Sweden's biggest party. After 1917 no other party managed to break the 30 percent barrier until 2010. The Social Democrats could thus hold government office continuously (aside from a brief break in 1936) from 1932 until 1976. So even when they were more estranged from each other, the center-right parties were often at least united by being in opposition.

What made the Social Democrats so strong? Structural conditions were helpful. Late but rapid industrialization is said to have fomented a strong working-class identity and a centralized set of industrial trade unions, which proved a huge asset for the party after its formation in 1889. In addition, the relatively late establishment of parliamentary democracy (seen as occurring when the Social Democrats first entered government in 1917) gave the party an early objective—constitutional reform—that facilitated an openness to progressive allies to their right, particularly on the issue of suffrage (achieved in a series of reforms in 1918–21). That pulled the party towards reformism and away from radicalism (Castles 1978: 15). All this happened in the context of a well-functioning state with stable borders, a homogeneous population, and a national church, which meant that the class cleavage was unchallenged as the basic dimension of political conflict (Therborn 1992: 6–7).

But the Social Democrats also did a lot to shape their own fate. The institutional ties between party and unions were keenly reinforced during the first decades of the twentieth century, not least to keep Communist influence out (Svensson 1994: 59–76). A national-level cooperation committee was established in 1931, but it may have been at local level, with the creation of Social Democratic "union clubs" and party ombudsmen in workplaces, that the Swedish Communists were most effectively prevented from gaining a foothold within organized labor. Svensson (1994) argues that such measures, which secured the electoral support of their core social constituency, permitted the Social Democrats to reach out to middle-class voters. This mitigated the strategic dilemma that confounded many comparable European social democratic parties (Przeworski and Sprague 1986).

Externally, strategy and policy worked consistently to the party's advantage. Indeed, in his comparative survey, Elvander (1980) concluded that such factors were much the most important in explaining the Swedish party's relative success compared to its Danish and Norwegian equivalents. Deals with the Agrarian Union in the 1930s are seen as facilitating successful reflationary policy at that desperate time for Europe. Having kept out of World War II, Sweden was well placed to prosper amid the subsequent recovery. The construction of a comprehensive welfare state, the design of which appealed to both working classes and middle classes, further boosted the party's electoral success (Esping-Andersen 1990).

We thus have a collection of features—five party-types (see Table 12.1); the dominance of the class cleavage; the two-bloc structure; Social Democratic predominance—that have often been used to characterize the Swedish party system until the 1970s and even the 1980s. To that list, one more feature can be added: stability (Arter 1999: 145–7). Sweden seemed especially relevant to the famous claim, made in 1967 by Lipset and Rokkan (1990: 134), that "the party systems of the 1960s reflect, with few but significant exceptions, the cleavage structures of the 1920s."

Table 12.1 The five-party model in Sweden: Average percentage vote by decade and party type

	Communist	Social Democratic	Agrarian	Liberal	Conservative	Total share
1920s	4.9	36.0	10.3	18.3	27.3	96.7
1930s	3.2	43.8	14.3	12.4	20.6	94.1
1940s	6.9	48.8	12.7	15.9	15.4	99.7
1950s	4.2	45.6	10.9	22.1	15.8	98.7
1960s	4.2	48.4	14.2	16.3	14.4	97.5
1970s	5.1	43.7	21.8	11.8	15.4	97.9
1980s	5.6	44.5	13.1	10.8	21.1	95.0
1990s	7.6	39.8	7.1	7.0	22.4	83.9
2000–10	6.6	35.0	6.9	9.3	23.8	81.6

Party names (years indicates change, italics indicate modern name):

• Communist party type—Swedish Social Democratic Left Party (1917), Communist Party of Sweden (1921), Left Party—the Communists (1967), *Left Party* (1990);

• Social Democratic—*Social Democratic Party* (1889);

• Agrarian—Farmers League (1913), merged with National Farmers Union (1922), *Center Party* (1957);

• Liberals—Liberal Party (1900), alliance with National Association of Free Thinkers (1902), merger into People's Party (1934), *Liberals* (1990);

• Conservative—General Electoral League (1902), National Organization of the Right (1938), Right Party (1952), *Moderate Party* (1969).

Some translations of older party names are the author's own.

Note: Figures are for elections to the lower chamber of parliament up to 1968, then to the unicameral parliament.

Sources: Särlvik (2002); Valmyndigheten (2013).

In fact, it was about then that other European party systems began to thaw. The early 1970s saw particularly turbulent electoral periods in neighboring Denmark and Norway, partly because of divisive moves to take these countries into the European Community. In Sweden, where the country's neutrality policy was interpreted by its Social Democratic governments as being incompatible with Community membership, little such turbulence was experienced.

A (Slowly) Thawing Party System

As we saw, the Social Democrats dominated Swedish governments for most of the twentieth century. They did not quite monopolize cabinet positions, however. The Agrarian Union formed a short-lived caretaker government in 1936 and governed in coalition with the Social Democrats in 1936–9 until the establishment of a wartime national government. In 1951–7 the two parties once again formed a coalition under Social Democratic leadership. After that, though, the Social Democrats held office alone for nearly two decades.

In the late 1960s, harder economic times raised challenges for the Social Democrats. However, we first examine an institutional change that weakened the party's position.

Institutional Change

The upper chamber that had been instituted in 1867 was indirectly elected (see Möller, this volume). The rise of the Social Democrats, plus the opening up of the franchise, meant that the chamber's composition gradually shifted leftwards. Its powers made it an increasingly vital prop for the Social Democrats, as Table 12.2 shows. It indicates the periods in which the Social Democrats controlled the median legislator—that is, the strategically vital central position on a single dimension of competition—between 1932 and 1970 in three parliamentary arenas: (a) the lower chamber, (b) the upper chamber, and (c) joint votes of both chambers. This control of the median legislator in each arena was either because the Social Democrats could command their own majority or, failing that, because of their combined strength with the Communists to their left.

In 1953–8, the Social Democrats lost control of the median legislator in the lower chamber, yet they retained office. This was because they could consistently still rely on their own majority in the upper chamber, *plus* control of the median legislator in joint votes of both chambers on national budgets, either through their own majority (1953–6) or with the Communists' implicit support (1956–8) (Bergman 2000: 199–200). Although the Social Democrats chose to retain the Center Party as their coalition partner during most of this period (creating a government that rested on majorities in all three parliamentary arenas), they could do so from a position of relative strength, with Communist support as their fall-back option.

Table 12.2 The Social Democrats' strength in the two parliamentary chambers

Year	Lower chamber		Upper chamber		Joint votes	
	Socialist majority	Social Democratic own majority	Socialist majority	Social Democratic own majority	Socialist majority	Social Democratic own majority
1932–6					*	
1937–40	X					
1941–4	X	X	X	X	X	X
1945–8	X		X	X	X	X
1949–52	X		X	X	X	X
1953–6	*		X	X	X	X
1957–8			X	X	X	
1958–60	X		X	X	X	
1961–4	X		X	X	X	X
1965–8	X		X	X	X	X
1969–70	X	X	X	X	X	X

Note: X indicates a majority in the chamber, or the two chambers combined, held by the Social Democrats and/or by the socialist parties (that is, the Social Democrats and the Communists combined). An asterisk (*) indicates that the forces of the socialist and center-right parties were evenly balanced.

Source: Adapted from Särlvik (2002: 250).

In 1969 the Social Democrats agreed to abolish the upper chamber. (It disappeared with the first election to the new unicameral parliament in 1970.) Särlvik (2002: 254) suggested that it had simply become difficult for the Social Democrats to defend a system of indirect election. Whatever their motives, the end of the upper chamber surely contributed to undermining their predominance (Immergut 2002).

Challenges to Social Democratic Governments

An early indication of trouble on the policy front, meanwhile, was a series of wildcat strikes in 1969–7 (Martin 1984: 248–54). The response of the Trade Union Confederation (LO) was to move leftwards, epitomized by the proposal, presented at the 1971 LO congress, to set up union-controlled "wage-earner funds" that would acquire increasing equity stakes in the biggest private companies.

This proposal, when adopted by the Social Democrats, was extremely contentious. In the 1973 election the party lost its hold of the median legislator, and in 1976 the center-right parties finally won a majority. Their three-party coalition, the first Swedish government in 40 years in which the Social Democrats did not participate, was headed by Torbjörn Fälldin of the Center Party (see also Bäck and Bergman in this volume). The Center had successfully exploited disquiet about nuclear power, a mainstay of the

Swedish grid but increasingly worrying for environmentally minded voters, to win a full quarter of the vote.

This marked a major change in the party system. During the 1960s, the Moderates' right-wing image had obstructed any alliance; the Center and liberal parties cooperated sufficiently closely for them to be seen periodically as the only realistic alternative to a Social Democratic government (and, indeed, for merger between them to be periodically discussed) (Möller 1986). With the formation of the three-party coalition in 1976, party competition was now more clearly about a centripetal battle for the median position in the legislative arena and, by extension, in the electoral arena.

The center-right coalition had a hard time in office. It faced difficult economic circumstances, although its collapse owed most to disagreement over nuclear power. A one-party liberal government was tolerated by the main parties for a year until the next election, in 1979. The center-right trio again won a majority, and their coalition was revived. However, Fälldin's second government fared little better than his first. The Moderates left in 1981 over their coalition partners' willingness to deal on tax policy with the Social Democrats.

For a short spell, Sweden appeared to have shifted toward a more polarized pluralism, with bilateral oppositions and without the Social Democrats' stabilizing predominance. As the economy deteriorated, however, normal service was soon apparently resumed. In the 1982 election, the Social Democrats returned to office, with their best score since 1968 and only nine seats short of their own majority. A new economic strategy, kickstarted by a big devaluation of the krona, seemed to be working, and the Social Democrats retained office in 1985.

Yet that election proved to be the last gasp of the five-party model. In 1988 a new party appeared in the parliament, the first such breakthrough since the 1930s. The Greens appeared to leap through a window of opportunity: according to one observer, "[N]ever before has a political issue so dominated an election campaign as the environmental issue did in 1988" (Bennulf 1995: 151; see also Bolin 2012: 105–44). At first, the Greens eschewed bloc affiliation. However, their twenty seats were insufficient to deprive the Social Democrats, with Communist support, of the median legislator.[3] The sixth parliamentary party had not yet changed significantly the Swedish party system.

THE 1990S: NEW PARTIES, NEW ISSUES, NEW DYNAMICS

In fact, in 1991 the Greens fell back below the 4 percent threshold for winning parliamentary seats. Yet it was far from a return to normality for the Swedish party system. In the context of a dangerously overheating economy and rising inflation, and even as the Greens dropped out, two other parties arrived in the parliament.

The Breakdown of Bloc Politics in the 1990s

One was actually quite an old party. The Christian Democrats had been formed in 1964, but had previously never threatened to win parliamentary seats. (Their leader had won a seat as part of an electoral pact with the Center Party in 1985, but that experiment was not renewed.) Now, however, they not only made the breakthrough into parliament; they also went straight into government. The earlier three-party center-right coalition became a four-party arrangement, this time with a Moderate Prime Minister. The other new parliamentary party, meanwhile, threatened to be more disruptive. New Democracy was a recently created, irreverent, populist, right-wing force. Opposition to immigration was not its primary issue, but its stance was sufficiently provocative, especially to the Liberals (the name having now been formally adopted by the party), to preclude any formal collaboration between New Democracy and the center-right government.

As Sweden's crisis deepened, polarized pluralism again seemed briefly to characterize the party system. In 1992 the government reached agreement with the opposition Social Democrats on two packages of crisis measures, designed to restore order to the public finances and, most immediately, to bolster the sinking currency. Such cross-bloc austerity deals might well have bolstered the radical oppositions on each flank of the spectrum. But New Democracy by then was falling apart, and, in any case, the Social Democrats declined to offer any more deals. They duly won back power in the 1994 election with over 45 percent of the vote.

Even before that election, center-right unity had crumbled. In the summer of 1994 the Center leader resigned from the cabinet over the construction of a bridge to Denmark. During the campaign, the Liberal leader then signalled his readiness to form a coalition with the Social Democrats, which would have been a first for Sweden. In the event, the Social Democrats demurred (Aylott 1995). Less than a year later, however, they struck a deal on parliamentary cooperation with the Center Party instead.

Once again, the customary order—the Social Democrats straddling the median position, a tame opposition to its left and a (now even more) fragmented opposition to its right—seemed to have been restored. The Greens had recovered their place in parliament in 1994, but again they did not threaten the Social Democrats' hold on the median legislator. Seared by its awful experience in government, the center-right bloc was divided. True, there was one especially tricky issue for the Social Democrats: that of European integration. The party leadership had provoked considerable internal opposition when, back in 1990 and in government, it proposed that Sweden should apply for membership of the European Community, abruptly reversing decades of party policy. Yet the issue was adroitly managed subsequently, through its being quarantined in a referendum that was held soon after the 1994 election (Aylott 1997).

The Revival of Bloc Politics from the Late 1990s

After the 1998 election, the Social Democratic Prime Minister, Göran Persson, would probably have preferred to renew his engagement with one of the middle parties. That proved impossible, however. After a term of painful spending cuts, the Social Democrats had suffered severe electoral losses. The two likeliest center-right collaborators, the Center and Liberals, also lost votes—so much so, in fact, that even a deal with *both* of them would not have secured the Social Democrats a parliamentary majority.

Instead, the Social Democrats reached agreement with the Left Party, which had almost doubled its vote, and the Greens. The policy influence that the deal brought those two parties was unprecedented. The Greens, moreover, were pulled more closely into the left bloc. After the 2002 election, the two "support parties" were again denied a full place in government by the Social Democrats (Aylott and Bergman 2011). They did, though, secure a more detailed and comprehensive agreement on the terms and areas of cooperation—a coalition deal in all but the sharing of cabinet jobs (see also Bäck and Bergman, and Persson in this volume).

Meanwhile, events were pushing the center-right parties closer to each other. In 2002 the Liberals had stumbled upon an issue, a demand for Swedish-language tests as part of the requirements for bestowing citizenship on immigrants, that was rather arcane, but which lit up their election campaign and dramatically improved their vote. Even though the issue was subsequently dropped, the party leadership's confidence had been boosted and its room to innovate enhanced. Indeed, to widespread surprise, the Liberals even initiated post-election talks with the Greens about tempting them into a middle-parties minority government.

The Center Party pulled the plug on that process, probably because its new leader was keen to re-establish its identity as a center-right party. She had declared repeatedly during the campaign that she could not envisage cooperation with the Social Democrats. Her party's sympathizers seemed to like it: the Center increased its vote for the first time in nine elections.

Most significant, however, was the dismal campaign and terrible result that the Moderates had endured in 2002. A big change in the party's elite was induced by this failure. Fredrik Reinfeldt became the new leader in 2003 and he immediately moved his party—the "New Moderates," as he called them—towards the political midfield. Several policy issues on which the Moderates had been isolated, such as reform of the labor and housing markets, were shelved. Ideological goals in general were deprioritized. Office-seeking became the de facto objective of party strategy.

What all this facilitated was a more advanced form of center-right cooperation: a pre-electoral coalition (Allern and Aylott 2009). Such an arrangement between opposition parties was not entirely novel. The Moderates and the Liberals, for instance, had worked out a joint manifesto before the 1991 election. However, the "Alliance for Sweden," launched by the the four center-right parties in 2004, was unprecedented in its scope. The initial aim was a common policy platform, which was developed over the next couple of years.

The Alliance was a huge success, and not just in its winning the 2006 election, thus ending 12 years of Social Democratic rule (Aylott and Bolin 2007). It also persuaded the new Social Democratic leader that her party had to emulate it. (The comparable success of a pre-electoral coalition in neighboring Norway in 2005, in which the Social

Democrats had joined with two other parties to win power, must also have been a per-suasive precedent.)

The 2010 campaign thus offered voters perhaps their clearest ever choice. Each of the parties in parliament had committed itself unequivocally to one of two pre-electoral coalitions, based on the traditional blocs. Although there were seven relevant parties in the system, each elector thus knew exactly which of the two competing teams of aspiring office-holders, and which of the two prime ministerial candidates, his or her vote would be for. Remarkably, Sweden had acquired a "modified two-party system," 40 years after the phrase was suggested (Ruin 1968). The arrangement, presented as an extension of the original five-party-type format, is summarized in Table 12.3.

Yet 2010 may have been the zenith of modern Swedish bloc politics. For one thing, the "red-Green" pre-electoral coalition went badly wrong (Aylott 2010). Most observ-ers felt that the association with the Left Party was electorally damaging to the Social Democrats, whose share of the vote in 2010 was their worst since 1914. The Moderates only just fell short of supplanting them as Sweden's biggest party.

Moreover, the party system was complicated still further by the arrival of an eighth party in parliament. The Sweden Democrats were formed in 1988 by elements from extreme right-wing organizations. From 2005 a new leader had softened the party's pol-icy and image, yet its origins and continuing hostility to immigration made the Sweden Democrats *persona non grata* for the other parties. The center-right Alliance, which continued in office, reached deals with opposition parties on two areas of policy: with the Greens on immigration; and with the Greens and the Social Democrats on Swedish military presence in foreign conflict zones. Otherwise, however, little significant leg-islation was possible, as neither bloc would countenance negotiation with the Sweden Democrats.

Table 12.3 Pre-electoral alliances in the Swedish election campaign in 2010, including party type

party type	(former) communist	social democratic	green	(former) agrarian	liberal	Christian democrat	conservative
party name	Left Party	Social Democrats	Greens	Center Party	Liberals	Christian Democrats	Moderates
pre-electoral coalition		Red–Greens				Alliance for Sweden	

Note: Additional party types to the five included in Table 12.1 are taken from Gallagher, Laver, and Mair (2011: 238–77). The two parties not included in Table 12.1 are the following (years indicates change, italics indicate modern name):

- the *Greens* (1981);
- Christian Democratic Rally (1964), *Christian Democrats* (1995).

THE SWEDISH PARTY SYSTEM: OSCILLATING WILDLY?

Swedish electoral politics can no longer be considered a bastion of comparative stability. As is clear in Table 12.4, the electoral volatility that Denmark and Norway experienced in the 1970s arrived, belatedly but with a vengeance, in the 1990s. We, though, are especially interested in the parties in the core of the party system, those who vie for control of government (Mair 2006: 65). For this reason, electorally promiscuous voters, and even the strongly fluctuating electoral fortunes of individual parties, need not necessarily presage a change in a party system.

In the late 1990s Sundberg (1999) argued that the Nordic party systems were actually more stable than was commonly supposed. Of course, numerous new parties had arrived and there were manifest signs of electoral dealignment (see the chapters by Oskarson and by Oscarsson and Holmberg, this volume). The five-party model was dead, in Sweden as elsewhere in the region (Arter 2012; Aylott 2011; Demker and Svåsand 2005). Yet Sundberg (1999: 238) argued that the three class-based parties still structured inter-party competition. He put the "enduring" Nordic party system down to the old parties' ability to adapt to new political circumstances.

There is still something to be said for the stability thesis in the Swedish case. As we saw in Table 12.1, the five old parties took pretty much the entire vote from the 1920s right up to the 1980s. As new parties arrived, the five-party oligopoly took a smaller share. Yet even in 2000–10 the quintet still took, on average, more than four of every five Swedish votes in parliamentary elections.

However, in other respects, we see profound change in the party system. First and foremost, Sweden no longer has anything approaching a predominant-party

Table 12.4 Mean aggregate electoral volatility in seven West European countries

	1950s	1960s	1970s	1980s	1990s	2000–9
Denmark	5.5	8.7	15.5	9.7	12.4	10.4
Finland	4.4	7.0	7.9	8.7	11.0	6.8
Germany	15.2	8.4	5.0	6.3	9.0	9.0
Iceland	9.2	4.3	12.2	11.6	13.7	12.4
Norway	3.4	5.3	15.3	10.7	15.9	13.7
Sweden	4.8	4.0	6.3	7.6	13.8	14.9
UK	4.3	5.2	8.3	3.3	9.3	6.0

Note: Aggregate electoral volatility is the sum of the percentage vote gains of all the winning parties (or the sum of the percentage vote losses of all the losing parties) compared to the previous election.

Source: Gallagher, Laver, and Mair (2011: 310).3

system. The abolition of the upper chamber was one blow to the Social Democrats' power. The other was long-term electoral decline, surely due to the development of a more heterogeneous, less class-based society, but probably also as a consequence of the bouts of economic problems under Social Democratic governments during the 1970s, 1980s, and 1990s. The period of change is reminiscent of the "oscillation" that Bille (1989) ascribed to the postwar Danish party system. Bilateral oppositions, characteristic of Sartori's category of polarized pluralism, emerged in Swedish party politics during troubled times, mainly around center-right governments in the 1970s and 1990s.

As late as 1994, the Social Democrats could win over 45 percent of the vote and choose one among several potential parliamentary collaborators. But the longer-term Social Democratic decline opened up the core of the system. From 1932, and excluding the national governments during World War II, the Social Democrats either governed alone or with the Center Party. From 1976, things became much more complex. Four new combinations of center-right parties held office up to 2014. The Social Democrats' deals with the Left and the Greens in 1998–2006 were not far short of constituting another coalition combination.

In the late 1990s, Sweden moved away from one-party predominance or polarized pluralism and towards a party system that, by 2010, offered a remarkable resemblance to ideal-typical two-party competition. As we saw, two pre-electoral coalitions emerged, encompassing the entire set of parties with parliamentary representation. What is more, the blocs on which the pre-electoral coalitions were based established a pattern of alternation in office. Between 1998 and 2006, the left bloc governed. After 2006, the right took over.

Relatedly, by 2010 the left-to-right dimension was as dominant as ever, having subsumed the dimensions that Arter, writing in the 1990s, reckoned were emerging in the system (1999: 155–7). The environment had become almost a valence issue.[4] The Greens had long since stopped being a single-issue party. Similarly, the Christian Democrats had become a moderate conservative party, with few policy positions, even on family-related issues, that could cause problems with its Alliance partners. As for the center-versus-periphery cleavage, the Center Party's surprising post-2002 strategy of rebranding itself not just as a firmly center-right party, but even sometimes as Sweden's neoliberal party, defused the potential for the divide between prosperous Swedish cities and a languishing, depopulating countryside to find much overt expression in party politics (cf. Bergman 2000: 197–8).

Figure 12.1 depicts one measure of how the parties have developed ideologically over the last three decades. An annual survey asks parliamentarians to place themselves on a left-to-right scale. Among other observations, the graph shows that while the Greens do enjoy a middle position between the center-right and center-left parties, they have become closer to the Social Democrats, due to the latter's rightwards drift. The Center and Liberal parties, meanwhile, which were not far from being equidistant between the Moderates and the Social Democrats in the late 1980s and

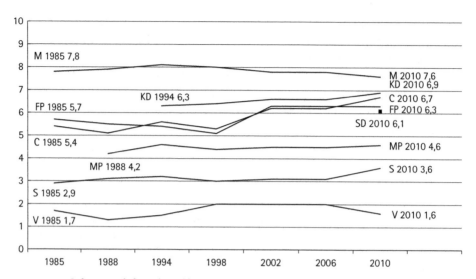

FIGURE 12.1 Subjective left–right self-placement by Swedish MPs, 1985–2010.
Mean values within parties on a scale from 0 (far left) to 10 (far right). Note that there was no survey conducted in 1991. Since 1994 the mandate period for the parliament has been four years; before that it was three. M = Moderates; FP = Liberals; C = Center Party; S = Social Democrats; V = Left Party; KD = Christian Democrats; MP = Greens; SD = Sweden Democrats.

Source: Swedish Parliamentary Surveys, Department of Political Science, University of Gothenburg
Thanks to Peter Esaiasson and Lena Wängnerud for help with these data.

1990s, are now much more closely aligned with the Moderates, who themselves have moved away from the flank, and the Christian Democrats. Perhaps above all, the two main parties, the Social Democrats and the Moderates, have moved closer to each other.[5]

Next Steps

The subsequent development of the party system will obviously be of interest to those whose lives are affected by the political outcomes that it mediates. It will also be worth watching for political scientists.

The Swedish system fits what is, according to some, a European pattern in which party systems have been increasingly "bipolar" (Gallagher, Laver, and Mair 2011: 231–3), with bloc-based competition replacing more fluid patterns of cooperation. Mair (2006: 69–70) suggested two main factors behind it. One was the "victory of democracy." The "anti-system parties" that Sartori (2005) had observed on both the far left and far right, which rejected the basic rules of the democratic game, had all but gone. The other factor was related to the parties themselves. Mair argued that they had experienced an "ascendancy of the party in public office"—in other words, domination by their representatives in parliament and government, rather than by their members or the extra-parliamentary organization. Parties' primary motivation in contemporary politics was assumed to be the retention of such public offices, rather than the pursuit of policy goals or the representation of a particular social group. That, Mair argued (2006: 70), meant that elections had become "a choice of persons"—most acutely, a choice between prime ministerial candidates.

Yet rigid bloc politics in Sweden may turn out to be a temporary phase. For one thing, parties are unlikely to stick with an alliance if it does not deliver collective benefits. That was what happened after the 2010 election, when the Social Democrats and Greens swiftly decommissioned their failed alliance with the Left Party. Despite the success of their Alliance, meanwhile, the price of loyalty to it could also be high for some center-right parties. Seemingly overshadowed in government by the Moderates, the Center Party and the Christian Democrats saw their support fall after 2010 to levels dangerously close to the threshold for parliamentary representation. These parties' post-Alliance strategies, whatever they are, might have to be implemented from outside parliament.

Finally, the success in 2010 of a "niche party" (Meguid 2005), the Sweden Democrats, suggested that an additional dimension of party competition—immigration and ethnic relations—might finally have established itself in the party system. The party was ostracized in parliament. Yet, paradoxically, the "*cordon sanitaire*" (cf. van Spanje 2010) seemed likely to work in its favor, as no other party seemed prepared to offer voters a lighter version—indeed, any version—of the Sweden Democrats' anti-immigration stance. That lack of competition on the immigration dimension might explain why support for the party in opinion polls appeared impervious to highly unflattering revelations about the behavior of some of its parliamentarians. There was little sign that the Sweden Democrats might collapse in the way that New Democracy had done two decades before.

In terms of parliamentary power, the significance of the Sweden Democrats' enduring parliamentary presence would be that it would become far harder for either bloc to win a majority of seats—precisely as in 2010. The sort of policy paralysis that this outcome induced was probably not sustainable beyond the 2014 election. Instead, the pressure for some sort of deal between the Social Democrats, the Greens, and the smaller center-right parties, and perhaps even with the Moderates, might become irresistible. In such a scenario, the Swedish party system will have oscillated once more—this time towards a new era of polarized pluralism and centrifugal competition. That might portend a very different style of politics to that which Swedes have become accustomed.

NOTES

1. Note that the chapter focuses exclusively on the Swedish party system at national level. Its features at local or European levels are disregarded.
2. In reality, party structures were somewhat unstable in the early part of that period.

3. In 1990, in an acute economic situation, the Communists did withdraw support from the Social Democratic government on a confidence vote, causing it to fall. However, with no viable alternative, the same Social Democratic Prime Minister quickly formed a new cabinet.

4. Two decades before, Bennulf (1992) had argued that an environmental dimension in the Swedish electorate was only barely distinct from the left–right one.

5. Another measure of placing parties in an ideological space, through content analysis of their election manifestos, confirms most of these trends, except that the Social Democrats are indicated to have moved back leftwards since the 1990s and the Moderates to have moved away from the right even more sharply (Volkens et al. 2013). Additional measurement options include asking voters or experts to place the parties.

References

Allern, E. H. and Aylott, N. (2009). "Overcoming the Fear of Commitment: Pre-electoral Coalitions in Norway and Sweden," *Acta Politica* 44: 259–85.

Arter, D. (1999). "Sweden: A Mild Case of 'Electoral Instability Syndrome'?" in D. Broughton and M. Donovan (eds), *Changing Party Systems in Western Europe*. London: Pinter, 143–62.

Arter, D. (2012). "'Big Bang' Elections and Party System Change in Scandinavia: Farewell to the 'Enduring Party System'?" *Parliamentary Affairs* 65/4: 822–44.

Aylott, N. (1995). "Back to the Future: The 1994 Swedish Election," *Party Politics* 1/3: 419–29.

Aylott, N. (1997). "Between Europe and Unity: The Case of the Swedish Social Democrats," *West European Politics* 20/2: 119–36.

Aylott, N. (2010). "Europe and the Swedish Election of September 19th 2010," Election Briefing 59. Sussex: European Parties Elections and Referendums Network.

Aylott, N. (2011). "Parties and Party Systems in the North," in T. Bergman and K. Strøm (eds), *The Madisonian Turn: Political Parties and Parliamentary Democracy in Nordic Europe*. Ann Arbor, MI: University of Michigan Press, 297–328.

Aylott, N. and Bergman, T. (2011). "When Median-Legislator Theory Fails: Why the Swedish Greens Allowed Themselves to Be Kept Out of Power in 1998 and 2002," in R. W. Andeweg and L. De Winter (eds), *Government Formation: Coalition Theory and Deviant Cases*. London: Routledge, 44–64.

Aylott, N. and Bolin, N. (2007). "Towards a Two-Party System? The Swedish Parliamentary Election of September 2006," *West European Politics* 30/3: 621–33.

Bennulf, M. (1992). "En grön dimension bland svenska väljare?" *Statsvetenskaplig Tidskrift* 95: 329–58.

Bennulf, M. (1995). "Sweden: The Rise and Fall of Miljöpartiet de gröna," in D. Richardson and C. Rootes (eds), *The Green Challenge: The Development of Green Parties in Europe*. London: Routledge, 94–107.

Berglund, S. and Lindström, U. (1978). *The Scandinavian Party System(s): A Comparative Study*. Lund: Studentlitteratur.

Bergman, T. (2000). "Sweden: When Minority Governments Are the Rule and Majority Coalitions the Exception," in W. C. Müller and K. Strøm (eds), *Coalition Governments in Western Europe*. Oxford: Oxford University Press, 192–230.

Bille, L. (1989). "Denmark: The Oscillating Party System," *West European Politics* 12/4: 43–58.

Bolin, N. (2012). *Målsättning riksdagen: Ett aktörsperspektiv på nya partiers inträde i det nationella parlamentet.* Umeå: Department of Political Science, Umeå University.

Castles, F. G. (1978). *The Social Democratic Image of Society: A Study of the Achievements and Origin of Scandinavian Social Democracy in Comparative Perspective.* London: Routledge & Kegan Paul.

Demker, M. and Svåsand, L. (2005). "Den nordiska fempartimodellen: En tillfällighet eller en fundament?" in M. Demker and L. Svåsand (eds), *Partiernas århundrade.* Stockholm: Santérus, 9–38.

Elvander, N. (1980). *Skandinavisk arbetarrörelse.* Stockholm: Liber Förlag.

Esping-Andersen, G. (1990). *The Three Worlds of Welfare Capitalism.* Cambridge: Polity Press.

Gallagher, M., Laver, M., and Mair, P. (2011). *Representative Government in Modern Europe,* 5th edn. New York: McGraw Hill.

Immergut, E. M. (2002). "The Swedish Constitution and Social Democratic Power: Measuring the Mechanical Effect of a Political Institution," *Scandinavian Political Studies* 25: 231–57.

Laakso, M. and Taagepera, R. (1979). "'Effective' Number of Parties: A Measure with Application to West Europe," *Comparative Political Studies* 12: 3–27.

Lipset, S. M. and Rokkan, S. (1990 [1967]). "Cleavage Structures, Party Systems, and Voter Alignment," in P. Mair (ed.), *The West European Party System.* Oxford: Oxford University Press, 91–138.

Mair, P. (2006). "Party System Change," in W. Crotty and R. Katz (eds), *Handbook of Political Parties.* London: Sage, 63–72.

Martin, A. (1984). "Trade Unions in Sweden: Strategic Responses to Change and Crisis," in P. Gourevitch, A. Martin, G. Ross, S. Borstein, A. Markovits, and C. Allen (eds), *Unions and Economic Crisis.* London: George Allen and Unwin, 190–359.

Meguid, B. M. (2005). "Competition Between Unequals: The Role of Mainstream Party Strategy in Niche Party Success," *American Political Science Review* 99/3: 347–59.

Möller, T. (1986). *Borgerlig samverkan.* Uppsala: Diskurs.

Przeworski, A. and Sprague, J. (1986). *Paper Stones: A History of Electoral Socialism.* Chicago: University of Chicago Press.

Rae, D. (1967). *The Political Consequences of Electoral Laws.* New Haven, CT: Yale University Press.

Ruin, O. (1968). *Mellan samlingsregering och tvåpartisystem: Den svenska regeringsfrågan 1945–1960.* Stockholm: Bonniers.

Särlvik, S. (2002). "Party and Electoral Systems in Sweden," in B. Grofman and A. Lijphart (eds), *The Evolution of Electoral and Party Systems in the Nordic Countries.* New York: Agathon, 225–69.

Sartori, G. (2005 [1976]). *Parties and Party Systems: A Framework for Analysis.* Colchester: ECPR Press.

Spanje, J. van (2010). "Parties Beyond the Pale: Why Some Political Parties Are Ostracized by their Competitors While Others Are Not," *Comparative European Politics* 8/3: 54–383.

Sundberg, J. (1999). "The Enduring Scandinavian Party System," *Scandinavian Political Studies* 22/3: 221–41.

Svensson, T. (1994). *Socialdemokratins dominans: En studie av den svenska socialdekokratins partistrategi.* Uppsala: Acta Universitatis Upsaliensis.

Therborn, G. (1992). "A Unique Chapter in the History of Democracy: The Social Democrats in Sweden," in K. Misgeld, K. Molin, and K. Åmark (ed.), *Creating Social Democracy: A Century of the Social Democratic Labor Party in Sweden.* Pennsylvania: Pennsylvania University Press, 1–34.

Valmyndigheten [Election Authority]. Various dates. Election data.

Volkens, A., Lehmann, P., Merz, N., Regel, S., Werner, A., with Lacewell, O. P., and Schultze, H. (2013). The Manifesto Data Collection: Manifesto Project (MRG/CMP/MARPOR). Berlin: Wissenschaftszentrum Berlin für Sozialforschung (WZB).

CHAPTER 13

THE PARTY ORGANIZATIONS

GISSUR Ó. ERLINGSSON, ANN-KRISTIN KÖLLN, AND PATRIK ÖHBERG

INTRODUCTION

To what extent have Swedish party organizations followed the alleged development from mass parties[1] to ever more centralized "electoral-professional" and so called "cartel" parties? If there has been such a development, how has it affected the quality of intra-party democracy? With these questions as points of departure, this chapter takes a bird's eye perspective on party organizational developments in Sweden, which—as Allern and Pedersen (2007) point out—is intrinsically connected to the development of representative democracy.

In order to paint our general picture, we review the existing literature and present data on party membership and on the share of party income provided by state subsidies over time. Additionally, party centralization, professionalization, and intra-party democracy will be assessed by a comparative and longitudinal account of how members of parliament (MPs), local politicians, and unelected candidates define their roles vis-à-vis their own party. Finally, new, longitudinal survey results from Swedish citizens will be presented, with regards to how they assess the quality and performance of Swedish party organizations.

What we observe, we maintain, lends strength to three overarching conclusions. First, little is left of the once-so-strong mass parties. Swedish party organizations have become increasingly professionalized and seem to be less connected with their own grass-roots members and civil society. As a consequence, parties run the risk of providing suboptimal linkages between citizens' preferences and policy outcomes. Second, some tendencies towards a cartelization of the Swedish party system are observed. And third, more optimistically, although political parties remain one of the most distrusted political institutions in Sweden, their reputation has gained in strength considerably throughout the last 15 years, and also, no conclusive evidence suggests that they have become less internally democratic.

* * *

The Swedish party system follows a long tradition of party organizations. On average, parties currently in parliament are 77 years old.[2] However, had this chapter been written twenty years ago our general assessment of Swedish party organizations would have been rather depressing. In the early 1990s, Sweden suffered an economic crisis and was perceived to have democratic problems. Turnout had plummeted. Citizens' trust in politicians and parties dropped and party membership was in rapid decline. As a consequence, academic and public debate was directed to the state of the party organizations. In 1995, a special issue of *Statsvetenskaplig tidskrift*—our national political science journal—addressed the "crisis of parties" (cf. Bäck 1995; Håkansson 1995; Pierre and Widfeldt 1995). In 1997, a governmental commission was appointed to analyze the state of Swedish democracy; and in 2000, a number of Scandinavian political scientists published a book named *Demokrati utan partier* [*Democracy Without Parties*] (Petersson et al. 2000). However, even though trust in parties remains at comparatively low levels,[3] voter turnout has risen and trust in politicians has become significantly stronger throughout the past decades (cf. Öhrvall in this volume). All in all, this development calls for a closer look at the state of party organizations in Sweden.

THE CONTEXT: TRANSFORMATIONS OF PARTY ORGANIZATIONS

In the course of the twentieth century, European parties have undergone substantial transformations. Party organizations first emerged as loosely tied groups of politicians in the early days of parliamentarianism. Characterized by a small yet strong network with little societal outreach and no ambitions to be socially inclusive, the first party model is commonly referred to as a *cadre party* (Katz and Mair 1995). By the mid-twentieth century, Western party organizations slowly developed towards the *mass party* model (Duverger 1955; Neumann 1956). As another theoretical model, the mass party represents rather well-demarcated interest groups; it has a large membership base, vital local organizations, and a party elite accountable to its members. These features assist mass parties to build strong ties to civil society. In the Swedish context specifically, parties of such type aided citizens to develop strong feelings of party identification in the 1950s and 1960s. Subsequently, for a long time Swedish voters were very loyal to their preferred party (see Oskarsson and Holmberg in this volume; cf. Oskarsson 1994).

In what followed, growing equality amongst citizens and the subsequent erosion of traditional class cleavages affected the appeal of mass parties. Gradually, parties lost incentives to build their politics on class rhetoric, and became increasingly interested in attracting the "median voter" (see Katz and Mair 1995: 12). Already in the 1960s, Kirchheimer (1966: 184) identified a tendency for mass parties to transform into more or less ideologically unfaithful "catch-all" parties. As Krouwel (2012: 45–6) argues, for example, becoming a catch-all organization nearly by definition implies a movement from the mass party model: parties became less dependent on having grass-roots members. Conversely, the parties increasingly got more dependent on state subsidies for their finances and on commercial media for campaigning. This also meant increased levels of professionalization within parties, as described by, for example, Panebianco (1988) and the concept of the *electoral-professional party* (cf. Håkansson 2005; Krouwel 2012).

Since the mid-1990s, scholars have identified an additional party model: the "cartel party" (Katz and Mair 1995, 2009; see also Detterbeck 2005). According to this model, parties have developed a stronger relationship to, and dependence on, the state at the expense of their ties with members and citizens. Research shows that declining party membership rates are common across western European parties (van Biezen et al. 2012; Whiteley 2011). In addition, the cartel party model identifies stronger inter-party collaboration so that existing parties retain their power. The almost evolutionary development of party models illustrates the parties' changing relationship to their members, to civil society, and to the state (cf. Harmel 2002; Krouwel 2006).

The changing nature of intra-party democracy as one aspect of party organizational life is often debated. While the earlier model of the catch-all party describes intra-party democracy as largely centralized with a strong party leader, some have argued that parties grant ordinary members larger direct influence in the cartel party model (Bolleyer 2009; Saglie and Heidar 2004). These new rules are more inclusive and democratic. With declining membership rates, there seems to have been a tendency within parties to introduce more democratic rules for their internal organization (Dalton et al. 2011), suggesting that increased professionalization and the unraveling of mass parties does not necessarily imply a deteriorating internal democracy.

PARTY ORGANIZATIONS IN SWEDEN: PROFESSIONALIZED, CARTELIZED, *AND* LESS INTERNALLY DEMOCRATIC?

More Professionalized Party Organizations?

Previous assessments of party organizational development in Sweden mirror much of what has been observed elsewhere in the general party literature. Most scholars agree that mass parties are practically eradicated in Sweden as elsewhere, and that today they have essentially taken on the character of more or less professionalized organizations that in part resemble the descriptions of the cartel party model (see Blyth and Katz 2005; Bäck and Möller 2001; Dahl 2011; Gidlund 2004; Gidlund and Möller 1999; Gilljam and Möller 1996; Håkansson 2005; Hagevi 2014; SOU 2004:22; Soininen and Etzler 2006). In this context, one ought also to note Nord's (2007) and Strömbäck's (2009) reflections on the professionalization of political marketing and campaigning in Sweden.

An important facet of the alleged changes in party organizations is that party elites have become less dependent on party members. It has been claimed that public subsidies and increased professionalization induce resistance to maintaining vital inner lives that offer members social activities. Conversely, parties have become more focused on maximizing votes (cf. Svensson 1994). Furthermore, in the Swedish context, some argue that the development has increased the distance between party elites and members, which in turn has been claimed to have resulted in deteriorating quality of internal democracy (cf. Gilljam and Möller 1996; Pierre and Widfeldt 1995).

To illustrate the development of party membership in Sweden, consider the upper and lower panel of Figure 13.1. It depicts data on parties' membership sizes, per party on an annual basis for the period 1960–2010. For presentational purposes the upper panel only shows the number of members enrolled in the Social Democratic Party, whereas the lower panel presents membership sizes of all other parties. It is obvious that Swedish parties have lost a substantial number of members. While Swedish parties pulled a combined number of 1,124,917 members in 1960 (or 22.62 percent of the electorate), reported figures in 2010 only amounted to 258,067 members across all parties (or 3.67 percent of the electorate). Counter to this general trend, the Green Party (Miljöpartiet, MP), the Left Party (Vänsterpartiet, V), and the Christian Democratic Party (Kristdemokraterna, KD) have either gained or maintained membership figures on a steady base. The case of the Social Democratic Party (Socialdemokraterna, S) is also noteworthy. Throughout this period S has always had the largest share of party members (for example more than 70 percent in 1990 alone), partly due to the cooperation with trade unions, where unionists automatically became members of the Social Democratic Party. However, in 1990 the S voided this collaboration, which resulted in a steep loss of more than 500,000 members (upper panel in Figure 13.1). These longitudinal comparisons illustrate that Swedish parties are no longer "mass parties."

With declining membership figures, membership dues are no longer particularly important for the economy of Swedish political parties (which they in fact were before the introduction of party subsidies in 1965; cf. Hjertqvist 2013). Since the 1960s, parties have increasingly become dependent on different kinds of public subsidies, and it is noteworthy that decisions as to more public funding are entirely controlled by the parties themselves (cf. Pierre and Widfeldt 1995). Hence, high public subsidies to political parties indicate tendencies toward party cartelization in Sweden (cf. Hagevi 2014).

Figure 13.2 demonstrates the economic dependence of Swedish parties on public subsidies. It depicts the percentage of total party income generated through subsidies throughout the period 1960–2010, averaged across parties.[4] Looking at the figure, we can see that state subsidies were introduced in the mid-1960s. Since then, the Swedish

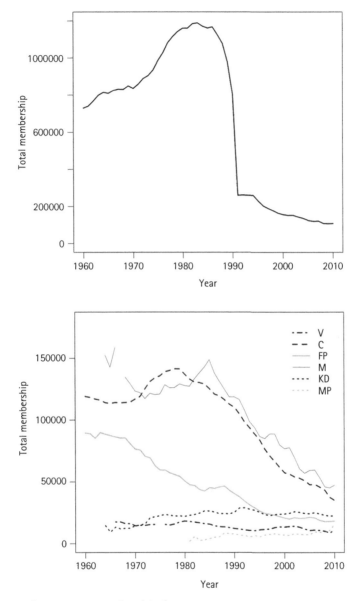

FIGURE 13.1 Declining party membership figures.

Note: Total membership figures for Swedish parties: Social Democratic Party (upper panel) and all other parties (lower panel), 1960–2010. For the Moderate Party and the Left Party some data points are missing.

Source: Data stem from the Party Organisation Dataset 1960–2010 (Kölln 2014a).

state has been co-financing parties substantially. However, the percentage of income provided by the state has been largely stable over time, as the figure shows. While this pattern does not straightforwardly corroborate the assumption of an ever-growing party–state relationship, it does show that Swedish parties, on average, have been heavily subsidized by the state during the last decades—on average, 53 percent of their annual

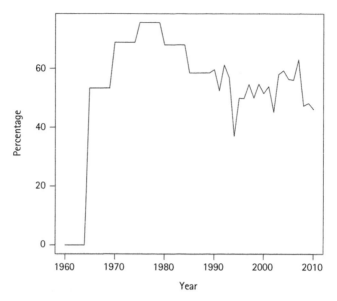

FIGURE 13.2 Share of party income provided by state subsidies, 1960–2010
Source: Data stem from the Party Organisation Dataset 1960–2010 (Kölln 2014a). Averages across all parties.

income.[5] Overall, members are clearly no longer an important source of income. Since members are not crucial for the economy of parties, the parties' incentives to recruit more members are quite limited.

This pattern is not only observable for Swedish parties, but also for parties in several other western European countries (Kölln 2014b). The development implies a movement away from mass-party-based democracy, which is in line with expectations derived from the literature on the emerging cartel party: ever fewer citizens are involved in political parties, and parties have become increasingly dependent on resources provided by the state.

As briefly mentioned before, the figures also lend support to the idea of cartelized structures where parties collaborate to gain joint advantages and retain power. The cartel argument, for the Swedish context, has recently been put forward strongly by Hagevi (2014). And interestingly, von Sydow (1989) argued along the cartel line of reasoning some 25 years ago when he observed that every time the individual Swedish parties had to make a constitutional choice, they opted for a vote that aided their parliamentary self-interest. Tendencies toward a cartelization of the party system are, and have been, observable in Sweden for a long period of time.

* * *

A telling indicator of the changing nature of Swedish representative democracy, party organizations, and increased professionalization is the decreasing number of politicians in local politics. A comparison of the number of local politicians today and 60 years ago is illuminating. Sweden had almost 2,500 municipalities, in which approximately 200,000 individuals were involved as politicians (in relation to 7.5 million inhabitants) before the far-reaching reforms of amalgamating municipalities took place between 1952 and 1974. Today, there are about 38,000 politicians (in relation to today's 9.5 million inhabitants).[6] The ratio "citizen per politician" has hence increased dramatically (SCB 2011).

Important consequences of this are discernible in local government and the local party organizations operating there. Ceteris paribus: from a mass-party perspective, the relationship between citizens, rank-and-file members, and elected politicians would be expected to work at its best in municipalities. The pure proximity between the groups leads one to expect a high probability of recurring interaction between citizens, rank-and-file members, and councilors (cf. Copus and Erlingsson 2013). However, we do not observe such widespread public participation in local affairs. Instead, a concentration of commissions in the hands of ever fewer individuals has taken place: the share of councilors with more than three commissions has increased dramatically. In 1999, 10 percent of the councilors held three or more commissions. In 2011, the share was up to 15 percent (SCB 2011). This implies that a concentration of powers has taken place in local government.

Several scholars (cf. Hagevi 1999; Isaksson 2002; Montin 2004, 2006) maintain that the concentration of commissions not only entails increased concentration of powers, but has also brought about a professionalization of local politics. The consequence is diminishing influence of lay politicians and party members. For example, Montin (2004: 65) notes that in practice, party groups in councils form the parties' respective policies autonomously, without much influence from rank-and-file members (cf. Bäck 2000). Similarly, Gidlund and Möller (1999), as well as Johansson et al. (2001), have demonstrated that the number of members actually showing up for party meetings has diminished radically. These scholars hence conclude that local organizations of Swedish parties have a hard time filling their purpose of channeling demands from ordinary citizens and civil society to local party elites. Therefore, they say, parties are no longer vital arenas for democratic debate and discussion (cf. Gilljam and Möller 1996). The problem of concentration of powers may be further exacerbated, since those members who choose to remain active are socially exclusive as regards gender, age, and ethnicity (cf. Gidlund and Möller 1999; Petersson et al. 2000; Soininen and Etzler 2006).

In sum, existing research demonstrates an increasing professionalization of Swedish parties also in local politics. Parallel to this, a concentration of power to ever fewer individuals at the top of local party organizations can be observed. In addition, individuals holding top positions are somewhat socially exclusive compared to the electorate as a whole, and scholars question whether local party organizations can channel the demands of the electorate or work as vital arenas for political debate.

* * *

Not surprisingly, indications of increased professionalization of parties are more pronounced at the national level, as Figure 13.3 displays. It depicts a steep increase in the proportion of MPs that best can be described as "professional politicians" between 1906 and 2010.[7]

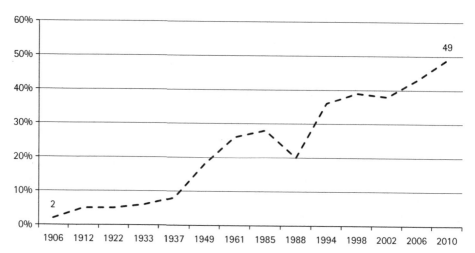

FIGURE 13.3 Proportion of professional MPs, 1906–2010 (percent).

Source: Esaiasson and Holmberg (1988) and Swedish Parliamentary Surveys 1985–2010

The combined effect of fewer members, fewer active politicians, and increasing professionalization can—as is done in Petersson et al. (2000)—be framed in terms of the parties losing touch with civil society and citizens. However, when conceptualized in terms of representativeness, Widfeldt (1999) does not find support for that assertion. Using data on average left–right self-placement, he compares MPs with voters, and finds no evidence of a decline in the political representativeness of parliamentarians (see also Esaiasson and Wängnerud in this volume). We will have reasons to return to citizens' opinions and attitudes towards parties and Sweden's representative democracy in this essay.

Does Increased Professionalization Imply Deterioration of Internal Democracy?

To what extent has the increased *professionalization* of Swedish parties and the alleged cartelization of them affected the quality of intra-party democracy? According to Gilljam and Möller (1996), there is *no doubt* that internal democracy has deteriorated over time. However, as Teorell (1998) correctly points out, it is difficult to give straightforward answers to this question: there are no older studies of intra-party decision-making processes. This makes longitudinal accounts almost impossible. When discussing changes in internal democracy, Teorell (1998) maintains that much of previous research is struck by a "nostalgic optical illusion": without *proving* the premise, scholars tend to *assume* that internal democracy was fine in the "golden ages" of the 1950s and 1960s. Present-day findings are evaluated against an *assumed* yardstick. Simply assuming that internal democracy was better earlier may be a mistake. For example, Loxbo (2013) argues—in an attempt to compare contemporary internal democracy to the situation in previous times—that in some instances, internal democracy was not more inclusive before.

* * *

But can *something* be said about changes in internal democracy? In light of the difficulties associated with measuring longitudinal changes, the degree of centralization of decision-making within parties may be viewed as a proxy for internal democracy (cf. Scarrow et al. 2000). In order to shed at least some light over the issue of centralization and internal democracy, we will consult three kinds of material. First, we take a look at how MPs and local politicians have developed their views on party representation in the past 35–45 years. Second, we take a snapshot of internal democracy by comparing views of unelected candidates to Parliament with those of MPs in 2010. And third, we take a look at the perceptions of citizens on issues related to internal democracy.

There is an assumption in the literature that party leaders in more professionalized parties prefer to centralize decision-making processes (Bolleyer 2009; Katz 2001). The premise here is that party elites prefer to have loyal foot soldiers in the local and national parliaments, not autonomous MPs or autonomous local politicians. That way unity can be ensured. We will examine the extent to which there has been a process of centralization towards stronger party leadership by analyzing two factors:

- MPs' and local politicians' perception of the importance of the individual representative to promote the policies of the party;
- MPs' perception on which factors are of importance to best influence the party group.

Over the years, MPs and local councilors have been asked how elected officials should act in Parliament in instances when their own understanding of a subject is in conflict with the party's or the voters', respectively. The question is inspired by Eulau et al. (1959) and Wahlke et al. (1962), and focuses on *principles of representation*. Politicians had to indicate in the questionnaires which principle they consider most important when their opinions are at odds with those of either their party or their voters. Since our focus is on a potential centralization of party structures, only the importance of the party and the importance of MPs' own opinions are reported.

Figure 13.4 shows how the proportion of MPs and local politicians are distributed between the importance of the party and own opinion. Between 1969 and 2002, the importance of one's own opinion among MPs fell from 71 percent to 53 percent. The importance of the party increased in the meantime from 24 percent to 38 percent. However, between 1985 and 2002 the importance of the party decreased slightly, and the opposite is true for one's own opinion during the same period. Still, small changes occurred after the 1980s, and the difference was more pronounced in the 1960s. On the local level, a similar pattern can be observed. In the 1960s the difference between the principles of representation was larger than they were from 1980s and onward. Nowadays, the party and one's own opinion are equally important.

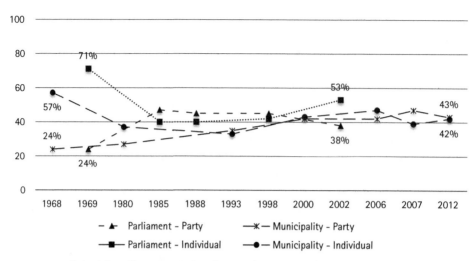

FIGURE 13.4 Principles of representation (percent).

Note: The numbers are taken from Gilljam et al. (2010), except 2012. The numbers from 2012 have been taken from Gilljam and Karlsson (2013): *Kommun- och landstingsfullmäktigeundersökningen (KOLFU) 2012* (University of Gothenburg: Department of Political Science and School of Public Administration).

How can this be interpreted? The figures are straightforward: when the 2000s are compared with the 1960s, party discipline has become considerably more pronounced. In a short-term perspective, however, styles of representation have been stable since the 1980s. It is not straightforward how to interpret the developments. Intra-party organizational changes are just one variable to consider. Institutional reforms—for example, large-scale municipal amalgamations in 1962–74, the introduction of the unicameral system in 1971, and the introduction of the preferential voting system in 1998—may also have affected the styles of representation. Nevertheless, party loyalty is much stronger today (and conversely, the individual mandate weaker), than in the 1960s.

An additional factor to consider is how MPs assess they can best influence their own party group. In the Parliamentary Surveys, MPs have been asked to consider seven factors that could be of importance to gain influence within the parliamentary group. The most interesting items here are: *support in own party* and *good relations with party leadership*. If the party elite has been affected by a process of centralization, one would expect support from the MPs' own party (i.e. party organization, rank-and-file members) to be less important in 2010 than in 1994, and good relations with the party leadership to have become more important.

Figure 13.5 indicates that MPs believe that a centralization in fact may have taken place. The importance of party support has declined since 1994 when 62 percent of the MPs stated it was very important to have support from the party organization. In 2010, less than half of the MPs considered inside support to be of great importance. Nevertheless, when we compare the importance of gaining influence with the other factors asked about: "support from the electorate" (29 percent), "successful in internal

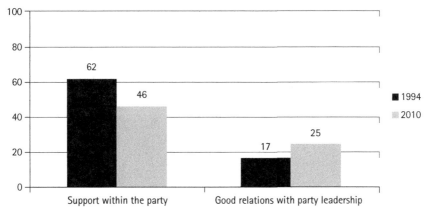

FIGURE 13.5 Very important factors to influence decisions in the party group (percent).

Source: The Parliamentary Surveys 1994 and 2010

debates" (19 percent), "good relations with media" (12 percent), "support from experts" (10 percent), and "good relations with other parties" (4 percent), support from the party organization is still the most important factor. Yet having good relations with the party leadership has gained in importance. One quarter of MPs in the 2010 Parliament said it was very important to have good relations with the party leadership, up from 17 percent in 1994.

However, note that these results may be driven by the proximity between MPs and leaders: MPs are a distinct group of individuals who have already succeeded in occupying influential positions. In contrast, persons who were candidates in the national election of 2010, but were ultimately *not* elected to Parliament, form a group of "unsuccessful" politicians with perhaps different views on the workings of intra-party democracy. As part of the Comparative Candidates Survey,[8] MPs *and* unelected candidates were asked to assess propositions on the state of intra-party democracy in their respective parties.

We employ three statements to obtain snapshot indicators of how the party elite and unelected candidates assess the situation; each statement has the answer categories of "totally agree," "agree," "neither," "disagree," and "totally disagree" assigned to it: (1) "Decision-making in my party is too top-down; the grass roots cannot make its voice heard"; (2) "The party leader is too powerful"; (3) "Pollsters and political strategists have too much influence over my party's decision-making." Table 13.1 reports the proportion of respondents that totally agree or agree with the statements.

The table shows that 29 percent of unelected candidates think that the grass roots cannot make their voices heard. MPs agree with the statement to a significant lesser extent: 20 percent agree. Still, the majority of MPs and unelected candidates think that the grass roots can indeed have a say (49 percent among MPs and 50 percent among unelected candidates). Regarding the influence of the party leader, there is no significant difference between the groups on how they evaluate his/her influence. So, a majority of

Table 13.1 Centralization of powers within the parties (totally agree + agree)

	Unelected candidates (n 1289)	MPs (n 176)	Difference
Grass roots cannot make their voices heard	29	20	9**
Party leader too strong	23	18	5
Pollsters are too influential	48	30	18***

* $p < 0.1$, ** $p < 0.05$, *** $p < 0.01$

respondents do not think that the party leader is too influential. However, considerable criticism against the influence of pollsters and political strategists can be noted, especially among unelected candidates. Almost half of the unelected candidates hold the view that pollsters and strategists are too influential. MPs are also more concerned about pollsters than about the influence of party leaders or possibilities for the grass roots to be heard.

* * *

As important and informative as opinions held by (un)elected representatives are, in the long run, opinions of ordinary citizens are ultimately what matters for the legitimization of representative democracy. How do Swedish citizens view political parties? Do they trust them? Do they think they can be influenced? And what do they think about the quality of intra-party democracy? First of all, relatively speaking, political parties stand out as one of the most distrusted institutions in Sweden. However, levels of trust have increased considerably since this question was first recorded by the SOM-institute in 1996. Secondly, in the Election Studies (Valundersökningarna), since 1968 Swedes have been regularly asked to assess the following statement: "Parties are only interested in citizen's votes, not their opinions." The all-time high was recorded in 1968 when 55 percent "disagreed" or "partly disagreed" with the statement, a figure which consistently dropped to its lowest point in 1998 when a mere 23 percent dissociated themselves fully or partly from this negative statement. However, parties have regained some of their former reputation. In 2010, 44 percent of the respondents disagreed or partly disagreed with the statement, which means that we are almost back to the same levels as in the early 1970s.

A similar pattern can be discerned when asking people specifically about "how parties work when it comes to channelling the demands and preferences of citizens." In 1999, a mere 24 percent answered "good" or "fairly good," whilst 61 answered "fairly bad" or "bad" (Petersson et al. 2000). Erlingsson and Persson (2014) repeated the same question in 2013, and found that 29 percent answered that parties are "good" or "fairly good" at channelling the demands of citizens. At the same time, the number of critical citizens has dropped to 48 percent, i.e. an increased satisfaction with parties' functionality. And when citizens are asked about the internal democracy of parties, a similar pattern

Table 13.2 Changes in citizens' view of parties

How do parties work when it comes to	Net-attitude 1999 (good *minus* bad)	Net-attitude 2013 (good *minus* bad)
... *allowing their members to affect the politics of the party?*	(−44)	(−22)
... *correctly channelling the demands and opinions of citizens*	(−37)	(−10)

Source: Petersson et al. (2000) and Erlingsson and Persson (2014)

emerges. Citizens were more positive in 2010 than in 1999: 22 percent of respondents in 2013 answered that parties are "good" or "fairly good" at granting their members influence, compared to 13 percent in 1999. Consequently, citizens are also less critical. In 2013, 39 percent said that parties are "fairly bad" or "bad," compared to 57 percent in 1999. This gives us a considerable net increase in trust for parties, as demonstrated in Table 13.2.

To sum up, citizens and politicians give slightly different directions for the path which parties' internal democracy has taken. Surprisingly, citizens are more positive in the 2010s than they were in the 1990s, while politicians indicate that the importance of internal party support has decreased just as the significance of the party leadership has increased over the years.

Conclusion

Although research on parties has been dubbed a "mature field" (Wolinetz 2007: 572), several high-profile scholars in Sweden have complained about the lack of research on political parties *as organizations*. In the early 1990s, Petersson (1993) wrote that the collected knowledge on decision-making and internal democracy of Swedish parties had vast blind spots (see also Möller 1993). In the late 1990s, Teorell (1998) concurred that we *still* know too little about how decisions are made within Swedish party organizations. About ten years later, Oscarsson (2009) yet again highlighted the rather poor state of research on Swedish party organizations when concluding that we lack knowledge about the leading actors in Swedish democracy: the political parties. Gidlund (2010) argues along similar lines.

Against this backdrop, we have provided a bird's eye view on the development and state of Swedish party organizations. The basis for this was formed by brief reviews of existing research in combination with a presentation of original data. Using popular concepts and themes in existing party literature as guides for the presentation, we have aimed to evaluate the extent to which Swedish parties have generally followed the alleged development from mass parties to more centralized, "electoral-professionalized" parties, and subsequently to "cartel" parties. Connected to this, the chapter also addressed whether or not such a development may have affected the quality of intra-party democracy.

First of all, it is unquestionable that mass parties—as they once were and typically have been described in the Swedish context—are practically eradicated. Throughout the past decades, membership figures have dropped dramatically. Simultaneously, party organizations have become increasingly professional both at the national as well as at the local level. The number of politicians has dramatically decreased, and individuals who choose to take on leading roles can more or less be described as "professional" politicians (i.e. paid, more or less full-time politicians, in contrast to the more layman-oriented type of politician frequent in older times). The concurrent developments of losing members and increasing professionalization may be coincidental or causal—such an assessment is beyond the scope of our contribution—however, our analyses support findings in previous research, that the era of the mass party model in Sweden is over. Ever more professionalized parties prevail.

Secondly, we have described a few tendencies toward a cartelization of the party system. In particular, this concerns the way parties have designed a system of public funding for themselves that has made them independent—at least economically—from having many paying party members. In addition, the Swedish system (similar to many other parliamentary systems) is designed in such a way that parties represented in the Riksdag, as well is in councils at subnational levels, can collectively determine their own levels of salaries, pensions, and other forms of compensation. Lastly, it is noteworthy that such a system allows parties that are "insiders" to adjust the rules of electoral contestation in favor of their own interests and at the expense of present (or future) competitors.

Thirdly, reviewing the existing literature and analyzing a few proxies for internal democracy, we cannot find support for the hypothesis that intra-party democracy has deteriorated in connection with a movement from mass parties to more professionalized or even cartelized parties. Although political parties remain one of the most distrusted public institutions in Sweden, this does *not* imply that the state of intra-party democracy is to blame. As authors such as Teorell (1998) and Loxbo (2013) point out, it may well be the case that it was more difficult to propose new ideas and to participate in parties during the heyday of the mass party. In that sense, today's quality of intra-party democracy might actually be higher than in the old days under the mass party model.

* * *

In line with much previous comparative work on parties in western Europe, we have shown that Swedish party organizations have undergone significant organizational changes throughout the past decades. However, although experiencing problems attracting members and recruiting suitable candidates for political appointments, they still organize politics and hence still are ultimately the upholders of representative democracy. Therefore, a key question—asked for example by Petersson et al. (2000)—is whether or not the transformations that parties have undergone pose a long-term threat to the legitimacy of representative democracy. Such a worry could be grounded in a Patemanian view of democracy, where active involvement of the many in common affairs is seen as creating legitimacy (Pateman 1970). However, in contrast to such a theory of legitimacy, no dramatic negative changes are observable in how the electorate views representative democracy.

First of all, although one of our most distrusted public institutions, faith in parties seems to be on the rise. Secondly, there has been a remarkable revival of trust in politicians in the last 10–15 years. Today, Swedish politicians enjoy the same levels of trust as did politicians in the 1960s and 1970s. Thirdly, a group of scholars have tried to assess whether Swedes (a) prefer a system where their active involvement in public affairs is required, i.e. some ideal-typical version of *participatory democracy*, over (b) a system where a selected elite of elected politicians take care of public affairs for them, i.e. some ideal-typical version of *representative democracy*. Their somewhat surprising finding, both from studies in 2001 and 2010, is that a majority of Swedes prefer the representative model over the participatory one. Further, support for the representative system is much more pronounced in 2010 than in 2001 (Esaiasson et al. 2011).

All in all, there is no doubt that Swedish parties have undergone significant transformations since the 1950s and 1960s. They have lost almost five out of six members, have become increasingly dependent on state subsidies, and have turned into professionalized, centralized, and somewhat cartelized organizations. And although there still is an ongoing scholarly as well as public debate about a "crisis of party," much indicates that this development does *not* seem to have affected the citizen's perception of the desirability of living under the current system of representative democracy where parties play a key role in organizing politics. In fact, turnout has been on the rise, as well as trust in parties and politicians, and so too has the citizen's preference for living under a primarily representative system.

Notes

1. In the Swedish discourse—the academic as well as the public debate—mass parties are often labeled *folkrörelsepartier*, i.e. "popular movement" parties (cf. Gidlund 1989, 2004).
2. Between the introduction of universal suffrage in 1921 and 1988 when the first new party entered the Swedish Riksdag, the same five parties were represented in Parliament. These are the Left Party (founded in 1917), the Social Democratic Party (1889), the Center Party (1913), the Liberal Party (formally 1934, but its roots go back to the *Frisinnade landsrörelsen*, founded in 1902), and the Moderate Party (1904). In 1988 the Green Party (founded in 1981) entered Parliament. The Christian Democratic Party (1964) gained representation in Parliament in 1991, and in 2010 the Sweden Democrats (1988) became party number eight in today's Riksdag. Between 1991 and 1994, New Democracy (1991) made a short appearance in Parliament; after it lost parliamentary representation it soon lost its relevance and its organization slowly dissolved. However, the formal dissolution only took place in 2000.
3. Parties remain one of the most, if not the most, distrusted institutions in Sweden. Ever since the introduction of the survey measure, at best 20 percent of Swedish citizens state that they have very or fairly much confidence in political parties (Holmberg and Weibull 2012).

4. The remainder were membership dues, donations, and other private sources of income.
5. This share of income provided by the state is common among several West European countries (Kölln 2014a).
6. Not all of them are *elected* officials though. There are approximately 14,000 politicians that hold elected office in Sweden (Gilljam et al. 2010).
7. MPs who were upon election to Parliament full-time employees of their parties, employed by a public sector organization to perform political work, or employed by lobbying organizations, were categorized as professional politicians. The definition is established within the framework of the Parliamentary Studies (see for example Esaiasson and Holmberg 1996).
8. See <http://www.comparativecandidates.org/>.

References

Allern, E. and Pedersen, K. (2007). "The Impact of Party Organisational Change on Democracy," *West European Politics* 30/1: 68–92.

Bäck, H. (1995). "Partikrisen, den nya politiken och den nya högern," *Statsvetenskaplig tidskrift* 96/1: 51–4.

Bäck, H. (2000). *Kommunpolitiker i den stora nyordningens tid*. Malmö: Liber.

Bäck, M. and Möller, T. (2001). *Partier och organisationer*. Stockholm: Norstedts Juridik.

Biezen, I. van, Mair, P., and Poguntke, T. (2012). "Going, Going, Gone …? The Decline of Party Membership in Contemporary Europe," *European Journal of Political Research* 51/1: 24–56.

Blyth, M. and Katz, R. (2005). "From Catch-All Politics to Cartelisation: The Political Economy of the Cartel Party," *West European Politics* 28/1: 33–60.

Bolleyer, N. (2009). "Inside the Cartel Party: Party Organisation in Government and Opposition," *Political Studies* 57/3: 559–79.

Copus, C. and Erlingsson, G. (2013). "Formal Institutions versus Informal Decision-Making: On Parties, Delegation and Accountability in Local Government," *Scandinavian Journal of Public Administration* 17/1: 51–69.

Dahl, S. (2011). *Efter folkrörelsepartiet: Om aktivism och politiska kursomläggningar i tre svenska riksdagspartier*. Stockholm: Stockholms universitet.

Dalton, R., Farrell, D., and McAllister, I. (2011). *Political Parties and Democratic Linkage: How Parties Organize Democracy*. Oxford: Oxford University Press.

Detterbeck, K. (2005). "Cartel Parties in Western Europe?" *Party Politics* 11/2: 173–91.

Duverger, M. (1955). *Political Parties*. New York: John Wiley and Sons.

Erlingsson, G. Ó. and Persson, M. (2014). "Ingen partikris, trots allt?" in A. Bergström and H. Oscarsson (eds), *Mittfåra och marginal*. Göteborg: Göteborgs universitet, SOM-institutet, 407–20.

Esaiasson, P., Gilljam, M., and Persson, M. (2011). "Medborgarnas demokratiuppfattningar," in S. Holmberg, L. Weibull, and H. Oscarsson (eds), *Lycksalighetens ö*. Göteborg: Göteborgs universitet, SOM-institutet, 269–77.

Esaiasson, P. and Holmberg, S. (1996). *Representation from Above: Members of Parliament and Representative Democracy in Sweden*. Aldershot: Dartmouth.

Eulau, H., Wahlke, C., Buchanan, W., and Ferguson, L. (1959). "The Role of the Representative: Some Empirical Observations on the Theory of Edmund Burke," *American Political Science Review* 53/3: 742–56.

Gidlund, G. (1989). "Folkrörelsepartiet och den politiska styrelsen: SAP:s Organisationsutveckling," in K. Misgeld, K. Molin, and K. Åmark (eds), *Socialdemokratins samhälle*. Stockholm: Tiden, 282–308.

Gidlund, G. (2004). "Folkrörelsepartiet och kunskapssamhället," in O. Ruin (ed.), *Politikens ramar och aktörer: En vänbok till Ingvar Carlsson*. Stockholm: Hjalmarsson och Högberg Förlag, 282–308.

Gidlund, G. (2010). "För partier i tiden," *Statsvetenskaplig Tidskrift* 112/5: 396–409.

Gidlund, G. and Möller, T. (1999). "Demokratins trotjänare," SOU 1999:30. Stockholm: Fakta Info Direkt.

Gilljam, M., Karlsson, D., and Sundell, A. (2010). *Politik på hemmaplan: Tiotusen fullmäktigeledamöter tycker om demokrati*. Stockholm: SKL Kommentus.

Gilljam, M. and Möller, T. (1996). "Från medlemspartier till väljarpartier," in *På medborgarnas villkor. En demokratisk infrastruktur*, SOU 1996:162. Stockholm: Fakta Info Direkt.

Hagevi, M. (1999). *Professionalisering och deltagande i den lokala representativa demokratin. En analys av kommunala förtroendeuppdrag 1999*. Göteborg: Göteborgs universitet, CEFOS.

Hagevi, M. (2014). "Kartellisering i nytt ljus: Slutsatser," *Statsvetenskaplig Tidskrift* 116/1: 159–69.

Håkansson, A. (1995). "Kris för de svenska partierna?" *Statsvetenskaplig tidskrift* 98/1: 45–50.

Håkansson, A. (2005). "Vad styr partiernas agerande?" in G. Erlingsson, A. Håkansson, and K. M. Johansson (eds), *Politiska partier*. Lund: Studentlitteratur, 61–107.

Harmel, R. (2002). "Party Organizational Change: Competing Explanations?" in K. R. Luther and F. Müller-Rommel (eds), *Political Parties in the New Europe*. Oxford: Oxford University Press, 119–42.

Hjertqvist, O. (2013). *Det politiska bidragsberoendet: Finansieringen av Sveriges politiska partier*. Stockholm: Timbro.

Holmberg, S. and Esaiasson, P. (1988). *De folkvalda: En bok om riksdagsledamöterna och den representativa demokratin i Sverige*. Stockholm: Bonnier.

Holmberg, S. and Weibull, L. (2012). "Förtroendet för staten," in L. Weibull, H. Oscarsson, and A. Bergström (eds), *I framtidens skugga*. Göteborg: Göteborgs universitet: SOM-institutet, 127–44.

Isaksson, A. (2002). *Den politiska adeln: Politikens förvandling från uppdrag till yrke*. Stockholm: Wahlström & Widstrand.

Johansson, F., Nilsson, L., and Strömberg, L. (2001). *Kommunal demokrati under fyra decennier*. Malmö: Liber.

Katz, R. S. (2001). "The Problem of Candidate Selection and Models of Party Democracy," *Party Politics* 7/3: 277–96.

Katz, R. S. and Mair, P. (1995). "Changing Models of Party Organization and Party Democracy: The Emergence of the Cartel Party," *Party Politics* 1/1: 5–28.

Katz, R. S. and Mair, P. (2009). "The Cartel Party Thesis: A Restatement," *Perspectives on Politics* 7/4: 753–66.

Kirchheimer, O. (1966). "The Transformation of Western European Party Systems," in J. LaPalombara and M. Weiner (eds), *Political Parties and Political Development*. Princeton: Princeton University Press, 177–200.

Kölln, A. (2014a). *Party Organisation Dataset 1960–2010*. Enschede: University of Twente.

Kölln, A. (2014b). "Party Decline and Response: The Effects of Membership Decline on Party Organisations in Western Europe, 1960–2010," PhD thesis, University of Twente.

Krouwel, A. (2006). "Party Models," in R. S. Katz and W. Crotty (eds), *Handbook of Party Politics*. London: Sage Publications, 249–69.

Krouwel, A. (2012). *Party Transformations in European Democracies*. New York: State University of New York Press.

Loxbo, K. (2013). "The Fate of Intra-Party Democracy: Leadership Autonomy and Activist Influence in the Mass Party and the Cartel Party," *Party Politics* 19/4: 537–54.

Möller, T. (1993). "Forskning om svensk politisk historia 1945–1980," in *Svensk politisk historia: En komprimerad litteraturöversikt*. Stockholm: HSFR.

Montin, S. (2004). *Moderna kommuner*. Malmö: Liber.

Montin, S. (2006). *Politisk styrning och demokrati i kommunerna: Åtta dilemman i ett historiskt ljus*. Stockholm: Sveriges kommuner och landsting.

Neumann, S. (1956). "Toward a Comparative Study of Political Parties," in S. Neumann (ed.), *Modern Political Parties*. Chicago: University of Chicago Press, 395–421.

Nord, L. (2007). "The Swedish Model Becomes Less Swedish," in R. Negrine, P. Mancini, C. Holtz-Bacha, and S. Papathanassopoulos (eds), *The Professionalisation of Political Communication*. Bristol: Intellect, 81–96.

Oscarsson, H. (2009). "Svensk partiforskning," available online at <www.henrikoscarsson.com/2009/02/svensk-partiforskning.html>, last accessed April 16, 2014.

Oskarsson, M. (1994). *Klassröstning i Sverige: Rationalitet, lojalitet eller bara slentrian*. Stockholm: Narenius & Santérus Förlag.

Panebianco, A. (1988). *Political Parties: Organization and Power*. Cambridge: Cambridge University Press.

Pateman, C. (1970). *Participation and Democratic Theory*. Cambridge: Cambridge University Press.

Petersson, O. (1993). *Svensk politik*. Stockholm: Publica.

Petersson, O., Hernes, G., Holmberg, S., Togeby, L., and Wängnerud, L. (2000). *Demokrati utan partier? Demokratirådets rapport 2000*. Stockholm: SNS Förlag.

Pierre, J. and Widfeldt, A. (1994). "Party Organizations in Sweden: Colossuses with Feet of Clay or Flexible Pillars of Government?" in R. S. Katz and P. Mair (eds), *How Parties Organize: Change and Adaptation in Party Organizations in Western Democracies*. London: Sage Publications, 332–56.

Pierre, J. and Widfeldt, A. (1995). "Partikris i Sverige?" *Statsvetenskaplig tidskrift* 98/1: 41–5.

Saglie, J. and Heidar, K. (2004). "Democracy within Norwegian Political Parties: Complacency or Pressure for Change?" *Party Politics* 10/4: 385–405.

Scarrow, S., Webb, P., and Farrell, D. (2000). "From Social Integration to Electoral Contestation: The Changing Distribution of Power within Political Parties," in R. Dalton and M. Wattenberg (eds), *Parties without Partisans: Political Change in Advanced Industrial Democracies*. Oxford: Oxford University Press, 121–56.

SCB (2011). *Förtroendevalda i kommuner och landsting*. Demokratistatistik rapport 12. Stockholm: Statistics Sweden.

Soininen, M. and Etzler, N. (2006). *Partierna nominerar: Exkluderingens mekanismer–etnicitet och representation*. SOU 2006:53. Stockholm: Norstedts Juridik AB.

SOU (2004). *Allmänhetens insyn i partiers och valkandidaters intäkter*. Stockholm: Fritzes.

Strömbäck, J. (2009). "Selective Professionalisation of Political Campaigning: A Test of the Party-Centred Theory of Professionalised Campaigning in the Context of the 2006 Swedish Election," *Political Studies* 57/1: 95–116.

Svensson, T. (1994). *Socialdemokraternas dominans: En studie av den svenska socialdemokratins partistrategi*. Uppsala: Statsvetenskapliga föreningen.

Sydow, B. von (1989). *Vägen till enkammarriksdagen: Demokratisk författningspolitik i Sverige 1944–1968*. Stockholm: Tidens Förlag.

Teorell J. (1998). *Demokrati eller fåtalsvälde?* Uppsala: Acta Universitatis Upsaliensis.

Wahlke, J., Eulau, H., Buchanan, W., and Ferguson, L. (1962). *The Legislative System: Explorations in Legislative Behavior*. New York: Wiley.

Whiteley, P. F. (2011). 'Is the Party Over? The Decline of Party Activism and Membership across the Democratic World," *Party Politics* 17/1: 21–44.

Widfeldt, A. (1999). "Losing Touch? The Political Representativeness of Swedish Parties, 1985–1994," *Scandinavian Political Studies* 22/4: 307–26.

Wolinetz, S. (2007). "Coping with Cornucopia: The Parties' Literature in the New Millennium," *International Political Science Review* 28/5: 571–84.

....

CHAPTER 14

POLITICAL PARTIES AND POLITICAL REPRESENTATION

....

PETER ESAIASSON AND LENA WÄNGNERUD

Introduction

....

"THE Swedish people's ancient right to tax itself is exercised by the Riksdag only." This passage from the Instrument of Government Act of 1809 signifies the pivotal position of the national parliament in Swedish political discourse. In the early nineteenth century, the Riksdag was portrayed as an institution through which free men could maintain autonomy vis-à-vis the monarchy (Metcalf 1977). Two centuries later, the new Instrument of Government Act of 1974 expresses an idea of the same purport but in the context of a modern democracy: "All public power in Sweden proceeds from the people" and "the Riksdag is the foremost representative of the people." According to official rhetoric then, the Swedish Riksdag and its members have for a long time been an instrument for the people to rule themselves.

Not only is the Riksdag associated with popular rule; it is also a model of institutional stability. Important for the representative relationship (Powell 2000), representatives have been chosen by means of a proportional electoral system since 1911, even before the introduction of universal suffrage in 1921 (Särlvik 2002). Although the electoral system has changed with regard to district sizes in 1921 (the average district magnitude increased from 4.1 to 8.1), electoral formula in 1952 (moving from d'Hondt to a modified Saint-Laguë), the introduction of a 4 percent electoral threshold in 1970, and the introduction of a (moderate) open list system in 1998 (Särlvik 2002; Hermansson in this volume), the only constitutional change that arguably moves the Riksdag from one category of representational system to another is the abolition of the upper chamber in 1970 (Petersson in this volume). And this constitutional change, moreover, was motivated by an urge to further strengthen the people's influence over governmental decision-making (von Sydow 1989; Petersson in this volume). Clearly, judging from both historical public discourse and institutional set-up, there is reason to expect political representation in

Sweden to illustrate how democratic principles can be applied within the realms of a nation state (Dahl 1989).

Of course, political realities fail to meet expectations of a flawless democracy. As emphasized by recent theorizing on representation, the system of government called representative democracy is generically more elitist and less egalitarian than commonly recognized in the formal speeches. To be precise, there is no escape from the fact that selection by elections is inherently advantageous for the resourceful (Manin 1997), that the selected few can shape the preferences of the represented (Disch 2011), and that it is an act of submission to entrust others with the right to decide common matters (Urbinati 2006; cf. Esaiasson and Narud 2013). Moreover, while the Constitution has remained stable over the years, other factors of importance for the representative relationship have changed dramatically. For example, Nicholas Aylott's chapter in this volume describes how a once orderly five-party system has evolved into an unwieldy eight-party system. Relatedly, as discussed in the section on electoral behavior, voters have become more volatile and less attached to political parties. A telling statistic is that the proportion of voters who change party between elections has increased from about 15 percent in the 1970s to above 30 percent in the 2010 elections (Oscarsson and Holmberg 2013: 164). Further complicating the representative relationship, an increasingly large number of social groups and interests demand attention from the representative system. As discussed in the final section of this book, in the new political landscape compromises may be hard to achieve.

Against this background of stability, change, and democratic challenges, this chapter takes stock of the long-term development of political representation in Sweden. Aware that the notion of political representation defies simplifications (e.g. Pitkin 1967: 9; Eulau 1967; Mansbridge 2003: 515), we will focus on three observable aspects of the phenomenon: party-based policy representation with special attention to congruence between the policy views of citizens and their representatives; the role of individual representatives in a party-based representative system with special attention devoted to gender; and citizen trust of representative institutions. These aspects represent areas where major changes have occurred in recent decades. In 1971 the number of women in the Riksdag was 14 percent; today, after the election in 2014, the number is 44 percent. As already mentioned, the once orderly five-party system has evolved into an eight-party system. Finally, citizen trust is included in order to get an indicator of legitimacy for the Swedish representational system in the wake of changes and challenges.

Our indicators of political representation are anchored in representation theory and real-world changes, but they are also chosen to demonstrate the richness of data available for analysis of long-term developments of the representative relationship in Sweden. Beginning in 1985, the Swedish National Election Studies (SNES) have surveyed members of the Riksdag after each parliamentary election. With a response rate of 89 percent and higher, this series of mail surveys, which is coordinated with the SNES voter surveys (Holmberg 1994), provides scholars with a unique opportunity to study representative processes with standardized individual-level data. The analyses that follow draw primarily on this data source.[1]

PARTY-BASED POLICY CONGRUENCE

In representative democracy, elected politicians are principally free to follow their own best judgment of how to act as long as they provide convincing justifications for their actions (Pitkin 1967: 209–10; Manin 1997). Accordingly, agreement between the policy preferences of citizens and their representatives at a certain point of time is not the only criterion for a well-functioning representative relationship. However, although democratic performances are ultimately to be judged retrospectively and dynamically, the static level of policy congruence is an important diagnostic statistic. In general, large deviations between the policy preferences of citizens and their representatives call for an explanation (Dahl 1989; Powell 2000; Soroka and Wlezien 2010).

As discussed in the introduction, several factors suggest that the level of policy congruence should be high in Sweden. To begin, political discourse lets the Riksdag and its members embody the idea of popular rule by the people. The discursive factor is backed up constitutionally with the PR-electoral system, which is generally believed to be conducive for policy congruence (Lijphart 1999; Powell 2000; but see Blais and Bodet 2006; Golder and Stramski 2010). Other mechanisms that induce congruence are also present. Oscarsson and Holmberg (in this volume) report a high level of issue voting (see also Bengtsson et al. 2013), and Naurin (2011: 39–66) documents that elected governments are typically committed to act on their campaign pledges. The combination of issue voting and fulfilment of election pledges should favor what Mansbridge (2003) calls promissory representation.

The single most important factor for congruence is the dimensionality of citizens' policy views. There is scholarly agreement that congruence is enhanced to the extent that citizens' policy preferences can be arranged along a single dimension such as left versus right (e.g. Downs 1957). Historically, Swedish politics is strongly organized around the left–right dimension (e.g. Holmberg and Oscarsson 2004), which adds to the factors that facilitate agreement between citizens and their representatives. However, recent developments in party politics have made Swedish politics less orderly. In particular, the emergence of viable niche parties such as the Greens and anti-immigration Sweden Democrats stresses issues that are less readily subsumed under the left–right divide.

We also want to draw attention to two further long-term changes in party competition (see Aylott in this volume). First, in 1985 the Liberal Party and the Center Party occupied a middle position in the ideological space. Over time, these parties have moved to the right and are now close to the ideological position of the Conservative Party. Second, the two major parties, the Conservatives and the Social Democrats, have converged over time. This means that having more parties (eight rather than five) does not necessarily lead to a less perspicuous party system. In fact, beginning with the 2002 parliamentary election, the Swedish party system resembles a two-party system with two dominant ideological blocs which offer less polarized policy alternatives than before and with the Sweden Democrats as an anti-establishment party.

Turning to empirical analyses on policy congruence in the changing political land-scape, Sören Holmberg has continuously mapped the relative ideological positions of citizens and their representatives. In an initial study from the late 1960s he found that representatives in all parties held more leftist policy views than their voters (Holmberg 1974, 1989). This finding had a significant impact in the public debate, and for a long period of time left-leaning party elites were seen as the repeating pattern in the representative relationship (e.g. Westerståhl and Johansson 1981: 87).[2] However, beginning with the 1985 Riksdag survey and in six consecutive studies, a different pattern emerges, one in which party elites are more polarized than party voters; left party representatives are more leftist whereas right party representatives are more rightist than their respective voters (e.g. Holmberg 1989, 2010). The pattern with more polarized party elites than party voters is found also at the local and regional level (Strömberg 1974; Karlsson 2013). The evidence suggests that the initial representative survey in the radical late 1960s captured a period effect, which, in the absence of replication studies was wrongly seen as typical for the representative relationship.

To look further into the representative relationship, Figure 14.1 shows a summary measure of the congruence between the policy views of citizens and their representatives from 1985 to 2010. While other studies in the field rely on indirect measures of party elite policy positions such as party voter subjective placement (e.g. Golder and Stramski 2010), expert surveys (e.g. Powell 2006), and manifesto data (e.g. Budge and McDonald 2007), this study uses the Riksdag surveys and the corresponding voter surveys that put identically worded questions on policy views to representatives and eligible voters after parliamentary elections from 1985 to 2010.

Results in Figure 14.1 represent the average percentage difference between representatives' and citizens' support for various policy propositions, and thus captures what

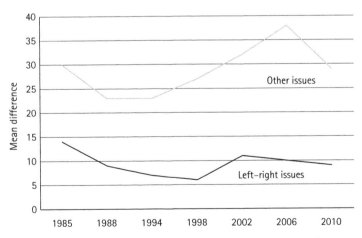

FIGURE 14.1 Average level of issue disagreement between MPs and eligible voters (difference in percent distributions).

Note: Computed from results presented in Holmberg (1989, 1996, 2002, 2004, 2010, 2014) and Esaiasson and Holmberg (1996). Number of issues (policy proposals) varies between 4 and 7 (left–right issues) and 8 and 16 (other issues).

Golder and Stramski (2010) call a many-to-one congruence relationship, and what Weissberg (1978) calls collective representation. Following Holmberg (1989) we report the averaged difference between representatives and voters' dichotomized responses to survey questions after don't knows and middle positions (3s on a 1 to 5 response scale) have been excluded. Zero (0) stands for perfect congruence and 100 for maximum policy difference over all issues.

We differ between two types of policy issues: "left–right issues" and "other issues." The former concerns proposals over taxation, state coordination of the economy, and social welfare policies. The latter type of issues concern a range of policy matters such as the environment (e.g. banning inner-city driving), energy supply (e.g. abolish nuclear power), migration, Sweden's relationship with the European Union, gendered relationships (e.g. quotation of high-ranking positions in the state administration), and moral issues (e.g. forbid all pornography).

The results fulfill high demands on consistency. At all seven points of observation, differences in policy views between citizens and their representatives are larger for "other issues" than for issues that relate to the left–right divide. Thus, as expected, the representatives deviate less from citizen preferences when citizen opinion can be arranged along a left–right dimension.

Moreover, the changing political landscape notwithstanding, issue agreement on left–right issues has remained largely stable over time. While differences in policy views were relatively lower in 1988, 1994, and 1998, there is no discernible trend in the data over the full period. For issues outside the left–right domain, however, there is a significant upward trend in the data ($\beta_{year} = .38$; SE = .150; p = .05; n = 7). This finding further underlines the importance of dimensionality for policy agreement. The less orderly eight-party system of today may have made it even more difficult than before to achieve issue agreement between citizens and their representatives on policy matters that cannot be attributed to the left–right divide.

Absent generally accepted criteria it is difficult to assess the level of congruence. It can be noted that differences in policy views are much larger than would be generated from a purely random model (a sample of 349 individuals who were drawn at random from the population of eligible voters would only rarely deviate more than 5 percent from the target population) (Holmberg 1989; Esaiasson and Holmberg 1996: 111). However, as selection by lottery is the best possible way to secure agreement, this comparison primarily tells us that the level of congruence falls short of a really high standard. Another criterion is to compute the number of issues displaying different majority positions among members and voters (Holmberg 1989). As it turns out, the majority position among representatives differs from citizen views in one fourth to one third of the policy issues. Overall, there appears to be little reason to characterize agreement as either strikingly high or alarmingly low. The most reasonable characteristic is perhaps that the level of agreement is midway between the high and the low.

ENTRANCE OF NICHE PARTIES

A major finding from the analysis above is that congruence is lower in issues that fall outside the left–right divide. These issues are stressed by niche parties like the Greens (the environment) and the Sweden Democrats (migration) (e.g. Meguid 2007). Does this mean that niche parties are succeeding without being in agreement with their voters on their profiled issues, or is it primarily established parties that diverge from their voters outside the left–right domain?

To begin to answer this question, Figure 14.2 compares within-party congruence on profiled issues that fall outside the left–right domain at the time of niche parties' entrance into parliament. For the Greens in the 1988 election, we focus on the issue of banning inner-city driving. For the Sweden Democrats in the 2010 election, the corresponding issue is on acceptance of fewer refugees into the country. As before, results show the difference between representatives and voters' dichotomized

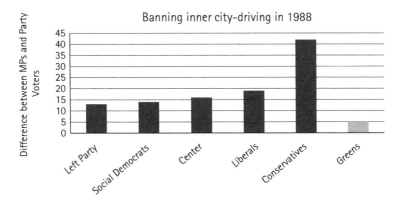

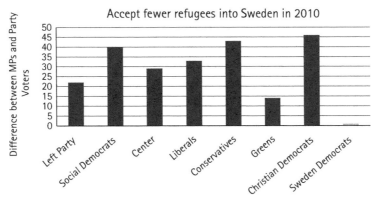

FIGURE 14.2 Average level of issue disagreement between members of niche parties and mainstream parties and their voters (difference in percent distributions).

Note: Compiled from Esaiasson and Holmberg (1996) and Holmberg (2014).

responses to survey questions after don't knows and middle positions have been excluded. Zero (0) stands for perfect congruence and 100 for maximum policy difference.

Once more, results are clear-cut. When they first made it into parliament, the Greens and the Sweden Democrats were in much closer agreement with their voters on their "own" issues than were the established parties on the same issue. The fact that the Sweden Democrats are in perfect agreement with their voters on the issue of accepting fewer refugees into the country is particularly noticeable as disagreement between parties and voters was higher for immigration issues than for any other issue domain from 1994 to 2006 (Dahlström and Esaiasson 2013). Thus, the emergence of viable niche parties that exploit new issues may have made it more difficult for established parties to achieve congruence with voters, but given that these new issues are politicized it would seem that niche parties contribute positively to the overall level of issue agreement. We return to this topic in the concluding discussion.

INDIVIDUAL-LEVEL REPRESENTATION

Thus far, our focus has been on parties as unitary actors. Given the programmatic strength and discipline of political parties, a collectivist approach is the natural starting point for analyses of the representative relationship, not only in Sweden but in most democratic systems. However, even though parties are the major actors, it may still matter which particular persons are elected. The reason for this is that the representative role can be broadly defined; Riksdag representatives and other elected MPs may function as champions of their party *and* of other interests as well.

A first illustration that loyalty to a party does not preclude members from promoting other interests—further examples will follow—is presented in Table 14.1. It shows the proportion of Riksdag members who report it to be "very important" for them personally to promote the interests of various representational categories in the 1985, 1998, and 2010 Riksdag surveys. Previous research has validated that these "self-defined champions" are more likely than other representatives to act on behalf of the interest in question (Esaiasson and Holmberg 1996: 61–8; Esaiasson 2000).

Interesting to note is that, over time, party loyalty has become stronger in the Riksdag. In 1985, 77 percent of Swedish MPs answered that their own party was very important to represent; in 2010 the corresponding figure was 86 percent. The category "own constituency" is also supported by more MPs in 2010 than in 1985, while individual voters are, from this perspective, losing ground: from 49 percent answering very important to represent individual voters in 1985 to 33 percent in 2010.

With respect to various forms of group representation the picture that emerges from Table 14.1 is rather stable: wage earners, women, immigrants, and young people are, at all surveyed occasions, highlighted as very important to represent by 20 to 29 percent of MPs. Groups such as pensioners, businessmen, farmers, religious people, and

Table 14.1 Proportion of MPs who view it as very important to champion various interests

Type of Interest	1985	1998	2010
Party representation			
Own party	77	80	86
Geographical representation			
Own constituency	44	46	50ˆ
Individual representation			
Individual voters	49	35	33
Group representation—underprivileged groups			
Wage earners	29	25	29
Women	24	31	28
Immigrants	NA	28	26
LBGT persons	NA	NA	20
Pensioners	17~	18	21
Young people	20	25	29
Unemployed/Long-term sick	NA	NA	31
Group representation—private business			
Businessmen	12	15	18ˆ
Farmers	8	9	9ˆ
Group representation—ideological interests			
Religious people (Christians)	NA	7	11
Teetotalers	NA	5	4ˆ
Burkean representation			
Personal views	34	33	39
Minimum n	331		301

Note: The survey question was worded as follows: "How important is it to you personally to promote the interests of the following groups and interests?"

~ Results are from the 1988 Riksdag survey; ˆ results are from the 2006 Riksdag survey.

teetotalers are, by Swedish MPs, perceived as less important but they still have their self-defined champions.

Taken together, what we have at hand is a complex situation: political parties in Sweden are losing members, voter volatility has increased, and on top of that, turnover in the Riksdag has increased. During the 1970s and 1980s there was, at each election, a turnover in about 20 percent of the seats in the Riksdag. Since 2002 turnover has been above 35 percent and the increase is most significant among MPs that voluntarily refrain from candidacy (Ahlbäck Öberg, Hermansson, and Wängnerud 2007). Thus various "objective" measures indicate a weakened position of political parties, but subjective measures such as those reported in Table 14.1 tell a different story—that political parties seem to have strengthened their grip over Riksdag members.

THE LINK BETWEEN DESCRIPTIVE AND SUBSTANTIVE REPRESENTATION

Theories of political representation vary in terms of how they view group representation. In the influential Responsible Party Model (e.g. Klingemann, Hofferbert, and Budge 1994) the importance of social background characteristics is toned down, whereas presence theories (Phillips 1995) strongly emphasize that everyday life experiences matter for political standpoints and priorities.

Presence theories present reasons for expecting a link between *descriptive* and *substantive* representation (Phillips 1995; Pitkin 1967). The idea is that who the representatives are, their individual characteristics, is of importance for the outcome of the parliamentary process. In what follows, we will focus on the increase in the number of women elected to the Riksdag (descriptive representation) and discuss gender differences in policy priorities and attitudes toward a number of concrete policy proposals (indicators of substantive representation). The rationale behind our focus on gender is that this is a well-researched area. However, we will also include a few results on the importance of being foreign-born. We will start by looking at data from official records (Statistics Sweden) for the number of women compared to foreign-born in the Riksdag over time. Included in Figure 14.3 is data from 1971 and onwards for women MPs and from 1982 and onwards for foreign-born MPs (percentages).

Today, the proportion of women (44 percent after the 2014 election) in the Riksdag almost equals the proportion in the population. From an international perspective this is quite exceptional. The average number of women elected to national parliaments

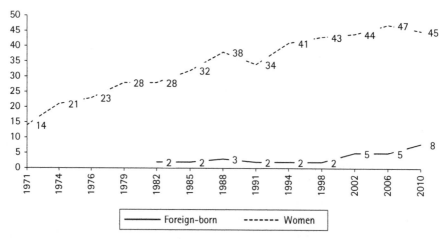

FIGURE 14.3 Number of women compared to foreign-born in the Riksdag, 1971–2010 (percent).

> *Note:* Statistics from official records (Statistics Sweden). Foreign-born includes all Members of Parliament born outside Sweden. The mandate period was three years until 1994, thereafter four years.

around the world is currently 21.7 percent. For Europe, the corresponding figure is 25.1 percent (figures from Inter-Parliamentary Union, situation as of February 2014). There are, in total, 11 countries in the world with more than 40 percent women elected to the national parliament.

The situation is different for the number of foreign-born in the Riksdag (8 percent after the election 2010). Figures from Statistics Sweden show that in 2010 15 percent of the Swedish population was born outside Sweden. Another 4 percent was born in Sweden by two foreign-born parents; 7 percent was born in Sweden by one parent foreign-born and one parent native-born. This means that in 2010 74 percent of the Swedish population was born in Sweden by two native-born parents. In sum, no matter how the comparison is made there is a clear numerical under-representation of foreign-born citizens in the Swedish parliament. At the same time it should be noted that there is, over time, and upward-going trend.

A number of studies show that the Swedish electoral system with proportional representation and large district magnitudes facilitates for the election of historically excluded social groups. The comparatively generous welfare state is also, particularly with regard to the election of women, an enabling factor (Wängnerud 2009 presents an overview). However, recent research points to the importance of active efforts by political parties. In the 1970s an increased representation of women became a political issue in Sweden—the major political parties started to craft strategies in order to spark changes. Currently regulations are most compelling within the Left Party, the Green Party, and the Social Democratic Party, whereas the Conservative Party, the Liberal Party, the Center Party, and the Christian Democratic Party to a higher degree rely on goal formulations (Freidenvall 2006; see also Dahlerup 2006). Recently the issue of being foreign-born has received increased attention by major political parties in Sweden, which in part can explain the slight upward trend in Figure 14.1 (Soininen 2011). The Swedish case is characterized by a stepwise development *accelerated* by strategies initiated by party leadership.

The core question in research on the theory of the politics of presence is, however, about changes on the political agenda. Phillips (1995: 47) states "It is representation ... with a purpose, it aims to subvert or add or transform." When Phillips concretizes what substantial changes to expect, she zeroes in on differences between women and men with regard to child care, the division of paid and unpaid labor, access to positions of power, and exposure to sexual violence:

> Women have distinct interests in relation to child-bearing (for any foreseeable future, an exclusively female affair); and as society is currently constituted they also have particular interests arising from their exposure to sexual harassment and violence, their unequal position in the division of paid and unpaid labour and their exclusion from most arenas of economic or political power. (Phillips 1995: 67–8)

Phillips emphasizes that women's interests are connected to how societies are organized, which means that the precise meaning of women's interests can vary over time and space. We should add that the notion of women's interests is controversial and that critics have noted that there is risk of both elitism—that is, that certain interests will be ascribed to women from a top-down perspective—and essentialism, by which gender is seen as a biological given, rather than a socially changeable category (Dietz 2003). One solution for avoiding pitfalls like elitism and essentialism is to perform analyses that take into account variations among women and to contrast definitions based on theory against opinions expressed by women themselves.

Results from the Swedish National Elections Study Program show that there is a pertinent gender gap in policy priorities among Swedish voters. In the election in 2010 more women than men emphasized social policy, health care, and elderly care, when they were asked to state what they consider the most important issues for their party choice. More men than women emphasized jobs and the economy. Over time, social policy becomes more highly prioritized by male voters and one can always dispute whether gender gaps are small or big—whether the glass is half-empty or half-full—but so far the most important conclusion is that even though changes occur, gender has an effect on political priorities among Swedish voters (Oskarson and Wängnerud 2013).

We will now turn to results from the Riksdag. The analysis in Table 14.2 covers 1985, 1994, and 2006. For each year, the table shows the ten most frequently cited areas in response to an open-ended question about the MPs' areas of particular interest. Two areas, social policy and employment policy (jobs), are shaded in gray. The shading accentuates a convergence of women's and men's priorities over time. What is not shown in Table 14.2 is the results for 2010, but for the two areas social policy versus jobs the 2010 situation looks like the situation in 1994, which means that gender gaps, in this particular area, "wax and wane" over time rather than disappear.

The types of rankings shown in Table 14.2 are, of course, affected by current events. Unemployment is higher in Sweden today than it was in the 1980s, and it is perhaps no surprise that jobs have become an issue of prime concern for elected representatives of both genders.

Research on priorities focuses on an early step of the parliamentary process and asks which issues get onto the political agenda in the first place. In contrast, research on attitudes examines what solutions are favored once an issue is on the political agenda. The next analysis deals with gender differences in relation to a number of concrete policy issues that have featured in Swedish political debate: reducing the public sector, providing more health care under private management, banning all forms of pornography, and introducing a six-hour workday for all workers. The issues included in the analysis are those that relate to the conflict between private and public spheres or otherwise distinguish themselves by their particular impact on the situations of women citizens. Reported in Figure 14.4 are the proportions of male and female MPs, and male and female voters, who support each proposal—ranking it as "good" or "very good."

Table 14.2 Policy priorities: Top ten issues among women and men in the Riksdag (ranked according to the percentage who mention each issue as an area of particular interest)

1985		1994		2006	
Women	Men	Women	Men	Women	Men
1. social policy	1. economy	1. social policy	1. economy	1. jobs	1. jobs
2. economy	2. jobs	2. education	2. jobs	2. social policy	2. social policy
3. education	3. business policy	3. jobs	3. foreign policy	3. education	3. foreign policy
4. jobs	4. environment	4. economy	4. business policy	4. environment	4. education
5. environment	5. foreign policy	5. environment	5. social policy	5. gender equality	5. economy
6. health care	6. taxes	6. foreign policy	6. environment	6. foreign policy	6. environment
7. business policy	7. education	7. culture	7. communications	7. justice/law	7. business policy
8. family policy	8. agriculture	8. business policy	8. education	8. culture	8. culture
9. foreign policy	9. social policy	9. gender equality	9. taxes	9. business policy	9. justice/law
10. peace	10. communications	10. taxes	10. peace	10. health care	10. communications

Note: The question reads: "Which area or areas in politics are you most interested in?" The question is open-ended and respondents were permitted to choose any area or areas. The table shows the ten most frequently cited areas. A detailed code schema was used to code the answers, which resulted in about 30 general policy areas. Number of respondents (women/men): 1985 (102/221); 1994 (128/186); 2006 (154/173).

Source: Riksdag Surveys, Department of Political Science, University of Gothenburg.

A few notes are of special importance in this section. First, party affiliation is obviously an aspect that must be considered when analyzing attitudes towards concrete policy issues. As one example, opinions on the issue of the six-hour workday have always been strongly divided along party lines. The gender differences found among MPs with regard to this issue are largely grounded in differences within the left/green bloc, particularly within the Social Democratic Party. That party affiliation is a critical factor among MPs is even more obvious with regard to reducing the public sector and providing more health care under private management. The situation changes with regard to banning all forms of pornography, which is still a gender-splitting issue across party lines. Another important result is that the gender gap currently is more distinct among voters than among MPs. When asked about banning all forms of pornography, 65 percent of women voters supported the proposal in 2010, and the number is also

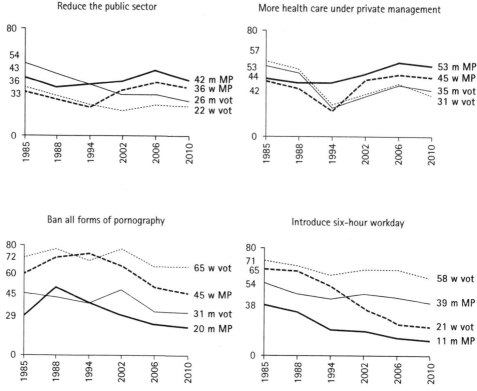

FIGURE 14.4 Attitudes: Proportions of women and men in the Riksdag and women and men voters who support specific proposals.

Note: The question reads as follows: "The following list covers a number of proposals that have featured in the political debate. What is your opinion of each of them?" For each proposal, the alternatives were "very good proposal," "good proposal," "neither good nor bad proposal," "bad proposal," and "very bad proposal." The table shows the percentages in favor (very good and good proposal, combined). The exact wording of each proposal: "reduce the public sector"; "provide more health care under private management"; "ban all forms of pornography"; and "introduce a six-hour workday for all workers." Number of respondents in the Riksdag surveys (women/men): 1985 (100/230); 1988 (126/203); 1994 (132/183); 2002 (145/175); 2006 (153/170). Election studies are based on a sample of approximately 2–3,000 respondents.

Source: Riksdag Surveys and Election Studies, Department of Political Science, University of Gothenburg.

high, 58 percent, for those who are in favor of implementing a six-hour workday for all workers.

To sum up, evidence from Sweden supports the assumption of a link between descriptive and substantive representation. Female MPs are closer to female voters than are male MPs in terms of policy priorities and attitudes towards a number of concrete policy proposals. Our finding is strengthened by research on policy promotion, parliamentary speeches, and, to some extent, by research on outcomes of the parliamentary process (Bäck, Debus, and Müller 2014; Wängnerud and Sundell 2012). The most important result however from the analysis in this section is that the size of the gender gap varies across time and across political domains. We also want to stress that trends toward a

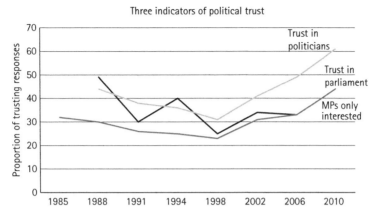

FIGURE 14.5 Citizen trust in politicians and representative institutions (percent trusting responses).

Note: Adapted from Oscarsson and Holmberg (2013) and Holmberg (2011).

diminished gender gap are stronger among MPs than among voters. This may reflect the increase in party loyalty among MPs noted previously (Table 14.1). A preliminary conclusion from this section would be that the room to maneuver for individual representatives is shrinking in tandem with the rise of more distinct bloc politics in the Riksdag.

TRUST IN PARLIAMENT

We started this chapter by quoting the Instrument of Government Acts of 1809 and 1974. The idea was to illustrate the central position assigned to the Riksdag in the official rhetoric on democracy. In line with this, trust in parliament and other measures of subjective legitimacy can be seen as central indicators of a well-functioning representative relationship. Figure 14.5 shows the development of citizen trust in politicians and the Riksdag during the eventful period 1985 to 2010.

What emerges is a fluctuating time series. Up until the late 1990s, citizen political trust was trending downwards (see also Holmberg 1999). However, beginning in the early 2000s there was a trend shift, and by 2010 the level of citizen support is just as high as at the beginning of the period, three decades ago.

These observations put the changes and challenges highlighted in this chapter into perspective. The unwieldy party system, the increasing voter volatility, the growing social diversity among representatives, and other factors under discussion would seem not to have fundamentally affected citizen evaluation of the representative relationship. Rather, the absence of a linear trend in the data suggests that citizen political trust is more strongly affected by alternative factors such as political and economic performance. At the very least, the observed shifts in political support at the millennium coincide more with economic indicators than with factors directly linked to political representation.

STABILITY AND CHANGE IN A MULTI-PARTY SYSTEM

Sweden is characterized by a stable framework for political representation. Since the abolition of the upper chamber in 1970 the only noteworthy constitutional change is the introduction of a moderate open-list system in 1998. So far, most studies point out that the open list affects career opportunities, enabling popular candidates to get re-elected and receive influential positions. More far-reaching effects, e.g. on policy promotion, have however been hard to detect (Davidsson 2006; Folke, Persson, and Rickne 2014).

The open list was introduced in an era of increased levels of turnover in the Riksdag and increased efforts by major political parties to recruit women and, to some extent, foreign-born representatives. Thus, the open list was just one of many changes that took place simultaneously in Sweden. The open list in combination with more newcomers and more representatives from historically excluded groups could have constituted a major challenge to the party-based system of political representation. A major finding of this chapter, however, is that Swedish political parties are successful survivors.

First, we want to stress the stability in policy agreement on left–right issues. We are able to compare agreement between MPs and voters on seven different occasions over a period of 25 years. The size of the mean difference does not change much between occasions, and the current trend is towards higher levels of agreement. This suggests that the core dimension in Swedish politics remains strong.

Secondly, we want to stress that overall policy agreement on issues outside the left–right divide is comparatively low. However, when MPs of niche parties (Greens and Sweden Democrats) are compared to their own voters there is a high level of agreement on profile issues such as environmental issues (Greens) and immigration issues (Sweden Democrats). Moreover, we find that women MPs are closer to women voters than are men MPs in policy priorities and standpoints on policy proposals where there are gender gaps in the population. Thus, the increased number of parties and the increased number of women has meant stronger agreement between *certain segments* of MPs and voters. Based on the findings in this chapter, we suggest that this agreement between certain segments on a limited number of issues may be more important for the functioning of the representative system than overall levels of agreement between all MPs and all voters on a wide range of issues.

For scholars of political representation the Swedish case is of double interest. First, in terms of substance Sweden is interesting because major parties seem to be able to adjust to external pressure such as increased voter volatility, and to internal pressure from individual representatives with new profiles. Second, in terms of analytical opportunities

Sweden is interesting because the data we have at hand—the unique series of Riksdag surveys—allows for analyses at three different levels: the system level, the party level, and the individual level. We learn from this chapter that future research should strive to develop more fine-tuned understandings of the flexibility of political parties in representative democracies. In meeting this analytical challenge, the Swedish case might play a central role.

Notes

1. To date, the Riksdag survey covers seven parliamentary elections from 1985–2010 (the 1991 election was not covered). An initial survey (face to face) was conducted in 1968/9, with Bo Särlvik as principal investigator, and in collaboration with Warren E. Miller and the ISR at the University of Michigan. The major publication from the 1968/9 study is Holmberg (1974). A master file from the 1985–2010 Riksdag surveys is available upon request from SNES at the University of Gothenburg.
2. Indeed, Conservative party leader Gösta Bohman referred to left-leaning party elites in his successful effort to move his party further to the right in the wake of the Reagan–Thatcher movement in the late 1970s (Ljunggren 1992).

References

Ahlbäck Öberg, S., Hermansson, J., and Wängnerud, L. (2007). *Exit riksdagen*. Malmö: Liber.

Bengtsson, Å., Hansen, K., Hardarson, O., Narud, H. M., and Oscarsson, H. (2013). *The Nordic Voter: Myths of Exceptionalism*. Colchester: ECPR Press.

Blais, A. and Bodet, M. A. (2006). "Does Proportional Representation Foster Closer Congruence between Citizens and Policymakers?" *Comparative Political Studies* 39: 1243–62.

Bäck, H., Debus, M., and Müller, J. (2014). "Who Takes the Parliamentary Floor? The Role of Gender in Speech-making in the Swedish Riksdag," *Political Research Quarterly* 67/3: 504–18.

Budge, I. and McDonald, M. (2007). "Election and Party System Effects on Policy Representation: Bringing Time into Comparative Perspective," *Electoral Studies* 26: 168–79.

Dahl, R. (1989). *Democracy and Its Critics*. New Haven: Yale University Press.

Dahlerup, D. (ed.) (2006). *Women, Quotas and Politics*. London: Routledge.

Dahlström, C. and Esaiasson, P. (2013). "The Immigration Issue and Anti-immigrant Party Success in Sweden 1970–2006: A Deviant Case Analysis," *Party Politics* 19: 343–64.

Davidsson, L. (2006). *I linje med partiet? Maktspel och lojalitet i den svenska riksdagen*. Stockholm. SNS Förlag.

Dietz, M. G. (2003). "Current Controversies in Feminist Theory," *Annual Review Political Science* 6: 399–431.

Disch, L. (2011). "Toward a Mobilization Conception of Democratic Representation," *American Political Science Review* 105: 100–14.

Downs, A. (1957). *An Economic Theory of Democracy*. New York: Harper.

Esaiasson, P. (2000). "How Members of Parliament Define their Task," in P. Esaiasson and K. Heidar (eds), *Beyond Westminster and Congress: The Nordic Experience*. Ohio: Ohio State University Press, 51–82.

Esaiasson, P. and Heidar, K. (eds) (2000). *Beyond Westminster and Congress: The Nordic Experience*. Ohio: Ohio State University Press.

Esaiasson, P. and Holmberg, S. (1996). *Representation from Above: Members of Parliament and Representative Democracy in Sweden*. Aldershot: Dartmouth.

Esaiasson, P. and Narud, H. M. (2013). "Between-Election Democracy: An Introductory Note," in P. Esaiasson and H. M. Narud (eds), *Between Election Democracy: The Representative Relationship after Election Day*. Colchester: ECPR Press, 1–14.

Eulau, H. (1967). "Changing Views of Representation," in I. de Sola Pool (ed.), *Contemporary Political Science: Toward Empirical Theory*. New York: McGraw Hill, 53–85.

Folke, O., Persson, T., and Rickne, J. (2014). "Preferential Voting and Promotions into Political Power: Evidence from Sweden," *Research Institute of Industrial Economics Working Paper Series*.

Freidenvall, L. (2006). "Vägen till Varannan damernas," PhD dissertation, Stockholm University, Stockholm.

Golder, M. and Stramski, J. (2010). "Ideological Congruence and Electoral Institutions," *American Journal of Political Science* 54: 90–106.

Holmberg, S. (1974). *"Riksdagen representerar svenska folket": Empiriska studier i representativ demokrati*. Lund: Studentlitteratur.

Holmberg, S. (1989). "Political Representation in Sweden," *Scandinavian Political Studies* 12: 1–36.

Holmberg, S. (1994). "Election Studies the Swedish Way," *European Journal of Political Research* 25: 309–22.

Holmberg, S. (1996). "Svensk åsiktsöverensstämmelse," in B. Rothstein and B. Särlvik (eds), *Vetenskapen om politik: Festskrift till professor emeritus Jörgen Westerstål*. Göteborg: Department of Political Science, 109–25.

Holmberg, S. (1999). "Down and Down We Go: Political Trust in Sweden," in P. Norris (ed.), *Critical Citizens: Global Support for Democratic Governance*. Oxford: Oxford University Press, 103–22.

Holmberg, S. (2002). "Necessarily Unrepresentative Political Parties," in D. Fuchs, E. Roller, and B. Wessels (eds), *Burger und Demokratie in Ost und West: Festschrift für Hans-Dieter Klingemann*. Wiesbaden: Westdeutscher Verlag, 481–94.

Holmberg, S. (2010). "Dynamisk representation," in M. Brothén and S. Holmberg (eds), *Folkets representanter: En bok om riksdagsledamöter och politisk representation i Sverige*. Gothenburg: Department of Political Science, 65–102.

Holmberg, S. (2011). "Förtroendet för Riksdagen 1986–2010," SOM Institute Working Paper 2011:16.

Holmberg, S. (2014). "Feeling Policy Represented," in Jacques Thomassen (ed.), *Elections and Democracy: Representation and Accountability*. Oxford: Oxford University Press, 132–52.

Holmberg, S. and Oscarsson, H. (2004). *Väljare: Svenskt väljarbeteende under 50 år*. Stockholm: Norstedts Juridik.

Klingemann, H.-D., Hofferbert, R., and Budge, I (1994). *Parties, Policies and Democracy*. Boulder: Westview Press.

Lijphart, A. (1999). *Government Forms and Performance in Thirty-Six Countries*. New Haven: Yale University Press.

Ljunggren, S. (1992). *Folkhemskapitalismen: Högerns programutveckling under efterkrigstiden*. Stockholm: Tiden.

Karlsson, D. (2013). "Åsiktsöverensstämmelse mellan väljare och valda i regionpolitiken," in A. Bergström and J. Ohlsson (eds), *En region för alla? Medborgare, människor och medier i Västsverige.* Gothenburg: SOM Institute.

Manin, B. (1997). *The Principles of Representative Government.* Cambridge: Cambridge University Press.

Mansbridge, J. (2003). "Rethinking Representation," *American Political Science Review* 97: 515–28.

Meguid, B. (2007). *Party Competition between Unequals: Strategies and Electoral Fortunes in Western Europe.* Cambridge: Cambridge University Press.

Metcalf, M. (1977). "The First 'Modern' Party System? Political Parties, Sweden's Age of Liberty and the Historians," *Scandinavian Journal of History* 2: 265–87.

Naurin, E. (2011). *Election Promises, Party Behavior, and Voter Behavior.* Basingstoke: Palgrave Macmillan.

Oscarsson, H. and Holmberg, S. (2013). *Nya svenska väljare.* Stockholm: Norstedts juridik.

Oskarson, M. and Wängnerud, L. (2013). "The Story of the Gender Gap in Swedish Politics: Only Partially Diminishing Differences," in S. Dahlberg, H. Oscarsson, and L. Wängnerud (eds), *Stepping Stones: Research on Political Representation, Voting Behavior, and Quality of Government.* Gothenburg: Department of Political Science, 59–76.

Phillips, A. (1995). *The Politics of Presence.* Oxford: Oxford University Press.

Pitkin, H. (1967). *The Concept of Representation.* Berkeley: University of California Press.

Powell, G. B. (2000). *Elections as Instruments of Democracy.* New Haven: Yale University Press.

Powell, G. B. (2006). "Election Laws and Representative Governments: Beyond Votes and Seats," *British Journal of Political Science* 36: 291–315.

Soininen, M. (2011), "Ethnic Inclusion or Exclusion in Representation? Local Candidate Selection in Sweden," in K. Bird, T. Saalfeld, and A. Wüst (eds), *The Political Representation of Immigrants and Minorities: Voters, Parties and Parliaments in Liberal Democracies.* London: Routledge, 145–63.

Soroka, S. and Wlezien, C. (2010), *Degrees of Democracy: Politics, Public Opinion, and Policy.* Cambridge: Cambridge University Press.

Strömberg, L. (1974). "Väljare och valda: En studie av den representativa demokratin i kommunerna," PhD dissertation, Department of Political Science, Gothenburg University.

Sydow, B. von (1989). *Vägen till enkammarriksdagen: Demokratisk författningspolitik i Sverige 1944–1968.* Stockholm: Tiden.

Särlvik, B. (2002). "Party and Electoral System in Sweden," in A. Lijphart and B. Grofman (eds), *The Evolution of Electoral and Party Systems in the Nordic Countries.* New York: Agathon Press, 225–69.

Urbinati, N. (2006). *Representative Democracy: Principles and Genealogy.* Chicago: Chicago University Press.

Wängnerud, L. (2009). "Women in Parliaments: Descriptive and Substantive Representation," *Annual Review of Political Science* 12: 51–69.

Wängnerud, L. and A. Sundell (2012). "Do Politics Matter? Women in Swedish Local Elected Assemblies 1970–2010 and Gender Equality in Outcomes," *European Political Science Review* 4: 97–120.

Weissberg, R. (1978). "Collective vs. Dyadic Representation in Congress," *American Political Science Review* 72: 535–47.

Westerståhl, J. and Johansson, F. (1981). *Medborgarna och kommunen,* Studier av medborgerlig aktivitet och representativt folkstyrelse. Stockholm: Ds Kn 1981:12.

CHAPTER 15

....

THE PARTIES IN GOVERNMENT FORMATION

....

HANNA BÄCK AND TORBJÖRN BERGMAN

INTRODUCTION

In any parliamentary democracy, like the Swedish one, a process of government formation commences after an election has been held or when a government resigns. This
chapter pays particular attention to the role of political parties in this process. In doing
so, we pick up where other chapters leave off, and we leave some aspects for other chapters. An example of the former is the chapter on competition in the party system (Aylott,
this volume), and an example of latter is the chapter on policy-making in the cabinet
(Persson, this volume). To illustrate the Swedish case, we focus on questions and problems which are central in the comparative literature on government formation. We start
by looking at the formation process. Next we discuss how the composition and size of
governments is determined, followed by an analysis of the distribution of ministerial
posts.

THE GOVERNMENT FORMATION PROCESS

"Formateurs" or Prime Ministerial Candidates from Large Parties Are Appointed

A "stylized" view of parliamentary government formation in parliamentary democracies is that it is as a stepwise process which starts with the Head of State choosing a
"formateur" who is given a first chance to form a government. This person then has to

negotiate with other party leaders to form a government which has the support of a parliamentary majority (Bäck and Dumont 2008).

The selection of who gets the first opportunity to form a government has also been in focus in the game-theoretical literature on coalition bargaining. One standard conclusion in this literature is that the party designated to go first in forming a government will be able to significantly shape bargaining. Another common argument is that the largest party is likely to be given the first chance of forming a government. Looking at data from the western European countries (and Sweden), we also see that this is the case: in about 70 percent of the cabinets formed over the postwar period, the PM was drawn from the largest party (see Table 15.1; Bäck and Dumont 2008).

One of the reasons why the PMs do not always come from the largest party is that a number of features may be important to consider when forming a government. In Sweden, the Social Democrats have almost always been the party controlling most seats in the Riksdag—however, the non-socialist parties have also been in power during some of the postwar period, and on those occasions the PM has come from one of the non-socialist parties, even though this party has not been the largest in the Riksdag. A reason for foregoing the principle of giving the largest party the "formateur" role is that in some situations, other parties have a better chance of forming a viable government.

Table 15.1 Heads of government in twelve western European countries

	Head of government (PM) comes from ...			PM's institutional powers	
	Largest party	Median party	Former PM party	Power index	Summary evaluation
Austria	90%	20%	80%	3–4	Weak
Belgium	70%	80%	75%	6–7	Medium
Denmark	68%	0%	68%	6–7	Medium
Finland	83%	33%	67%	5	Weak
Germany	78%	57%	79%	14	Strong
Iceland	53%	40%	27%	4	Weak
Ireland	64%	64%	36%	8	Medium/strong
Italy	90%	68%	79%	3–5	Weak
Luxembourg	88%	88%	75%	6	Weak
Netherlands	73%	64%	55%	4	Weak
Norway	63%	31%	44%	3–5	Weak
Sweden	67%	67%	60%	4–6	Weak/medium
All (average)	73%	49%	63%	6	–

Note: Data on which parties become heads of government (1970–2006) from Bäck and Dumont (2008); information about PM's institutional powers (1945–2000) is drawn from Strøm et al. (2003). For countries with two scores on the power index, this illustrates a change over time (with early years described first).

Most coalition scholars would argue that parties' ideological positions are important to take into account when explaining why certain coalitions form, and when analyzing formateur selection. For example, we may expect that "centrally" located parties have a better chance of forming a viable government. Assuming that parties that are likely to be successful in forming a cabinet are often chosen to get the first chance to do so, median parties should become "formateurs." Looking at Table 15.1, we see that parties holding "median" positions are more likely to include the PM. Sweden here scores a bit higher than the average, with 67 percent of the PMs coming from the median party. In most cases, the Social Democrats have also held the "median" position in the Riksdag, but there are cases where they have lost this "stronghold," for example in the period from 1976–81 and in 1991 when the Center Party held this position. The "median" position is dependent on the alignment of the parties, and this in turn is dependent on the precise measurement used, be it expert surveys or manifesto data, but comparisons of different measurements show that the general picture is quite valid for Sweden. In a comparative perspective, Sweden has an unusually strict left–right alignment in party competition, which also makes it relatively easy to pinpoint the median party (Bergman 2000; see also Aylott in this volume).

Prior governmental experience can also advantage a party, especially if there is a more or less formal institution that says that the outgoing PM is given the first chance of forming a new government and/or the previous government is not formally obliged to resign after a general election. Bäck and Dumont (2008) suggest that this is most likely to occur in systems where the Head of State (in Sweden the Speaker; see next section) has a predominantly ceremonial role in government formation. Table 15.1 shows that about 60 percent of the Swedish and West European PMs came from the party holding this post in the incumbent cabinet. Hence, Sweden does not stand out here, but we note that from 1945 until a new voting rule came into use in 1975, it was common that the dominant party, the Social Democrats, alone or with the Center Party, simply remained in power after an election (Bergman 2000). This brings us to a closer examination of the institutional context (see also the chapters by Petersson and Möller in this volume).

Freestyle Bargaining and Tolerating the Speaker's Candidate for PM

Examining the formation process more closely, we note that Sweden is a constitutional monarchy, but that the King lost his political powers when parliamentarism was firmly established in 1917. However, it was not until 1969 that the first revisions were made to harmonize the Swedish Constitution with existing practices. The Instrument of Government of 1974 transferred the monarch's role in cabinet formation to the Speaker of the unicameral (since 1971) Riksdag (Bergman 1992). Before 1975, the King himself acted as something of an "informateur" listening to the advice of the party leaders. Since 1975, the Speaker of the Riksdag consults with all party leaders, and in this respect the

Speaker has a role which corresponds to that of the Head of State in many other western European countries. However, the decision rule that is used is more uncommon.

One of the most important institutional features of Swedish parliamentary democracy is what is known as "negative" parliamentarism (Bergman 1995). When formation rules require that a new government must have an explicit level of legislative support in the parliament, they can be seen as an expression of "positive" parliamentarism. In negative parliamentarism, the coming to power of a new government is based on the tolerance of a parliamentary majority, though not necessarily on its active support. Within the category of negative parliamentarism, Swedish formation rules are unusual. A candidate for PM is suggested by the Speaker, and before a new cabinet can assume power it must be proven that an absolute majority tolerates this candidate. The candidate can form a cabinet if not more than half of the members of the Riksdag vote against him or her. Conversely, if a PM resigns, the cabinet resigns with him.

Perhaps because of the institutional rules, it should be noted that Swedish government formation is largely a process of "freestyle bargaining" among the party leaders, without direct participation by the Speaker (Bergman 2000). The Swedish government formation process has also been described as comparatively "short": during a few weeks the composition of the cabinet is decided (Bergman 2000).

THE COMPOSITION AND SIZE OF THE GOVERNMENTS ARE DECIDED UPON

Single-Party Social Democratic Governments and Non-socialist Alliances

In Table 15.2 we describe the governments that have formed during the postwar period. Here we illustrate the fact that Swedish cabinets have to a large extent been minority single-party governments. Another important feature is that cabinets, at least since the 1960s, have followed a bloc political pattern: either the Social Democrats have governed by themselves with the support of one or more of the "socialist" parties (Greens or Left Party), or the "non-socialist" parties (Center Party, Liberals, Christian Democrats, Moderates) have coalesced. It was only in the early and mid-1950s that we saw cooperation across the "blocs" when the Social Democrats governed with the Center party (Agrarian Party) under the leadership of PM Tage Erlander.

However, the "blocs" have not been unitary actors. In fact, the center-right bloc was for a long time derided by the Social Democrats for their internal competition and lack of a coherent government alternative. In the 2006, 2010, and 2014 election campaigns, the tables turned and their firm pre-electoral alliance became a feature often stressed by the same center-right parties—such alliances are however not something uniquely Swedish (see the chapter by Aylott in this volume).

Table 15.2 Swedish Cabinets, 1945–2013

Cabinet	PM's party	Date in–Date out	Parties included ("bloc" character)	Minority cabinet	Connected coalition	Percent female ministers
Hansson	Social Democrats	31.07.45–06.10.46	Social Democrats	Yes	–	0 (0)
Erlander I	Social Democrats	11.10.46–19.09.48	Social Democrats	Yes	–	5 (1)
Erlander II	Social Democrats	19.09.48–01.10.51	Social Democrats	Yes	–	11 (3)
Erlander III	Social Democrats	01.10.51–21.09.52	Social Democrats, Center Party	No	Yes	0 (0)
Erlander IV	Social Democrats	21.09.52–26.09.56	Social Democrats, Center Party	No	Yes	5 (1)
Erlander V	Social Democrats	26.09.56–26.10.57	Social Democrats, Center Party	No	Yes	4 (1)
Erlander VI	Social Democrats	31.10.57–01.06.58	Social Democrats	Yes	–	7 (1)
Erlander VII	Social Democrats	01.06.58–18.09.60	Social Democrats	Yes	–	5 (1)
Erlander VIII	Social Democrats	18.09.60–20.09.64	Social Democrats	Yes	–	5 (1)
Erlander IX	Social Democrats	20.09.64–15.09.68	Social Democrats	Yes	–	12 (3)
Erlander X	Social Democrats	15.09.68–14.10.69	Social Democrats	No	–	8 (2)
Palme I	Social Democrats	14.10.69–20.09.70	Social Democrats	No	–	11 (2)
Palme II	Social Democrats	20.09.70–16.09.73	Social Democrats	Yes	–	16 (5)
Palme III	Social Democrats	16.09.73–19.09.76	Social Democrats	Yes	–	17 (4)
Fälldin I	center Party	07.10.76–05.10.78	Center Party, Liberal Party, Moderates	No	Yes	24 (5)
Ullsten	Liberal Party	13.10.78–16.09.79	Liberal Party	Yes	–	29 (6)
Fälldin II	center Party	11.10.79–08.05.81	Center Party, Liberal Party, Moderates	No	Yes	23 (5)
Fälldin III	center Party	19.05.81–19.09.82	Center Party, Liberal Party	Yes	Yes	28 (5)
Palme IV	Social Democrats	07.10.82–15.09.85	Social Democrats	Yes	–	23 (5)
Palme V	Social Democrats	15.09.85–01.03.86	Social Democrats	Yes	–	26 (7)
Carlsson I	Social Democrats	12.03.86–18.09.88	Social Democrats	Yes	–	33 (8)
Carlsson II*	Social Democrats	18.09.88–15.09.91	Social Democrats	Yes	–	36 (18)

Table 15.2 Continued

Cabinet	PM's party	Date in–Date out	Parties included ("bloc" character)	Minority cabinet	Connected coalition	Percent female ministers
Bildt	Moderates	03.10.91–18.09.94	Center Party, Mod., Liberals, Chr. Dem.	Yes	Yes	38
Carlsson III	Social Democrats	06.10.94–18.03.96	Social Democrats	Yes	–	50
Persson I	Social Democrats	21.03.96–20.09.98	Social Democrats	Yes	–	42
Persson II	Social Democrats	20.09.98–15.09.02	Social Democrats	Yes	–	49
Persson III	Social Democrats	15.09.02–17.09.06	Social Democrats	Yes	–	52
Reinfeldt I	Moderates	05.10.06–19.09.10	Center Party, Mod., Liberals, Chr. Dem	No	Yes	42
Reinfeldt II	Moderates	19.09.10–14.09.14	Center Party, Mod., Liberals, Chr. Dem	Yes	Yes	57
		Total average	66% ("socialist") 24% "non-socialist")	72%	100%	26%

Note: Bäck (2010); Bäck, Persson, Vernby, and Wockelberg (2009); Bergman (2000), updated by the authors. Coalition governments are marked in gray. Party positions (which constitute the basis for the connected cabinet variable) from Huber and Inglehart's (1995) expert survey have been used to measure whether a coalition is connected. Here the parties are placed (from left to right) accordingly: Left Party, Social Democrats, Green Party, Center Party, Liberal Party, Christian Democrats, Moderates. Share of female ministers is calculated as the proportion of women of all appointments during the life of the cabinet.

*PM Carlsson II reigned in February 1990 but returned to power shortly thereafter. This reshuffle has not been included in the list of cabinets because it does not meet the strict cross-national criteria that we use. A new cabinet is only recorded when there is a new (a) party composition, or (b) a new Prime Minister, or (c) after a general election.

To sum up thus far: the fairly strict left–right competition, the favorable position that this provides for the median party (often the Social Democrats), and the size of the largest party (the Social Democrats), provides much of the explanation of the historical record of frequent minority governments. To this, we can add the permissive government formation rules. Next we look more closely at the "support parties" that remain outside the cabinet. But to introduce this, we first make some comparisons and provide a research context.

Minority Governments and Support Party Arrangements

As mentioned, Sweden has often been governed by minority cabinets during long periods since the 1950s, but is this exceptional? In order to make this clear, we have to take a comparative perspective, and in Figure 15.1 we therefore present the percentage of cabinets that are minority cabinets (and the percentage of cabinets that are coalition cabinets) over the postwar period in sixteen western European countries. This figure shows clearly that Sweden, along with some other countries, like Denmark and Spain, is exceptional in this respect, with over 70 percent of the cabinets being minority governments, whereas many other western European countries, like Austria, Belgium, and Germany, have almost no minority cabinets. Why is this the case?

One of the most prominent studies focusing on explaining minority governments is Kaare Strøm's (1990) *Minority Government and Majority Rule*. His argument, simply put, is that in systems where (institutional) oppositional influence is high, minority governments are more likely to form, since parties may view it as unnecessary to be in office when they can influence policy from outside cabinet (Strøm 1990). As argued by Bergman (2000), internal structures in the Swedish Riksdag, such as the system of sixteen standing committees, all authorized to take legislative initiatives, provide opportunities for the opposition to exercise influence over policy, thereby reducing the incentives to participate in cabinet (see Mattson in this volume). Parties represented in the Riksdag but not in the government are thus not necessarily without influence over policy-making, which is likely to have contributed to the high frequency of minority cabinets (see Rasch and Tsebelis 2011 for similar arguments regarding Denmark and Norway).

A related explanation focuses on the idea that "investiture requirements hinder the formation of minority governments [. . .] because it requires a prospective government to pass a formal vote in the legislature before it can take office" (Martin and Stevenson

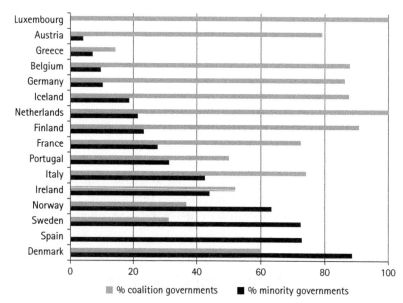

FIGURE 15.1 Coalitions and minority governments in sixteen western European countries.

Note: Cabinets formed between 1945 and 2010. Data from Andersson, Bergman, and Ersson (2014).

2001: 36). Bergman (1993, 1995) suggests that the regularity of minority governments in Sweden can be explained by the fact that the Swedish Constitution prescribes a *negative* parliamentary system. As described above, in this type of system a proposal for a new government only needs implicit support of a majority, which may make it easier for parties to acquire the support of other parties without including them in government. Martin and Stevenson (2001) and Mitchell and Nyblade (2008) show that investiture rules influence the likelihood of minority governments when looking at western Europe. Hence, this institutional feature is likely to be part of the explanation for the frequent occurrence of Swedish minority cabinets.

Together with the potential for "opposition influence" and the permissive institutional rules, a complementary way of explaining the "puzzle" of minority governments points to the existence of "support" parties. In the context of Danish government formation, for example, Damgaard (1969) found that if parties involved in more or less permanent cooperation with governing parties were counted as a part of government's parliamentary basis this removed the discrepancy between the theory and empirical practice in many cases of minority governments. This is known as the "majority government in disguise" argument (Sjölin 1993: 84; see also Strøm 1990). Currently, the comparative literature does not have a very good handle on the "support party" concept or its empirical manifestation. But we can suggest here a "narrow" and a "broad" definition and exemplify this definition in the case of Sweden. Support party relations based on written and public agreements ("contracts") meet a strict and narrow definition. The broad definition is somewhat vaguer, but also of more empirical applicability: a "support party" is a party which by its behavior directly contributes to the existence of a minority government, whether this behavior is to vote in favor or abstain in favor of a government (cf. Bergman 1995: 29).

Bale and Bergman (2006: 422) suggest that certain systems are characterized by "contract parliamentarism," where minority governments have relationships with their "support parties" that are "so institutionalized that they come close to being majority governments." Hence, here we are dealing with the narrow definition of a support party relationship. In contrast, following the broader definition, explicit (or tacit) support by some of the opposition parties is not uncommon, for example, in Denmark and Norway, where several minority center-right coalitions have been helped into government by populist radical-right parties, and Sweden has a long tradition of the Left Party enabling Social Democrat single-party governments. What Bale and Bergman (2006) suggest is particular with some recent cabinets in Sweden and New Zealand is that here we find minority cabinets which have an explicit written contract with one or more parties that remain outside cabinet, publicly committing the partners "beyond a specific deal or temporary commitment." In some cases, as after the Swedish 2002 election, support parties also appoint representatives to serve in the administration. The agreement which was signed by the Left Party, Greens, and Social Democrats in 2002 was very long and detailed, and covered a range of policy areas, and this agreement also included the setting up of a "coordination office" in the finance ministry including all parties in the "support coalition" (see Persson in this volume).

Table 15.3 Support party arrangements for Swedish minority Cabinets, 1970–2013

Cabinet	Parties included	Support parties	Investiture vote support (votes in favor, from 1975)	Policy agreement (areas/broad)	Policy agreement (public/ formal)	Positions in government chancellery	Type of support party coalition
Palme II	Social Democrats	Left	N/A				No blocking majority
Palme III	Social Democrats	Left	N/A				No blocking majority
Ullsten	Liberal Party	Social Dem., Center	39				No blocking majority
Fälldin III	Center Party, Liberal Party	Moderates	102				No blocking majority
Palme IV	Social Democrats	Left	179				No blocking majority
Palme V	Social Democrats	Left	N/A				No blocking majority
Carlsson I	Social Democrats	Left	178				No blocking majority
Carlsson II	Social Democrats	Left	175				No blocking majority
Bildt	Center Party, Mods, Liberals, Chr. Dem.	No	163				(3 bloc)
Carlsson III	Social Democrats	Left 1994, from 1995 Center Party	180	On budget and defence	Yes	Yes	Explicit but not written
Persson I	Social Democrats	Center Party	178		Yes (cont.)	Yes	Explicit but not written
Persson II	Social Democrats	Left+Green	N/A	Broad agreement	Yes	Yes	Contract-based
Persson III	Social Democrats	Left+Green	N/A	Comprehensive (except EU, defence)	Yes	Yes	Contract-based
Reinfeldt II	Center Party, Mods, Liberals, Chr. Dem	No	N/A				(3 bloc)

Note: Investiture vote support implies that the formateur is elected unless 175 or more MPs vote against. In the table we record only the votes in favor of the formateur. The categories in the "Type of support party column" are explained in the text. The table refers to the moment of government formation, and does not necessarily apply during the full tenure of each government.

But there are many support party relations that do not fit the narrow definition. Table 15.3 illustrates the cases of support party arrangements in Sweden, including the ones that can be identified on a basis of a broad definition. Of the fourteen minority governments that formed between 1970 and 2010, the first eight managed to form because one or more parties preferred to allow them to form instead of using the option to join forces with the other opposition parties to block the formation of a government. In Table 15.3 we label this a "no blocking majority" situation. Such relationships do not include a formal contractual agreement. One such case was in 1978 when the Social Democrats abstained from voting against a Liberal one-party cabinet (Ullsten) as the lesser evil among other alternatives—primarily to prevent a cabinet that included the Moderate Party. This was also the case when the Left Party declared that it preferred Social Democratic cabinets over center-right ones (Palme and Carlsson cabinets until 1995). When this was no longer an option, the Social Democrats first made an explicit agreement with the Center Party that secured the state budget. Later they signed comprehensive contracts with both the Left Party and the Greens. With our broad definition of a support party, only twice have the minority cabinets not had an explicit support party. This occurred when Sweden had its first right-wing populist party (New Democracy) in parliament in 1991 and again when the second such party, the Sweden Democrats, entered parliament in 2010. While in both cases the new party could be counted as more favorable towards the center-right government, the populist parties were not reliable and trusted support parties either. Rather they were a third force (a third "bloc") in government formation.

All in all, we suggest that the more narrowly defined, contractual, "support party arrangements" are a particularly interesting characteristic of the Swedish case, even though there are of course also examples elsewhere (as in the above-mentioned case of New Zealand). We now turn to look more closely at the ministerial positions in Swedish cabinets.

THE SELECTION AND IMPORTANCE OF CABINET MINISTERS

The Swedish PM's Institutional Powers—from Weak to Medium Powers

This section focuses mainly on the selection of cabinet ministers, but we begin with a discussion on the role or "importance" of the Prime Minister in cabinet. The PM position is clearly not only of symbolic value, but how much power does the Swedish PM have compared to other western European countries? Bergman and colleagues (2003: 179–80) identify a number of sources of PM influence: the ability to (1) appoint and (2) decide the jurisdiction of cabinet members; (3) dismiss other cabinet members; (4)

instruct ministers; (5) prevent ministers from bringing issues to the attention of the cabinet (agenda control); and (6) significantly influence cabinet decision-making.

Hence, appointment and dismissal powers can be identified as some of the most important powers of the PM, clearly distinguishing the PM from the other cabinet members. In Sweden, it is up to the PM to select the other members of the cabinet (Bergman 2000), whereas in most of western Europe the PM proposes the other cabinet members, but the Head of State makes the formal appointment. However, in many coalitions there are strong conventions saying that the party leaders of coalition partners can themselves in practice decide who should be their ministerial candidates (e.g. Bergman et al. 2003: 184). Other rules are also important, such as the PM's ability to determine ministerial jurisdictions—in countries, like Sweden, where the PM has such powers, the PM can easily shift policy areas between ministries and thereby exercise power (see Persson in this volume).

Bergman et al. (2003) have constructed an index of PM powers, which includes a number of features, such as the powers discussed above, but also other formal rules and the personnel resources at the disposal of the PM. According to this index, described for twelve western European countries in Table 15.1, institutionally powerful PMs are found for example in Germany (UK and Spain are examples not presented here), whereas institutionally weak PMs are found for example in Finland and the Netherlands. Bergman et al. (2003: 190) note that "Thanks to increased staffing, the institutional powers of the Swedish prime minister have increased," giving Swedish PMs a "medium" level of power. Thus, Swedish Prime Ministers are "first among equals," but their influence is typically circumscribed in coalition cabinets where they have to negotiate the distribution of portfolios with party leaders from other parties.

A Proportional and "Salient" Allocation of Ministerial Portfolios

Most comparative studies on how ministerial portfolios are allocated have focused on predicting *how many* portfolios each party gets. The "proportionality principle" is the main hypothesis, predicting that: "The percentage share of ministries received by a party participating in a governing coalition and the percentage share of that party's coalition seats will be proportional on a one-to-one basis" (Browne and Franklin 1973: 457). Several empirical tests looking at western European cabinets have confirmed that the proportionality relationship is associated with an extremely high explained variance, and it has been described as one of the strongest relationships in the social sciences (Warwick and Druckman 2006).

Table 15.4 presents the coalition governments formed in Sweden during the postwar period. Each party represents a row in the table. Column four presents the party's share of the government's legislative support; that is, the proportion of seats that the party contributes to the coalition. Column six presents how large the deviation is from

Table 15.4 Distribution of portfolios in Swedish coalition governments

Government	Year (formed)	Party	Leg. seats (percent)	Ministerial posts (percent)	Deviation (prop.)	Ministerial posts (e.g.)
Erlander III	1951	Social Democrats	0.79	0.73	−0.06	PM, Finance, Foreign, Defense, Justice, Social
Erlander III	1951	Center Party	0.21	0.27	0.06	Education, Agriculture
Erlander IV	1952	Social Democrats	0.80	0.73	−0.07	PM, Finance, Foreign, Defense, Justice, Social
Erlander IV	1952	Center Party	0.20	0.27	0.07	Education, Agriculture
Erlander V	1956	Social Democrats	0.85	0.77	−0.08	PM, Finance, Foreign, Defense, Justice, Social
Erlander V	1956	Center Party	0.15	0.23	0.08	Education, Agriculture
Fälldin I	1976	Center Party	0.48	0.42	−0.06	PM, Foreign, Social, Agriculture
Fälldin I	1976	Liberal Party	0.22	0.26	0.04	Finance, Labor, Education
Fälldin I	1976	Moderates	0.31	0.32	0.01	Defense
Fälldin II	1979	Center Party	0.37	0.35	−0.02	PM, Social, Agriculture
Fälldin II	1979	Liberal Party	0.22	0.25	0.03	Finance, Foreign, Labor, Education
Fälldin II	1979	Moderates	0.42	0.40	−0.02	Defense, Justice
Fälldin III	1981	Center Party	0.63	0.56	−0.07	PM, Defense, Social, Agriculture
Fälldin III	1981	Liberal Party	0.37	0.44	0.07	Finance, Foreign, Labor, Education
Bildt	1991	Moderates	0.47	0.40	−0.07	PM, Foreign, Defense, Justice, Education
Bildt	1991	Center Party	0.18	0.25	0.07	Labor, Agriculture
Bildt	1991	Liberal Party	0.19	0.25	0.06	Finance, Social
Bildt	1991	Christian Dem.	0.15	0.10	−0.05	
Reinfeldt I	2006	Moderates	0.55	0.50	−0.05	PM, Finance, Foreign, Defense, Justice, Labor
Reinfeldt I	2006	Center Party	0.16	0.18	0.02	Agriculture
Reinfeldt I	2006	Liberals	0.16	0.18	0.02	Education
Reinfeldt I	2006	Christian Dem.	0.14	0.14	0	Social
Reinfeldt II	2010	Moderates	0.62	0.56	−0.06	PM, Finance, Foreign, Defense, Justice, Labor
Reinfeldt II	2010	Center Party	0.13	0.16	0.03	Agriculture
Reinfeldt II	2010	Liberals	0.14	0.16	0.02	Education
Reinfeldt II	2010	Christian Dem.	0.11	0.12	0.01	Social

Note: Data on seats and portfolio shares from Warwick and Druckman (2006) and Bäck, Persson, Vernby, and Wockelberg (2009), updated by the authors. "Leg. seats" refers to the parties' share of the parliamentary seats controlled by the government. "Deviation" is the difference between seat and portfolio share. "Ministerial posts" only describes selected posts.

perfect proportionality. In the Erlander III government, the deviation was −0.06 for the Social Democrats and 0.06 for the Center party, which means that the Center party was overrepresented in the government. In other Swedish governments, the distribution is slightly more proportional, but overall there seems to be a slight overrepresentation of small parties in Swedish cabinets, just as has been shown in research on other western European governments (Warwick and Druckman 2006).

Generally speaking, one can say that in comparison with the governments of many other countries, Swedish governments display a relatively high correspondence between the legislative seats a party contributes to the government and the share of ministerial posts the party gets. Why are ministerial posts distributed with such proportionality? Looking more in-depth at the Swedish non-socialist coalition government in 1976 (Fälldin I), and the center-right coalition that formed after the 1994 German election (by PM Kohl), Bäck, Meier, and Persson (2009) show that parties seem to emphasize the importance of a proportionality principle if they can gain from doing so. Thus, they do not blindly follow an internalized norm of proportionality, but this principle appears as a well-established "bargaining convention."

In most early analyses of portfolio allocation, all ministerial posts are assumed to be of the same importance; that is, a minister of culture weighs the same as a PM post. Of course this is not very realistic, as argued by Warwick and Druckman (2006), who have therefore measured the importance of various posts by conducting an expert survey in fourteen western European countries. The results show that the PM is, in most cases (also in the Swedish case), twice as important as an average ministerial post, and that other important posts in most countries are the posts of Foreign Minister and Finance Minister. Even when these "weights" are considered, the relationship between seat shares and portfolio shares remains strong (Warwick and Druckman 2006).

Parties may also potentially value various ministerial posts differently, and this question was first studied by Budge and Keman (1990), who focused on the fact that parties from different party families (conservative, liberal, religious, agrarian, and socialist parties) are likely to obtain certain ministerial posts. For example, they expected that the parties from an agrarian party family prefers the post of Minister of Agriculture. They also predict that the liberal parties should aim to get the post of Finance or Justice Minister. Conservative parties are expected to obtain the posts of Foreign Minister and Defense Minister, and socialist parties are likely to want the posts of Minister of Social Affairs and Minister of Labor.

Table 15.4 shows the distribution of some selected ministerial posts in the Swedish coalition governments that have formed in the postwar period (see last column). If we first take a look at the Finance Minister post, we can see that in all cases where the Liberal Party has been part of the government, except in the Reinfeldt administrations, they have received this post, giving some support to Budge and Keman's (1990) prediction about liberal parties. When we look at the Defense Minister post, we see that in most cases where the Moderates have been part of the government they have received this post, giving support to the party family hypothesis. Conservative parties should, according to Budge and Keman, also obtain the post of Foreign Minister, but here the results are less clear—this post has been held by the Center Party, the Liberals, and Moderates in the bourgeois governments. As for the post of Justice Minister it should largely be held by Liberals according to Budge and Keman, but in most Swedish non-socialist cabinets the Moderates have held this post. Very clear support is given to the hypothesis about agrarian parties—according to this hypothesis, the Center Party should hold the post of Minister of Agriculture, which they have in all Swedish coalition governments. As for socialist parties, the hypothesis that they should receive the post of Minister of Social Affairs and Minister of Labor is also given some support here—in the few coalition governments that have included the Social Democrats, they have received both of these posts.

Another hypothesis in the literature says that the more important (or "salient") a policy area is for a party, the more likely it is that the party will hold the ministerial post that controls this policy area. Bäck, Debus, and Dumont (2011) argue that the parties' electoral manifestos give us information on which ministerial posts the parties aim to control: if a party dedicates a large proportion of their manifesto to a specific policy area, then we can expect that the party perceives this policy area as important, and the party is thus likely to aim to hold the ministerial post controlling this policy area. Evaluating this hypothesis, the authors show that parties in western European cabinets (including Swedish ones) are to a high extent allocated the ministerial posts that control the policy areas that are stressed in the parties' manifestos.

Women in Cabinet and Ministers with a "Political Insider" Background

In the comparative literature, less is known about the social background of ministers. Bäck, Persson, Vernby, and Wockelberg (2009) analyze how socially representative the Swedish ministers are, and conclude that even though Swedish cabinets are fairly equal in composition between men and women nowadays, it was not until the 1970s that the share of female ministers started to increase more rapidly (see also the last column in Table 15.2). The first woman to become a minister was Social Democrat Karin Koch-Lindberg, in 1947. On average, about 25 percent of all ministers appointed during the postwar period have been women, compared to an average of 6.2 percent in postwar cabinets (1945–85) in western Europe reported by Thiébault (1991). Former PM Ingvar Carlsson claims that his Social Democratic predecessor, Olof Palme, was the first to acknowledge the gender dimension when appointing ministers. Carlsson made a promise in the 1994 election campaign to appoint as many women as men to cabinet and kept this promise (Bäck, Persson, Vernby, and Wockelberg 2009).

Bäck, Persson, Vernby, and Wockelberg (2009) also analyze the recruitment of members of parliament (MPs) to the cabinet, which has been seen as a defining feature of parliamentary systems. Previous comparative research has found that the parliament is the main career path for becoming a minister; for example, De Winter (1991) finds that 75 percent of western European ministers (1945–85) have been MPs before becoming ministers. For the years 1945–2007, Bäck, Persson, Vernby, and Wockelberg (2009) find that about 60 percent of appointed ministers had been MPs. This suggests that Sweden has had a relatively low proportion of ministers with a parliamentary background compared to many other countries. Despite these comparatively low figures, Swedish PMs frequently underline the importance of parliamentary experience among their ministers. However, whether parliamentary experience is seen as important varies across PMs, and Social Democratic PM Göran Persson stressed the need to broaden the ministerial recruitment base to outside parliament.

Concluding Discussion

To conclude, we have shown in this chapter that Swedish cabinets stand out in some ways in a comparative perspective. First, many of the postwar governments have been minority, single-party governments and when coalitions have formed, they have had a clear-cut "bloc" political character. Part of the explanation as to why Sweden has had so many minority cabinets is the institutional setting where government formation takes place, such as the negative formation rules. The strict left–right competition and the favorable position that this provides for the median party (often the Social Democrats) and the size of the largest party (often the Social Democrats) provides much of the remaining explanation for the historical record of frequent minority governments. Add to this the potential for "opposition influence" and the support party arrangements, and we have a fairly good explanation of the historical record. Of these elements, the role of the support parties is the least explored. We have seen very clear "support party arrangements" after some elections, where policy agreements have been reached and publicly announced, and even in some cases, offices are given to parties that are formally part of the opposition. How "truly unique" the Swedish case is in this respect is however something for future comparative research to determine.

Second, Swedish cabinets are very gender-equal in comparison with cabinets in many other countries, in the sense that a large share of ministers are women (in some cabinets around 50 percent). As described by Esaiasson and Wängnerud (in this volume), Sweden also stands out when looking at female representation in parliament. How can we explain this pattern? Several explanations for cross-country patterns in the share of female ministers have been proposed in the literature, focusing for example on political and socioeconomic factors and diffusion effects. Looking at cabinet members in Latin America, Escobar-Lemmon and Taylor-Robinson (2005) hypothesize and show empirically that women are more likely to be appointed to cabinet by leftist presidents and in cases of intense partisan competition. Why Sweden has such a high proportion of female cabinet members is of course difficult to determine, and part of the explanation may be found in the "culture" or norms of Swedish society, inducing Swedish PMs to take gender into account when appointing cabinet members. The potential election advantage from such a strategy is also always present. We suggest that also on this point more comparative research is needed.

Lastly, we should discuss one recent feature of Swedish politics, which we have not focused on much in this chapter: the presence of a right-wing populist party, the so-called Sweden Democrats—a party that entered parliament after the 2010 election (see the chapter by Aylott in this volume). How this party has and will influence government formation is difficult to say at this point. While programmatically advocating a mix of welfare policies, they also have a more radical anti-immigration stance that separates them from the other parties (Backlund 2013; Jungar and Ravik Jupskås 2014). In the more general literature on populist radical right-wing parties, such parties have often been described as "pariah" parties due to their "anti-democratic" tendencies. Previous research shows that the mainstream western European parties' responses have been variable, ranging from ignorance and isolation to inclusion as formal coalition partners holding cabinet portfolios. So far, the "mainstream" parties have treated the Sweden Democrats as a sort of "pariah" party, a party which is not allowed even to negotiate over cabinet participation, but it is difficult to say what will happen in the future—we could perhaps see similar developments as in some other countries, where populist radical right-wing parties lose their "pariah" status when their electoral support increases (see e.g. De Lange 2008). If the Sweden Democrats make electoral gains in coming elections, government formation might become a complex matter also in Sweden, as indicated by the formation in late 2014.

References

Andersson, S., Bergman, T., and Ersson, S. (2014). "The European Representative Democracy Data Archive, Release 3," <www.erdda.se>. Main sponsor: Riksbankens Jubileumsfond (In2007-0149:1-E).

Bäck, H. (2010). "Den svenska regeringsbildningen i ett jämförande perspektiv," in J. Hermansson (ed.), *Regeringsmakten i Sverige: Ett experiment i parlamentarism, 1917–2009*. Stockholm: SNS, 33–55.

Bäck, H., Debus, M., and Dumont, P. (2011). "Who Gets What in Coalition Governments? Predictors of Portfolio Allocation in Parliamentary Democracies," *European Journal of Political Research* 50: 441–78.

Bäck, H. and Dumont, P. (2008). "Making the First Move: A Two-Stage Analysis of the Role of Formateurs in Parliamentary Government Formation," *Public Choice* 135: 353–73.

Bäck, H., and Meier, H. E., and Persson, T. (2009). "Party Size and Portfolio Payoffs: The Proportional Allocation of Ministerial Posts in Coalition Governments," *Journal of Legislative Studies* 15: 10–34.

Bäck, H., Persson, T., Vernby, K., and Wockelberg, H. (2009). "In Tranquil Waters? Swedish Cabinet Ministers in the Post-War Era," in K. Dowding and P. Dumont (eds), *The Selection of Ministers in Europe: Hiring and Firing*. London: Routledge, 159–78.

Backlund, A. (2013). "Placing Radical Rights in Political Space: Four Methods Applied to the Case of the Sweden Democrats," PESO Research Reports, 1:2013, Södertörns högskola.

Bale, T. and Bergman, T. (2006). "Captives No Longer, but Servants Still? Contract Parliamentarism and the New Minority Governance in Sweden and New Zealand," *Government and Opposition* 41: 449–76.

Bergman, T. (1992). "Multiple Goals and Constitutional Design: How the Swedish King Lost his Formal Powers," *Statsvetenskaplig Tidskrift* 95: 209–33.

Bergman, T. (1993). "Formation Rules and Minority Governments," *European Journal of Political Research* 23: 55–66.

Bergman, T. (1995). "Constitutional Rules and Party Goals in Coalition Formation: An Analysis of Winning Minority Governments in Sweden," PhD thesis, Department of Political Science, Umeå University.

Bergman, T. (2000). "When Minority Cabinets Are the Rule and Majority Coalitions the Exception," in W. C. Müller and K. Strøm (eds), *Coalition Governments in Western Europe*. Oxford: Oxford University Press, 192–230.

Bergman, T., Müller, W. C., Strøm, K., and Blomgren, M. (2003). "Democratic Delegation and Accountability: Cross-National Patterns," in K. Strøm, W. C. Müller, and T. Bergman (eds), *Delegation and Accountability in Parliamentary Democracies*. Oxford: Oxford University Press, 109–220.

Browne, E. C. and Franklin, M. N. (1973). "Aspects of Coalition Payoffs in European Parliamentary Democracies," *American Political Science Review* 67: 453–69.

Budge, I. and Keman, H. (1990). *Parties and Democracy: Coalition Formation and Government Functioning in Twenty States*. Oxford: Oxford University Press.

Damgaard, E. (1969). "The Parliamentary Basis of Danish Governments: The Patterns of Coalition Formation," *Scandinavian Political Studies* 4: 30–57.

De Lange, S. L. (2008). "From Pariah to Power: The Government Participation of Radical Right-Wing Populist Parties in West European Democracies," dissertation, University of Antwerp.

De Winter, L. (1991). "Parliamentary and Party Pathways to the Cabinet," in J. Blondel and J. Thiébault (eds), *The Profession of Government Minister in Western Europe*. Basingstoke: Macmillan, 44–69.

Escobar-Lemmon, M. and Taylor-Robinson, M. M. (2005). "Women Ministers in Latin American Government," *American Journal of Political Science* 49: 829–44.

Huber, J. and Inglehart, R. (1995). "Expert Interpretations of Party Space and Party Locations in 42 Societies," *Party Politics* 1: 73–111.

Jungar, A.-C. and Ravik Jupskås, A. (2014). "Populist Radical Right Parties in the Nordic Region: A New and Distinct Party Family?" *Scandinavian Political Studies* 37/3: 215–343.

Martin, L. W. and Stevenson, R. T. (2001). "Government Formation in Parliamentary Democracies," *American Journal of Political Science* 45: 33–50.

Mitchell, P. and Nyblade, B. (2008). "Government Formation and Cabinet Type," in K. Strøm, W. C. Müller, and T. Bergman (eds), *Cabinets and Coalition Bargaining: The Democratic Life Cycle in Western Europe*. Oxford: Oxford University Press, 782–802.

Rasch, B. E. and Tsebelis, G. (eds) (2011). *The Role of Governments in Legislative Agenda Setting*. London: Routledge.

Sjölin, M. (1993). *Coalition Politics and Parliamentary Power*. Lund: Lund University Press.

Strøm, K. (1990). *Minority Government and Majority Rule*. Cambridge: Cambridge University Press.

Strøm, K., Müller, W. C., and Bergman, T. (eds) (2003). *Delegation and Accountability in Parliamentary Democracies*. Oxford: Oxford University Press.

Thiébault, J. (1991). "The Social Background of Western European Cabinet Ministers," in J. Blondel and J. Thiébault (eds), *The Profession of Government Minister in Western Europe.* London: Macmillan, 19–30.

Warwick, P. V. and Druckman J. (2006). "The Paradox of Portfolio Allocation: An Investigation into the Nature of a Very Strong but Puzzling Relationship," *European Journal of Political Research* 45: 635–65.

SECTION 4

ELECTORAL BEHAVIOR

SECTION EDITORS
SÖREN HOLMBERG AND
HENRIK OSCARSSON

....

CHAPTER 16

INTRODUCTION

Electoral Behavior

....

SÖREN HOLMBERG AND HENRIK OSCARSSON

IN Sweden, systematic studies of electoral behavior started early. As early as 1911 in pre-democratic times, Statistics Sweden conducted its first Electoral Participation Survey. That was ten years before voting rights were extended to all adults of both genders in 1921. At every election since then, Statistics Sweden has produced highly reliable data on turnout in different demographic and occupational groups. Studies of voting behavior in addition to electoral participation and including party choice came early to Sweden as well. The first election surveys were done by Gallup in the mid-1940s followed by the premiere investigations done by the Swedish National Election Studies (SNES) and Statistics Sweden in 1954/6. Since then some twenty national and European elections as well as four nationwide referendums have been covered by SNES.

Based on this extended and internationally unique material, the section focuses on four central aspects of elections and voting behavior. These four focused aspects are voter turnout, class voting, ideological voting, and election campaigning.

From a normative democratic vantage point, turnout should be high and evenly spread among different societal groups. Richard Öhrvall analyzes the extent to which this has been true in Sweden during the last hundred years—using data on voter turnout that are more sketchy for older times and more detailed in recent periods. Sweden is of special interest—not as an average case, but as sort of an outlier with comparatively high levels of turnout, at least since the late 1940s.

The Sociological Model of voting behavior emphasizing socioeconomic determinants of party choice has become less relevant over the years, in Sweden as well as in most electoral democracies. Compared to forty or fifty years ago, voting in the 2000s is less structured by which social and economic group people belong to. Class voting is a good illustration. As Maria Oskarson demonstrates in her chapter, the relationship between occupational class and party choice is less pronounced in today's Swedish elections compared to what it was in the 1950s and 1960s. But class voting is still substantial and of importance in present-day Sweden. As a matter of fact, class voting in the last

Swedish elections, although weaker than before, has been stronger than in any other known established democracy. Thus, Oskarson's analysis of Swedish class voting is a study of a true outlier.

Strong or weak class voting is not a topic explicitly addressed by normative democratic theory. However, if anything, we would think that lower levels of socioeconomic voting are easier to accommodate normatively, especially if they are accompanied by higher levels of voting inspired by ideology and issues. Voters and parties in the Responsible Party Model should be rational and put policies and performance center stage come election time. Issue voting, not class voting, should characterize the behavior of democratic citizens on election day. Henrik Oscarsson and Sören Holmberg examine whether or not Swedish voters have lived up to this ideal during the last fifty years. Swedish voting behavior is from a comparative perspective extremely unidimensional and structured by the ideological left–right dimension. So even in this chapter the Swedish case is somewhat of an outlier.

Election day is the big day in a democracy. And the preceding election campaign is the largest and most important *agora* in a well-functioning democracy. Voters and parties and candidates and media meet and exchange ideas and inform each other, resulting in better knowledge and more reasoned decision by voters come the election. In theory, at least, that is the way it should be. The extent to which Swedish election campaigns fulfill these expectations is analyzed by Jesper Strömbäck in the last chapter of the section. And, as with the other chapters, Strömbäck's subject is also kind of an outlier. Compared internationally, Swedes are less involved in election campaigns through personal contacts with parties or candidates than is the case in most other democracies. Indirect contacts via media are more essential in Sweden.

To sum up, the menu in this section consists of four studies of Swedish exceptionalism. A study of turnout where Swedes are exceptionally participatory. A study of class voting where Swedes are exceptionally old fashioned and still vote according to the occupational class they belong to. A study of ideological voting where Swedes are exceptionally influenced by the classic left–right divide. And last, a study of election campaigns where Swedes have exceptionally little personal contact with parties and candidates.

Thus, Sweden as exceptional and as an outlier—that is the name of the game in this section on Swedish electoral behavior.

CHAPTER 17

···

VOTER TURNOUT

···

RICHARD ÖHRVALL

THE right to vote is fundamental to a representative democracy. Voter turnout is often seen as an indicator of the state of democracy; a high turnout is assumed to give legitimacy to the democratic system. Voting is also often considered the most equal form of political participation. All those entitled to vote have one and only one vote and they are all given the same weight. However, the right to vote is not exercised to the same extent within all population groups. As stated by Lijphart (1997), "Voting is less unequal than other forms of participation, but it is far from unbiased."

A substantial amount of literature has been devoted to the question of who votes and why. It has for a long time been a well-established fact that better educated and wealthy people are more likely to vote (Lijphart 1997). Differences in turnout between different groups therefore tend to give more weight to the opinions of those with higher socioeconomic status. There is also a link between voter turnout and political equality.

If political equality was the only concern, one could argue that low turnout might not be a problem if the turnout was equally low across all groups. Then election results could still be considered unbiased. However, empirical studies have shown that higher turnout is associated with more equal participation. That is what Tingsten stated with his "law of dispersion" (1937). By studying comparative data on voter turnout among men and women, age groups, and social classes, he reached the conclusion that as turnout increases it becomes more equal. And conversely, differences in turnout levels between different population groups increase as voter turnout decreases.[1]

Against this backdrop, the decrease in voter turnout that has taken place in many democracies over the last decades has raised concern. The decline has also renewed the academic interest in voter turnout. In this context, Sweden provides an interesting case with a high electoral participation which has once more increased in recent years. The main purpose of this chapter is to describe voter turnout in Sweden, and more precisely to study whether differences between different population groups also exist in a high-turnout context and whether such differences correlate with the general level of turnout.

The chapter proceeds as follows: First, the key survey for analyzing electoral participation in Sweden is presented. After that, a broad picture of Swedish voter turnout over the last hundred years is painted. The rest of the chapter is devoted to studying differences in voter turnouts between different population groups: by sex and age, socioeconomic status, citizenship and country of birth, and political interest and motivation. The final section sums up the main results.

High-Quality Surveys
of Voter Turnout

Overall voter turnout and turnout in different geographical areas can be deduced from statistics over the election results; it contains information on the number of people entitled to vote and the number of votes cast, and the turnout is simply the ratio between those two figures. However, in order to study differences in turnout between different population groups, we have to use other statistics. The main data source for studying voter turnout in Sweden is the Electoral Participation Survey conducted by Statistics Sweden. The statistical results presented in this chapter are based on that survey.

The survey has a long tradition; it was carried out for the first time in 1911 and it has covered every election to the Riksdag since then. It is thereby one of the oldest surveys in Sweden. The design of the study has changed over the years, but it has consistently produced high-quality estimates of voting rates in different population groups. The information on voting is validated using the electoral rolls. During the first decades it was a complete enumeration of voter turnout among all who were entitled to vote. The information on voting was retrieved from electoral rolls together with information about sex (from 1921 when women were entitled to vote) and occupation.

The complete enumeration was a laborious and dreary task; millions of records were manually processed in order to retrieve the necessary information. In 1944, Statistics Sweden's Electoral Participation Survey implemented a sample survey design. This fundamental change was made possible after the statistical invention of the sample survey theory was established in the 1930s, most notably by Neyman (1934). Another major change occurred two decades later: in the survey conducted in 1964, the sample was the same as in the then newly established Labor Force Survey (LFS). Thereby, information gathered through the LFS could be used when analyzing voter turnout, e.g. employment and socioeconomic status.

Samples from the LFS still serve as the backbone of the Electoral Participation Survey today. They are complemented with additional samples in order to cover population groups that are entitled to vote but not included in the LFS, e.g. elderly and Swedish citizens residing abroad. Since the Swedish national statistical system is based to a large extent on register statistics, a lot of information can also be retrieved from different registers and used in the survey, e.g. information on age, gender, country of birth, education, and income. Further improvements have been made over the most recent decades. The sample size has increased: the 2010 survey included over 100,000 observations, and more advanced statistical methods have been introduced. Still, in one fundamental aspect, the survey is the same today as when it started in 1911: the information on voting is retrieved from electoral rolls. It is worth stressing that this information does not come from any survey questions, which tend to be plagued by measurement errors, but rather from registers. Hence, estimates of voter turnout in population groups defined by register information can be based on a sample without nonresponse.[2]

THE SWEDISH ELECTORAL SYSTEM

Cross-country studies of voter turnout have mainly focused on institutional factors (Franklin 2004). From what is known, Sweden seems to have institutional arrangements that in almost all aspects promote turnout. The electoral system is proportional, which tends to facilitate turnout to a larger extent than majoritarian systems (Blais 2007; Blais and Aarts 2006). The costs of voting are also relatively small: electoral rolls are produced based on a national population register, which is updated daily. Hence, no one has to register in order to be able to vote. Voter cards are sent to all entitled to vote. It has been shown in previous research that registration laws increase the costs of voting and thereby decrease turnout (Highton 1997; Wolfinger and Rosenstone 1978).

In Sweden, elections to the Riksdag are held every four years, and on the same day as elections to county and municipal councils. The election day takes place on the third Sunday in September.[3] Historically, the rationale behind the choice of date was that this was a time of year when the harvest was reaped and the whole country was free from snow (Oscarsson and Håkansson 2001). Even today it is a suitable time to hold elections; in spring and summer people are often away from home during holidays or on vacation, and the winters are dark and cold and therefore not ideal for political campaigning. It is also reasonable to expect that the cost of voting is lower if the election takes place on a Sunday when most people do not work (cf. Franklin 2004).

Furthermore, Sweden has a very generous system for early voting. When the system was introduced in 1940, only persons with specific reasons had the right to vote in advance, but since 1969 the regulation has been more liberal. The popularity of early voting has increased over time, from 14 percent of the voters in 1970 to 37 percent in 1985. After a decline to 30 percent in 2002 it has increased again, reaching over 40 percent in the 2010 election. Today, early voting starts almost three weeks before election day, and votes can be cast at numerous public places, e.g. public libraries and town halls. In the 2010 election, more than 3,300 polling stations for early voting were available in Sweden's 290 municipalities. In the literature, different results have been reached on whether early voting has any effect on turnout (Franklin 2004; Blais 2007). Dahlberg et al. (2008) have studied the effects of availability of early voting on the propensity to vote in Sweden. They found a small but positive effect of better access to early voting on the likelihood to vote.

All things considered, the only adjustment to the Swedish institutional arrangements that is likely to improve voter turnout is to introduce mandatory voting. Previous research shows that mandatory voting leads to higher turnout, but the mechanisms are not clear and there is uncertainty regarding how strong sanctions must be in order to increase the propensity to vote (Blais 2007). Implementation of mandatory voting was discussed in Sweden in the early twentieth century (Tingsten 1937). However, today it is not an issue that is discussed or suggested by any of the major political parties.

One Hundred Years of Voting

Over the last hundred years, electoral participation in Sweden has increased. In the 1911 election to the Riksdag (parliament), 57.0 percent of those entitled to vote participated. As mentioned, this was the first election covered by Statistics Sweden's Electoral Participation Survey. It was also the first election to the Riksdag where somewhat equal voting rights for men were applied. Still, it should be noted that more than a fifth of all men of voting age were still not entitled to vote, due to debts, convictions, not fulfilling military service, etc. In addition, no women were permitted to vote. It was not until 1921 that women were entitled to vote in an election to the Riksdag for the first time.[4] Sweden was thereby the last of the Nordic countries to give women and men equal voting rights. In the 1921 election, the criteria regarding debts were also abolished, thereby reducing the share of Swedish citizens of voting age who were not entitled to vote to 1.8 percent.[5] Hence, 1921 can be seen as the starting point of Swedish electoral democracy

In the 1921 election, turnout was only 54.2 percent (see Figure 17.1). Over the following decades election participation increased. Turnout did not increase in every single election, but there was a general trend of increasing rates. The highest voting rate was reached in the 1976 election to the Riksdag, when 91.8 percent of those entitled to vote participated. After reaching that peak, electoral participation decreased, especially in the 1988 and 1998 elections. The decrease was cause for concern and a publicly funded investigation was launched. One of the results of this investigation was a couple of scientific contributions that gave better understanding about voting behavior in Sweden (e.g. Bennulf and Hedberg 1999; Westholm and Teorell 1999). Still, the decrease continued, and in the 2002 election only 80.1 percent voted. That is the lowest turnout since 1958. However, since 2002 a break in the trend has occurred and in the last two elections voting has increased. In the most recent election to the Riksdag in 2010, 84.6 percent voted.

Before 1970, national and local elections were held separately. During that period, turnout was lower in local elections than in national elections. In the 1960s the difference was between 3 and 8 percentage points (Oscarsson 2001). A change back to separate election days has been an issue in the Swedish public debate. The main argument for such a change is that local political issues drown in national political campaigns.

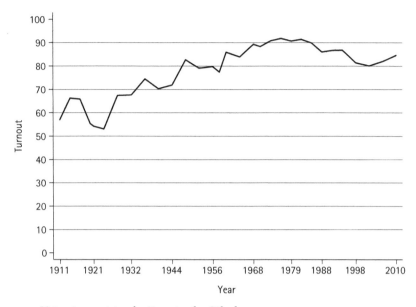

FIGURE 17.1 Voter turnout in elections to the Riksdag, 1911–2010.

Source: Statistics Sweden.

However, separate election days would most likely lead to a lower turnout in the local elections; according to Oscarsson (2001), between 10 and 20 percentage points lower.

Having the same election day as the national elections has helped to increase voter turnout in local elections. In the 1970s, turnout in local elections was only slightly lower than in national elections. At that time, the differences between the different types of elections were less than 2 percentage points, but it has increased somewhat in more recent years and in the 2010 election it was close to 4 points. The difference, and why it increases, is mainly due to lower and decreasing turnout among foreign citizens. Since 1976, foreign citizens have been entitled to vote in elections to municipal and county councils if they have been registered residents in Sweden for a continuous period of three years before election day. However, citizens of EU member states, Iceland, or Norway only have to be registered in Sweden to be allowed to vote. In the elections to the Riksdag, only Swedish citizens are entitled to vote. Swedish citizens residing abroad are only entitled to vote in elections to the Riksdag but not in local elections. Voter turnout in that group is very low, so it helps reduce the difference in turnout between the different elections.

Among Swedish citizens residing in Sweden the differences in turnout in the different elections are minuscule. This is because most people who make the decision to vote do so in all elections they are entitled to vote in. Of those Swedish citizens who voted in the 2010 election to the Riksdag, more than 98 percent also voted in the municipal elections (Öhrvall 2012).[6]

Since Sweden became a member of the European Union in 1995, elections have also been held to the European Parliament. The first EU election was in 1995. The turnout was only 41.6 percent, and in the following two elections it decreased even further. In the 2009 election, the voter turnout increased by 7.6 percentage points to 45.5 percent. It was not only the first time participation increased in a Swedish election to the European Parliament, but also the first time that Sweden had a turnout that was above the total turnout for the European Union.

Within Sweden the differences in voter turnout between different regions are fairly small, at least at the municipal level (see Figure 17.2). In 1976, when the total turnout in the election to the Riksdag was 91.8 percent, no municipality had a turnout below 85 percent. The difference between the municipality with the lowest turnout and the highest was 11 percentage points. In 2010, that difference had increased to 20 points.

As mentioned, turnout was 84.6 percent in the most recent election to the Riksdag in 2010. In other words, 15.4 percent did not, for some reason, vote. From an international perspective, this is a small share of the population that decided to not use the right to vote. If those nonvoters are dissatisfied citizens who lack confidence in the democratic system, that share might still be considered large enough to be concerned about. However, recent research shows that consistent nonvoters constitute a small share of the Swedish electorate. Oscarsson and Holmberg (2013) studied validated voting for a sample over three consecutive elections, and found that only 6 percent did not vote in any of those three elections. The remaining 94 percent voted in at least one election, and of them 73 percent voted in all three elections.[7] So, most people vote in a given election and

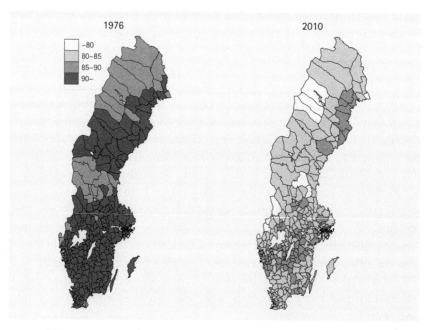

FIGURE 17.2 Voter turnout in elections to the Riksdag, by municipality, 1976 and 2010.

Source: Statistics Sweden.

many of those who do not are likely to vote in the following one. Even so, there might still be differences in turnout between different population groups.

How does Swedish turnout rank internationally? André Blais (2007) has compiled information on voter turnout in all democratic legislative elections in all democracies during the period 1972–2004.[8] This study includes 533 elections in 106 countries. The average voter turnout for all these elections was 76 percent. Among those countries, Sweden ranked sixteenth with an average turnout of 88 percent. At the very top of the list were Malta, Australia, and Belgium. In another comparison by Holmberg and Oscarsson (2004), Sweden ranked eighteenth of 172 countries when average turnout from 1945 to 2003 was studied. If new democracies and countries with mandatory voting are excluded, Sweden advances to fourth place. In yet another study conducted in 2012 by Öhrvall (2012), voter turnout in the most recent parliamentary election in all European countries was compared. There Sweden ranked seventh out of 45 countries (three of the countries with higher turnout have mandatory voting).

Another finding in this literature is that since World War II there has been a general international trend of decreasing turnout, and the decline seems to have become accentuated over recent decades (Blais 2007; IDEA 2002). However, turnout is not declining in all countries and in all elections. Of 45 European countries studied in 2012, turnout in the most recent election was lower than in the previous election in 26 countries (Öhrvall 2012). In the remaining 19 countries the turnout increased. Sweden is found among the countries with increasing turnout. So, even if there are a few countries with even greater turnout, Swedish turnout is comparatively high. Furthermore, as mentioned, participation increased in the most recent Swedish election.

Demographic Characteristics and Turnout

In 1921, when women were allowed to vote in an election to the Riksdag for the first time, only 47 percent did so. The turnout among men was 15 percentage points higher. Over the following decades that gap decreased; in 1948 it was 4 percentage points and in 1960 it was only 2 points. At the end of the 1960s the gap became even smaller, and after that there was a period when it was not possible to determine from the sample surveys whether women or men had a higher turnout. In the 1988 election, a statistically significant higher turnout among women than among men was found for the first time. Since then, turnout has been slightly higher among women. Still, the difference has been very small at only around 1 percentage point (see Figure 17.3).

However, if both age and sex are studied simultaneously, bigger differences emerge. Among younger and middle-aged persons, women are more likely to vote than men. In Figure 17.4, this relationship is illustrated for the 2010 election to the Riksdag. In that election, turnout among women was 3–5 percentage points higher in age groups up to

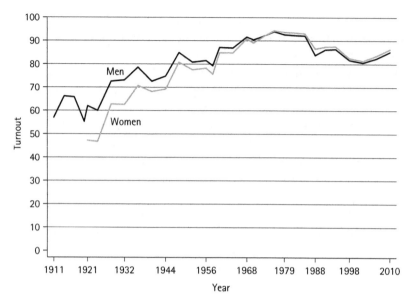

FIGURE 17.3 Voter turnout in elections to the Riksdag, by sex, 1911–2010.

Note: The statistics are based on complete enumeration until and including the election in 1960. After that, the figures are based on survey samples and thereby have some statistical uncertainty (still, the confidence intervals are less than ±1 percentage point). The surveys for the years 1973–85 do not include persons of 75 years and older.

Source: Statistics Sweden.

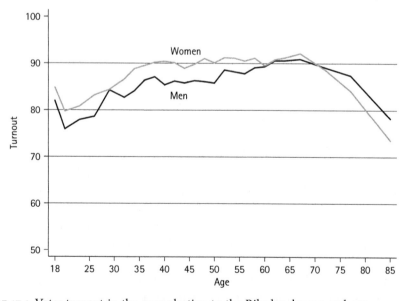

FIGURE 17.4 Voter turnout in the 2010 election to the Riksdag, by sex and age.

Source: Statistics Sweden.

Note: The estimates are based on a survey sample and calculated for small age intervals. They therefore have some statistical uncertainty. The confidence intervals vary, but they are consistently less than ±2 percentage points.

50 years of age. In the age group 60–74, turnout is about the same for women as for men. It is only among those aged 75 years and older that men vote to a higher degree. This pattern is not unique to Sweden; similar results have been found by Bhatti and Hansen (2012b) in studies of Danish elections.

Figure 17.4 also illustrates that the relationship between age and turnout is curvilinear. Turnout is relatively low during early adulthood, then gradually increases before reaching a plateau in middle age and finally declines with old age. This is a well-established finding dating back as early as the 1930s (Wolfinger and Rosenstone 1980; Bhatti et al. 2012). The increase in turnout in the early phase of the life cycle can be associated with getting a job, forming a family, and in other ways strengthening the social network, something that is attributed to higher turnout. In the later phase of the life cycle those networks tend to deteriorate and physical infirmities are also more common (Bhatti et al. 2012). Apart from this *life-cycle effect*, it is also possible to find a *generational effect* when younger generations replace older ones (Wass 2007).

This relationship between age and participation is also confirmed by statistics on early Swedish elections. Information on voter turnout by age is available from the election to the Riksdag in 1944 and onwards. Since then, the lowest turnout has always been among the youngest and the elderly. The most remarkable change has been among those 75 years and older. In 1944, the difference between those 75 years and older and those 50–64 years of age was 37 percentage points. In 1970, that difference was only 10 points.

It is worth mentioning that during the period from 1973 to 1982 when the voter turnout was above 90 percent, the differences between the different age groups was lower than ever before or since. When the turnout declined in the 1988 and 1998 elections, it did so mainly among people under 50 years of age. On the other hand, the increase in turnout in recent years has been stronger in those age groups with a comparatively low turnout, thereby decreasing the differences. However, turnout is still lower among the youngest and the oldest.

As can be seen in Figure 17.4, the relationship is not perfectly curvilinear. Some of the fluctuations are random noise because the estimates are based on a sample survey, but a more striking divergence can be seen among the youngest persons. Among the very young, turnout is higher among 18 years old than among their slightly older peers. From age 18 to 20 voter turnout drops off, before gradually increasing again by age. This phenomenon has been observed in Finland and Denmark as well (Bhatti et al. 2012), and it has been analyzed in more detail by Bhatti and Hansen (2012a) using data from the 2009 local elections in Denmark. They reach the conclusion that those who are 18 years old are more likely to live at home and thereby their propensity to vote is positively influenced by their parents. After leaving the nest, that positive influence wears off. They also find a substantial effect on voter turnout by being enrolled in school. Since the turnout by age has a similar pattern in Sweden as in Denmark, it is likely that similar mechanisms are in place in both countries.

In recent years, young first-time voters have been given more attention. Several researchers have argued that voting should be seen as a habit, and as such the early, formative years are of particular importance. Those who vote the first time can form a habit that is maintained over following elections (Plutzer 2002; Aldrich et al. 2011). It has been argued by Franklin (2004) that the decline in voter turnout in old democracies is partly due to generational effects. The argument is as follows. In the 1970s the voting age was lowered to 18 years in many democracies. Hence, according to Franklin, many face their first election at a time when they are less likely to vote, and thereby form a habit of abstaining. Other researchers have also argued that the lowering of the voting age has had a negative effect on turnout (e.g. Blais and Dobrzynska 1998). However, in Sweden the voting age was lowered from 20 to 19 in 1969 and then from 19 to 18 in 1975, but the decline in turnout did not come until the late 1980s.[9] It should also be noted that the increase in the general turnout in the 2006 and 2010 elections to the Riksdag was even stronger among first-time voters. In 2010, their turnout was 80 percent, only 5 points lower than among other voters. That difference was twice as big in 2002.

At the other end of the age scale we find senior citizens. Their turnout has not been given much attention in the existing literature. However, Bhatti and Hansen (2012b) have recently analyzed turnout among the elderly. They find a rapid demobilization of seniors from around age 65 to 67 and that women demobilize earlier than men. The reason for the decline is, according to them, that seniors withdraw from the labor market and thereby disrupt their social ties. An additional factor is that they also tend to live alone more often than people in other age groups. The latter explanation seems to be more in line with Swedish data than the former. The decline in turnout seems to come later in life among Swedes than what was seen among Danes. In the 2010 election to the Riksdag the voting rate among 70- to 74-year-olds was 88.8 percent. In other words, their turnout is still very high even if they left the labor market several years earlier. It is not until age 80 years and older that turnout declines rapidly.

In the Danish study, as well as in Swedish data, turnout drops faster for women than for men. Bhatti and Hansen (2012b) argue that this is because women lose their social network earlier. This is due to the fact that women, on average, are younger than their spouses, and that they also live longer. Therefore, they are more likely to live alone at a given age, and especially when they become elderly. In addition, older generations of women are less educated and have a lower affiliation to the labor market than men do. These explanations also seem reasonable for the Swedish situation. However, among younger Swedish generations women are more educated than men, so the gender difference among the elderly might change with time.

Generational effects have been suggested by some researchers as an explanation for the declining turnout in old democracies. Blais et al. (2004) have studied Canadian elections and reached the conclusion that the main reason for the decline in turnout is lower turnout of the post-baby-boomers, i.e. in younger generations. A similar result was found by Miller and Shanks (1996) when analyzing the decline in the United States. In a study by Persson et al. (2013) it was concluded that a generational effect can also be found in Sweden, but that it is more moderate than in other countries with a lower general turnout.

SOCIOECONOMIC DIFFERENCES

In the literature on voter turnout, the effects of the individual's resources have been stressed by many (e.g. Verba and Nie 1972; Wolfinger and Rosenstone 1980; Verba et al. 1995). In Sweden a close relationship between socioeconomic resources and participation has also been found. During the first half of the twentieth century, official statistics on voter turnout were presented only by sex and occupation. The latter was aggregated into three social classes. The highest participation rate was found in the first class, or the upper class, and the lowest in the third, or the working class, with the middle class in-between. Throughout that time the differences in turnout between the groups varied, but the relationship was the same: higher socioeconomic status was associated with higher turnout. The same pattern can also be found in more recent elections. In the 2010 election to the Riksdag, the turnout was 82 percent among blue-collar workers and 94 percent among white-collar workers.[10] The gap was a bit smaller in the early 1990s when overall turnout was higher.

A relationship can also be found between the propensity to vote and educational attainment. Previous research has shown that education together with age is the socio-demographic factor that has the strongest correlation with the propensity to vote (Blais 2007). In that aspect Sweden is no exception. Statistics on education and turnout are only available for the election in 1968 and then in 1988 and onwards. The result is the same for all those elections: higher education is associated with higher turnout. In the 2010 election to the Riksdag, turnout was 79 percent for people with primary and lower secondary education, 86 percent with upper secondary education, and 94 percent with post-secondary education. The increase in turnout in recent elections has led to a more equal turnout, but the changes are small and the differences are bigger today than they were in the early 1990s. The strong correlation between education and the propensity to vote can be found even when controlling for a wide set of other demographic and socioeconomic factors (Öhrvall 2012). However, this does not prove any causal relationship. Using data on Swedish elections, Persson (2012) argues that it is not the skills promoted by education that have positive effects on political participation. Instead, he finds support for a model that suggests that education influences individuals' social status, which in turn influences political participation. It might also be the case that both educational choice and voter turnout are due to pre-adult factors (Persson 2013). Pre-adult factors include family socioeconomic status, cognitive ability, political socialization in the family environment, and other factors.

An individual characteristic closely related to educational attainment is level of income. It is therefore no surprise that a clear relationship can also be found between income and the likelihood to vote. People with higher income tend to vote to a higher degree. If those eligible to vote are divided into quintiles by income, it can be shown that the turnout is higher in the first quintile than in the second, and so on. This is true for the 2010 election and all previous elections for which data are available. In 2010 the difference in turnout between the first and the fifth quintile was 17 percentage points.

IMMIGRATION, CITIZENSHIP, AND VOTING

During the second half of the nineteenth century and the first decades of the twentieth century, Sweden experienced a substantial emigration, mainly to North America. It was only after World War II that immigration took off. Postwar industry was booming and there was a lack of workers. Most immigrants came from the neighboring Nordic countries, but also from other parts of Europe. The number of foreign-born persons increased from 100,000 in 1945 to 538,000 in 1970. After that, immigration shifted in character, and a large share of those who came to Sweden were refugees fleeing oppression in other parts of Europe, but also more distant places. Hence, "foreign-born persons" is not a homogenous group; it includes people from different parts of the world who have migrated to Sweden for different reasons, and have arrived in Sweden at different times when the economy has been in different states. Immigrants during more recent decades have had a more difficult time finding a job and thereby integrating into Swedish society.

Today around 1.4 million people in Sweden were born in another country, i.e. 15 percent of the population. Among those entitled to vote in elections to the Riksdag, the percentage is lower: 11 percent in the 2010 election. The difference is mainly because some foreign-born are not Swedish citizens and are thereby not entitled to vote. Some of those foreign citizens are, however, allowed to vote in local elections. In 1976, foreign citizens were for the first time entitled to vote in elections to municipal and county councils. About 60 percent of them also used that right, a slightly higher percentage than expected beforehand (Hammar 1979: 107). One reason might be the interest the expanded voting rights caused and all the information campaigns launched. Also, as mentioned, the overall voting rate in that election was record-high. Since then, voter turnout among foreign citizens has decreased in almost every election. In the 2010 elections to the municipal councils the turnout was only 36 percent, i.e. a decline of 24 percentage points since 1976. This can be compared with a decline of 9 percentage points for total turnout. If we only consider the most recent elections, the turnout among foreign citizens seems to have stabilized, but at a comparatively low level.

Since 1976, the share of foreign citizens among those entitled to vote in elections to municipal councils has increased by 2 points to 5 percent in the 2010 elections (Öhrvall 2012). There are also substantial changes within the group. Many foreign citizens become Swedish citizens after living in the country for a number of years.[11] Among Swedish citizens, foreign-born persons have a considerably lower turnout. Furthermore, this difference has increased over the last two decades. In the 1991 election to the Riksdag, 77 percent among foreign-born voted. Among those born in Sweden, turnout was 87 percent, i.e. a difference of 10 percentage points. In the 2010 election, the corresponding difference was 14 percentage points. Still, the 2010 election constitutes a break in the trend: compared to the 2006 election, turnout among foreign-born increased by 6 percentage points, more than twice the increase among people born in Sweden.

As mentioned, immigrants do not constitute a homogenous group. Hence, it is not surprising that voter turnout differs depending on country of birth. Turnout is especially low among immigrants from Asia, Africa, and parts of Europe outside of the EU. Conversely, those born in Nordic or EU countries, North America, or South America vote to a relatively high degree. The variation in turnout in the 2010 election ranges between 71 percent among immigrants from Europe outside of the EU and 81 percent among those from the Nordic countries. Still, even if such differences can be found, voting rates among the foreign-born are lower than among the Swedish-born, regardless of country of birth.

Some previous studies suggest that turnout among immigrants increases over time, i.e. people who have stayed a longer time in Sweden tend to vote to a higher extent (Öhrvall 2012, 2006). Among those who have been in Sweden less than ten years, turnout in the 2010 election to the Riksdag was 64 percent. That figure can be compared to 70 percent among those who stayed 10–20 years, and 78 percent among them who stayed more than 25 years. As mentioned, immigration has shifted in character over the years. But even when taking this into account there seems to be a positive effect over time (Öhrvall 2012). Still, more research is needed in order to know more about the mechanisms and if they work in different ways for different groups of immigrants.

The percentage of foreign-born persons in the Swedish population has increased significantly over the last 50 years. As a consequence, the number of Swedish-born with both parents born abroad has also increased. In the 2010 election to the Riksdag, that group constituted 2.5 percent of those entitled to vote. An interesting question is whether the lower propensity to vote among the foreign-born is carried on by their children. Previous research has emphasized the importance of the parents for their children's political participation (Verba et al. 1995; Bhatti and Hansen 2012a). This implies that children of immigrants should also have a lower propensity to vote. On the other hand, they have grown up in Sweden and taken part in Swedish education, and are therefore more likely to be integrated into Swedish society than their parents.

In the 2010 election to the Riksdag, turnout among Swedish-born persons with both parents born abroad was 8 percentage points lower than among other Swedish-born persons. However, they vote to a higher degree than foreign-born persons. It should be noted that the Swedish-born with two foreign-born parents are relatively young. As mentioned earlier, younger persons vote to a lesser extent. Still, even when controlling for age and a large set of other factors, a sizable difference in voter turnout between Swedish-born persons with two foreign-born parents and other Swedish-born persons can still be found (Öhrvall 2006).

Political Interest and Motivation

Socioeconomic explanations have dominated research on political participation (e.g. Verba and Nie 1972). However, according to the *Civic Voluntarism Model* presented by Verba et al. (1995), political participation is not only affected by resources but also by mobilization and motivation. A person can be mobilized in many different ways, and of particular importance are the individual's networks. The family can constitute one such network that can promote voting. It is known from many studies that married persons tend to vote to a higher degree than unmarried persons (Wolfinger and Rosenstone 1980).

In the Swedish Electoral Participation Survey, statistics over turnout by civic status have been published since the 1944 election to the Riksdag. In all elections since then, turnout among married persons has consistently been higher.[12] Back in 1944, the gap was 22 points. As the general turnout increased, the gap decreased. In the 2010 election, the difference was 10 points. Two comments are worth making: First, there is of course a correlation between age and marriage, but even after controlling for age, a positive effect of marriage on the propensity to vote has been found in studies of the Swedish electorate (Öhrvall 2012). Second, it does not seem to be the marriage per se that affects turnout, but rather to be living together with someone else. Furthermore, this effect of living together with someone else seems to be stronger among men than among women (Öhrvall 2012). This is in line with other research that emphasizes the role of an individual's network in general and the role of the family in particular (e.g. Bhatti and Hansen 2012b).

Another network that can help mobilize turnout is the workplace. Studies have shown that employed persons are more likely to vote than those outside the workforce. In the 2010 election to the Riksdag, that difference was about 10 percentage points, and it has been about that magnitude over the last two decades.

Motivation is also a factor that gets empirical support. In a study based on the Swedish National Election Studies, Oscarsson and Holmberg (2013) find that people who are more motivated also have a higher propensity to vote. Among the indicators of motivation used are political interest and party identification. However, as argued by Blais (2007), the link is trivial and it begs the question of why some people are more interested than others in politics.

Conclusions

Sweden has a voter turnout that is relatively high, both in comparison with other countries and in relation to earlier times. Still, even in this high-turnout context, resources are a crucial aspect in order to figure out who is more likely to vote. Voting rates are substantially lower among single persons, blue-collar workers, unemployed and people outside the labor force, and among those with lower education levels and lower incomes. Conversely, voting is more frequent among married people or cohabitees, white-collar workers, the employed, the well educated, and those with higher incomes. Furthermore, voting rates are relatively low among the very young and the very old. In addition, foreign citizens and those who are born abroad are comparatively less inclined to vote.

Women vote to a slightly higher degree than men, and that difference becomes even bigger when other factors are taken into account, especially income. The relationships between other variables and likelihood to vote also depend on whether other variables are considered at the same time. The negative effects on the propensities to vote by being foreign-born or foreign citizens are reduced when controlling for sex, age, and civil status. But even after taking a wide set of factors into account, there are still considerable differences.

A more general conclusion is that higher turnout is associated with a more equal participation. This finding lends further support to the law of dispersion, formulated by Tingsten (1937). The decrease in voting that took place between 1994 and 2002 led to a more unequal voter turnout. This is because the decline in voting was more prominent in those groups where the voting rates were relatively low to begin with. However, turnout has increased again in the most recent elections. This increase has been greater within those groups that have a lower turnout. Hence, this has led to a more equal voter turnout. Still, it is worth noting that some differences in voting rates between different groups are larger now than they were at the beginning of the 1990s, e.g. by level of education and income. This further underlines the value of studying voting rates in different population groups even in countries with a high general turnout.

NOTES

1. Of course, to some extent this is simple arithmetic; at very high levels of turnout, no large population group can have a very low level of participation. However, the law formulated by Tingsten is to be seen more generally across different population groups of different sizes.

2. Even if the Electoral Participation Survey is a high-quality survey with a comparatively big sample size, it is limited in scope since it mainly contains register information. Other surveys provide richer material based on survey responses on questions related to elections and voting. A key data source for analyzing Swedish voter turnout is the Swedish National Election Studies. It has been conducted since 1956 in collaboration between Statistics Sweden and the University of Gothenburg. The sample size has varied over the years, but has usually been between 3,000 and 4,000. The main mode of data collection is through face-to-face interviews, but some information is also gathered from registers, and validated voting is retrieved from the electoral rolls (Oscarsson and Holmberg 2013).

3. From the 2014 elections and onwards, the elections to the Riksdag will take place on the second Sunday in September.

4. In municipal elections, equal voting rights for women and men were implemented in 1918.

5. If foreign citizens are included the share was 2.2 percent.
6. The estimate does not include Swedish citizens residing abroad, who are only entitled to vote in the elections to the Riksdag.
7. The distribution was: 6 percent nonvoters in all three elections, 6 percent voted in one election, 14 percent in two elections, and 74 percent voted in all three elections. The elections studied took place in 2002, 2006, and 2010. More detailed information is presented by Oscarsson and Holmberg (2013).
8. Democracy is defined by Blais as countries having a score of 1 or 2 on the Freedom House ratings of political rights in the year the election was held (Blais 2007).
9. Similar and other arguments against Franklin's hypothesis are presented by Blais (2007).
10. The figures refer to employed Swedish citizens 18–64 years of age.
11. The period of required residency varies depending on different factors, but in most cases you are required to have been resident in Sweden for at least five years.
12. The category unmarried includes divorced, widows, and widowers. In more recent years, married includes registered same-sex partners.

References

Aldrich, J. H., Montgomery, J. M., and Wood, W. (2011). "Turnout as a Habit," *Political Behaviour* 33: 535–63.

Bennulf, M. and Hedberg, P. (1999). "Utanför demokratin: Om det minskande valdeltagandets sociala och politiska rötter," in E. Amnå (ed.), *Valdeltagande i förändring*, SOU 1999:132. Stockholm: Fakta Info Direkt, 75–136.

Bhatti, Y. and Hansen, K. M. (2012a). "Leaving the Nest and the Social Act of Voting: Turnout among First-Time Voters," *Journal of Elections, Public Opinion and Parties* 22: 380–406.

Bhatti, Y. and Hansen, K. M. (2012b). "Retiring from Voting: Turnout among Senior Voters," *Journal of Elections, Public Opinion and Parties* 22: 479–500.

Bhatti, Y., Hansen, K. M., and Wass, H. (2012). "The Relationship between Age and Turnout: A Rollercoaster Ride," *Electoral Studies* 31: 588–93.

Blais, A. (2007). "Turnout in Elections," in R. J. Dalton and H. Klingemann (eds), *Political Behaviour*. Oxford: Oxford University Press, 621–35.

Blais, A. and Aarts, K. (2006). "Electoral Systems and Turnout," *Acta Politica* 41: 180–96.

Blais, A. and Dobrzynska, A. (1998). "Turnout in Electoral Democracies," *European Journal of Political Research* 33: 239–61.

Blais, A., Gidengil, E., Nevitte, N., and Nadeau, R. (2004). "Where Does Turnout Decline Come From?" *European Journal of Political Research* 43: 221–36.

Dahlberg, S., Oscarsson, H., and Öhrvall, R. (2008). *Förtida röstning i Sverige*. Gothenburg: University of Gothenburg.

Franklin, M. N. (2004). *Voter Turnout and the Dynamics of Electoral Competition in Established Democracies since 1945*. Cambridge: Cambridge University Press.

Hammar, T. (1979). *Det första invandrarvalet*. Stockholm: Liber Förlag.

Highton, B. (1997). "Easy Registration and Voter Turnout," *Journal of Politics* 59: 565–75.

Holmberg, S. and Oscarsson, H. (2004). *Väljare: Svenskt väljarbeteende under 50 år*. Stockholm: Norstedts Juridik.

IDEA (2002). *Voter Turnout Since 1945: A Global Report*. Stockholm: IDEA.

Lijphart, A. (1997). "Unequal Participation: Democracy's Unresolved Dilemma," *American Political Science Review* 91: 1–14.

Miller, W. E. and Shanks, M. (1996). *The New American Voter*. Cambridge, MA: Harvard University Press.

Neyman, J. (1934). "On the Two Different Aspects of the Representative Method: The Method of Stratified Sampling and the Method of Purposive Selection," *Journal of the Royal Statistical Society* 97: 558–625.

Öhrvall, R. (2006). "Invandrade och valdeltagande," in H. Bäck and M. Gilljam (eds), *Valets mekanismer*. Malmö: Liber, 61–78.

Öhrvall, R. (2012). *Svenskt valdeltagande under hundra år*. Stockholm: Statistics Sweden.

Oscarsson, H. (2001). "Mot ett lägre valdeltagande i kommunvalen?" in H. Oscarsson (ed.), *Skilda valdagar och vårval?* SOU 2001:65. Stockholm: Fritzes, 75–98.

Oscarsson, H. and Håkansson, N. (2001). "Val på våren?" in H. Oscarsson (ed.), *Skilda valdagar och vårval?* SOU 2001:65. Stockholm: Fritzes, 229–40.

Oscarsson, H. and Holmberg, S. (2013). *Nya svenska väljare*. Stockholm: Norsteds Juridik.

Persson, M. (2012). "Does Type of Education Affect Political Participation? Results from a Panel Survey of Swedish Adolescents," *Scandinavian Political Studies* 35: 198–221.

Persson, M. (2013). "Review Article: Education and Political Participation," *British Journal of Political Science*, FirstView Article, <http://journals.cambridge.org/action/displayAbstract?fromPage=online&aid=9072274&fileId=S0007123413000409>.

Persson, M., Wass, H., and Oscarsson, H. (2013). "The Generational Effect in Turnout in the Swedish General Elections, 1960–2010," *Scandinavian Political Studies* 36: 249–69.

Plutzer, E. (2002). "Becoming a Habitual Voter: Inertia, Resources, and Growth in Young Adulthood," *American Political Science Review* 96: 41–56.

Tingsten, H. (1937). *Political Behaviour*. London: P. S. King.

Verba, S. and Nie, N. H. (1972). *Participation in America: Political Democracy and Social Equality*. New York: Harper and Row.

Verba, S., Shlozman, K. L., and Brady, H. E. (1995). *Voice and Equality: Civic Voluntarism in American Politics*. Cambridge, MA: Harvard University Press.

Wass, H. (2007). "The Effects of Age, Generation and Period on Turnout in Finland 1975–2003," *Electoral Studies* 26: 648–59.

Westholm, A. and Teorell, J. (1999). "Att bestämma sig för att vara med och bestämma: Om varför vi röstar—allt mindre," in E. Amnå (ed.), *Valdeltagande i förändring*, SOU 1999:132. Stockholm: Fakta Info Direkt, 137–204.

Wolfinger, R. E. and Rosenstone, S. J. (1978). "The Effect of Registration Laws on Voter Turnout," *American Political Science Review* 72: 22–45.

Wolfinger, R. E. and Rosenstone, S. J. (1980). *Who Votes?* New Haven, CT: Yale University Press.

CHAPTER 18

THE NEVER-ENDING STORY OF CLASS VOTING IN SWEDEN

MARIA OSKARSON

EVEN though predictions of the demise of class voting have been around for some 40 years, class voting is still a viable characteristic of Swedish politics. Undoubtedly class voting has changed and weakened, but the story of class voting in Sweden has still not reached its end.

From a comparative perspective, class voting has been a characteristic trait of voting behavior in Sweden for as long as it has been studied. Already in 1937 Herbert Tingsten had stated the importance of class position in his book *Political Behaviour*, based on voting patterns in constituencies of different social composition (Tingsten 1937). In the seminal book *Electoral Behavior: A Comparative Handbook* (1974) edited by Richard Rose, Sweden is found to be the country where occupation has the strongest impact on partisanship (tie with Finland) (Rose 1974). In a recent comparative study of class voting in Europe, Sweden is found to still have the strongest class voting, in spite of a recent decrease (Jansen 2011).

This chapter presents a broad description of the development of class voting in Sweden. The ambition goes somewhat beyond simple description, however, and also presents and applies a wider frame for understanding the development of the relationship between class position and party choice. To establish this frame the chapter begins with a reflection on the theoretical basis for class voting.

A CONTEXTUAL FRAME FOR UNDERSTANDING CLASS VOTING

That the social position of a voter correlates with his or her party choice is one of the most long-lasting and well-documented facts in electoral research and political sociology (Alford 1963; Rose 1974). One explanation often presented understands class voting as an expression of class identification, derived through socialization in the family, the social surroundings, and at the workplace. In this view, class identification is closely related to party identification in the traditional sense, and basically politically "empty." Of course this is a valid conception of how individuals relate to politics, but as with party identification, this alignment between the social and the political does not come about by chance. It is formed in a certain political context. Once formed, it could be spread or upheld by mechanisms of socialization. The question then is how is the alignment between social groups and political parties formed from the beginning?

In 1967 Seymour Martin Lipset and Stein Rokkan introduced what has become known as the *social cleavage model* in the book *Party Systems and Voter Alignments* (Lipset and Rokkan 1967). The introductory chapter presents a theoretical foundation for the process through which groups, along a number of social cleavages anchored in a society's historical development, were aligned to political parties. The model states that four social cleavages resulting from historical processes in relation to the national and the industrial revolutions, respectively, have structured the party systems in the Western world. Depending on historical experiences and constitutional decisions at formative moments, combinations of one or more of the cleavages along religious lines (especially the Catholic church vs the state), center/periphery (nation state elites vs geographically peripheral elites), rural/urban (landowners vs industry), or class (employers vs workers) came into shaping the party systems at the time of democratization. Once groups along these social cleavage lines were aligned to the parties, the connection tended to remain through political socialization as well as through party strategies and organization. Even though the relation between social position and party choice has been studied from many different theoretical perspectives, the social cleavage model remains highly central (Nieuwbeerta 1995; Nieuwbeerta and Ultee 1999; Franklin et al. 1992; Knutsen 2007; Deegan-Krause 2007). This connection between people's social position and party choice tends to be more or less institutionalized in the party systems. The social cleavages of a society are in most cases reflected in the origin of the party systems (Lipset and Rokkan 1967).

A central point in the social cleavage model was that the party systems were not a mere reflection of the social cleavage structure. The alignment process could take different routes depending on the institutional context at certain points in the democratization process, and the parties once founded were actors seeking survival and thus had an interest in keeping the alignments to the voters. The parties were seen as actors defining and articulating the relevant political cleavages for the voters. This last point was further pronounced by Giovanni Sartori in his article "The Sociology of Parties: A Critical Review" in 1969, where he stated that "The party is not a 'consequence' of the class. Rather, and before, it is the class that receives its identity from the party" (Sartori 1969/1990; Przeworski and Sprague 1986; Bartolini and Mair 1990).

This political perspective, or "party choice thesis," states that the importance of social cleavages for party choice does not only depend on the nature or strength of the cleavages, but also on how the parties relate to the cleavages, and what policies they actually stand for (Oskarson 1994, 2005; Evans 2000; Evans and Tilley 2012; Jansen et al. 2012; Kriesi 1998). What this implies is quite simply that if there is no party that could be perceived as representing the policy interests of a certain group better than other parties, it is less likely that the group will vote in a coherent pattern. Cleavage voting in this perspective refers to the interplay between social structural groups and political parties, or in Lipset and Rokkan's terminology "Social Cleavages and Political Alignments" (Lipset and Rokkan 1990 [1967]).

A political perspective on cleavage voting also links the study of cleavage voting to the discussion about how the working conditions of parties and party strategies have changed. The parties are said to be transforming from "mass parties" mobilizing along cleavage lines, to "catch-all" or "cartel" parties striving to mobilize all groups in society (Kitschelt 1994; Kirchheimer 1997 [1966]; Katz and Mair 1997; Enyedi and Deegan-Krause 2010). Of course these trends are interrelated—if voters are less inclined to vote in accordance with social position, the rational response for parties is to tune down the group appeal and rather appeal to the "median voter" (Downs 1957).

However, class voting cannot be understood only from the structural aspect of social cleavages and party systems. In order to fully understand the linkage between class position and party preference we also have to consider the mechanisms at the individual level, forming the rationale for a person to vote in accordance with her class position. Apart from the criteria of an existing social cleavage and an organization representing positions along this cleavage, the political alignment of social cleavages also has to have a conscious and normative component (Bartolini and Mair 1990; Oskarson 1994). The individual should somehow identify herself with the position, and be guided by it when it comes to political considerations. If these criteria are not fulfilled, the correlation between class position and party preference would either be spurious or simply habitual and even unconscious.

The discussion above has stated that class voting includes several central aspects—structural as well as individual; social as well as political—as illustrated in Figure 18.1.

	Society	Politics
Structural level	Class structure	Party system
Individual level	Class identification	Perception of class interests / ideology

FIGURE 18.1 A contextual frame of analysis for class voting.

In order to understand the nature and development of class voting, ideally all aspects should be considered—the class structure and its composition; how clearly and distinctively the party system represents the social structure; the degree and patterns of class identification; and whether or how this is reflected in perception of class interests and ideology. From this perspective, these four aspects explain why class voting differs between different countries or over time. Furthermore, change in any of these aspects would change the level of class voting.

In the next section, the characteristics and development of each aspect of Swedish class voting will be discussed. The chapter continues with a general description of the trends in the correlation between individuals' class position and party choice. It then proceeds with a consideration of how the different aspects outlined in Figure 18.1 provide an understanding about the development of class voting in Sweden.

DEVELOPMENT OF CLASS VOTING IN SWEDEN

Even though class voting is not as strong in Sweden today as it was in the 1930s, 1940s, and 1950s, it still lingers on with a persistence that is among the strongest in the Western democratic world.[1]

The question of how to measure the relation between social position and party choice has been highly debated. The most widely used measure was for a long time the Alford index of class voting, a simple index indicating the proportion of the working class voting for left parties minus the proportion of the middle class voting left (Alford 1962; Nieuwbeerta 1995; Nieuwbeerta and Ultee 1999; Manza 1995). For many years this index was more or less the definition of class voting. Even if we accept the crudeness in applying dichotomous variables for both class and party vote, one serious drawback remains. The Alford index does not take into account general shifts in party popularity, and thus risks mixing changes in the correlation between class and vote with changes in party popularity. However, for ease of interpretation and as an introductory description of the development Figure 18.2 presents the Alford index for the period 1956–2010.

Sometimes decrease in class voting is considered a quite recent phenomenon in Swedish, or for that matter, western European voting. This is a description in need of some correction. The largest decrease actually occurred in the mid-1960s, some fifty years ago. According to an analysis by Bo Särlvik, the Social Democrats' vote was approximately 75 percent drawn from the working class for the entire period between 1936 and 1956, whilst the elections of 1964 and 1968 resulted in a significant increase of middle-class votes without losing strong support among the working class, thereby compensating for the changing social composition due to decrease of the working-class proportion (Särlvik 1974). In other words, the decrease of class voting in terms of the difference in left voting between the working class and the middle class took its start in the mid-1960s.

A quite steep decrease occurred between 1960 and 1970. Apart from the election of 1973, the index show a quite steady level of class voting from 1964 up until 1991, when it clearly

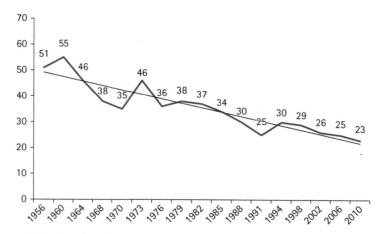

FIGURE 18.2 Alford's index of class voting, 1956–2010.

Source: Swedish National Election studies 1956–2010. Alford's index is the difference in left voting (Left Party and Social Democrats) between the working class and the middle class. The regression equation is y=-1,71x+50,93. R^2=0,84.

decreased, only to regain some ground in the following election of 1998. In the latest elections the tendency to a slight decrease has continued. The trend line in the diagram actually shows a quite steady decline by an average of 1.7 percentage points between every two elections.

Of course the diagram is oversimplified.[2] The divide between working class and middle class could perhaps rather be stated "the working class vs all other groups" since the homogeneity of the middle class could well be questioned. The definition of the working class makes more sense here, since it follows the organizational divide in the Swedish labor market and incorporates groups generally organized under the LO trade organization, which in turn has a close relation with the Social Democratic Party. Also, to collapse the Swedish party system into two blocs is doubtful. Furthermore, by employing these simple dichotomies, compositional effects are not accounted for, neither within the classes nor within the party system.

EFFECTS OF CHANGES IN SOCIAL COMPOSITION

Parties closely linked to social groups are quite vulnerable to changes in the social structure. If a party's core groups decrease in size, this might be directly reflected in the vote share of the party, unless it manages to attract new voter groups. If, on the other hand, the party does succeed in attracting new groups, the risk is that the "core voters" no longer recognize the party and thus abandon it. This is what is sometimes labeled "the Electoral Dilemma" (Przeworski and Sprague 1986). In Sweden the electoral dilemma has been highly present.

In the 1950s Sweden was at the height of industrialism. Even though the welfare state had taken on some of its basic traits, the welfare service sector was still small. Towards the end of the 1960s the welfare service sector started to expand, not least by providing employment for women in the public sector. There was a rapid expansion of higher education, and increasingly higher specialization and qualifications in the labor market, transforming Sweden from an industrial society to the knowledge society of today.

The expansion of the middle layers, not least in the public sector, has been central for the change in the simple 2x2 conception of class voting, as this group has tended to quite evenly split between the left and right. For the more traditional "core groups" the class voting pattern has been more stable, as depicted in Figure 18.3, where Social Democratic voting amongst industrial workers, voting for the agrarian Center Party among farmers, and voting for the Conservative Party amongst higher professionals are illustrated.

Support for the Social Democratic Party among industrial workers has decreased over the period, not least since the last peak in 1994. As this group is also decreasing in size, industrial workers are definitely not a sufficient base for the Social Democratic Party. In the election of 2010 only 13 percent of the total support for the Social Democrats came from the shrinking industrial working class, compared to 35 percent in 1976. At the same time, the Social Democratic Party has retained quite steady support among the lower and middle salariat, two groups increasing in size on the Swedish labor market. In the election of 2010 these groups actually provided 15 and 24 percent respectively to

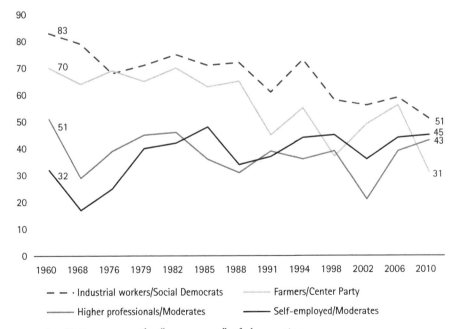

FIGURE 18.3 Voting among the "core groups" of class voting.

Source: SNES surveys. Note that the election years of 1956, 1964, 1970, and 1973 are missing. The entries for the years 1976–2010 is from the report Forsberg et al. (2011). The entries for 1960 and 1968 is from Oskarson (1994).

the overall vote for the Social Democrats, as compared to 8 and 15 percent respectively in 1976 (Holmberg and Oscarsson 2004; Oscarsson and Holmberg 2013).

Very much the same decreasing trend in support from the traditional core groups is found for the agrarian Center Party. Up until the election of 1988, between 60 and 70 percent of the farmers voted for the Center Party, but since then the support has decreased. As the farmers are a small and shrinking group, only a small minority of Center Party voters today are occupied in farming. Today the Center Party voters are mainly middle class outside the agriculture sector. Higher professionals on the other hand show quite steady support for the Moderate Party. In spite of some temporal variations, a base level of around 40 percent is clearly visible in Figure 18.3. Self-employed and smaller businessmen have finally evolved into a strong group for the Moderate Party, with a support of around 40 percent in every election since 1979.

Other important compositional changes are of course the entry of women into the labor market, as well as the expansion of the public sector. In the 1980s there was a discussion of the public/private split as an emerging cleavage crosscutting the class cleavage (Holmberg and Gilljam 1987; Holmberg and Oscarsson 2004). This is mainly relevant in the salariat, where public-employed tend to vote "left" to a slightly higher degree than those in private employment. The tendency to a public/private split is also an important partial explanation for the gender gap in Swedish politics, where women tend to vote left to a somewhat higher degree than men and to vote for the conservative Moderate Party to a clearly lower degree than men, to a degree reflecting the gender composition of the public and private sectors (Oscarsson and Holmberg 2013; Oskarson and Wängnerud 1995; Oskarson 1994; Holmberg 1981).

Many of the compositional changes in the class structure affect young people the most. They take up the "new" occupations on the labor market, whilst older generations to a higher degree reflect the labor market of previous decades. Also, during the last decades we have witnessed an increase in education, where younger generations tend to have a higher educational level both in terms of years and as a proportion of a cohort that actually have more than compulsory education. This is probably an important explanation behind the clear generational pattern that can be found in class voting, where every new generation of voters follows the class voting pattern to a lower degree than the proceeding generation (Oskarson 1994; Oscarsson and Holmberg 2013).

Another aspect of changes in the social composition is the actual living conditions linked to different class positions and how they differ. In the comparative study of Paul Nieuwbeerta the conclusion is that changes in class voting within countries over time are linked to improvement in the standard of living, but not to income differences or the size of the manual working class. Union density showed various results, mainly due to different country-specific traits in labor organization (Nieuwbeerta 1995). For the Swedish part it is sometimes claimed that improved standard of living and decreasing class differences in actual living conditions are what lie behind the decreasing class voting. The first factor finds support in Nieuwbeerta's analyses, whilst a decrease in economic inequality is more dubious as an explanation for decreasing class voting.

CLASS IDENTIFICATION

A key factor for understanding the mechanisms behind class voting is how the voter perceives her own social position and whether she identifies with her class. Class identification is a core concept in political sociology, and is generally found to capture something else, or maybe something more, than "objective" class position, based on labor market position (Hout 2008; Evans and Kelley 2004; Andersen and Curtis 2012; Savage and Warde 2010). It refers mainly to a cognitive orientation towards the social position, and is not necessarily linked to a conception of shared interests or ideology. The degree to which class identification is politicized is an empirical question in its own sense. As discussed in the introduction, class identification could be perceived more or less in the same way as party identification, as something to which you are socialized into but without any deeper political foundation. This kind of socially rather than politically based identifications could be expected to weaken and dealign when the formative moments of the linkage are several generations back. However, class identification could also be linked to a perception of shared interests and thus give rise to a political understanding of class belonging in the present. In Sweden the link between class and party identification is generally close, due to the clear left–right dimension in the party system based on the class cleavage (Petersson 1982). However, the degree to which they correlate should and will be seen as an empirical question here.

The concept of class identification is still a relevant concept in the Swedish context. In a survey conducted in 2008, sociologists Mattias Bengtsson and Tomas Berglund found that 24 percent of the respondents identified themselves as working class, 51 percent as middle class, and 17 percent as upper middle class. Of those in working-class occupations, 44 percent identified as working class, 43 percent as middle class, and only 7 percent as upper middle class. In "intermediate occupations" 20 percent identified as working class, 58 percent as middle class, and 13 percent as upper middle class. Among professionals only 4 percent identified themselves as working class and 32 percent as upper middle class (Bengtsson and Berglund 2010). This means that not only is the concept of class identification relevant in Sweden; it also relates clearly to position on the labor market. However, it is not only labor market position that matters for the individual's class identification. Family background and household composition is also relevant for class identification, as is shown by Bengtsson and Berglund (2010) as well as Karlsson (2005), Oskarson (1994), and Holmberg (1981). For the working class, working-class identification is also found to be closely linked to union membership. There is as well a generational pattern in the sense that working-class identification is considerable higher, and more strongly linked to actual class position, among earlier generations, whilst middle-class identification is more independent of birth cohort (Oskarson 1994). In more longitudinal analyses, the relation of class identification to position on the labor market is quite stable. Oskarson (1994) found decreasing working-class identification in working-class positions on the labor market between 1968 and 1988, whilst the middle-class identification among those occupied in middle-class positions remained more or less the same (Oskarson 1994). Lena Karlsson has studied class identification for the period between the years 1993 and 2000 and finds steady, if not strengthened, associations between the position on the labor market and class identification (Karlsson 2005).

When it comes to the importance of class identification for class voting, it is clear that it is central. To identify in line with the actual class position re-enforces the probability of voting in accordance with your class position, whilst "cross-class identification" undermines the class voting pattern (Oskarson 1994; Karlsson 2005). The link between actual position on the labor market and class identification is accordingly a relevant explanatory factor for decreasing class voting. Factors such as intergenerational social mobility, dual-income households with heterogeneous class positions, and decreasing union membership all serve to explain why the linkage between class position and party vote has decreased, not the least within the working class.

ATTITUDES AND IDEOLOGY

Attitudes and ideology are clearly linked to party choice in Sweden and elsewhere (Oscarsson and Holmberg 2013; Thomassen 2005). That left–right attitudes are strong predictors for party choice is discussed in Henrik Oscarsson's chapter in the present volume. In a longitudinal analysis Henrik Oscarsson and Sören Holmberg find the highest correlations between left–right position and party choice in the period 1979–88. A slight increase in the correlation was found between the elections of 2006 and 2010 (Oscarsson and Holmberg 2013).

However, strong links between ideology or political attitudes and party choice do not necessarily imply that issue attitudes and/or ideological orientations have replaced class position as an important cue or antecedent for party choice, as is sometimes assumed (Knutsen and Kumlin 2005). In the political perspective of class voting applied here, attitudes and ideological orientation could be seen as at least potentially rooted in class positions and class identity. This is really inherent in the general understanding of how class matters for politics, ever since *The Political Man* by Lipset (1981 [1960]) or *The American Voter* by Campbell et al. (1960). The class differences in political orientations are seen as reflecting different material interests concerning inequality and redistribution, which lead voters to support different parties, pursuing different policy solutions on these matters. In spite of the face validity of this model, it has more rarely been empirically employed.

There are however some exceptions relevant for the Swedish case (Svallfors 2006; Brooks and Svallfors 2010). For economic left–right issues as well as issues related to the welfare state there are quite clear class differences in Sweden (Bengtsson et al. 2013; Svallfors 2006; Brooks and Svallfors 2010). In other issue areas, such as immigration or the environment, the class differences are slightly smaller and also found to be more related to education than labor market position. There is more limited longitudinal research on how the association between class position and ideological orientations has evolved over time, and accordingly to what degree a weakening link between class position and ideology lies behind the decrease in class voting. Maria Oskarson finds a decrease in the ideological linkage between class position, class identification, and party choice for the period 1968 to 1988 (Oskarson 1994). In the most recent book from the Swedish Election Study Program, Henrik Oscarsson and Sören Holmberg present a very complex causal model of party choice which considers both the direct and indirect effects (through ideology and other factors) of "socioeconomy" on the bloc vote for the entire period 1985–2010. The conclusion is that the total effect of socioeconomic factors actually is stronger in 2010 than in 1985. The factor "socioeconomy" in this analysis does however include multiple indicators and should not be interpreted as only class position (Oscarsson and Holmberg 2013).

Party System Polarization

Class voting cannot be understood exclusively from the side of the voters or the demand side as it is often labeled. In order to understand the alignment between individuals, social groups, and parties we also have to consider what alternatives the party system actually offers to voters, and how the parties—that is the "supply side"—relate to the class cleavage Also here two perspectives could be applied. If we understand the class–party link as mainly a question of social identification rather than representation of interests, ideology, and party positions, the link could be conceived of as direct references or pleas to different groups. The perspective generally applied to understanding the link between individuals in different class positions and parties—the political choice perspective—focuses on ideology and policy positions, and the distinctiveness between parties in class-relevant policy positions, i.e. left–right polarization in the party system (Evans and Tilley 2012, 2011; Jansen 2011; Jansen et al. 2012; Elff 2007, 2009; Oskarson 2005; Evans 2000). Geoffrey Evans and James Tilley conclude that ideological convergence on the left–right dimension between the main parties is the main explanation for decrease in British class voting (Evans and Tilley 2012, 2011). In a comparative study Giedo Jansen, Geoffrey Evans, and Nan Dirk de Graaf conclude that it is not primarily the left–right positions of left-wing parties that matter for the level of class voting, but the left–right polarization in the full party system (Jansen et al. 2012). The same conclusion is reached in the more limited comparative analysis presented in the book *The European Voter* from 2005 (Oskarson 2005; Thomassen 2005). Sweden is included in these comparative studies and does not deviate from the general pattern.

Another aspect of how development in the party system might affect the alignment between class position and party choice is presented in the book *Class Politics and the Radical Right* (2013) edited by Jens Rydgren. The book departs from the findings that populist right parties in Europe attract strong support from among the working class. For Sweden, Oskarson and Demker show in their chapter "Another Kind of Class Voting" that one explanation for the strong working-class support for the populist-right Sweden Democrats is that as the left–right distinction between the two major parties (Social Democrats and Moderate Party) has decreased, it leaves more room for other ideological dimensions, such as the authoritarian–libertarian dimension, to be politicized (Oskarson and Demker 2013). And people in working-class positions with generally lower education tend to lean toward the authoritarian end more than other groups (Bengtsson et al. 2013; Berglund and Oskarson 2010).

Conclusion

In spite of repeated claims made about the demise of class voting, in Sweden class voting still lingers on. People occupied in blue-collar occupations or unqualified service occupations still vote for the left parties to a much higher degree than managers or professionals do. It is still too early to abandon class voting as an important factor behind party choice in Sweden. For the last decades the levels of class voting in Sweden has actually been quite stable, and considerably higher than in most comparable countries. Even though structural changes and generational replacement have weakened and blurred the ties between class position and voting, the Swedish party system has been clearly aligned to the class cleavage in Sweden, structuring material interests and political attitudes along the ideological left–right dimension. Whether class voting will be a continuing story for Swedish voting behavior depends to a large degree on whether this alignment will be maintained and kept vital also in the postindustrial knowledge society characterizing Sweden in the twenty-first century.

Notes

1. Analyses of class voting in Sweden have mainly been based on the Swedish National Election Studies (SNES) commencing in 1956 and covering all general elections since then. The standards for coding occupation as well as for construction of class schemes have changed over time. For 1956–66 an older standard was used. For the studies dated 1968–2006, a coding scheme and class scheme were constructed by Bo Särlvik and Olof Peterson, along much the same theoretical foundations as those behind the Goldthorpe scheme. Since the study in 2006, SNES has used ISCO codes for occupations and for example the European Socioeconomic Standard as a class scheme. A key based on occupational codes for moving between the class schemes used before and after 2006 has been constructed by Maria Oskarson (see Oskarson 2007).
2. Detailed analyses of class voting in Sweden are presented (in Swedish) in Holmberg (1981, 1984, 2000), Holmberg and Oscarsson (2004), Oscarsson and Holmberg (2008), and Oskarson (1994).

References

Alford, R. B. (1962). "A Suggested Index of the Association of Social Class and Voting," *Public Opinion Quarterly* 26: 417–25.

Alford, R. B. (1963). *Party and Society: The Anglo-American Democracies.* Westport: Greenwood Press.

Andersen, R. and Curtis, J. (2012). "The Polarizing Effect of Economic Inequality on Class Identification: Evidence from 44 Countries," *Research in Social Stratification and Mobility* 30: 129–41.

Bartolini, S. and Mair, P. (1990). *Identity, Electoral Competition and Electoral Availability: The Stabilization of European Electorates 1885–1995.* Cambridge: Cambridge University Press.

Bengtsson, M. and Berglund, T. (2010). "Social rörlighet och klassidentifikation," in M. Oskarson, M. Bengtsson, and T. Berglund (eds), *En fråga om klass: Levnadsförhållanden, livsstil, politik.* Malmö: Liber, 30–41.

Bengtsson, M., Berglund, T., and Oskarson, M. (2013). "Class and Ideological Orientations Revisited: An Exploration of Class-based Mechanisms," *British Journal of Sociology* 64: 691–716.

Berglund, T. and Oskarson, M. (2010). "Klass och ideologiska dimensioner," in M. Oskarson, M. Bengtsson, and T. Berglund (eds), *En fråga om klass: Levnadsförhålanden, livsstil, politik.* Malmö: Liber, 184–97.

Brooks, C. and Svallfors, S. (2010). "Why Does Class Matter? Policy Attitudes, Mechanisms, and the Case of the Nordic Countries," *Research in Social Stratification and Mobility* 28: 199–213.

Campbell, A., Converse, P. E., Miller, W. E., and Stokes, D. E. (1960). *The American Voter.* New York: Wiley.

Deegan-Krause, K. (2007). "New Dimensions of Political Cleavage," in R. J. Dalton and H.-D. Klingemann (eds), *The Oxford Handbook of Political Behavior.* Oxford: Oxford University Press, 538–56.

Downs, A. (1957). *An Economic Theory of Democracy.* New York: Harper & Row.

Elff, M. (2007). "Social Structure and Electoral Behaviour in Comparative Perspective: The Decline of Social Cleavages in Western Europe Revisitied," *Perspectives on Politics* 5: 277–94.

Elff, M. (2009). "Social Divisions, Party Positions and Electoral Behaviour," *Electoral Studies* 28: 297–308.

Enyedi, Z. and Deegan-Krause, K. (eds) (2010). *The Structure of Political Competition in Western Europe.* London: Routledge.

Evans, G. (2000). "The Continued Significance of Class Voting," *Annual Review of Political Science* 3 401–17.

Evans, G. and Tilley, J. (2011). "How Parties Shape Class Politics: Explaining the Decline of the Class Basis of Party Support," *British Journal of Political Science* 42: 137–61.

Evans, G. and Tilley, J. (2012). "The Depoliticization of Inequality and Redistribution: Explaining the Decline of Class Voting," *Journal of Politics* 74: 963–76.

Evans, M. D. R. and Kelley, J. (2004). "Subjective Social Location: Data from 21 Nations," *International Journal of Public Opinion Research* 16: 3–38.

Forsberg, M., Hedberg, P., and Oscarsson, H. (2011). "Väljarnas partier 1956–2010" [The Parties of the Voters 1956–2010], *Swedish National Election Surveys (SNES).* Gothenburg: Department of Political Science, University of Gothenburg.

Franklin, M. N., Mackie, T., and Valen, H. (eds) (1992). *Electoral Change: Responses to Evolving Social and Attitudinal Structures in Western Countries*. Cambridge: Cambridge University Press.

Holmberg, S. (1981). *Svenska väljare [Swedish Voters]*. Stockholm: Liber.

Holmberg, S. (1984). *Väljare i förändring*. Stockholm: Liber.

Holmberg, S. (2000). *Välja parti*. Stockholm: Norstedts Juridik.

Holmberg, S. and Gilljam, M. (1987). *Väljare och val i Sverige*. Stockholm: Bonniers.

Holmberg, S. and Oscarsson, H. (2004). *Väljare: Svenskt väljarbeteende under 50 år*. Stockholm: Norstedts juridik.

Hout, M. (2008). "How Class Works: Objective and Subjective Aspects of Class since the 1970s," in A. L. A. D. Conley (ed.), *Social Class: How Does It Work?* New York: Russell Sage Foundation, 25–64.

Jansen, G. (2011). *Social Cleavages and Political Choices: Large-Scale Comparisons of Social Class, Religion and Voting Behavior in Western Democracies*. Nijmegen: Radboud University of Nijmegen.

Jansen, G., Evans, G., and Graaf, N. D. D. (2012). "Class-Voting and Left-Right Party Positions: A Comparative Study of 15 Western Democracies, 1960–2005," *Social Science Research* 42: 376–400.

Karlsson, L. (2005). *Klasstillhörighetens subjektiva dimension: Klassidentitet, sociala attityder och fritidsvanor*. Umeå: Sociologiska institutionen, Umeå universitet.

Katz, R. S. and Mair, P. (1997). "Party Organization, Party Democracy, and the Emergence of the Cartel Party," in P. Mair (ed.), *Party System Change: Approaches and Interpretatations*. Oxford: Clarendon Press, 93–119.

Kirchheimer, O. (1997 [1966]). "The Catch-All Party," in P. Mair (ed.), *The West European Party System*. Oxford: Oxford University Press, 50–60. Originally published in J. Lapalombara and M. Weiner (1966), *Political Parties and Political Development*. Oxford: Oxford University Press, 177–200.

Kitschelt, H. (1994). *The Transformation of European Social Democracy*. Cambridge: Cambridge University Press.

Knutsen, O. (2007). "The Decline of Social Class?" in R. J. Dalton and H.-D. Klingemann (eds), *The Oxford Handbook of Political Behaviour*. Oxford: Oxford University Press, 457–80.

Knutsen, O. and Kumlin, S. (2005). "Value Orientations and Party Choice," in J. Thomassen (ed.), *European Voter: A Comparative Study of Modern Democracies*. Oxford: Oxford University Press, 125–66.

Kriesi, H. (1998). "The Transformation of Cleavage Politics: The 1997 Stein Rokkan Lecture," *European Journal of Political Research* 33: 165–85.

Lipset, S. M. (1981 [1960]). *The Political Man: The Social Bases of Politics*. Baltimore: Johns Hopkins University Press.

Lipset, S. M. and Rokkan, S. (eds) (1967). *Party Systems and Voter Alignments*. New York: Free Press.

Lipset, S. M. and Rokkan, S. (1990 [1967]). "Cleavage Structures, Party Systems, and Voter Alignments," in P. Mair (ed.), *The West European Party System*. Oxford: Oxford University Press, 91–111.

Manza, J., Michael, H., and Brooks, C. (1995). "Class Voting in Capitalist Democracies since World War II: Dealignment, Realignment, or Trendless Fluctuation?" *Annual Review of Sociology* 21: 137–62.

Nieuwbeerta, P. (1995). *The Democratic Class Struggle in Twenty Countries 1945–1990.* Amsterdam: Thesis Publishers.

Nieuwbeerta, P. and Ultee, W. (1999). "Class Voting in Western Industrialized Countries, 1945–1990: Systematizing and Testing Explanations," *European Journal of Electoral Research* 35: 123–60.

Oscarsson, H. and Holmberg, S. (2008). *Regeringsskifte: Väljarna och valet 2006.* Stockholm: Norstedts juridik.

Oscarsson, H. and Holmberg, S. (2013). *Nya svenska väljare.* Stockholm: Norstedts juridik.

Oskarson, M. (1994). *Klassröstning i Sverige: Rationalitet, lojalitet eller bara slentrian.* Stockholm: Nerenius & Santerus.

Oskarson, M. (2005). "Social Structure and Party Choice," in J. Thomassen (ed.), *The European Voter: A Comparative Study of Modern Democracies.* Oxford: Oxford University Press, 84–105.

Oskarson, M. (2007). "Att koda klass," Valundersökningarnas klasschema jämfört med European Socio-economic Classification (ESeC). Göteborg: SOM-institutet.

Oskarson, M. and Demker, M. (2013). "Another Kind of Class Voting: The Working-Class Sympathy for Sweden Democrats," in J. Rydgren (ed.), *Class Politics and the Radical Right.* London: Routledge, 173–89.

Oskarson, M. and Wängnerud, L. (1995). *Kvinnor som väljare och valda.* Lund: Studentlitteratur.

Petersson, O. (1982). "Klassidentifikation," in K. Asp (ed.), *Väljare Partier Massmedia.* Stockholm: Liber, 19–32.

Przeworski, A. and Sprague, J. (1986). *Paper Stones: A History of Electoral Socialism.* Chicago: University of Chicago Press.

Rose, R. (ed.) (1974). *Electoral Behavior: A Comparative Handbook.* New York and London: Free Press.

Särlvik, B. (1974). "Sweden: The Social Bases of the Parties in a Developmental Perspective," in R. Rose (ed.), *Electoral Behavior: A Comparative Handbook.* New York: Free Press, 371–434.

Sartori, G. (1990 [1969]). "The Sociology of Parties: A Critical Review," in P. Mair (ed.), *The West European Party System.* Oxford: Oxford University Press, 150–82.

Savage, M., Silva, E., and Warde, A. (2010). "Dis-identification and Class Identity," in E. Silva and A. Warde (eds), *Cultural Analysis and Bourdieu's Legacy: Settling Accounts.* New York: Routledge, 60–74.

Svallfors, S. (2006). *The Moral Economy of Class: Class and Attitude in Comparative Perspective.* Stanford: Stanford University Press.

Thomassen, J. (ed.) (2005). *The European Voter: A Comparative Study of Modern Democracies.* Oxford: Oxford University Press.

Tingsten, H. (1937). *Political Behaviour: Studies in Electoral Statistics.* Stockholm: P. S. King & Son.

CHAPTER 19

....

ISSUE VOTING STRUCTURED BY LEFT–RIGHT IDEOLOGY

....

HENRIK OSCARSSON AND SÖREN HOLMBERG

IN most normative models of representative democracy, issue voting is conceived as positive: parties' policy proposals should matter for voters on election day. In a representative party-based democracy, voters are supposed to support parties based mainly on their policy positions. Policies and issues should be the centerpiece of election campaigns. Elections are fought over issues that voters, parties, and leaders think are important. Consequently, a well-working representative democracy is a system where elections produce a high degree of issue congruency between voters and parties (Holmberg 2011; Rosema et al. 2011).

The main focus in this chapter is to analyze to what extent issues—parties' policy positions and voters' issue standpoints—matter for voting behavior in Sweden. Is issue voting becoming more important over time? How well can voters' attitudes on political issues explain party choice? To what extent are voters' issue standpoints structured by stable ideological predispositions? We summarize the findings from systematic analyses of the role of issues and ideology on Swedish voting behavior for the past six decades.

IDEOLOGICAL LEFT–RIGHT VOTING

....

In comparative analyses, the Swedish party system stands out as one of the most unidimensional systems in the world. In fact, it comes close to being the real-life replica of the simplified model of a multi-party system most students of political science know from Anthony Downs' classic book *An Economic Theory of Democracy*. A traditional left–right dimension has been structuring party competition and voting behavior in Sweden since at least the 1880s, and it is still overwhelmingly dominant in explanations of political change. The mental representation of parties lined up from left to right along a single continuum is predominant also among younger generations. Left–right ideological predispositions keep bringing stability, order, and congruence to political attitudes and behavior, perhaps more so than in any other political system (Dahlberg and Oscarsson 2006; Dahlberg 2009; Oscarsson 1998; Bengtsson et al. 2013; Granberg and Holmberg 1988).

The covariation between left–right orientation and party choice has always been strong in Sweden, and there is little change over time. According to SNES, the correlation between voters' self-placements along an eleven-point left–right scale (0–10) and party choice has varied between eta=.71–.77 in the period 1979–2010. The strong relationship means that most opinion changes, party switching, and government turnovers can be explained by the parties' positioning and maneuverings along the left–right dimension—the "super-issue" of Swedish election campaigns (Oscarsson and Holmberg 2013).

Consequently, ideological cycles—trends and shifts towards left or right—are fundamental to understanding political change in Sweden. Here, the most intriguing in a forty-year perspective is the clear opinion shift from the left to the right that has taken place in the electorate. Figure 19.1 shows the development of the proportion of Swedish voters that place themselves to the left of center (0–4) or to right of the center (6–10) in the period 1968–2010. In 1968, 43 percent of the voters had a left-leaning ideological identification and only 31 percent positioned themselves to the right of center. Forty years later, in 2010, the picture was reversed, with 47 percent right-leaners and 34 percent left-leaners. In 2010 the Swedish voters were as much right-leaning as they were

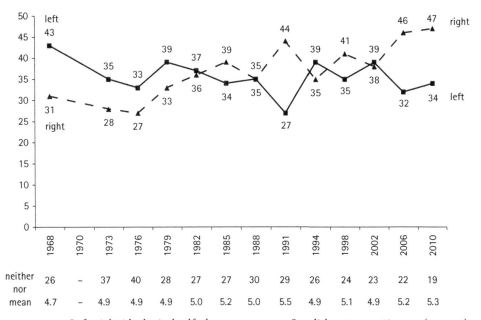

FIGURE 19.1 Left–right ideological self-placement among Swedish voters, 1968–2010 (percent).

Note: Results come from the Swedish National Election Studies 1968–2010 and are based on respondents' self-placements on an eleven-point left–right scale from 0 "far to the left" to 10 "far to the right" with a center point 5 "neither left nor right." The numbers of "don't know" responses vary between 3–10 percent and are not included in the analyses.

left-leaning in 1968. Hence, in this period, there has been an apparent ideological shift to the right among Swedish voters. Consequently, the electoral fortunes of left-wing parties in general, and the Social Democratic party in particular, have declined over time. The slow and gradual rightward spin of the political turntable is visible in its consequences for coalition building, party collaboration, and government turnovers.

Interestingly, the proportion of the electorate that position themselves in the center of the left–right dimension has decreased over time. In 2010 only 19 percent of the voters identified themselves as "neither left nor right." And the proportion of "don't knows" (3–10 percent) showed no signs of increasing. Left and right are still functioning concepts in the mindset of Swedish voters. The old ideological left–right dimension is still very much alive. Since the Swedish election studies are designed as panels between elections, we know that there is a high degree of stability in ideological left–right orientations: the panel stability of voters' left–right self-placements averages at a high r=.75, and high levels of panel stability are also found among younger cohorts. Left–right identifications are being effectively reproduced among the young. Therefore, we do not foresee any dramatic change in the standing of the left–right dimension in Swedish politics.

The main reason is that, although the left–right distinction is constantly being deemed outdated and obsolete, no other ideological compass or heuristic tool that is as effective seems to exist. The spatial metaphor is reinvented and reproduced as a useful tool of communicating between citizens and elites. Most scholars agree that the meaning of the labels "left" and "right" is slowly changing as it is complemented with new ideological dimensions. The left–right dimension in Sweden has been so dominant that it has had a great tendency to absorb new rivals: emerging political issues—such as euro-skepticism, gender equality, green values, and nuclear energy—have started out as oblique dimensions in their own right, but have all ended up more strongly correlated, and thus more aligned with, the "imperialist" left–right dimension (Oscarsson 1998). The absorptive power of the spatial distinction is exceptional in the Swedish case.

The idea of decreasing ideological distances between parties over time, and whether there is an ongoing depolarization in the Swedish party system, is under constant scrutiny and vivid debate. Different data produce different answers to the question of polarization. Analyses of party manifestoes, voters' emotional attachment to parties, and roll calls all tell somewhat different stories about the development of the degree of party system polarization. However, according to Swedish voters, the relative ideological left–right distance between the Social Democrats and the Conservatives was perceived to be larger in the 1970s when our time series started (see Figure 19.2) than in more recent elections. The converging tendencies are clearly visible in the 2006 and 2010 elections. If one uses this way of measuring the degree of polarization—in the eyes of the voters—there is a weak tendency toward left–right depolarization, at least when it comes to the two main political alternatives in Swedish politics. Perceptions of voters may, as always, be more or less correct, but at the end of the day it is voter perceptions of the reality that we believe matter the most for explaining political behavior at the polls.

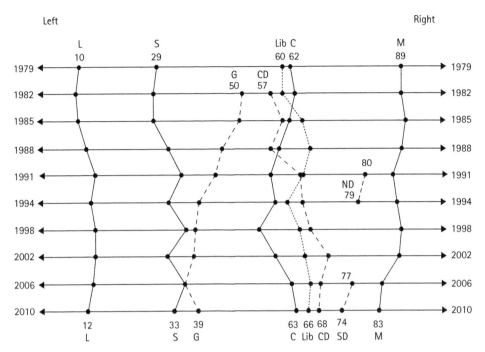

FIGURE 19.2 Voters' perceptions of Swedish parties' average left–right positions, 1979–2010 (means).

> *Note*: Data are from Swedish National Election Studies 1979–2010. All eligible party voters are included in the analysis. The scale runs from 0 "far to the left" to 10 "far to the right" with a mid-point 5 "neither left nor right." Parties' average positions are multiplied by 10 to avoid decimals. V = Left Party, S = Social Democrats, MP = Greens, C = Center Party, FP = Liberals, KD = Christian Democrats, M = Conservatives, NYD = New Democracy, SD = Sweden Democrats.

The classic five-party system survived much longer in Sweden than in other Nordic countries. However, since the late 1980s the party system has developed from a five- to a seven-or-eight-party system, as the Left Socialist, Social Democratic, Center Agrarian, Liberal, and Conservative parties have been complemented with Green, Christian Democratic, and populist parties (Bengtsson et al. 2013). The Swedish electorate has had a clear and quite stable perception of the left–right orderings of the parties along the dimension (see Figure 19.2).

The new parties have been formed on the basis of new and conflicting political dimensions, but they have also eventually come to find a distinct place in the left–right ordering to which Swedish voters are so accustomed. The Green Environmental Party started out in the very center of Swedish politics but has gradually moved to the left in the eyes of the voters. And the Christian Democrats were perceived as a center party in the early 1980s but are now farther to the right in the continuum. The populist party New Democracy was firmly perceived to be a right-wing party in the period 1991–4. And the most recent party in the Swedish Riksdag, the anti-immigrant Sweden Democrats, is also positioned clearly to the right by most Swedish voters.

It is obvious that the tendency for a "two-party system within the multi-party system" has been stronger after the forming of the Alliance for Sweden in 2004—an electoral coalition between the Center Party, Liberal Party, Christian Democrats, and the Conservative Party. In the two elections in 2006 and 2010, the four Alliance parties have moved closer to each other while the Green Party has moved closer to the Social Democrats and the Left Party. This tendency toward a stronger bloc division is also visible in trends on what government coalitions voters prefer after the election. The proportion of voters that would prefer a government that includes parties from both blocs was down to only 13 percent in the election of 2010. Whether a strong bloc division will linger in Swedish politics also after 2014 remains to be seen. With eight parties in the parliament, of whom several are close to the 4 percent threshold, the future of the Swedish party system is unclear.

THE EVOLUTION OF ISSUE VOTING

If you let Swedish voters speak for themselves, issues are becoming increasingly important as justifications for their party choice. The proportion of respondents in the Swedish National Election Studies that refer to concrete and specific political issues when asked to justify their choice of party is higher today than 20 years ago. Responses to open-ended questions about the rationale behind the party choice are of course infused with post-rationalization and social satisficing effects. But such self-reported motivations about the prominence of issues are not unimportant given our normative reference point.

Modernization theory predicts a simultaneous decline over time in social group-based voting and an increase in issue voting (Thomassen 2005). Weakening party identification and cognitive mobilization will make individuals able to form opinions on political issues more independently from interest groups and parties. An increased social mobility will pave the way for more electoral mobility as fewer voters use their party choice to manifest group belongings. The party choice gradually becomes more of a real choice between alternatives. Competition between parties will in turn be more issue-oriented as class struggle is replaced with an ideological struggle and a battle of campaign agendas. As a result, issue voting will become more important over time.

In the period 1950–80 the expectations of Modernization theory were met in the case of Sweden. To begin with, the strong class voting in the 1950s and the early 1960s was not accompanied by strong issue voting. There was a relatively weak relationship between Swedish voters' attitudes towards specific political issues and voting, as a large share of voters habitually supported parties whose policies aligned with their own social class or occupational status. However, as class voting declined in the 1960s and 1970s, the dealigned voter's issue standpoints became increasingly correlated with party choice. Results in Figure 19.3 illustrate the rising importance of issues in Swedish elections in the early period.

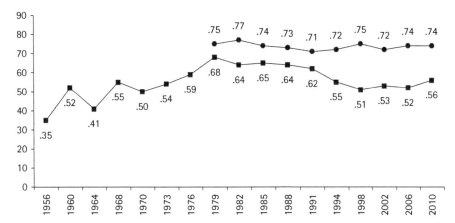

FIGURE 19.3 Ideological left–right voting in Swedish elections, 1956–2010. Correlations between left–right issues and party choice (mean eta) and left–right self-placements and party choice (eta).

Note: The results are mean etas based on analyses of variance treating party voting groups (5 to 8 parties) as the independent variable and three left–right issue questions with the strongest relationship to party choice as the dependent variables. The left–right issue questions are not exactly the same throughout the years.

However, the Swedish record on issue voting was set already in 1979–82, and that is now more than thirty years ago. Issue voting peaked in the period 1979–88. At that time, there were still lively political discussions of socialist reforms such as socialization, state ownership of banks, and wage earners' funds (Gilljam 1988). Attitudes on left–right issues discriminated effectively between groups of party sympathizers. As in many other countries, an ideological depolarization followed after the end of the Cold War and the fall of the Berlin Wall. In Sweden, one effect was a decreased correlation between classic left–right issue position and party choice. The overall strength of issue voting declined in the early 1990s, since many of the new political issues and issue dimensions—such as internationalism, immigration/integration, green ideology, Christian values, and gender equality—still are comparably weakly correlated to party choice in comparison with traditional social and economic left–right issues. The 2010 election may be the start of a new spring for left–right issue voting, as the SNES reveals an increasing correlation between attitudes on left–right issues and party choice. The left–right divide in Swedish politics has become more important, not less important, in recent elections.

FROM IDEOLOGY TO ISSUES

The relationship between voters' subjective left–right placements and party choice has, as already said, always been very strong in Sweden. An interpretation of this strong association is that the discussions that take place during Swedish elections have been effective in activating values and beliefs associated with left–right ideology. Issue congruency between voters and parties can also be regarded as a positive outcome of elections: voters have successfully matched their own attitudes with the parties' policies. Election campaigns play an important role in that political preferences have been shown to be more structured and aligned with left–right orientations during election years than between election years.

Voter preferences on concrete political issues that are on the political agenda should preferably be embedded firmly in stable long-term beliefs and ideological predispositions. The typical understanding in contemporary electoral research is that voters' left–right ideology is a stable predisposition or orientation that causally precedes attitudes towards more concrete political issues and campaign issues. Ideology—such as left–right orientations—serves as a heuristic cost-saving device that makes it possible for voters to form opinions about political issues and parties' policies (Aardal and van Wijnen 2005). Voters' manifest attitudes towards particular concrete policy proposals—such as "lower taxes" or "accept fewer immigrants"—are assumed to be derived from more stable latent values or belief systems. Or, in Anthony Downs' own words, ideological orientations are used as "yardsticks" for developing attitudes on specific issues (Downs 1957).

The correlation between issue attitudes and party choice can be analyzed extensively with data from the Swedish National Election Study. The SNES 2010 study included more than forty items on voters' attitudes towards specific policy proposals (Oscarsson and Holmberg 2013). Results illustrate how important left–right ideology is in explanations of party choice. The top six policy proposals that display the strongest association (eta>.50) with party choice were all closely related to the traditional left–right dimension such as state intervention, tax levels, public vs private welfare service, and the size of the public sector. More precisely, proposals such as "sell off state owned business and utilities to private interests," "abolish the tax reduction for domestic and domestic-related services," and "increase the proportion of health care run by private interests" displayed the highest correlations. Another set of classic left–right issues also showed high correlations with party choice (etas just below .50), such as "cut taxes," "reduce social benefits," and "reduce the size of the public sector." Right-wing voters are much more positive than left-wing voters to policy proposals about a strengthened market economy, privatization, and a reduced public sector.

Issues that represent competing dimensions of ideological predispositions display a much lower correlation with party choice. However, they are not unimportant if you want to give the full picture of issue voting in the Swedish context. Using dimensional analysis techniques, such as factor analysis, scholars have repeatedly identified a set of latent issue dimensions that serve to structure voters' attitudes on particular issues (Holmberg and Oscarsson 2004; Petersson 1977; Holmberg 1981). The results serve to structure also the analyses of the impact of issues on party choice. In past analyses, up to nine different issue dimensions have been included (Oscarsson and Holmberg 2013). The party voters' positions along the nine dimensions are shown in Figure 19.4.

The analysis serves as a snapshot illustrating the conflict structure of the Swedish party system. Results show convincingly that there are two issue dimensions that

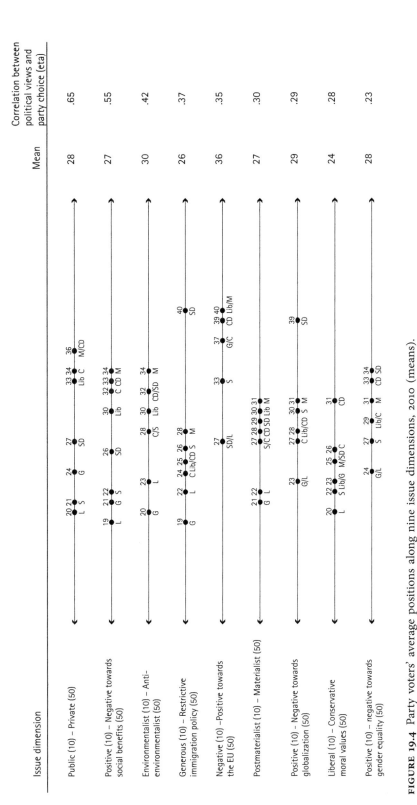

FIGURE 19.4 Party voters' average positions along nine issue dimensions, 2010 (means).

Note: Results are from SNES 2010. L = Left, S = Social Democrats, G = Greens, C = Center, Lib = Liberals, CD = Christian Democrats, C = Conservatives, SD = Sweden Democrats.

dominate the structuring of party choice in Sweden, and both are closely related to left–right orientations: the private–public dimension (eta=.65) and the welfare state dimension (eta=.55). Both issue dimensions show a similar line-up of parties from left to right; the only difference is that Green Party voters position themselves to the right of Social Democratic voters along the private–public dimension, and to the left of Social Democratic voters along the welfare state dimension.

The remaining seven issue dimensions show weaker correlation with party choice. Among those, the green environmental dimension has the strongest relationship with voting behavior (eta=.42). Here, the Green Party voters have the greenest attitudes while the Conservative Party voters have the "grayest" issue standpoints.

The xenophobic immigration dimension comes close with a eta=.37, and here the Sweden Democratic voters have clearly more restrictive attitudes than other groups of party voters. The Green Party and the Left Party voters are the most positive in their attitudes towards immigration. The weakest correlation with party choice has the gender equality dimension. Here, Left Party and Green Party voters are the most positive and the Sweden Democrat and Christian Democratic voters are the most negative.

The party voters' average positions along the issue dimensions tell a story about what issues motivated them to vote the way they did. There are no big surprises in the patterns. Left voters are the most pro welfare programs and a strong welfare regime, and are also the most liberal on the social ethics dimension. Social Democratic voters are more pragmatic as they do not have flank positions on any of the issue dimensions. Green voters are most environmentalist, but also the voter group with the most postmaterialist values and the most generous issue standpoints on immigration issues. Results also show that Left and Green voters are the most pro gender equality and globalization.

Center Party voters position themselves in the center on all issue dimensions. Liberal and Conservative voters have flanking positions along the EU dimension. Christian Democratic voters are the most morally conservative, and also share the flank position with Conservative voters along the public–private dimension as they are most positive towards private solutions in the welfare system.

Conservative voters oppose social benefits more than other groups of party voters, are the most anti-environmental, the most positive towards the European Union, and have the most pronounced material values. Sweden Democrats have flanking positions along four of the issue dimensions, as they are most negative towards immigration, globalization, the European Union (together with Left voters), and gender equality.

The ideological positioning of the two large parties' voters along the nine dimensions gives an idea of the political domains in which there are large ideological distances in Swedish politics today. Along the two left–right issue dimensions, the distance between the Social Democratic and Conservative voters is relatively large, 15 units along the public–private dimension and 12 units along the welfare dimension. Along all the other issue dimensions, however, there are much shorter distances. Along the EU dimension 7 units, immigration, gender, and postmaterialism 4 units, globalization 1 unit, and ethics and moral dimension 0 units.

ISSUES THAT EXPLAIN PARTY SWITCHING

It is clear that the left–right issue dimension alone does not suffice if you want to explain the electoral fortunes and misfortunes of specific parties that mainly compete along other ideological dimensions. Although left–right is dominant, the smaller parties also compete for votes along conflicting issue dimensions and in policy domains that are crucial to their electoral fortunes.

Table 19.1 illustrates the relative usefulness of the nine ideological issue dimensions in analyzing party switching. If we begin with party shifting from the red–green parties

Table 19.1 Effects of the positioning along nine issue dimensions on the probability of shifting from red–green parties in 2006 to Alliance parties in 2010, and shifting from non-Sweden Democratic Party in 2006 to Sweden Democratic Party in 2010 (logistic effects)

Issue dimension	Model 1 From Red–Green 2006 to Alliance 2010			Model 2 From Non-SD 2006 to SD 2010		
	multivariate	bivariate	R^2	multivariate	bivariate	R^2
public (1)–private (5)	1.42***	1.56***	.15	.14	-.21	.00
Pro (1)–con (5) social benefits	.96***	1.13***	.11	-.49**	-.15	.00
Pro (1)–con (5) globalization	.22	.26**	.01	.18	1.13***	.02
Moral liberal (1)–moral conservative (5)	.36*	.37**	.01	.26	.21	.00
Generous (1)–restrictive immigration (5)	-.40	.40***	.02	1.17***	1.43***	.04
Green (1)–gray (5)	.46***	.48***	.03	.32	.58***	.01
Pro (1)–con (5) gender equality	.39**	.43***	.02	.03	.32*	.00
Postmaterialist (1)–materialist (5)	.17	.38**	.02	-	-	-
Con (1)–pro (5) European Union	.28	.36***	.02	-.47**	-.77***	.02

Note: Results are from a series of logistic regression analyses with party switching from Left Party/Social Democratic Party/Green Party 2006 (0) to Center Party/Liberal Party/Christian Democratic Party 2010 (1) as dependent variable (model 1) and from non-Swedish Democratic Party (0) to Sweden Democratic Party 2010 (1) as dependent variable (model 2). The nine issue dimensions are coded from 1 to 5 and entered as independent variables in the regression analyses. See Oscarsson and Holmberg (2013) for more details. All results but for the postmaterialism–materialism dimension come from the combined pre- and post-election survey. The Pseudo R^2-values for the multivariate analyses are .24 for model 1 and .05 for model 2.

(Left Party, Social Democratic Party, and the Greens) to the Alliance parties (Center Party, Liberals, Christian Democratic Party, and the Conservatives) in 2010, it becomes obvious that the two variants of the left–right dimension show the strongest correlations with party change. Red–green voters in 2006 that were relatively positive towards private market solutions and somewhat skeptical of the welfare system had a higher propensity to shift to an Alliance party in 2010.

In addition to the two left–right dimensions, three other issue dimensions show significant relationships with the tendency to switch party from the red–greens to the Alliance. The relevant dimensions deal with environmental issues, gender equality, and social ethics. Red–green voters from the election in 2006 who leaned toward gray, not green, solutions to environmental problems, tended to be less in favor of increased gender equality, and held a more moral conservative attitude, had an independent propensity to move over to an Alliance party in 2010.

The success of the Sweden Democrats, however, is only very weakly related to the left–right divide. The main factor behind the electoral gains for the SD Party is instead one very specific issue—immigration. Vote changes to the Sweden Democrats in 2010 are very strongly related to a restrictive view on refugee admittance and a negative attitude to immigration. Sweden Democrats gained votes in the election despite public opinion becoming less negative toward refugees and immigration between 2006 and 2010. A larger share of immigration-negative citizens voted SD in 2001 than in 2006.

The regression analyses indicate that two other issue dimensions as well had some independent impact on the vote switching to the Sweden Democrats, weaker effects compared to the effects of the immigration dimension, but independent effects nevertheless. These two dimensions are the EU dimension and the left–right welfare dimension. On top of a negative view on immigration, party changes to SD in 2010 were related to a critical attitude to EU membership and a positive opinion on the Swedish welfare state.

Issue Ownership

Parties' competition for votes is not only a positional game. Since parties' policies are derived from mostly stable party ideologies, it is not possible to change them quickly. Short-term, party ideology severely limits the possibilities for parties to maneuver to more favorable positions along issue dimensions in order to win more electoral support. Therefore, party competition is also a struggle for agenda setting. On some issues, parties have competitive advantages and are perceived as having the best policies. In other words, parties possess ownership over certain issues (Martinsson 2009; Green and Jennings 2012; Holmberg 1981; Budge and Farlie 1983). If a party manages to propel advantageous issues to a higher position on the public agenda and play down the importance of disadvantageous issues, this may serve as a short cut to electoral gains. Here, a Downsian matching of parties' policy positions and voter preferences—ideological proximity—is not sufficient to produce large effects on voting; it needs to be combined with positive judgments of the party's competence in handling the issues.

The idea of issue ownership is a key concept in electoral research (Martinsson et al. 2013; Budge and Farlie 1983; Petrocik 1996; Holmberg 1981). Traditionally, issue ownership has been regarded as a very stable phenomenon. It takes a long time to establish a reputation among voters that you are the party that is best at handling specific political domains. However, the Swedish case provides numerous examples of situations where smaller parties have been able to "steal" issues from each other, overtaking the position of the party that is believed to have the best policies (Martinsson et al. 2013). These results show that there is much larger variation in parties' ownership of issues than previously conceived.

The most important domains of Swedish politics—unemployment, social welfare, and the Swedish economy—turn out to be the most stable in terms of issue ownership. Since the election in 1979, the SNES has systematically studied how voters judge issue ownership over a wide range of issue areas. In Figure 19.5 we highlight how Swedish voters have assigned ownership between the two main parties—the Conservatives and the Social Democrats—in three of the most electorally important issue domains in Swedish politics. Former Social Democratic issue ownership on the economy and specifically on unemployment was lost to the Conservatives in the elections of 2006 and 2010. On the other hand, Social Democratic ownership on social welfare was not lost to the Conservatives, indicating that the economy, especially unemployment, trumped welfare as decisive election issues when the Alliance ousted the Social Democratic government in the Swedish elections of 2006 and 2010.

Ideologically Motivated Swedish Voters

Citizens' ideological predispositions and standpoints on classic left–right issues remain among the most potent explanations for political behavior in a party-centered Swedish political system. In analyses of behaviors such as party choice, party switching, and government turnovers, it is always campaign issues that rest most heavily on stable ideological orientations that tend to surface as the most important factors. Political change in Sweden is to a large extent explained by parties' and voters maneuvering along a unidimensional continuum from left to right. In a Swedish context, parties still compete for votes mainly with ideology. And here, issues about state regulations, size of public sector, tax levels, and organization of social welfare remain among the most decisive explanations in analyses of issue voting.

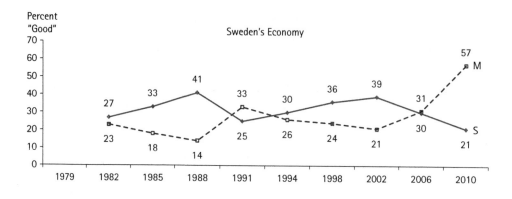

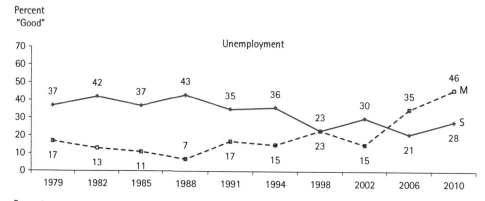

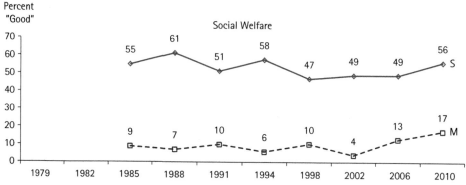

FIGURE 19.5 Proportion of Swedish voters assessing Social Democratic Party/Conservative Party politics as "Good" for Unemployment, Sweden's Economy, and Social Welfare, 1979–2010 (percent).

Note: Results are from the SNES 1979–2010. Open-ended questions were used to tap respondents' attitudes towards the parties' policies in up to eighteen different domains. S = Social Democrats, M = Conservatives.

Issue voting has become more important over time as ideological predispositions have slowly replaced class and occupational status as a structuring force behind political behavior at the polls. However, the effects of issue voting may have peaked in the mid-1980s. After 1990, a left–right depolarization of the party system, enlargement of the party system, and weakening party identification are believed to be slowly bringing new competing explanations to the table. Some of these explanations are believed to be structural, such as complementary ideological dimensions, and some are thought to be affecting party choice due to short-term voter perceptions of issue ownership, leader evaluations, and retrospective evaluations of government performance and economic development. It is still, however, quite unclear whether there is a distinct decrease in the strength of issue voting in the Swedish case because of these developments.

REFERENCES

Aardal, B. and Wijnen, P. van (2005). "Issue Voting," in J. Thomassen (ed.), *The European Voter*. Oxford: Oxford University Press, 192–212.

Bengtsson, Å., Hansen, K. M., Narud, H.-M., Hardarson, O., and Oscarsson, H. (2013). *The Nordic Voter: Myths of Exceptionalism*. London: ECPR Press.

Budge, I. and Farlie, D. (1983). *Voting and Party Competition*. London: John Wiley & Sons.

Dahlberg, S. (2009). *Voters' Perceptions of Party Politics: A Multilevel Approach*. Gothenburg: University of Gothenburg, Department of Political Science.

Dahlberg, S. and Oscarsson, H. (2006). "En europeisk partirymd?" [A European Party Space], in H. Oscarsson and S. Holmberg (eds), *Europaval*. Göteborg: Göteborgs universitet, Statsvetenskapliga institutionen, 153–78.

Downs, A. (1957). *An Economic Theory of Democracy*. New York: Harper & Row.

Gilljam, M. (1988). *Svenska folket och löntagarfonderna: En studie i politisk åsiktsbildning*. Lund: Studentlitteratur.

Granberg, D. and Holmberg, S. (1988). *The Political System Matters: Social Psychology and Voting Behavior in Sweden and the United States*. Cambridge: Cambridge University Press.

Green, J. and Jennings, W. (2012). "The Dynamics of Issue Competence and Vote for Parties In and Out of Power: An Analysis of Valence in Britain, 1979–1997," *European Journal of Political Research* 51: 469–503.

Holmberg, S. (1981). *Svenska väljare* [Swedish Voters]. Stockholm: Liber.

Holmberg, S. (2011). "Dynamic Representation from Above," in M. Rosema, S. A. H. Denters, and K. Aarts (eds), *How Democracy Works: Political Representation and Policy Congruence in Modern Societies. Essays in Honour of Jacques Thomassen*. Amsterdam: Pallas Publications, 53–76.

Holmberg, S. and Oscarsson, H. (2004). *Väljare: Svenskt väljarbeteende under 50 år* [*Voters: Fifty Years of Voting Behavior in Sweden*]. Stockholm: Norstedts.

Martinsson, J. (2009). *Economic Voting and Issue Ownership: An Integrative Approach*. Gothenburg: University of Gothenburg, Department of Political Science.

Martinsson, J., Dahlberg, S., and Christensen, L. (2013). "Change and Stability in Issue Ownership," in S. Dahlberg, H. Oscarsson, and L. Wängnerud (eds), *Stepping Stones*. Gothenburg: University of Gothenburg, Department of Political Science, 129–44.

Oscarsson, H. (1998). "Den svenska partirymden: Väljarnas uppfattningar av konfliktstrukturen i partisystemet 1956–1996" [The Swedish Party Space: Voters' Perceptions of the Conflict Structure of the Party System 1956–1996], dissertation, Göteborg University, Department of Political Science.

Oscarsson, H. and Holmberg, S. (2013). *Nya svenska väljare* [*The New Swedish Voter*]. Stockholm: Norstedts Juridik.

Petersson, O. (1977). *Väljarna och valet 1976* [*Voters and the Election 1976*]. Stockholm: Statistiska centralbyrån.

Petrocik, J. R. (1996). "Issue Ownership in Presidential Elections, with a 1980 Case Study," *American Journal of Political Science* 40: 825–50.

Rosema, M., Denters, S. A. H., and Aarts, K. (eds) (2011). *How Democracy Works: Political Representation and Policy Congruence in Modern Societies: Essays in Honour of Jacques Thomassen.* Amsterdam: Pallas Publications.

Thomassen, J. (ed.) (2005). *The European Voter.* Oxford: Oxford University Press.

CHAPTER 20

SWEDISH ELECTION CAMPAIGNS

JESPER STRÖMBÄCK

INTRODUCTION

IN any electoral democracy, election day is the most important day. Never do ordinary citizens have as much and as equal influence over politics as then, and nothing embodies the democratic norm of political equality as much as the institution of one person, one vote (Dahl 2006). This presupposes, of course, that elections are free and fair.

For elections to be democratically meaningful, they not only have to be free and fair. They also have to be preceded by election campaigns where political parties and candidates campaign intensively to win support, where the media devote resources and space to covering the election campaigns, and where voters have ample opportunities to learn about the issues at stake and compare the parties and candidates running for office. Democracy requires free and fair elections, but the quality of elections hinges on the quality of election campaigns.

The three most important sets of actors in an election campaign are voters, political parties and candidates, and the media. The outcome of any election depends on the interactive relationships and interdependencies between this set of actors. The purpose of this chapter is thus to describe and analyze Swedish election campaigns, with a focus on how voters learn about politics and the issues at stake during election campaigns; how Swedish news media cover election campaigns; how Swedish parties plan and run their election campaigns; and finally the importance of Swedish election campaigns in terms of campaign effects.

The focus will be on national election campaigns, as there is most research in this area and as elections to local and regional parliaments as well as the European Parliament are often considered second-order national elections by the parties as well as by the media and voters (Maier, Strömbäck, and Kaid 2011; Reif and Schmitt 1980).

A Brief Background: High Turnout, Increased Electoral Volatility

As a background, it should be noted that election campaigns in Sweden are quite short, and that people vote in national as well as regional and local elections on the same day every fourth year. Election day is always on the third Sunday in September—from 2014 the second Sunday in September—and it is not until mid-August that the parties begin the most intensive phase of campaigning and the media start covering the election campaign more extensively. To gain parliamentary representation, a party has to win at least 4 percent of the votes. Voter turnout is high: in the 2002, 2006, and 2010 elections, 80, 82, and 85 percent turned out to vote (Oscarsson and Holmberg 2013). The record was set in 1976, however, when electoral participation was almost 92 percent.

It is also important to understand, with regard to election campaigns in Sweden, that electoral behavior has become increasingly volatile during the last decades. Between the elections in 1956 and 1960, only 11.4 percent of the voters switched parties. Between the elections in 2006 and 2010, 32.6 percent switched parties. The share of voters switching parties *during* the election campaigns similarly increased from 7.3 percent in 1968 to 17.3 percent in 2010, while the share of voters deciding which party to vote for during the election campaign increased from 18 percent in 1964 to 53 percent in 2010. Some studies suggest that around 12–13 percent of the voters decide which party to vote for as late as on election day (Holmberg, Näsman, and Wännström 2012). The record in terms of electoral volatility was set in 2006, when 58 percent decided which party to vote for during the election campaign and 37.1 percent switched party compared to the preceding election (Oscarsson and Holmberg 2013).

This trend toward increasing electoral volatility can partly be explained by an increasing number of political parties and thus a greater supply of parties. From the first democratic election in 1921 until 1988, the same five parties were represented in parliament: the Left Party, the Social Democratic Party, the Center Party, the Liberal Party, and the Moderate Party. In 1988, the Green Party won parliamentary representation, which they lost in 1991. In 1991, the Christian Democratic Party and the New Democrats entered parliament. In 1994, the New Democrats lost parliamentary representation and eventually dissolved, while the Green Party returned. In 2010, the Sweden Democrats entered parliament for the first time. Since 2010, Sweden thus has had eight parties in parliament. The Center Party, the Liberal Party, the Moderate Party, and the Christian Democratic Party form a center-right bloc—and the government between 2006 and 2014—while the Left Party, the Green Party, and the Social Democratic Party form a center-left bloc. The Sweden Democrats are considered a xenophobic and nationalistic party that none of the established parties wants to deal with.

The key explanation behind the increased electoral volatility, aside from a greater supply of parties to vote for, is a long-term trend towards decreasing party identification. In 1968, 65 percent described themselves as identifying with a particular party while 39 percent described themselves as strongly identifying with a particular party. In 2010, only 28 and 17 percent, respectively, described themselves as identifying or strongly identifying with a particular party. The share of voters identifying with a particular party has in fact declined in almost every election since 1968 (Oscarsson and Holmberg 2013).

Taken together, the increasing electoral volatility and decreasing party identification suggests that election campaigns in Sweden have become increasingly important (Petersson et al. 2006). More is at stake, and the parties stand to win more as well as to lose. Voters also perceive elections as increasingly important: in 2010, 84 percent said the election outcome matters greatly, which is more than in any election before (Oscarsson and Holmberg 2013).

Mediated Politics: Learning about Politics through the Media

On a general level, Swedish voters can be described as quite interested in politics. According to the annual SOM-surveys, around 50–55 percent consider themselves to have an interest in politics (Weibull, Oscarsson, and Bergström 2012). According to surveys—that are likely to overestimate the share of party members—only about 6 percent are members of any party however, and party membership has declined sharply during the last decades (Weibull, Oscarsson, and Bergström 2012; DS 2013:19). International comparisons of citizen involvement during election campaigns also suggest that Swedes follow politics from the sidelines rather than actively engage in party politics or election campaigning. For example, the Comparative Study of Electoral Systems (CSES) in 2006 showed that only 3 percent of Swedes actively showed support for a particular party or candidate during the most recent election campaign by, for instance, attending a meeting, putting up a poster, or in some other way. In the US, the corresponding share was 31 percent, while the average across twenty-four democracies was 10 percent. The same study showed that only 7 percent were contacted by anyone from a party trying to persuade them to vote in a particular way, in contrast to around 50 percent in countries such as Ireland, the US, and Brazil, and an average of 21 percent across twenty-three nations (Petersson et al. 2006).

The Swedish National Election Study suggests a somewhat more active engagement, however. In the national elections between 1982 and 2010, between 11 and 17 percent claim that they tried to convince someone to vote for a particular party. However, the share of voters who participated at a rally was only 8–9 percent during the last two elections—down from 10–13 percent in previous elections—while less than 10 percent claim that they had a personal visit in their home or were called on by someone working for a party, and during the last two campaigns, only 5 percent claim that they were in personal contact with campaign workers at their workplace (Oscarsson and Holmberg 2013; Oscarsson 2013).

Thus, only a small minority is actively engaged in and has personal contact with the parties in Swedish election campaigns. Instead, most voters follow the election campaigns and get political information from the news media. As an example, in conjunction with the 2010 national election, a panel survey by the research institute DEMICOM asked voters what they thought was their most important source of information about politics. The results showed that 45 percent mentioned TV, 25 percent daily newspapers, 16 percent the Internet, 9 percent radio, 4 percent interpersonal communication with friends, and 2 percent tabloids (Strömbäck and Shehata 2013). Although regular newspaper readership has declined significantly during the last decade, and there is evidence of increasing gaps in news consumption based primarily on age and political interest (Strömbäck, Djerf-Pierre, and Shehata 2013), regular news media consumption also shows that Swedes are quite avid news consumers (see Figure 20.1).

In addition to regular news media, research also shows that special election programming in TV—such as debates between party leaders and Question Time with each of the party leaders—attract large audiences (Oscarsson 2013; Petersson et al. 2006; Strömbäck and Shehata 2013). Although audiences here too have declined, in 2010, People Meter-studies showed that close to 1.4 million Swedes watched the traditional final debate in public service TV between all the party leaders, while surveys suggest that 57 percent watched the whole or parts of that debate (Oscarsson 2013; Strömbäck and Shehata 2013). The only kind of campaign communication that matches this is

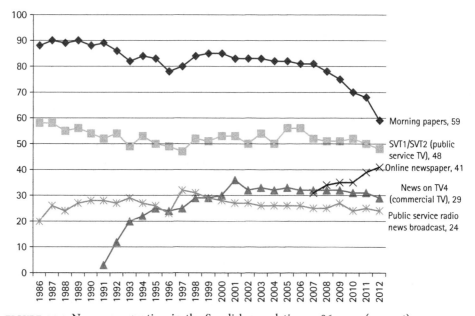

FIGURE 20.1 News consumption in the Swedish population, 1986–2012 (percent).

Source: The national SOM-survey 1986–2012.

Note: News consumption via TV, radio, and morning papers is operationalized as consumption at least five days a week. News consumption via online magazines and evening papers is operationalized as least three days a week.

exposure to televised political advertising, which was used in national elections for the first time in 2010, and which 69 percent were exposed to (Oscarsson and Holmberg 2013; Johansson and Grusell 2013).

Overall, one key feature of Swedish election campaigns is thus that they are heavily mediated, in the sense that most voters experience them indirectly and are exposed to them primarily through the media. Although controlled party communication through televised political advertising and the Internet has become more important over time, the media that matter most are still traditional news media, either in their traditional or their digital formats. This is of major importance for the parties when they plan and run their campaigns, and suggests that success in influencing media coverage of the election campaigns might be necessary—if not sufficient—for success on election day.

ELECTION NEWS COVERAGE IN SWEDEN

The discussion thus far suggests that election campaigns in Sweden have become more important as electoral volatility has increased and party identification has declined, but also that they are heavily mediated by the mass media. A key question is thus how Swedish media cover election campaigns.

Generally speaking, election campaigns are considered good news, and the national news media devote extensive space to covering the campaigns (Asp 2006, 2011; Strömbäck 2008a, 2013). The national news media that are considered most important are the public service television news programs *Rapport* and *Aktuellt*, the commercial television news program *TV4 Nyheterna*, the public service radio news program *Ekot*, the daily newspapers *Dagens Nyheter* and *Svenska Dagbladet*, and the newsstand tabloids *Aftonbladet* and *Expressen*. In 2010, the three television news programs (*Rapport, Aktuellt, TV4 Nyheterna*) and the most important radio news program (*Ekot*) devoted altogether around 16 hours to the election campaigns,[1] while the daily newspapers and the tabloids published more than 2,000 articles.[2] In addition, the public service channels broadcast more than 40 hours of special election programming while the commercial television channel TV4 broadcast around 14 hours (Asp 2011). Although there is evidence suggesting that more than in the past the amount of election news depends on the news value assigned to a particular election—and less on a high news value ascribed to national elections per se—there is little doubt that Swedish news media devote quite extensive space and resources to covering election campaigns and that they offer voters ample opportunities to find news about the campaigns (Asp 2006, 2011).

In terms of the content of Swedish election news, there is evidence that the character has changed during the last decades. One framework for analyzing this is the theory of the mediatization of politics (Asp 1986; Mazzoleni and Schulz 1999; Strömbäck 2008a, 2008b).

At heart, mediatization refers to a social change process in which media have become increasingly influential in and integrated into different spheres of society. In the context of politics, it has been defined as a long-term process through which the importance of the media and their spillover effects on political processes, institutions, organizations, and actors have increased (Strömbäck and Esser 2014). According to this theory, one of the key dimensions is related to the media coverage of politics and current affairs, and the extent to which it is guided by media logic as opposed to political logic (Strömbäck 2008b; Strömbäck and Esser 2009, 2014). The more media cover politics and elections in ways that are designed to suit media logic—shaped by the media's understanding of journalistic professionalism, commercial imperatives, and media technologies—the more mediatized it is (Esser 2013; Strömbäck and Esser 2014).

One key indicator of this is the degree to which political news is interpretive rather than descriptive. A development towards more interpretive journalism has been documented in many Western democracies (for an overview, see Salgado and Strömbäck 2012), and with respect to Sweden, one major historical study of current affairs coverage in Swedish public broadcasting characterizes the rise of interpretive journalism as "the most significant change in political news journalism" (Djerf-Pierre and Weibull 2008: 209). In their historical study of special election programs on TV, Esaiasson and Håkansson (2002) also found a clear trend towards more interpretive and autonomous journalism. Although content analyses of the extent to which election news is characterized by an interpretive rather than descriptive journalistic style only go back to 1998, in the elections campaigns since then, around 40 percent of all news stories have been characterized by an interpretive journalistic style (Strömbäck 2009a, 2013).

Another—and related—key indicator of mediatization is related to the media's framing of politics. Within this field of research, a distinction is usually made between the framing of politics as a strategic game and the framing of politics as issues. When media frame politics as a strategic game, they portray politics as being about opinion polls, winners and losers, electoral success, campaign strategies and tactics, and the images of politicians, while also tending to use the language of wars and sport. In contrast, when media frame politics as issues, they focus on the substance of issues and issue positions, on real-life conditions with relevance for issue positions, or on what has happened or what someone has said and done to the extent that it is depicted as relevant for the political issues (Aalberg, Strömbäck, and de Vreese 2012; Cappella and Jamieson 1997; Patterson 1993). An emphasis on the framing of politics as a strategic game is generally considered an expression of media logic and an indication of mediatization (Strömbäck and Dimitrova 2011; Zaller 2001), since it allows the media a greater degree of independence from political actors while also being better suited to traditional news values such as drama and conflict. Another framing that is also often considered as an expression of media logic and mediatization is scandal framing, where the media focus on real or alleged scandals or gaffes.

Research on the framing of politics in Swedish media during election campaigns dates back to the 1998 election, and shows that the issue framing of politics increased between 1998 and 2002, but that it has decreased since then. In the 2002, 2006, and 2010 election campaigns, on average 59, 49, and 44 percent of all news stories framed politics as issues. In 2010, on average 44 percent of the news stories on the election framed politics as substance, 54 percent as a strategic game, and 2 percent as scandals (Strömbäck 2004, 2009a, 2013). Overall, the commercial TV news and the tabloids have a stronger tendency to frame politics as a strategic game or as scandals compared with public service news and daily newspapers. As part of the framing of politics as a strategic game, Swedish media also display a strong interest in publishing the results of opinion polls—with an increase from 88 in 2002 to 121 in 2010—and in more or less sweeping references to what "public opinion" thinks or unidentified "polls" show (Strömbäck and Jendel 2013).

The issue related to the news media's coverage of election campaigns that is most widely discussed is, however, the question of partisan bias. This question has been extensively studied by Asp (2006, 2011) for every election since 1979. His analyses start from the notion that parties can be part of news stories as objects (of other's comments) or as active subjects. He summarizes the data in an "actor treatment index," constructed on the basis of the extent to which the parties receive media attention and the extent to which their mention is either positive or negative.

The results show that in every election campaign there is some party or parties that receive more favorable coverage whereas other parties receive more unfavorable coverage. What is more important, however, is that different parties receive favorable and unfavorable coverage in different election campaigns (Asp 2006, 2011). Hence, there is no evidence for a systematic bias favoring some party or parties across different election campaigns. Moreover, there is a tendency for a party that receives positive treatment in one election campaign to receive more negative treatment in the next campaign.

The tendency with respect to the treatment of the two governing alternatives (the center-right versus the center-left blocs) is rather similar. Although the left-wing parties have tended to receive more negative coverage on the whole than the center or right-wing parties, this tendency is not particularly strong, and the treatment of the two blocs has varied between elections. There is also a tendency that parties in government receive more scrutiny and criticism than parties in opposition, regardless of whether they belong to the left or right. Research also shows that the media tend to join together with respect to the coverage of individual parties as well as of the governing alternatives, so that different parties or governing alternatives receive a roughly similar treatment in different media.

Taken together, this research suggests that the Swedish media do not display any systematic partisan bias, despite the fact that journalists are more leftist than Swedes in general, while at the same time, most media in terms of ownership are private and more rightist (Asp 2012; Strömbäck, Nord, and Shehata 2012).

The problem—to the extent that there is a problem—is thus not partisan bias. The problem is rather what has been conceptualized as structural bias.

The concept of structural bias can be traced back to Hofstetter (1976: 34), who suggested that structural bias "occurs when some things are selected to be reported rather than other things because of the character of the medium or because of the incentives that apply to commercial news programming." Graber (2005: 236) similarly concludes that "Political bias reflects ideological judgments, whereas structural bias reflects the circumstances of news production." When different news media treat a particular party favorably or unfavorably in a similar manner, no matter their linkages to political predispositions among owners or journalists, this thus suggests that structural rather than partisan bias is at work. Or, phrased differently, that media logic rather than political logic is governing the news coverage.

Evidence for this can be found in studies linking the treatment of the parties to the framing of politics. In news stories where an issue frame is dominant, all parties except the xenophobic and nationalistic Sweden Democrats receive more or less neutral coverage, but when politics is framed as a strategic game, parties that are perceived as not doing well receive more negative coverage (Strömbäck and Jendel 2013). This suggests that the news value of individual parties is influenced by how they are doing in the battle for public opinion and votes, not just in those news stories that explicitly focus on the results of opinion polls but also in news stories that in broader terms frame politics as a strategic game. This may result in either upward or downward spirals for different parties, and helps to explain why different parties get more favorable or unfavorable coverage in different election campaigns.

Combined with the notion that election news often has an interpretive journalistic style and frames politics as a strategic game, this suggests that Swedish election campaigns are not only heavily mediated but also mediatized. While this is not unique of Sweden (Esser 2008; Esser and Strömbäck 2014), this poses another challenge for Swedish parties when they plan and run their election campaigns.

Political Campaigning in Sweden

The discussion thus far suggests that election campaigns in Sweden have become both more important and more unpredictable. Still, it is not clear exactly how important they are—or are perceived to be by the parties. To date, there are only few studies related to how important the parties perceive the campaigns to be.

Two of these investigate internal party documents from the two major parties—the Social Democrats and the Moderate Party—between 1964 and 1991. These studies suggest that both parties consider ideology and policy preferences together with the media coverage as most important when explaining voter behavior (Ekengren and Oscarsson 2011, 2013). According to these results, it is not mainly how the parties run their campaigns and what campaign techniques they use that matter but the positioning of the parties with respect to the issues that are salient in the media coverage of the campaigns and in the minds of voters (Ekengren and Oscarsson 2011). Another study, based on a survey among members of parliament (MPs) of all parties, similarly found that the most important factors when explaining election outcomes are perceived to be the party leader, the party's policies on different issues, how the media cover the election, and the party's ideology. The only factors related to campaign strategies and tactics that a majority of MPs consider very important are effective identification of target groups and door-to-door canvassing and meeting directly with voters (Strömbäck, Grandien, and Falasca 2013). This is consistent with an earlier study of Swedish MPs, which found that the two most important factors when explaining what party Swedish voters vote for were perceived to be the media coverage of the election campaigns and the image of the party leaders. For example, while 64 percent of MPs perceived the media coverage of the election campaigns to be very important, only 16 percent perceived the parties' campaign activities as very important (Holmberg 2010).

At the same time, studies also suggest that parties have increased their staff working with media management, public relations, and political marketing activities (Nord 2007), and for each election, they increase their campaign budgets. Between 2006 and 2010, for example, the total campaign budget for all parties in parliament is estimated to have increased from 180 to 259 million Swedish kronor (Johansson and Grusell 2013). While this is nothing compared to what election campaigns might cost in countries such as the United States, the development over time suggests that all parties do consider the campaigns to be increasingly important.

Two useful frameworks when analyzing political parties and their campaigning are the theories of *political market orientation* and the *professionalization of political campaigning*. Political market orientation deals with the parties' grand strategy, which has been defined as "the policy-level decisions an organization makes about goals, alignments, ethics, and relationship with publics and other forces in its environment" (Botan 2006: 225). According to the theory, there are three types of parties: product-oriented, sales-oriented, and market-oriented (Lees-Marshment 2001a, 2001b; Lees-Marshment, Strömbäck, and Rudd 2010; Newman 1994). The defining features of a *product-oriented party* is that it believes strongly in its own ideas and policies, and that these are formed internally in processes where only members and activists have a say and where the party's core ideology is important. A product-oriented party "argues for what it stands for and believes in. It assumes that voters will realize that its ideas are the right ones and therefore vote for it" (Lees-Marshment 2001a: 696). This type of party does not change its ideas or "product" even if it fails on election day.

A sales-oriented party is similar to product-oriented parties in the sense that it designs its ideas and policies in internal processes where only members and activists have a say, but it also believes that all ideas and policies (the political product) need to be sold as effectively as possible. A sales-oriented party consequently focuses on selling its arguments to voters, and uses various campaign strategies and tactics to that end. Following Lees-Marshment (2001a: 696), a sales-oriented party "does not change its behaviour to suit what people want, but tries to make people want what it offers."

A market-oriented party, in contrast, uses market intelligence such as opinion polls and focus groups to identify voters' perceived wants and needs, and seeks to design its policies, ideas, and behavior to meet those wants and needs and thus provide voter satisfaction. In contrast to sales-oriented parties, a market-oriented party does not try to make people want what it offers, but rather to offer what people perceive they want. Similar to sales-oriented parties, a market-oriented party tries to make effective use of different campaign strategies and tactics, but most importantly, it seeks to become as effective as possible in terms of identifying and meeting voters' perceived wants and needs.

These party types are of course ideal types, and should be thought of as positions along a continuum from product orientation through sales orientation to market orientation rather than as discrete categories (Strömbäck, Lees-Marshment, and Rudd 2012). In reality there are few pure product-oriented, sales-oriented, or market-oriented parties, and no party is likely to go all the way in terms of designing its ideas and policies to satisfy voters' wants and needs. It is more likely that they try to identify and change policies that might repel important target groups. Comparative research also suggests that there are few truly market-oriented parties. Instead, most parties could be classified as sales-oriented and leaning more or less towards either product or sales orientation (Lees-Marshment, Strömbäck, and Rudd 2010).

With respect to Sweden, studies similarly suggests that most parties are sales-oriented, but that some—the Left Party and the Green Party—tend towards product orientation whereas the Moderate Party after their electoral failure in 2002 has tended towards market orientation, although they do not describe themselves that way (Strömbäck 2010). There is in addition a tendency for parties that have faced major electoral failures to become more market-oriented as a means to recover, but once they have become more successful, they tend to go back to a sales orientation. The degree of market orientation may thus vary across time and elections (Strömbäck, Lees-Marshment, and Rudd 2012).

In contrast to political market orientation, the professionalization of campaigning deals with campaign strategies and tactics, defined as "campaign-level decision making involving maneuvering and arranging resources and arguments to carry out organizational grand strategies" and "the specific activities and outputs through which strategies are implemented," respectively (Botan 2006: 226). In very general terms, professionalization refers to a process of change that "brings about a better and more efficient—and more reflective—organization of resources and skills in order to achieve desired objectives" (Negrine 2007: 29) in the context of electoral success.

Following the party-centered theory of political campaigning (Gibson and Römmele 2001, 2009), the professionalization of political campaigning is often operationalized as the use of various campaign strategies and tactics, such as opinion polls and focus groups, direct mail and telemarketing, opposition research, permanent campaigning, and the use of campaign professionals such as public relations and media consultants (Gibson and Römmele 2001, 2009; Nord 2013; Strömbäck 2009b). It is assumed that the more parties make use of various campaign strategies and tactics, the more professionalized their campaigning. One drawback of this approach is that it does not account for the fact that parties can be more or less professionalized in *how* they use various campaign strategies and tactics, but making reliable assessments of how skillful and professional they are in using different campaign strategies and tactics is exceedingly difficult. Measuring how much the parties use different campaign strategies and tactics can thus be considered the best possible—if not the perfect—approach.

The results from Swedish studies show that some campaign strategies and tactics are used by more parties than others and that some parties are more professionalized than others, but also that no Swedish party can be considered as running fully professionalized campaigns (Nord 2013; Strömbäck 2009b). The most recent study, covering the election campaigns in 2010, included the use of eleven campaigns strategies, and the more the parties used each of them, the higher their score. The maximum score for each campaign strategy or tactic was 3; a party that made full usage of all campaign strategies and tactics would thus get 33. The results for each campaign strategy and tactic are displayed in Table 20.1 (adapted from Nord 2013).

If full usage of all campaign strategies and tactics is assumed to equal fully professionalized campaigns, the degree of professionalization can be calculated by dividing the total score with the maximum possible score (33). Following this approach, the bottom line shows the degree of campaign professionalization for each party in 2010. These results suggest that the Social Democrats ran the most professionalized campaign, followed by the Moderate Party and the Center Party.

Comparing the degree of professionalization in 2006 and 2010, research suggests that all parties have become more professionalized, but that the ranking of the parties

Table 20.1 Professionalization of political campaigning in the 2010 election

	Left Party	Green Party	Social Democrats	Center Party	Liberal Party	Christian Democrats	Moderate Party	Sweden Democrats
Permanent campaigning	1	1	2	2	2	1	2	1
External campaign HQ	1	1	2	2	2	1	2	1
Campaign consultants	1	1	1	1	1	1	1	0
Opinion polls	0	1	2	2	1	0	2	0
Focus groups	1	1	2	2	0	0	2	0
Opposition research	0	1	2	2	2	1	2	0
Reverse opposition research	1	1	2	2	2	1	2	0
Social media	2	2	3	1	1	2	2	3
Door-to-door canvassing	1	0	3	2	2	2	3	0
Televised advertising	1	1	1	2	1	2	2	2
Telemarketing & direct mail	2	1	3	1	1	1	2	1
Total	11	11	23	19	15	12	22	8
Degree of professionalization	33	37	70	58	45	36	67	24

is the same (Nord 2013; Strömbäck 2009b). In both years, the larger parties ran more professionalized campaigns than the others. Size thus matters, and is often a good proxy for the availability of resources. The exception is the Center Party, which is the richest party in Sweden since it sold the newspaper consortium it owned in 2005. This helps to explain why this party in both 2006 and 2010 ran more expensive and professionalized campaigns than other similarly sized parties.

Equally important is that none of the Swedish parties can be considered fully professionalized in terms of their political campaigning. Comparing the sophistication and skill by which Swedish parties make use of different campaign strategies and tactics with their counterparts in countries such as the United States and the United Kingdom would probably also reveal that Swedish parties are less professionalized than parties in such countries.

One reason for this is that Swedish parties have fewer financial resources than parties in countries that are larger or where private fundraising is integral to the party-political system. An equally important reason is that even though Swedish parties have lost members during the last several decades, they retain and want to cultivate the image of being grass-roots organizations where the internal arena and internal democracy are highly important. Increasing centralization is thus viewed with skepticism, while increasing professionalization requires increasing centralization. This is also a reason why Swedish parties seldom hire external campaign professionals except when it comes to producing advertising material; instead they prefer to have that competency in-house. A third and related reason is that Swedish parties and Swedish politics in general place great emphasis on the importance of policies, which also helps to explain why internal party documents as well as surveys among MPs show that the parties place greater weight on policies and ideas than on campaign strategies and tactics when trying to explain voter behavior and election outcomes (Ekengren and Oscarsson 2011, 2013; Strömbäck, Grandien, and Falasca 2013). In essence, Swedish political culture and the history and character of political parties serve as breaks in the process of professionalizing how election campaigns are planned for and conducted (see also Nord 2007, 2013; Nord and Strömbäck 2003; Strömbäck 2010).

Election campaigns may have become both more important and more unpredictable, but it is not mainly through more professionalized campaigns that they are thought to be decided. It is rather through having policies and ideas and a party leader that resonate with important target groups, can mobilize supporters, and can influence how the media cover the election, that election outcomes are thought to be decided.

CAMPAIGN EFFECTS IN SWEDEN

In the literature on campaign effects, the main focus tends to be on campaign effects on the final election outcome (Erikson and Wlezien 2012). The more people change their vote intention during the campaigns (as a result of exposure to the election campaigns), the larger the campaign effects are assumed to be. As noted already by Lazarsfeld, Berelson, and Gaudet in their landmark study *The People's Choice* (1948), such conversion effects are however not the only type of campaign effects. Other important effects are activation and reinforcement effects. Equally important is that such an approach only takes aggregate changes into consideration, neglecting what might be considerable effects on the individual level. For the dynamics and nature of election campaigns, it matters greatly, however, whether many people change vote intention, even if such conversion effects would cancel each other out. The end result is that campaign effects tend to be underestimated.

In the Swedish case, there is rather limited research on campaign effects. Comparing people's vote intention before the election campaigns and their actual votes, the National Election Studies show, however, that there is considerable movement. As a case in point, Table 20.2 shows how many percentage points each of the parties lost or won during the 2002, 2006, and 2010 election campaigns (Oscarsson and Holmberg 2013: 173).

These results—and the same holds true for earlier elections—show that most parties win and lose votes during the election campaigns, and that there are, in that sense, important campaign effects. In some elections there is more movement, in others less. Two general patterns can be discerned from the historical data. First, smaller parties tend to win while larger parties tend to lose votes during the election campaigns. One reason is that the smaller parties receive a visibility during election campaigns that they otherwise do not have. Another reason is that many people vote strategically, not least to help smaller parties that might otherwise lose parliamentary representation while being crucial for either the center-left or the center-right blocs to win governing power. Second, there has been a tendency toward greater changes during more recent election campaigns. Between 1968 and 2010, the share of voters switching parties during the final weeks before election day increased from 7.3 to 17.3 percent (Oscarsson and Holmberg 2013). Most party switchers tend to switch parties within the center-left or the center-right bloc, respectively, but in the last elections, between around 8 and 12 percent changed party across this dividing line (Oscarsson and Holmberg 2013).

Table 20.2 The parties' wins and losses during the election campaigns, 2002–10 (percent)

	2002	2006	2010	Average 1968–2010
Left Party	−1.1	+0.2	+0.9	+0.6
Social Democrats	−2.4	−2.6	+0.1	−1.2
Green Party	+2.1	+0.6	−0.9	+0.0
Center Party	−0.2	+1.3	+2.1	+0.2
Liberal Party	+4.1	−0.7	−0.2	−0.1
Christian Democrats	+0.0	+0.2	+1.0	+0.6
Moderate Party	−2.4	+0.8	−3.6	−0.5

Apart from campaign effects on voting, other research shows that Swedish election campaigns have considerable activation and reinforcement effects. Illuminating in this respect is a four-wave representative panel survey during the 2010 election, running from May to September (Strömbäck and Shehata 2013). For example, looking at uncertain voters who placed themselves to the left on the left–right ideological continuum in May, in June 16 percent had a preference for one of the parties belonging to the center-left bloc. That share grew to 22 percent in August and 63 percent in September. Even more noteworthy is the activation and mobilization of uncertain voters who placed themselves to the right on the left–right ideological continuum in May. In June, 13 percent had a preference for one of the parties belonging to the center-right. That share grew to 32 percent in August and 82 percent in September. Similar changes could not be detected among those who placed themselves in the middle of the ideological continuum, although they also formed a party preference during the course of the longer campaign, eventually favoring the center-right bloc. Leftist voters were also more likely to expose themselves to campaign communication from center-left parties while rightist voters were more likely to expose themselves to campaign communication from center-right parties, suggesting a dynamic of activation as well as selective reinforcement. Analyses also show significant effects on party choice based on exposure to campaign communication from either the left or right, under control for a number of other potentially relevant influences such as earlier party preference or ideological belonging (Strömbäck and Shehata 2013).

Aside from campaign effects that directly impinge on voting, research also shows a number of mobilization effects that are democratically encouraging. For example, in 2010, political interest as well as news media consumption and interpersonal discussions about politics and trust in Swedish politicians increased between May and September. Also important is that the mobilization effects, in general, were stronger among younger than among older voters (Strömbäck and Shehata 2013). The role of the media, in this context, is however dual. On the one hand, there is a correlation between news media consumption and political interest, where political interest contributes to news media consumption and exposure to mediated campaign communication, which in turn contributes to increasing political interest (Strömbäck and Shehata 2010, 2013). On the other hand, more detailed analyses also show that exposure to news that frames politics as a strategic game reduces both political interest and political trust, in contrast to news that frames politics as issues (Shehata and Strömbäck 2013a). What this suggests is that the Swedish news media contribute to a political mobilization in election campaigns, but that this holds particularly true for those who are exposed to issue-framed news and that the mobilizing effects would be stronger if the tendency to frame politics as a strategic game was weaker. Interestingly, while Swedish election campaigns contribute to higher trust in politicians, research also suggests that they contribute to lower trust in Swedish journalists as well as in different media (Strömbäck and Shehata 2013).

Although more research on different forms of campaign effects in the Swedish context is needed, the overall conclusion is nevertheless that Swedish election campaigns do have substantially meaningful effects in terms of conversion as well as activation, reinforcement, and political mobilization. Relevant in this context, considering that Swedish election campaigns are so heavily mediated, is also research showing that the Swedish news media can have significant agenda-setting and framing effects (Shehata 2010; Shehata and Strömbäck 2013a, 2013b; see also Asp 2011). Thus, Swedish political parties are right in assuming that the media coverage is important both when shaping and explaining election outcomes.

DISCUSSION AND CONCLUSION

Before every election there is a lot of talk and speculation about the outcome and how important the election campaigns are. After the dust has settled it is often concluded that there were no major surprises. Partly this is because changes seldom take place overnight: instead they develop more incrementally over the course of the long election campaign during the year before election day (Erikson and Wlezien 2012). Equally important is that there is often too much focus on aggregate changes in party choice and too little focus on individual-level changes in party choice and other campaign effects such as activation, reinforcement, and mobilization effects. If different kinds of effects, on the individual as well as the aggregate level, are taken into consideration, there is little doubt that Swedish election campaigns matter not just for the parties, but also for individuals, the media, and—ultimately—democracy.

From a democratic perspective, Swedish election campaigns also work quite well. During election campaigns, the playing field is leveled and all parties receive quite extensive media coverage, not only in regular news programs but also through the special election programming. Not least important is that each party leader gets one hour of Question Time on public service radio and TV, and that all party leaders are included in the televised debates. This assures that all parties have a chance of reaching out to voters and that voters have easy access to information about all parties. It is also important in this context that money probably means less in Swedish election campaigns than in many other countries. Whether the introduction of televised political advertising in 2010 will change remains to be seen.

The fact that election campaigns contribute to increasing political interest, news media consumption, and political trust are also signs that Swedish election campaigns work quite well. Election campaigns are supposed to mobilize citizens politically, and whatever flaws Swedish election campaigns have and whatever improvements are possible and desirable, the fact is that Swedish election campaigns mobilize people politically and that citizens perceive the outcome of elections as important. Without this, electoral turnout would be lower and the quality of Swedish democracy weaker.

NOTES

1. During the last four weeks before election day.
2. This also includes Göteborgs-Posten.

REFERENCES

Aalberg, T., Strömbäck, J., and Vreese, C. H. de (2012). "The Framing of Politics as Strategy and Game: A Review of Concepts, Operationalizations and Key Findings," *Journalism* 13/2: 162–78.

Asp, K. (1986), *Mäktiga massmedier: Studier i politisk opinionsbildning.* Stockholm: Akademilitteratur.

Asp, K. (2006). *Rättvisa nyhetsmedier: Partiskheten under 2006 års medievalrörelse.* Göteborg: JMG/Göteborgs universitet.

Asp, K. (2011). *Mediernas prestationer och betydelse: Valet 2010.* Göteborg: JMG/Göteborgs universitet.

Asp, K. (2012). "Journalistkårens partisympatier," in K. Asp (eds), *Svenska journalister 1989–2011.* Göteborg: JMG/Göteborgs Universitet, 101–8.

Botan, C. (2006). "Grand Strategy, Strategy, and Tactics in Public Relations," in C. H. Botan and V. Hazleton (eds), *Public Relations Theory II.* New York: Lawrence Erlbaum, 199–222.

Cappella, J. N. and Jamieson, K. H. (1997). *Spiral of Cynicism: The Press and the Public Good.* Chicago: University of Chicago Press.

Dahl, R. A. (2006). *On Political Equality.* New Haven: Yale University Press.

Djerf-Pierre, M. and Weibull, L. (2008). "From Public Educator to Interpreting Ombudsman: Regimes of Political Journalism in Swedish Public Service Broadcasting, 1925–2005," in J. Strömbäck, M. Ørsten, and T. Aalberg (eds), *Communicating Politics: Political Communication in the Nordic Countries.* Göteborg: Nordicom, 195–214.

DS 2013:19 (2013). *Svenska framtidsutmaningar: Slutrapport från regeringens Framtidskommission.* Stockholm: Fritzes.

Ekengren, A.-M. and Oscarsson, H. (2011). "Party Elites' Perceptions of Voters and Public Opinion," *Scandinavian Political Studies* 34/2: 101–22.

Ekengren, A.-M. and Oscarsson, H. (2013). "Party Elites' Perceptions of Voting Behavior," *Party Politics* 19/4: 641–64.

Erikson, R. S. and Wlezien, C. (2012). *The Timeline of Presidential Elections. How Campaigns Do (and Do Not) Matter.* Chicago: University of Chicago Press.

Esaiasson, P. and Håkansson, N. (2002). *Besked ikväll! Valprogrammen i svensk radio och TV.* Stockholm: Stiftelsen Etermedierna i Sverige.

Esser, F. (2008). "Dimensions of Political News Cultures: Sound Bite and Image Bite News in France, Germany, Great Britain, and the United States," *International Journal of Press/Politics* 13/4: 401–28.

Esser, F. (2013). "Mediatization as a Challenge: Media Logic Versus Political Logic," in H. Kriesi, S. Lavenex, F. Esser, J. Matthes, M. Bühlmann, and D. Bochsler (eds), *Democracy in the Age of Globalization and Mediatization.* Basingstoke: Palgrave Macmillan, 155–76.

Esser, F. and Strömbäck, J. (eds) (2014). *Mediatization of Politics: Understanding the Transformation of Western Democracies.* Basingstoke: Palgrave Macmillan.

Gibson, R. and Römmele, A. (2001). "Changing Campaign Communications: A Party-Centered Theory of Professionalized Campaigning," *Harvard International Journal of Press/Politics* 6/4: 31–43.

Gibson, R. and Römmele, A. (2009). "Measuring the Professionalization of Political Campaigning," *Party Politics* 15/3: 265–93.

Graber, D. A. (2005). *Mass Media and American Politics*, 7th edn. Washington, DC: CQ Press.

Hofstetter, C. R. (1976). *Bias in the News: Network Television News Coverage of the 1972 Election Campaign*. Columbus: Ohio State University Press.

Holmberg, S. (2010). "Riksdagsledamöternas väljarkännedom," in M. Brothén and S. Holmberg (eds), *Folkets representanter: En bok om riksdagsledamöter och politisk representation i Sverige*. Göteborg: Göteborgs universitet, Statsvetenskapliga institutionen, 123–44.

Holmberg, S., Näsman, P., and Wännström, K. (2012). *Väljarnas röst*. Stockholm: SVT.

Johansson, B. and Grusell, M. (2013). "'Och nu blir det reklamfilm': Politisk reklam i svenska valrörelser," in J. Strömbäck and L. Nord (eds), *Kampen om opinionen: Politisk kommunikation under svenska valrörelser*. Stockholm: SNS Förlag, 64–88.

Lazarsfeld, P. F., Berelson, B., and Gaudet, H. (1948). *The People's Choice: How the Voter Makes Up His Mind in a Presidential Election*, 2nd edn. New York: Columbia University Press.

Lees-Marshment, J. (2001a). "The Marriage of Politics and Marketing," *Political Studies* 49/4: 692–713.

Lees-Marshment, J. (2001b). *Political Marketing and British Political Parties: The Party's Just Begun*. Manchester: Manchester University Press.

Lees-Marshment, J., Strömbäck, J., and Rudd, C. (eds) (2010). *Global Political Marketing*. London: Routledge.

Maier, M., Strömbäck, J., and Kaid, L. L. (eds) (2011). *Political Communication in European Parliamentary Elections*. Farnham: Ashgate.

Mazzoleni, G. and Schulz, W. (1999). "Mediatization of Politics: A Challenge for Democracy?" *Political Communication* 16/3: 247–61.

Negrine, R. (2007). "The Professionalisation of Political Communication in Europe," in R. Negrine, P. Mancini, C. Holtz-Bacha, and S. Papathanassopoulos (eds), *The Professionalisation of Political Campaigning*. Bristol: Intellect, 27–45.

Newman, B. I. (1994). *The Marketing of the President: Political Marketing as Campaign Strategy*. Beverly Hills: Sage Publications.

Nord, L. (2007). "The Swedish Model Becomes Less Swedish," in R. Negrine, P. Mancini, C. Holtz-Bacha, and S. Papathanassopoulos (eds), *The Professionalisation of Political Campaigning*. Bristol: Intellect, 81–96.

Nord, L. (2013). "Jakten på den perfekta kampanjen: Professionaliseringen av de svenska partierna," in J. Strömbäck and L. Nord (eds), *Kampen om opinionen: Politisk kommunikation under svenska valrörelser*. Stockholm: SNS Förlag, 35–63.

Nord, L. and Strömbäck, J. (2003). *Valfeber och nyhetsfrossa: Politisk kommunikation i valrörelsen 2002*. Stockholm: Sellin & Partner.

Oscarsson, H. (2013). "Väljarnas valrörelser," in J. Strömbäck and L. Nord (eds), *Kampen om opinionen: Politisk kommunikation under svenska valrörelser*. Stockholm: SNS Förlag, 270–95.

Oscarsson, H. and Holmberg, S. (2013). *Nya svenska väljare*. Stockholm: Norstedts juridik.

Patterson, T. E. (1993). *Out of Order*. New York: Vintage.

Petersson, O., Djerf-Pierre, M., Holmberg, S., Strömbäck, J., and Weibull, L. (2006). *Media and Elections in Sweden*. Stockholm: SNS Förlag.

Reif, K. and Schmitt, H. (1980). "Nine Second-Order National Elections: A Conceptual Framework for the Analysis of European Election Results," *European Journal of Political Research* 8/1: 3–44.

Salgado, S. and Strömbäck, J. (2012). "Interpretive Journalism: A Review of Concepts, Operationalizations and Key Findings," *Journalism* 13/2: 144–61.

Shehata, A. (2010). "Unemployment on the Agenda: A Panel Study of Agenda-Setting Effects during the 2006 Swedish National Election Campaign," *Journal of Communication* 60/1: 182–203.

Shehata, A. and Strömbäck, J. (2013a). "Mediernas effekter under valrörelser," in J. Strömbäck and L. Nord (eds), *Kampen om opinionen: Politisk kommunikation under svenska valrörelser*. Stockholm: SNS Förlag, 239–69.

Shehata, A. and Strömbäck, J. (2013b). "Not (Yet) a New Era of Minimal Effects: A Study of Agenda Setting at the Aggregate and Individual Levels," *International Journal of Press/Politics* 18/2: 234–55.

Strömbäck, J. (2004). *Den medialiserade demokratin: Om journalistikens ideal, verklighet och makt*. Stockholm: SNS Förlag.

Strömbäck, J. (2008a). "Swedish Election News Coverage: Towards Increasing Mediatization," in J. Strömbäck and L. L. Kaid (eds), *Handbook of Election News Coverage Around the World*. New York: Routledge, 160–74.

Strömbäck, J. (2008b). "Four Phases of Mediatization: An Analysis of the Mediatization of Politics," *International Journal of Press/Politics* 13/3: 228–46.

Strömbäck, J. (2009a). "Den medialiserade valbevakningen," in L. Nord and J. Strömbäck (eds), *Väljarna, partierna och medierna: En studie av politisk kommunikation i valrörelsen 2006*. Stockholm: SNS Förlag, 127–67.

Strömbäck, J. (2009b). "Selective Professionalisation of Political Campaigning: A Test of the Party-Centred Theory of Professionalised Campaigning in the Context of the 2006 Swedish Election," *Political Studies* 57/1: 95–116.

Strömbäck, J. (2010). "Political Market-Orientation in a Multi-Party System: The Swedish Case," in J. Lees-Marshment, J. Strömbäck, and C. Rudd (eds), *Global Political Marketing*. London: Routledge, 52–64.

Strömbäck, J. (2013). "Den medialiserade valrörelsejournalistiken," in J. Strömbäck and L. Nord (eds), *Kampen om opinionen: Politisk kommunikation under svenska valrörelser*. Stockholm: SNS Förlag, 119–49.

Strömbäck, J. and Dimitrova, D. V. (2011). "Mediatization and Media Interventionism: A Comparative Analysis of Sweden and the United States," *International Journal of Press/Politics* 16/1: 30–49.

Strömbäck, J., Djerf-Pierre, M. and Shehata, A. (2013). "The Dynamics of Political Interest and News Media Consumption: A Longitudinal Perspective," *International Journal of Public Opinion Research* 25/4: 414–35.

Strömbäck, J. and Esser, F. (2009). "Shaping Politics: Mediatization and Media Interventionism," in K. Lundby (eds), *Mediatization: Concepts, Changes, and Consequences*. New York: Peter Lang, 205–23.

Strömbäck, J. and Esser, F. (2014). "Mediatization of Politics: Towards a Theoretical Framework," in F. Esser and J. Strömbäck (eds), *Mediatization of Politics: Understanding the Transformation of Western Democracies*. Basingstoke: Palgrave Macmillan, 3–28.

Strömbäck, J., Grandien, C., and Falasca, K. (2013). "Do Campaign Strategies and Tactics Matter? Exploring Party Elite Perceptions of What Matters When Explaining Election Outcomes," *Journal of Public Affairs* 13/1: 41–52.

Strömbäck, J. and Jendel, L. (2013). "Medierna och opinionsmätningarna," in J. Strömbäck and L. Nord (eds), *Kampen om opinionen: Politisk kommunikation under svenska valrörelser.* Stockholm: SNS Förlag, 150–76.

Strömbäck, J., Lees-Marshment, J., and Rudd, C. (2012). "Political Party Market Orientation in a Global Perspective," in J. Lees-Marshment (eds), *Routledge Handbook of Political Marketing.* London: Routledge, 79–92.

Strömbäck, J., Nord, L., and Shehata, A. (2012). "Swedish Journalists: Between Professionalization and Commercialization," in D. H. Weaver and L. Willnat (eds), *The Global Journalist in the 21st Century.* New York: Routledge, 306–19.

Strömbäck, J. and Shehata, A. (2010). "Media Malaise or a Virtuous Circle? Exploring the Causal Relationships between News Media Exposure, Political News Attention and Political Interest," *European Journal of Political Research* 49/5: 575–97.

Strömbäck, J. and Shehata, A. (2013). "Kampanjeffekter under svenska valrörelser," in J. Strömbäck and L. Nord (eds), *Kampen om opinionen: Politisk kommunikation under svenska valrörelser.* Stockholm: SNS Förlag, 207–38.

Weibull, L., Oscarsson, H., and Bergström, A. (2012). "I framtidens skugga," in L. Weibull, H. Oscarsson, and A. Bergström (eds), *I framtidens skugga.* Gothenburg: SOM-Institute, 11–40.

Zaller, J. R. (2001). "The Rule of Product Substitution in Presidential Campaign News," in E. Katz and Y. Warshel (eds), *Election Studies: What's Their Use?* Boulder: Westview Press, 247–70.

SECTION 5

PUBLIC ADMINISTRATION

SECTION EDITOR
GÖRAN SUNDSTRÖM

....

CHAPTER 21

INTRODUCTION

Public Administration

....

GÖRAN SUNDSTRÖM

THIS section discusses Swedish public administration at the central level. It contains four chapters. In the first—"The Swedish Administrative Model"—Patrik Hall examines four characteristics which together form the backbone of what is often referred to as the Swedish administrative model. These four characteristics are dualism (i.e. the relatively high degree of autonomy that Swedish state agencies enjoy in relation to the government), openness, decentralization, and corporatism. Each is considered in terms of its historical and constitutional foundations as well as the various tensions surrounding them: between the culture of administrative autonomy and the government's steering ambitions; between openness and managerialism; between decentralization and standardization; and between corporatism and lobbying. Hall argues that while the oldest features (the dualism and the openness) are still highly institutionalized, the younger ones (decentralization and corporatism) have weakened in recent decades. However, he also argues that administrative practices linked to the dualism and the openness have changed quite rapidly during the same years, giving these features the appearance of façades; government "talk" remains intact while actual government changes.

In the second chapter—"Administrative Reform"—Göran Sundström analyzes Swedish administrative reform from the mid-1970s until today. He shows that Sweden has embraced most New Public Management ideas, but while Sweden was an early mover regarding ideas about management (especially ideas about steering and control) the neoliberal part of the NPM package took root quite late in Sweden, from around 1990. In recent years Sweden has also embraced some "post-NPM" ideas, i.e., "whole of government," partnership, network governing, and governance. However, in programmatic terms these ideas have not been particularly pronounced. Sundström argues that the development can be understood partly as rational problem-solving. However, there are also observations supporting the argument that the development can be understood as rule-following. There are also clear signs pointing at a path dependency. Regarding effects, the reforms have, according to the reformers themselves, brought about a more effective and result-oriented administration. However, critics argue that the reforms have created a more fragmented state and that they have eroded trust. They also contend that the administration has become more silent and that the reforms have generated so much paperwork that it has precluded the agencies from carrying out their ordinary work.

In the third chapter—"The Public Servant"—Peter Ehn discusses Swedish public servants and the question whether they are to be considered traditional bureaucrats or "managers," modeled after the private sector. Ehn shows that nowadays Swedish public servants can hardly be characterized as old-fashioned bureaucrats, but neither as fully fledged managers. Instead, Ehn prefers to see them as "private servants." The privatization of public servants is expressed partly by an extensive alignment between the public and private sectors regarding the statutory regulation of working conditions. Also, Ehn argues, new public-management-inspired reforms have created a situation where Swedish public servants have come to regard the agencies as formal organizations in their own right. They tend to see themselves as just another worker in any organization, whether it be public or private. There is a limited and decreasing understanding of the specific requirements that such a position entails.

In the final chapter of this section—"Governing the State"—Bengt Jacobsson and Göran Sundström discuss the way the Swedish government governs the administration. They argue that demands put on governments to govern are high in modern democracies but that governing has proven difficult. The difficulties can be explained by the fact that modern states possess a complexity unparalleled in any other organization. According to the authors, ambiguity, conflicting interests, compromises, and the risk of overload reveal governments as everything but those rational, coordinated, and problem-solving entities that they routinely are presented as. However, this does not mean that states are ungovernable. Governments are often able to govern state activities, but they do it in other ways than those implied by contemporary management models with their hierarchical, top-down-oriented, command-and-control methods. Based on a multitude of empirical studies in Sweden, Jacobsson and Sundström discuss six strategies that the Swedish government uses when governing state agencies: creating formal organizations, positioning, fostering competition, distancing, forming communication channels, and storytelling. These strategies allow the government to strike a balance between basic demands on efficiency (avoiding overloading) and democracy (being able to influence issues for which it may become accountable, including issues which have previously been delegated to agencies).

CHAPTER 22

THE SWEDISH ADMINISTRATIVE MODEL

PATRIK HALL

INTRODUCTION

FOLLOWING World War II, Sweden earned the reputation of being one of the most modernized countries in the world. This adherence to a modernist ideology is clearly recognizable in Sweden's public administration, where public managers are eagerly pursuing the latest trends of fashionable management models such as LEAN, TQM, and project management. However, in terms of its administrative organization of the state apparatus, Sweden is often still considered to be one of the most traditional systems in the world. For instance, the ban on ministerial rule in administrative rulings goes back a long way and is primarily motivated on historical grounds rather than on principles of governing rationality. According to one review of Swedish public administration, the structure of the central government has remained "intact" for 350 years (Molander et al. 2002: 148). This has left the relatively small government with poor instruments to govern its administration. In a somewhat more optimistic vein, Andersson (2004) claims that some ancient traits of the Swedish system of government obviously have survived, but this is dependent upon a capacity to adjust where actors adapt these traits to new circumstances.

In this chapter, the Swedish administrative model will be described in terms of both the issue of governability of the Swedish state and the tension between traditional norms and modern practices. The structure will be chronological, starting with the oldest characteristics before briefly sketching the key tensions revolving around these traits. Thus, the chapter will provide an overview of the tensions between governing ambitions and the Swedish culture of administrative autonomy, openness and managerialism, decentralization and standardization, and corporatism and lobbying (Premfors et al. 2009). The final section of the chapter will be devoted to a succinct discussion regarding continuity and change in the Swedish administrative model.

DUALISM—GOVERNMENT AND AUTONOMY

Constitutional Foundations and Cultural Realities

Unlike most other countries, the Swedish central state is not organized into a large number of ministries, each one headed by a minister with autonomous power. Instead, Sweden has a distinctly dualistic structure. Government departments are small and organized in a clearly delimited organization headed by the Prime Minister—the government office (*regeringskansliet*). The bulk of central government activities, typically performed by large ministries in other countries, are undertaken by 370 semi-autonomous state agencies.

It is often claimed that the relative autonomy of Swedish state agencies was established already in the seventeenth century during the administrative reforms of Chancellor Axel Oxenstierna. It can at least be argued that the system of relatively autonomous agencies, in terms of liberty from detailed intervention by the monarch, was founded in the political upheaval following the death of Charles XII in 1718 and the fall of absolutism which resulted in the constitution of the "Age of Liberty" in 1720; the fallout from these events gave primacy to the parliament in terms of decision-making (Hallberg 2003). Why the dualistic system survived following constitutional changes (such as the democratic and parliamentary breakthrough in the early twentieth century) is not an issue to be discussed here (Andersson 2004). Rather, the issue is its enduring capability to persist in modern times, together with the problems and opportunities of dualism.

The strongest formal statements of dualism in the contemporary constitution are, first, that government decisions are settled collectively, resulting in an indirect ban on individual ministers governing their subordinate agencies, and second, that the government must not interfere in particular cases of the agencies (the Instrument of Government ch. 7, art. 3; ch. 12, art. 2). This actually lays a somewhat weak foundation for administrative dualism, and this foundation has never been particularly strong (cf. SOU 1983:39; SOU 2008:118). It grants the agencies discretion only in matters of individual decision-making (Bull and Sterzel 2013: 283). Instead, the rule regarding collective decision-making has the most immediate effect upon governmental culture. This requires a high degree of coordination among the ministries, making the Swedish government an organization characterized by negotiations (Larsson 1995). The individual ministers are thus quite weak, particularly in relation to the Prime Minister, and specifically in times of coalition government, when ministers may represent small parties with little parliamentary support. Collective decision-making also rules out possible alliances between ministers and agencies. Nevertheless, this negotiation machinery makes the government office a collective actor with strong action capabilities.

Historically, the division between a small government office—which, at the time of writing, employs only 2 percent of state personnel (and far below 1 percent of all public employees in Sweden)—and large agencies provides the strongest empirical foundation for dualism in Sweden. It is simply impossible for this small center to provide detailed government over the vast public landscape. As Jacobsson and Sundström point out in their chapter of this volume, the government solves this problem by delegation. "Small is beautiful," exclaims Page (2012: ch. 5) in a comparative investigation of political/bureaucratic relationships, where he argues that Sweden, due to this historical structure, is the state with the most clear division of policy/operations task in his comparative survey. Thus, the limited governmental level paradoxically seems to imply clear, coherent, and delimited political direction. Sweden has even been recalled as a role model for the international wave of "agencification" (Wettenhall 2005) since its historical structure presupposes the policy/operations divide that NPM reformers have eagerly tried to obtain (Verschuere 2009).

A historical–institutional explanation for the enduring importance of dualism in Sweden is that it has been a strategic resource for actors in new historical situations (Thelen 2004). The "ban on ministerial rule" is probably the most well-known constitutional article among Swedish political journalists—it has resulted in the fall of at least one cabinet minister as well as in severe accusations against many other ministers (Bäck and Larsson 2008: 176). The opposition uses every opportunity to blame ministers for this "fault." However, given the dualistic structure, it is equally true that individual ministers—as well as the government—may claim non-responsibility (Molander et al. 2002: 64; see also Hood 2010) for controversial decisions or outright mistakes made by the agencies (Bäck and Larsson 2008: 191-6). The agencies, in turn, may be quite confident about this culture of autonomy. Observers of Swedish politics often point to the comparatively autonomous actions of individual agency staff members in Sweden, although agencies often (rhetorically or not) request clearer guidance from the government (ibid.). Thus, even if the constitutional foundations for dualism remain somewhat fictitious, a culture of autonomous action prevails since it suits different actors.

The Tension between Government and Autonomy

Autonomy is a multidimensional concept, which may relate both to the government and to other social forces such as business interests (Carpenter 2001; Verhoest et al. 2004; Groenleer 2009; Verhoest et al. 2012). In Sweden, the small government office's ability to effectively govern the large agencies has been a matter of concern (see Chapter 23 by Sundström in this volume). The large agencies and the culture of dualism have led to repeated, but often unsubstantiated, complaints regarding the "ungovernability" of the Swedish state (cf. Molander et al. 2002). The brief observations below will discuss issues that illustrate the tension between government and the culture of autonomy: managerial autonomy, EU membership, and informal versus formal forms of governing.

Managerial autonomy in Sweden has increased during recent decades. The agency top-managers (directors general, DGs) have full discretion in issues on internal organization and recruitment (similar to local governments). The OECD (2009) considers Sweden a world leader in relation to HRM issues. This is a result of rather recent changes (see Ehn's chapter in this volume). Before the 1980s a significant part of government business revolved around detailed interventions in the agencies' internal organization and staff recruitment. On the other hand, what Verhoest et al. (2004) call "structural autonomy" (i.e. the existence of some form of governing or at least supervisory board) has decreased in recent years. The majority of agencies (60 percent, according to the Swedish Agency for Public Management 2014:4) are now exclusively governed by the respective DG. This development has weakened the "Swedish model" of corporatism, since organized interests were formerly represented in the boards. Thus, today, autonomy for Swedish agencies primarily means managerial autonomy. On the other hand, these formally clearer lines of accountability between the government and the DGs may in practice reinforce government control.

The government, and especially the Prime Minister, holds wide discretion in the procedure of appointing new DGs; a state of fact which is routinely questioned by the parliamentary opposition. A claim has repeatedly been raised that the government uses this discretion to politicize the agencies by appointing party-affiliated managers. Investigations have proved that this claim is vastly exaggerated (Sandahl 2003) and that most contemporary DGs lack both political and government background (Lemne and Larsson, forthcoming). A single, government-appointed leader may be both more dependent on and more easily controlled by the government. Managerial autonomy has increased, but recruited managers are seemingly more loyal to the government than before.

The strongest formal challenge towards agency autonomy in recent years has been Sweden's membership in the European Union. While the knowledge resources of the agencies are in high demand within the EU system, agencies are not allowed to make any autonomous decisions within the EU institutions. Unsurprisingly, the autonomous culture of Swedish agencies led to misapprehensions and conflicts in the early days of EU membership:

> Some of my experts thought that they only represented themselves and their expertise. It was extremely dangerous; they could sit with the Commission, together with experts from other nations, and figure out regulation about stuff which was insane from a Swedish, political perspective. In order to get a grip on this we had to introduce a new management system where it was not allowed to go to Brussels without some form of instruction from the government, usually with quite strict demands of reporting back. This was an important change. (Interview with the former DG of the Swedish Environmental Protection Agency)

This new situation has resulted in a closer collaboration between the government departments and the agencies, at least in certain policy sectors. In a formal sense, agencies operating within policy areas strongly regulated by the EU—or operating at the core of the internal market (such as the Swedish Customs and the Competition Agency)—have, in fact, become more autonomous from the government and instead more subordinate to the EU institutions (Jacobsson and Sundström 2009). In most cases, however, the informal cooperation between government and agencies has increased due to the international work which makes (at least part of) the agencies more of a governmental staff unit. It is still too early to ascertain the actual influence of EU membership upon Swedish agency autonomy—nevertheless, we know that relations are changing as Sweden evolves de facto from a parliamentary democracy to a system built on separation of powers between the EU and the state (Bergman 2004).

The most interesting but also most problematic question concerns how policy autonomy has developed in recent years. In plain terms: how much political decision-making is made by the bureaucracy? The level of policy autonomy for local municipalities and counties is easy to define, as these levels are free to expand the scope of their activities within the limits set by the Local Government Act. However, the level of policy autonomy for agencies is less clear-cut. Empirically, these matters are difficult to study since agencies do not like to confess they have policy autonomy; conversely, their counterparts in governmental departments do not like to admit they are not in control. There is reason to believe that the nature of the task may be a decisive factor (Bach 2012). Tasks with high political saliency are usually more strongly monitored by the government, while tasks with lower saliency may indicate the government's control is more pro forma. The following quotation from an earlier DG of a politically salient agency illustrates forms of informality that may have been a pattern in government–agency relations during the lengthy Social Democratic period in power:

> I have worked at the Ministry, and I understood that Bror Rexed [the DG in the 1960s and 1970s], and thus the National Board of Health and Welfare, received an important political role; government bills were virtually written at the agency. Where Bror had a group of young, talented men around him—those were the ones he actually governed. ... The relation towards the ministry has changed. This agency is very close to politics. It is not an agency which may work for itself in its own little corner. When I first came to the agency, many of the staff had direct and personal contacts with officials in the ministry. I didn't approve. Of course, you must exchange information, but this reduced my capacity of making decisions. I could decide, "Now we've been working with sexual mutilations for three years; I think that is enough." Then somebody called the ministry and said, "She is going to terminate the program—it is insane!" Consequently, it became an issue in the Parliament, and subsequently bounced back to me as a Governmental instruction. (Interview with former DG of the Board of Health and Welfare)

This indicates not only a quite strong degree of informality, but also that the relationship has changed, possibly as a result of reform models (such as NPM), but maybe also because of the weakened dominance of the Social Democrat party.

NPM-inspired steering models are devoted to role separation between policy development, public administration, and monitoring—a role separation between politics and management which is more rhetorically embraced than ever before. At the same time, as already indicated, this policy/operations divide may fit the historical Swedish system remarkably well. Nonetheless, increased formalization may also endanger politicians' ability to govern informally. Perhaps, without too much attention being paid, politicians have been reduced to a somewhat impotent position of formal goal-setters. There is a tension between the political side, which may prefer more traditional and informal ad hoc modes of governing, and the bureaucratic side, which seems to emphasize formalized control and management systems (Ullström 2011). However, in terms of political ideology, there is also evidence—following an increased body of empirical material on center-right government—that non-Social Democratic governments in Sweden are more inclined to purify roles and to enhance formalized relations between government and agencies. Both the Bildt government (1991–4) and the Reinfeldt government (2006–14) have pursued clearer rules and boundaries for public administration (cf. The Government 2010).

The most evident sign of the NPM trend within public administration in Sweden is that control over the inputs of agencies has been replaced by a focus on outputs. Agencies are primarily expected to devote their attention to government goals, as stated in their letters of appropriation and in agency instructions, the fulfillment of which are controlled according to an increasingly demanding performance regime. In other words, in Sweden, agencies are (at least formally) at present governed by a performance-based regime similar to those in many other "agencified" countries (Jacobsson and Sundström 2009). The government is also issuing more detailed instructions on the roles and functions of the agencies. In addition, the monitoring of agency operations has increased through the development of inspection and audit agencies where the separation between executing and monitoring policy has become more important than ever before (Johansson and Lindgren 2013). This is a subjection to the "audit society" trend (Power 1997), a consequence of far-reaching devolution where the government judges it necessary (and is demanded by media and public opinion) to take on a more supervisory role towards authorities on subordinate levels.

To sum up, Sweden's administration is characterized by a historical (rather than a constitutional) dualism implying a relatively autonomous bureaucracy. However, the delineation between this large bureaucracy and a small political core has been noted as a success factor since it provides a clear division between policies and operations which so many reform models call for (Page 2012). Furthermore, some aspects of managerial autonomy have been strengthened in recent years. On the other hand, there are reasons to believe that the DGs more than before are the extended arms of the government. Furthermore, EU membership reduces agency autonomy; informal contacts have seemingly become more sensitive or, at least, more centralized; detailed requirements upon the agencies' work have increased; and an NPM-inspired performance regime has been established. The risk of ungovernability seems to be exaggerated; instead, given that the autonomous culture of the Swedish administration seems to have been an important prerequisite for effective action, recent reforms arguably go too far in the other direction.

OPENNESS

Constitutional Foundations

The most well-known feature of the Swedish administrative model is likely the tradition of openness based on the 1766 Freedom of Information Act, in which public access to all government documents was granted in principle—the so-called "principle of public access" (*Offentlighetsprincipen*). The reason for the extraordinary progressivity regarding freedom of information was the strong dominance of the Riksdag during the Age of Liberty (1720–72), a period of strong parliamentary rule when all the power was vested in the Riksdag's representatives. However, even after the return of authoritarian rule (1772–1809), a strongly progressive Freedom of Information Act was adapted, and the principle of public access was reinstituted.

In the current Freedom of the Press Act, there is a whole chapter devoted to "the public nature of official documents." Here, it is stated that Swedish citizens shall enjoy free access to official documents and that any restrictions in this right must be "scrupulously specified in a provision of a special act of law" (ch. 2, art. 2). It is also stated that requests for copies of official documents "shall be dealt with promptly" (ch. 2, art. 13) and that the authority is not allowed either to inquire regarding the reasons for the request or to investigate the identity of the person making the request (art. 14).

Furthermore, the culture of openness is strongly promoted by public employees having the same rights of free speech as every other citizen. Most important in this regard is the informant protection for whistleblowers within public administration; for instance, managers have no right to research the identity of an employee who has leaked information to, for example, the press. Violation of this clause may lead to one year's imprisonment (ch. 3). Thus, Sweden has a very strong constitutional foundation for open government and transparency in public affairs, which is also a cornerstone of the autonomous culture within public administration.

The Tension between Openness and Managerialism

When Sweden entered the EU, there were fears that the principle of public access was threatened by the more secretive continental tradition towards public access to official documents. These fears proved to be exaggerated. Sweden (at least initially) contributed to increased transparency within the EU (Hillebrandt et al. 2014). Instead, the greatest challenge toward open government policies in recent years has been the privatization of public sector organizations. Private actors fulfilling public services have been unwilling to submit to the public administration transparency (Stolt et al. 2011). At the time of writing, a government proposal is under way regarding informant protection for whistleblowers in privately delivered welfare activities (SOU 2013:79).

A document is defined as official if it is "held by a public authority" and "has been received or drawn up by such an authority" (Freedom of the Press Act, ch. 2 art. 3). This implies, for instance, that all email correspondence to and from the authority is official. The consequence is an obvious delicacy in the production of "documents" within all public organizations in Sweden. A former DG of the National Audit Office, Inga-Britt Ahlenius, has referred to the right to public access as a right to "inspect empty cupboards." Her main argument (*Dagens Nyheter*, April 23, 2004) is that the "threat" of the right of immediate access to documents implies that the "really important" discussions and decisions are not recorded at all. Hence, the tendency in Swedish media is to study easily accessible but politically insipid documents, such as copies of restaurant bills of Swedish decision-makers incurred while on duty. Ahlenius has received support from political science professor Lennart Lundquist (1998), who argues that "economism" has become the overwhelmingly dominant value of the Swedish public sector. This implies that democratic values of open government—such as public access and freedom of speech—must give way to corporate values of efficiency and loyalty to management. Lundquist claims that even if the constitutional foundations for freedom of speech and information are strong, the sanctions against violations of these freedoms are ineffectual. The effect of this situation is a "silent" public administration where civil servants prioritize loyalty to the managers—"managerialism" rather than acting as the "guardians of democracy." The obstacle, in Sweden as well as elsewhere, in validating the claims of a declining public ethos in favor of "economism" is the lack of empirical data. The claim that Sweden is worse than comparable jurisdictions in recording the processes behind sensible political decisions *because of* the principle of public access is not empirically validated by Ahlenius nor anyone else. It could rather be argued that the most important effect of the principle of public access is preventive and acts as an important corrective against eventual corruption (Hansson 2014).

What is likely, though, is that the dominant center of attention to efficiency and service delivery has been instigated within public management. The increasing importance of media image for public organizations, the rapid proliferation of information technology in society, and the very fast expansion of the number of communication officers in public organizations are vital aspects of this discussion. Image management has become a central component of all public organizations in Sweden due to new self-perceptions of corporate identity. However, this image management is something distinct from the liberal regulation of openness. Externally, image management consists of producing an organizational brand and marketing the activities of public organizations toward the customer group of citizens, rather than of accurately describing what takes place within them. Internally, the communication strategies of public organizations demand organizational uniformity and collective allegiance to managerial goals, something which often conflicts with diversity among employees as safeguarded by freedom of speech. To claim that Swedish civil servants' freedom of speech is endangered is an overstatement, but it seems reasonable to conclude that the Swedish tradition of openness has been affected by the modern obsession with image management (Hall 2012).

THE FRAGMENTED WELFARE STATE

Constitutional and Historical Foundations

Even if Sweden is a "unitary state" it has had a long tradition of local self-government, which is inscribed in the first paragraph of the Instrument of Government. Local self-government is effectuated on two levels: municipalities and county councils (the latter mainly responsible for health care), with municipalities traditionally being the unit with the strongest democratic legitimacy. Municipalities (and county councils) are not only democratic instruments of self-determination but also—as stated in the first chapter of the Instrument of Government—parts of public administration. They have the right to levy taxes. One of the most, perhaps the most, important tensions within Swedish politics is the one between municipalities as self-determined democratic units and their ever-increasing role as the extended arm of the government in implementing the welfare state.

Sweden's rise to global peak position in terms of public sector expenditure (peaking at 63 percent of GDP in 1985) was very rapid. The most important expansion took place between 1965 and 1985, and it mainly concerned the local and regional level of government—what Tarschys (1983) labeled "the public revolution." The result is that the composition of the different levels has changed over the years, as shown in Table 22.1.

Based on these figures, it is clear that devolution has become the most important feature of the Swedish administrative model. Given that the Swedish welfare state is commonly conceived as one of the best examples of a centralized welfare state model, this is somewhat paradoxical. However, it is important to make a distinction between the social insurance systems, which are centralized and unified (and increasingly so during recent years), and the organization of welfare state service delivery. Education up to high-school level, child care, elderly care and services for the disabled, social security, the enforcement of environmental regulations, and new responsibilities for integration are all services which have become decentralized to the local government level.

Table 22.1 Distribution of public employees on different government levels, 1979 and 2009 (percent)

Employer/part of employed personnel	1979	2009
State	33.5	18
County councils (*landsting*)	28	19
Municipalities (*kommuner*)	38.5	63
Sum	100% (N=1 203 798)	100% (N=1 222 500)

Source: *Statistical Yearbook of Sweden*, Swedish Statistics (SCB)

The responsibility for health care lies with the county councils, as does the expanding responsibility for regional development.

The Tension between Decentralization and National Standardization

What characterizes many of these public services is that they are maintained by professionals. Consequently, professional cultures, socialized by common and specialized degree programs, bring unity to the welfare state. Furthermore, this professional administration was previously regulated, often in detail, by large national "reform bureaucracies" with a (Social Democratic) political character (Lindvall and Rothstein 2006). These two features—reform-oriented regulatory bureaucracies and strong professionalism—provided unity in an otherwise fragmented public administration. However, these reform-oriented bureaucracies are today reduced to almost nothing. In recent years, many national agencies have transformed into audit agencies with the single function of analyzing performance, and even more multipurpose agencies hold performance monitoring as one of their key tasks. In other words, central guidance mechanisms of the civil service have diminished over the years, and local and regional governments are often forced to work out such guidance on their own. Simultaneously, increasing variation between municipalities, following the 1991 Local Government Act and the privatization of public service delivery (mainly in the form of subcontracting), has had consequences on the unity of welfare professionalism. Furthermore, many of the newly delegated functions such as elderly care and services for the disabled (a rapidly developing sector) lack a strong professional foundation. The problem of governing this massive organization in a time of declining party membership has also increased (Bäck and Larsson 2008: ch. 11).

The decentralization reforms were, however, welcomed by the municipalities and county councils. They now have more freedom to self-organize and to develop independent policies, even though the majority of municipal activities are nationally regulated and monitored. Evidence of this local and regional autonomy can be witnessed as these organizations—predominantly the larger ones—often hold leading positions in public sector development, such as in privatization reforms within education, health care, and elderly care. The largest counties and municipalities are also the largest workplaces in Sweden (one fifth of the Swedish workforce is employed therein), and they, rather than the national agencies, are also leading actors in organizational modernization.

However, the other side of the decentralization coin is that municipalities in recent years have been delegated increased workloads without any influence over this delegation, possibly with decreasing ability to manage these new assignments. The local decision-makers' basic claim, which undoubtedly has some validity, is that increasingly unsolvable problems are dumped on the municipalities without accompanying resources, since municipalities are not allowed to raise taxes over a specific level

(Strandberg 2008). The Swedish period of decentralization seems to have come to an end with the focus now shifting instead toward national standardization. Public opinion seems to be an important factor in this process. Responsibility for education and health care is decentralized, which creates differences, but the acceptance of differences has been in decline during recent years. The ministers are held accountable even if formal responsibility resides on the local level. Thus, the government increasingly uses binding regulation to force local government to comply with national policy—for instance, in the form of "patient rights" within health care, increasing standardization of education, and legally binding obligations for municipalities to receive and house immigrants. This "recentralization" trend reinforces already existing ambiguities regarding responsibility and accountability between the state and local governments.

STAKEHOLDER INFLUENCE—FROM FORMALIZED CORPORATISM TO INFORMAL LOBBYING

Historical Foundations

One of the most significant traits of what was once called "the Swedish model" was the high degree of formal influence of organized interests in the government policy process. This formalized relation has been distinguished as a stabilizing force and referred to as "the spirit of Saltsjöbaden" (*Saltsjöbadsandan* after a summit in the small town of Saltsjöbaden in 1938 where the labor market organizations jointly decided to regulate industrial conflict measures and to establish mitigating institutions). From a political-science perspective, Sweden between the 1930s and the early 1980s has been referred to as a corporatist state (Rothstein 1992). The regulation of industrial conflict measures, which led to comparatively peaceful relations on the labor market, implied stability in state–society relations and made ambitious political reforms possible.

One important form of stakeholder influence within administrative affairs has been the formal role of organized interests in the legislative process, which is even safeguarded in the constitution:

> In preparing Government business, the necessary information and opinions shall be obtained from the public authorities concerned. Information and opinions shall be obtained from local authorities as necessary. Organizations and individuals shall also be given an opportunity to express an opinion as necessary. (The Instrument of Government, ch. 7, art. 2)

What is referred to here is mainly the Swedish tradition of policy-making through governmental consultations at the early stages of the policy process—consultations which often were (and still are) expected to provide legislators with sharp suggestions on regulation and policy recommendations (Ruin 1974). Aside from often being represented in the specially designated investigating commissions themselves, organized interests such as trade unions, Employers' Federations, and trade associations always have opportunities to give opinions on commission reports that are broadly remitted.

Another important link between state and society within policy formulation and implementation was the formalized representation of organized interests in agency boards with executive power. This was most strongly emphasized not only in the boards of the "reform bureaucracies" such as the Labor Market Board, where the strongest labor market organizations were all represented, but also in sectorial agencies such as the Forest Agency which included organized interests within their remit in their boards. In fact, in 1977 all state agencies but twelve had boards (Tarschys 2012: 301). The common denominator of these interactions between the state and organized interests, as interpreted by political scientists, has been consensus around the idea of "the strong state" (Lindvall and Rothstein 2006).

The Tension between Corporatism and Lobbying

The formal representation of labor market organizations came to an end when the Swedish Employers' Federation unilaterally decided to withdraw from all government agency boards in 1991. The reason for this dramatic measure has been an issue for debate among students of Swedish politics (Rothstein and Bergström 1999; Johansson 2000), but it seems clear that the federation felt themselves increasingly held hostage in the "strong state" model and wished to employ other channels of influence, inspired by US business models (cf. Barley 2010), for instance, through lobbying and think tanks. Even more important was the decision by the Employers' Federation to withdraw from the general agreement negotiations. Today, Swedish industrial negotiations are, with a few exceptions, strongly decentralized. In Sweden, as elsewhere, the greatest loss in terms of power has thus been suffered by the trade unions.

It may be true that Sweden is no longer a corporatist state, but this does not mean that the influence of organized interests has disappeared. On the contrary, informal network relations within all types of policy sectors are strongly promoted by the government, which now often makes it mandatory for national agencies to interact with "relevant stakeholders." The sector-based interests within certain policy areas are arguably as strong as ever. The difference from the past is that the current relations are more informal than before. In this more informal environment, the toolkit of lobbyism has also become more multifold. One central resemblance remains, though; namely, that the goal, at least on the part of the government, is still to preserve or generate consensus and stability. As opposing views are often hard to handle in informal relationships, the common reaction by central network actors is to exclude opposing views. Furthermore, common professional background is often vital for reaching consensus between public organizations and organized interests. For instance, I have been been observing "dialogues" regarding restrictions of hazardous chemicals between the Swedish Chemicals Agency and representatives of the textile industry: important preconditions for reaching consensus are the exclusion of actors with opposing views (i.e. environmental organizations) and the involved actors have a high level of knowledge and competence in chemistry (see also Pierre and Sundström 2009).

The term "stakeholder influence" is an adequate description of how to envisage the relation between state and society in Sweden today. The business language has colonized descriptions of political relations through concepts such as "relevant actors," "partnerships," "stakeholders," and "networks." As with the older language of corporatism, it is liberated from all forms of conflicts and opposing interests. Consensus still serves as the overarching rationale for state–society relations, as was the case in the corporatist system. However, the ability to observe power games is more restricted today since relations have become delegated and deformalized.

CONCLUDING DISCUSSION

As I have shown in this chapter, there is no unitary "administrative model" in Sweden; instead, there is (as in all advanced societies probably) a contradictory one. The development within central areas of the Swedish public sector seems to refute a key theoretical proposition of the neo-institutional model. While neo-institutionalism emphasizes adaptation to legitimized global norms regarding organization while stating that administrative practices are always deemed problematic or sometimes even impossible to change (Pollitt 2001), the opposite seems to be true of Sweden. Despite decades as a member of the EU, Sweden remains characterized by undisputed institutional norms, where the oldest norms (i.e. dualism and openness) are arguably the most prominent. On the other hand, administrative practices have changed rapidly in recent decades, giving some of the institutional norms the appearance of façades. In other words, discourses of government remain intact while actual government changes.

Regarding the management of national agencies, a principal-agent model of government has been applied, which is more in line with the Westminster model than any Swedish traditions. The most obvious feature of this is the persistent performance regime, which has replaced the earlier models of input management. Pollitt and Bouckaert (2011) place Sweden, together with the other Scandinavian countries, in between the Anglo-Saxon NPM model and the continental neo-Weberian one. However, in terms of administrative reforms (especially privatization), Sweden has clearly moved in the NPM direction more than any of the other Scandinavian countries (see Sundström's Chapter 23 in this volume). While political scientists claim that the Wilsonian boundary between politics and bureaucracy broke down long ago, in Swedish practice this boundary seems to be more emphasized than ever before. In this respect, the Swedish dualism is maintained, and perhaps it is particularly apt to introduce NPM in Sweden simply due to this dualist tradition. Still, the speed by which older administrative practices have been substituted by new ones, of Anglo-Saxon origins, is striking.

As a whole, ideas of national peculiarity should not be overstated in a time of unprecedented convergence, harmonization, and standardization, which are all, of course, reinforced by EU membership. Convergence is not merely a "useful myth" (Pollitt 2001) but an existing reality in Swedish public administration, where managers eagerly study and adapt to the mainstreaming business re-engineering programs for the public sector and its policies, benchmark themselves in relation to "competitors" and "partners," and constantly "process-orient" or "LEAN" their organizations. The university is perhaps one of the most striking examples: During less than two decades, Swedish universities have made an astonishing journey from a traditional institution characterized by collegial guardianship and rule by professors to corporate management (Hall 2012).

The "useful myths" are rather the institutional norms which describe the Swedish public administration model. It is true that traits such as dualism and transparency have shown a remarkable survival capacity. On the one hand, this provides public administration with a robust, cultural foundation. On the other hand, there is a risk that the enduring norms will fail to encompass changing practices. Even if state–society relations have changed, it seems as though it is only there that one of the central norms of the "Swedish model" has survived in practice: the norm of consensus as a precondition for stability—especially on the labor market. This norm survives because important interests are vested in it. Hence, Sweden remains a state with a strong labor regulation, a generous social insurance system, and high taxes.

The Swedish state rests on some remarkably ancient constitutional and political traditions. Still, there is reason to conclude that Sweden can be classed as a modernist rather than a traditionalist regarding its administrative model. Sweden was a modernist country in the 1950s and 1960s, when the universal welfare model was rolled out. But it is an equally modernist country now, when large parts of the state are rolled back (Bergh and Erlingsson 2009).

REFERENCES

Ahlenius, I.-B. (2004). "Rätten att granska tomma skåp," *Dagens Nyheter*, April 23.

Andersson, C. (2004). "En tudelad stat? Dualismens överlevnad i den svenska staten 1718–1987," dissertation, Stockholm University, Department of Political Science.

Bach, T. (2012). "The Involvement of Agencies in Policy Formulation: Explaining Variation in Policy Autonomy of Federal Agencies in Germany," *Policy and Society* 31: 211–22.

Bäck, H. and Larsson, T. (2008). *Governing and Governance in Sweden*. Lund: Studentlitteratur.

Barley, S. R. (2010). "Building an Institutional Field to Corral a Government: A Case to set an Agenda for Organization Studies," *Organization Studies* 31: 777–805.

Bergh, A. and Erlingsson, G. (2009). "Liberalization without Retrenchment: Understanding the Consensus on Swedish Welfare State Reforms," *Scandinavian Political Studies* 32: 71–93.

Bergman, T. (2004). "Sweden: Democratic Reforms and Partisan Decline in an Emerging Separation-of-Powers System," *Scandinavian Political Studies* 27: 203–25.

Bull, T. and Sterzel, F. (2013). *Regeringsformen: En kommentar*. Lund: Studentlitteratur.

Carpenter, D. P. (2001). *The Forging of Bureaucratic Autonomy: Reputations, Networks and Policy Innovation in Executive Agencies 1862–1928*. Princeton: Princeton University Press.

The Government (2010). Prop. 2009/10:175.

Groenleer, M. L. P. (2009). "The Autonomy of European Union Agencies. A Comparative Study of Institutional Development," unpublished doctoral thesis, University of Leiden.

Hall, P. (2012). *Managementbyråkrati: Organisationspolitisk makt i svensk, offentlig förvaltning*. Malmö: Liber.

Hallberg, P. (2003). *Ages of Liberty: Social Upheaval, History Writing and the New Public Sphere in Sweden 1740–1792*. Stockholm University: Department of Political Science.

Hansson, A. (2014). "Tjänstemannen är nyckeln," in B. Jacobsson (ed.), *I medborgarnas tjänst: Essäer om förvaltningspolitik*. Södertörns högskola: Förvaltningsakademin, 25–36.

Hillebrandt, M. Z., Curtin, D., and Meijer, A. (2014). "Transparency in the EU Council of Ministers: An Institutional Analysis," *European Law Journal* 20: 1–20.

Hood, C. (2010). *The Blame Game: Spin, Bureaucracy, and Self-Preservation in Government*. Princeton: Princeton University Press.

Jacobsson, B. and Sundström, G. (2009). "Between Autonomy and Control: Transformation of the Swedish Administrative Model," in P. G. Roness and H. Sætren (eds), *Change and Continuity in Public Sector Organizations*. Bergen: Fagbokforlaget, 103–25.

Johansson, J. (2000). *SAF och den svenska modellen: En studie av uppbrottet från förvaltningskorporatismen 1982–1991*. Uppsala: Acta Universitatis Upsaliensis.

Johansson, V. and Lindgren, L. (eds) (2013). *Uppdrag offentlig granskning*. Lund: Studentlitteratur.

Larsson, T. (1995). *Governing Sweden*. Stockholm: Swedish Agency for Administrative Development.

Lemne, M. and Larsson, T. (forthcoming). "Regeringens utnämningsmakt i teori och praktik," unpublished manuscript.

Lindvall, J. and Rothstein, B. (2006). "Sweden: The Fall of the Strong State," *Scandinavian Political Studies* 29: 47–63.

Lundquist, L. (1998). *Demokratins väktare: Ämbetsmännen och vårt offentliga etos*. Lund: Studentlitteratur.

Molander, P., Nilsson, J.-E., and Schick, A. (2002). *Does Anyone Govern? The Relationship between the Government Office and the Agencies in Sweden*. Stockholm: SNS.

OECD (2009). *Government at a Glance 2009*. OECD Publishing.

Page, E. C. (2012). *Policy without Politicians: Bureaucratic Influence in Comparative Perspective*. Oxford: Oxford University Press.

Pierre, J. and Sundström, G. (eds) (2009). *Samhällsstyrning i förändring*. Malmö: Liber.

Pollitt, C. (2001). "Convergence—the Useful Myth?" *Public Administration* 79: 933–47.

Pollitt, C. and Bouckaert, G. (2011). *Public Management Reform: A Comparative Analysis. New Public Management, Governance, and the Neo-Weberian State*. Oxford: Oxford University Press.

Power, M. (1997). *Audit Society: Rituals of Verification*. Oxford: Oxford University Press.

Premfors, R., Ehn, P., Haldén, E., and Sundström, G. (2009). *Demokrati och byråkrati*. Lund: Studentlitteratur.

Rothstein, B. (1992). "Explaining Swedish Corporatism: The Formative Moment," *Scandinavian Political Studies* 15: 173–91.

Rothstein, B. and Bergström, J. (1999). *Korporatismens fall och den svenska modellens kris.* Stockholm: SNS.

Ruin, O. (1974). "Participatory Democracy and Corporativism: The Case of Sweden," *Scandinavian Political Studies* 9: 171-84.

Sandahl, R. (2003). "Förtjänst och skicklighet—om utnämningar och ansvarsutkrävande av generaldirektörer," Ds 2003:7. Expertgruppen för studier i offentlig ekonomi.

SOU (1983:39). "Politisk styrning—administrativ självständighet," governmental report.

SOU (2008:118). "Styra och ställa: Förslag till en effektivare statsförvaltning," governmental report.

SOU (2013:79). "Stärkt meddelarskydd för privatanställda i offentligt finansierad verksamhet," governmental report.

Stolt, R., Blomqvist, P., and Winblad, U. (2011). "Privatization of Social Services: Quality Differences in Swedish Elderly Care," *Social Science & Medicine* 72: 560-7.

Strandberg, U. (2008). "Kommunal självstyrelse," in I. Mattson and O. Pettersson (eds), *Svensk författningspolitik.* Stockholm: SNS, 191-213.

Swedish Agency for Public Management (Statskontoret) (2014:4). "Myndigheternas ledningsformer—en kartläggning och analys."

Tarschys, D. (1983). *Den offentliga revolutionen.* Stockholm: Liber.

Tarschys, D. (2012). "Ett rekviem över hundra verksstyrelser med begränsat ansvar," in *Vänbok till Sten Heckscher.* Stockholm: Iustus Förlag, 299-308.

Thelen, K. (2004). *How Institutions Evolve: The Political Economy of Skills in Germany, Britain, the United States, and Japan.* Cambridge: Cambridge University Press.

Ullström, A. (2011). "Styrning bakom kulisserna: Regeringskansliets politiska staber och regeringens styrningskapacitet," dissertation, Stockholm University, Department of Political Science.

Verhoest, K., Peters, B. G., Bouckaert, G., and Verschuere, B. (2004). "The Study of Organizational Autonomy: A Conceptual Review," *Public Administration and Development* 24: 101-18.

Verhoest, K., Thiel, S. V., Bouckaert, G., and Lægreid, P. (eds) (2012). *Government Agencies: Practices and Lessons from 30 Countries.* Basingstoke: Palgrave Macmillan.

Verschuere, B. (2009). "The Role of Public Agencies in the Policy-Making Process: Rhetoric versus Reality," *Public Policy and Administration* 24: 22-46.

Wettenhall, R. (2005). "Agencies and Non-departmental Public Bodies: The Hard and Soft Lenses of Agencification Theory," *Public Management Review* 7: 615-35.

CHAPTER 23

ADMINISTRATIVE REFORM

GÖRAN SUNDSTRÖM

INTRODUCTION

IN recent years, administrative reform has become a much-discussed policy field in Swedish public debate. Developments within Swedish schools, health care, the police, elderly care, and other policy fields have led the media to examine and discuss public sector steering and control systems and how they result in undesirable, sometimes almost bizarre effects. The right of privately owned but publicly financed service providers to make and take out profits within welfare areas such as schools and elderly care has also been debated extensively in the media.

Actually, the debate about administrative reform has been of such proportions and intensity that it became one of the issues determining the outcome of the parliamentary election in 2014. We have not said this about the above policy field since the historic election in 1976, when the center-right parties took over government after forty-four years of Social Democratic rule. Administrative reform has for a long time been a quite invisible policy field in Sweden. Certainly, there have, as will be shown here, been many far-reaching programs and decisions within this field during the past thirty years, but they have not been particularly contentious among the political parties. Swedes have witnessed changes of government in 1991, 1994, and 2006; however, these changes have not led to the abandonment or redirection of established policies (Premfors et al. 2009). And the great reform wave, known as New Public Management (NPM), has hardly been debated in Sweden; in fact, the concept has only very recently appeared in the Swedish media and become known to the Swedish people.

All of this is noteworthy, not only because this policy field contains important issues but also because it is a very broad field. Administrative reform can be defined as deliberate and government-wide changes to the structure and processes of public sector organizations (Pollitt and Bouckaert 2011: 2). Thus, it targets the whole (or at least large parts of) the public administration—it is a policy that goes "crosswise" to all other policy fields, and therefore one would think that they are of great concern to many people. At the same time, decisions within this policy field are directed at the organization and work of the administration, and not at more citizen-oriented matters, i.e. education, environment, health, and defense. From the citizens' point of view, it is thus a more indirect policy.

This chapter contains an analysis of Swedish administrative reform from the mid-1970s until today. The discussion reflects central administrative reform, and three questions guide the presentation:

(1) How can the policy field be described in terms of dominating ideas and decisions taken?
(2) How can the development be explained?
(3) What are the effects of the reforms?

The text is divided into three main sections corresponding to the questions above. Thus, first, the ideas and decisions will be described, then the explanations for the development discussed, and, finally, the effects of the reforms analyzed. The chapter ends with a summary. The text is based on official documents—government bills, commission reports, and agency reports—and research reports.

IDEAS AND DECISIONS

The term "administrative reform" (*förvaltningspolitik*) is quite new in the Swedish language. It was not used in the public debate or in research until the latter part of the 1980s. Acceptance of the concept came from increasingly systematic and persistent attempts, toward the end of the 1970s, to comprehensively reform the administration. During this period, various institutional arrangements characterizing traditional policy fields—such as a responsible minister, specific agencies, commissions of inquiry, and government bills—started to emerge within administrative reform. Sweden is, in this respect, similar to many other comparable countries (Pollitt and Bouckaert 2011: 5–9).

Decentralization

When the center-right government came into power in 1976 it immediately initiated a range of commissions of inquiry to examine various issues linked to the administration's organization and work. Besides measures to cut expenses, simplify working methods, and make the administration more service-oriented (Tarschys 1983), the government also introduced a more conscious and comprehensive decentralization strategy. A number of commissions were initiated to advance decentralization. Local and regional government independence was to be strengthened by decreasing rules and grants and reducing monitoring and control activities by the state vis-à-vis local and regional government. The aim was also to increase democracy by moving decisions closer to the citizens (SOU 1978:52).

This decentralization strategy was continued and intensified when the Social Democrats regained power in 1982. A government department for administrative reform was now established: *Civildepartementet*. It was meant to be a department "for citizens against the agencies" (Mellbourn 1986: 20). "Renewal" (*förnyelse*) became a catchword, and it was to be accomplished through decentralization and increased service. Ideas about one-stop shops called "citizen offices" emerged. The idea was to concentrate local and state services in one place to improve access and service. These efforts were later intensified during the 1990s, but it was not until 2004 that these activities were made permanent (SOU 2008:34).

In the mid-1980s the need for citizens to make choices was also pronounced. Choice should, however, exist *within* the public sector and be seen as part of the emphasis on decentralization and increased service. In the Renewal program the government expressed major doubts about the market's ability to handle complex welfare services like health care and education (The Government 1985: 11–14). According to the program, health care was an example of a welfare service highly unsuited for the creation of markets; extremely ill patients suffering from pain, for example, do not make rational choices, the government argued.

An important part of the struggle to make the administration more service-minded was the efforts to change the mindset of the civil servants through storytelling. Thus, the minister in charge of administrative reform gathered all heads of agencies and explained that it was now urgent that the traditional civil servant, with his/her formal and cautious way of interpreting rules, was replaced by a new type of civil servant; a reflexive and innovative type, relying more on his/her own judgment and giving the best possible service to the citizen in each specific case (Mellbourn 1986: 31–2). The government also stressed the importance of the agencies using simple and easily understandable language when communicating with citizens. New service clauses were added to various general laws and ordinances directed towards the administration.

An important part of the Social Democratic government's decentralization strategy was to increase user influence. Partly, this was a way for the government to counter growing demands for privatization of public services, but it was also a way to strengthen democracy (The Government 1985: 4, 8; Mellbourn 1986: 41). In 1986 the government presented the bill "Active Public Influence in Local and Regional Government" (The Government 1986). User influence was to be tested in child care, schools, recreational activities, and health care. Additionally, local authorities were to be decentralized.

Managerialization

In the mid-1980s the relation between politicians and officials became a main issue within administrative reform. This discussion was linked to the construction and implementation of management by results, formally introduced in 1988 (Sundström 2003,

2006). The aims of this steering model were twofold: to strengthen the governments' steering capacity in relation to the agencies and to improve efficiency and creativity among the agencies. Central to the new strategy was to clarify the border between politics and administration. Politicians should concentrate less on details and technical issues and instead decide on policies and goals. The agencies were to be given more freedom to choose the means to realize policies and goals. In addition, follow-ups and evaluations should be used more frequently.

The introduction of management by results meant that a number of decisions were delegated from the government to the agencies, regarding organization, localization, resourcing, and personnel (recruitment, salaries, training, etc.). Also, the management of agencies changed. In order to clarify control and responsibility lines, the number of agencies with a lay board was gradually reduced, while those led solely by a director general increased (Premfors et al. 2009: 167). New budget documents were also introduced. Each year the government was to "place an order" with each agency regarding both activities to be carried out (goals) and results to be accomplished (results requirements), as well as information about activities actually carried out and results accomplished (reporting-back requirements). The agencies were to report back their activities, as well as their costs and results. This information should form a basis for new objectives and results requirements.

Management by results was partly modeled after the private sector. However, neither the model's basic ideas nor the methods introduced in its name were at all new. They were clearly, and highly, related to program budgeting, which had been tried out in Sweden already during the 1960s and early 1970s (Sundström 2003, 2006; cf. Pollitt and Bouckaert 2011: 6, 9). It had then been proven hard to realize, and when the ideas and methods were now introduced again—albeit with new labels—no references were made to program budgeting and lessons learned earlier.

Even though management by results remained strong through the whole 1990s—and was considered a strength when Sweden joined the European Union (Jacobsson and Sundström 2006: ch. 5)—there was a reaction in the mid-1990s to what the critics called "the economism" (Lundquist 1998). Voices were raised, claiming that the "companization"—i.e. attempts to make agencies similar to private companies and civil servants to managers—had had an undesirable effect. A number of "affairs" contributed to this criticism and to the matter appearing on the political agenda (Johansson 2002). A commission of inquiry (SOU 1997:57) argued that the role of the civil servant needed to be revitalized and clarified and that future administrative reforms needed to proceed from the values of democracy and rule of law, and not only from the value of efficiency. This call for a strengthened "public ethos" among public officials was supported by the government (The Government 1998). A new agency was established in 1999 to encourage a common administrative culture and ethics, and to support civil servants' further training in these matters.

In 2006 the government appointed a new commission of inquiry to review management by results. The Governing Inquiry, as it came to be called, presented its report in 2007 (SOU 2007:75). Its criticism was severe. It stated that there had been a strong conviction among responsible reformers that the steering model was correct and superior. Problems had generally been seen as a sign that efforts should be increased further. The problems had time after time been regarded as temporary and had thus not led to any deeper analyses of and challenges to the model's basic assumptions. The contrast to active learning was striking; observations made in evaluations at one point had never been compared with observations made in earlier evaluations. Over time, the same general successes had been reported (and stressed), the same problems noted (and toned down), and the same solutions suggested (without linking them to observed problems and without commenting that they had been suggested several times before).

The commission argued that observed setbacks no longer could be regarded as an implementation problem but that instead were to be regarded as a model problem. Thus, recurring problems to do with distinguishing political goals from non-political means, with formulating clear goals, with connecting activities to effects, and with calculating the cost of the effects, should not been seen as solvable problems, but as governing premises. In 2008, the government decided to reform management by results. Generally, governing was to be more "strategic" and adapted to the character of different activities (Statskontoret 2013). The red–green government, that came into power in 2014, has declared that it will proceed with this reform and work out a new "post-NPM-oriented" steering-model which "allows the professionals to be professional" (The Government 2014).

In parallel with management by results being de-emphasized, the government started to discuss the benefits of a "network administration." The state needed to solve problems together with various external actors: companies, interest organizations, professional experts, individual citizens, etc. (Österberg 2005). This idea was in line with the established corporative model, with its strong belief in consensus and cooperation (see Hall's chapter in this book). However, while the traditional model was highly centralized and formalized, the government now emphasized that the exchange between public and private actors should take place at arm's length from the political center. It implied complex and more informal exchanges between many different types of organizations.

Even though many state agencies in recent years have been urged by the government to cooperate with various types of private organizations (Pierre and Sundström 2009), this networking idea has perhaps been most pronounced at the regional level, where it has been supported by an idea of competition. Today, each region is to develop on the basis of its own prerequisites. They have, in competition with other regions (including regions outside Sweden), to attract companies, researchers, and investors by creating premises for new thinking, innovation, and cooperation. Public actors are to inform, cooperate, and support regional private actors, sometimes by creating common growth programs and formal agreements (Säll 2011). This regionalization has also meant that the regional political level has strengthened its position in relation to the central state. The County Boards (*länsstyrelserna*)—which are regulating, coordinating, and monitoring state agencies at the regional level—have gradually lost their responsibility for regional development policies to regional actors.

Marketization

In the late 1980s Sweden ran into a severe economic crisis and a paradigm shift occurred in Swedish economic policy. Keynesianism was abandoned and instead the Social Democrat government introduced far-reaching austerity measures in a slowing-down economic climate. Now, combatting inflation became the priority. This economic paradigm shift had a major influence on administrative reform. In 1990 the Social Democratic government argued that the administration's tasks, roles, and financing needed to be clarified. Activities open to competition were to be handed over to the private sector, the purchaser role separated from the producer role, and contracts and procurements tried as alternatives to publicly driven activities. There were to be general reassessments of public undertakings, and competition and market forces were to be used systematically as means toward increased efficiency and shrinking of the public sector (Premfors et al. 2009: 290–1). Market forces were also to be used more *within* the public sector—e.g. for agencies' choices of premises and recruitments. Furthermore, agencies were now allowed to place their funds in interest-bearing accounts and to raise loans at market rates from the Swedish National Debt Office for investments outside the state budget (ibid.: 291–2).

When a center-right government came into power in 1991 this marketization strategy was intensified. The government wanted to start a "freedom of choice revolution" and create conditions for the public sector as similar to the market and as neutral to competition as possible (ibid.: 292). Several markets were deregulated, e.g. communications, finance, education, and care as well as in the electricity and housing markets, and the government announced the sale of thirty-five state-owned companies. Private alternatives were to be encouraged also within "softer" policy fields, e.g. health, care, and education. A couple of years later the government issued general directives to all existing and future commissions of inquiries, which stated that the public undertaking to be examined by the commission was to be questioned per se and without prejudice (ibid.: 294).

This marketization strategy was not to be revoked by the Social Democrats when they regained power in 1994. In their first draft budget they instead stressed the continuity and improvements of recent administrative reforms:

> Major changes have been introduced from the beginning of the 1980s, and important results have been achieved. This renewal expressed in principles and guidelines has given a good foundation for the administration's organization and management. It must now continue and achieve high-impact results in practical operations. State finances require continued savings and structural changes in the administration. There is an ongoing extensive reassessment of public undertakings. (The Government 1994: Appendix 1, 71)

Even when finances, in the latter part of the 1990s, came in balance, the Social Democratic government stated that the general reassessment policy directed toward public undertakings remained (The Government 2001: 10).

In 2006 a center-right government—the Alliance—came into power. The Alliance continued to stress the need to reassess public undertakings and to rely on market mechanisms as a means to solve social problems. The Alliance also tried to redefine whom the public sector should serve. Previously, Swedish governments had emphasized that the public sector should serve the public in general or the citizens, but now the government argued that its main purpose also is to serve Swedish private industry. This is expressed in the title of the Alliance's bill of administrative reform from 2010, called *Public Management for Democracy, Participation, and Growth* (The Government 2010). Here a substantial value—growth—is put on an equal level as process values typical for administrative reform, i.e. democracy and participation. The bill strongly underlines the administration's importance for the function of the market:

> The public sector is, as for example the World Bank has shown, decisive for sustainable, economic growth. A properly working and accessible public administration together with well managed public finances, free entrepreneurship with proper competition, well defined ownership and free trade are the prerequisites for a strong and healthy Sweden. Furthermore, the State has an important role in supporting social institutions by rules and supervising bodies to ensure the existence and development of a market economy. (ibid.: 23)

In the bill, companies—in contrast to other organizations—have just as high priority as citizens. It may be noted that a search in the bill for expressions containing the term "companies" shows 206 hits. The same search in the Social Democratic bill on administrative reform from 1998 only shows 45 hits. Corresponding figures for the term "market" are 117 and 15 respectively.

EXPLANATIONS

How can the development of Swedish administrative reform be explained? In the international discourse on administrative reform development, three different interpretations are particularly common. These interpretations—which can be described as reform stories—are rooted in three popular new institutional schools: rational choice, sociological, and historical institutionalism (Premfors 1996; Barzelay and Gallego 2006). What stories emerge when applying these perspectives to the Swedish case?

Rational Problem-Solving

The first story is peddled by the government and the agencies responsible for developing and evaluating administrative reform. It is also told by the Organization for Economic Cooperation and Development (OECD) (Premfors 1996: 2–3). According to this story, all OECD countries endured a welfare state crisis in the 1970s due to the oil shocks. The public sector was now considered too costly and unapproachable, and it was argued that the distance between politicians and bureaucrats had grown excessively wide. This kind of criticism was also present in Sweden, where it found support on both sides of the political spectrum (Mellbourn 1986: 8–11; Tarschys 1983: 150).

Governments all over the world now set up major commissions of inquiry to find appropriate solutions to the problems identified. And they all came up with similar solutions stressing the need to decentralize decision-making, gain better control over public spending, introduce new management styles, and make the administration more service-oriented. However, given the complexity of both the problems and the solutions, the measures proposed were piecemeal and partial. The reformers underscored the need to progress slowly. This way of explaining the development as a gradual process of rational problem-solving is often found in Sweden (see Jacobsson and Sundström 2001: 4–7). Government documents and agency reports frequently claim that the government, after specifying the problems in the late 1970s and early 1980s, appointed various commissions of inquiry—especially important are the Government Commission on Public Policy Planning (Förvaltningsutredningen, SOU 1979:61) and the Government Commission on Central Government–State Agency Relations (Verksledningskommittén, SOU 1985:40)—whose thorough investigations came up with adequate solutions. However, the reforms were presented rather abstractly, leaving considerable leeway for the implementing agencies to refine models and methods continuously while executing them (Brunsson 1990).

Later on, so this story goes, the reformers found that initial reforms were not radical enough; they needed to be complemented with reforms aimed at changing the structure of the incentives of the public servants and their organizations. The norm was the market, and the measures taken included, as a first option, outright privatization, or otherwise the creation of as market-like conditions as possible within and around all public organizations. This kind of development sequence—starting with decentralization, followed by managerialization, and ending with marketization—is clearly present in the interpretations of the development in Sweden. As shown above, Sweden was an "early mover" of decentralization and management ideas. Regarding the more neoliberal parts of the NPM package, emphasizing the market and competition, reforms did not take off in earnest until Sweden experienced a deep financial crisis in 1990. Since then, however, the gap to other countries has been reduced and perhaps even closed.

This brings us to a final point in this story: the idea that there has been a trend toward *convergence* of administrative reform among OECD countries. And this convergence is regarded as a necessity. The OECD countries have all introduced NPM reforms because they are the most adequate given the problems. However, some countries have been quicker to develop, launch, and refine NPM reforms than others. Thus, in this story there are leaders (or heroes) and laggards (Premfors 1996: 3; Bach and Bordogna 2011: 2282). The leaders have been the Anglo-Saxons, particularly New Zealand and Australia, but also the United Kingdom and the United States (Sahlin-Andersson 2001). The laggards—rarely singled out—have been described as being in a sorry state of nonmodernity but not hopelessly lost. They can be saved if they reform themselves like the leaders. And in that struggle, the OECD has been most helpful by providing a forum for reformers to meet and exchange ideas and experiences, and by publishing comparative reports on OECD countries, showing how far each of them has come along the path to the land of plenty. Swedish reformers have, without doubt, been influenced by the OECD. Since the 1970s, they have participated in these meetings, and they often refer to OECD reports when discussing administrative reform (Lerdell and Sahlin-Andersson 1997; Sundström 2003: 309–10).

Rule-Following

The second account of administrative reform development questions the presence of instrumental rationality in all human action. In this story, human action is instead viewed as responses to environmental expectations. When actors, e.g. public organizations, face legitimacy problems, they typically look around for other actors that they perceive as modern and correct and try to imitate them. Action is in this way rule-driven (Meyer and Rowan 1977; March and Olsen 1989). This story singles out two kinds of actors as role models for national reformers: the private company and other countries.

It is not hard to find observations supporting the claim that Sweden was in a crisis of legitimacy toward the end of the 1970s. As mentioned above, the oil shocks of the 1970s resulted in the public sector being criticized for being too costly and bureaucratic. Thus, its legitimacy was clearly on the wane. Nor is it difficult to find observations substantiating the assertion that the reformers in Sweden have looked at private industry. For example, many reforms have been dressed in a linguistic form previously unknown to public servants but used for a long time by private companies, e.g. results, products, effects, ratios, managers, annual reports, contracts, customers, etc. Already in 1978, Tarschys claimed that the Swedish agencies had "come to be regarded as a kind of business, and the thinking about the administration has received many impulses from business research" (Tarschys 1978: 33).

In the mid-1980s, Pihlgren argued that "there is a clear trend towards 'business thinking' and a desire within many public organizations to work under the same conditions as the private industry"; a "corporate culture" was spreading in public organizations (1985: 7, 90). About the same time, Czarniawska (1986) found when interviewing 43 directors-general that private business played an important symbolic role for public administration and had come to be regarded as a role model and inspiration. The directors-general wanted to see reforms drawn from the private sector, which was characterized as "the more beautiful sister" (p. 103). And according to Tarschys (SOU 1985:40, 218) and Brunsson (1990: 109), the Government Commission on Central Government–State Agency Relations—the most important commission of inquiry on administrative reform during the 1980s—was clearly inspired by private industry when it proposed the introduction of management by results into central government.

Around 1990, Ehn (1998) found after interviewing some one hundred public servants at various levels within central government that the "market-oriented" public servant had gained ground at the expense of his/her "rule-oriented" counterpart and the former had private industry as a role model. Then, from the 1990s onward, the massive introduction of controllers and economic-administrative units within each agency, full of professionals trained in business management and leadership, was taken as evidence that the public administration was imitating private industry, and also as an explanation for why reforms like management by results have continued to flourish within central government (Ehn 1998: 79; Hall 2011). And as Hall points out, Swedish reformers have seldom asked the people whether they really want to see market forces applied to yet another welfare area; they seem to take that for granted (Hall 2011: 297).

But what about other countries? It is not hard to find researchers who claim that Swedish reformers have been inspired by countries like New Zealand, Australia, the United Kingdom, and the United States (see, e.g., Sahlin-Andersson 2001). However, empirical evidence supporting this claim is not easily found. Directors-general and other public servants seem keener to single out private companies as role models rather than other countries. Likewise, the government and commissions of inquiry have, when proposing administrative reforms, made little reference to other countries, at least not during the 1980s and 1990s (Sundström 2001: 38–9). And there are few studies on Swedish reformers' participation in meetings arranged by international organizations like the OECD, the World Bank, and the International Monetary Fund. However, a 1997 study indicates that the OECD has played an important role in spreading other countries' reform ideas to Sweden; moreover, it shows that Swedish reformers visited various Anglo-Saxon countries during the 1980s and 1990s (Lerdell and Sahlin-Andersson 1997).

Also, this second story predicts *convergence* among the OECD countries. However, it is a convergence of the way reformers talk about reforms (Pollitt 2001). Because reform is about increasing legitimacy, what counts is appearance. Politicians and reformers have to be able to present political programs and policies showing that they have embraced the latest reform. Still, whether this "talk" eventuates in decisions, changed behavior, and desired effects is quite another thing. In this story, decoupling (or hypocrisy) is instead an important phenomenon whose presence supports the idea that reforms are embraced (too) quickly and (too) uncritically.

Decoupling is quite common in studies of administrative reform in Sweden, especially in those on management by results. For example, research shows that politicians keep "meddling" in administration even though the steering model urges them to stick to goals; politicians do not formulate goals according to the steering model; agencies do not report back results in accordance with the model, and the government does not use result data when deciding on new policies. The steering model has been described as a symbolic ritual—something that few public servants are concerned with and which goes alongside ordinary activities (Jacobsson 1989; Ehn and Sundström 1997; Brunsson 2006; SOU 2007:75).

Path Dependency

The third account of administrative reform development stresses the importance of historical and structural determinants. While the other two stories perceive organizations—states in this case—as relatively homogenous, this story emphasizes historically conditioned power struggles within states. Such struggles will produce different reform trajectories among countries. Thus, convergence is not to be expected, but rather *divergence* (Premfors 1996).

The basic idea of this story is that developments within policy areas sometimes are marked by path dependencies (see, e.g., Thelen 2003; Pierson 2000), which can be divided into two rather distinct periods. The first—called critical juncture—has constituting qualities and is typified by agency, choice, and contingency. These junctures are followed by periods of institutional reproduction characterized by adaptation to institutional incentives and constraints. The reproduction is driven by "positive feedback," implying that the course of events is not only maintained but also reinforced over time.

Applying a path dependency perspective to Swedish administrative reform development is rather fruitful. Administrative reform has a quite interesting history in Sweden, going back to the early 1960s, when program budgeting was introduced into the Swedish state (Sundström 2003, 2006). Program budgeting, which has striking similarities with later management models, was developed and introduced by two strong agencies—the Swedish National Audit Office and the Swedish Agency for Public Management—in cooperation with the Ministry of Finance's Budget Department. These agencies were actually created in the early 1960s with the specific task of developing, introducing, and refining new and modern management and accounting techniques. And they saw a chance to fulfill that task when they imported program budgeting from the United States in the early 1960s. Throughout that decade and the 1970s, they invested heavily in steering and accounting techniques which derived from program budgeting. This meant that the adaptation of NPM ideas and techniques went quite smoothly when they became fashionable in the early 1980s, not only because many of the "new" ideas and techniques were in fact already in place and deeply institutionalized, but also because the two agencies had strong incentives to push for reforms as it gave them plenty of work, considerable prestige, and credit for their past work.

The initially strong position of these agencies meant that, at an early juncture, they took control of administrative reform development in Sweden. Studies show that these agencies—and from 1998 also the Swedish National Financial Management Authority—have not only had strong positions in the development of administrative reform but have also been responsible for executing and evaluating the reforms. By wearing more than one hat, they have had every possibility of controlling the development. This group of organizations—and individuals—has been small and homogenous, and matters have primarily been discussed within it. In this way, how these actors viewed problems and solutions has been increasingly strengthened. Thus, tendencies toward uniformity in thought have clearly been present—a uniformity that enhanced the embracing of NPM reforms during the 1980s and 1990s, especially the management-oriented ones. This explains why Sweden was an early mover of these reforms and a late mover of more neoliberal NPM reforms, and a really slow mover concerning what has been called "post-NPM" ideas, i.e., ideas about the "whole of government," networking, (meta)governance, etc. (Christensen and Lægreid 2007).

This explanation for the development is supported by the fact that the reforms generated much more debate during (the few and short) periods when this policy field was more pluralistically organized, for instance, in the early 1980s, when the government created the Ministry of Public Administration (Civildepartementet) and when the Ministry of Justice was partly responsible for administrative reform at the end of the 1990s. The lack of a more pluralistic organization might also help explain why there has generally been such a strong party political consensus on administrative reform in Sweden. Even if specific matters have been debated, changes of government have not resulted in any significant policy changes. According to this historical structural interpretation, the responsible public servants have not wanted to, or have maybe been unable to, present politicians with alternatives.

Effects

What are the effects of the above reforms? This is a tricky question because the effects of reforms are notoriously hard to establish. The impacts of the reforms also vary between policy fields and agencies. For example, Niklasson and Pierre (2012) argue that in Sweden, older agencies have resisted NPM reforms more than newer agencies. However, some general effects are relatively easy to prove—for instance, the reforms have led to a smaller state, at least in terms of the number of agencies. Thus, between 1990 and 2007, the number of agencies decreased from close to 1,400 to only 468 (SOU 2008:118, Appendix 8, 251). In 2014, there were 365 agencies (SCB 2014). The number of state employees has also decreased, but to nowhere near the same extent, from 264,000 in 1995 to 248,000 in 2013 (Arbetsgivarverket 2014). And between 1995 and 2005, the volume of state activities, measured in terms of consumer expenditure, only dropped by a few percent (SOU 2008:118, Appendix 8, 253). Thus, the agencies have generally become far fewer, but also much larger.

Some observers—foremost the government and the agencies responsible for developing and implementing administrative reforms—also argue that the reforms have made public administration more service-minded and results-oriented (see Sundström 2003). However, empirical studies supporting this claim are hard to find. A larger study from 2011 on the effects of increased competition within welfare services, such as schools, health care, and elderly care, shows that there is a remarkable lack of knowledge of the effects of increased competition (Hartman 2011).

Critics argue that the reforms have brought about a more fragmented state (Brunsson and Sahlin-Andersson 2000; SOU 1997:57). The agencies have gradually transformed into "normal" organizations with their own goals, recruitment policies, logos, home-pages, etc. Their identities have changed; they do not see themselves as part of a bigger whole—the state—anymore, but as organizations in their own right. Likewise, public servants consider themselves employed by agencies, not by the government or the state (see Ehn's chapter in this book).

Critics also contend that the new incentive structures, based on public choice and principal-agent theories, create a low-trust culture (Lindgren 2006; cf. Gregory 2006: 155). Public administration professionals complain that rigid and excessive steer-ing and control systems leave them with too little room to make their own professional judgments (Zaremba 2013; Ahlbäck Öberg and Widmalm 2012). Voices have also pro-tested that public servants, e.g. doctors, teachers, and police officers, are spending an inordinate amount of time filling in papers instead of treating patients, teaching pupils, and chasing villains (Ivarsson Westerberg 2004; Hall 2011). And since decoupling, according to the critics, is widespread—i.e. accounts are not used when new decisions about activities are taken—all this paperwork seems like wasted time (Lindgren 2006).

Finally, critics also argue that Swedish public servants have generally become less willing to blow the whistle, i.e. to use their right to inform outsiders and the media about their own agency's dubious decisions or improper behavior. The efforts to copy private business in general and the introduction of new management models in particular—which, among other things, has resulted in the public servants hav-ing become more dependent on their immediate superior—have created a situation where public servants have lost the sense of what it means to work as a state employee (Lundquist 1998; cf. Suleiman 2003).

CONCLUSIONS

This chapter has discussed administrative reform development in Sweden from the mid-1970s until today. Three questions were posed. How can the policy field be described in terms of dominating ideas and decisions taken? How can the development be explained? What are the effects of the reforms?

Regarding the first question, NPM has clearly not passed Sweden by. On the contrary, Sweden has embraced most of its ideas and practices, especially the *management-ori-ented* part of NPM, and particularly the various ideas about steering and control. The *neoliberal* part of NPM, emphasizing the market and competition, took root later in Sweden (from around 1990). In recent years, Swedish administrative reform has also embraced some "*post-NPM*" ideas. However, these ideas have not figured that promi-nently in policy programs. It should be noted that even though the development can be described as a sequence—starting with decentralization, followed by managerialization, then marketization, and ending with post-NPM—it does not mean that these reform packages have replaced each other in an orderly way. There has seldom, or never, been a decision to abolish already-executed administrative reforms. Instead, they have been stacked on each other, leading to ever greater *goal complexity* (cf. Lægreid and Pedersen 1994).

As for the explanations, the development can partly be understood as *rational problem-solving*, where reforms are to be conceived as genuinely Swedish solutions to genuinely Swedish problems, devised by Swedish commissions of inquiry, decided by the Swedish government, and then implemented and continually refined by Swedish agencies. However, the development can also be seen as *rule-following*, where reformers have quite uncritically imitated other countries and, foremost, private industry in order to strengthen the legitimacy of Swedish public administration. Finally, observations strengthen the argument that the development should be understood as *path dependency*, where a small group of administrative units and public servants early on gained a strong position allowing them to control the development of administrative reform from the end of the 1960s to the present day.

Finally, with regard to the effects, the reforms have made central government a bit *smaller*. Some also argue that Swedish public servants have become *more service-minded* and *results-oriented*. However, there is scarce empirical evidence to support this claim. Critics contend that the reforms have brought about a more *fragmented* state, that new incentive structures have started to *erode the previously so prominent high-trust culture* within Swedish central government, and that the Swedish public servant has generally become *more silent*, i.e. fewer are prepared to be whistleblowers. Still, empirical evidence is also here somewhat scant. The critics are on more solid ground when asserting that the reforms have generated *more control activities and paperwork*, and that the latter has largely precluded the agencies from carrying out their ordinary work.

References

Ahlbäck Öberg, S. and Widmalm, S. (2012). "Professionalism nedvärderas i den marknadsstyrda staten," *Dagens Nyheter*, October 26.

Arbetsgivarverket (2014). "Antal kvinnor och män," <http://www.agv.se/nyheter-press/fakta-om-staten/medarbetare/antal-kvinnor-och-man/>.

Bach, S. and Bordogna, L. (2011). "Varieties of New Public Management or Alternative Models? The Reform of Public Service Employment Relations in Industrialized Democracies," *International Journal of Human Resource Management* 22/11: 2281–94.

Barzelay, M. and Gallego, R. (2006). "From 'New Institutionalism' to 'Institutional Processualism': Advancing Knowledge about Public Management Policy Change," *Governance* 19/4: 531–57.

Brunsson, N. (1990). "Individualitet och rationalitet som reforminnehåll," in N. Brunsson and J. P. Olsen (eds), *Makten att reformera*. Stockholm: Carlsson, 86–117.

Brunsson, N. (2006). *Mechanisms of Hope: Maintaining the Dream of the Rational Organization*. Copenhagen: Copenhagen Business School Press.

Brunsson, N. and Sahlin-Andersson, K. (2000). "Constructing Organizations: The Example of Public Sector Reforms," *Organizations Studies* 21/4: 721–46.

Christensen, T. and Lægreid, P. (2007). *Transcending New Public Management*. Aldershot: Ashgate.

Czarniawska, B. (1986). "Förvaltningschefer—politiker eller ledare?" in N. Brunsson (ed.), *Politik och ekonomi: En kritik av rationalitet som samhällsföreställning.* Lund: Doxa Ekonomi, 75–108.

Ehn, P. (1998). "Maktens administratörer: Ledande svenska statstjänstemäns och politikers syn på tjänstemannarollen i ett förändringsperspektiv," dissertation, Stockholm University, Department of Political Science.

Ehn, P. and Sundström, G. (1997). "Samspelet mellan regeringen och statsförvaltningen," in *Det svåra samspelet: Resultatstyrningens framväxt och problematic,* SOU 1997:15.

The Government (1985). "Den offentliga sektorns förnyelse," Skr. 1984/85:202.

The Government (1986). "Aktivt folkstyre i kommuner och landsting," Prop. 1986/87:91.

The Government (1994). "Förslag till statsbudget," Prop. 1994/95:100.

The Government (1998). "Statlig förvaltning i medborgarnas tjänst," Prop. 1997/98:136.

The Government (2001). "Regeringens förvaltningspolitik," Skr. 2000/01:151.

The Government (2010). "Offentlig förvaltning för demokrati, delaktighet och tillväxt," Prop. 2009/10:175.

The Government (2014). "Ny styrning bortom New Public Management." Press release, October 23.

Gregory, R. (2006). "Theoretical Faith and Practical Works: De-autonomizing and Joining-Up in the New Zealand State Sector," in T. Christensen and P. Lægreid (eds), *Autonomy and Regulation: Coping with Agencies in the Modern State.* Cheltenham: Edward Elgar, 137–61.

Hall, P. (2011). *Managementbyråkrati: Organisationspolitisk makt i svensk offentlig förvaltning.* Malmö: Studentlitteratur.

Hartman, L. (ed.) (2011). *Konkurrensens konsekvenser: Vad händer med svensk välfärd?* Stockholm: SNS Förlag.

Ivarsson Westerberg, A. (2004). "Papperspolisen: Den ökande administrationen i moderna organisationer," dissertation, Stockholm School of Economics.

Jacobsson, B. (1989). *Konsten att reagera: Intressen, institutioner och näringspolitik.* Stockholm: Carlssons.

Jacobsson, B. and Sundström, G. (2001). "Resultat utan lärande—erfarenhet från tre decennier av resultatstyrning," Score Working Paper, 2001:15.

Jacobsson, B. and Sundström, G. (2006). *Från hemvävd till invävd: Europeiseringen av svensk politik och förvaltning.* Stockholm: Liber.

Johansson, P. (2002). "Vem tar notan? Skandaler i svensk offentlig sektor," report nr 39, Förvaltningshögskolan, Göteborg University.

Lægreid, P. and Pedersen, O. K. (1994). *Forvaltningspolitik i Norden.* Oslo: Jurist- og Okonomiforbundets Forlag.

Lerdell, D. and Sahlin-Andersson, K. (1997). "Att lära över gränser," SOU 1997:30.

Lindgren. L. (2006). *Utvärderingsmonstret: Kvalitets- och resultatmätning i den offentliga sektorn.* Lund: Studentlitteratur.

Lundquist, L. (1998). *Demokratins väktare.* Lund: Studentlitteratur.

March, J. and Olsen, J. P. (1989). *Rediscovering Institutions: The Organizational Basis of Politics.* New York and London: Free Press.

Mellbourn, A. (1986). *Bortom det starka samhället: Socialdemokratisk förvaltningspolitik 1982–1985.* Stockholm: Carlssons.

Meyer, J. W. and Rowan, B. (1977). "Institutionalized Organizations: Formal Structure as Myth and Ceremony," *American Journal of Sociology* 83: 340–63.

Niklasson, B. and Pierre, J. (2012). "Does Agency Age Matter in Administrative Reform? Policy Autonomy and Public Management in Swedish Agencies," *Policy and Society* 31/3: 195–210.

Österberg, S.-E. (2005). "Statlig förvaltning—ökad nytta för medborgare och företag." Speech at ESV-dagen, October 25.

Pierre, J. and Sundström, G. (2009). *Samhällsstyrning i förändring.* Malmö: Liber.

Pierson, P. (2000). "Increasing Returns, Path Dependence, and the Study of Politics," *American Political Science Review* 94/2: 251–67.

Pihlgren, G. (1985). *Management i förvaltningen: Effektivitet och förnyelse.* Lund: Liber.

Pollitt, C. (2001). "Convergence: The Useful Myth?" *Public Administration* 79/4: 933–47.

Pollitt, C. and Bouckaert, G. (2011). *Public Management Reform: A Comparative Analysis—New Public Management, Governance, and the Neo-Weberian State.* Oxford: Oxford University Press.

Premfors, R. (1996). "Reshaping the Democratic State: Swedish Experiences in a Comparative Perspective," Score Working Paper 1996:4.

Premfors, R., Ehn, P., Haldén, E., and Sundström, G. (2009). *Demokrati och byråkrati.* Lund: Studentlitteratur.

Sahlin-Andersson, K. (2001). "National, International and Transnational Constructions of New Public Management," in T. Christensen and P. Lægreid (eds), *New Public Management—The Transformation of Ideas and Practice.* Burlington: Ashgate, 42–72.

Säll, L. (2011). "Kluster som teori och politik. Om den regionala tillväxtpolitikens diskursiva praktiker," Karlstad University Studies, 2011:56. Karlstad: Universitetstryckeriet.

SCB (2014). Årsstatistik <http://www.myndighetsregistret.scb.se/Arsstatistik.aspx>.

SOU 1978:52. *Lägg besluten närmare människorna.* Final report from Decentraliserings-utredningen.

SOU 1979:61. *Förnyelse genom omprövning.* Final report from Förvaltningsutredningen.

SOU 1985:40. *Regeringen, myndigheterna och myndigheternas ledning.* Final report from Verksledningskommittén.

SOU 1997:57. *I medborgarnas tjänst: En samlad förvaltningspolitik för staten.* Final report from Förvaltningspolitiska kommissionen.

SOU 2007:75. *Att styra staten—regeringens styrning av sin förvaltning.* Final report from Styrutredningen.

SOU 2008:34. *Lättare att samverka—förslag om förändringar i samtjänstlagen.* Report from Utredningen om utveckling av lokal samverkan och service.

Statskontoret (2013). "Flexibilitetens fördelar och faror—perspektiv på regeringens myn-dighetsstyrning," Statskontoret.

Suleiman, E. (2003). *Dismantling Democratic States.* Princeton: Princeton University Press.

Sundström, G. (2001). "Ett relativt blygsamt förslag: Resultatstyrningens framväxt ur tre pers-pektiv," Score Working Paper 2001:2.

Sundström, G. (2003). "Stat på villovägar. Resultatstyrningens framväxt i ett historisk-institutionellt perspektiv," dissertation, Department of Political Science, Stockholm University.

Sundström, G. (2006). "Management by Results: Its Origin and Development in the Case of the Swedish State," *International Public Management Journal* 9/4: 399–42.

Tarschys, D. (1978). *Den offentliga revolutionen.* Lund: Liber.

Tarschys, D. (1983). "Kampen mot krångel och onödig byråkrati," in B. Rydén (ed.), *Makt och vanmakt: Lärdomar av sex borgerliga regeringsår.* Stockholm: SNS.

Thelen, K. (2003). "How Institutions Evolve: Insights from Comparative Historical Analysis," in J. Mahoney and D. Rueschemeyer (eds), *Comparative Historical Analysis in the Social Science*. New York: Cambridge University Press, 208–40.

Zaremba, M. (2013). *Patientens pris: Ett reportage om den svenska sjukvården och marknaden*. Stockholm: Weyler Förlag.

CHAPTER 24

THE PUBLIC SERVANT

PETER EHN

INTRODUCTION

FOR over two decades, New Public Management (NPM) has characterized administrative reform in Sweden (just as it has in many other Western countries). These—and other—reforms have changed the conditions for Swedish public servants. This chapter describes and discusses these changes. Is the public servant still to be considered a traditional bureaucrat, or is he/she mainly to be described as a "manager" modeled after the private sector?

The chapter is divided into four sections. First, the Swedish formal public employment model is introduced. Second, the background of Swedish public servants is described. Third, the recruitment of public servants is discussed, where the issue of politicization is given special attention. Finally, the chapter ends with some concluding remarks.

THE PUBLIC EMPLOYMENT MODEL

In Sweden, the division of labor between local and regional government, state agencies, and government departments implies a huge difference in the size of the organizations involved. The government departments have around 4,700 employees (including Swedish missions abroad), which can be compared to about 231,000 employees in state agencies and over 1 million employees in local and regional government (Regeringskansliets årsbok 2012; Statskontoret 2013). Between 1985 and 2009, expenditure cuts, privatization, decentralization, and other changes halved the number of central government employees (SAGE 2009). In 2011, around 5 percent of the total number of employees in Sweden worked for the state (Statskontoret 2013).

With regard to the state, commissions of inquiry support the government departments in their policy-making by providing advice and expertise, while semi-autonomous state agencies implement government policies. This semi-autonomy is expressed in several ways (see Hall's chapter in this book). For one thing, Swedish agencies are, unlike in most other countries, responsible for virtually all decisions regarding their own internal organization and work. This also includes employment policies.

The Private Sector as a Role Model

The transformation of the Swedish administrative system from a traditional career-based bureaucracy to what has been labeled a "post-bureaucratic" system started before the NPM era (Demmke and Moilanen 2012). A first important step was taken already in 1965 with the introduction of collective bargaining and the right of public servants to strike. The alignment of public and private sector working conditions then continued through the Public Employment Act (Lag om offentlig anställning) in the mid-1970s. Now collective bargaining was, with a few exceptions, allowed throughout the public sector, and hardly any differences remained between public and private sector working conditions.

The collective bargaining did not originally exclude the politicians from the wage-bargaining process. The government and the Riksdag, the Swedish parliament, were still responsible for central government pay levels. Not until the mid-1990s did the public sector wage system become fully decentralized with the introduction of frame budgeting and the creation of the Swedish Agency for Government Employers (SAGE), a member organization for state agencies.

SAGE differs from other agencies in that it is a member organization solely run by its members—the agencies, the Government Offices, and other state employers (SAGE 2009). SAGE develops a common employment policy for the agencies and is also responsible for negotiations of central agreements with labor unions. The main reason for establishing SAGE was to stop, or rather to protect, the government and the Riksdag from becoming involved in the bargaining process (Andersson and Schager 1999).

With the introduction of frame budget with cash limits, government employers received the same incentives as their private counterparts to keep costs low in central agreements. As a consequence, the government and the Riksdag no longer needed to approve central agreements due to budgetary considerations (ibid.). After this reform, the government could delegate employer responsibility entirely to the agencies. Henceforth, the agencies were (under certain budgetary limits) fully independent in deciding the size and structure of the workforce and wages (Gustafsson and Svensson 1999).

In practice, the central negotiations between SAGE and the unions result in central agreements that provide a basis for local parties to negotiate individual salaries and working conditions within the needs and circumstances of each agency. In 1989, a system of individual pay replaced the former system where public servants' positions had been pay-graded. Individual pay is to be set according to the difficulties and responsibilities of the position, the performance of the public servant, and the labor market situation (SAGE 2009).

Reduced Employment Security

In Sweden, there is no specific public servant status. Public servants' working conditions are, with few exceptions, not regulated in public law. On the whole, the public sector is regulated by the same general labor laws as other sectors of the labor market. However, some specific regulations can still be found, for example, concerning working disputes in some agencies.

Today, there is no lifelong employment guarantee for public servants. If it is necessary to make savings, permanent employed public servants may also be dismissed. However, some small groups do enjoy greater employment security: for example, senior judges, who can only be removed from their posts if they commit a crime or otherwise prove to be obviously unsuitable (SAGE 2009).

For heads of agencies (directors-general), a part of the government policy has since the 1980s been to reduce job security. Just like judges, directors general cannot be dismissed that easily. However, they can be reassigned "to an equivalent position." The government has also restricted the length of their appointment (Premfors et al. 2009: 187). Earlier, directors-general could remain in their posts for over a decade, sometimes for decades. Today, the normal length is six years, to which three more years can be added. Thus, no director-general or county governor is supposed to have his/her appointment longer than nine years.

Here it should also be noted that public servants are not given precedence when applying for vacant public administration posts. They compete on equal terms with applicants from other sectors (SAGE 2009).

Employment Security and the Integrity of the Public Servant

In general, the decentralization of the employment policy has been regarded as successful. However, as for the integrity of the public servant, some observers have questioned the consequences of the decentralization.

As Patrik Hall shows in his chapter in this book, Swedish public servants have a broad freedom of expression. They have a general right to inform outsiders of the work of the agencies and government departments, and the law forbids superiors from investigating who has leaked information.

Today, the head of the agency forms his/her own team. These persons are appointed by the director-general, on whom they are therefore dependent for their career and salary. In many other European countries, the public servants' integrity is strengthened by having a relatively independent position in relation to their immediate department head in the ministry. A public servant is employed and promoted by the decision of someone other than the immediate department head. Nor can the department head alone decide the public servant's salary (Krus/Ehn 2011).

Against this background, some debaters have questioned the willingness and courage of public servants to use the right to inform outsiders and the media (see, e.g., Lundquist 1998; Ehn and Sundström 1997: 96). Also, the increased use of temporary employments in the public sector can add to a more silent public administration. Statistics from 2011 show that over 18 percent of state employees have temporary jobs (Lejon 2013: 168–9); they are taking greater risks than their permanent counterparts when deciding to criticize the activities or the management of their organizations. They are not just jeopardizing their career development and their salary increase but also run the risk of their current employment contract not being extended (ibid.: 168).

On the whole, the alignment between the public and private sector concerning employment regulation has led to a situation—so the critics argue—where public servants today have (too) little understanding of their duties and responsibilities (SOU 1997:57; Lundquist 1998). This lack of understanding and knowledge has also been noticed by the government, which has made efforts to strengthen the so-called public ethos among public servants. The latest ethos project ran in 2010–11 and aimed to increase the understanding of what it means to be a state employee and of questions about basic democratic values, ethics, and treatment (Krus/Ehn 2011).

The Background of Public Servants

In Sweden, the representativeness of politicians—especially members of the Riksdag—has often been debated. The argument is that they should not only reflect citizens' opinions but also their social and economic background. Moreover, this argument has been applied to public administration and public servants. At least for senior public servants, it has been contended that they, in practice, not only implement policies but also take part in the creation of policies and therefore should be representative of the citizens in general (Kingsley 1944; Dolan and Rosenbloom 2003).

International studies show little representativeness among senior public servants (e.g. Lægreid and Olsen 1978; Aberbach, Putnam, and Rockman 1981). Generally, this group comes from the socially and economically more privileged groups in society. For Sweden, one might expect a slightly different picture. In a society where egalitarian values have for a long time characterized political discussion and social life in general, a more even social distribution of senior public sector appointments would perhaps be expected. But is that the case? To answer this question, the background (gender, age distribution, education, ethnicity, and social class) of Swedish public servants will be described in the following sections.

A More Gender-Equal Administration

Positive gender discrimination has been possible since the beginning of the 1980s, when the first law on gender equality was passed. However, it has not been proven that positive discrimination has had the desired effect on equality. Nevertheless, the government has decided that such discrimination should continue to be an option.

The government has also used other means to increase gender equality. Besides additional information, more training, recruiting campaigns, and the annual appropriation directions (where the government can determine the goals, assignments, and reporting-back requirements for each agency) have been used extensively in central government to support the gender-equality work (Premfors et al. 2009: 181).

As for numbers, women have taken over the public administration. Today, the majority of central government employees are women (51 percent in 2010). Thus, in terms of percentages, men and women are quite equal. However, they are not equally spread over policy fields. For example, in the defense sector, more than three out of four employees are men, compared to social protection, where almost the same share are women (SAGE 2012).

Also, in the Government Offices, women are in the majority (60 percent in 2012). However, among the heads of units, men still dominate (55 percent), but this domination is waning. In 2000, three quarters of the Government Offices' heads were men (Regeringskansliets årsbok 2012).

To be appointed director-general was historically more or less the preserve of men. This too has changed. In the late 1980s, only 10 percent of directors-general were women, and a little more than 20 years later, in 2010, their percentage had increased to 34 percent (Larsson and Lemne 2013: 83).

Moreover, the position of county governor (*landshövdingar*) has, in terms of gender distribution, changed dramatically during the last forty years. In 1973, there were no female county governors at all. In 1998, every third county governor was a woman, and today women are in the majority; 13 of the 21 governors are women (Ehn 1998b).

An Aging Administration

With regard to age, public servants deviate in two aspects from the labor market in general—the share of older employees is higher and the share of younger employees is lower. In 2010, 27 percent of central government employees were 55 years of age or older, compared to 21 percent of all employees in Sweden. At the same time, only 3 percent of the public servants were under 25, compared to 11 percent of all employees. The comparatively low percentage of younger central government employees is mainly due to educational qualifications being a prerequisite. A large number of central government positions require a post-secondary school education (SAGE 2012).

In the Government Offices, the average age of the employees has stabilized in recent years to around 45 (Regeringskansliets årsbok 2012). The directors-general of the agencies had an average age of 54 in 1990 (Ehn 1998a). These figures can be compared with the county governors, whose average age in 2010 was 57 when appointed (Larsson and Lemne 2013). The post of county governor has traditionally been used as a retirement position for politicians who, at the end of their careers, want to withdraw from the political fighting (Ehn 1998b).

A More Educated and Educationally Diverse Administration

The public servants are more educated compared to employees in the rest of the Swedish labor market. In 2010, almost three out of four of the Government Offices' employees had a post-secondary school education, compared to four out of ten within the labor market in general, and of the 10 percent of public servants with expert or senior managerial duties in the Government Offices, 97 percent had a post-secondary education. Just a few percent of the employees in the Government Office had only a pre-secondary school education (SAGE 2012).

The high educational level within the state can mainly be explained by the fact that most universities in Sweden are public institutions and represent a large part of the state (and thus the bulk of the public servants), and to become a researcher or a teacher at a university, it is, of course, necessary to have an academic degree. However, this does not fully explain the high educational level within the state. Numerous other state activities require highly educated staff. Perhaps it is most evident in the Government Offices (Premfors et al. 2009: 183).

Even though in Sweden the educational demands on public officials are quite high, there has never been such a thing as a special education, examination, or a test for recruitment to central government. Nevertheless, in Sweden, as in most other countries, legal studies used to be the natural educational route to traditional public servant positions. For many years, the lawyer was the dominant profession in the Swedish administration (Petersson 1994). In fact, until the mid-1960s, a legal degree was practically a requirement for obtaining a public servant position in the Government Offices (Premfors et al. 2009).

However, already in the second half of the nineteenth century, a gradual change started to occur at the agency level when, during the course of industrialization, there was a shift toward professional knowledge, and more and more engineers and economists were employed in central government (Torstendahl 1985). After World War II, when the public sector rapidly developed and social engineering became a characteristic of the welfare state, new professional groups entered central government. Social and behavioral scientists were needed in planning positions. Public servants who were trained sociologists, political scientists, and ethnogeographers entered central government. These new professional groups generally had a less traditional view of their role as public servants and also a better understanding of political preferences (Esping 1994: 88).

In the Government Offices, the dominating educational backgrounds today are social scientists (including economists) and lawyers. The last category has, in recent years, had somewhat of a revival in government departments. This comeback is, to some extent, due to Swedish membership of the European Union (EU), which is mainly a rule-producing organization, thus requiring legal expertise to manage EU legal documents and adapt them to Swedish regulations (Premfors et al. 2009: 183).

Also, among directors-general, the dominating educational backgrounds are lawyers and social scientists. Almost three out of four directors-general had such a background in 1998, which is the latest data we have for the heads of the agencies (Statskontoret 1999: 57–8).

In addition to social scientists and humanists, technicians have gained ground in recent years as a group of central government employees. Technological changes have always had a strong impact on politics and public administration. The information and communications technology (ICT) revolution—with the introduction of PCs, the Internet, and email—has rapidly changed the work conditions within public administration. ICT has also led to new types of jobs. For example, nowadays within public administration, ICT experts of various kinds are quite numerous. At the same time, ICT has made many public servants with assisting duties redundant. Thus, their numbers have gradually decreased.

One category of public servants who have increased in number, partly as a result of ICT, is public relations staff (SOU 2007:107). Today, meetings between public servants and citizens often take place on the Internet. Consequently, the Government Offices' and the state agencies' external communication has changed dramatically. The latter are not just represented on the Internet with homepages; they are also active in social networks, like Facebook and Twitter. It has become increasingly imperative for agencies to be publicly seen, and accordingly it is important how they are presented (Fredriksson et al. 2013; Fredriksson and Pallas 2013; Erlandsson 2008). Here public relations officers and press secretaries play vital strategic roles. It is no coincidence that the heads of public relations units are often members of the agencies' management teams (Krus/ Ehn 2011).

A Socially Diverse Administration

Historically, the Government Office has been dominated by upper-class people. However, seen over a longer time period, there has been an equalization of the public servants' social and economic background. Still, as late as the beginning of the 1990s, there was a considerable imbalance in the social background of senior public servants. For example, in government departments, only 11 percent of the directors (heads of units) came from a working-class background, while 53 percent were from an upper class. The corresponding figures for directors-general were 17 and 36 percent, respectively (Ehn 1998a: 73).

Despite the picture of Sweden as a modern and egalitarian welfare state, which stands in sharp contrast to stereotyped bureaucracies of other kinds, such as the British civil service or the German Beamtentum, Swedish public servants' social background still shows similarities to that of their British and German counterparts (Ehn et al. 2003). One obvious reason for the social imbalance among the senior public servants is that these positions, in practice, require an academic degree, and as there is still a clear imbalance in the recruitment to higher education, this will be reflected in the composition of senior public servants.

A More Ethnically Homogenous Administration

Sweden is an immigrant country with almost 16 percent of its approximately 9.6 million inhabitants born in another country, 4 percent born in Sweden with both parents born abroad, and 6 percent with one parent born abroad (Statistics Sweden). The percentage of the population with a foreign background can be compared with countries like the United States or Germany and is higher than, for example, the United Kingdom or France.

Statistics from SAGE for 2012 show that around 15 percent of state employees have a foreign background. Among the newest employees, the figure is as high as 24 percent. The percentage of public servants with a foreign background is increasing over time, and at a rate faster within the state sector compared to the labor market in general. The highest percentage of public servants with a foreign background can be found in universities. A high figure can also be found within the field of social protection, where it is relatively common for direct contact between public servants and citizens. It is considered important that employees at these kinds of agencies, which have a lot of contact with the general public—like the Swedish Social Insurance Agency—mirror the composition of the population (SAGE 2013).

Statistically, the Government Office has over time become better at mirroring the ethnic diversity of the Swedish population. However, this positive development has seen one important exception: namely, in the category of public servants with managerial duties, where very little has happened. This category of employees represents 6.8 percent of all state employees. Among public servants with an ethnic Swedish background, the share was 7.5 percent in 2012. Among public servants with a foreign background, the share has been stable at around 3 percent (SAGE 2013).

How Representative is the Swedish Administration?

As shown above, the answer to the question posed in the headline is simply: not very representative—at least not for senior public servants. Compared to the population in general, senior public servants are more often upper-middle-class, educated, ethnic

Swedish men. Senior public servants clearly form an "elite" in terms of their social and educational background.

The discussion about the representativeness of public servants has had a long history, even if it has never been very intensive. When democracy was established in early twentieth-century Sweden, the traditional bureaucracy's role under the new democratic regime began to be debated. At the same time as democracy was introduced, the political status and role of public servants were very strong and influential. Sweden could at that juncture be described as a "bureaucratic state" (*ämbetsmannastat*).

When the Social Democratic Party came to power in the early 1930s, with the ambition to build a strong welfare state, it tried to avoid using the traditional bureaucracy, mainly the county administrative boards, and instead opted for the municipalities and newly formed agencies; for example, the Public Employment Service (Ehn 1998b; Rothstein 1986). Many leading Social Democrats were at that time very suspicious of the existing bureaucracy, which they saw as a defender of the pre-democratic society.

Another sign that leading politicians did not trust public servants was the large-scale introduction of lay boards into the agencies during the twentieth century, by the end of which the vast majority of the agencies had one (Lewin 1994). Certainly, there were several reasons for the introduction of these boards, e.g. increased efficiency and expert knowledge, but one important reason was to strengthen democratic control over the agencies. The governments simply did not trust the public servants to manage the agencies by themselves (Söderlind and Petersson 1986: 90; Ehn 1998b: 56).

Also later on, the public administration was, from time to time, criticized for not being sensitive to—or even opposing—the government's wishes and policies. Some critics have argued that a more socioeconomic and politically representative public administration is needed in order to implement the government's policy, or more formally, the will of the people (e.g. Helldén 1966; Ehn 1998a: 122).

Twentieth-century discussion about the representativeness of public servants mainly focused on socioeconomic and political factors. Today, this discussion has a slightly different focus. It is not so much about the lack of working-class public servants, or the political sympathies of public servants; rather, it concerns the gender balance in top positions. More recently, the question of ethnic representation has also gained more attention (e.g. Rönnqvist 2008).

THE RECRUITMENT OF PUBLIC SERVANTS

The main principle for the recruitment of public servants at all levels within the public administration—government departments, agencies, county councils, and municipalities—is a process based on merit and competence. The overwhelming majority of public servants are recruited on this basis.

The government or the Prime Minister appoints all employees within the Government Office (The Government 1996: §§ 5, 34). The Prime Minister usually delegates these decisions to government departments, i.e. to the ministers. Regarding state agencies, the government appoints directors-general, members of agency boards, members of agencys' advisory councils, and a few other senior officials, while all other employees are appointed by the agency on delegation from the government. The earlier distinction between statutory civil servants, white collar and blue collar, has been abolished. Accordingly, and as mentioned earlier, there is no special examination or any other central recruitment procedure for central government jobs. Some traditional career patterns still exist, e.g. for judges, prosecutors, and staff at the Swedish Ministry for Foreign Affairs. But also in these cases, each agency or government department is responsible for appointments and training (SAGE 2009).

The criteria for appointing staff to central government positions are stated in the Swedish constitution: namely, merit, competence, and other objective factors should be decisive. Of these factors, competence is given precedence. What this competence consists of is determined by the agency on an individual basis and is specified in the requirements for each post (SAGE 2009).

The recruiting process is transparent in that applications and supporting documentation are public documents. An agency's employment decision can also be contested by lodging an appeal with the government or a central authority—Statens överklagandenämnd.

The Extent of Politicization

Even if the Swedish recruitment system is basically meritocratic, there are formal political appointees, but relatively few. They are concentrated in the Government Office and are state secretaries, political advisors, and other staff employed under the Government Office's agreement on politically appointed staff, for example, information officers.

The state secretary is a very important strategic position within the Government Office. As the second most important politician within the government department, they sometimes, but not always, act like a junior minister. However, of greater importance to the inner workings of the Government Office is that they are responsible for running the government department.

The political advisors are a very complex category of public servants (Ullström 2011). Some work mostly externally, maintaining contact with their party and other organizations around the country as well as with the media. Others work more internally, and can play an important interministerial role, especially during coalition governments.

The Directors-General—Politically Appointed?

For a number of agencies, the appointment of the director-general is of great strategic importance to the government. The media and political scientists have long discussed whether heads of agencies are, *in practice*, politically appointed or not (e.g. Ehn 1998a;

Sandahl 2003). Having been a politician is not a prerequisite for being accused of being politically appointed—or to accuse the government of making a political appointment. It can be enough to have worked in an organization with relatively strong links with a party in government, or to have (or have had) close links with politicians working in the Government Office. Sweden is a small country, many of whose most senior public administration figures have come to know each other quite well and have developed extensive elite networks.

An answer to the question whether directors-general are politically appointed or not is that it depends. The agencies are disparate both in size and importance. Many of them are of minor political interest to the government and therefore the appointment of their directors-general is also less politically controversial; in most cases, their recruitment can be regarded as meritocratic.

For agencies of greater political importance—for example, the Public Employment Service—it is more commonly held that the directors-general have been politically appointed. During the long era of Social Democratic rule from the early 1930s to the early 1990s (with a break from 1976–82), it was more or less an unspoken fact that the head of that agency should be a Social Democrat (Rothstein 1986).

Of course, every government strongly denies having politically appointed any directors-general. Nevertheless, the opposition parties, by and large, do not accept that argument, and therefore discussions about political appointments are frequently held in the Riksdag's Committee on the Constitution (see, e.g., the Committee on the Constitution 1997). Some external observers argue that this scrutiny of the government is a good thing, while others contend that the opposition is merely trying to score political points when it reports ministers to the Committee on the Constitution.

Because the recruitment system is based on competence and merit, directors-general are not expected to resign if a new government comes to power after a general election. Moreover, the director-general's image is clearly that of a public servant, and not of a political appointee. Another consequence of this formally meritocratic, but, in some cases, de facto political, appointment system is that there is no clear-cut division between a meritocratic and political appointment (cf. Pierre and Ehn 1999: 253–4).

Studies show that the percentage of directors-general with a political background has decreased over time. In the late 1980s, 42 percent of them had a political background; ten years later, the figure had dropped to 33 percent. Since then, the figure has continued to dwindle, and in 2010, it was down to 19 percent (Larsson and Lemne 2013). Having a political background does not mean that the person concerned has to be politically affiliated with a government party. Directors-general with a political past can be appointed by a previous government, and it is not uncommon for a government to appoint persons affiliated with an opposition party (Ehn 1998a). This was quite prevalent during the period from 1976 until around 2000. In 1976, an agreement was signed between the outgoing Social Democratic government and the new center-right government, stipulating that the outgoing state secretaries should be guaranteed equivalent appointments; for example, a director-generalship. One consequence of this agreement was that new governments tended to appoint state secretaries who had worked for the previous government. This agreement is now abolished (Ehn 1998a).

The fact that Sweden does not have a spoils system means that a new government has to mainly rely on directors-general appointed by its predecessors. As mentioned above, they cannot be reassigned that easily during their six-year appointment. Partly as a consequence of these rules, a deep mutual respect has developed between politicians and directors-general (see Jacobsson and Sundström's chapter in this book). The government normally places great confidence in the directors-general fulfilling their duties in accordance with government policy (albeit impartially and with integrity), while directors-general are usually very loyal to the government (Tarschys 2008: 33).

When a new center-right government came to power in 2006, some changes were made to the recruitment policy for heads of agencies. The parties in the new government had criticized the Social Democratic government for the way it handled these recruitments. They argued that its predecessor had not followed the recruitment criteria stated in the constitution; namely, merit and competence should be decisive factors. Instead, they accused the Social Democratic government of having used a nontransparent and informal recruitment process whereby persons close to the Social Democratic Party—and especially the Prime Minister—were favored (see Sundström 2009).

Thus, the new center-right government decided that all vacant director-general posts (and corresponding positions) should be publicly advertised. Furthermore, a requirement profile for the advertised positions should always be drawn up. However, the government does not have to choose any of the applicants; it has always the possibility of selecting someone else (The Government 2009).

One problem for the government when advertising senior public servant positions is the Swedish principle of public access to official documents. As a main principle, all documents that public agencies—including the Government Office—receive are public. That also applies to application papers or even just applications of interest. Often these persons already hold senior positions in another agency or company. Therefore, it can be in their interest to keep their application confidential; public access, on the other hand, could jeopardize, or at least create problems for, their appointment. To overcome this difficult situation, the government has decided that for a small number of appointments, e.g. directors-general, the principle of secrecy should be applied.

County Governors: A Special Case

The new recruitment policy does not apply to one group of heads of agencies, namely, county governors, for whom the government still uses the more informal model of handpicking suitable persons. County governors, whose formal position is otherwise equivalent to that of directors-general, have much more often than directors-general been politicians. In a 1998 study, Ehn found that at the time of their appointment over 75 percent of county governors held a political position as a minister, member of the Riksdag, local or regional politician, or state secretary (Ehn

1998b). In a later study, the percentage had slightly decreased to 67 percent (Larsson and Lemne 2013).

Politicization: A Summary

Sweden's dualistic structure of central government, with small policy-formulating government departments and large semi-autonomous policy-implementing agencies, creates a basis for a specific Swedish discussion about politicization. The crucial question in this debate is: how independent should the agencies be? In the Swedish context, this discussion has partly been linked to the established model for steering the public administration, namely, management by results. This steering model is based on the idea of a sharp division between politics and administration (see Sundström's chapter in this book). Consequently, it is important to maintain a dividing line between the government's and the agencies' tasks, and political appointments can, in this respect, be regarded as a way for the government to secretly and illicitly cross the dividing line between politics and administration. On the other hand, the opponents of the rational view of politics built into management by results argue that it is wrong—from a democratic constitutional perspective—not to allow the government to choose who will head the politically important agencies. It prevents the government from carrying out the political program it has presented to the Swedish electorate and for which it has received a mandate in democratic elections. The critics even argue that the introduction of management by results has made it more important for the government to appoint people to leading public administration positions, as management by results implies that the government should delegate all "means" (decisions about internal organization, appointments below the heads of agencies, training, location, resources, etc.) to the agencies and concentrate on the formulation of "goals."

CONCLUSIONS: FROM TRADITIONAL BUREAUCRAT TO PRIVATE SERVANT

So, who is the Swedish public servant today? Is he/she a traditional bureaucrat or has he/she been transformed into a modern manager, modeled after the private company? As the discussion in this chapter has hopefully shown, he/she is neither. Nowadays, the public servant is definitely not an old-fashioned bureaucrat, but nor have the influences of NPM made him/her a fully fledged manager. Instead, the contemporary Swedish public servant is perhaps best characterized as a "private servant."

The "privatization" of the public servant is shown mainly in two different ways. Firstly, there has been an alignment between the public and private sector regarding the statutory regulation of working conditions. Today, the public and private sector differ very little in this regard.

Secondly, the government's delegation of decisions to the agencies regarding internal organization, human resources policies, and financial and operational issues, in combination with managing by results, has created a situation where public servants at the agency level have come to regard the agency as a formal organization in its own right. More than ever, public servants see themselves as just another worker in any organization, whether it be public or private. They do not see the agency as part of a bigger whole—as part of the state.

Generally, the public servant of today seems to have a quite limited understanding and knowledge of the specific requirements that such a position entails. Clearly, something has been lost during the transformation from a traditional bureaucracy to a more privatized public sector.

REFERENCES

Aberbach, J. D, Putnam, R., and Rockman, B. (1981). *Bureaucrats and Politicians in Western Democracies*. Harvard: Harvard University Press.

Andersson, P. and Schager, N. H. (1999). "The Reform of Pay Determination in the Swedish Public Sector," in R. Elliot, C. Lucifora, and D. Meurs (eds), *Public Sector Pay Determination in the European Union*. Basingstoke: Palgrave Macmillan, 240–84.

Committee on the Constitutions (1997). Report 1997/98:KU25.

Demmke, C. and Moilanen, T. (2012). *The Future of Public Employment in Central Public Administration*. Maastricht: EIPA.

Dolan, J. and Rosenbloom, D. H. (2003). *Representative Bureaucracy: Classic Readings and Continuing Controversies*. Armonk, NY: M. E. Sharpe.

Ehn, P. (1998a). "Maktens administratörer," dissertation, Department of Political Science, Stockholm University.

Ehn, P. (1998b). "I skärningspunkten: Landshövdingarna och den central och regional samordningen," SOU 1998:168.

Ehn, P., Isberg, M., Linde, C., and Wallin, G. (2003). "Swedish Bureaucracy in an Era of Change," *Governance* 16/3: 429–58.

Ehn, P. and Sundström, G. (1997). "Samspelet mellan regeringen och statsförvaltningen," in *Det svåra samspelet: Resultatstyrningens framväxt och problematik*, SOU 1997:15.

Erlandsson, M. (2008). "Regeringskansliet och medierna: Den politiska exekutivens resurser och strategier för att hantera och styra massmedier," *Statsvetenskaplig tidskrift* 110: 335–49.

Esping, H. (1994). *Ramlagar i förvaltningspolitiken*. Stockholm: SNS.

Fredriksson, M. and Pallas, J. (2013). "Med synlighet som ledstjärna: En analys av vilka principer som styr kommunikationsarbetet i nationella förvaltningsmyndigheter," Research Report 2013:1, Uppsala University, Division of Media and Communication Science.

Fredriksson, M., Pallas, J., and Wehmeier, S. (2013). "Public Relations and Neo-institutional Theory," *Public Relations Inquiry* 2/2: 183–203.

The Government (1996). "Förordning med instruktion för Regeringskansliet Svensk författningssamling," 1996:1515.

The Government (2009). Written communication from the Government, 2009/10:43.

Gustafsson, L. and Svensson, A. (1999). *Public Sector Reform in Sweden*. Malmö: Liber ekonomi.

Helldén, A. (1966). *Regeringsmakt och demokrati*. Stockholm: Liber.

Kingsley, J. D. (1944). *Representative Bureaucracy: An Interpretation of the British Civil Service*. Yellow Springs, OH: Antioch Press.

Krus/Ehn, P. (2011). "I statens tjänst—en roll med många bottnar." Stockholm: Krus.

Lægreid, P. and Olsen, J. P. (1978). *Byråkrati og beslutninger*. Oslo: Universitetsforlaget.

Larsson, T. and Lemne, M. (2013). *Regeringens utnämningsmakt i teori och praktik—om att utse generaldirektörer och landshövdingar*. Stockholm: Ministry of Finance, ESO (forthcoming).

Lejon, B. (2013). "Statstjänstemannen och arbetsmiljön," in Å. Casula Vifell and A. Ivarsson Westerberg (eds), *I det offentligas tjänst: Nya förutsättningar för tjänstemannarollen*. Malmö: Gleerups, 165–84.

Lewin, L. (1994). "The Rise and Decline of Corporatism: The Case of Sweden," *European Journal of Political Research* 26: 59–79.

Lundquist, L. (1998). *Demokratins väktare*. Lund: Studentlitteratur.

Petersson, O. (1994). *Swedish Government and Politics*. Stockholm: Fritze.

Pierre, J. and Ehn, P. (1999). "The Welfare State Managers: Senior Civil Servants in Sweden," in E. C. Page and V. Wright (eds), *Bureaucratic Elites in Western European States*. Oxford: Oxford University Press, 249–65.

Premfors, R., Ehn, P., Haldén, E., and Sundström, G. (2009). *Demokrati och byråkrati*. Lund: Studentlitteratur.

Regeringskansliets årsbok (2012). Stockholm: Regeringskansliet.

Rothstein, B. (1986). *Den socialdemokratiska staten*, Arkiv avhandlingsserie. Lund: Arkiv Förlag.

Rönnqvist, S. (2008). *Från diversity management till mångfaldsplaner: Om mångfaldsidéns spridning i Sverige och Malmö stad*, Lund Studies in Economic History 48. Lund: Lund University.

SAGE (2009). *Central Government and Delegated Employer Responsibility: The Swedish Model*. Stockholm: SAGE.

SAGE (2012). *Facts on Swedish Central Government as Employer*. Stockholm: SAGE.

SAGE (2013). *Utländsk bakgrund i staten 2012*. Stockholm: SAGE.

Sandahl, R. (2003). *Förtjänst och skicklighet—om utnämningar och ansvarsutkrävande av generaldirektörer*. Stockholm: Ministry of Finance, ESO, Ds 2003:7.

Söderlind, D. and Petersson, O. (1986). *Svensk förvaltningspolitik*. Uppsala: Diskurs.

SOU 1997:57. *I medborgarnas tjänst: En samlad förvaltningspolitik för staten*. Final report from Förvaltningspolitiska kommissionen.

SOU 2007:107. *Opinionsbildande verksamhet och små myndigheter*. Stockholm: Fritzes.

Statskontoret (1999). "Det viktiga valet av verkschef: En jämförande studie av verkschefsutnämningar," Statskontoret, report 1999:21.

Statskontoret (2013). "Den offentliga sektorn i korthet—utvecklingen 2012." Statskontoret.

Sundström, G. (2009). "'He Who Decides': Swedish Social Democratic Governments from a Presidentialisation Perspective," *Scandinavian Political Studies* 32/2: 143–70.

Tarschys, D. (2008). "Differentierad styrning," in *Underlagsrapporter till 2006 års förvaltningskommitté*, SOU 2008:119, 6–70.

Torstendahl, R. (1985). "Byråkratisering och industrikapitalism," in *Tvärsnitt* 4.

Ullström, A. (2011). "Styrning bakom kulisserna: Regeringskansliets politiska staber och regeringens styrningskapacitet," dissertation, Department of Political Science, Stockholm University.

....

CHAPTER 25

GOVERNING THE STATE

....

BENGT JACOBSSON AND GÖRAN SUNDSTRÖM

INTRODUCTION

....

IN modern representative democracies, such as the Swedish one, the demands put on governments to govern are high. They are responsible and accountable not only for state activities, but also for what is happening in the entire society. And therefore they should have the tools and resources required to govern.

However, the governing of states has proven difficult. The difficulties can be explained by the fact that modern states possess a complexity unparalleled in any other organization (Matthews 2013). Many of the problems that states have to handle are "wicked"; they are inherently ill-defined, unstable, and contested, and therefore in a sense unsolvable (Rittell and Webber 1973; Head 2008). It is extremely difficult to trace and isolate the effects of specific activities on indistinct and moving targets such as poverty, crime, and unemployment, not least since such problems often are influenced by a lot of factors in the hands of a lot of actors—they are typically "many hands problems" (Thompson 1980).

Furthermore, the goals of state organizations are often both ambiguous and conflicting (Pfeffer and Salancik 1978; March and Olsen 1976, 1989). States are de facto multiorganizational and consist of many separate organizations often with very different ambitions, strategies, and goals. And politics is to a considerable extent about making compromises between all these ambitions and goals, and compromises are almost per definition vague; they are elusively created in order to get support from different political actors. Generally, politicians want to keep room for maneuver and adjust their policies as processes evolve.

To this should be added that states handle an enormous amount of issues. The demand put on contemporary governments to decide on detailed policies vastly exceeds the supply. Governments constantly run the risk of becoming overloaded, and therefore they generally try to keep decisions and activities—also policy-making—away from them, by pushing issues downwards to officials at lower levels within the state (Page 2008, 2012).

Ambiguity, conflicting interests, compromises, and the risk of overload reveal governments as everything but those rational, coordinated, and problem-solving entities that they routinely are presented as. It is obvious that the governing of states is a most complex task. And it has become more complex in recent decades as states have become strongly influenced by agendas in the European Union, other international organizations, standards organizations, nongovernmental organizations, etc. Today, a myriad of organizations, associations, and professions all over the world are involved in issuing rules aimed at states (Brunsson and Jacobsson 2000).

This complexity does not mean that states are ungovernable. Our impression is that governments often are able to govern and control state activities. However, they do it in other ways than those implied by contemporary management models with their hierarchical, top-down-oriented, command-and-control methods. In our understanding, governing must meet two basic and potentially contending demands: it should be effective and democratic. In order to avoid overload (i.e. be effective), the government has to delegate a lot of decisions of various kinds to the administration, thus generally giving administrative units a rather high degree of autonomy. At the same time, in order to avoid democratic illegitimacy, it has to be able to influence decisions for which it can become accountable, and also such issues that previously may have been delegated. How do governments manage to strike a balance between these two demands?

We argue, based on a multitude of empirical studies in Sweden, that governing is primarily about organizing policy fields. Each policy field has its own basic organizational structure in which the administration performs its daily activities (Sørensen 2006; Kooiman 2003; Torfing and Triantafillou 2009). These organizational structures are not rearranged on a regular basis by the politicians. The basic structure of a policy field can be relatively stable for years or even decades. Then suddenly, due to a change in government, new technologies, a redefinition of a problem, a scandal, a catastrophe, or some other reason, it can become subject to reform—there is an opportunity to "set the stage" in a new way. And when this happens it becomes crucial for the politicians to think things through carefully, not only because it may take some time for such a reform opportunity to come again, but also because the manner in which a field is organized is of great importance for how the problems that the government wants to attend to are handled (Lægreid and Verhoest 2010: 6–7; Seidman 1998: 12–13).

When setting the stage for policy fields the main question occupying the government—in relation to the administration—is less about how to create a complying than about how to create a responsive system. How can the government ensure that an administration, given an extensive discretionary authority, has the ability to orient and adapt to changing conditions, while at the same time not losing sight of the government's policy line? The administration must be able to see how the problems it has to handle change over time and take new forms. Likewise, it needs to be able to see how ways to attack problems at hand change over time and take new forms. It cannot generally expect detailed top-down directives from the government telling them these things.

In the following we will discuss six strategies that the Swedish government uses when setting the stage and trying to achieve a responsive administration: *creating formal organizations, positioning, fostering competition, distancing, forming communication channels*, and *storytelling*. We want to stress that these strategies are analytical constructions. They are simplifications and *our* conceptualizations of various governing practices that we have observed. They should thus be conceived as "emergent strategies" (Mintzberg and McHugh 1985; Mintzberg 1978) or as "strategies in use," rather than "espoused strategies."

Creating Formal Organizations

A first and very basic strategy used by the government when it wants to attend social problems is to *create formal organizations*, with assignments, managers, rules to follow, and resources. Generally, the government has to protect and nurse a wide range of goals and values, and for those goals and values the government considers most important it sets up administrative units of various kinds, e.g. ministries (for example, as when the government set up the Ministry of the Environment in 1987 in order to address increasingly high-profile environmental issues), agencies (for example, as when it set up The Equal Opportunities Ombudsman (*JämO*) in 1980 to battle gender-based discrimination), departments inside ministries or agencies (for example, when it set up a department for financial audit inside the National Audit Office in 1986), or commissions of inquiry.

The creation of such units implies specific institutional conditions for the collection of information and development of knowledge about the problems that the units have been commissioned to handle. For example, by establishing an agency, stakeholders within the policy field at hand get a distinct "key player" to turn to with information and feedback. Also, the agency will recruit people with specific expertise, sometimes paired with a considerable amount of passion for the problem at hand. But also persons who initially may not be that committed tend to gradually socialize into the values and attitudes that are represented within the agency (Miles 1978).

Of course, the same logic applies for situations when the government dismantles an administrative unit. Such a measure can be taken as an indicator that the government gives less priority to the problem that the unit has handled, which for example many critics maintained was the case when the government shut down the Animal Welfare Agency in 2007 (Carlbom 2007). The government can also transfer the responsibility for certain activities from one unit (which perhaps is shut down) to another unit, as a way of redefining a problem. This was for example the case when the government closed the Swedish Integration Board in 2007 and relocated the responsibility for newly arrived refugees to the Public Employment Service, thus making the refugee policy a more distinct part of the employment policy (Qvist 2015).

POSITIONING

When setting up administrative units the government also often makes sure that the units are exposed to influence from other organizations. We call this strategy *positioning*. We distinguish between external and internal positioning.

External positioning refers to situations where the government exposes administrative units to influences from organizations outside the state. These organizations are working with the same social problem as the unit. However, being private corporations, interest organizations, unions, etc., they typically view the problem from a distinct perspective, and they tend to protect specific values in line with that perspective. Applying positioning means that the unit becomes answerable to these other external organizations and required to accommodate their ideas and opinions (Hood 1998: 60–4, 2004: 6–7). Thus, the unit is exposed to alternative ways of looking at problems and solutions, and it has to reassess its own established ways of thinking and acting. Agency expertise is handled by counter-expertise. The stakeholders become a kind of policy watcher who can ring the "fire alarm" when an administrative unit proposes action that they perceive to be at odds with the government line (McCubbins and Schwartz 1984; Page 2012: 5).

External positioning is used frequently by the Swedish government, and has been used for a long time. For example, when the government reformed its work safety policy in the mid-1970s, and introduced a framework law, it gave the National Board of Occupational Safety and Health a highly autonomous position in relation to the government. However, to the extent that the Board wanted to fill out the law with more specific rules and regulations, it was instructed to do so in cooperation with worker and employer organizations. The agency was thus created as an arena, where various interests could meet regularly and discuss perceived problems and find common solutions to those problems (Jacobsson 1984). The same can be said about Swedish forest policy. The Swedish Forest Agency has been assigned to balance the two overall objectives stated in the Forestry Act—which principally just say that the forest should be big and green—and "work out detailed objectives to the extent to which it is required." However, the agency has been instructed by the government to do so in cooperation with all relevant stakeholders. And that meant that the agency came to cooperate with no less than 17 stakeholder organizations when it worked out detailed goals in 2004 (Sundström 2010).

These two examples show that external positioning can be applied along several dimensions (see, e.g., Héritier and Lehmkuhl 2008; Feldman and Khademian 2000). It can be applied at different *levels*. Sometimes the government establishes boards or councils within agencies and populates them with external stakeholders (occupational safety). But it can also decide to include external stakeholders in specific projects run by bureaucrats lower down in the agency (forest policy). Positioning can also be applied within different *policy phases* (Hood 1998: 63). Sometimes the government grants stakeholders access to early stages of the policy process in order to make them participate in the initiation and discussion of new policy programs and law proposals which are then presented to the government (occupational safety). Stakeholders are often also involved at a later stage of the policy process, when agencies are to implement policies and programs (forest policy). The government can also decide on *working methods* or "rules of the game" (Torfing and Triantafillou 2009: 10). Sometimes the government decides in some detail about the form for exchange between an agency and its stakeholders—for example, how to make decisions, when and how to report results from the cooperation, how to create incentives for external actors to participate in the agency's work, etc. (occupational safety). In other cases, the government delegates these questions to the agency and the stakeholders (forest policy). The same applies for decisions about *which actors* should be granted access to policy and implementation processes. Sometimes the government points out which stakeholders the agency in question should meet (occupational safety). On other occasions it merely urges the agency to try to include all relevant stakeholders (forest policy).

Internal positioning means that administrative units are exposed to the influence of other administrative units. The government makes the division of tasks among administrative units ambiguous and creates partly overlapping responsibilities between them. The units involved are not working on exactly the same policy problem and are not protecting the same value. Instead they are working on adjacent problems and protecting different values.

Thus, even though administrative units pursue different policies, different goals, and different values, and are led by different ministers, their fields of responsibilities are often unclear. Policies are partly overlapping, as are goals and values. Action taken by one unit will affect other units. They are therefore mutually dependent (Landau 1969; Bendor 1985). While at the same time competing for resources, definitions of problems, the government's attention, and so on, they are quite willing to supervise each other.

In this way overlaps—or "loosely coupled" organizations (Landau 1991: 7)—will help to uphold efficiency and prevent malfunctions within the administration (Lerner 1986; Miranda and Lerner 1995). Following this kind of reasoning, rivalry between administrative units can be perceived as something essentially good. This is not always evident to researchers and reformers. This is for example the case with those critics who characterize the state as permeated by a "silo mentality." However, silos exist for good reasons (Page 2005: 141). As mentioned earlier in this chapter, for those goals and values the government considers most important it sets up administrative units of various kinds. Such units imply specific institutional conditions for the collection of information and the development of arguments in defense of the values at stake. Thus, through specialization each unit will be able to sharpen its arguments when competing with other units for resources, problem definitions, and solutions. And hopefully, the best argument will come out victorious. However, the claim that "silos" are good is based on the assumption that the units—or the officials populating them—are not protecting their "turfs," seeking to maximize their own self-interest. Instead, they must be protecting their "views" (ibid.: 143).

Overlap, or internal positioning, is a well-known organizational technique within the Swedish central state. The government often uses it in tandem with external positioning.

For example, when the Swedish Forest Agency specified the forest law through the forest sector objectives, as was discussed above, two other state agencies were among the seventeen organizations taking part in the creation of the objectives. One was the Swedish Environmental Protection Agency, which obviously has a stake in forest policy, as the policy states that Swedish forests should not only be big (the production value) but also green (the environmental value).

Internal positioning is, however, most developed and institutionalized inside the Swedish Government Office (Premfors and Sundström 2007). Here, the so-called joint drafting procedure is essential. This rule states that issues that affect the area of competence of several ministers must be prepared in consultation with members of their staffs and that all the government departments involved must be in agreement about an appropriate course of action before the matter is brought to the government for decision. This procedure is meant to ensure that issues are thoroughly discussed, and that arguments based on different values are expressed, before decisions are taken.

FOSTERING COMPETITION

A third strategy that the government uses in order to promote a reflexive and creative administration is to foster competition (Hood 1998: 55). Just as in other OECD countries, competition has been induced within a range of policy fields in Sweden during recent decades, especially within social welfare areas such as schools, health care, and care of the elderly. These policy fields have been organized so that they do not only contain "internal" but also "external" competition. That is, citizens are not only free to choose among different *public* schools, doctors, and nursing homes, but also *private* ones. However, from a governing perspective the aim with competition is the same: to make the units more responsive in order to increase efficiency, creativity, and quality.

In contrast to positioning, where "voice" (discussion, argument, and deliberation) is the prime mechanism for preventing failure and increasing quality, here the prime mechanism is "exit" (Hirschman 1970). The risk of being abandoned by their "customers," who can choose other service providers, is to spur administrative units (as well as the private providers) to make necessary changes.

An interesting case where the Swedish government has introduced the idea of competition in recent years is regional policy. Historically, Swedish regional policy has been directed by an "equalization goal." However, from the end of the 1990s this goal was de-emphasized in favor of a "development goal" (SOU 1995:27). Each region was to develop more from its own prerequisites. They had in competition with other regions (including regions outside Sweden) to attract companies, researchers, and investors by creating premises for new thinking, innovation, and cooperation. In this work, public regional actors—not least the government's own regional main player, the County Boards (*länsstyrelserna*)—should take an active part. They were to inform, cooperate with, and support regional players, sometimes by creating common growth programs and formal agreements (Säll 2011; Pierre 2009). Thus, regional policy is an example of positioning and competition being used in tandem and in a kind of sequence. The government has stressed the need for a more network-oriented regional administration that should solve societal problems together with various "inside" players: companies, interest organizations, professional experts, individual citizens, etc. in the region—thus, positioning. But it should do that in order to attract "outside" players: investors, companies, researchers, etc. from other regions and elsewhere—thus, competition.

The government often tries to strengthen competition by instructing various control units to promote benchmarking activities and to make, and publish, comparisons and ranking lists. Care of the elderly is a good example. Here, the government has decided to use "open comparisons" (*öppna jämförelser*), which is a monitoring system with nationally defined indicators describing different aspects of various welfare services at local and regional level. The aim is to increase efficiency and quality by stimulating learning and cooperation between municipalities and regions. The aim is also to support freedom of choice for patients and users by providing them with accessible, timely, relevant, user-friendly, and reliable information. In addition, the indicators are meant to facilitate evaluation of health care and social services (see Odén 2013).

Competition is often applied at the later stages of the policy process, among service providers. However, it can also be applied at other stages of the policy process. For example, in recent years the government has established a range of smaller and specialized "evaluation agencies," which compete not only with evaluation units within traditional multifunctional agencies but also with the fast-growing market of private evaluation bureaus (Johansson and Lindgren 2013: 14).

Distancing

In order to strike the balance between efficiency (avoiding overload) and democratic legitimacy (being able to influence decisions for which it can become accountable) the government often uses a strategy which we call *distancing*, which implies that the government organizes administrative units at different lengths from itself.

The government sometimes organizes administrative units far from itself, which has been called "hands off"-strategy (Sørensen 2006: 101–2). Here, the aim is to direct claims of responsibility and accountability downwards in the administration. This strategy is achieved by giving units a high level of autonomy. The more autonomy agencies are given, the lower the risk that the government gets the blame if something goes wrong. One example would be when the Swedish Central Bank was given its independent status in 1999, which means that the Executive Board of the Bank nowadays makes the monetary policy decisions without instruction from any other parties, including the government and parliament. This means that it has become much harder for the government to govern the Bank and to influence monetary policy. However, it also means that media attention has shifted from the government to the Bank when things have gone wrong, decreasing the government's need to govern.

The same can be said about export of Swedish military equipment (Andersson 2010). Decisions to allow such export were earlier taken by the government, and these decisions were prepared by an agency—the War Material Inspectorate (KMI)—located inside the Ministry of Foreign Affairs; a rather unusual organizational arrangement. However, the government's decisions were often criticized by the opposition. In 1996 a major reform was conducted where these decisions were delegated to a new agency—the Swedish Inspectorate of Strategic Products (ISP)—organized outside the ministry, thus obtaining the same legal autonomy as other agencies in Sweden. This meant that the opposition was no longer able to criticize the government to the same extent and as directly as before. Thus, just as in the case of the Central Bank, the government's ability to govern the export of military equipment decreased after 1996, but so did its need to govern as accountability was pushed downwards to the agency.

Thus, the "hands-off" strategy implies a situation where the government tries to reduce its need to govern. An opposite strategy is the "hands-on" strategy, where the government tries to increase its ability to govern. One example of this strategy is the way the government nowadays uses public commissions of inquiry. Sweden has a long and strong tradition of analyzing and discussing reform ideas in big commissions of inquiry where representatives from different spheres of society—political parties, NGOs, companies, researchers, etc.—have participated as members and experts. These commissions' assignments are formulated in directives decided by the government. However, formally the commissions are organized as (temporary) agencies, and traditionally they have enjoyed almost the same autonomous position in relation to the government and the ministries as permanent agencies. In recent years the government has, however, changed its use of commissions. One of the most distinctive and debated changes is the development from multi-member to single-member commissions. And critics have argued that single-member commissions are working much closer to the government than traditional multi-member commissions and that this is threatening traditional and vital core values in the Swedish administrative model, e.g. qualitative decision-making, anchoring, and consensus-seeking.

This development is particularly noticeable in the case of so-called national coordinators. Sweden's first national coordinator was set up in 2002, with the assignment to coordinate the government's policy on drugs (see Crole-Rees 2005). The coordinator was instructed to facilitate contacts and exchanges between various actors responsible for implementing the government's drug policy. But the coordinator was also to "serve as the government's spokesman in drug policy with the task of illuminating and actively propagating the government's policy by participating in the drug policy debate and initiating public discussions on various issues" (ibid.). Thus, during the period July 2003 to June 2004 the coordinator appeared personally in some two hundred events and meetings, nationally and internationally, spreading the government's message and forming public opinion (ibid.: 11). In addition, the coordinator was instructed to submit suggestions continuously to the government on how to refine the government's drug policy.

On the whole, the coordinator arrangement implied a new way of using commissions of inquiry, where a more immediate and informal link between the commission and the government and the government department is one of the most important changes. And all this was accomplished within the existing system of public commissions of inquiry—no formal changes of the system were made. Since 2002 the Swedish government has set up a range of national coordinators within various policy fields.

Forming Communication Channels

If the government succeeds in its basic design of policy areas it will not have to interfere so much in the administration's daily work. However, this does not mean that the administration, once the government has set the stage, becomes a player piano. The government continues to govern the administration also after the stage has been set. And it must do so, *because politics is inherently elusive.* Issues which at one point in time have been regarded as "technical," and therefore have been delegated to the administration, can suddenly—for various reasons—become "political." In such cases the government must, in order to keep its democratic legitimacy, be able to influence the issues at hand. Thus, there have to be some communication channels between politicians and the administration that ensure that the administration keeps to the government's policy line also in times of turbulence, uncertainty, and unpredicted change. Politicians and bureaucrats must be able to maneuver and interact, without putting the established institutional structure at risk. In our studies, we have seen many examples of this, not least after Sweden joined the EU. The requirement to speak with one voice in interaction with European and global counterparts has required open and informal communication channels (Jacobsson and Sundström 2006).

There are many different more or less formal communication channels available in the Swedish central administration (Niemann 2013; Page 2012; Jacobsson 1984; Jacobsson and Sundström 2006; Premfors and Sundström 2007). Some of them are formed by the government as some kind of interorganizational routines: for instance, regular (weekly) meetings between politicians and bureaucrats within the ministries; regular (yearly, and sometimes more frequent) dialogues between politicians and leaders of agencies; recurrent dialogues between bureaucrats in ministries and agencies about budget issues; exchanges between agencies and ministries in preparation of negotiations in the European Union, etc. Some regular communication channels are less strategically orchestrated; for instance, when ministers and administrators meet at conferences, seminars, dinners, etc. However, such meetings are frequent and are of great importance. Generally, the Swedish state is quite small, and people working in a specific policy field know one another quite well, which means that is it is quite easy to pick up the phone (Niemann 2013; Page 2012: 93, 97–8). Indeed, the frequent use of informal contacts was pointed out as "the Swedish central government's special hallmark" by the Swedish Power Inquiry in 1989 (Petersson 1989: 16).

Thus, there are numerous and reasonably open channels of communication between the political and administrative spheres. This close interaction makes it possible for Swedish officials (both within government departments and agencies) to act in ways that are consistent with what the political leadership wants. As a first option they try to do that with the minimum involvement of politicians. To accomplish such *anticipatory behavior* they rely heavily on experience from frequent (previous) interaction with politicians (cf. Page and Jenkins 2005: 128). Such interaction means that over time they get to know their superiors quite well and can anticipate their will, and that they adjust their behavior accordingly. Another technique used by officials to ascertain the political leadership's preferences on a particular policy issue is to look for "cues" in documents, statements, and speeches made by ministers (ibid.: 131–4).

Sometimes officials also turn directly to the political leadership for guidance—they "*invite authority*." However, the guidance they get seldom comes in the form of detailed instructions and orders but rather as broader intentions and visions—"steers"—often sought out in discussions between the politician and the official (ibid.: 136, 140–3; Niemann 2013: 121–2).

Anticipatory behavior and "steers" do not always help to keep issues away from the government. Sometimes they are brought up to the political level to be authoritatively decided—they are *repoliticized*. Issues are sometimes "hoisted"; that is, pushed up from the administrative to the political level by actors on the former level (Jacobsson and Sundström 2006: 176–7; Page 2012: 12). This is done either because officials perceive the issues as highly political or because units or officials on the same level, and with overlapping responsibilities, fail to agree on a course of action. Issues are sometimes also "lifted," which means that actors on the political level take the initiative and pull issues up from the administrative level. The political level gets informed about ongoing activities on lower levels by reading documents produced by the administrative units themselves but also by external public and private supervising actors, not least the media. Frequent informal exchanges between politicians and officials also create opportunities for actors on the political level to "listen in to" what is going on further down in the administration (Jacobsson 1984; Page 2012: 12).

In sum, the presence of numerous and frequently used communication channels between Swedish politicians and officials makes the relation between the two *highly dynamic*. In practice there is no clear line between politics and administration. Instead, everything, even the tiniest issue, can become—and quite often become!—of interest for the politicians. In such situations the mechanisms we have discussed ensure that the politicians can influence the issues at hand.

STORYTELLING

A final strategy that the government uses when deciding on a policy field's basic organizational structure is *storytelling*. Rationalistic ideals are hard to match in the everyday practices of governmental organizations (with ambiguities, fragmentation, etc.). However, when practices fail to meet rationalistic ideals politicians can suggest reforms. Policy reform and organizational reform are fundamental features of societal change. It has even been suggested that they have become routine in the modern world (Brunsson 1989). Reform is a direct product of a desire for (or dream of) rationality and progress, and it is specifically ambiguities and decoupling that trigger reform. Reforms typically have the ambition to make the world less ambiguous and more coupled. Thus, reformers—organizational and political leaders—need stories (see, e.g., Neuhauser 1993; Czarniawska 1997; Boal and Schultz 2007; Elgie 2003; Rhodes 2005; Morrell 2006).

Swedish politicians have excellent opportunities to tell stories. All reforms of some magnitude follow specific policy stages in Sweden, and in each of these stages the government has the opportunity to present a story, telling all actors involved—*not least the administration*—what the reform is all about: the nature of the problem, possible and preferred solutions, what has been tried before, who the relevant actors are and how they are connected, etc. (cf. Sørensen 2006: 101). Normally, the rhetoric is presented in formal documents such as government bills. However, politicians may also issue press releases, arrange press conferences, write articles in the media, and stress specific aspects of policies in TV and radio interviews (Erlandsson 2008; Eriksson et al. 2013). For example, during their time in power in 2006–14 the former center-right government connected its efforts to reform the field of development cooperation to a story that problems in the existing system were a consequence of an old-fashioned way of thinking. The minister in charge gave speeches and wrote articles where she depicted the Swedish development cooperation as hopelessly outdated and stated that actors within this policy field were generally indifferent to results (cf. Carlsson 2006). During her time as minister she delivered—according to the government's website—105 speeches, 36 announcements, and 98 opinion articles, and close to a thousand press releases.

From a governing perspective the importance of the media cannot be overestimated. Indeed, officials inside the Government Office claim that it is barely possible nowadays to put forward proposals that cannot be presented as attractive press releases (Premfors and Sundström 2007: 10). Studies also show that it is relatively easy for Swedish ministers to reach out with messages through the media (Petersson and Carlsberg 1990: 175; Eriksson et al. 2013; Strömbäck 2012). In recent years the government has increased its capacity to spread information and handle the media. In the early 1970s there was only one person employed in the Government Office working on external information and issues related to the media. By 2008 that figure had risen to 141 (Erlandsson 2008: 340). Today, every government department has a unit for information.

Stories spread by politicians have some basic characteristics which make them successful (e.g. Morrell 2006: 371–2). Thus, good stories contain promises about some kind of positive change ("novelty") and appear possible to pursue ("credibility"). Often they also contain distinct characters (such as "winners" and "heroes") and plots. Good stories also often contain "magic concepts." Such concepts are fashionable and have "a high degree of abstraction, a strongly positive normative charge, a seeming ability to dissolve previous dilemmas and binary oppositions and mobility across domains" (Pollitt and

Hupe 2011: 642). In the case of development cooperation "results," "quality," "perfor-mance," "transparency," and "accountability" are examples of such magic concepts used by the minister in charge.

Not only have Swedish politicians excellent opportunities to tell stories, but studies also show that the Swedish administration is all ears when ministers talk. Swedish offi-cials read government bills and other governmental documents very carefully, and they listen hard to what ministers say when they launch reforms (Jacobsson 1984: 183–6; Ehn and Sundström 1997: 98; Premfors and Sundström 2007: 134).

Conclusions

In this chapter we have shown how the Swedish government manages to strike a bal-ance between basic demands on efficiency (avoiding overload) and democracy (being able to influence issues for which it may become accountable, including issues which previously may have been delegated to agencies). We have shown how the government creates organizational arrangements which, once in place, require less of recurrent and detailed steering and control by the government. The government does not seek to control all aspects of governing. To a much larger extent than is usually understood it delegates policy-making to the administration; it uses the administration to fend off issues that it does not want to deal with. However, when unexpected issues emerge and become regarded as "political" (by politicians or officials), there are mechanisms ensur-ing that the government can influence the issues, more or less directly.

The strategies we have discussed may not be used all the time. Together, they provide a kind of stable framework in which everyday life can take place. How a policy field is organized does not totally determine what happens within the field. However, it surely increases the probability that some actions take place (and not others), that some issues are taken care of (but not others), and that some ideas (and not others) influence both actions and identities among administrative units and officials—and surrounding non-state actors—within the field.

There is one central ingredient that needs to be present in political systems in order for these strategies to be successful, and that is *trust*. Swedish politicians are able to del-egate policy-making to Swedish officials because they know that these officials, most of the time, understand and accept that issues, which at one point in time can be perceived as small, technical, and "administrative," at other times can be perceived as highly politi-cal. In such situations the politicians trust the officials to do their best to act in accord-ance with what they believe is the will of their political superiors or else hand over the issues to the politicians. The politicians also trust that the officials in such situations will do their best to assist them with expertise and advice.

The strategies outlined here are firmly rooted in empirical studies of the relation between political and administrative units in Sweden, but they may be relevant for other cases as well. We do not think that the Swedish case is a blueprint for understanding governing in general, but we believe that our understandings may be fruitful also in other contexts.

References

Andersson, C. (2010). "Completed Responsibility? Delegation, Organization, and Accountability in Swedish Export of Military Equipment," in G. Sundström, L. Soneryd, and S. Furusten (eds), *Organizing Democracy: The Construction of Agency in Practice.* Cheltenham: Edward Elgar, 32–47.

Bendor, J. (1985). *Parallel Systems: Redundancy in Government.* Berkeley: University of California Press.

Boal, K. B. and Schultz, P. L. (2007). "Storytelling, Time, and Evolution: The Role of Strategic Leadership in Complex Adaptive Systems," *The Leadership Quarterly* 18/4: 411–28.

Brunsson, N. (1989). "Reforms as Routines," in N. Brunsson and J. P. Olsen (eds), *The Reforming Organization.* Bergen: Fagbokforlaget, 33–47.

Brunsson, N. and Jacobsson, B. (2000). *A World of Standards.* Oxford: Oxford University Press.

Carlbom, M. (2007). "Kort liv för utskälld myndighet," *Dagens Nyheter*, February 19.

Carlsson, G. (2006). "Ny myndighet för bättre bistånd," Speech in Karlstad, November 8.

Crole-Rees, R. (2005). "Nätverk på vems villkor? En studie av nationell samordning inom narkotika- och psykiatripolitiken," Master's thesis, Stockholm University, Department of Political Science.

Czarniawska, B. (1997). *Narrating the Organization: Dramas of Institutional Identity.* Chicago: University of Chicago Press.

Ehn, P. and Sundström, G. (1997). "Samspelet mellan regeringen och statsförvaltningen," in *Det svåra samspelet: Resultatstyrningens framväxt och problematik.* Report to Förvaltningspolitiska kommissionen, SOU 1997:15.

Elgie, R. (2003). "Governance Traditions and Narratives of Public Sector Reform in France," *Public Administration* 81/1: 141–62.

Eriksson, G., Larson, L., and Moberg, U. (2013). *Politikernas arena: En studie om presskonferenser på regeringsnivå.* Lund: Studentlitteratur.

Erlandsson, M. (2008). "Regeringskansliet och medierna: Den politiska exekutivens resurser och strategier för att hantera och styra massmedier," *Statsvetenskaplig tidskrift* 110: 335–49.

Feldman, M. S. and Khademian, A. M. (2000). "Managing for inclusion: Balancing control and participation," *International Public Management Journal* 3: 149–67.

Head, B. W. (2008). "Wicked Problems in Public Policy," *Public Policy* 3/2: 101–18.

Héritier, A. and Lehmkuhl, D. (2008). "Introduction: The Shadow of Hierarchy and New Modes of Governance," *Journal of Public Policy* 28/1: 1–17.

Hirschman, A. O. (1970). *Exit, Voice, and Loyalty: Responses to Decline in Firms. Organizations, and States.* Cambridge, MA: Harvard University Press.

Hood, C. (1998). *The Art of the State: Culture, Rhetoric, and Public Management.* Oxford: Oxford University Press.

Hood, C. (2004). "Controlling Public Services and Government: Toward a Cross-National Perspective," in C. Hood, O. James, B. G. Peters, and C. Scott (eds), *Controlling Modern Government: Variety, Commonality and Change.* Cheltenham: Edward Elgar, 3–21.

Jacobsson, B. (1984). *Hur styrs förvaltningen: Myt och verklighet kring departementets styrning av ämbetsverken.* Lund: Studentlitteratur.

Jacobsson B. and Sundström, G. (2006). *Från hemvävd till invävd: Europeiseringen av svensk förvaltning och politik*. Stockholm: Liber.

Johansson, V. and Lindgren, L. (eds) (2013). *Uppdrag offentlig granskning*. Lund: Studentlitteratur.

Kooiman, J. (2003). *Governing as Governance*. London: Sage.

Lægreid, P. and Verhoest, K. (2010). "Introduction: Reforming Public Sector Organizations," in P. Lægreid and K. Verhoest (eds), *Governance of Public Sector Organizations: Proliferation, Autonomy, and Performance*. Basingstoke: Palgrave, 1–20.

Landau, M. (1969). "Redundancy, Rationality, and the Problem of Duplication and Overlap," *Public Administration Review* 29/4: 346–58.

Landau, M. (1991). "On Multiorganizational Systems in Public Administration," *Journal of Public Administration Research and Theory* 1/1: 5–18.

Lerner, A. (1986). "There Is More Than One Way to Be Redundant," *Administration & Society* 18/3: 334–59.

March, J. G. and Olsen, J. P. (1976). *Ambiguity and Choice in Organizations*. Bergen: Universitetsforlaget.

March, J. G. and Olsen, J. P. (1989). *Rediscovering Institutions: The Organizational Basis of Politics*. New York and London: Free Press.

Matthews, F. (2013). *Complexity, Fragmentation and Uncertainty: Governing Capacity in an Evolving State*. Oxford: Oxford University Press.

McCubbins, M. D. and Schwartz, T. (1984). "Congressional Oversight Overlooked: Police Patrol versus Fire Alarms," *American Journal of Political Science* 28: 167–79.

Miles, Jr, R. E. (1978). "The Origin and Meaning of Miles' Law," *Public Administration Review* 38/5: 399–403.

Mintzberg, H. (1978). "Patterns in Strategy Formation," *Management Science* 24/9: 934–48.

Mintzberg, H. and McHugh, A. (1985). "Strategy Formation in an Adhocracy," *Administrative Science Quarterly* 30: 160–97.

Miranda, R. and Lerner, A. (1995). "Bureaucracy, Organizational Redundancy, and the Privatization of Public Services," *Public Administration Review* 55/2: 193–200.

Morrell, K. (2006). "Policy as Narrative: New Labour's Reform of the National Health Service," *Public Administration* 84/2: 367–85.

Neuhauser, P. C. (1993). *Corporate Legends and Lore: The Power of Storytelling as a Management Tool*. New York: McGraw-Hill.

Niemann, C. (2013). "Villkorat förtroende: Normer och rollförväntningar i relationen mellan politiker och tjänstemän i Regeringskansliet," dissertation, Stockholm University: Department of Political Science.

Odén, E. (2013). "Öppna jämförselser inom äldreomsorgen: Praktiken i Eskilstuna och Nyköping," Master's thesis, Stockholm University, Department of Political Science.

Page, E. C. (2005). "Joined-Up Government and the Civil Service," in V. Bogdanor (ed.), *Joined-Up Government*. Oxford: Oxford University Press, 139–55.

Page. E. C. (2008). "Delegation, Detail and Discretion: Bureaucracy and the Construction of Policies," in U. Sverdrup and J. Trondal (eds), The Organizational Dimension of Politics. Bergen: Fagbokforlaget, 206–33.

Page, E. C. (2012). *Policy without Politicians: Bureaucratic Influence in Comparative Perspective*. Oxford: Oxford University Press.

Page E. C. and Jenkins, B. (2005). *Policy Bureaucracy: Government with a Cast of Thousands*. Oxford: Oxford University Press.

Petersson, O. (1989). *Maktens nätverk*. Stockholm: Carlssons.

Petersson, O. and Carlberg, I. (1990). *Makten över tanken: En bok om det svenska massmedi-asamhället*. Stockholm: Carlssons.

Pfeffer, J. and Salancik, G. R. (1978). *The External Control of Organizations: A Resource Dependency Perspective*. New York: Harper and Row.

Pierre, J. (2009). "Tillväxtpolitikens styrningsproblem," in J. Pierre and G. Sundström (eds), *Samhällsstyrning i förändring*. Malmö: Liber, 72–89.

Pollitt, C. and P. Hupe (2011). "Talking about Government: The Role of Magic Concepts," *Public Management Review* 13: 641–58.

Premfors, R. and Sundström, G. (2007). *Regeringskansliet*. Malmö: Liber.

Qvist, M. (2015). "Activation Reform and Inter-Agency Co-operation: Local Consequences of Mixed Modes of Governance in Sweden," *Social Policy & Administration*, online version, 2015-02-27.

Rhodes, R. A. W. (2005). "Everyday Life in a Ministry: Public Administration as Anthropology," *American Review of Public Administration* 35/1: 1–23.

Rittel, H. W. J. and Webber, M. M. (1973). "Dilemmas in a General Theory of Planning," *Policy Science* 4/2: 155–69.

Säll, L. (2011). *Kluster som teori och politik: Om den regionala tillväxtpolitikens diskursiva prak-tiker*, Karlstad University Studies 2011:56. Karlstad: Karlstad University.

Seidman, H. (1998). *Politics, Position, and Power: The Dynamics of Federal Organization*. Oxford: Oxford University Press.

Sørensen, E. (2006). "Metagovernance: The Changing Role of Politicians in Processes of Democratic Governance," *American Review of Public Administration* 36/1: 98–114.

SOU 1995:27. *Regional framtid*. Final report from Regionberedningen. Fritzes.

Strömbäck, J. (2012). "Journalistiken och politiken," in L. Nord and J. Strömbäck (eds), *Medierna och demokratin*. Lund: Studentlitteratur, 263–89.

Sundström, G. (2010). "In Search of Democracy: The Process behind the Swedish Forest-Sector Objectives," in G. Sundström, L. Soneryd, and S. Furusten (eds), *Organizing Democracy: The Construction of Agency in Practice*. Cheltenham: Edward Elgar, 79–93.

Thompson, D. F. (1980). "Moral Responsibility of Public Officials: The Problem of Many Hands," *American Political Science Review* 74/4: 905–15.

Torfing, J. and Triantafillou, P. (eds) (2009). *Interactive Policy Making, Metagovernance and Democracy*. Colchester: ECPR Press.

SECTION 6

SUBNATIONAL GOVERNMENT

SECTION EDITOR
ANDERS LIDSTRÖM

CHAPTER 26

··

INTRODUCTION

Subnational Government

··

ANDERS LIDSTRÖM

SOME scholars have characterized Sweden as a *decentralized unitary state* (Loughlin 2000; Ansell and Gingrich 2003). Others have referred to the political system as hourglass-shaped (Peterson 1998). Both these conceptualizations attempt to characterize a somewhat paradoxical combination. On the one hand, the state is centralized, with all powers collected in the hands of Parliament and with a type of welfare model that emphasizes uniformity, equality, and primarily public provision of services. The unitary state has a long tradition, emanating from unification in the sixteenth century, and has not really been challenged since. Over the years, it has been a convenient tool used by autocratic kings, conservative governments, and Social Democrats to rule the country. On the other hand, centralization is combined with strong local government as concerns functions, resources, personnel, and fiscal powers. These are in charge of practically all public welfare services, have more resources per inhabitant than in any other country (with the exception of Denmark), employ 23 percent of the workforce (or 81 percent of all public employees), and can decide on local income tax rates without having to consult any other level of government.

Although this is a seeming anomaly, it is a requirement for the welfare model that characterizes Sweden and the other Nordic states (Esping-Andersen 1990). Centralization and universality is only one side of the coin. In order to avoid the pitfalls of bureaucratization and rigorous standardization, national welfare services need to be adjusted to specific local circumstances. Central government has entrusted local elected politicians with the task of implementing key national welfare services. This requires capable public providers with local democratic legitimacy (cp. Hansen and Klausen 2002). Trust between levels is enhanced by the strong dominance of the same political parties at all levels of government. Apart from implementing national welfare policies, local government also carries out collective services that are generated locally, such as road maintenance, parks, recreation, and cultural facilities.

The four chapters in this section study the features of subnational government in a Swedish setting in more detail, based on the most recent research in the field. First, Stig Montin outlines the system of local and regional government with a particular focus on the internal working of subnational governments ("Municipalities, Regions and County Councils: Actors and Institutions"). One important observation is that Swedish local government has retained its basic structure with regard to formal democratic institutions, despite growing pluralism in how welfare services are provided. These forms include internal delegation, corporatization, contracting out, and consumer choice.

David Feltenius continues the analysis in the following chapter with a focus on the horizontal relationships of Swedish subnational government ("Subnational Government in a Multilevel Perspective"). Not least their important position in the welfare system provides local and regional levels of government with a strategic position in negotiating the distribution of powers and resources between levels. In addition, the European Union became increasingly relevant to subnational government after Sweden joined in 1995.

The next chapter, by Lars Niklasson, highlights how subnational governments have been transformed through reforms over the last few decades ("Challenges and Reforms of Local and Regional Governments in Sweden"). Particular attention is paid to the role played by different central government interests in the reform processes, and how this may partially explain why the nature of the changes has varied.

Finally, Anders Lidström concludes with a comparative overview ("Swedish Local and Regional Government in a European Context"). This chapter positions Swedish subnational government in comparison with other European systems of local and regional government and highlights the various aspects that make Swedish local and regional government different. It is argued that many of these differences, such as decentralized responsibility for welfare services and representative democracy through strong political parties, may be regarded as a reflection of the core values of the Scandinavian welfare model.

REFERENCES

Ansell, C. and Gingrich, J. (2003). "Trends in Decentralization," in B. E. Cain, R. J. Dalton, and S. E. Scarrow (eds), *Democracy Transformed? Expanding Political Opportunities in Advanced Industrial Democracies*. Oxford: Oxford University Press, 140–63.

Esping-Andersen, G. (1990). *The Three Worlds of Welfare Capitalism*. Cambridge: Polity Press.

Hansen, T. and Klausen, J. E. (2002). "Between the Welfare State and Local Government Autonomy," *Local Government Studies* 28/4: 47–66.

Loughlin, J. (2000). "Regional Autonomy and State Paradigm Shift in Western Europe," *Regional and Federal Studies* 10/2: 10–34.

Peterson, O. (1998). *Kommunalpolitik*. Stockholm: Norstedts juridik.

CHAPTER 27

MUNICIPALITIES, REGIONS, AND COUNTY COUNCILS

Actors and Institutions

STIG MONTIN

INTRODUCTION

LOCAL self-government has been recognized as a distinctive feature of the Swedish political system for many decades, and still is. The principle of the decentralized model was set down as early as 1862 when the first Local Government Act was introduced. Yet, Sweden is a unitary state, which means that the real world of local self-government is a negotiated order in the shadow of central government and the Parliament (*Riksdagen*). Although the institutional setting of local governance has fundamentally remained the same for 150 years, the role of municipalities and county councils has expanded dramatically during the development of the welfare state, especially since the 1950s. However, from the 1980s we have witnessed a third era of change and reform which, to some extent, challenges the fundamental image of local self-government and local representative democracy.

The first era of change was during the 1960s and 1970s when municipalities were amalgamated and turned into local welfare institutions with substantial financial, legal, political, and professional resources. Mainly as a response to this expansion and resource growth, decentralization measures were carried out expressed as a period of experimenting with "free communes" during the 1980s and after that giving municipalities freedom to organize political and administrative functions (which was laid down in the new Local Government Act in 1991 (LGA 1991)), decentralization of responsibility for primary and secondary education, and the transformation of central government subsidies (from earmarked to general subsidies) in 1993. Since the late 1980s a third era of reforms can be identified. The overall direction has been movement towards the adaptation of market mechanisms as drivers for development (purchaser–provider split, competition, customer choice, privatization, and performance management), as well as increased demands for citizen involvement in handling complex policy matters and intermunicipal cooperation in order to cope with operational and strategic issues. Local government responsibility for welfare, education, economic development, and broader issues related to sustainable development has increased, but so has central government control and supervision; for example, concerning public purchasing, education, and health care. Several changes that have taken place in legislation directed at municipalities and county councils can be regarded as adaptation to EU legislation concerning the free movement of money, people, goods, and services.

Hence, circumstances for local governance have become continuously more complex. Municipalities and county councils are actors in a multilevel government system, and they are themselves multi-organizational units characterized by challenges concerning how to cope with specialization and coordination. From this point of view, two fundamental tensions can be distinguished. The first tension is between national equality and local self-government (autonomy). More specifically, on the one hand people should have equal access to high quality of services independent of where they live. On the other hand, political priorities should make a difference and service production should be adapted to local needs (Karlsson and Montin 2013). The second tension is specifically related to the increased complexity of local governance: the municipality can be described as a tension between, on the one hand, a coherent territorial and functional unit steered and controlled by a party-based representative democratic system that regards citizens mainly as voters; and on the other hand, a customer-oriented setting of professionalized, self-managed units collaborating with neighboring municipalities and (especially in larger municipalities) a substantial number of private providers.

Both of these tensions will be elaborated on in this chapter, with a special focus on the latter. First, an overview of the local and regional government systems will be provided, followed by an institutional overview. Emphasis is then placed on the relationship between politics and administration, increased organizational complexity, new citizen–local-government relations, and how the local system is coordinated. Finally, main development tendencies are summarized.

Local Self-Government

Local self-government in Sweden is mainly defined by a clause of "general powers" in the Local Government Act (LGA 1991: 900): municipalities and county councils may themselves attend to matters of general concern which are connected with the area of the municipality or county council or with their members and which are not to be dealt with solely by the state, another municipality, another county council, or some other body (LGA 1991: ch. 2, section 1).

The principle of local self-government has always been strong in Sweden and has been further emphasized in the Constitution. Local self-government is a principle, but has never has been clearly defined. What local self-government actually means in a specific historical moment is a negotiated order, negotiated primarily between the political parties and between central government and the Swedish Association of Local Authorities and Regions (SALAR). Reviewed over time, the strongest tendency is decentralization; however, occasionally, and within specific policy areas, central government control has simultaneously increased. Over a period of several years, certain praxis has developed which has recently been constitutionalized. Accordingly, in the revised Constitution from 2010, there is a chapter of six articles on local authorities that has been added which includes both democratic self-government and its restrictions (Instrument of Government, ch. 14). It primarily clarifies that decision-making powers are exercised by elected assemblies, that "local authorities are responsible for local and regional matters of public interest on the principle of local self-government," and that the "local authorities may levy tax for the management of their affairs." In addition to the principles stated in the Constitution, the Planning and Building Act states that "planning the use of land and water areas is a matter for the municipality" (The Planning and Building Act 1987: 10), which is generally referred to as the municipal "planning monopoly."

On the other hand it is also stated that detailed rules concerning responsibilities are laid down in law, that "local authorities may be obliged to contribute to costs incurred by other local authorities if necessary to achieve an equal financial base" (a system of financial equalization), and, more generally, that "regulations regarding grounds for change in the division of the realm into local authorities are laid down in law." Finally, a principle of proportionality is stated: "Any restriction in local self-government should not exceed what is necessary with regard to the purpose of the restriction" (Instrument of Government, ch. 14).

One particularly important central government instrument is the system of financial equalization which was introduced in the mid-1960s (and has been reformed several times). Simply speaking, it means that resources from richer municipalities and regions are redistributed to poorer municipalities and regions ("the Robin Hood tax"). The basic idea is that all citizens should have equal access to services independent of residence. Critics of the system argue that a municipality does not enjoy its just rewards for reducing unemployment or strengthening local growth, which is regarded as unfair. On the other hand, the equalization system is fundamental for people who live in sparsely populated areas and in municipalities suffering from the negative effects of economic globalization.

LOCAL AND REGIONAL, AND POLITICAL AND ADMINISTRATIVE INSTITUTIONS

The term "local government" includes municipalities and county councils, whose territories overlap but have different areas of responsibilities. Municipalities are thus not subordinated to county councils. While municipalities are responsible for a wide range of activities, the county councils' primary responsibility is health and medical care (about 90 percent of the budget). In four cases (Västra Götaland, Skåne, Halland, and Gotland) the county councils are called regional councils. The difference between regional councils and other county councils is that the former have broader responsibilities. In addition to health and medical care, they are responsible for regional development and infrastructure planning (see Lars Niklasson's chapter in this section).

To a large extent, the areas of responsibility and the content of responsibilities are regulated by national legislation, which in most cases consists of "framework legislation." Simply speaking, this means that substantial objectives are set in the legislation and local governments are then free to choose the means to achieve these objectives. Additionally, national government agencies are continuously "filling up" framework legislation with recommendations and instructions, and supervise specific sectors and policy areas at local government level. Broadly speaking, in terms of budget, about 80 percent of all municipal responsibilities are mandatory.

Municipalities and county councils are jurisdictional units (spheres of authority), governed by councils (assemblies) and standing committees, including an executive committee. The municipal political organization varies as concerns the number of committees and their relationships to each other, but the basic structure is regulated in the Local Government Act.

Although the organizational structure differs between municipalities, the system of party-based representative democracy is the same. In accordance with this system, every member of the council and standing committees represents a political party. The political parties nominate candidates for election. During the last few decades there have been three observable trends in the local, party-based representative system: a decreasing number of local representatives in councils and standing committees (from approximately 70,000 in 1980 to less than 40,000 in 2013), an increasing number of political parties represented in municipal councils (from usually six or seven in the 1988–91 to more than eight in 2011–14 in most councils), and escalating political conflicts. Most of the political parties are local branches of national parties, such as the Left Party, the Social Democratic Party, the Green Party, the Liberal Party, the Center Party, the Christian Democrats, the Moderate Party, and the Sweden Democrats (a newish party based mainly on xenophobia). In several municipalities there are also local parties.

There are several types of political majorities formed after the elections. In the 1990s one third of the municipalities had a one-party majority (mostly Social Democrats); however, this model has decreased to about 7 percent of the current 290 municipalities. Minority control, which is a model in which a minority party depends on other political parties case by case, has become more common (from 6 to 17 percent). A fairly common parliamentary situation is "grand coalitions" (one third of the municipalities) and in a few cases these coalitions are across the left–green bloc and the right-wing bloc. In approximately one fifth of the municipalities there is a single political party who can tip the balance, and this proportion has been the same since the 1990s. More conflicts occur in this latter parliamentary situation than in the other models (Gilljam and Karlsson

2012). Hence, although political complexity has increased, it does not appear to have become more difficult to form functioning majorities in the municipalities.

The *municipal council* consists of at least twenty-one members, the number of members being regulated and related to the number of residents entitled to vote. The regular and deputy members of the council are directly elected (nominated by political parties) at general elections. The council decides on matters concerning principal issues or matters of major importance, especially objectives, targets and guidelines, budget, and taxation.

The *executive committee* is the municipal "government." It is a coalition government because the members are proportional to the elected members of the council. In the Swedish system there is no formal mayor. In some municipalities the chair of the municipal council is called "mayor," but this is not in a modern sense. The actual position of the chair of the executive committee, who is usually a full-time salaried politician (*kommunalråd*), can be described as an informal executive mayor. The Swedish assembly government system is sometimes referred to as "quasi-parliamentarism" (Bäck 2005), which means that the executive committee is elected proportionally in relation to the distribution of mandates in the assembly, but the chair and the vice chair of all standing committees are appointed by the majority.

The overall duty of the executive committee is to direct and coordinate local government activities, and supervise the activities of the other committees and the municipal enterprises. Furthermore, the executive committee prepares or pronounces on business to be transacted by the council, takes charge of financial administration, gives effect to council decisions, and generally performs the tasks entrusted to it by the council. Due to the prominent role of the executive committee, most decisions taken in the council are previously settled in the committee. Thus, ever since the 1960s, the council has recurrently been described as more or less a registration unit for decisions already made in the executive committee. However there are variations. In some municipalities the political party groups are more dynamic and active in council than in others.

The standing committees are, to some extent, autonomous in relation to the council and to the executive committee. Neither the council nor the executive committee is allowed to intervene when standing committees execute their authority according to national legislation, such as the Education Act, the Social Services Act, and environmental legislation. The logic behind this "dualism" is that the standing committees are primarily responsible for implementing national policies and laws, while the municipal council makes overall priorities concerning financial and other conditions for this implementation. For example, school legislation, national curricula, and central government agencies state the substantial goals for education and carry out evaluations and inspections, while the municipality is the formal responsible authority for providing the preconditions for achieving these goals (hires teachers, provides premises, etc.).

Municipalities and county councils are organized in different ways. Variations have increased since the 1990s and there is no overall or systematic categorization at hand. Broadly speaking, there are five different models. The still most common way to organize standing committees and administration is according to a *sector model*. This is a model where each committee is responsible for one or more sectors (such as education, social services, culture, construction, and environment) and the administration and service business is subordinated to the committees. However, the actual distribution of responsibility differs between municipalities. There is no universal definition of, for example, an education committee.

Secondly, in the 1980s, a sub-municipal reform was introduced and several municipalities became organized according to a *territorial model*. By 1991, twenty-three municipalities had divided their territories into sub-units governed by sub-municipal or sub-city councils. They were mainly granted authority for "soft" sectors such as culture, leisure, primary education, and social services. In some counties there were sub-county councils responsible for primary health care. However, by the beginning of the twenty-first century most of the municipalities and all county councils had abolished these sub-units. However, the three largest cities (Stockholm, Gothenburg, and Malmö) have retained this territorial model.

Thirdly, several municipalities and county councils chose a *functional model*. One of the most important changes in the 1991 LGA was that municipalities and county councils became entitled to decide on their own political and administrative organization. The only compulsory bodies left are the council and the executive committee (and also an election committee). Different organizational structures were implemented across the country. At the time, one of the most popular organizations was termed the "purchaser/provider model," which basically means that one type of committee was responsible for purchasing and financing, while another type of committee was responsible for the "production" of services (Montin 1992). Although the label as such has almost disappeared, the principle of division of functions has survived and further developed (especially in larger municipalities) into a system where "ordering" committees make contracts with internal or external providers. For larger municipalities and county councils this financing/production split is the most common form and the discussion is no longer so focused on the pro and cons of this organizational logic. Instead, questions are raised as to how politically responsible committees can follow up and control external providers.

Fourthly, several smaller municipalities have established a *centralized model*. In this model all standing committees have been abolished and authority has been moved to the executive board.

Last but not least, an increasing number of municipalities and county councils have more recently developed institutionalized collaboration by introducing a *joint committees model*. An example is when two or more municipalities have a joint committee for secondary education. In general there is a strong tendency toward intermunicipal cooperation and collaboration. There are great variations in the size of municipalities, from Stockholm (approximately 900,000 inhabitants) to Bjurholm (3,000 inhabitants). The system of financial equalization prevents these variations from impacting on welfare services. However, there are significant incentives for small municipalities to cooperate. Small municipalities often do not possess the necessary professional resources to meet citizen needs and demands and to fulfill the increasing expectations stated in national laws, regulations, and more general political goals. Intermunicipal cooperation is common between municipalities and between county councils and has increased since the

1990s. Cooperation takes different, more or less institutionalized, forms such as joint committees, intermunicipal associations, agreements, projects, and networks. Motives for cooperation have expanded over time (Gossas 2006). First they mainly concerned joint service delivery—for example, public transport, energy supply, waste management, and emergency services. Subsequently, cooperation has been initiated on the grounds that it will increase regional identity and regional economic growth. Especially in the latter sense, cooperation has been encouraged by central government. Special priorities have been placed on projecting infrastructure (especially for public transport), coordination between municipal land use planning, regional transport planning, and regional growth programs. However, institutional factors such as the municipal land use planning monopoly and the constitutional principle of local self-government in general have been regarded as obstacles to intensified cooperation (Rader Olsson and Cars 2011). In several municipalities the principle of local self-government, often described in terms of "local identity," imposes limits on the extent of collaboration. There is a recurrent debate on the issue of a new amalgamation reform, but so far most municipal politicians reject this idea.

Politics and Administration

Issues concerning the relationship between politics and administration, or more specifically, the relationship between politicians and professional managers and administrators have been discussed since the 1970s. Broadly speaking, there are two contradictory images supported by empirical evidence. The first image is that municipal professional administrators (*tjänstemän*) are powerful and thus pursue policies that politicians react to and follow. A different image is that politicians enjoy ultimate power. As employers they can always dismiss managers from their positions. The power of the municipal manager is delegated power.

Due to the complexity of the municipal organization, there are different categories of professional administrators. In direct relationship to the executive board and to the standing committees there are two types of positions that may be distinguished. First, there are those who handle strategic tasks such as preparing plans, budget, and other decisions, especially the municipal officer (*kommundirektör*). Secondly, there are managers at different levels, such as chief administrative officers and middle managers. A comparative case study on planning processes indicates that what could, on the surface, be interpreted as the power of professional planners is actually a process of anticipation. Very few professional planners propose anything that has not formally or informally gained acceptance among leading politicians. The interaction within planning processes can be described as "politicians influence professional administrators, who in their turn influence politicians" (Bengtsson 2012). Research based on a national survey covering council members from all Swedish municipalities reveals that political strength in relation to local administrators varies to a great extent according to the size of the municipality, which means that the political role of administrators is stronger in smaller than in larger municipalities (Karlsson 2013). The political context, such as the degree of political dispute and public attention paid to it, is also important. The level of attention paid by the public to a particular policy issue is positively associated with a more reflective approach among politicians, which means that they are more open to influence from professional administrators and planners (Lundin and Öberg 2014).

One particular relationship, which has increasingly become of interest, is that between the chair of the executive committee (CEC) and the municipal officer (MO), who may be described as having "overlapping roles" (Bergström et al. 2008). They are at the apex of two pyramids: the political and the administrative. The CEC has been defined as an informal mayor, which means that she or he does not have a formal mandate, but the position is in practical terms at least as powerful as formal mayors in other European local government systems (Bäck 2005). Swedish local governance, like other local government systems, is characterized by weak formal institutions and hence strong informal processes (Karlsson 2012; Copus and Erlingsson 2013).

The powerful positions of CECs and MOs have developed gradually due to the process of professionalization and the expansion of municipal activities. In order to balance the knowledge advantage of administrators, the number of full-time and part-time politicians has increased, which has contributed to a hierarchization of the political organization. According to the LGA, all representatives are equal. There are no special formal rules related to whether representatives are part-time politicians or full-time politicians. In practice, however, there is a major difference between being an unsalaried lay politician and a part- or full-time salaried politician. Over the decades, the number of representatives has continuously decreased, but the number of part- and full-time employed politicians (*kommunalråd*) has increased. This can be interpreted as a trend towards informal political professionalization (Montin 2005). Generally speaking, lay politicians, who are supposed to be the carriers of local democracy, have lost much of their day-to-day political control. Some policy matters have become strategic and are now in the hands of salaried politicians. Other matters have been delegated further down in the administrative and professional organization.

In municipalities and county councils/regions, only political units (the council and standing committees) have decision-making power, not individual politicians or managers/administrators. The latter are still hardly mentioned in the Local Government Act. All municipal employees are recognized as "assisting" standing committees in terms of handling daily matters and implementing political decisions only. Recently, SALAR has suggested that the relationship between political and administrative leaders ought to be regulated, and the issue is also under consideration in a review of the Local Government Act (Government Directive 2012) commissioned by central government. However, so far advocates of regulation have failed to make their argument strong enough to actually challenge the old institutions, especially if a formal demarcation will bring restrictions for leading politicians. The traditional principle of political sovereignty has been heavily challenged by rather different NPM ideals of how to manage a modern municipality, and several large municipalities have formed informal demarcations between political and professional managers. The old image of political sovereignty still represents the basic ideal of local democracy, and establishing formal demarcations would, for many local politicians, be considered as giving too much power to the professional administration.

INCREASED COMPLEXITY

Until the 1990s, social services were almost completely provided in-house in what was part and parcel of the local welfare state. Schools (primary and secondary) were also almost exclusively municipally managed. Municipalities and county councils were regarded as important institutions in the universal welfare state guided by values of national equality, and for that reason local welfare services would be held together. The future wave of corporatization, contracting out, and customer choice was not foreseen at the time. An important driver behind the change was increasing professionalization along with financial problems by the end of the 1980s.

Professionalization has become a trademark in local government. In this respect there is a historically important difference between municipalities and county councils. Due to fact that health and medical care have always been the primary responsibility of the county councils, medical professions have always been strong. In the municipalities, on the other hand, a cultural shift took place during the 1960s and 1970s which has been described as a transformation from "administration by laymen" to "administration by professionals" (Strömberg and Westerståhl 1984). Professionalization has increased ever since. By the late 1980s, managers received more responsibility in terms of balancing needs and resources and this was further facilitated by the new LGA in 1992. In relation to this internal delegation, the idea was to develop a "new" role for the elected representatives. Arms-length political control was introduced, such as management by objectives (MbO), management by results (MbR), and purchaser/provider models. Politicians should be able to focus on strategic issues rather than on time-consuming, day-to-day politics. Today, nearly all municipalities have some type of MbO/MbR, and most municipalities use some type of internal contract system. Along with this, internal managerialism initiatives were gradually taken in order to increase management autonomy by creating municipal companies and contracting out welfare services.

Public utilities, such as electricity, public transport, and refuse collection have, to a great extent, been privatized or contracted out. Other public utilities such as municipal housing, water and waste disposal, real estate management, and private company services have, to a large extent, been transformed into municipal corporations. Since the 1980s corporatization has occurred in two waves. From the end of the 1980s to the mid-1990s there was a first wave, when a couple of hundred corporations were established. The second wave was from 2007 and the number of completely and partly owned municipal companies rose to more than 1,700 in 2012, which on average would be about six companies in each municipality. However, most corporations are situated in larger cities and their business mainly consists of private company services and real estate management. In terms of employment, the largest corporations are within the area of energy and water supply. Between 2004 and 2009, total turnover of municipal corporations increased by 27 percent.

Private entrepreneurs within "soft" sectors, such as hospital care, elderly care, primary and secondary education (free schools), and preschools have increased substantially since the 1990s. All private providers gain their revenue from taxes, which means that "privatization" stands for management but not financing and regulation. Purchase from private health and medical care providers increased 10 percent between 2001 and 2010. The increase will continue due to the regulated freedom of establishment of private primary care providers from 2010. From 2000 to 2010, private care for elderly and disabled people increased by approximately 12 percent. The number of private primary schools increased by 10 percent between the late 1990 and 2010 and the number of free secondary schools increased by 20 percent. In total, the costs for purchasing from private providers in municipalities and county councils increased from EUR 9.22 to 13.74 billion between 2007 and 2011 (Swedish Government Official Report 2013:53).

In addition, a "system of choice" (*lagen om valfrihet*) regarding services within health (primary health care) and social (home-help) services for elderly and disabled persons was introduced in 2009. This system of choice means a procedure where the individual is entitled to choose the supplier to perform the service with whom a contracting authority (municipality or county council) has approved and concluded a contract. This legislation is compulsory for county councils but voluntary for municipalities. In 2014 a government commission suggested that all municipalities should be obliged to create conditions for users to choose between various providers of home-help services. Approximately 180 of the 290 municipalities had introduced this system by 2014.

Hence, management of municipal soft sectors has been subjected to rather extensive change, mainly since 2006 when the right-wing Alliance government intensified the market-oriented approach. This has caused intensive political discussions, especially concerning the opportunities for private providers of education, health care, and social care to generate profit for their owners (which are often venture capital corporations). One specific issue that has been discussed is whether the introduction of free schools and freedom of choice of schools has caused increased social and economic segregation. According to some studies, differences between individual schools and municipalities in terms of results have increased since the 1990s and this can be related to the freedom of choice system. However, according to other studies this development would have taken place anyhow, and still others argue that recent reforms within the education sector provide opportunities to break this trend. Hence, primary and secondary education is a matter of tension between national equity and local self-government, as well as ideological conflicts concerning to what extent local governance should be controlled by consumer choice and the logic of the market.

Standing committees execute the political responsibility of public care and services at local government level, irrespective of whether public or private suppliers provide the service. This means that a committee must "ensure that activities are conducted in accordance with the goals and guidelines resolved by the assembly and with the provisions applying to the activities." It is also stated that the politically responsible committee will ensure that "checks are sufficient" and that "the activities are otherwise carried out in a satisfactory way" (LGA 1991, ch. 6, section 7). This includes in-house as well as private providers. In order to fulfill political responsibility and accountability, an overall control of output is necessary. When it comes to private providers it is stated that the assembly "shall ensure that the municipality … is guaranteed an opportunity to check and follow up on the activity." However, according to several reviews there is a lack of systematic control and follow-up of private provider activities (Swedish Government Official Report 2013:53).

In order to place emphasis on local political responsibility and accountability, an expert committee appointed by central government has recently proposed a change in the Local Government Act consisting of a formal requirement for the municipal council to adopt a program for how to follow up and control in-house and external providers of welfare (Swedish Government Official Report 2013:53). This proposal is in line with the intensified orientation towards performance scrutiny (supervision, inspections, evaluations, quality measurements, benchmarking, etc.) now taking place at national level (Johansson and Montin 2014). National agencies, such as the Inspectorate of Health and Social Care and the Schools Inspectorate, have been commissioned to increase their scrutiny of public and private providers. Furthermore, SALAR, together with the National Board of Health and Welfare, are developing national quality standards, and several interest groups and private consultants are establishing ranking lists of municipalities and service providers. In general, there is widespread recognition of a growing "audit society" in Sweden with a specific focus on health care, social services, and education. For example, in a review of the development within education commissioned by central government it is critically remarked that " 'decentralized management by objectives' has been replaced by a 'centralized performance-based management' " (Swedish Government Official Report 2014:5, p. 30).

CITIZENS AND LOCAL GOVERNMENT

Since 1970, elections to municipal councils, county/regional councils, and the Riksdag are held on the very same day. In this respect, the Swedish system is quite unique. In most other European democracies, national and local elections are held on separate election days. As in many other countries, a general trend away from voting and participating in political parties toward other forms of citizen participation can be observed at local and regional government level. Several political parties have proposed, from time to time, separate election days; however, faced with the possible constitutional and political consequences of making such a reform, most parties have ended up supporting the status quo. The primary argument has been that in countries where election days are separate, election turnout is lower than in Sweden (Montin 2007). However, less challenging initiatives have been taken in order to increase citizen participation at local government level.

During the 1980s, central government and many local political leaders argued that collective user involvement (voice) should be an important measurement for improving small-scale local democracy. It was sometimes regarded as a "school in democracy" and as a possible entrance into more large-scale democracy and would thus increase the number of members in local branches of political parties. Research indicated that user-boards in schools could have a positive impact on learning processes about democracy, given that the relationship between municipal institutions and the user-boards was characterized by dialogue and cooperation (Jarl 2005). However, user democracy went out of fashion and instead was gradually more or less replaced by ideas of competition between service producers and "freedom of choice." By way of introduction, "internal competition" was launched as a soft version; however, in the 1990s political support for opening up to private competitors in education, health services, medical services, and care of the elderly became increasingly apparent. The focus changed from citizens as end-users toward citizens as consumers (Elander and Montin 1995). According to recent analysis of citizen surveys between 1992 and 2010, it has become more common that citizens prefer a mixed welfare model (public–private mix of providers), especially in municipalities where welfare services are, to a large extent, carried out by private actors (Edlund and Sevä 2013).

In addition to voting, citizen participation has had a long tradition in Sweden. For example, participation and mobilization within democratic organizations (popular movements) was important for the development of national democracy and the building of the welfare state. Some organizations have lost their attraction, while other types of political organization have increased their membership. Political participation through digital channels has increased. A historically more recent phenomenon, which began in the late 1970s and increased in the 2000s, is the idea of inviting citizens to take part in different policy processes (M. Karlsson 2013). In Sweden the contemporary concepts used are citizen dialogues or plain citizen perspectives. Various forms of contacts between citizens and local politicians and professionals can be found behind this label, such as service priorities, safety walks, development of new services, urban renewal, and spatial planning.

It should be noted that citizen dialogues differ from previous ideas of participatory democracy, which were often described as bottom-up-initiated activities. Nowadays they can be framed as institutional capacity building (Smedby and Neij 2013), and initiatives are often taken from local governments themselves. Thus, it is not about changing the decision-making system, but recruiting citizens as co-creators of local policy.

The ideal of the individual, rational consumer of services and the concept of the collectively oriented citizen involved in local matters are quite different and place rather contradictory expectations on the inhabitants of a municipality. However, they can be regarded as two different ingredients in the same discourse, and this discourse is the distribution of risk and responsibility. In the first case, citizens are encouraged to make their own choices and also bear responsibility for making wrong choices. This can be interpreted as ways of privatizing politics. In the second case, people are encouraged to take part, but also to undertake co-responsibility for dealing with common issues.

Political Coordination

Corporatization, contracting out, and the rising number of free schools have led to increasing institutional complexity of public service provision. However, municipal policy formation has not echoed such complexity. First, still the most important institution for holding it all together is the political party. In the council and the standing committees the members constitute party groups (naturally depending on the number of mandates). The overall municipal organization of the political party coordinates the policy-making, and controls the political positions among its members. In this process, the leading councillors (*kommunalråd*), such as the chair of the executive committee, possess decisive power. However other full- or part-time politicians are important in the policy process in positions such as political secretaries. However, the political party usually means a rather distinguished elite. For instance, council party groups can become detached from party organization and grass-roots party members (Copus and Erlingsson 2013).

Second, according to a comparative and longitudinal study of local government leaders there are, on the one hand, tendencies toward increasing contacts between local political leaders and civic organizations, such as neighborhood organizations and the public in general. Contacts with regional government actors have also increased. However, these contact patterns are not entirely new. What nowadays are referred to as governance networks have always been common at local government level, but the phenomenon has increased (Hall et al. 2009). On the other hand, the internal, informal local government power structure, which was empirically discovered in the mid-1980s, was thought to be similar to that found in 1999 and in 2005:

> The core triangle of the Swedish local power elite includes its administrative and political executive as well as its local party organizations. Thus, local governance equals local government: those most frequently contacted for support within the local elite group are also the most powerful according to the formal organization of local government. (Szücs and Strömberg 2006: 53)

There are no reasons to suspect that any fundamental change in this respect has taken place since 2005. Although governance networks have become more extensive, the iron triangle of local government still remains.

Summary

Two tensions were outlined in the introduction: that between central control and local self-government, and between coherence and fragmentation in local governance. In this concluding section some of the main tendencies are summarized in relation to these tensions.

First, after an era of decentralization, central state control began to increase in the 1990s and has developed further after the millennium shift. This is especially true in "soft" sectors like health care, social services, and education, the main argument being that the quality of decentralized services tends to become less equal. Local self-government is still widely recognized as a basic value, which means that only a few forms of central state control are related to sanctions or other types of coercion. However, Sweden has tended to follow other nations in the EU into the development of an audit society.

Second, due to increasing internal delegation, corporatization, contracting out, and the expansion of free schools and consumer choice, there is extensive pluralism of welfare services, sometimes referred to as fragmentation. On the other hand, the basic structure of formal democratic institutions has not been changed and the fundamental political–administrative power structure is also fairly intact. However, the local institutional settings of the political–administrative elite are mainly informal. According to contemporary discussions on these matters, the trend is development toward a formalization of the relationship between politics and administration.

A third theme is the contemporary development of the relationship between local/regional public authorities and citizens. These have developed along two parallel but also interrelated pathways. The first is increasing expectation of citizens as rational consumers (customers) of publicly financed services, and the second is increasing expectation of citizen participation in local policy-making, especially in urban renewal processes, spatial planning, and sustainable development. Although these two constructions of citizens may be seen as conflicting—one that privatizes politics while the other is oriented toward collective active citizenship—it appears that both of them are combined at municipal level.

Fourth, although intermunicipal cooperation has a long history, it has begun to be regarded as increasingly important for mobilization of common resources. Initiatives for cooperation are taken from below, but are also encouraged by central government. However, there are also tensions in this process. On the one hand, municipalities cooperate for resource mobilization and for strategic reasons in order to facilitate regional growth; on the other hand, the values of local self-government are considered to be very important, especially among citizens and politicians in smaller municipalities.

References

Bäck, H. (2005). "Borgmästarens makt," *Kommunal ekonomi och politik* 9/1: 7–36.

Bengtsson, M. (2012). *Anteciperande förvaltning: Tjänstemäns makt i kommunala policy-processer om vindkraft*. Göteborg: Förvaltningshögskolan, Göteborgs universitet.

Bergström, T., Magnusson, H., and Ramberg, U. (2008). "Through a Glass Darkly: Complexity in Swedish Local Government," *Local Government Studies* 34/2: 203–20.

Copus, C. and Erlingsson, G. Ó. (2013). "Formal Institutions versus Informal Decision-making: On Parties, Delegation and Accountability in Local Government," *Scandinavian Journal of Public Administration* 17/1: 51–69.

Edlund, J. and Sevä, I. J. (2013). "Is Sweden Being Torn Apart? Privatization and Old and New Patterns of Welfare State Support," *Social Policy & Administration* 47/5: 542–64.

Elander, I. and Montin, S. (1995). "Citizenship, Consumerism and Local Government in Sweden," *Scandinavian Political Studies* 18/1: 25–51.

Gilljam, M. and Karlsson, D. (2012). "Tungan på vågen-partier i svenska kommuner," in J. Björkman and B. Fjaestad (eds), *Tungan på vågen: Vågmästare och balanspartier*. Göteborg: Makdam Förlag, 107–36.

Gossas, M. (2006). *Kommunal samverkan och statlig nätverksstyrning*, dissertation, Örebro Studies in Political Science 13. Örebro: Örebro Universitet.

Government Directive (2012). *En kommunallag för framtiden* [*A Local Government Act for the Future*], Instruction to Commission, Dir. 2012:105.

Hall, P., Kettunen, P., Löfgren, K., and Ringholm, T. (2009). "Is There a Nordic Approach to Questions of Democracy in Studies of Network Governance?" *Local Government Studies* 35/5: 515–38.

Jarl, M. (2005). "Making User-Boards a School in Democracy? Studying Swedish Local Governments," *Scandinavian Political Studies* 28/3: 277–94.

Johansson, V. and Montin, S. (2014). "What if Performance Accountability Mechanisms Engender Distrust?" *Urban Research & Practice* 7/2: 213–27.

Karlsson, D. (2012). "The Hidden Constitutions: How Informal Political Institutions Affect the Representation Style of Local Councils," *Local Government Studies* 39/5: 1–22.

Karlsson, D. (2013). "A Democracy of Scale: Size and Representative Democracy in Swedish Local Government," *Scandinavian Journal of Public Administration* 17/1: 7–28.

Karlsson, D. and Montin, S. (2013). "Solving Municipal Paradoxes: Challenges for Swedish Local Democracy," in Wilhelm Hofmeister (ed.), *Panorama: Insights into Asian and European Affairs. Local Politics and Governance*. Singapore: Konrad Adenauer Stiftung, 125–36.

Karlsson, M. (2013). *Covering Distance*, Örebro Studies in Political Science 33. Örebro: Örebro University.

LGA (1991). Swedish Local Government Act (Law 1991:900).

Lundin, M. and Öberg, P. (2014). "Expert Knowledge Use and Deliberation in Local Policy Making," *Policy Sciences* 47: 25–49.

Montin, S. (1992). "Recent Trends in the Relationship between Politics and Administration in Local Government: The Case of Sweden," in R. Batley and A. Campbell (eds), *The Political Executive: Politicians and Management in European Local Government*. London: Frank Cass, 31–43.

Montin, S. (2005). "The Swedish Model: Many Actors and Few Strong Leaders," in R. Berg and N. Rao (eds) *Transforming Local Political Leadership*. Basingstoke: Palgrave Macmillan, 116–30.

Montin, S. (2007). "Mobilizing for Participatory Democracy? The Case of Democracy Policy in Sweden," in T. Zittel and D. Fucks (eds), *Participatory Democracy and Political Participation: Can Participatory Engineering Bring Citizens Back In?* London: Routledge, 187–201.

Planning and Building Act (1987). (Law 1987:10).

Rader Olsson, A. and Cars, G. (2011). "Polycentric Spatial Development: Institutional Challenges to Intermunicipal Cooperation," *Jahrbuch für Regionalwissenschaft* 31: 155–71.

Smedby, N. and Neij, L. (2013). "Experiences in Urban Governance for Sustainability: The Constructive Dialogue in Swedish Municipalities," *Journal of Cleaner Production* 50: 148–58.

Strömberg, L. and Westerståhl, J. (1984). "The New Swedish Communes," Research Reports 1984:1, Department of Political Science, University of Gothenburg.

Swedish Government Official Report (2013). *Privata utförare—kontroll och insyn,* Delbetänkande av utredningen om en kommunallag för framtiden, SOU 2013:53.

Swedish Government Official Report (2014). Staten får inte abdikera—om kommunaliseringen av den svenska skolan. SOU 2014:5.

Szücs, S. and Strömberg, L. (2006). "The Untouchables: Stability among the Swedish Local Elite," in S. Szücs and L. Strömberg (eds), *Local Elites, Political Capital and Democratic Development: Governing Leaders in Seven European Countries.* Wiesbaden: VS Verlag für Sozialwissenschaften, 39–70.

CHAPTER 28

SUBNATIONAL GOVERNMENT IN A MULTILEVEL PERSPECTIVE

DAVID FELTENIUS

INTRODUCTION

CENTRAL–LOCAL government relations in Sweden developed towards decentralization from the late 1970s and onwards. Power has been transferred from the central to the regional and local levels to such an extent that Sweden has been classified as a decentralized unitary state (Loughlin 2000; Ansell and Gingrich 2003). At the same time, power has been transferred both upwards from central to European level, and horizontally from public actors to private actors (Cope et al. 1997; Kersbergen and Waarden 2004). This transfer of power both vertically and horizontally has created a suitable environment for the emergence of a style of governing referred to as multilevel governance (MLG) (Piattoni 2010). This style has not replaced the conventional style of governing emanating from representative democracy; rather it should be regarded as a complement of growing importance. The aim of this chapter is to describe and analyze subnational government in Sweden from an MLG perspective. How is MLG evident, considering subnational government in relation to (a) the welfare state and (b) the European Union (EU)? What are the implications of MLG for subnational government in general, as well as its relationships with other tiers of government in particular?

In this chapter, MLG refers to "negotiated, non-hierarchical exchanges between institutions at the transnational, national, regional, and local levels" (Peters and Pierre 2001: 131). In addition, at each of these levels a similar exchange is believed to exist between both official and private actors, such as concerns business interests (Peters and Pierre 2001).[1] An important assumption in the literature on MLG is that it represents a *new* system of governing (Rhodes 1996; Smith 1997). Although differences between new and old are often exaggerated in this context, it is important to emphasize that MLG is not about central–local government relations in general. In fact, it has some characteristics that are different, such as the emphasis on "negotiated" and "nonhierarchical" exchanges between institutions at different territorial levels.

Instead of being controlled from the central level, the exchange between institutions is ad hoc, and differs with respect to the policy field in question (Peters and Pierre 2004). That is, the rules of the interaction are negotiated and agreed upon by the participating actors (Smith 2003). Accordingly, there are no particular laws or formal rules that determine the outcome of the negotiations.[2] This informal nature of the exchange is believed to create a style of governing that is flexible and able to adapt to ongoing changes in society which is considered to be the chief strength of MLG (Peters and Pierre 2004). Another major strength of MLG is associated with mobilization of actors. This is particularly evident in the case of the EU, where subnational actors can bypass the nation state and participate directly in the decision-making process at European level (Piattoni 2010).

The concept of MLG is primarily associated with Gary Marks' work on the EU (Marks 1992, 1993). Accordingly, previous studies and discussions on subnational government and MLG in Sweden have mainly focused on the European dimension (Larsson and Bäck 2008; Montin 2010, 2011). One of the main concerns of this chapter is to illustrate that MLG can also be relevant for consideration in a national policy context.[3] This is in accordance with Pierre and Stoker's understanding of the concept, which refers to different institutional levels regardless of whether they are inside or outside the nation state (Pierre and Stoker 2002: 30). In seeking to illustrate that MLG is of relevance both within and outside the nation state, this chapter will consider subnational government in relation to (a) the welfare state and (b) the EU. It should be acknowledged that the welfare state, in some instances, also includes a European dimension, though, generally speaking, it remains in the jurisdiction of the nation state. Before exploring subnational government and MLG in relation to the EU and the welfare state, the institutional setting will be introduced.

Subnational Government in Sweden

Two Tiers of Government

Subnational government in Sweden consists of two levels: the regional and the local. In the latter case, there are 290 municipalities which are headed by directly elected councils. These councils are, in their turn, responsible for electing the executive and other committees. The political–administrative organization at the regional level is the county councils, twenty in number, also headed by a directly elected council. The county councils in Skåne, Halland, and Västra Götaland (and the municipality of Gotland) have officially received the status of regions from 2011 and 2012 with responsibility for regional development. Even though regions have been introduced in some parts of the country, the metaphor of the political system in Sweden in terms of an "hourglass" still holds true (Petersson 2000). This metaphor refers to the circumstance that the country has strong central and local-level political systems, and yet a weak system at regional level.

In discussing the importance of the role played by the subnational level in Sweden, the following concepts provide points of departure: "function" (tasks performed), "discretion" (degree of maneuverability) and "access" (influence on central government) (Page and Goldsmith 1987; Goldsmith and Page 2010). The function of subnational government in Sweden is mainly about providing welfare services. Municipalities are responsible for elderly care, care for the disabled, and education (preschool, compulsory school, and upper secondary school). County councils and regions are foremost responsible for health care; however, the task of regional development has grown in importance over the years (Larsson and Bäck 2008; Lidström 2011). In financial terms, the functions performed by subnational government are extensive. According to figures for 2013, operating costs for municipalities were SEK 546 billion and SEK 280 billion for county councils (SKL 2015). According to calculations from earlier figures, this represents 25 percent of GDP or about 44 percent of total public expenditure (Lidström 2011).

Discretion

Although the responsibilities of subnational government are extensive, there is no overall regulation of them in the Constitution. Instead, each specific policy field is regulated through ordinary legislation which may be more or less detailed. By closely examining these laws, it is possible to estimate the degree of discretion afforded to subnational government. The overall trend in this respect, from the late 1970s and onwards, is toward less detailed laws even though the 1990s provided a mixed pattern of centralization and decentralization (Feltenius 2007). Another important aspect of the discretion held by subnational government is the financing of welfare service provision. Subnational government does not rely on grants from central government to any major extent. Instead, local income taxes are the main source of revenue for local authorities. In 2006, it was estimated that this tax revenue comprises about 70 percent of the total revenue sources (Lidström 2011).

Even though the Constitution does not entail any regulation of the tasks performed by subnational government, it defines the principle of local-self-government. This principle states that local authorities are "responsible for local and regional matters of public interest … By the same principle, the local authorities are also responsible for other matters laid down in law" (Instrument of Government, chapter 14, article 2). This formulation implies that municipalities and county councils are free to make decisions on matters of public interest for their citizens. For example, this has resulted in the involvement of subnational government in tasks such as promoting trade and industry within their geographical area. Additionally, it is on the grounds of this principle that subnational governments' involvement in EU affairs may be legitimized.

Access

Considering the access of subnational government to the decision-making process at central level they are able, along with other interests in society, to participate in the process of referral. However, there are no formal procedures for deliberations with central government. Such deliberations are primarily assumed to take place within the parties represented in the Swedish Parliament. Since these parties, to a great extent, are represented at the regional and local levels as well, they are able to accommodate interests from different territorial levels (Bäck and Johansson 2010: 206).

In addition to the accommodation that takes place within parties, attention must also be paid to the role played by the Swedish Association of Local Authorities and Regions (SALAR). The aim of the organization, broadly speaking, is to represent the interest of subnational government. One expression of this is SALAR's function as a lobby organization promoting the interest of subnational government vis-à-vis the central government, the EU, and the media. Another expression is that the organization functions as a mediator between the different levels of the political system. SALAR's contacts with central government have been considered to be of vital importance for the actual government and division of responsibilities between the central, regional, and local levels (Montin 2008).

In fact, contacts between SALAR and the government are so close that the organization receives state grants for performing certain, agreed-upon tasks. This sum has increased over the last couple of years. For instance, in 2012 SALAR received SEK 1,345.7 million from central government. Of these funds, SEK 454.1 million was intended for the organization itself and its activities. The remaining sum was to be distributed by the organization to its individual members, i.e. municipalities and county councils, for the performance of certain agreed-upon tasks (SKL 2013). Even though contacts are extensive, neither SALAR nor its negotiations with the central government are mentioned in the Constitution. This creates a suitable environment for MLG, which will later become evident when examining subnational government and the welfare state.

SUBNATIONAL GOVERNMENT AND THE WELFARE STATE

A Negotiated Order

The hierarchical relationship between central and local government began to loosen its grip from the late 1970s onwards due to reform promoting decentralization (Strandberg 1998). Framework laws were introduced in several policy fields which stipulated the broader aims without detailed regulation (Esping 1994). In effect, a more fragmented welfare state developed where the content and organization of welfare differed among municipalities. Accordingly, the term *welfare state*, referring to one single welfare regime applied in the same manner across the country, has been challenged by the term *welfare municipality* (Trydegård and Thorslund 2001).

The distribution of political power at different territorial levels of the welfare state has fostered MLG, where governance takes place through an interaction between these levels (Blomqvist 2008). One expression of this is negotiation between central and subnational government on welfare policy. Those negotiations have resulted in agreements in several policy fields such as care of the elderly and health care. Common to these policies is that they all are governed by framework legislation. The Social Services Act, adopted in 1981, targets care of the elderly and disabled people; at the same time, the Swedish Health and Medical Service Act adopted in 1982 targets health care.

Elderly care. Negotiations between the central government and SALAR are evident both in preparing broader aims within care of the elderly, and in preparing and implementing specific projects. One illustration of the latter is the central government's concern for the seriously ill elderly in the country. In supporting this group, negotiations resulting in annual agreements have been held with SALAR since 2010. According to the agreement for 2013, SEK 1.1 billion will be distributed to local governments in a result and performance-based model. Among the results to be achieved, and reported in special registers, are improvements in drug therapy and preventive and palliative care. SALAR's responsibility concerns the disbursement of grants to municipalities along with the responsibility for implementing specific aims (Statskontoret 2013; Socialdepartementet 2013).

Another example involves negotiations with the aim of improving staff competence within elderly care (*Kompetensstegen*). Instead of allowing government authorities responsibility for distributing this grant, the central government appointed a special working group consisting of representatives from other ministries along with SALAR, labor unions, and pensioners' organizations (Statskontoret 2009). In the first stage, the task of the working group was to develop policies and strategies for the distribution of funds. In the second stage, the work consisted of preparing government decisions on individual applications for funding (SOU 2007:88: 10). At the local level, there are reports of similar cooperation in implementing the project. For instance, in the municipality of Avesta, a steering committee was established consisting of politicians, civil servants, and representatives of pensioners' organizations (Wolff and Sjöstrand 2009).

Health care. The most well-known negotiations taking place within health care were christened the *Dagmaröverenskommelsen*, named after Dagmar whose name-day happened to coincide with Parliament's approval of the first agreement in 1984. These negotiations concern the issue of how state grants are to be distributed within health care. In the first agreement from 1984, it was concluded that state grants should be distributed to county councils on a per capita basis instead of fee for service (Karlberg 2011). Since then, negotiations have continued, and in 2012 an agreement was reached that SEK 158 million would be distributed to specific projects concerning e-health and a national register for open comparisons (Socialdepartementet 2012b). In addition to this type of overarching agreement, there are several other negotiations between SALAR and the central government on narrower issues. One example is *Kömiljarden*, with the aim of improving citizens' accessibility to health care (Socialdepartementet 2012a).

Ensuring Subnational Government Complies

A common theme in the policy literature on negotiations is how to ensure that actors comply with agreements (Whitehead 2003; Jacobsson 2004; Héritier and Lehmkuhl 2008). One of few studies dealing with Sweden concerns the Patient Choice Recommendation (PCR), partly negotiated with the government and formally issued by SALAR in 2000. It is evident from the study that implementation of this recommendation was not without its controversies. Some county councils were reluctant to accept the recommendation, but in the end they complied. Of particular importance was the role played by SALAR which functioned as an arena for naming and shaming those who did not comply (Fredriksson et al. 2012).

The results from this study also stress the fact that implementation of this recommendation took place in the shadow of the hierarchy (Scharpf 1997). It is evident from the case of the PCR that central government occupied a strong position. This is due to the fact that central government is able to threaten the other party with the possibility of regulation by law (Fredriksson et al. 2012). This result is in agreement with one of the most common criticisms of governance, namely that the concept focuses too much on cooperation and consensus within policy networks. Accordingly, it tends to neglect the existence of power differences between actors and their consequences for policy-making (Arts and Tatenhove 2004; Koppenjan 2007).

In summary, it is evident from this section that MLG is also of relevance in discussions concerning subnational government and the welfare state. Governance of welfare policy does not solely take place in a hierarchical manner through legislation and state grants. Instead, governance takes place through negotiations between central and subnational government, resulting in agreements. Some interest has been devoted to this issue by studying how subnational units comply with agreements. Generally speaking, this development has not been paid any major attention by scholars. In the Swedish context, the concept of MLG has primarily been applied to subnational government and its relations with the EU—a topic that will be considered next.

SUBNATIONAL GOVERNMENT AND THE EU

Activity in EU-Related Affairs

Sweden's formal status as a member of the EU since 1995 has created an additional political level that is of importance to subnational government. Areas of cooperation in the

EU have evolved to include large parts of local government operations, something that is not unique to local government in Sweden (John 1997; Borghetto and Franchino 2010). In a 2010 survey, it was reported that on average, 60 percent of the points on the agenda of the municipal councils are influenced by the EU, while the corresponding figure for county council assemblies is 50 percent. The discrepancy is explained by the circumstance that health care—in other words, the main county council function—does not involve the EU to any great extent (SKL 2010).

Among the specific EU policy areas affecting the subnational level is regional policy. The goal of the EU's regional policy is to strengthen economically disadvantaged regions of Europe (Goldsmith 1993, 2003). For this purpose, structural funds are used as an important tool. Sweden received SEK 19 billion over the period 2000–6 for interventions in regional development (Statskontoret 2005). Regional policy has been paid the greatest attention in the literature, but there are other policies worth mentioning. One example is environmental policy, where the EU requires that municipalities apply environmental rules correctly in environmental impact statements and environmental assessments. Another example is the EU's food and agricultural policy with its requirements for the municipal supervisory organization. Sweden has repeatedly been examined by the EU Commission, which has expressed criticism concerning municipalities' lack of appropriate resources (Statskontoret 2005).

As a result of this development, subnational government's EU-related activities have increased. This is evident from surveys performed in 1999 and 2006 estimating the share of municipalities with "high" and "moderate" degrees of EU activity. In 2006, about 80 percent of Swedish municipalities belonged to one of these categories. This figure represents an increase compared with the survey performed in 1999. In that year, the figure was about 60 percent (Berg and Lindahl 2007). One expression of this increasing activity is the development of regional offices in Brussels. They are of vital importance for coordinating the subnational-level activities in EU-related matters (Jeffery 1997; Bomberg and Peterson 1998; Hooghe 1995). For instance, one important task is to coordinate activity on the EU transnational programs which involve actors from different countries and are governed directly by the EU Commission. In 1999, it was estimated that about 87 percent of the Swedish municipalities belonged to an organization with an office in Brussels. Today, all municipalities are reported to have some kind of representation at the EU level (Berg and Lindahl 2007: 26). Examples of this are North Sweden (a regional office representing Västerbotten and Norrbotten) and South Sweden (a regional office representing Småland and Blekinge).

Subnational government is not only represented at the European level through their regional offices, but also through their association SALAR. In addition to the EU-related activities carried out in their main office in Stockholm, SALAR also maintains an office in Brussels. Among the responsibilities of this office are, according to the organization's website, supporting politicians in the EU Committee of the Regions, monitoring developments within relevant policy fields, and transferring information back to the national level.

Coordinating Swedish activity within the EU Committee of the Regions is an important part of SALAR's international work. The President of SALAR, Anders Knape, considers the Committee of the Regions to be the only formal channel for subnational government to exert direct influence on EU decision-making.[4] The importance attributed to the Committee by SALAR is also reflected in the activities of the Swedish delegation. It is regarded as one of the most active delegations compared with other countries (Domorenok 2009). Nomination to the Swedish delegation is carried out by SALAR, and the final decision is made by central government. During the period 2011–15, both SALAR's President and second Vice President were included in the delegation to the Committee of the Regions.

How efficiently SALAR is able to perform the role as a mediator between subnational government and the EU remains to be seen. Drawing from research findings on the EU activity of local government associations in other countries, it is evident that their activity level is dependent on financial, staffing, and informational resources, in addition to structural conditions such as whether a local government association represents the entire subnational level in the country, or just parts of it (Callanan 2012). Based on these factors, SALAR has every opportunity to become a strong force at the EU level. Even so, there has been criticism from regional and local actors that SALAR has been passive in connection with the development of the Structural Funds Program for 2007–13 (Berg and Lindahl 2007). This criticism may be an expression of how difficult it is for SALAR to represent the voice of the entire subnational level with its different goals and interests.

Vertical and Horizontal Cooperation

Sweden's membership in the EU has changed the old logic of central–local government relations in terms of hierarchy. One expression of this is the notion that EU regional policy has enabled regions and municipalities to "bypass" central government, since they can turn directly to EU institutions (Goldsmith 1993; Tatham 2008). However, this does not exclude the possibility of cooperation between subnational actors and central government on EU-related matters (Tatham 2010; Callanan 2011). In the Swedish context, there has been a development toward a more nonhierarchical cooperation between central and subnational government on EU-related matters. The Swedish government was actually caught unprepared by the subnational level's involvement in European affairs and had not adopted any formal policy. Accordingly, subnational government was free to develop its own relationships with the EU. Today, central government has come to accept the activities of subnational actors in Brussels, and these activities are regarded as a part of a national partnership. Clearly, cooperation is in the interest of both central and subnational government if Sweden is to be successful in obtaining funding from the EU (Jerneck and Gidlund 2001).

One example of this type of cooperation is provided by the EU employment policy and the practice of the open method of coordination (OMC). This method aims to link processes of policy-making at national and at European levels (Jacobsson and Johansson

2001; Borrás and Jacobsson 2004; Jacobsson 2004). A consequence of this method is that the subnational level is given a more prominent role in the policy process. In a proposal from the European Commission on a new strategy for growth and employment (2010–20), participation by subnational government was emphasized. It is clearly stated in the proposal that the strategy should be implemented in partnerships between subnational authorities, parliaments, civil society, and business interests (COM 2010).

The EU's emphasis on the involvement of subnational actors is not solely restricted to the growth and employment policy field. This area represents one example of a more general ambition (Callanan 2002, 2012). This may promote the further growth of cooperation in networks of representatives of different tiers of government. Whether this will be the case or not remains to be seen, since it also depends on the responses from central and local governments in Europe.

Subnational government's EU-related activities have not only fostered the development of networks within a vertical tier; they have also fostered cooperation along a horizontal tier with local business and civil society. This cooperation was already established in some municipalities before Sweden's EU membership (Lundqvist 1998; Pierre 1998), but has since grown in importance. According to a survey performed in 1999, about 2/3 of all municipalities cooperated with local business on EU-related matters (Berg 1999). In some instances, this cooperation is referred to in terms of partnerships. According to a mapping performed in 2005, seven different types of partnerships existed, five of which had direct links to the EU (Gorpe 2006).

Partnerships have attracted research from a variety of perspectives, such as that of democracy (Peters 1998; Elander 1999). In the case of Sweden, it has been reported that the dominance of civil servants gives networks a technocratic character. In addition, networks tend to prioritize performance rather than democratic values such as accountability (Bache and Olsson 2001). Other perspectives applied are partnership and gender equality (Hudson and Rönnblom 2007; Hedlund 2008). For example, the issue of women and their presence in the partnerships has attracted attention, as it has been reported that partnerships with a focus on business development are dominated by men (Hedlund 2008).

Geography, Size, and Influence

One important topic in the Swedish context of varied geographical circumstances including large cities and sparsely populated areas is whether all types of municipalities possess the preconditions to devote equal attention to, and participation in, EU-related affairs (Berg 1999; Ström 1999, 2000; Berg and Lindahl 2007). Studies have shown that, as the activities of subnational government in EU-related matters have increased, a center–periphery pattern has been reinforced. Major cities have especially increased their activity level due to what has been referred to as resource push (i.e. favorable economic conditions for devoting resources to international activities) (Berg and Lindahl 2007). An example of how this relationship appears is seen in how municipalities in the center tend to be more active in shaping their own EU policies, and maintain their own officials to monitor EU affairs, compared to smaller municipalities on the periphery (Berg 1999).

To what extent these imbalances can be offset by the fact that municipalities are represented through regional offices in Brussels is worth discussion. Moreover, imbalances can be offset by what has been referred to in terms of "resource pull" (i.e. the resources that can be obtained from international activity). It has been noted that an important exception to the center–periphery pattern is the large-scale EU activity in the sparsely populated northern parts of Sweden. This activity can be explained by the circumstance that this part of the country is targeted by EU regional policy, which strengthens their opportunities to obtain funding (Berg and Lindahl 2007).

Size, geography, and influence have also been considered in the debate on regions in Sweden. It has been argued that the regional level in Sweden must be strengthened to be able to compete in a context of "Europe of the Regions." In seeking to improve the impact of the regional level, SALAR has campaigned for merging county councils across the entire country into larger geographical units, and thus, regions (Feltenius 2008). Such a proposal was also submitted in 2007 by the Committee on Public Sector Responsibilities (SOU 2007:10). The committee's proposals, however, never materialized, and today responsibility for regional development is handled by various institutions in different parts of the country. This opaque regime at the regional level has been referred to in terms of a "regional mess" (McCallion 2008).

Summarizing this section, it can be concluded that Sweden's membership of the EU has changed the old logic of central and local government relationships in terms of "hierarchy." Subnational government can "bypass" the nation state and exert influence directly on the EU policy process. For instance, subnational governments participate in networks on different policy matters such as regional and employment policy. Once again, SALAR has proved to play an important role as mediator between different levels. However, subnational government is not represented in the EU through SALAR only; on the contrary, almost every county council and municipality is represented in Brussels through their own regional offices. This presence suggests that there is an element of competition between regions and municipalities in making their voices heard at EU level.

Concluding Remarks

The purpose of this chapter has been to describe and analyze subnational government in Sweden from a perspective of multilevel governance (MLG). The concept of MLG is defined here in terms of negotiated, nonhierarchical exchanges between institutions at different territorial levels. Previous studies on subnational government in Sweden from an MLG perspective have mainly focused on the EU, but MLG can also be applied within a national context. Accordingly, one of the main concerns of the chapter has been to illustrate that the concept of MLG is relevant for consideration both in a European and a national context.

In the case of the EU, it is evident that subnational government has increased its activities at this level. Some expressions of this include participation in transnational programs, the Open Method of Coordination, and the Committee of the Regions. There is no lack of research devoted to the issue of EU membership and its consequences for the subnational level. However, many studies were conducted not long after Sweden joined the EU, and more recent studies are scarce. In particular, there is a lack of evaluations of the country's 20 years of membership in the EU and its consequences for subnational government.

Of particular interest would be to broaden our knowledge concerning the "regional mess" in Sweden, and its effect on subnational government participation in, and influence on, the European arena. Throughout the 1990s and thereafter, there has been an extensive debate on substituting larger regions for county councils. One of the primary motives behind this proposal was that it would foster the influence of subnational government at the EU level. Today, the debate on regions has lost its previous intensity due to a government decision that there will not be a reform throughout the country directed from the central level. Clearly, the consequences of this decision for subnational government and the EU are matters that deserve further attention.

The concept of MLG is not only important to consider in relation to the EU, but also in the national context of the welfare state. This has been illustrated by negotiations between SALAR and the central government within policy fields such as elderly care. In sharp contrast to the amount of literature concerning subnational government and the EU, very little is known about the negotiations between subnational and central government. In which policy areas of the welfare state are they practiced and to what extent? What about development and content over time? How do they differ compared with the exchange between different tiers of government back in the early days of the welfare state? Of particular importance here is whether negotiations really are that non-hierarchical and unaffected by formal rules as described by the concept of MLG. In the absence of formal rules governing negotiations, informal rules might have developed. How these rules affect power relationships between actors, set the limits for what is possible to achieve, and relate to the overall political system are some issues that deserve further attention.

Regardless of whether MLG concerns the EU or the welfare state, the role played by SALAR has proven to be of vital importance. In both instances, SALAR mediates between different tiers of government. There is little knowledge on how this function is exercised in practice with regard to the association's relationship with its members. How is the mandate to SALAR from its members constructed? Is it carried out within a narrow or wide circle of members? What opportunities are there for SALAR's members to demand accountability for the activities performed both at the EU level and the national level? These questions are not only a concern for the association and its members, but also for the functioning of representative democracy. In the end, the mandate to SALAR originates from the voters in each subnational unit.

NOTES

1. This definition is similar to one of the earliest notions of MLG by Gary Marks in the early 1990s (Marks 1993: 392).
2. However, negotiations take place within a legal framework which, on a more general level, sets limits for what it is possible to achieve.
3. For other such examples, see Painter (2001); Reigner (2001); Baldersheim and Ståhlberg (2002).
4. According to a statement made by SALAR's president (2007–15), Anders Knape, on the organization website.

REFERENCES

Ansell, C. and Gingrich, J. (2003). "Trends in Decentralization," in B. C. Cain, R. J. Dalton, and S. E. Scarrow (eds), *Democracy Transformed? Expanding Political Opportunities in Advanced Industrial Democracies*. Oxford: Oxford University Press, 140–63.

Arts, B. and Tatenhove, J. van (2004). "Policy and Power: A Conceptual Framework between the 'Old' and 'New' Policy Idioms," *Policy Sciences* 37/3–4: 339–56.

Bache, I. and Olsson, J. (2001). "Legitimacy through Partnership? EU Policy Diffusion in Britain and Sweden," *Scandinavian Political Studies* 24/3: 215–37.

Bäck, H. and Johansson, V. (2010). "Sweden," in M. Goldsmith and E. C. Page (eds), *Changing Government Relations in Europe: From Localism to Intergovernmentalism*. London: Routledge, 198–209.

Baldersheim, H. and Ståhlberg, K. (2002). "From Guided Democracy to Multi-Level Governance: Trends in Central-Local Relations in the Nordic Countries," *Local Government Studies* 28/3: 74–90.

Berg, L. (1999). *Aktiva kommuner? En studie av de svenska kommunernas aktivitet i EU-frågor.* Göteborg: Göteborg University, Centre for European Research.

Berg, L. and Lindahl, R. (2007). *Svenska kommuners och regioners kanaler till Bryssel: Subnationella nivåers försök att påverka EU:s policyprocess.* Rapport 1651–8942; 2007:7. Stockholm: Svenska institutet för europapolitiska studier.

Blomqvist, P. (2008). "Den svenska välfärdspolitiken," in L. Bennich-Björkman and P. Blomqvist (eds), *Mellan folkhem och Europa*. Malmö: Liber, 235–60.

Bomberg, E. and Peterson, J. (1998). "European Union Decision Making: The Role of Subnational Authorities," *Political Studies* 46/2: 219–35.

Borghetto, E. and Franchino, F. (2010). "The Role of Subnational Authorities in the Implementation of EU Directives," *Journal of European Public Policy* 17/6: 759–80.

Borrás, S. and Jacobsson, K. (2004). "The Open Method of Co-ordination and New Governance: Patterns in the EU," *Journal of European Public Policy* 11/2: 185–208.

Callanan, M. (2002). "The White Paper on Governance: The Challenge for Central and Local Government," *Administration* 50/1: 66–85.

Callanan, M. (2011). "EU Decision-Making: Reinforcing Interest Group Relationships with National Governments?" *Journal of European Public Policy* 18/1: 17–34.

Callanan, M. (2012). "Subnational Collective Action: The Varied Patterns of Mobilisation of Local Government Associations," *Local Government Studies* 38/6: 753–75.

COM (2010). "Europe 2020: A Strategy for Smart, Sustainable and Inclusive Growth," Final. Brussels: Communication from the Commission.

Cope, S., Leishman, F., and Starie, P. (1997). "Globalization, New Public Management and the Enabling State," *International Journal of Public Sector Management* 10/6: 444–60.

Domorenok, E. (2009). "The Committee of the Regions: In Search of Identity," *Regional and Federal Studies* 19/1: 143–63.

Elander, I. (1999). "Partnerskap och demokrati," in A. Brink and E. Amnå (eds), *Globalisering*. Stockholm: Fritzes, 327–64. SOU 1999:83.

Esping, H. (1994). *Ramlagar i förvaltningspolitiken*. Stockholm: SNS Förlag.

Feltenius, D. (2007). "Relations between Central and Local Government in Sweden During the 1990s: Mixed Patterns of Centralization and Decentralization," *Regional and Federal Studies* 17/4: 475–74.

Feltenius, D. (2008). "Från splittring till enighet: Om Sveriges Kommuner och Landstings ståndpunkt i regionfrågan," *Kommunal ekonomi och politik* 12/2: 37–65.

Fredriksson, M., Blomqvist, P., and Winblad, U. (2012). "Conflict and Compliance in Swedish Health Care Governance: Soft Law in the 'Shadow of Hierarchy,'" *Scandinavian Political Studies* 35/1: 48–70.

Goldsmith, M. (1993). "The Europeanisation of Local Government," *Urban Studies* 30/4–5: 683–99.

Goldsmith, M. (2003). "Variable Geometry, Multilevel Governance: European Integration and Subnational Government in the New Millenium," in K. Featherstone and C. M. Radaelli (eds), *The Politics of Europeanization*. Oxford: Oxford University Press, 112–33.

Goldsmith, M. and Page, E. C. (2010). *Changing Government Relations in Europe: From Localism to Intergovernmentalism*. London: Routledge.

Gorpe, P. (2006). *Svenska partnerskap: En översikt. Rapport 1 till Organisationsutredningen för regional tillväxt*. Stockholm. SOU 2006:4.

Hedlund, G. (2008). *Regionala partnerskap, kön och demokrati*. Örebro: Örebro Universitet, Centrum för urbana och regionala studier.

Héritier, A. and Lehmkuhl, D. (2008). "The Shadow of Hierarchy and New Modes of Governance," *Journal of Public Policy* 28/1: 1–17.

Hooghe, L. (1995). "Subnational Mobilization in the European Union," *West European Politics* 18/3: 175–98.

Hudson, C. and Rönnblom, M. (2007). "Regional Development Policies and the Constructions of Gender Equality: The Swedish Case," *European Journal of Political Research* 46/1: 47–68.

Jacobsson, K. (2004). "Between Deliberation and Discipline: Soft Governance in EU Employment," in U. Mörth (ed.), *Soft Law in Governance and Regulation: An Interdisciplinary Analysis*. Cheltenham: Edward Elgar, 81–101.

Jacobsson, K. and Johansson, K. M. (2001). "Välfärdspolitik i EU," in K. Jacobsson, K. M. Johansson, and M. Ekengren (eds), *Mot en europeisk välfärdspolitik? Ny politik och nya samarbetsformer i EU*. Stockholm: SNS Förlag, 9–42.

Jeffery, C. (1997). "Regional Information Offices in Brussels and Multi-Level Governance in the EU: A UK–German Comparison," in C. Jeffery (ed.), *The Regional Dimension of the European Union: Towards a Third Level in Europe?* London: Frank Cass, 183–203.

Jerneck, M. and Gidlund, J. (2001). *Komplex flernivådemokrati: Regional lobbying i Bryssel*. Malmö: Liber ekonomi.

John, P. (1997). "Europeanization in a Centralizing State: Multi-level Governance in the UK," in C. Jeffery (ed.), *The Regional Dimension of the European Union: Towards a Third Level in Europe?* London: Frank Cass, 131–46.

Karlberg, I. (2011). *Från Vasa till vårdval: Om ansvar och styrning av svensk hälso- och sjukvård.* Lund: Studentlitteratur.

Kersbergen, K. van and Waarden, F. van (2004). "'Governance' as a Bridge between Disciplines: Cross-disciplinary Inspiration Regarding Shifts in Governance and Problems of Governability, Accountability and Legitimacy," *European Journal of Political Research* 43/2: 143–71.

Koppenjan, J. F. M. (2007). "Consensus and Conflict in Policy Networks: Too Much or Too Little?" in E. Sørensen and J. Torfing (eds), *Theories of Democratic Network Governance.* Basingstoke: Palgrave Macmillan, 132–52.

Larsson, T. and Bäck, H. (2008). *Governing and Governance in Sweden.* Lund: Studentlitteratur.

Lidström, A. (2011). "Sweden: Party-Dominated Subnational Democracy under Challenge?" in J. Loughlin, F. Hendriks, and A. Lidström (eds), *The Oxford Handbook of Local and Regional Democracy in Europe.* Oxford: Oxford University Press, 261–82.

Loughlin, J. (2000). "Regional Autonomy and State Paradigm Shift in Western Europe," *Regional and Federal Studies* 10/2: 10–34.

Lundqvist, L. J. (1998). "Local-to-Local Partnerships among Swedish Municipalities: Why and How Neighbours Join to Alleviate Resource Constraints," in J. Pierre (ed.), *Partnerships in Urban Governance: European and American Experience.* Basingstoke: Macmillan, 93–111.

Marks, G. (1992). "Structural Policy in the European Community," in A. M. Sbragia (ed.), *Euro-Politics: Institutions and Policymaking in the "New" European Community.* Washington, DC: Brookings Institution, 191–224.

Marks, G. (1993). "Structural Policy and Multi-Level Governance in the EC," in A. W. Cafruny and G. G. Rosenthal (eds), *The State of the European Community*, vol. 2: *The Maastricht Debates and Beyond.* Boulder, CO: Lynne Rienner, 391–410.

McCallion, M. S. (2008). "Tidying Up? 'EU'ropean Regionalization and the Swedish 'Regional Mess,'" *Regional Studies* 42/4: 579–92.

Montin, S. (2008). "Den lokala politiken," in L. Bennich Björkman and P. Blomqvist (eds), *Mellan folkhem och Europa.* Malmö: Liber, 171–92.

Montin, S. (2010). "Kommunerna och flernivåstyrningen i EU," in P. Tallberg and M.-L. von Bergmann-Winberg (eds), *Flernivåstyrning: Framgångsfaktor för kommuner, regioner och staten.* Kristianstad: Region Skåne, 121–47.

Montin, S. (2011). "Swedish Local Government in Multi-Level Governance," in H. Reynaert, K. Steyvers, and E. van Bever (eds), *The Road to Europe: Main Street or Backward Alley for Local Governments in Europe?* Brugge: Vanden Broele Publishers, 71–92.

Page, E. and Goldsmith, M. (eds) (1987). *Central and Local Government Relations: A Comparative Analysis of West European Unitary States.* London: Sage Publications.

Painter, M. (2001). "Multi-Level Governance and the Emergence of Collaborative Federal Institutions in Australia," *Policy and Politics* 29/2: 137–50.

Peters, B. G. (1998). "'With a Little Help From Our Friends': Public–Private Partnerships as Institutions and Instruments," in J. Pierre (ed.), *Partnerships in Urban Governance: European and American Experience.* Basingstoke: Macmillan, 11–34.

Peters, B. G. and Pierre, J. (2001). "Developments in Intergovernmental Relations: Towards Multi-Level Governance," *Policy and Politics* 29/2: 131–5.

Peters, B. G. and Pierre, J. (2004). "Multi-Level Governance and Democracy: A Faustian Bargain?" in I. Bache and M. Flinders (eds), *Multi-Level Governance*. Oxford: Oxford University Press, 75–89.

Petersson, O. (2000). *Statsbyggnad*. Stockholm: SNS Förlag.

Piattoni, Simona (2010). *The Theory of Multi-Level Governance: Conceptual, Empirical, and Normative Challenges*. Oxford: Oxford University Press.

Pierre, J. (1998). "Local Industrial Partnerships: Exploring the Logics of Public–Private Partnerships," in J. Pierre (ed.), *Partnerships in Urban Governance: European and American Experience*. Basingstoke: Macmillan, 112–39.

Pierre, J. and Stoker, G. (2002). "Towards Multi-Level Governance," in P. Dunleavy, A. Gamble, R. Heffernan, I. Holliday, and G. Peele (eds), *Developments in British Politics 6*. Basingstoke: Macmillan, 29–46.

Reigner, H. (2001). "Multi-Level Governance or Co-administration? Transformation and Continuity in French Local Government," *Policy and Politics* 29/2: 181–92.

Rhodes, R. A. W. (1996). "The New Governance: Governing without Government," *Political Studies* 44/4: 652–67.

Scharpf, F. (1997). *Games Real Actors Play: Actor-Centered Institutionalism in Policy Research*. Boulder, CO: Westview Press.

SKL (2010). *EU i lokalpolitiken: en undersökning av dagordningar från kommuner, landsting och regioner*. Stockholm: Sveriges kommuner och landsting.

SKL (2013). *Årsredovisning 2012*. Stockholm: Sveriges kommuner och landsting.

SKL (2015). "Kommunernas/Landstingens kostnader och intäkter." Information from SKL's homepage at <www.skl.se>.

Smith, A. (1997). "Studying Multi-Level Governance: Examples from French Translations of the Structural Funds," *Public Administration* 75/4: 711–29.

Smith, A. (2003). "Multi-Level Governance: What It Is and How It Can Be Studied," in B. G. Peters and J. Pierre (eds), *The Handbook of Public Administration*. London: Sage Publications, 377–86.

Socialdepartementet (2012a). "Fortsatta insatser för att förbättra patienters tillgänglighet till hälso- och sjukvård ("kömiljarden") 2013," Överenskommelse mellan staten och Sveriges Kommuner och Landsting.

Socialdepartementet (2012b). "Godkännande av Dagmaröverenskommelsen 2012," March 8.

Socialdepartementet (2013). "Överenskommelse 2013—De mest sjuka äldre," February 18. Stockholm: Regeringskansliet, Socialdepartementet. Informationsstencil.

SOU 2007:10. "Hållbar samhällsorganisation med utvecklingskraft," Slutbetänkande av Ansvarskommittén.

SOU 2007:88. "Att lära nära: Stöd till kommuner för verksamhetsnära kompetensutveckling inom omsorg och vård av äldre," Betänkande av Kompetensstegen.

Statskontoret (2005). *EU:s påverkan på kommuner och landsting*. Stockholm: Statskontoret.

Statskontoret (2009). *Kompetensstegens organisation: Effektiv hantering av stöd till kommuner?* Stockholm: Statskontoret.

Statskontoret (2013). *Sammanhållen vård och omsorg om de mest sjuka äldre: Uppföljning av överenskommelsen mellan regeringen och SKL*, Delrapport 4. Stockholm: Statskontoret.

Strandberg, U. (1998). *Debatten om den kommunala självstyrelsen 1962–1994*. Hedemora: Gidlund.

Ström, L.-I. (1999). *Den kommunala revolutionen: Svenska kommuners förändring under två decennier*. Östersund: Statens institut för regionalforskning.

Ström, L.-I. (2000). "Swedish Municipalities and the European Union," in J. Gidlund and M. Jerneck (eds), *Local and Regional Governance in Europe: Evidence from Nordic Regions*. Cheltenham: Edward Elgar, 97–123.

Tatham, M. (2008). "Going Solo: Direct Regional Representation in the European Union," *Regional and Federal Studies* 18/5: 493–515.

Tatham, M. (2010). "'With or Without You?' Revisiting Territorial State-Bypassing in EU Interest Representation," *Journal of European Public Policy* 17/1: 76–99.

Trydegård, G.-B. and Thorslund, M. (2001). "Inequality in the Welfare State? Local Variation in Care of the Elderly—The Case of Sweden," *International Journal of Social Welfare* 10: 174–84.

Whitehead, M. (2003). "'In the Shadow of Hierarchy': Meta-Governance, Policy Reform and Urban Regeneration in the West Midlands," *Area* 35: 6–14.

Wolff, S. and Sjöstrand, A. K. (2009). *Utvärdering av kompetensstegen i Avesta kommun*. Falun: Dalarnas forskningsråd.

CHAPTER 29

CHALLENGES AND REFORMS OF LOCAL AND REGIONAL GOVERNMENTS IN SWEDEN

LARS NIKLASSON

INTRODUCTION

THE purpose of this chapter is to give a general overview of the challenges and reforms of local and regional governments (*kommuner* and *landsting*) in Sweden after World War II, with a focus on the period after 1970. Building on the detailed descriptions in the other chapters of this section, I will summarize the major waves of reform that have occurred, beginning with the consolidation of local governments and ending with the major attempt to redesign the public sector and especially the role of local and regional governments after 2007. Finally, I will analyze the drivers of reform in order to discuss how these issues may develop in the future. In doing this, I will indicate important scholarly contributions and also suggest new areas for research.

My own original argument about these challenges and reforms is that they may, to a large extent, be explained by motives and struggles at the central rather than the local level. There is something of a popular understanding that local and regional policies are designed in response to local and regional needs. While this is partly true, I will argue that it is more illuminating to think of local and regional governments as being designed in response to central government needs. This point should come as no surprise to the scholar, since formal decisions about roles and responsibilities are, of course, made by Parliament and are influenced by the experiences of local and regional actors. Nevertheless, the importance of the central level has been underestimated, as well as under-researched.

My main argument will be that there are factions (policy networks) within the central government which have different opinions on what the local, regional, and central government (i.e. agencies) should do. These factions have been visible during the past decades when reforms were made in several partially opposite directions. In particular, the role of agencies as an alternative to local welfare production has been overlooked in the analysis of local and regional governments. My main source of information about these conflicts is that I have taken part as an analyst in exchanges in the central Government Offices where some of these recent battles were fought.

The roles of local and regional governments have changed over time. Focusing on the period after World War II, three major themes or waves of reform can be distinguished. The first was consolidation, the second was decentralization, and the third was collaboration and regionalization. All these waves have been driven by concerns for efficiency, while concern for democracy has been largely a counterweight to some of the actions taken in the name of efficiency, with a few interesting exceptions. In reality, the events are even more complex than this, if we take into account that a wide variety of approaches have been tried across various policy areas. By necessity, the overview provided cannot describe all the detail or even all the research on these events. Needless to say, it is slightly simplified in order to make it easier to follow. The themes of the waves are still relevant today and can be observed in the politics of reform, which will be discussed after the historical overview.

First Wave: Consolidation

The decades after World War II were a period when the welfare state was built up, with the local and regional governments as key instruments of the expansion. The Swedish welfare state reached some level of organizational maturity in 1974, when local and regional governments were consolidated as powerful actors in a system of government-provided welfare. The chapters in this volume by Stig Montin and Anders Lidström describe the unique characteristics of the Nordic countries, with strong subnational governments operating as what may be labeled semi-autonomous implementers of national policies (cf. Granberg 2004).

It is generally held that the Nordic welfare states combine a generous welfare state with strong traditions of local independence. The local governments build on the traditions of free and equal men meeting at the "ting" to decide on common affairs. Their birth can be dated to 1862 when there was a major reform to design local units based on the older cities and parishes. With the building up of the welfare state in the 1940s came the necessity of further consolidation to create powerful units to become instruments of national political ambitions. The groundwork was laid in the 1940s, with mergers following in the 1950s and again in the 1960s and 1970s. This key formative process has been the subject of much research, recently by Peder Nielsen (2003) and Markus Gossas (2006) and previously by Gunnel Gustafsson (1980) and others. Nielsen contrasts the case for consolidation with the case for secession as a few of the consolidated local governments have been split up in recent years. Gossas contrasts consolidation with collaboration (networking), which has always been an alternative and was the dominant theme of the third wave (below).

The welfare state was built pragmatically on local experiences and was most of all an expansion of scope where the volume of services such as education and health care expanded in the 1950s and 1960s. For example, compulsory schooling was prolonged, and previously parallel systems were integrated to become a comprehensive type of school, illustrating the belief in equal services for all. Schools are an important part of what local governments do, and they are typical in that there was always a mix of responsibilities with the central government, a kind of "multilevel governance," "intergovernmental relations," or even "federalism," to use an American term applied to relationships between levels of government. While the Constitution of Sweden is not federal, it scores higher than some federal countries (e.g. Australia) when it comes to the fiscal autonomy of the subnational levels. This mix of roles was not just about the regulation, but also the operation of schools where teachers in the local schools were employed by the central government. This was to change in the second wave of reform.

Local governments became increasingly important in welfare services, housing, infrastructure, and other areas. It was generally the central government which added tasks and responsibilities to the local government mandates, often combined with funding to make sure that all local governments played along and set up local public housing corporations, etc. Interestingly, housing is an area where the government supported alternative providers from the start, in the form of cooperatives related to the labor movement. They are seldom referred to as private, but nevertheless indicate that there are traditions of nonpublic providers in the Swedish welfare state.

The expansion of local and regional welfare states was also reflected in the professionalization of staff. Higher education expanded dramatically in the 1960s to provide local and regional governments with teachers, nurses, welfare workers, and others. Day care (kindergarten) expanded and created a need for new types of staff. This was also an era of large-scale immigration to Sweden, which was eventually met with new services in skills development, language training, etc.

It gradually became obvious that there was going to be a problem with local governments that were too small to fund and operate the welfare services desired by central government. The process of mergers began in the 1950s and reached its peak in 1974 when the number of local governments was reduced to less than 300, i.e. about a quarter of what existed before and about a tenth of what was in place in 1945. Consolidation of regional governments took longer and mainly concerned the integration of health care run by the larger cities with surrounding regions. However, there was a strong conflict among the political parties as consolidation was supported by the Social Democrats and the Communists, while the non-socialist parties were opposed to it. This would eventually lead to a counter-reaction.

Public support was generally strong for these moves as it was regarded as essential that the welfare state be based on local traditions, even though it was not as local as before. The key values of consolidation were instrumental efficiency and economies of scale.

Concerns for local variety and closeness to the voters were played down and resurfaced later as unresolved issues and important drivers for later waves of reform.

It is important to note that not all welfare activities are the responsibility of local and regional governments. They are important as producers and funders of services, where the services are regulated by the national government and mainly financed through taxes collected at the local and regional levels. However, the general systems of fiscal transfers such as pensions and support for the unemployed and those who are ill are operated by other organizations. The pensions system is based on a national basic pension with some complementary pension schemes (for example, by the local and regional governments for their white-collar workers). Transfers to the ill and the unemployed were originally organized by independent regional associations, similar to the welfare systems in some continental countries. Over time, they became more integrated into the welfare state and developed services such as training and skills development as instruments to help their clients back to work. They were also transformed into government agencies and are now a consolidated part of national government rather than local or regional governments (*Arbetsförmedlingen* and *Försäkringskassan*). Hence, they provide an example of services kept at arm's length from local and regional welfare production, a relationship which was questioned in more recent times and was central to the third wave of reform. In other words, consolidation meant the consolidation of many parts of the welfare state into the local and regional governments, but not all of it.

Note also that regional and local governments are independent of each other since they are constitutionally at the same level, i.e. not in a hierarchical relationship to each other. The Swedish Constitution mentions two levels of government, not three. However, Swedes often refer to them as making up different levels of the public sector but, as will be described later, there are other public actors at each level or arena, often central government agencies. The horizontal relationships at the various levels became an important issue later, as indicated in the chapter in this volume by David Feltenius.

Relationships with other actors were no big issue in the early years of the welfare state, but gradually became more important, especially for regional governments. When the elected regional governments were consolidated as providers of health care and some other services in the 1960s and 1970s, they began to articulate the view that they should play the leadership role at the regional level. This later led to a reduced role for the county administrative boards (*länsstyrelsen*), the prefecture-like agencies operating regionally under the central government, which originally held the leadership role at regional level (below).

To summarize, the major challenge of the first period was to build up the welfare state. Local and regional governments became implementers of most welfare services, which created a need for consolidation. These mergers created mini-states with broad mandates and considerable autonomy at local level. For regional governments, consolidation led to the seeking of a larger role. Comparing the two levels, developments meant that democratic values such as closeness and accountability were traded for efficiency at the local level, while the case for democratic leadership was building up at the regional level. Here, efficiency and democracy seemed to point in the same direction, though it later led to a discussion of how many layers of democratic leadership there can be in a unitary state.

SECOND WAVE: DECENTRALIZATION

The consolidation of local and regional governments in the early 1970s was followed in the late 1970s and early 1980s by a backlash of criticism. Partially this was a counter-reaction to the previous period of consolidation, which was regarded by some as a loss of working democracy at the local level. Partially it was a political critique of the Social Democrats and some aspects of the welfare state. This contributed to a change of government in 1976 when the new, non-socialist government pursued a mix of reform and continuation, the theme of which was the necessity of decentralization. When the Social Democrats returned to power in 1982 they adopted the reform agenda and made the renewal of the public sector one of their main aims.

The 1980s was a busy period of reform. A series of measures were taken by governments in the 1980s to decentralize the public sector. One type of measure was to deregulate and assign more autonomy to local governments. Some national regulations were removed and local governments were invited to become "free communes" with further reductions in regulation. There was also the beginning of lump-sum funding in the system of fiscal transfers from the central government, as opposed to earmarked funding for specific purposes.

These reforms coincided with early elements of what was later to be called New Public Management, advocating a greater emphasis on control of outputs produced by local and regional governments rather than their inputs or processes. Eventually, local governments were allowed greater space to decide on their own organization (1991). Very few offices and boards for specific purposes are mandatory, which opened up for internal mergers as concerns decision-making; for example, creating divisions for child-related issues rather than separate structures for schools, day care, and sports.

Some policies aimed at introducing market-like measures into the operation of the public sector; for example, through the separation of purchasers and providers, where the roles were played by different organizations within local governments. Purchaser boards defined the needs and concluded contracts with providers, who often were the operative divisions of local government and sometimes also private providers. The number of private providers was initially low, but has increased in various service areas since the 1980s.

There were some examples of devolution, where national responsibilities were transferred to local and regional levels. The most important was to hand over the employment of teachers to local governments in the early 1990s, which gave local governments full responsibility for the operation of public sector schools (with a few minor exceptions) under national regulation. This was contested by the teachers' unions but generally desired by the local governments. More bitter fights took place in the mid-1980s over labor market policy, which many local governments wished to take over and integrate with other policies for local development. Several minor steps were taken, which are principally interesting since they weakened the previously mentioned National Labour Market Board (*Arbetsförmedlingen*), which was a very powerful government agency with local operations. Programs for immigrants and unemployed youth were turned over to local governments. Some other programs were to be decided jointly by the regional Labor Market Boards and the county administrative boards. The regional governments were not yet powerful enough to claim a role in this setup; however, tensions over roles at the regional level would soon lead to a third phase of reform.

With a non-socialist government in 1991 came a further set of decentralizing policies, this time empowering citizens in relation to local and regional governments. The prime example was the introduction of "voucher schools," opening the public funding system to independent schools. This was subsequently followed by similar models for the care of senior citizens. These reforms illustrate that decentralization is a very broad theme which can take many forms and that the original forms did indeed change later, from a focus on local governments to a focus on citizens' choice, the latter being pursued by national government sometimes against the wishes of local governments (cf. Feltenius 2010).

The reforms were combined with a stronger focus on control by the central government. The agencies for schools and health care were upgraded to play a stronger role in overseeing the quality of services. They were later to be followed by similar agencies in many areas, including inspection and evaluation of the agencies for the ill and the unemployed. In other words, decentralization was about partly contradictory transfers of power, where some transfers gave greater autonomy to local and regional governments, while other transfers gave more power to citizens and the controlling agencies of central government.

Studies on the effects of these reforms came about ten years later. A rather early overview of the debate on the effects of citizens' choice and privatization was given by Paula Blomqvist and Bo Rothstein (2000), recently followed by a more controversial overview by Laura Hartman (2011). While the first complained about a lack of nuance among adherents and critics, the latter took a rather one-sided negative view on the effects and was, in turn, criticized for applying a narrow view to motives, causality, and side effects.

Decentralization was combined with a few cases of secession, where consolidated local governments were partly broken up after local protests. A different kind of reform to strengthen local democracy was to recreate a more local level in the consolidated local (and regional) governments. Many large cities introduced semi-independent boards for subdivisions of the local governments (*kommundelsnämnder*), where geographical area often coincided with the old local governments which were now merged (Jönsson, Rubenowitz, and Westerståhl 1995). This was often done with independent villages or even small cities near the big cities. Most of these reforms were later abandoned, mainly because it was difficult to divide up responsibilities while at the same time maintaining overall responsibility with local government. The political majority of the subdivisions were generally the same as with the local government, which ensured smooth relationships within local government but sometimes looked strange to the citizens when it was obvious that the citizens of the smaller unit had voted for another majority. Another criticism was that division by function (service) was more efficient than division by geography. This debate resurfaced later at the regional level.

To summarize, the 1980s and early 1990s saw a combination of reactions against the previous centralization and an element of economic thinking to drive reforms in a new direction. The challenges were about efficiency and empowerment of citizens, through choice as well as through more local democracy. Decentralization went hand in hand with New Public Management, even though they did not always imply the same reforms. Efficiency was still the dominant value while the concern for democracy was seen in the efforts to recreate local subdivisions, and also in the various instruments of New Public Management which were often justified as means to regain political control over the agenda while delegating implementation to civil servants. One of the ideas of the time was that politicians should stop "rowing" and focus on "steering" instead. The reforms were mainly about local governments and the services they provided, but some similar thinking was found in the regional governments. Similar reforms of the services provided by the agencies came later and partly as a reaction against the horizontal collaboration across the levels of government in the third wave of reform.

THIRD WAVE: COLLABORATION AND REGIONALIZATION

The 1990s opened up two new themes of reform while the previous themes were still more or less present. The theme of consolidation was lurking in the background but resurfaced in the new millennium as a discussion about the need for further mergers of regional governments and/or of local governments. This has been one of the top issues over the past five years, where the proponents of consolidation see a need to merge units to take advantage of new economies of scale, for example in health care and infrastructure (Statens vård- och omsorgsutredning 2011). They also point to the problem of the gentrification of the countryside, making it increasingly difficult for small local governments to finance services or even find staff to provide services for their decreasing number of inhabitants. The relationship between democracy and the size of local governments has been analyzed by Folke Johansson et al. (2007).

The theme of decentralization is also still present, mainly as an alternative or complementary strategy to consolidation, but there are also some believers in very local communities, especially in rural areas (Berry 2013). Reforms in line with the theme of decentralization are primarily about instruments such as citizens' choice and voucher schemes, but there is also talk about reinvigorating local democracy. The contrary forces of centralization are equally present, and the ongoing problems of weak finances and continued need for reform make local governments more dependent on central government. The government agencies for schools and health care are putting pressures on local and regional governments, especially when there are social rights awarded to citizens in the form of certain welfare rights or the right to be treated fairly. For example, pupils and parents are increasingly taking legal action against schools and local governments, with the support of the agency for schools.

The pressures for increased efficiency along the lines of New Public Management are still there. In addition to this, e-government has become a big issue when local governments use the Internet to communicate with their citizens in areas such as choice of service providers, feedback to parents about their children in school, and also processing a variety of applications for services. The development of e-government locally, and the subsequent diversity of strategies, will most likely reinforce variety and give rise to a new discussion about how much diversity and decentralization there should be in the welfare state (Jansson 2013; cf. Åström 2004).

Yet, there was also a new theme of reform that emerged in the 1990s, or rather had been in the background for a long time and finally surfaced in the 1990s. This was the theme of collaboration between public and, to some extent, private organizations. Although there is a long tradition of cooperation across the public sector, networking and partnerships (and regions, as discussed later) were new buzzwords which entered the scene at the time when Sweden decided to join the EU (early 1990s). This period was a very turbulent time, with one government resigning over the economy and another government letting the currency float. Cutbacks and reform were high on the agenda in the mid-1990s with rising unemployment. This led to some specific effects such as expansion of programs for the unemployed, which in turn led to an abundance of overlapping systems of skills development and training, funded by all levels of government without coordination designed at central level (Statskontoret 2003). Eventually this created a need for collaboration and consolidation at local and regional levels.

This wave of reform differed from previous events in that the roles were reversed. The central government played a less visible role, primarily opening up for collaboration at the other levels, though it sometimes entered into contractual relations with local governments, for example in urban policy (*Storstadspolitiken*) (Statskontoret 2002; Hertting 2003). Some would say that the encouragement of local and regional networking is itself evidence of a weak national government stepping down from its previous role. One interpretation is that Sweden fell into the crisis of the strong government (Rothstein and Vahlne Westerhäll 2005), similar to what is generally referred to as government overload and incapacity to govern. A different and compatible interpretation is that national politics could not handle the conflicting policy networks, which were evident in the increasingly complex compromises where responsibilities were divided among local governments and national agencies with local operations, as well as between various organizations operating at the regional level. The Government Offices as well as the major parties were riddled with conflict over the themes discussed in this chapter, and collaboration was the easy solution for all parties, in line with international concepts such as "governance" and "joined-up government" (Niklasson 2011 and see below).

At the local level, there is now extensive collaboration across local governments for joint service production (Gossas 2006) and also with the other levels of government (see below and the chapter in this section by Feltenius). Markus Gossas argues that local governments are increasingly separated from their territory as they collaborate within many different constellations of local governments to find efficient service provision. At the same time, the central government has increasingly played the theme of collaboration in relation to local governments, which is not as open and flexible as it may sound. Martin Qvist argues that collaboration in the area of services for refugees is limited by tradition and professional norms, which implies that the central government does not have a working strategy for the design of the processes of collaboration (Qvist 2012).

There is also extensive collaboration by local governments with the EU structural funds and others to fund projects in various areas, often to develop new services and to do things in new ways (cf. Bache and Olsson 2001). According to critics, there is now a risk of the hollowing out or "projectification" of the public sector in general and local governments in particular.

Two Kinds of Regionalization

Interestingly, the collaboration wave has exerted the strongest impact on the regional level of government, which is much more complex than the national and local levels due to the large number of organizations operating there. In addition to the elected regional governments (*landsting*) there were not only the previously mentioned, prefecture-like agencies (*länsstyrelsen*), but also regional branches of agencies for infrastructure, labor market policy, and many more, as well as the public universities and the partnerships of the EU structural funds. In areas such as skills development and support for start-up companies, many organizations did/do similar things for overlapping groups of clients. In other areas, the roles are intertwined, for example in infrastructure planning where local and regional governments are responsible for planning while the funding involves the government agencies for infrastructure (now merged into one agency).

There were two interrelated developments at regional level in the 1990s which were parallel reactions to these complexities. One was a drive for stronger regional governments, especially in the regions in the south of Sweden. The other was to give regional governments the mandate to coordinate central government agencies, i.e. to collaborate at the regional level. The decision to build a bridge across the Oresund straight from Malmö to Copenhagen (Denmark) coincided with strong feelings of Europeanness, where the future was seen to lie in cooperation with Copenhagen and Hamburg (Germany), rather than with Stockholm, the capital of Sweden far away in the north. Regional autonomy and devolution of mandates from national government were regarded by many politicians as the way of the future, in a "Europe of the Regions."

One aspect was a strong drive among local and regional governments to simplify administrative structures and to play a larger role in economic development and other policy areas. Local governments in the south of Sweden believed that they stood a better chance of increasing efficiency, as well as giving a boost to democracy, if the national government backed down, especially at the regional level (Johansson and Niklasson 2013). This was partly driven by the contradictions of the old administrative structures. One of the most contested compromises in the 1980s was that the county administrative boards ("prefectures") maintained the leadership role at the regional level, while its board was made up of local politicians. Especially in the south, they were beginning to feel like hostages to a national agency and started to make plans for a leadership role for the elected regional government (Johansson and Niklasson 2013). Their political influence was strong at the time and they managed to convince the national government to start a series of devolution experiments. These experiments began informally in 1995 and formally in 1999, when the old counties in the south and west were merged into new regions. The leadership role was turned over to elected bodies in four regions and eventually in almost all regions.

This regionalization or devolution was the outcome of a long debate over what democracy should mean at the regional level, described by Tobias Krantz (2002). It was a rich and fruitful debate with no obvious conclusion. Basically there are three competing visions indicating each level as a basis for democracy. The traditional Swedish model is that the national level (Parliament) is the true bearer of democracy, which is important for the equal treatment of all citizens, for accountability as well as for the drive to change society top-down, all of which are important prerequisites for the welfare state. Another tradition is of course that there should be extensive space for local self-rule and democracy within the overall national system of democracy. The difficult question is then how to handle the regional level.

Traditionally, regional governments were given self-rule within a system dominated by the national level, like local governments. In the 1990s, the proponents of a "regional demos" became very influential and managed to achieve devolved powers and the official leadership role for the elected regional governments in the two merged regions and on the island of Gotland. This was in conflict with the proponents of a "national demos" as well as with the proponents of a "local demos." The latter argued that regional democracy would, in the end, limit the local level and confuse the voters. Their alternative was that the regional leadership role should be held by a body consisting of local governments jointly with the regional government, hence opting for regional governments grounded in the tradition of local democracy. This is the model that was tried in one region as an experiment and then opened up for any region interested in 2002 (Mörck 2008).

Parallel with this debate over the true meaning of regional democracy, the national government made networking and collaboration an official element of their policies for economic development in a wider sense. After decades of debate over "the regional mess," the government in the mid-1990s encouraged actors in all regions to form partnerships to coordinate their instruments for economic development. The government indicated that it wanted to see the participation of almost all agencies with regional and local activities in areas such as education, business development, and infrastructure planning.

Collaboration and networking meant that organizations (government agencies) were allowed to adapt their programmes to each other and to their partners at the regional and local levels, while staying within the goals and regulations set by the national government. This horizontal coordination is a kind of decentralization of national government which gave an extra boost to devolution by providing the elected regional politicians with more room to influence and coordinate the national agencies. Interestingly, this was often appreciated by the civil servants in the agencies who found that coordination by elected politicians provided them with a strategic agenda which was largely absent when the leadership role was held by the prefecture-like agencies (*länsstyrelsen*) (Statskontoret 2004b).

Horizontal coordination across organizational boundaries means that organizations belonging to all levels of government adapt their programs to each other. To some extent this is a continuation of Swedish pragmatism, but it also raises some fundamental questions about power and accountability, where the effect may be that the civil servants rather than politicians coordinate and make important decisions. Another critical issue is who influences whom. Critics argue that the national government has increasingly designed networking arrangements in ways that limit the independence of local governments (Qvist 2012; cf. Hedlund and Montin 2009). Another criticism is that roles and responsibilities are not always compatible, for example where local and national organizations are involved in the planning of new railways (Wänström 2009).

The positive aspect is that collaboration opens up a holistic perspective on the public sector, often combined with a client focus (Statskontoret 2004a). The proponents of collaboration see it as a way to counter the fragmentation of the public sector which follows from New Public Management, especially the focus on objectives for individual agencies. Collaboration is a soft form of territorial coordination which could solve the problem of various agencies and organizations making contrary demands on citizens in a specific region. Interestingly, the focus of the debate at the turn of the century shifted to another need for coordination; the need to coordinate each service from a national perspective, which is maximized through functional specialization. These opposite principles for the design of the public sector are now laid on top of each other, making the structure even more confusing. Strong tensions are building up in the Swedish system of government, indicated for example by the publication of a volume with the provocative title "Are regions necessary?" (Rakar and Tallberg 2013).

The government set up a committee to study the roles played by various levels of government (Ansvarskommittén 2007). It proposed further regionalization but has not been endorsed by national government. The committee made a very ambitious attempt to scrutinize the operations of the public sector. It came up with many observations on how the allocation of responsibilities could be made more efficient, but the comments from leading politicians indicate that some of them had wanted more radical suggestions, even the abolition of the regional governments (a long-time proposal from the Conservatives, now with some surprising support from Social Democrats). Still, the criticism and non-action by the government indicates that these issues are very sensitive and not yet solved. The irony is that there was, finally, a solution to the "regional mess," but the central government did not like it.

In the last couple of years, actors at the regional and local levels have tried to circumvent the deadlock on the proposals by the committee. The central government encouraged the merger of regions while it studied the future structure of the regional branches of the central government agencies, especially the prefecture/county administrative boards (*länsstyrelsen*). The central government also centralized control of its two key agencies with local operations (*Arbetsförmedlingen* and *Försäkringskassan*), which has made it more complicated to collaborate at local and regional levels.

There was an implication that central government would adjust its structure of agencies to merged regions, which stimulated intense bargaining among the regions. However, only one possible merger remains, concerning four regions in the south, scheduled to take place with the elections in 2018. The last committee also proposed an end to hybrid organizations where the local and regional governments collaborate. This has opened up the possibility of mergers with the elected regional governments in several regions, where the hybrid organization will become a regional development agency within much bigger organizations primarily devoted to health care. A key issue is how trust is built between local and regional governments in order for them to regard this move as a win–win situation (Johansson and Niklasson 2013).

To summarize, the past two decades began with strong encouragement for regions and collaboration under regional leadership and ended with a national government that has taken back control over its agencies and reduced the space for local and regional action. At the same time, devolution to regional governments is now permanent and more regional governments will play the leadership role after mergers with the hybrid organizations. The effects of all these moves remain, of course, to be seen in the future (cf. Lidström 2010), but it is safe to say that decentralization is not as popular as it was in the 1980s and that mergers and consolidation are high on the agenda again.

National Politics behind the Reforms

One way to understand the complex politics involved is to identify competing policy networks or epistemic communities within and around the national government (Niklasson and Tallberg 2010). These conflicts cut across political parties and have much to do with specific ministries and the way they have organized the implementation of their policies through government agencies or subnational levels of government. The presence of a "regional mess" of organizations based on different strategies and logics, as well as the bitter fights over regional policies in the past decade, illustrate that there are several groups competing for power.

There are proponents of devolution to elected regional bodies (the regional demos), as well as to regional bodies based on local governments (the local demos), though the latter group appears to be the weakest right now. There are also proponents of the prefectures/county administrative boards as well as proponents of centralization in the form of national control over welfare policy in general and the agencies for labor market policy and for social security especially (the national demos), which seem to be the strongest right now and are probably the strongest opponents of decentralization and regionalization. Conflicts over reform have to be settled in the Government Offices, where the "centralizing" ministries have veto powers.

Predictions of where these conflicts will lead can be made from three stylized institutional perspectives which are popular as explanations in the social sciences (Hall and Taylor 1996). One perspective (rational choice institutionalism) focuses on the rules of the game and the games that are played. In this perspective, politics is about bargaining within central government and with the proponents of regional and local governments. More specifically, explanations in this perspective would point to the strong position of the Center Party as a partner to the Social Democrats in the mid-1990s, influencing decentralization and regionalization. The recent move to centralization could be explained by the strong position of the Ministry of Finance (together with the Ministries of Labor and Health and Social Affairs) in the present government coalition, where the Center Party plays a lesser role, primarily controlling ministries with a pro-regional agenda (Industry and Agriculture).

Another perspective (historical institutionalism) focuses on path dependence. This perspective points to continuity and how each step restricts the options available at a future point in time. Ironically, there appeared to be inevitable development toward regionalization, crowned by the proposals from the committee in 2007 (Ansvarskommittén). Subsequent events have rather shifted track, which needs an alternative explanation.

The third perspective (sociological institutionalism) focuses on the drive for legitimacy and the ideas that dominate. In the 1990s there was much enthusiasm about a "Europe of the Regions" and the need for territorial coordination. With the cutbacks in the late 1990s, the government shifted its focus to equal treatment across the regions and a subsequent interest in streamlining government agencies. The initial focus was on stimulating economic growth but shifted to the survival of the welfare state instead. Austerity forced the Social Democrats to make a choice as concerns core values and this produced a shift in values which later governments have reinforced. The non-socialist coalition used the new rhetoric to take control of the national Labor Market Board (*Arbetsförmedlingen*) and subsequently of the social insurance agency (*Försäkringskassan*). Continued regionalization was not a preferred option. Rather it was control from the center, continued New Public Management, reform of the programs run by government agencies, and, possibly, a desire to privatize some of their operations.

To summarize the politics of challenges and reforms of local and regional governments, there has been a remarkable shift in the direction of events since the 1970s. After consolidation under central control there was a period in the 1980s and 1990s when local governments were much favored. Decentralization was a way of dealing with cutbacks and challenges for national government. Influenced by the EU, the proponents of regions managed to build up a case in the early 1990s for regionalization, largely due to the influence of the Center Party. This changed when crisis hit the welfare state in the late 1990s and the Social Democrats began to opt for centralization—a strategy followed by the non-socialists in 2006. The main focus of reform over the last few years has been on government agencies and the transfer systems of the welfare state. The role of the regions is rather unclear and the few developments seem to be about as minor as national government can accept.

It would be too strong to say that this is the story of the rise and fall of the regions. There is much enthusiasm at regional level that the regional mess will be managed in a better way and that regions may even bring consistency and an improved focus on economic growth to the public sector. It remains to be seen how these forces will play out in the future. There is a need for more research into the politics of reform of local and regional governments. There is also a great opportunity to follow the events at regional level when the regional governments merge with other organizations.

REFERENCES

Ansvarskommittén (2007). *Hållbar samhällsorganisation med utvecklingskraft?* SOU 2007:10. Stockholm: Swedish Government.

Åström, J. (2004). *Mot en digital demokrati? Teknik, politik och institutionell förändring.* Örebro: Örebro University.

Bache, I. and Olsson, J. (2001). "Legitimacy through Partnership? EU Policy Diffusion in Britain and Sweden," *Scandinavian Political Studies* 24/3: 215–37.

Berry, M. (2013). *Sockentänk: En studie av två deltagardemokratiska experiment i Ydre kommun.* Linköping: Linköpings universitet.

Blomqvist, P. and Rothstein, B. (2000). *Välfärdsstatens nya ansikte: Demokrati och marknadsreformer inom den offentliga sektorn.* Stockholm: SNS Förlag.

Feltenius, D. (2010). "Decentraliserad äldreomsorg under förändring," *Scandinavian Journal of Public Administration* 14: 61–85.

Gossas, M. (2006). *Kommunal samverkan och statlig nätverksstyrning.* Stockholm: Institutet för framtidsstudier.

Granberg, M. (2004). *Från lokal välfärdsstat till stadspolitik: Politiska processer mellan demokrati och effektivitet.* Örebro: Örebro University.

Gustafsson, G. (1980). *Local Government Reform in Sweden.* Lund: Gleerup.

Hall, P. and Taylor, R. (1996). "Political Science and the Three New Institutionalisms," *Political Studies* 44: 936–57.

Hartman, L. (ed.) (2011). *Konkurrensens konsekvenser: Vad händer med svensk välfärd?* Stockholm: SNS Förlag.

Hedlund, G. and Montin, S. (eds) (2009). *Governance på svenska.* Stockholm: Santérus Academic Press.

Hertting, N. (2003). *Samverkan på spel: Rationalitet och frustration i nätverksstyrning och svensk stadsdelsförnyelse.* Stockholm: Égalité.

Jansson, G. (2013). *En legitim (elektronisk) förvaltning? Om IT-utveckling och förändring i offentlig förvaltning.* Linköping: Linköping University.

Johansson, F., Karlsson, D., Johansson, B., and Norén Bretzer, Y. (eds) (2007). *Kommunstorlek och demokrati.* Stockholm: Sveriges Kommuner och Landsting (SKL).

Johansson, J. and Niklasson, L. (2013). *Kommunernas region—kommunernas inflytande i regionen.* Stockholm: Sveriges Kommuner och Landsting (SKL).

Jönsson, S., Rubenowitz, S., and Westerståhl, J. (eds) (1995). *Decentraliserad kommun: Exemplet Göteborg.* Stockholm: SNS Förlag.

Krantz, T. (2002). *Makten över regionen: En idékritisk studie av svensk regiondebatt 1963–1996,* dissertation, Acta Universitatis Upsaliensis. Uppsala: Uppsala University.

Lidström, A. (2010). "The Swedish Model under Stress: Waning of the Egalitarian, Unitary State?" in H. Baldersheim and L. E. Rose (eds), *Territorial Choice: The Politics of Boundaries and Borders.* Basingstoke: Palgrave Macmillan.

Mörck, J. (2008). *Regionalt samhällsbyggande i otakt. En studie av den varierande framväxten av samverkansorgan,* dissertation. Örebro: Örebro Universitet.

Nielsen, P. (2003). *Kommunindelning och demokrati: Om sammanläggning och delning av kommuner i Sverige,* dissertation, Acta Universitatis Upsaliensis. Uppsala: Uppsala University.

Niklasson, L. (2011). "Strategies to Join Up Resources across Levels and Sectors of Government: A 12 Country Comparison," in E. Ongaro, A. Massey, M. Holzer, and E. Wayenberg (eds), *Policy, Performance and Management in Governance and Intergovernmental Relations.* Cheltenham: Edward Elgar.

Niklasson, L. and Tallberg, P. (2010). "Forming a Regional Policy in Sweden: Where Will the Contradictory Policies Lead?" Paper for the 32nd Conference of the European Group for Public Administration (EGPA), September 8–10, Toulouse.

Qvist, M. (2012). *Styrning av lokala integrationsprogram: Institutioner, nätverk och professionella normer inom det svenska flyktingmottagandet.* Linköping: Linköpings universitet.

Rakar, F. and Tallberg, P. (eds) (2013). *Behövs regioner?* Stockholm: Reglab/SKL.

Rothstein, B. and Vahlne Westerhäll, L. (eds) (2005). *Bortom den starka statens politik?* Stockholm: SNS Förlag.

Statens vård- och omsorgsutredning (2011). *Statens roll i framtidens vård- och omsorgssystem: En kartläggning.* SOU 2011:65. Stockholm: Swedish Government.

Statskontoret (2002). *Tillsammans i storstaden: En studie av offentlig samverkan inom ramen för de lokala utvecklingsavtalen.* Stockholm: Statskontoret.

Statskontoret (2003). *Kommunernas ansvar för vuxnas lärande: Vad bör staten göra?* Stockholm: Statskontoret.

Statskontoret (2004a). *Det regionalpolitiska experimentet: Lärande nätverk för regional utveckling?* Stockholm: Statskontoret.

Statskontoret (2004b). *Regionalt ansvar på försök i Skåne och Västra Götaland: Bättre samordning och effektivare resursutnyttjande?* Stockholm: Statskontoret.

Wänström, J. (2009). *Samråd om Ostlänken: Raka spåret mot en bättre demokrati?* Lund: Arkiv.

CHAPTER 30

SWEDISH LOCAL AND REGIONAL GOVERNMENT IN A EUROPEAN CONTEXT

ANDERS LIDSTRÖM

Introduction

In comparative local government system literature Sweden is, often together with the other Nordic countries, regarded as a special case as concerns local government. It has been emphasized how it differs in terms of responsibilities, central–local government relations, and systems of finance. Indeed, many scholars have suggested that the Nordic countries form a category of their own, or even a separate type of local government system. For example, Bennett (1993) claims that local government in Scandinavia is unique with its combination of a hierarchical relationship with central government, a certain amount of autonomy, and a form of internal organization that emphasizes collective responsibility.

Based on a historical argument, Loughlin et al. have stressed how systems of subnational government are connected to specific state traditions (Loughlin and Peters 1997; Loughlin 2001; Loughlin, Hendriks, and Lidström 2011). The Scandinavian countries combine features from other European state traditions: for example, there is a resemblance to the Anglo-Saxon tradition found in the UK, Ireland, the US, and Canada, and from a long history of self-reliant communities that have developed into contemporary local self-government. It corresponds to the German state tradition (with Germany, Austria, and the Netherlands as major examples) with regard to some corporatist features, and it is also similar to the French tradition (with France, Italy, Spain until 1978, and Portugal) in terms of central control and uniformity. Similar conclusions about the uniqueness of Nordic local government have been reached by Bours (1993), Norton (1994), Lidström (2003), Heinelt and Hlepas (2006), and Heinelt and Bertrana (2011), despite the application of different criteria.

Scandinavian uniqueness also features in other classifications of types of societies and ways of organizing economies. For example, these countries are regarded as social democratic or universalistic welfare states (Esping-Andersen 1990; Huber and Stephens 2001; Sellers and Lidström 2007), as coordinated market economies (with Germany) (Hall and Soskice 2001), and they have also common traits with regard to their planning systems (Nadin and Stead 2008).

However, there are also scholars who have suggested that Swedish and Nordic local government is a less distinct category. In a well-cited anthology, Hesse and Sharpe (1991) have assessed the status of local government in twenty countries, with a particular focus on their functional and political roles and their performance. Sweden and the other Nordic countries are seen as belonging to a joint North and Middle European group. The common denominator is decentralized local government with considerable autonomy and a concern with local democracy. At the time of writing, this was regarded as "the model for the future" (Hesse and Sharpe 1991: 608). The category is very heterogeneous as it includes both unitary and federal states, which have different relationships to their local governments. Nevertheless, as shown by Kersting and Vetter (2003), the distinction still has considerable explanatory relevance with regard to the paths of local government reforms occurring in Europe.

Goldsmith (1992) has also claimed that differences between local government in the Nordic and other countries should not be exaggerated. They share, with Germany, the Netherlands, and Great Britain, responsibility for the welfare state which they carry out through large and professionalized local authorities. Hence, they contrast with the clientelistic/patronage model, which is mainly represented by local government in southern Europe, and an economic development model found in the US, Canada, and Australia. In their studies of central–local government relations, Page and Goldsmith (1987) and Page (1991) also locate the Swedish and other Nordic local government systems as parts of a larger northern European category, in contrast to local government in southern Europe. Although basing his analysis on the Page and Goldsmith model, John (2001) found that these distinctions were not so clear-cut. In a later analysis, Goldsmith and Page themselves also came to a similar conclusion. Contemporary tendencies toward convergence have changed the picture (Goldsmith and Page 2010).

Despite the differences, there appears to be a consensus among scholars about similarities between the local government systems in Sweden, Denmark, and Norway. Less commonly observed, these are also similar to local government in Finland which originates from a time when Finland was still part of Sweden. The question of whether local government in Sweden is different from other European systems outside the Nordic countries largely depends on the criteria used in the comparisons (Lidström 1998). However, the issue of Swedish exceptionalism requires closer scrutiny. This chapter aims at relating the Swedish system to a European context by studying the extent to which the Swedish model of local government is different from systems elsewhere in Europe, mainly outside the Nordic countries. We will carry this out on the basis of findings from comparative research literature on local government.

The analysis will concern the following features which have all been proposed as possible distinguishing features: constitutional protection, structure, functions, access to central government, and systems for democratic decision-making. The main differences will be clarified, and concerns as to why such differences have occurred will be discussed as well as what their implications are.

Constitutional Status

Many scholars have referred to a constitutional guarantee as one sign of local government enjoying a strong position in the national political system (cp. Norton 1994; Sellers and Lidström 2007). The underlying assumption is that such protection would establish a formal barrier for a temporary parliamentary majority to make drastic changes in the status of local government. In Sweden, the position of local government has been regulated in the Constitution since 1974, when it was emphasized in the first paragraph of the Instrument of Government that local self-government was a fundamental part of Swedish democracy. In addition, the types of local government and the right to taxation were also mentioned in the Constitution. A recent revision in effect from 2011 has emphasized this further, by including a separate chapter on local self-government and by stressing that Parliament should be restrictive in circumscribing local self-government.

The extent to which local and regional government is protected by the Constitution varies between countries. The European Charter of Local Self-Government, which has been ratified by all the member states of the Council of Europe, explicitly demands that local self-government should be acknowledged in the Constitution when appropriate. In line with the European Charter, most countries mention local autonomy of self-government in general terms, often in an initial paragraph in the constitution. It usually specifies that local government has its own functions or its responsibility for local matters. Even federal countries such as Switzerland and Germany emphasize local self-government, although the right to establish Local Government Acts rests with the länder/cantons. Exceptions include the UK, which has no written constitution, and Norway, which does not mention local government in its constitution.

Local self-government is more explicitly described in the Swedish Constitution than in the constitutions of most other European countries; however, there are also countries with more detailed regulation (Davidsson 2004). For example, the length of the local election period is mentioned in the constitutions of the Netherlands, Czech Republic, and Hungary. Methods for selecting the executive board or mayor are specified in the Netherlands, Portugal, Spain, and Austria. In the Netherlands it is stated that mayors are appointed through a royal decree and that the mayor is the chair of the council. The functions of local government are constitutionally regulated only in Luxembourg and Austria. This is most detailed in the Austrian Constitution, where Article 118:3 specifies eleven tasks that local government carries out on behalf of the federal level.

Constitutional regulation may be toothless if no effective means are available for ensuring that rules are followed. Swedish constitutional protection is weak in this sense, as there is no constitutional court to which local authorities can refer when they believe that central government is breaching the Constitution. Although there are other mechanisms, these are not as strong as a constitutional court would be. In contrast, federal decisions that are regarded as reducing local self-government may be taken to the German constitutional court by a local authority. A corresponding rule exists in the constitutions of the German länder. The Austrian constitution imposes a similar regulation.

Hence, compared to most other European countries, Swedish local government enjoys relatively strong constitutional regulation in favor of local self-government, but the absence of a constitutional court is likely to reduce the impact of this regulation. Indeed, an evaluation carried out by the Council of Europe in 2005 reported on several cases where central government actions vis-à-vis local government could be questioned as to whether they were in line with the Constitution. This included the regulation of municipal housing and a centrally imposed limit on local tax levels (SKL 2005).

STRUCTURE

In most countries, the structure of local government reflects both historical traits and more recent adjustments. Sweden has a two-tier structure of municipalities and county councils. The municipalities originate from a parish organization with medieval roots that were transferred into municipalities with non-ecclesial functions in 1862. Through two amalgamation reforms during the 1950s and 1970s, the number of municipalities was reduced from 2500 to the present-day 290. The second tier consists of 21 county councils/regional councils. County councils were also established in 1862 for self-governing tasks that required larger populations. Recently, regional councils have emerged as a label for county councils with extended functions (see just below). There are no specific provisions for the governance of metropolitan areas in Sweden.

Compared to other European countries, Sweden does not stand out with regard to the structure of its local government system. Most countries of a similar size as Sweden have two tiers (Hoorens and Dexia 2008; Loughlin et al. 2011). However, there are exceptions. Finland has a municipal level only and deals with problems that require a larger scale through intermunicipal cooperation. Larger states, particularly in southern Europe, tend to have three subnational levels. France is an example, with 36,000 municipalities, 100 *departements*, and twenty-six regions.

In many respects, the Swedish amalgamation reforms were a model for other countries in the 1970s. Their primary driving force was a wish to establish units of local government that were sufficiently large to carry the welfare services developed within the welfare state (see Niklasson in this volume). Subsequently, corresponding territorial reforms were implemented in most other countries in the northern part of Europe (Baldersheim and Rose 2010). Attempts at such reforms have also been made in several southern European countries such as Spain, Italy, and France, although the municipalities were able to resist these changes. One consequence is that Swedish municipalities are on average among the largest in Europe, with a mean size of 32,000 inhabitants. Most other countries have smaller municipalities. Only in the UK, Ireland, the Netherlands, Denmark. and Lithuania are larger in terms of average municipal population size (Loughlin et al. 2011).

On the other hand, Sweden was a latecomer as regards regional reform. Beginning mainly in the 1980s, several waves of regionalization have swept through Europe. Existing regional levels have been given new functions, in particular the responsibility for regional economic development. In addition, entirely new regional levels have been established and previous county councils have been amalgamated into larger units. The explicit emphasis by the European Union on allocating development resources to the regional level of government has been an important driver, together with demands for self-government by ethnic minorities. Indeed, the dominating concept of how economic development should be achieved has moved from an emphasis on central government redistribution to the "new regionalist" stress of the regions' own responsibility for their development (Keating and Loughlin 1997; Keating et al. 2003). This process came later to Sweden and has only been applied piecemeal (Lidström 2010; Hörnström 2013). A few county councils have been empowered by central government to change to regional status with extended responsibilities for economic development. Skåne and Västra Götaland are the results of amalgamations of county councils but Halland and Gotland managed to retain their original borders. At further six county councils are given regional status in 2015 and an additional three in 2017. The issue of amalgamation of county councils is also back on the policy agenda.

In Sweden, just as in the rest of Europe, self-governing and democratically elected institutions addressing specific problems of metropolitan areas are rarely found (Hoffmann-Martinot and Sellers 2007). The common pattern is a fragmented municipal structure in which each municipality focuses on their own locality, combined with an indirect level of government for the metropolitan area as a whole. There are exceptions, such as the Greater London Authority, although the travel-to-work area around London is larger than the GLA area. However, a significant exception in Sweden is that the urban municipal structure is less fragmented than in comparable countries (Hoffmann-Martinot and Sellers 2005).

FUNCTIONS

Swedish local authorities have both mandatory and voluntary functions. The mandatory functions are regulated in legislation and are formally carried out on behalf of central government. At municipal level, these include education, social services, planning, building permits, and environmental protection. Municipalities have a planning monopoly, i.e. they have the right (within the law) to decide for what purpose the land in

the municipality should be used. County councils and regions have compulsory responsibility for health care, but also for public dental care and care of the disabled. In addition, local government has a general competence, which allows both tiers to voluntarily
carry out functions that are not the responsibility of other public authorities. Such functions include recreational and cultural facilities and economic development policies.
There are no hierarchical relationships between the two tiers of government, but county
and regional councils are in charge of coordinating public health activities.

To a large extent, the functions of local government are similar in all the European
countries (Marcou 2007). However, the main difference between Sweden and, in particular, local government in southern Europe is extensive responsibility for welfare services (see Rothstein's and Lindbom's contributions to this volume). Sweden shares this
with the other Nordic countries and also, to some extent, with local government in the
Netherlands and Germany. Not only are the functions comprehensive—for example,
including municipal kindergartens and extensive public responsibility for social services and health care—in financial terms they are also relatively generous. This is changing, with an increasing share of welfare services being carried out by private contractors
(but still financed by taxes) and through pressure to reduce costs and improve service
efficiency. Nevertheless, there are still significant differences in functions.

There are also other differences. Together with Hungary and Germany, Sweden has
no municipal police force (Marcou 2007). All municipalities have the same responsibilities, which means that most of Europe differs from Spain where larger municipalities
are in charge of, for example, social welfare and public transport not only for their own
population but also for those living in their smaller neighbors. At regional level, there
is a greater variety of function between local authorities in different countries (Heinelt
and Bertrana 2011). Swedish county councils are unique in the way they are dominated
by just one type of function, i.e. the responsibility for health care, which represents
about 90 percent of their expenses. However, contrary to regional levels in most other
European countries, they have no legislative powers, no supervisory, control, or evaluation of municipal activities function, no role in distributing resources to municipalities,
and very limited coordinating function. The four Swedish regions, on the other hand,
have the additional responsibility for economic development and also a stronger coordinating role (Lidström 2011b).

One consequence of the responsibility for a relatively generous public welfare system is that Swedish local government deals with comparatively large-scale financial
resources. Total local government spending represents 25 percent of GDP and 44 percent of total public expenditure (Lidström 2011a). In Europe, the local government share
of the economy is larger only in Denmark; however, Denmark has additional responsibilities as provider of pensions. The other Nordic countries, the Netherlands, and Italy
have local government sectors that represent about 15–20 percent of GDP. The English
and French systems spend about 11–12 percent of the GDP, whereas local government
in, for example, Germany, Ireland, Belgium, and Portugal spend less than 10 percent
of GDP (Hoorens and Dexia 2008). Indeed, if capacity is regarded in a broader sense,
by also including measures of autonomy and corporate representation, Swedish local

government is the strongest in the Western world, very closely followed by Denmark and Finland (Sellers and Lidström 2010). Although this gives Swedish local government an important position in the country's economy, local authorities make their budgets and decide on local tax levels without prior consultation with central government. However, by law, local government budgets must be balanced.

Swedish exceptionalism is also a feature of the political culture of the country. As shown by Ronald Inglehart and colleagues, people in Sweden and the other Nordic countries are more secularized and tend, to a larger extent, to believe in postmaterial values such as well-being, self-expression, and democracy (Inglehart and Welzels 2005, 2010). When combining the two dimensions of secularization and postmaterialism on the basis of data from ninety-seven countries, Sweden comes out as a particularly extreme country, with the highest figures for both dimensions.

Other studies, using data from the European Social Survey, not only confirm this picture but also show that Nordic exceptionalism is extended to other issues. Citizens in the Nordic countries express stronger support for the key values underpinning the welfare system, such as universalism and equality (Edlund 2007). They also hold more gender-equality-friendly attitudes than other Europeans. Nordic citizens have more generalized trust, i.e. tend to trust their fellow citizens more than citizens in other European countries do. Trust for national political and legal institutions is also higher in the North. Indeed, in the Nordic countries it is common to refer to the state as "the society," which underlines that the state is not regarded as an adversary (Ervasti et al. 2008). Despite the tendencies during recent years towards marketization and cuts in the welfare services (cp. Montin in this volume), citizens' support for public welfare remains stable (Svallfors 2011).Trust in other citizens and in political institutions is also fairly stable (Holmberg and Weibull 2011; Rothstein 2011).

ACCESS TO CENTRAL GOVERNMENT

Local government access to central government has traditionally followed different patterns in the northern and in the southern European countries. In the north it has tended to be organized in collective forms, whereas in the south it depends on how well individual local politicians are connected to national policy-makers (Page and Goldsmith 1987, although the conclusion has been slightly modified in Goldsmith and Page 2010). A strong mayor may make a difference for the local community in southern Europe. Individual access does not play the same role in Sweden, but instead the collective voice of the Swedish Association of Local Government and Regions (SALAR) has a strategic position (see Feltenius in this volume). This organization was established in 2007 when the separate local government associations for municipalities and county councils were amalgamated. All local authorities are members of SALAR. It has an annual budget of EUR 75 million and a staff of 450 employees. SALAR is involved in formal and informal consultations with central government, both with relevant ministers and with key administrative staff.

Local government associations exist in all of Europe and indeed in an increasing number of countries, currently 115, in the world (Lidström 2013). From a comparative perspective, Swedish SALAR stands out as very strong. In an index of corporate representation for local government, developed by Sellers and Lidström (2007) on the basis of empirical literature, Sweden turns out as one of six countries in the Western world with the strongest representation of this type.

Another important point of access to central government in Sweden is through the political parties (Bäck and Johansson 2010). In Sweden, all elected politicians have to represent a political party, and since about 95 percent of local councillors represent a party that is also present in the Parliament, the party system itself functions as a link between central and local levels of government. Since 1970, local and national elections are held on the same day, which further emphasizes the connection between the different levels. Not only do central and local politicians from the same party campaign for each other in the elections, there are also well-developed forms of interaction between politicians from the different levels. For example, it is common that parties arrange national conferences for local politicians, where policies are presented and discussed and where there are good opportunities to meet the party's key politicians at central level. There is a considerable element of trust between local and central politicians, without which central government would be hesitant to allocate and maintain responsibility for major welfare services to the local level. However, this is under challenge as there are currently leading national politicians who are questioning local government responsibility for both education and health care.

Although political parties may have similar integration functions in other countries, there are several mechanisms that may reduce their impact. First, in most countries, local elections are held on separate days. Second, political parties are not necessarily relevant to local politics. Independent candidates are permitted in most other countries. An attempt to measure and compare the significance of political parties in local decision-making in seventeen European countries has been made on the basis of survey responses from the leading politicians at local level, politicians such as mayors and executive committee chairpersons. Party significance turns out to be highest of all in Sweden, and very low in France, Germany, Ireland, the Netherlands, Poland, and Switzerland (Fallend et al. 2006). Indeed, in another comparative overview, the integrative capacity of the local party system stands out as very high in the Nordic countries as compared to those in Germany, Japan, the Netherlands, France, Great Britain, Canada, and the US (Vetter 2000).

DEMOCRATIC DECISION-MAKING

The fall of the Iron Curtain and the breakdown of communism led to an increase in the number of democratic states in Europe. Although Russia and Belarus are still classified as authoritarian in the Economist Democracy Index, and there is concern about the state of democracy in several western and eastern European countries (the Economist Intelligence Unit 2013), democracy at both national and local levels is stronger than ever. As mentioned above, the European Charter of Local Self-Government, which emphasizes fundamental democratic and self-governing rights at a local level, has now been ratified by all the member states of the Council of Europe.

In practice, the models and methods used to realize the will of the people at local level vary between countries (Hendriks 2010; Loughlin et al. 2011). However, in most local authorities, an elected council is the primary decision-making body. This council appoints an executive board, a set of committees, and/or a mayor, although there is a tendency in an increasing number of countries to allow the citizens to elect the mayor directly. In Switzerland, and in some smaller municipalities in Spain, local decisions are to a large extent taken in municipal assemblies where all the voters have the right to participate (Ladner 2011).

Swedish local government is based on the principles of representative democracy and elected councils (see Montin in this volume). In several respects, democracy in Swedish local government has distinctive traits that emphasize representation rather than direct democracy: a prominent role for political parties and collective rather than individual, executive power.

First, local councils are comparatively large. On average, a Swedish municipal council has forty-five members, varying between thirty-one and 101 depending on population size, which is larger than the councils in most other European countries (Lidström 2003). County and regional councils vary in size from forty-five to 149 members. As councillors are elected through proportional representation, the opportunities of fairly small parties to win representation are good, which rewards activism in all parties, independent of size. The executive board and the various committees are also composed in proportion to the strength of the parties in the council. This facilitates coalition-building and may also promote a more consensus-oriented political culture, in particular in the smaller and less politicized municipalities. This contrasts with local government systems where the councils are smaller (such as in France and Spain) and where relations between the political parties are more antagonistic (such as in the United Kingdom). However, the number of councillors in the smallest Swedish municipalities may be reduced, as a new act coming into effect from 2015 will permit councils consisting of only twenty-one councillors.

Second, and as mentioned previously, local and national elections are consistently held on the same day, every four years. In most other European countries it has been regarded as a disadvantage to combine these elections, and although there is a debate about this in Sweden, the combined election day has been retained. This has been seen as a way of linking national and local issues in a system where the local level has extensive responsibility for the national welfare system. In addition, it has also been regarded as a way of enhancing voter turnout. The general pattern in other European countries is that local turnout increases when, for some reason, national and local elections coincide (Lidström 2003).

Third, political parties dominate local decision-making in Sweden. As already emphasized, it is compulsory for councillors to represent a political party. Between the elections, all powers are in the hands of the elected representatives. There are no means for citizens to recall their mandates during an election period. In most other European countries there are provisions for running as an independent candidate in elections, and these can be fairly significant, not least as representatives of alternative voices in local politics (Copus et al. 2012).

Fourth, decisions in local authorities are taken collectively, in councils and boards, and there is practically no scope for individual politicians to make their own decisions, which again emphasizes the role of the political parties. Although the chairperson of a Swedish municipal executive committee may be a prominent figure, and informally may have a powerful role, he or she has no formal individual decision-making powers. Voters may indicate their support for a specific candidate at the elections, but there is no room for individual mandates in Swedish local government.

This contrasts strongly with the role of the mayors in many mid- and southern European countries, who usually enjoy decision-making powers of their own as well as often belonging to the council and committees. In addition, the mayor is the political leader as well as the head of the administrative organization, which in Sweden is divided between two functions—the politically appointed chairperson and a professional chief executive officer. The individual mandate is particularly strong in the countries where the mayor is directly elected. Originating in southern Germany after World War II, the model of directly elected mayors has spread to many other countries, including the rest of Germany, Poland, Hungary, and parts of England and Austria. In these countries, the mayor not only enjoys individual decision-making powers and a role in preparing and implementing council decisions, he/she also has a direct mandate from the citizens (Berg and Rao 2005; Denters and Rose 2005). The model is a clear case of policy diffusion, as it has spread without being superimposed by any international organization. However, it has not yet reached Sweden—indeed, indirectly or directly elected mayors have not even been proposed by any political party in Sweden.

Further, collectivism is a principle that characterizes the Swedish system of government more generally. Apart from a role for the Speaker of the Parliament in government formation and the powers of the Prime Minister to select ministers and dissolve Parliament, all decisions in the Parliament and the government are taken collectively. Hence, political collectivism may be regarded as a key element in the Swedish political culture, which may also partly explain why it has resisted more individualist models of decision-making.

Fifth, there are only weak instruments of direct democracy in Swedish local government. The political parties, and in particular the Social Democratic Party, have been reluctant to accept such instruments, as these may constrain the parties' overarching control of local policy-making. However, from 1977, advisory referendums have been permitted and may be initiated by a council majority. As a part of a constitutional reform, means of direct democracy were further strengthened with the introduction of an extended local citizens' initiative from 2011. If 10 percent of the local electorate sign a petition for a referendum, and this is not rejected by two thirds of the councillors, an advisory referendum must be held. The referendum has to concern a matter that is a responsibility of the local authority and may be initiated at either municipal or county council/regional level. Despite being advisory only, the parties usually declare beforehand under which conditions they will comply with the results of the referendum. This may include a certain level of turnout. Several citizen-initiated referenda have been carried out, and there is good reason to expect this instrument will be used more frequently in the future.

However, the means of direct democracy used in Swedish local government is still far from the types of binding referenda that are frequent in countries such as Germany and Austria, and in particular in Switzerland. In the city of Zürich alone, there have been 850 referenda on local issues between 1934 and 2008, in addition to those on cantonal and federal matters (Ladner 2011). Nevertheless, the recent reforms in Sweden may mean a step towards a further strengthening of direct democracy at the expense of traditional, party-dominated representative democracy.

SUMMARY AND CONCLUSIONS

The Swedish system of local government complies with all the components of a minimum definition of local government. Local authorities operate in a clearly defined territory, execute a certain amount of self-government or autonomy, possess authoritative powers over their citizens, and use directly elected decision makers and/or municipal assemblies (Lidström 1998). Hence, Swedish local government shares a set of traits that are common to all other European local government systems. However, this chapter has aimed at highlighting the extent to which Swedish local government differs, primarily by relating this system to a European context and research findings from literature on comparative local government. This analysis has showed that Swedish local government, in many ways, stands out as unique.

Its uniqueness lies in the combination of local responsibility for costly, tax-financed national welfare policies, strong and mainly nationally organized political parties at a local level, consistent decision-making collectivism, and a type of representative democracy that leaves little room for means of direct democracy. This clearly distinguishes Sweden from countries with less extensive welfare responsibilities (such as the southern European), weaker political parties (such as the southern and East European), mayoral systems (such as the southern and mid-European), Westminster-type conflict enhancing systems (such as the UK or Ireland), and/or systems with more extensive use of direct democracy (such as Switzerland and Germany). There are also significant differences as compared to local government in the other Nordic countries. For example, Swedish local government has two tiers (only one in Finland), no mayors (in contrast to Denmark), and is constitutionally regulated (in contrast to Norway).

These features of Swedish local government may be regarded as logically intertwined as they stress decentralized responsibility for welfare services combined with representative democracy through strong political parties. Central government needs to be able to trust that local government is able carry out its responsibilities for its extensive and costly welfare system in an efficient and effective manner. The dominant position of the national political parties at a local level ultimately ensures that local government complies with expectations from the center. Collective decision-making and weak means of direct democracy ensure that power is firmly in the hands of the political parties. This has established a political culture that is not easily changed.

However, many features of this culture are under challenge. Over the last few decades, the welfare system has become less generous with more elements of means testing and more emphasis on effectiveness and efficiency. Private entrepreneurs increasingly carry out welfare functions on behalf of local government. This is a welfare system that, at the same time, has to deal with growing gaps in wealth between Swedish citizens and an increase in the number of elderly people. Although still supported by the middle class, if the quality of services is eroded, this class may increasingly turn to private alternatives and question why they have to pay for public services that they do not use (Pierson 1998; Kautto et al. 2001).

Political parties and representative democracy are also under challenge (Arter 2006). As elsewhere in Europe, Swedish political parties find it difficult to recruit new members. In the smaller municipalities, there may also be problems finding candidates for public office. The major parties in Sweden are now largely financed through public means and less by their own members. This may contribute to undermining the legitimacy of representative democracy and open up the possibility of direct democracy as an alternative. The previously mentioned citizens' initiative is one example of a new means that adds to the pressure imposed on Swedish political parties.

Although changes are taking place, the core values of the political culture of Swedish local government have resisted fundamental transformation (Montanari et al. 2007; Ervasti et al. 2008). Local government has followed an institutional logic of path dependency which has favored solutions in line with the dominating culture, rather than with fundamentally different alternatives. Whether Swedish local government will be able to resist these pressures in the future remains to be seen, and this also calls for more systematic research explicitly addressing the partly conflicting tendencies and the tensions that occur when public welfare meets private provision and traditionally strong political parties have to deal with more instances of direct democracy (cp. Baldersheim and Wollmann 2006).

References

Arter, D. (2006). *Democracy in Scandinavia: Consensual, Majoritarian or Mixed?* Manchester: Manchester University Press.

Bäck, H. and Johansson, V. (2010). "Sweden," in M. J. Goldsmith and E. C. Page (eds), *Changing Government Relations in Europe*. Abingdon and New York: Routledge, 198–209.

Baldersheim, H. and Rose, L. E. (eds) (2010). *Territorial Choice: The Politics of Boundaries and Borders*. Basingstoke: Palgrave Macmillan.

Baldersheim, H. and Wollmann, H. (2006). "An Assessment of the Field of Comparative Local Government Studies and a Future Research Agenda," in H. Baldersheim and H. Wollmann (eds), *The Comparative Study of Local Government and Politics: Overview and Synthesis*. Opladen and Farmington Hills: Barbara Budrich Publishers, 109–31.

Bennett, R. J. (1993). "European Local Government Systems," in R. J. Bennett (ed.), *Local Government in the New Europe*. London and New York: Belhaven Press, 27–48.

Berg, R. and Rao, N. (eds) (2005). *Transforming Local Political Leadership*. Basingstoke: Palgrave Macmillan.

Bours, A. (1993). "Management, Tiers, Size and Amalgamations of Local Government," in R. J. Bennett (ed.), *Local Government in the New Europe*. London and New York: Belhaven Press, 109–29.

Copus, C., Wingfield, M., Steyvers, K., and Reynaert, H. (2012). "A Place to Party? Parties and Nonpartisanship in Local Government," in K. Mossberger, S. E. Clarke, and P. John (eds), *The Oxford Handbook of Urban Politics*. Oxford: Oxford University Press, 210–30.

Davidsson, L. (2004). *Kammare, kommuner och kabinett*, SNS författningsprojekt. Stockholm: SNS Förlag.

Denters, B. and Rose, L. E. (eds) (2005). *Comparing Local Governance: Trends and Developments*. Basingstoke: Palgrave Macmillan.

Edlund, J. (2007). "Class Conflict and Institutional Feedback Effects in Liberal and Social Democratic Welfare Regimes: Attitudes towards State Redistribution and Welfare Policy in Six Western Countries," in S. Svallfors (ed.), *The Political Sociology of the Welfare State: Institutions, Social Cleavages and Orientations*. Stanford: Stanford University Press, 30–79.

Ervasti, H., Fridberg, T., Hjerm, M., and Ringdal, K. (eds) (2008). *Nordic Social Attitudes in a European Perspective*. Cheltenham: Edward Elgar.

Esping-Andersen, G. (1990). *The Three Worlds of Welfare Capitalism*. Princeton: Princeton University Press.

Fallend, F., Ignits, G., and Swianiewicz, P. (2006). "Divided Loyalties? Mayors between Party Representation and Local Community Interests," in H. Bäck, H. Heinelt, and A. Magnier (eds), *The European Mayor*. Wiesbaden: Verlag für Sozialwissenschaften, 245–71.

Goldsmith, M. J. (1992). "Local Government," *Urban Studies* 29/3–4: 393–410.

Goldsmith, M. J. and Page, E. C. (eds) (2010). *Changing Government Relations in Europe*. Abingdon and New York: Routledge.

Hall, P. and Soskice, D. (eds) (2001). *Varieties of Capitalism: The Institutional Foundations of Comparative Advantage*. Oxford: Oxford University Press.

Heinelt, H. and Bertrana, X. (eds) (2011). *The Second Tier of Local Government in Europe*. London and New York: Routledge.

Heinelt, H. and Hlepas, N.-K. (2006). "Typologies of Local Government Systems," in H. Bäck, H. Heinelt, and A. Magnier (eds), *The European Mayor: Political Leaders in the Changing Context of Local Democracy*. Wiesbaden: VS Verlag für Sozialwissenschaften, 21–42.

Hendriks, F. (2010). *Vital Democracy: A Theory of Democracy in Action*. Oxford: Oxford University Press.

Hesse, J. J. and Sharpe, L. J. (1991). "Local Government in International Perspective: Some Comparative Observations," in J. J. Hesse (ed.), *Local Government and Urban Affairs in International Perspective*. Baden-Baden: Nomos Verlagsgesellschaft, 603–21.

Hoffmann-Martinot, V. and Sellers, J. (2005). "Conclusion: The Metropolitanization of Politics," in V. Hoffmann-Martinot and J. Sellers (eds), *Metropolitanization and Political Change*. Wiesbaden: VS Verlag für Sozialwissenschaften, 425–43.

Hoffmann-Martinot, V. and Sellers, J. (2007). "Metropolitan Governance," in United Cities and Local Governments (eds), *Decentralization and Local Democracy in the World*. Barcelona: UCLG, 256–84.

Holmberg, S. and Weibull, L. (2011). "Förtroendekurvorna pekar uppåt," in S. Holmberg, L. Weibull, and M. Oscarsson (eds), *Lycksalighetens ö*. Göteborg: Göteborgs universitet, SOM-institutet, 45–64.

Hoorens, Dominique and Dexia-Crédit local de France (2008). *Sub-national Governments in the European Union: Organisation, Responsibilities and Finance*. La Défense: Dexia.

Hörnström, L. 2013. "Strong Regions within the Unitary State: The Nordic Experience of Regionalization," *Regional and Federal Studies* 23/4: 427–43.

Huber, E. and Stephens, J. (2001). *Development and Crisis of the Welfare State*. Chicago: University of Chicago Press.

Inglehart, R. and Welzel, C. (2005). *Modernization, Cultural Change, and Democratization*. New York: Cambridge University Press.

Inglehart, R. and Welzel, C. (2010). "Changing Mass Priorities: The Link between Modernization and Democracy," *Perspectives on Politics* 8/2: 551–67.

John, P. (2001). *Local Governance in Western Europe*. London: Sage Publications.

Kautto, M., Fritzell, J., Hvinden, B., Kvist, J., and Uusitalo, H. (eds) (2001). *Nordic Welfare States in the European Context*. London and New York: Routledge.

Keating, M. and Loughlin, J. (eds) (1997). *The Political Economy of Regionalism*. London and Portland: Frank Cass.

Keating, M., Loughlin, J., and Deschouwer, K. (2003). *Culture, Institutions and Economic Development: A Study of Eight European Regions*. Cheltenham: Edward Elgar.

Kersting, N. and Vetter, A. (eds) (2003). *Reforming Local Government in Europe*. Opladen: Leske + Budrich.

Ladner, A. (2011). "Switzerland: Subsidiarity, Power-sharing, and Direct Democracy," in J. Loughlin, F. Hendriks, and A. Lidström (eds) (2011). *The Oxford Handbook of Local and Regional Democracy in Europe*. Oxford: Oxford University Press, 196–220.

Lidström, A. (1998). "The Comparative Study of Local Government Systems: A Research Agenda," *Journal of Comparative Policy Analysis* 1/1: 97–115.

Lidström, A. (2003). *Kommunsystem i Europa*, 2nd edn. Lund: Liber.

Lidström, A. (2010). "The Swedish Model under Stress: Waning of the Egalitarian, Unitary State?" in H. Baldersheim and L. E. Rose (eds), *Territorial Choice: The Politics of Boundaries and Borders*. Basingstoke: Palgrave Macmillan, 61–79.

Lidström, A. (2011a). "Sweden: Party-Dominated Subnational Democracy under Challenge," in J. Loughlin, F. Hendriks, and A. Lidström (eds), *The Oxford Handbook of Local and Regional Democracy in Europe*. Oxford: Oxford University Press, 261–82.

Lidström, A. (2011b). "Regional Self-Government and Democracy," in T. Herrschel and P. Tallberg (eds), *The Role of the Regions*. Kristianstad: Region Skåne, 21–34.

Lidström, A. (2013). "Local Government Associations in the World: Promoting Democratic Local Governance," in G. S. Cheema (ed.), *Democratic Local Governance: Reforms and Innovations in Asia*. Tokyo: United Nations University Press, 73–88.

Loughlin, J. (ed.) (2001). *Subnational Democracy in the European Union: Challenges and Opportunities*. Oxford: Oxford University Press.

Loughlin J., Hendriks, F., and Lidström, A. (eds) (2011). *The Oxford Handbook of Local and Regional Democracy in Europe*. Oxford: Oxford University Press.

Loughlin, J. and Peters, B. G. (1997). "State Traditions, Administrative Reform and Regionalization," in M. Keating and J. Loughlin (eds), *The Political Economy of Regionalism*. London: Routledge, 41–62.

Marcou, G. (2007). *Local Authority Competences in Europe*. Strasbourg: Council of Europe.

Montanari, I., Nelson, K., and Palme, J. (2007). "Convergence Pressures and Responses: Recent Social Insurance Development in Modern Welfare States," *Comparative Sociology* 6/3: 295–323.

Nadin, V. and Stead, D. (2008). "European Spatial Planning Systems, Social Models and Learning," *disP—The Planning Review* 44/172: 35–47.

Norton, A. (1994). *International Handbook of Local and Regional Government: A Comparative Analysis of Advanced Democracies*. Aldershot: Edward Elgar.

Page, E. C. (1991). *Localism and Centralism in Europe: The Political and Legal Bases of Local Self-Government*. Oxford: Oxford University Press.

Page, E. C. and Goldsmith, M. (eds) (1987). *Central and Local Government Relations*. Beverly Hills: Sage Publications.

Pierson, C. (1998). *Beyond the Welfare State? The New Political Economy of Welfare*, 2nd edn. Cambridge: Polity Press.

Rothstein, B. (2011). "Social tillit, lycka, välfärdsstat och korruption," in S. Holmberg, L. Weibull, and M. Oscarsson (eds), *Lycksalighetens ö*. Göteborg: Göteborgs universitet, SOM-institutet, 65–84.

Sellers, J. and Lidström, A. (2007). "Decentralization, Local Government and the Welfare State," *Governance* 20/4: 609–32.

SKL (2005). *Om lokal och regional demokrati i Sverige*. Stockholm: Sverige kommuner och landsting.

Svallfors, S. (2011). "A Bedrock of Support? Trends in Welfare Attitudes in Sweden 1981–2010," *Social Policy & Administration* 45/7: 806–25.

The Economist Intelligence Unit (2013). "Democracy Index 2012: Democracy at a Standstill," report. London: The Economist Intelligence Unit.

Vetter, A. (2000). "Urban Democracy," in O. W. Gabriel, V. Hoffmann-Martinot, and H. V. Savitch (eds), *Urban Democracy*. Opladen: Leske + Budrich, 433–52.

SECTION 7

SWEDEN'S INTERNATIONAL RELATIONS

SECTION EDITOR
OLE ELGSTRÖM

CHAPTER 31

....

INTRODUCTION

Sweden's International Relations

....

OLE ELGSTRÖM

RESEARCH on Swedish foreign policy has primarily focused on four recurrent themes: Sweden's policy of neutrality, its relations with Russia, Swedish internationalism, and its efforts to promote allegedly universal values. In each theme, we find—in domestic and external political narratives—one or several dominant and prevalent conceptions of Swedish policy. Together, they form a good picture of the foreign policy *roles* (Holsti 1970; Harnisch et al. 2011: 7–15) that Sweden is perceived to play.

Each of the four themes is covered by the chapters in this section. The task of the authors has been to reconstruct these predominant narratives, but also to challenge them. To what extent are they still valid? Have changes in external and internal environments resulted in competing role prescriptions and/or in changed role interpretations and behavior? To what extent do domestic and external role conceptions coincide?

Ulf Bjereld and Ulrika Möller examine the modern history of Sweden's foreign policy through the lens of neutrality. Sweden's identity is still closely associated with its *neutrality role*, which during the Cold War linked a policy of non-alliance with internationalism. The traditional policy of neutrality has, however, been replaced by a postneutrality policy after the collapse of the bipolar world order. While still not partaking in military alliances, Sweden's involvement in a political alliance, the EU, as well as its increasing cooperation with NATO, implies a substantial change in its security policy.

Sweden's relations with Russia and the Baltic Sea states are analyzed by Rikard Bengtsson. His focus is on Sweden's visions for interaction with the states around the Baltic Sea, on the development of regional institutions, and on the roles played by Sweden in the region. While distrust vis-à-vis Russia remains strong, mirroring its traditional arch-enemy image, Sweden today plays the role of *multilateral cooperation agent*, inter alia by a *proactive* role in and through the European Union.

In her analysis of Swedish internationalism and development aid, Annika Bergman Rosamond highlights Sweden's role as an *internationalist state*, with a commitment to universal justice and equality as a dominant self-image, reflected in its foreign assistance, norm promotion, and multilateralism. She explores the extent to which this policy of international human rights' support and solidarity is still prevalent in the discourses of Sweden's non-socialist governments and finds a shift toward liberal, market-oriented internationalism, corresponding to a global normative trend. Still, global solidarity remains a discursive marker of Swedish discourse and practice, and external descriptions of Sweden's policy often reiterate the traditional picture of Sweden as a "good international citizen."

The chapter by Lisbeth Aggestam and Adrian Hyde-Price critically reflects on Sweden's role as a "force for the good." It examines the politics of Swedish military activism and finds a marked change from traditional peacekeeping in recent Swedish participation in military operations. While Sweden's traditional liberal internationalist role is still an important driving force, its military activism also reflects instrumental purposes: a desire for influence and an interest in collective milieu shaping. The authors also highlight the precarious balance between a continued commitment to international military action and its national territorial defense.

Is it then possible to discern any *specific Swedish traits* in its foreign policy? The combination of nonalignment with an active internationalist stance seems to be one example of "Swedish exceptionalism"; while there are other neutral states, and other states that act as "norm entrepreneurs," the combination is rare, if existing. However, increasing Europeanization and global trends have challenged this role combination, making Sweden more of an ordinary European small state.

References

Harnisch, S., Frank, C., and Maull, H. W. (eds) (2011). *Role Theory in International Relations.* Abingdon: Routledge.

Holsti, K. (1970). "National Role Conceptions in the Study of Foreign Policy," *International Studies Quarterly* 14/3: 233–309.

CHAPTER 32

SWEDISH FOREIGN POLICY

The Policy of Neutrality and Beyond

ULF BJERELD AND ULRIKA MÖLLER

In this chapter we are concerned with the *policy of neutrality* Sweden developed during the Cold War, and with the *postneutrality policy* that evolved after the collapse of the bipolar world order. We describe the chronology and characteristics of these policies in order to identify the main differences between them, and to detect any consistent trends. In both periods, competing conceptions of Sweden's appropriate international role have implications for Sweden's relationship with Western powers and its possible contributions to international peace and security.

Sweden has not been to war with another state since 1814—one of the longest continuous periods of peace experienced by any state in the world. It is sometimes claimed that this historically unique long peace is the result of longstanding and intentional neutrality. However, on several occasions it has actually been coincidental political circumstances and luck that have kept Sweden out of military conflict (Cramér, 1989: 68; Bjereld et al. 2008: 25–7). Furthermore, although the policy of neutrality Sweden implemented during the Cold War was used to prevent hostilities, it was by no means an inherently peace-promoting policy. A strong military capacity was instead seen as crucial in order to maintain the credibility of the neutrality policy, and the need to ensure the independence of Swedish defense was cited to justify substantial arms exports.

In addition to bolstering the credibility of the policy of neutrality, the Swedish military capacity during the Cold War was important in giving teeth to the "international activism" that emerged as inherent to the policy of neutrality (Ferreira-Pereira 2007; Doeser 2008). In the context of the dismantling of Swedish national defense in the post-Cold-War era, it has remained Sweden's political ambition to maintain sufficient military capacity to contribute to international missions. As Sweden has become a postneutral state, the pattern of Swedish foreign policy, i.e. contributing to international peace-supporting missions, has persisted. In 1992, Sweden began its long-term engagement in the Balkan area, through participation in the European Union Force in Bosnia and Herzegovina, specifically in Operation Althea (EUFOR) and Kosovo Force

(KFOR). In 2001, Sweden initiated its protracted participation in the International Security Assistance Force (ISAF) in Afghanistan, and in 2011, Sweden agreed to participate in the Operation Unified Protector (OUP) for the establishment of a no-fly zone over Libya. The previous emphasis on peacekeeping, mainly through the United Nations (UN), has been combined with an increased preparedness to engage in crisis management and peace enforcement. This may be seen in the context of Sweden's extended security cooperation as a member of the EU since 1995 and as a party to the Partnership for Peace (PfP) implemented by the North Atlantic Treaty Organization (NATO) since 1994. In addition to these security engagements, Sweden also envisions strengthened Nordic defense cooperation. While the abovementioned operations were supported by the UN, they have all been carried out under the leadership of the EU (EUFOR) or NATO (KFOR, ISAF, OUP). Sweden's participation in these international missions—under NATO leadership—indeed illustrates how the shift in Swedish foreign policy from one of neutrality to postneutrality is profound in certain regards.

In the following, we describe the chronology and characteristics of this shift in order to identify the main differences, and to detect any existing trends, between the policies of neutrality and of postneutrality. The chapter ends with a discussion of (1) how this change in foreign policy should be understood and (2) whether the change should be seen as completed, or whether Swedish foreign and security policies instead remain in a phase of gradual transformation. Sweden shares the experience of gradually shaping a policy of neutrality into one of postneutrality with other European states, such as Finland, Austria, and Ireland. We will make some comparisons with other cases when appropriate, beginning in the next section, where we make conceptual clarifications.

HISTORICAL AND CONCEPTUAL POINT OF DEPARTURE

Neutrality is a judicial concept in international law as well as a political tool for states in international politics. It is also a theoretical concept applied in the study of international politics and in foreign policy analysis. While in the current world order it might be relevant to ask whether neutrality is really a dead concept (Goetschel 1999; Agius and Devine 2011), we suggest that it remains useful in analyzing the foreign policy of former neutrals. While the elasticity of neutrality as a political tool represents a potential challenge to its use as a theoretical concept (Devine 2011; Lödén 2012), analyzing the shifting role and meaning of the concept is essential in order both to grasp the differences between policies of neutrality and to understand the process of shifting from neutrality to postneutrality.

The right to invoke neutrality in war was first acknowledged by the Congress of Vienna in 1815, and the rights and duties of neutral states in war were further established by the Hague Conventions of 1899 and 1907. As a political tool in international politics, *neutrality* is a principle states can invoke in war, implying *nonparticipation* and *impartiality* according to the rules of the Hague Conventions (Cramér 1998). An additional concept related to neutrality as a form of state conduct is *nonbelligerency*, still implying nonparticipation but, unlike impartiality, implying that the state could *favor one side over another*. In addition to wartime neutrality, there is also the option of *permanent neutrality*, implying that a state has codified neutrality as a form of conduct *in both war and peace*. Swiss neutrality, recognized by the Congress of Vienna, is the best-known example of this.

Furthermore, a *policy of neutrality* can be implemented in times of peace even when a state is not permanently neutral. This less robust codification through legal means comes with freedom to make adjustments, but also demands that the state be capable of demonstrating credibility in its neutrality commitment in order to convince the international community (Carlsnaes 1988; Möller and Bjereld 2010). *Military nonalignment* is another term often associated with neutrality as both wartime conduct and formal policy. Military nonalignment can be described as the core of a policy of neutrality, in that it is a necessary condition to enable the invoking of neutrality in war, as well as a necessary condition for a policy of neutrality. However, it is customary for a policy of neutrality to go beyond such a thin version to a thicker nation-specific version regarding the particular foreign and security policy stance of a state. Through such national interpretations, a policy of neutrality can emerge that serves the strategic interests and normative considerations of the state deploying it (Neal 2007; Möller and Bjereld 2010).

Sweden has a long tradition of using neutrality as a political tool in its external relations. As a great power in northern Europe, Sweden signed a treaty of neutrality in 1632 with the small Catholic states Trier and Köln in exchange for their recognizing its claims as rightful and not assisting the Habsburg imperial power. When the great power period had passed, Sweden's declaration of neutrality in 1834 instead represented an attempt to ensure survival in the face of possible war between England and Russia (Cramér 1998: 171, 173; af Malmborg 2001: 30, 92). This illustrates the strategic use of neutrality both for the purpose of national great-power politics, and to ensure security in a position of relative weakness. In addition to the use of neutrality as a *strategic instrument of security*, neutrality has also been used as a *prescriptive principle of policy*. Regarding the extent of interference with the foreign policies of other states, Sweden's policy of neutrality during the Cold War was "low profile" with Östen Undén as foreign minister, but emerged as "loudly critical" with Olof Palme as Prime Minister. Neutrality as a prescriptive principle has thus led to different policy approaches with regard to Sweden's appropriate stance.

It is certainly also noteworthy that neutrality in the context of armed conflict has been inconsistently applied in dealings with other states throughout the history of Sweden's external relations. To illustrate, when Sweden issued an official declaration of neutrality at the outbreak of World War I (1914–18), Germany was told that the interpretation would be benevolent, while Germany's opponents were told it would be strict. When the war turned to favor the Western powers, so did Sweden's approach. In the interwar period (1919–39), Sweden was a member of the League of Nations and therefore included in a system of collective security. During World War II (1939–45), Sweden again claimed official neutrality, which proved difficult to uphold in practice. As during World War I, deviations from neutrality corresponded to the course of the war, initially being to the advantage of Germany and later to the advantage of the Western powers (Bjereld et al. 2008: 25–7). Sweden's political use of neutrality has relied on the fact that it has not been codified from Sweden's conduct in either war or peace in accordance with international law. Evaluations of historical instances of discrepancy in the application of neutrality, especially during World War II, differ depending on whether the yardstick is neutrality as a strategic instrument of security or neutrality as a prescriptive principle of policy. To illustrate, the harshest criticism of Sweden's neutrality casts it in terms of moral weakness; in defense, it is emphasized that Sweden stayed out of the war due to its use of—and deviations from—neutrality. The transformation of the Swedish policy of neutrality into one of postneutrality was also facilitated by the policy's nonlegal status. The concept of "postneutrality" is commonly used to refer to the adaptations implemented by European states that adopted a policy of neutrality in response to the post-Cold-War setting (Cramér 1998: 643; Möller and Bjereld 2010; Agius and Devine 2011; Agius 2011). While the term is useful in comparing states with similar backgrounds of using neutrality to shape their foreign policy, we suggest that the concept also captures the presence of some degree of ongoing policy transformation. In the cases of Sweden and Finland, it is sometimes assumed that the endpoint of this transformation phase would be membership in NATO (Christiansson 2010; Miles 2014).

DEVELOPING A POLICY OF NEUTRALITY: SWEDEN'S SECURITY POLICY DURING THE COLD WAR, 1946–90

Sweden's policy of neutrality emerged during the Cold War (1946–90) as a specific characteristic of its foreign policy. The development of this policy can be described as a response to the emerging bipolarity of the Cold War. In the years immediately after World War II, Sweden became a member of the United Nations (1946), participated in implementing the Marshall Plan (1947), and joined the Council of Europe (1949). Discussions were also held between Sweden, Denmark, and Norway about establishing a regional security solution. The idea of a Nordic defense alliance was not realized largely due to disagreement on its relationship with the Western defense alliance. With the experience of German occupation during World War II, Norway insisted on establishing such a link between the alliances, while Sweden argued that a Nordic defense alliance should be independent of the great power blocs. The failed attempt to create a regional security solution resulted in different paths of security for the Nordic countries: Norway and Denmark became members of NATO, while Sweden forged its policy of neutrality. While it was not the result of a common strategy, there was nevertheless a specific label for the emerging security solution in Scandinavia. "The Nordic balance" captured how, with Finland leaning towards the Eastern bloc and Norway and Denmark leaning towards the Western bloc, Sweden's neutral position kept the superpowers apart in the Nordic region. Sweden implemented a so-called third way policy to maneuver between and independently of the two superpower alliances.

Sweden did not codify any policy of permanent neutrality, but relied instead on the formulation: "nonalignment in peace in order to remain neutral in wartime" (*"alliansfrihet i fred, syftande till neutralitet i krig"*) as a decisive guiding principle. The formulation implies two central political obligations to ensure the credibility of the chosen foreign policy stance. First, political ties and commitments that could confine Sweden's option of neutrality in the event of war had to be avoided. Second, the pursued policy had to enhance confidence in neutrality in the international arena, especially among the superpowers (Ferreira-Pereira 2006, 2007: 466; Bjereld et al. 2008).

To protect Sweden from hegemonic superpower ambitions, pursuing a credible policy of neutrality was prioritized. Refraining from political and military alliances and sustaining self-sufficient and dissuasive military defense became the cornerstone of strategic beliefs regarding how this credibility was to be upheld (Bjereld et al. 2008; Ferreira-Pereira 2006, 2007; Dalsjö 2014). The Swedish government therefore refrained from making any official political and military commitments, in order to uphold the credibility of its policy of neutrality. The government nevertheless expected help from the Western bloc if Sweden was drawn into a war, and the military was secretly authorized to prepare for wartime cooperation. Even in peacetime, there was intense intelligence cooperation with Western powers. Additional collaboration included expanding airports to accommodate NATO aircraft, securing communication lines between Sweden, Norway, and Denmark, and together with Norway, coordinating airforce reporting and recognition systems and planning a joint military weather service. Though secret, this collaboration with the West likely undermined the credibility of Sweden's policy of neutrality in at least two respects. First, the Soviet Union was likely aware of most of these activities and might well have concluded that Sweden would abstain from neutrality in wartime even if not attacked. Second, the collaboration likely helped strengthen ties between Sweden and the Western bloc, which could have reduced actual Swedish readiness to stay neutral in the event of war (Bjereld et al. 2008).

The initial years of Sweden's policy of neutrality were characterized by "small-state realism" without normative ambitions. The late 1960s brought substantial change in this regard through an "active foreign policy" that made its breakthrough with Palme's criticism of US warfare in Vietnam. It was not just the USA that was targeted by Swedish criticism. Sweden also criticized the Soviet Union for intervening in Czechoslovakia in 1968 and Afghanistan in 1979. Even dictatorships in the Third World were criticized for violating human rights. In particular, the apartheid regimes of Rhodesia (today's Zimbabwe) and South Africa as well as military dictatorships in Latin America were criticized. In the Middle East, Sweden began to support the Palestinian Liberation Organization, while condemning the Israeli occupation of Palestinian territories. In the UN General Assembly, Sweden had usually voted with other Western states; instead,

Sweden now to a greater extent voted with the Third World countries (Bjereld 1995; Demker 1998). Sweden also explicitly supported Third World demands for a new economic world order.

Sweden's frequent condemnation of the world's injustice gave rise to the somewhat ironic description of Sweden as a "moral superpower." Yet the active diplomacy also became an additional factor bolstering the credibility of the policy of neutrality. In this guise, the policy became something of a virtue rather than a means to an end, even outside Social Democratic circles. This is proven by the fact that the conservative/liberal governments of 1976–82 continued to maintain a high profile on international matters. This conferring of virtue on neutrality as a foundation of Swedish security policy helped amass support for Sweden's international role (Doeser 2008; Makko 2012). However, this virtue was also contested, indicating that there were competing conceptions of the role Sweden should play in the international arena. Furthermore, describing neutrality as more of a moral virtue than as a strategic necessity also made the policy more vulnerable to accusations of deviation from principle. As mentioned, Swedish security policy did include the option of less virtuous and more instrumentally oriented preparations in the event of war.

The overall goal of Swedish security policy during the Cold War can be described as intended to defend the country's independence, i.e. Sweden's ability to maintain and develop its society according to its own values. In order not to be drawn into any possible wars, the country acted in peacetime so as not to complicate—or rule out—neutrality in the event of war. This policy of neutrality, with military nonalignment at its core, was the most important component of Swedish security policy.

The Swedish policy of neutrality may be compared with the Finnish policy of neutrality that evolved in the 1950s under President Kekkonen, which should be seen in the context of the Treaty of Friendship, Cooperation, and Mutual Assistance agreed with the Soviet Union in 1948. While Sweden strove to maintain political autonomy through its policy of neutrality during the Cold War, Finland had to use the same means to maintain both its political autonomy and territorial integrity. The Swedish policy of neutrality during the Cold War also differed from Austrian neutrality in that it was not imposed by external forces (Cramér 1989: 105).

Domestic debate in the aftermath of the Cold War with regard to the policy of neutrality revealed two competing self-images. According to *the first self-image*, during the Cold War, Sweden had implemented a consistent and intentional policy, enabling it to remain neutral in the event of a major war in Europe. Nonalignment in peace, based on a strong military defense, would convince the world that Sweden had both the will and the ability to defend its neutrality if war came. The policy of neutrality was a security policy meant to defend the country's independence, even at a time of increasingly complex interdependence. By treating the two superpower blocs impartially and by implementing foreign and security policies based on international law and a strong UN, Sweden not only enhanced its own ability to stand outside any major war, but also helped strengthen peace throughout Europe. Swedish security policy helped create shared security. Swedish nonalignment did not mean isolation, but was instead part of creating a more secure world in general. The Swedish neutrality line was developed through domestic political consensus, in which the government and the opposition agreed on the policy's main thrust. The neutrality line was strongly supported by Swedish public opinion and was also appreciated by the outside world as actively advancing detente in Europe.

According to *the second self-image*, however, Sweden's policy of neutrality was an illusion. Sweden was in fact and in practice an informal member of the Western alliance. If war came to Europe, none of the belligerent parties would have any interest in respecting Sweden's neutrality, and Sweden would not be able to avoid being drawn into the military hostilities. To prevent such a development, the Swedish military and the political leadership had agreed that, in peacetime, Sweden would take measures to facilitate military assistance from Western states if war broke out in Europe. Taking such measures in peacetime increased the opportunities for Sweden to prevent the Soviet Union from occupying the country during wartime. It was, after all, in the Western bloc that Sweden "belonged." The leading politicians and the military knew about the cooperation and the preparation measures, though the Swedish people knew nothing. The official neutrality line was immoral and undemocratic, because cooperation with the Western states was carried out in secret, beyond visibility and control. The Swedish people were lulled into a false sense of security by politicians who, for electoral reasons, did not want to admit the truth. The policy of neutrality was a chimera: if war came to Europe, Sweden would have no real opportunity to stand outside the conflict or to defend its neutrality.

BECOMING POSTNEUTRAL: SWEDEN'S SECURITY POLICY AFTER THE COLD WAR, 1991–THE PRESENT

The end of the Cold War dramatically changed the structural conditions affecting Sweden's foreign and security policies. The formula for the Swedish security doctrine during the Cold War was based on the risk that a major war could occur in Sweden's immediate neighborhood, and that neutrality would prevent Sweden being drawn into it. But what if there were no longer any such risk of war? Sweden was no longer situated as a neutral buffer state between two superpower blocs, between the NATO member states of Norway and Denmark, on one hand, and Finland with its agreement with the Soviet Union, on the other. The "Nordic balance" had become less relevant in characterizing the security situation in northern Europe (Ferreira-Pereira 2007: 47; Bjereld et al. 2008: 315). Instead of a grotesque, yet stabilizing, balance of terror, Sweden's security context was now characterized by nation state disintegration, democratization processes, identity crises, and regional or ethnic war (as far away as Somalia and Rwanda, and as close as Yugoslavia). The new wars differed from the old ones in that there was little risk that great power involvement in them would spread conflict to Sweden's neighborhood and threaten its territorial integrity (Bjereld et al. 2008; Doeser 2008; Möller and Bjereld 2010). In the early 1990s, the likelihood of a major war in Europe appeared minimal. How reasonable was it for Sweden to continue designing its peacetime defense policies in the same way as before, with striving for neutrality in wartime a key consideration?

After the end of the Cold War, the Swedish policy of neutrality was domestically challenged in a completely different way. The battle was taken up mainly by the liberal Folkpartiet and the conservative Moderaterna, the parties that, even during the Cold War, had wanted Sweden to adopt a more Western-oriented foreign policy—albeit within the neutrality policy framework. Still, the political parties could not fully articulate their criticism in public during the Cold War, since this could have undermined the credibility of the Swedish neutrality policy. Liberals and conservatives simply had to clench their fists in their pockets, while still putting a good face on things. However, the end of the Cold War meant that these parties could freely air their feelings about the Swedish policy of neutrality.

There has been some critical assessment of the normative dimension of the neutrality policy. On the one hand, some considered the policy real and sincere, seeing it as expressing political commitment. Through nonalignment, Sweden gained independence that enabled it to criticize both superpowers—the United States for its actions during the Vietnam War and the Soviet Union for its interventions in Czechoslovakia and Afghanistan. On the other hand, others, who considered the neutrality policy a chimera, tended to see it as expressing isolationism and inaction in the face of events in the world beyond its borders. Certainly, it is true that in peacetime Sweden had already taken steps to facilitate military assistance from the West should war occur. It is also true that these measures were carried out in secret, beyond public visibility and democratic control.

After the end of the Cold War, intense domestic political debate broke out concerning Sweden's policy of neutrality. Critics argued that Sweden's cooperation with the Western powers during the Cold War meant that the policy of neutrality had been illusory, and that Sweden had in practice been part of the Western alliance NATO. The government decided to set up a special commission on neutrality, to investigate whether Sweden's cooperation with the Western powers had indeed violated its neutrality policy. In its report, the Neutrality Commission (1994) pointed out that the cooperation had *not* led to a departure from the policy of neutrality, since the measures included in the strategy were meant only as a fallback. These measures would only have been initiated if Sweden had first been attacked by the Soviet Union and the neutrality thus violated; if Sweden was not attacked, the rules of neutrality would instead have been followed. The Neutrality Commission therefore argued that the Swedish policy of neutrality was a responsible one. On the other hand, the Neutrality Commission claimed that former Prime Minister Tage Erlander did not tell the truth—or conveyed a "knowingly false impression" of what was actually occurring—when, in a parliamentary debate with Conservative leader Jarl Hjalmarson in autumn 1959, he asserted that "preparations and negotiations for military cooperation with members of a superpower alliance are thus excluded" (SOU 1994:11: 307–8). It is also important to remember that Sweden's peacetime cooperation with the Western powers was voluntary and entailed no binding reciprocal defense obligations. This means that Sweden's freedom of action would have persisted, at least in formal terms, if war had struck Europe. However, the collaboration with the West eroded the credibility of Sweden's policy of neutrality in at least two respects. First, the Soviet Union was likely well aware of what was going on and perhaps interpreted it as indicating that Sweden would refrain from neutrality and interact with the Western powers in a war situation even if Sweden were not itself attacked. Second, Sweden's collaboration with the West strengthened the friendship between Sweden and the Western powers, which in itself could reduce the Swedish desire for neutrality in a war situation. In addition, collaboration with the Western bloc was naturally carried out in secret, making it questionable from a democratic point of view. The choice was not between collaborating secretly and collaborating openly; instead, the choice was between collaborating secretly and not collaborating at all.

Criticism of the neutrality policy gave rise to two not entirely compatible arguments for political change. First, liberals and conservatives asserted that the policy of neutrality had become empty and meaningless since there was no longer any real risk of war and therefore no need of neutrality towards belligerents. Second, liberals and conservatives argued that in the unlikely event of war in Sweden's neighboring countries—for example, if Russia attacked any of the newly formed Baltic States—neutrality, for moral and ideological reasons, should not be a Swedish option. The idea was that if Russia attacked any Baltic state, Sweden should be able to support that state, albeit not with military force, politically and economically in a way not strictly compatible with the law of neutrality. The political situation after the Cold War was deemed to be such that Sweden could provide such support without risking direct involvement in the hostilities.

In connection with Sweden's decision to apply for membership of the European Union, the latter argument was rhetorically reiterated: would Sweden as an EU member really remain neutral if another EU state were attacked? The Social Democrats acted defensively in the debate, arguing that the neutrality policy would remain unchanged even if or when Sweden joined the EU. However, the party refused to clarify its position as to whether it really meant that Sweden would indeed remain neutral if another EU member state were attacked.

In parallel with the debate on the future of Swedish neutrality policy, in 1994 Sweden began to participate in NATO's new cooperation program Partnership for Peace (PfP). In this program, NATO's sixteen member states interacted with a number of non-member countries to increase both NATO's and its partners' ability to participate in international crisis management operations. Sweden's participation was described as an effort to help construct European security structures and expand opportunities for peace-support operations. The program did not require that non-member cooperation partners become involved in the NATO countries' mutual defense guarantees.

Even within the EU, the common elements of foreign, security, and defense policies were strengthened. EU membership meant that Sweden became part of the EU's Common Foreign and Security Policy (CFSP), which entailed coordinating foreign policy positions, forming joint crisis-management forces, and issuing stronger statements of solidarity between member states in times of crisis or war. In the case of the

EU, neither would it be reasonable to speak of a formal military alliance or of any mutual defense guarantees. However, although the Swedish policy of neutrality began to be openly questioned in public debate, despite Sweden's closer cooperation with NATO within the PfP framework and despite Sweden's entry into the EU, support for military nonalignment remained strong among the Swedish public. In 1994, 70 percent of respondents to a large survey believed it was a good idea that "Sweden should in peacetime pursue a nonaligned policy, in order to remain neutral in wartime"; only 7 percent felt it was a bad idea. In the same survey, 15 percent of respondents said that it was a good idea that "Sweden should apply for membership in NATO," while more than three times as many—48 percent—felt that it was a bad idea. Toward the end of the 1990s, the liberal Folkpartiet became the first party to suggest that Sweden should seek NATO membership. The conservative Moderaterna argued that NATO membership was indeed a "natural step" for Sweden to take, but that it should ideally be done along with Finland and the Baltic States.

In the continuing debate on Swedish NATO membership, purely geopolitical arguments did not figure prominently. Because the risk of war was considered almost negligible, it was difficult to claim with any credibility that NATO membership would weaken or strengthen Sweden's security in any significant way. Instead, it was ideological and power-political arguments that dominated the debate. NATO supporters argued that Swedish membership would be an expression of Sweden's European identity and allow Sweden to influence by far the world's most powerful defense organization. NATO critics argued that Swedish membership would reinforce the new boundaries drawn between the West and the rest of the world and that, by such membership, Sweden would lose its freedom of action in foreign and security policy issues.

Another way to characterize the debate is that it was fairly easy for NATO critics to formulate the disadvantages of Swedish NATO membership. Why join the NATO military alliance when there is no threat, public opinion is unambiguously opposed to the move, and Sweden would become aligned with NATO's nuclear doctrine? Why change the security arrangements when Sweden has had peace for 200 years, especially given that NATO is an outdated organization adapted to the Cold War world order and logic? Moreover, Sweden should not be in the same defense alliance as that superpower, the USA. On the other hand, NATO critics found it more difficult to identify the benefits of nonalignment. Yes, it gave freedom of action, but what should this freedom be used for?

Despite NATO supporters' difficulties in asserting themselves in the debate, the explicit neutrality option was steadily phased out of the security policy doctrine. The government's foreign policy declaration in February 2003 did not mention the word "neutrality" but referred only to Sweden's nonalignment. This change was based on a political agreement between the Social Democrats, the Center Party, the Christian Democrats, and Moderaterna, all of which rallied behind the narrow formulation "Sweden is militarily nonaligned," combined with a declaration that Sweden should implement its security policy in cooperation with other states. The expression was a pure description of reality and said nothing about how Sweden could or should behave in wartime. However, the gradual shedding of the word "neutrality" from the Swedish security policy doctrine had little or no impact on Swedish public opinion. In the 2012 SOM survey, 17 percent of respondents agreed that "Sweden should apply for membership in NATO," while 45 percent thought it was a bad idea (Bjereld 2013).

Sweden's ever closer cooperation with NATO was manifested in participation in ISAF, which acted in connection with the US-led coalition that toppled the Taliban government in Afghanistan. It is a peacekeeping operation deployed under a UN Security Council mandate (Resolution 1386) and an agreement between ISAF and the Afghan government. Sweden has participated in ISAF since January 1, 2002, contributing approximately 330 troops to the Force. Domestically, Sweden's participation in ISAF is controversial in that, although based on a UN mandate, the operation is led by NATO. The ISAF mission has expanded over time and critics have warned that its mission is about to change from one of peace to one of war. In addition, many people believe that, in practice, it has become increasingly difficult to distinguish ISAF's UN-based business from that of the US-led coalition Enduring Freedom, the official name of the forces that overthrew the Taliban government. Through ISAF, Swedish forces became militarily engaged to an extent unprecedented on any of its previous international missions, including the UN operation in the former Belgian Congo in 1963 (Agrell 2013).

Sweden also participated in OUP enforcing the no-fly zone established over Libya by UN Security Council Resolution 1973, which gave UN member states the right to use "all necessary means" to protect Libyan civilians. Democratic uprisings in Tunisia and Algeria had spread even to Libya. The city of Benghazi, where the opposition had taken power, was facing assault by Libyan government troops, and the outside world perceived considerable risk of humanitarian catastrophe. Resolution 1973 was followed by immediate military intervention by the Western powers, initially mostly from France and the USA. Even Sweden welcomed the resolution, and a large parliamentary majority—240 in support versus 18 opposed—approved Sweden's sending of Gripen planes to monitor the UN-agreed no-fly zone over Libya. The OUP brought the Swedish Air Force into military action for the first time since the abovementioned mission in the Congo in 1963, and Sweden became party to a military mission accused of manifesting "mission creep," i.e., it was claimed that the military activities exceeded the UN mandate to protect civilians and that NATO-led forces had become a party to the conflict (Lödén 2012).

The EU's Lisbon Treaty, which entered into force on December 1, 2009, contains not only one but two declarations of member state solidarity. According to the declaration articulated in Article 222: "The Union and its Member States shall act jointly in a spirit of solidarity if a Member State is the object of a terrorist attack or the victim of a natural or man-made disaster. The Union shall mobilize all the instruments at its disposal, including the military resources made available by the Member States …." The declaration expressed in Article 42 concerns what will happen if a member state is the victim of armed aggression in its territory: "If a Member State is the victim of armed aggression on its territory, the other Member States shall have towards it an obligation of aid and assistance by all the means in their power, in accordance with Article 51 of the United Nations Charter. This shall not prejudice the specific character of the security and defence policy of certain Member States," the latter implying that nonaligned or neutral EU countries can remain so even in the future.

Finland experienced an even more liberating structural change than did Sweden through the collapse of the bipolar world order, which eliminated Finland's political ties to the Soviet Union and enabled closer transatlantic security cooperation. While the Finnish and Swedish transitions towards postneutrality are largely similar, Finland has in some regards gone further in integrating itself with the European political and security community. Like Sweden, Finland has joined NATO's Partnership for Peace and has become a member of the EU; unlike Sweden, Finland also decided to join the EMU. As EU members, Finland and Sweden have become equally engaged in the evolving European security architecture, perhaps especially concerning the capacity for international crisis management. Like Sweden, both Finland and Ireland remain militarily nonaligned, though Finland has been the most open to the prospect of future membership in NATO (Goetschel 2011; Gebhard 2013; Lödén 2012).

Concluding Discussion

There has been a gradual transformation of Sweden's *policy of neutrality* into one of *postneutrality*. The change can be seen as a consequence of the inappropriateness of the former alternative in the post-Cold-War structural setting with regard to Sweden's international role. While Sweden no longer describes its foreign and security policies in terms of neutrality, and carries out close security cooperation with the United States and with NATO, Sweden has remained militarily nonaligned and continues to reject membership in NATO. How can this paradoxical political stance be explained? Welch (2005) argues that foreign policy change occurs "when decision makers perceive that their current policies are incurring painful costs; that a failure to change policy is virtually certain to result in further painful costs; and that at least one option open to them holds forth the possibility of an acceptable outcome" (Welch 2005: 46). The transition towards a postneutral foreign policy may be seen in the context of the painful costs of remaining dedicated to the policy of neutrality once the step to join the EU had been taken. The gradual Europeanization of the Swedish foreign and security policies made a dedicated policy of neutrality increasingly problematic. The image of Sweden as a state that constructively engaged in matters of international peace and security could not be maintained through a policy of neutrality but required a transformation towards a stronger European commitment and towards engagement with the "new" NATO.

When it comes to the core of a policy of neutrality—military nonalignment—the political cost of change still remains greater than that of the status quo due to the discrepancy between the political elite and public opinion on the question of membership in NATO (Möller and Bjereld 2010; Miles 2014). An advantage for Sweden of being "inside the fence" but remaining "outside the walls" (Ferreira-Pereira 2006, 2007) consists of the opportunity to continue between the policies of neutrality and of postneutrality in the form of autonomous norm entrepreneurship with regard to international norms that serve the interests of small and medium-sized states (cf. Björkdahl 2008, 2013). The resilience of military nonalignment can also be seen in the context of its remaining strategic attractiveness as a means to maintain Sweden's national autonomy. However, some argue that the natural endpoint of the transition to a policy of post-neutrality is membership in NATO—an issue somewhat defused by the absence of any military threat to Sweden. Certainly, Russia's policy toward Ukraine and the Crimea has raised deep concerns and revitalized the Swedish defense debate, but it is still not considered to present a direct threat of war against Sweden. However, NATO has undergone a process of expansion and of evolution into an organization for broad cooperation on security policy issues. Also, the most recent surveys point in the direction of a public opinion less skeptical toward the prospect of Swedish membership. It is therefore not impossible that Sweden might eventually choose to apply for membership, given that its national autonomy would not be adversely affected.

REFERENCES

Agius, C. (2011). "Transformed Beyond Recognition? The Politics of Post-Neutrality," *Cooperation and Conflict* 46/3: 370–95.

Agius, C. and Devine, K. (2011). "'Neutrality: a Really Dead Concept?' A Reprise," *Cooperation and Conflict* 46/3: 265–84.

Agrell, W. (2013). *Ett krig här och nu: från svensk fredsoperation till upprorsbekämpning i Afghanistan 2001–2014*. Stockholm: Bokförlaget Atlantis.

Bjereld, U. (1995). "Critic or Mediator? Sweden in World Politics, 1945–90," *Journal of Peace Research* 32/1: 23–35.

Bjereld, U. (2013). "Fortsatt starkt Nato-motstånd i svensk opinion," in L. Weibull, H. Oscarsson, and A. Bergström (eds), *Vägskäl*, SOM Report 59. Göteborg: Göteborgs universitet, SOM-institutet, 611–15.

Bjereld, U., Molin, K., and Johansson, A. W. (2008). *Från igelkott till världssamvete: En bok om Sverige under kalla kriget*. Stockholm: Santérus.

Björkdahl, A. (2008). "Norm Advocacy: A Small State Strategy to Influence the EU," *Journal of European Public Policy* 15/1: 135–54.

Björkdahl, A. (2013). "Ideas and Norms in Swedish Peace Policy," *Swiss Political Science Review* 19/3: 322–37.

Carlsnaes, W. (1988). *Energy Vulnerability and National Security: The Energy Crises, Domestic Policy Responses and the Logic of Swedish Neutrality*. London and New York: Pinter Publishers.

Christiansson, M. (2010). "Solidarity and Sovereignty: The Two-Dimensional Game of Swedish Security Policy," *Baltic Security and Defence Review* 12/2: 26–49.

Cramér, P. (1989). *Neutralitetsbegreppet: Den permanenta neutralitetens utveckling*. Stockholm: Norstedts.

Cramér, P. (1998). *Neutralitet och europeisk integration*. Stockholm: Norstedts juridik.

Dalsjö, R. (2014). "The Hidden Rationality of Sweden's Policy of Neutrality during the Cold War," *Cold War History* 14/2: 175–94.

Demker, M. (1998). "A Magic Moment in Swedish Foreign Policy: Voting YES to Algerian Self-Determination in 1959," *Cooperation and Conflict* 33/2: 130–51.

Devine, K. (2011). "Neutrality and the Development of the European Union's Common Security and Defence Policy: Compatible or Competing?" *Cooperation and Conflict* 46/3: 334–69.

Doeser, F. (2008). "In Search of Security after the Collapse of the Soviet Union: Foreign Policy Change in Denmark, Finland and Sweden, 1988–1993," PhD thesis, Department of Political Science, University of Stockholm.

Ferreira-Pereira, L. C. (2006). "Inside the Fence but Outside the Walls: Austria, Finland and Sweden in the Post-Cold War Security Architecture," *Cooperation and Conflict* 41/1: 99–122.

Ferreira-Pereira, L. C. (2007). *Inside the Fence but Outside the Walls: The Military Non-aligned States in the Security Architecture of Post-Cold War Europe.* Bern: Peter Lang.

Gebhard, C. (2013). "Is Small Still Beautiful? The Case of Austria," *Swiss Political Science Review* 19/3: 279–97.

Goetschel, L. (1999). "Neutrality, a Really Dead Concept?" *Cooperation and Conflict* 34/2: 115–39.

Goetschel, L. (2011). "Neutrals as Brokers of Peacebuilding Ideas", *Cooperation and Conflict* 46/3: 312–33.

Lödén, H. (2012). "Reaching a Vanishing Point? Reflections on the Future of Neutrality Norms in Sweden and Finland," *Cooperation and Conflict* 47/2: 271–84.

Makko, A. (2012). "Advocates of Realpolitik: Sweden, Europe and the Helsinki Final Act," PhD thesis, Department of History, University of Stockholm.

Malmborg, M. af (2001). *Neutrality and State-Building in Sweden.* Wiltshire: Palgrave.

Miles, L. (2014). "Political Entrepreneurship as Painful Choices: An Examination of Swedish (Post)-Neutrality Security Policy," in I. N. Aflaki, E. Petridou, and L. Miles (eds), *Entrepreunership in the POLIS: Understanding Political Entrepreneurship.* Aldershot: Ashgate, 133–50.

Möller, U. and Bjereld, U. (2010). "From Nordic Neutrals to Post-Neutral Europeans: Differences in Finland's and Sweden's Policy Transformation," *Cooperation and Conflict* 45/4: 363–86.

Neal, J. G. (2007). "Contemporary Irish Neutrality: Still a Singular Stance," *New Hibernia Review* 11/1: 74–95.

SOU (1994:11). *Om kriget kommit … Förberedelser för mottagande av militärt bistånd 1949–1969.* Betänkande av Neutralitetspolitikkommissionen.

Welch, D. A. (2005). *Painful Choices: A Theory of Foreign Policy Change.* Princeton: Princeton University Press.

CHAPTER 33

···

SWEDEN AND THE BALTIC SEA REGION

···

RIKARD BENGTSSON

THE Baltic Sea region has undergone fundamental changes since the end of the Cold War. Being primarily defined as an area of East–West confrontation and ideological competition for half a century, the region has in the last two decades transformed into a zone of cooperation and joint problem-solving. At the same time, great challenges remain for the full realization of the region's potential; indeed, a return to a more conflict-prone situation cannot be excluded. This is reflected in two main and partly contradictory features characterizing the region. On the one hand, the region has developed a dense web of institutional dynamics and linkages—all littoral states except Russia are members of the European Union (EU), a majority of the littoral states are members of the North Atlantic Treaty Organization (NATO), regional institutions like the Council of the Baltic Sea States (CBSS) have been developed, Nordic–Baltic cooperation has been launched, and intra-Nordic cooperation has been reformed and intensified in important ways, not least in the security and defense areas. On the other hand, tensions and conflicts of various intensity between Russia and parts, or all, of the region continue to be a prominent feature of regional politics. In short, relations between Russia and the rest of the countries of the region are characterized by a challenging mix of distrust and advanced interdependence. The exact nature of the respective bilateral relations varies according to a complex set of interest-based normative and historical parameters.

These two features succinctly capture Sweden's relationship to the Baltic Sea region and therefore form the basis of the disposition of this chapter. Whereas the centrality of (distrust vis-à-vis) Russia is a generic feature of Swedish foreign policy, regional institutions-based cooperation is of more recent origin, primarily in the post-Cold-War period. From a strategic foreign policy perspective, the institutions-based approach to Baltic Sea regional cooperation can be viewed as a formula for Sweden to multilateralize relations with Russia while simultaneously reaping economic and security benefits that stem from regional and European-level interdependencies. Arguably, Sweden has played two prominent roles in the post-Cold-War Baltic Sea context—as regional integrator and as normative critic of Russia. Further, these roles are increasingly enacted through European channels, primarily the EU.

The remainder of this chapter consists of four substantive parts and a conclusion. After a general explanation of change and continuity in Swedish foreign policy, focused on the changing nature of military nonalignment and underlining the centrality of EU membership for foreign policy reorientation, the chapter introduces six main elements that define Swedish post-Cold-War Baltic Sea policy. The third and fourth sections follow a more detailed analysis of relations with Russia and the development of institutions-based regional cooperation, respectively. The chapter concludes with a discussion of the two roles pointed out above and some reflections on a possibly changing third role—that of Sweden as a security provider or consumer in the Baltic Sea region.

CHANGE AND CONTINUITY IN SWEDISH FOREIGN POLICY

As is discussed at length elsewhere in the volume, the time since the end of the Cold War has been transformative for Swedish society in a number of ways. The key driver of change is naturally Swedish membership in the European Union, a change predicated on the end of the Cold War and the transformed security environment in Europe (for discussions on structural change and the role of policy entrepreneurs, see Gustavsson 1998; Doeser and Eidenfalk 2013). In the realm of foreign policy and international relations, this change is most importantly reflected in the fact that foreign policy is no longer built on strategic neutrality between superpowers (see Bjereld and Möller in this volume) or primarily defined in terms of international solidarity focused on the Third World (as discussed in Bergman Rosamund's chapter). Rather, while maintaining the cornerstone of nonalignment, the defining trait is to seek to develop security together with others within a European frame of reference centered on the EU and in close cooperation with NATO (Carlsnaes 2005; Dahl 2012). This is clearly evident in the government's annual foreign policy declarations to the Riksdag (for example, see Swedish Government 2014), and concretely in terms of participation in operations and missions within the auspices of the EU and NATO. Substantial parts of the discursive change can be attributed to the center-right coalition government in office since 2006, but the process clearly has deeper roots, and the majority of EU missions/operations predate the non-socialist coalition. Swedish proactive engagement in NATO's partnership arrangement as well as frequent participation in exercises and in a number of operations also testifies to the shift. To be sure, Sweden's operational engagement reflects a longstanding tradition of participation in international peacekeeping operations, but the NATO flag is an indication of Sweden's reorientation in international relations.

The end of the Cold War and the subsequent fall of the Soviet Union brought fundamentally new geopolitical realities to the Baltic Sea region, including the return of a number of states that had been part of the Soviet Union. A key feature of Swedish foreign policy in the first few years of the post-Cold-War period was thus to support the fragile democracies on the eastern shore of the Baltic Sea, while also trying to arrange relations with Russia in an orderly fashion. The first steps of developing regional institutions were taken in the first half of the 1990s, at the same time, interestingly enough, that Sweden and Finland (and Norway) were completing negotiations for EU membership. All in all, this meant a focus on the regional and European context, in clear contrast to previous times. The 1991–4 center-right government under the leadership of Prime Minister Carl Bildt is associated not least with the support and assistance of the Baltic states, but it ought to be mentioned that it was the preceding Social Democratic government led by Ingvar Carlsson that applied for EU membership and the subsequent Social Democratic government headed by Göran Persson that further developed the parallel ambition of regional and European integration in the second half of the 1990s and the first half of the 2000s. It is thus a fair conclusion that reorientation of Swedish foreign policy has been embraced by large segments of the political spectrum. The centrality of Russia has remained a constant throughout the period, irrespective of government orientation. Having said that, there has been some ideological variation in the generally consensual nature of foreign policy, at least at the level of debates in the United Nations General Assembly (UNGA). As shown by Brommesson and Ekengren (2013), there are distinct differences between the center-right government of 1991–4 and the Social Democratic government that followed (1994–8), much less so between the Social Democratic government prior to the 2006 election and the center-right coalition that took office thereafter (Brommesson and Ekengren 2013: 14–16). The reasons for this may be manifold, ranging from the changing nature of the global order to the changing character of the UNGA debates, but it seems reasonable to conclude that the effect can also be ascribed to Sweden's gradual integration into the EU; over time the EU has become the natural point of reference for foreign policy, irrespective of government.

Often discussed in terms of Europeanization, Swedish foreign policy is thus arguably crafted at the interface of national and European-level processes (see further Brommesson's chapter in this volume). Meanings of Europeanization vary, but typically entail both processual aspects (how policy is formulated) and substantive ones (reciprocal processes in which member states both contribute to and are affected by policy developments at the European level (for discussions on Europeanization, see for instance Wong and Hill 2012; Michalski 2013). Europeanization is an inherent feature of policy-making in the EU invoking key questions about agenda-setting, leadership, and forms of influence. In relation to third countries (i.e. outside the EU), this process entails prospects as well as challenges: if perceived as credible by outside actors, common policy formulation renders individual member states less vulnerable and collectively stronger, but such an outcome most often requires quite advanced compromises to reach common positions. This is not least characteristic for the EU's Russia policy, which is conceptualized quite differently by the different member states—while a number of countries argue for developing and strengthening the common approach to Russia, member states have shown themselves to have dramatically different perspectives on how a policy should be framed (returning to the issue of mistrust versus advanced interdependence) and not least executed in relation to Russian foreign policy behavior.

This chapter rests on two premises: first, that Sweden's relations with Russia are intimately related to relations with the rest of the Baltic Sea states; second, that Baltic Sea dynamics cannot be understood in isolation from the processes of European integration. Hence, I argue that two interrelated sets of dynamics are at play. One concerns the transformation of Sweden's relations with Russia from the bilateral nature of historical times to a multilayered and multilateralized relationship in which the bilateral relations of various Baltic Sea states interact with European-level processes of engagement—and confrontation—with Russia. These higher-order processes most obviously concern the EU (membership and subsequent deepened integration and institutional embeddedness), but naturally also include NATO (membership or close partnership). These defining features of European integration in the Baltic Sea region contribute to underlining the difference between Russia and the rest of the Baltic Sea (for a discussion of these increasingly sharp lines of exclusivity, see Bengtsson 2009). They also mean that Sweden's relations with Russia can no longer be understood in solely bilateral terms.

The other set of linkages between regional (Baltic Sea) and European processes concerns the development of a dense institutional landscape, which is increasingly tied to, some would say subordinate to, EU structures of regional cooperation. As is analyzed later in the chapter, especially since the end of the Cold War, a great number of organizations have been set up in the region, some sector-specific in orientation, others with a broad mandate, some involving Russia, others exclusively for EU members. Over time, EU-level initiatives, which need to be understood as parts of a broader EU policy landscape, have taken on a defining role in the institutional setup in the Baltic Sea context, in effect proposing an organizational division of labor in the region and in so doing connecting specific aspects of regional problem-solving to all-European issues and dynamics. In terms of foreign policy formulation, this means that it is increasingly difficult to talk of a policy directed exclusively at the Baltic Sea. Rather, such an approach is increasingly part of processes concerning European development, welfare, competitiveness, soft security, etc.

In effect, this means that for any EU member in the region, relations with Russia and regional cooperation are not only interrelated but also take place within the larger policy realm of European integration. Regional relations are in that sense a second-tier order situated in European (and, for that matter, global) political processes. Where does this leave Sweden? What are the defining elements of Swedish relations to the Baltic Sea region? What characterizes Swedish policy towards Russia? What has been the role of Sweden in the institutional development of relevance to the region?

In addressing these questions, the subsequent analysis is informed by two sets of theoretical perspectives—internationalism and role theory. Drawing on the work of Goldmann (1994: 2), *internationalism* can be defined as "a set of beliefs to the effect that if there is more law, organization, exchange, and communication among states, this will reinforce peace and security." Transformed into policy, this means among other things promoting institutionalized cooperation, multilevel (governmental and nongovernmental) interaction and strong governance structures. Of specific relevance for our analysis is Bergman Rosamund's concept of "adjacent internationalism," which refers to a "normatively informed political process that provides a point of unification for Nordic commitments to international, European and adjacent forms of solidarity, democracy and stability" (Bergman 2006: 78; see also Bergman Rosamund's chapter in this volume). The key contribution of *role theory* is its dynamic understanding of the complex links between perceptions and behavior. Roles refer in this context to (durable but not permanent) patterns of expected, appropriate behavior. In distinguishing between role conceptions (actor self-images), role prescriptions (the expectations of others), and role performance (policy behavior by a given actor), role theory helps to illuminate continuity and change in patterns of interaction (for an overview of role theory, see Harnisch et al. 2011).

KEY ELEMENTS OF SWEDISH POLICY TOWARD THE BALTIC SEA REGION

As a point of departure for the subsequent analysis, it may be worthwhile to point to six interrelated key elements that define current Swedish policy towards the Baltic Sea region. First, the explicit acknowledgment of the relational nature of security is a defining dimension of present-day Swedish policy. It is now explicitly stated that security is constructed together with others: "Sweden's security is built in solidarity with others. Threats to peace and security are deterred collectively and in cooperation with other countries and organizations" (Swedish Government 2013a). This reflects a quite fundamental change in approach compared to previous times—while formal nonalignment remains, security cooperation and exchange have increasingly come to define Swedish relations with individual Baltic Sea states and also with institutions such as NATO.

Second, of more direct relevance to our area of interest is the normative commitment towards the security and well-being of the Nordic and Baltic states. In clear contrast to previous policy, the Swedish Riksdag in June 2009 approved the government's proposal for a unilateral solidarity declaration to the effect that Sweden would not remain passive should a neighbor be attacked or face a disaster of some sort, adding that it expects others to support Sweden in corresponding ways. The 2014 government's statement on foreign policy, delivered to the Riksdag in February 2014, repeats this fundamental point: "Our security policy and our declaration of solidarity remain firmly in place. Sweden will not remain passive if another EU Member State or Nordic country suffers a disaster or an attack. We expect these countries to act in the same way if Sweden is similarly affected. We must be in a position to both give and receive support, civilian as well as military" (Swedish Government 2014). It ought to be added that the Nordic governments in April 2011 agreed on a parallel Nordic declaration of solidarity. Debates on the necessity and contents as well as limits to solidarity have been quite vocal in recent years, not least related to discussions about the defense capabilities of varying countries, including Sweden, but few question the fundamental logic that the region, Russia excluded, approximates a security community, or zone of stable peace centered on a high degree of trust among the parties concerned (Kacowicz et al. 2000; Bengtsson 2000a, 2000b).

Third, in the same vein, support for the independence and sovereignty of the Baltic states represents a key trait of the post-Cold-War foreign policy. It was manifested as support for their membership in the EU (and, one could argue, in NATO, by underlining their absolute right to choose their security-political orientation on their own). Engagement with the Baltic states largely took institutional expression in the context of already existing Nordic institutions and not least in the form of bilateral support—monetary and technical assistance as well as concrete equipment to key state functions.

Fourth, a key aspect underpinning Swedish policy is the realization and conceptualization that regional and EU dynamics are linked, with a clearer EU primacy over time—after the entry into the EU of the three Baltic states and Poland and the subsequent development of the EU Baltic Sea strategy, the regional dynamics cannot be understood isolated from EU developments. Sweden has indeed promoted this development, most notably through pushing the EU strategy for the Baltic Sea region (see "Regional Institutional Dynamics" below). Fifth, contrary to popular belief in times of globalization and "the Pacific century," the Baltic Sea remains of key importance to Swedish economic development—46 percent of Swedish trade and 33 percent of its aggregated FDI is with the region (Statistics Sweden 2014; UNCTAD 2014). This economic interdependence carries both welfare and security implications. Sixth and finally, relations with Russia are complex and ambiguous, defined by economic interaction and practical cooperation coexisting with historical distrust (Bengtsson 2000a) and normative and security competition, in turn reflecting the intricate dynamics of interactions across the boundaries of zones of stable peace.

As these brief observations highlight, Swedish Baltic Sea policy contains elements of both continuity and change. The activist foreign policy that was previously aimed at other parts of the world remains in principle (as shown by Bergman Rosamund in this volume), but is now primarily operationalized through the interface of European and Baltic Sea political processes. Security policy has been reformed to encompass active responsibilities and expectations concerning other Baltic Sea states (be it through solidarity mechanisms or concrete military and non-military security cooperation). Russia, lastly, features as a constant concern of Swedish security planners, but is, as will be discussed in more detail in the next section, a more complex issue of prospects and problems compared to the past.

RELATIONS WITH RUSSIA

Relations with Russia have historically been at the center of Swedish foreign policy attention. Reflecting the asymmetries in size and power, Russia (and the Soviet Union) has been the key determinant of Swedish security (this is true also for the other Nordic states, especially Finland), whereas the contrary naturally does not apply: Sweden and the other Nordics have been relevant to the extent that they have been parts of a larger European dynamic, be it in the context of NATO or previous alliance formations or through policies of nonalignment (Etzold and Haukkala 2011: 249). Often characterized as the historical arch-enemy of Sweden, Russia has thus been the primary, though not always the only, focus of consecutive defense planning, and Sweden has repeatedly sought reassurances from other great powers in looser or tighter form (see further Åselius 1994; Rystad, Böhme, and Carlgren 1995; Bengtsson 2000a). Principally speaking, Russia (and the Soviet Union) has been the crucial factor determining Swedish security.

The Swedish Cold War policy of neutrality was in effect a way of managing relations with the Soviet Union and the Warsaw Pact (see further Bjereld and Möller in this volume). As was afterwards made public, it was known to all sides at the time—and, most importantly, known to the Soviets—that Sweden sought and received reassurance from the West while maintaining a public policy of neutrality. Hans Lödén argues that "the Soviets acquired a general appreciation about Sweden's Western military cooperation [but] nevertheless preferred to handle and deal with [Sweden as] an unorthodox neutral before an orthodox NATO member" (Lödén 2012: 247). Sweden's active foreign policy during the Cold War can be ascribed to its need to demonstrate credibility in order to balance its ideological leaning to the democratic West with a nonaligned security-political posture between the two military blocs in Europe (see further Möller and Bjereld 2010).

Swedish relations with Russia generally underwent an improvement in the aftermath of the dissolution of the Soviet Union, in parallel with Sweden's support of the Baltic states' independence. Sweden was the first country to open a consulate-general in Kaliningrad, reflecting the economic and political relevance attached to the enclave. Moreover, trade with Russia has increased substantially (imports from Russia grew from 0.8 percent to 4.4 percent in the period 2000–13, exports to Russia from 0.6 percent to 2.1 percent during the same years; Statistics Sweden 2014), and Sweden has increasingly come to rely on Russian oil for automobile fuel, featuring as Russia's seventh oil export destination in 2013 (EIA 2014). As developed in the next section of the chapter, the primary vehicle for Sweden's Russia policy has been institution-building, in effect embedding bilateral relations in a regional context. The enhanced "European reflex" on the part of Sweden can be found also in the context of engaging Russia. Sweden has been a clear proponent of the Northern Dimension cooperation scheme among the EU, Norway, Iceland, and Russia as well as of developing a coherent Russia policy at the level of the EU. The latter point is not least illustrated by Swedish attempts to place cooperation with Russia on the agenda during its two EU Council Presidencies thus far (2001 and 2009). Generally speaking, these efforts have reaped limited success, which may be explained by intra-EU dynamics (quite different interests, dependencies, and historical relations between EU states and Russia) as well as variation in Russia's ambitions and commitment.

Alongside attempts at constructive engagement, Swedish policy towards Russia has also contained strong criticism, generally focused on the lack of human rights and liberal democracy and the presence of generic corruption. More specifically, Sweden has for instance been a critic of the Russian treatment of the Chechen opposition, which has provoked Russian anger and accusations of protecting Chechen terrorists.

Significantly, during the 2008 Georgia crisis the Swedish government was among the harshest critics of Russia within the EU. Foreign Minister Bildt even compared Russian aggression to that of Germany in the Sudeten district in Czechoslovakia prior to World War II, which deeply upset the Russian government—diplomatic relations deteriorated to an all-time low when Russia de facto declared Foreign Minister Bildt *persona non grata* in the fall of 2008. But in international politics memory is sometimes short, and by spring 2010 Prime Minister Reinfeldt and Foreign Minister Bildt paid a state visit to Moscow (the first since 2000). The parallel with the Ukrainian crisis in early 2014 is obvious—again Sweden took a strong position within the EU, based on international law and with reference to historical parallels. Sweden has attempted an agenda-setting rather than a mediating role, which fits into a broader picture of active Swedish engagement in the eastern neighborhood of the EU, first in the form of the European Neighborhood Policy (ENP) and later through the Eastern Partnership (EaP), a platform for closer cooperation with six eastern neighbors, including Ukraine, promoted by Sweden and Poland.

The words of the government in February 2013 are illuminating in this respect: "We welcome constructive cooperation [with Russia] concerning the Baltic Sea and the Arctic. We have close economic relations ... But at the same time, we are increasingly concerned to see that respect for human rights is deteriorating, that the scope of civil society is shrinking and that the country's leaders appear to give priority to modernising the armed forces ahead of modernising Russian society" (Swedish Government 2013a). A year later, heavily influenced by the evolving Ukrainian crisis, the wording was stronger: "in country after country in our eastern European neighborhood we see unacceptable Russian pressure and threats, based on the faulty logic of the zero-sum game, being brought to bear on those who seek closer cooperation with the EU. —We want to see a relationship with Russia that rests on respect for international rules, institutions and principles. —The EU must call attention to the unacceptable human rights abuses, not least against LGBT people, and the increasing repression of civil society" (Swedish Government 2014).

In conclusion, despite elements of concrete cooperation and periods of improvement, the historic distrust (Bengtsson 2000a) remains a key feature in Swedish perspectives on Russia. In the works of the parliamentary defense commissions on threat assessments, Russia has figured prominently also in the post-Cold-War period, increasingly so since the turn of the millennium due to increases in Russian defense spending in recent years and not least the events in Georgia in late summer of 2008. Simultaneously, attention has increasingly focused on societal problems and domestic weaknesses in Russia, which may challenge stability in the region, and on Russian exploitation of its energy position for foreign policy purposes, rather than territorial aggression in the traditional sense. Debates concerning the 2013 report from the parliamentary defense commission ahead of a new defense decision in 2015 are illuminating in this sense. Having said that, the crisis in Ukraine in early 2014 will again increase concerns about Russian territorial ambitions and military intentions in its immediate neighborhood, including the Baltic states.

In recent years, Russian military exercises in the Baltic Sea, and not least its military modernization program, have cast renewed concern about Russian intentions in the greater security realm, a line of thought strongly reinforced by Russian behavior towards Ukraine and potential parallels with the Baltic states. It may thus be concluded that the strategic importance of the Baltic Sea remains. During the Cold War it held the clear East–West divide (with a special position and role for Sweden to uphold the so-called Nordic balance). Now, as the most important maritime route for energy transport in the world after the Hormuz and Malacca straits, the Baltic Sea encompasses a key dependence for Russia to reach open waters for its energy exports, of crucial importance to its economic welfare and viability. What this implies in terms of security and cooperation in the Baltic Sea region is largely a matter of assumption and perspective—either it induces a temptation for Russia to unilaterally use all available means to secure its sea lines of communication, or it induces Russia into further regional cooperation to secure a benign environment and enhanced security and safety in the region.

Irrespective of perspective, it must be noted that Russia holds the key to most of the challenges in the Baltic Sea context, be they environmental issues, maritime transport, or organized crime, just to mention a few. Taken together, a complex policy dilemma appears: how to strike the right balance between realizing economic and welfare potentials (institutional engagement) and maintaining a security policy with longstanding historical underpinnings.

REGIONAL INSTITUTIONAL DYNAMICS

A central trait of Swedish policy towards the Baltic Sea region concerns its promotion of institutions-based cooperation for joint problem-solving. This feature reflects an awareness of Sweden's relative smallness and a conceptualization of key challenges as in need of common solutions given their predominantly transnational nature. The approach has been a prominent feature of consecutive Swedish governments irrespective of party affiliation, although the means for achieving desired goals have differed substantially.

A principal expression of this policy approach is the development of intergovernmental cooperation through regional institutions. Such organizations date way back in the Nordic context (see the chapter by Brommesson in this volume) and also in a Baltic Sea perspective in specific sectors, not least regarding the marine environment, most importantly through the Baltic Marine Environment Protection Commission (or the Helsinki Commission—HELCOM), which was originally agreed in 1974 (and brought into force in 1980), then renewed in 1992 (and brought into force in 2000) (HELCOM

2014). As an expression of practical cooperation across the East/West divide during the Cold War, HELCOM has helped to inspire newer initiatives, some of which have subsequently attained great political significance. Perhaps most important of these is the Council of the Baltic Sea States (CBSS), which in parallel to HELCOM includes all littoral states as well as Russia as members (and subsequently the EU in its own right). The CBSS was originally set up on a Danish–German initiative in 1992 but substantially developed during the 1995–6 Swedish Presidency, resulting in the so-called Visby Declaration aimed at addressing common soft security challenges to the region, such as cross-border crime, and stimulating people-to-people contacts (Council of the Baltic Sea States 2014). Swedish prioritization of the CBSS is also reflected in hosting the CBSS secretariat since its establishment in 1998. Stepping up regional cooperation served two purposes for Sweden in the mid-1990s—a functional one reflecting the nature of challenges and potentials in the region, and as a balance weight to the supranational elements of EU cooperation. Developing the CBSS thus coincided with Swedish entry into the EU and reflects longstanding Swedish hesitancy towards supranationalism. Getting the CBSS to realize its full potential proved quite difficult, and after the entry of the Baltic states into the EU, the CBSS has—in line with Swedish ambitions—reoriented itself into a project-based organization. As an intergovernmental forum involving both Russia and EU members, however, it retains its political significance.

Much the same can be said about the Northern Dimension (ND), which reflects not least Swedish–Finnish ambitions to develop the EU's Russia policy around issues of common concern. ND cooperation started out as a foreign policy instrument of the EU but was reshaped in 2006 into a shared policy of Russia, Norway, Iceland, and the EU, reflecting the changing EU dynamics after the 2004 enlargement as well as a desire by the EU side to get greater Russian engagement. The ND is organized in the form of four so-called partnerships—on transport and logistics, environment, public health and social well-being, and culture—with markedly different financial preconditions, political relevance, and substantive progress (for further information on the ND, see Northern Dimension 2014).

Another key feature of the institutional approach of successive Swedish governments concerns EU enlargement in general and the inclusion of the Baltic states and Poland in European integration structures in particular (with the EU and NATO as the most prominent ones), again reflecting support for the independence of the Baltic states from the early 1990s onwards and the related longstanding argument of fundamental interest to Sweden itself, namely the right of any country to choose the security political path it sees fit. Enlargement has figured prominently in Swedish EU policy since the beginning of the Swedish membership itself, but was especially evident in connection to the 2001 EU Council Presidency, in which enlargement was one of the key priorities of the Swedish Presidency; the European Council in Gothenburg in June 2001 concluded major steps on the path of the eastern enlargement. Swedish governments have continued to push the enlargement agenda since 2004, with a focus on membership prospects for the Balkan countries as well as Turkey, not least in recent years when the multiple

European crises have challenged European solidarity and largely crowded out proactive regional and global foreign policy initiatives.

Third, Sweden has played a leadership role in promoting the various ideas of a Baltic Sea strategy for the EU. Not only did Swedish MEPs take part in the Baltic Intergroup that launched the original idea in 2005 in the European Parliament, but the Swedish government made the strategy a priority for its second EU Council Presidency—picking up the issue in 2007 to bring it to conclusion during its fall 2009 Presidency. The EU Strategy for the Baltic Sea Region (EUSBSR) has subsequently come to be the centerpiece of regional (Baltic Sea) integration, implying that regional developments are linked to a great degree to European-level dynamics and developments. The focus on the strategy can be understood from a functionalist–institutionalist perspective: most of the challenges in the region, be they environmental issues, maritime transport, or security issues, require joint action in the region, and, as we have seen, Sweden has a longstanding focus on international organization and institutional solutions. The strategy also aims at economic development in the region, and specifically at reducing the development gap between the western and eastern shores of the region, which is a fundamental interest for Sweden given the deep economic interdependence in the region. From an organizational perspective, it can be concluded that the rise of the EUSBSR has implied a division of labor in the region to the effect that the institutions referred to above—HELCOM, CBSS, ND—have (along with many others) become agents of implementation of EU-level policy development (in part for dealing with Russia, which holds the key to most challenges of the region but remains outside of the EUSBSR as it is framed as a so-called macro-regional (internal) strategy of the EU) (see Bengtsson 2011; Dühr 2011). For Sweden, this coincides with its own growing acceptance (even appreciation?) of supranational rather than intergovernmental integration, evident for instance in the government's 2013 report to the Riksdag on new directions for the EUSBSR (Swedish Government 2013b).

Fourth and finally, both developments in Arctic cooperation and the promotion of the Eastern Partnership together with Poland signal a Swedish conceptualization of relating Baltic Sea internal developments to the greater neighborhood (again linking the regional and European dimensions), spanning the whole spectrum of security, economic, and environmental issues.

In conclusion, an institutions-based approach to regional integration and governance has become the key feature of Swedish Baltic Sea policy—as such, Sweden's approach is clearly one inspired by the logic of adjacent internationalism. This is somewhat of a change compared to previous periods in foreign policy history, when institutional "anchorage" has been limited—the transformation fundamentally reflects changed geopolitical preconditions and encompasses an increasing willingness to engage in Baltic Sea and European developments rather than just immediate Nordic cooperation. Also, in the Nordic context proper, significant changes have occurred in just the last few years, with institutional reform and the expansion of cooperation into the security and defense sector. Here, it seems, there is a significant element of continuity in seeking cooperative solutions for the region. It must be noted, however, that there is a principal difference in the means for achieving regional cooperative goals—whereas in the early phase of the post-Cold-War period engagement was sought through intergovernmental regional institutions, in more recent times the European level of cooperation has become the primary driver for regional outcomes.

Conclusions: What Roles for Sweden in the Baltic Sea?

Where does this leave us in terms of Swedish approach to and role in Baltic Sea developments? Two prominent roles follow from the analysis above. The first one—regional integrator—greatly reflects the logic of adjacent internationalism and involves regional agenda-setting, institution-building as well as embedding the regional dynamics in the overall European dynamics. It has been a recurrent theme of successive Swedish governments. In relation to the Baltic states it has also included sovereignty-oriented support in forms ranging from political assistance to financial aid. A second role—that of normative critic—is primarily found in relation to Russia and includes criticism of both Russian domestic developments and its foreign policy outlook and behavior. From a Swedish perspective, the two sides (domestic and foreign policy) mirror each other as they are reproducing uncertainty and lack of trust. These two roles are mutually reinforcing—promoting regional integration through institutional means facilitates an outspoken stance on Russia, which simultaneously reinforces the promotion of liberal values at the heart of internationalism. Regional integration involving Russia is thus also a means for trying to influence Russian developments in a desired direction, thereby reducing uncertainty and distrust. Both roles have been accentuated during the post-Cold-War period (as Sweden gradually departed from its policy of neutrality) and are increasingly played out through EU channels.

An additional third role can perhaps be discerned—that of security provider—which in a sense has a longer history but which has been challenged in recent years. While not providing collective defense assurances, Sweden sought during the Cold War to contribute to the stability of the Baltic Sea through its nonaligned posture and strong defense (upholding the so-called Nordic balance between NATO allies Denmark and Norway, and Finland with its special relationship with Soviet Union). After the Cold War, security provisions also included civilian measures, defense-related support to the capabilities of the Baltic states, and not least the unilateral solidarity declaration. Over time, problem-ridden defense reform and reduced spending have come to impact negatively on Sweden's role as security provider, rendering the recipient part of the solidarity declaration more prominent. "Will Sweden become a net consumer of security—or will Svea [i.e. Sweden] wake up and seek to assume its traditional role as a stabilizing power in the Baltic Sea?" asks Charly Salonius-Pasternak, motivated by the observation that weakening military capability is at odds with Sweden's previously strong role in the region as well as with recent statements of foreign policy ambitions and not least the solidarity declaration. Salonius-Pasternak argues: "Fundamentally, Sweden no longer has a military capable of defending itself or securing the Baltic Sea around it.— ... while the Swedish "Solidarity Declaration" is a strong sign of political commitment if a neighbour is threatened or attacked, Sweden has very little military capability to send abroad during an escalating regional crisis" (Salonius-Pasternak 2013: 1), a condition that contributes to increasing talk of a security vacuum in the region, at a time when the Russian military expenditures are increasing substantially and the Ukrainian developments show that security and stability in Europe cannot be taken for granted. At the same time, Sweden ranks fourth, just after the big three, France, Germany, and the UK, in consecutive editions of the European Foreign Policy Scoreboard's annual assessment of leadership in EU foreign policy, where Sweden especially promotes policy on Russia and "wider Europe" and multilateral issues, respectively (ECFR 2014). Are these two observations at odds with each other? Not necessarily. Rather, both reflect a reorientation of Swedish security policy, now anchored in—some would say dependent on—European cooperation structures, primarily the EU regarding foreign policy, and NATO as well as Nordic partners in defense policy. Salonius-Pasternak concludes: "A country that for centuries had contributed to regional stability has become a consumer of security in less than half a decade" (Salonius-Pasternak 2013: 2). At the same time, Sweden is among the leaders regarding both the regional foreign policy of the EU (enlargement and neighborhood policies, especially the Eastern Partnership) as well as promoting the EU's global engagement, as evident, for instance, in successfully pushing for the development of an EU global strategy (an idea approved by the European Council in December 2013 but that still awaits concrete substance).

In closing, Sweden's roles in the Baltic Sea region are a reflection of Swedish ambitions, structural preconditions, and the actions of others. What does this imply for the future? Sweden's European cooperation reflex seems ingrained and is likely a constant for the foreseeable future, as is the approach to regional institutions-based cooperation—no major differences can be expected due to changes in government. The open factor is Russia—irrespective of how the Ukrainian crisis evolves in the longer term, it has made perceptions about Russia more uncertain. What this means in terms of changing Swedish role conceptions remains to be seen, in the end reflecting a choice faced also by others, including the EU, between embarking on an internationalist approach focused on common interests and cooperative security or a realist approach centered on normative competition.

REFERENCES

Åselius, G. (1994). *The "Russian Menace" to Sweden: The Belief System of a Small Power Security Elite in the Age of Imperialism*. Stockholm: Almqvist & Wiksell International.

Bengtsson, R. (2000a). "Trust, Threat, and Stable Peace: Swedish Great Power Perceptions 1905–1939," dissertation, Department of Political Science, Lund.

Bengtsson, R. (2000b). "Towards a Stable Peace in the Baltic Sea Region?" *Cooperation and Conflict* 35/4: 355–88.

Bengtsson, R. (2009). "I den stabila fredens gränsland: EU:s utvidgning och den europeiska grannskapspolitiken," in M. Jerneck (ed.), *Fred i realpolitikens skugga*. Lund: Studentlitteratur, 259–70.

Bengtsson, R. (2011). "Norden in the Arctic and Baltic Sea Region," in T. Tiilikainen and K. Korhonen (eds), *Norden—Making a Difference? Possibilities for Enhanced Nordic Cooperation in International Affairs*. Helsinki: FIIA, 53–67.

Bergman, A. (2006). "Adjacent Internationalism: The Concept of Solidarity and Post-Cold War Nordic–Baltic Relations," *Cooperation and Conflict* 41/1: 73–97.

Brommesson, D. and Ekengren, A.-M. (2013). "What Happens When a New Government Enters Office? A Comparison of Ideological Change in British and Swedish Foreign Policy 1991–2011," *Cooperation and Conflict* 48/1: 3–27.

Carlsnaes, W. (2005). "Transatlantic Relations, European Security and Swedish Foreign Policy: What Kind of Wine in What Kind of Bottles?" *Security Dialogue* 36: 402–6.

Council of the Baltic Sea States (2014). "Council of the Baltic Sea States" [homepage], <http://www.cbss.org/>, last retrieved March 19, 2014.

Dahl, A.-S. (2012). "Partner Number One or NATO Ally Twenty-Nine: Sweden and NATO Post-Libya," Research Paper No. 82. Rome: NATO Defense College.

Doeser, F. and Eidenfalk, J. (2013). "The Importance of Windows of Opportunity for Foreign Policy Change," *International Area Studies Review* 16/4: 390–406.

Dühr, S. (2011). "Baltic Sea, Danube and Macro-Regional Strategies: A Model for Trans-National Cooperation in the EU?" Notre Europe Study and Research 86. Paris: Notre Europe, Jacques Delors Institute.

ECFR (2014). "European Foreign Policy Scorecard 2014," <http://www.ecfr.eu/scorecard/2014>, last retrieved March 19, 2014.

EIA (2014). "Country Analysis Russia," <http://www.eia.gov/countries/analysisbriefs/Russia/russia.pdf>, last retrieved March 21, 2014.

Etzold, T. and Haukkala, H. (2011). "Is There a Nordic Russia Policy? Swedish, Finnish and Danish Relations with Russia in the Context of the European Union," *Journal of Contemporary European Studies* 19/2: 249–60.

Goldmann, K. (1994). *The Logic of Internationalism: Coercion and Accommodation*. London: Routledge.

Gustavsson, J. (1998). "The Politics of Foreign Policy Change," dissertation, Department of Political Science, Lund.

Harnisch, S., Frank, C., and Maull, H. W. (eds) (2011). *Role Theory in International Relations: Approaches and Analyses*. London: Routledge.

HELCOM (2014). "Baltic Marine Environment Protection Commission" [homepage], <http://helcom.fi/>, last retrieved March 19, 2014.

Kacowicz, A. M., Bar-Siman-Tov, Y., Elgström, O., and Jerneck, M. (eds) (2000). *Stable Peace among Nations*. Lanham: Rowman & Littlefield.

Lodén, H. (2012). "Reaching a Vanishing Point? Reflections on the Future of Neutrality Norms in Sweden and Finland," *Cooperation and Conflict* 47/2: 271–84.

Michalski, A. (2013). "Europeanization of National Foreign Policy: The Case of Denmark's and Sweden's Relations with China," *Journal of Common Market Studies* 51/5: 884–900.

Möller, U. and Bjereld, U. (2010). "From Nordic Neutrals to Post-Neutral Europeans: Differences in Finnish and Swedish Policy Transformation," *Cooperation and Conflict* 45/4: 363–86.

Northern Dimension (2014). "EEAS Northern Dimension" [homepage], <http://eeas.europa. eu/north_dim/index_en.htm>, last retrieved March 19, 2014.

Rystad, G., Böhme, C.-R., and Carlgren, W. (eds) (1995). *In Quest of Trade and Security: The Baltic in Power Politics 1500–1990*. Lund: Lund University Press.

Salonius-Pasternak, C. (2013). "Will Sweden Become a Net Consumer of Security—or Will Svea Wake Up and Seek to Assume its Traditional Role as a Stabilizing Power in the Baltic Sea?" FIIA Comment 19 (November 2013), available at <http://www.fiia.fi/fi/publication/382/will_sweden_become_a_net_consumer_of_security/>, last retrieved May 19, 2015.

Statistics Sweden (2014). "Foreign Trade—Exports and Imports of Goods," <http://www.scb. se/ha0201-en>, last retrieved February 27, 2014.

Swedish Government (2013a). "Statement of Government Policy in the Parliamentary Debate on Foreign Affairs 2013," <http://www.regeringen.se/content/1/c6/20/90/53/c7791e9a.pdf>, last retrieved February 27, 2014.

Swedish Government (2013b). "Ny inriktning för EU:s strategi för Östersjöregionen," Regeringens skrivelse 2013/14:29, <http://www.regeringen.se/sb/d/16997/a/226897>, last retrieved March 11, 2014.

Swedish Government (2014). "Statement of Government Policy in the Parliamentary Debate on Foreign Affairs 2014," <http://www.government.se/sb/d/5304/a/234235>, last retrieved February 27, 2014.

UNCTAD (2014). UNCTADStat database, <http://unctad.org/en/Pages/Statistics.aspx>, last retrieved April 29, 2014.

Wong, R. and Hill, C. (eds) (2012). *National and European Foreign Policies: Towards Europeanization*. London: Routledge.

....

CHAPTER 34

SWEDISH
INTERNATIONALISM
AND DEVELOPMENT AID

....

ANNIKA BERGMAN ROSAMOND

INTRODUCTION

....

SCHOLARLY inquiries into Swedish internationalism tend to center on the country's longstanding social democratic legacy (Aigus 2006; Bergman 2007; Lawler 2005). While social democratic ideology remains a key marker of Swedish internationalism, it has been challenged by the electoral victories of the center-right coalition in 2006 and 2010. Despite being different in their ideological roots, both the social democratic and liberal variants of internationalism exhibit strong commitments to global justice, solidarism, and peaceful settlement of conflict within and beyond borders (Schouenborg 2012). The practical expressions of these ambitions are, for example, comparably generous provisions of overseas development assistance (ODA) (Bergman 2006, 2007), strong activism within the United Nations (UN), support for international peace support, human rights, and "gender cosmopolitanism," including promoting women's security and protection beyond borders (Bergman Rosamond 2013). Sweden's self-narrative, although somewhat mythical (Bergman 2007; Ryner 2002), is that of a state ethically committed to the well-being of citizens and non-citizens alike (Bergman Rosamond 2011, 2013). However, this self-perception has been tarnished by the growing discomfort amongst the Swedish electorate with immigration, as suggested by the electoral success of *Sverigedemokraterna*, a right-wing populist party, in 2010. The overall objective of this chapter is to provide an assessment of Swedish internationalism by unpacking its social democratic roots as well as its liberal expressions, as pursued by the center-right coalition that governed from 2011 to 2014, *the Alliance for Sweden* (my translation). The chapter is intellectually situated within scholarship on Swedish (and Nordic) internationalism (Lawler 2013; Aigus 2006; Browning, 2007; Bergman 2007). Christine Aigus (2006), for example, has studied the connection between Swedish internationalism, social democracy, and the defense doctrine of neutrality, which will be discussed in greater detail later. The empirical focus is Sweden's commitment to a more equitably distributed international income through generous provisions of overseas development assistance.

The chapter commences by discussing the liberal roots of Western internationalism as theory and practice, and how it relates to the Swedish context. It then moves on to examine the distinct features of Sweden's social democratically inspired internationalism, with its focus on solidarism within and beyond borders and the country's longstanding tradition of neutrality (and nonalignment), all of which are closely linked to internationalism (Aigus 2006; Bjereld and Möller in this volume). The chapter then provides a brief investigation into the internationalist tradition of the Alliance by comparing and contrasting it with its social democratic counterpart. The inquiry below will show that the two traditions share certain commitments to international justice and solidarism while framing their discursive commitments in somewhat different language. Instructive here is the center-right's attempts to add pro-market and entrepreneurial elements to Swedish aid policy, taking more of a neoliberal stance on development. In sum, by discursively studying a select few policy documents and figures as well as tracing variations and similarities across the party spectrum, the chapter demonstrates the contemporary connections and disjunctions between Sweden's social democratic and liberal internationalist traditions. As already noted, the emphasis here is on the country's provision of foreign assistance, which is often viewed as a key component of social democratic internationalism (Pratt 1990). The idea is to show that the levels of such assistance have not significantly fluctuated over time, but that the discourses pursued by the center-right government are more pronouncedly rooted in liberal ideology. The conclusion contends that Sweden's social democratically inspired internationalist tradition has recently been challenged by the shift toward liberalism as a source of ideological inspiration (Ryner 2002; Aigus 2007), and intolerance toward newcomers, as well as the shift towards military internationalism in Swedish foreign and security policy (Aggestam and Hyde-Price in this volume).

LIBERAL AND SOCIAL DEMOCRATIC ATTRIBUTES OF INTERNATIONALISM

Western internationalisms are ideologically associated with liberalism and its broad cosmopolitan assumption that all human beings are part of a shared moral order and that we have obligations beyond our own sovereign selves. However, Fred Halliday (1988: 188; see also Lawler 2005) has argued there are different internationalisms ranging from liberal, hegemonic to revolutionary traditions, all of which concede that "we both are and should be part of a broader community than that of the nation or the state." Adam Smith stressed the importance of global trade and commerce in seeking to curb

the tension and conflict between states. Immanuel Kant's (1991) liberal cosmopolitanism emphasized republican and responsible governments, rule of law, free trade, and
a commitment to social harmony as well as hospitality to non-citizens as a route to
perpetual peace. American President Woodrow Wilson, known for his liberal internationalist ideas during the interwar period, reiterated Kant's ideals; in particular, the
need for domestic change and progressive foreign policy to prevent callous national
interests from dominating national foreign policies. To achieve this goal and make way
for a more orderly or even just international society, states needed to promote binding
international law, institutions, the principle of self-determination, global communications, negotiations, and peaceful and dialogic settlement of disputes (Bergman 2002).
As Ian Clark and Chris Reus-Smit (2013: 38–9) have argued, "liberal internationalism
is an ordering project, a set of ideas and attendant practices designed to organize the
political life of the globe in distinctive ways … (l)iberal internationalism is a procedural doctrine, prescribing the sovereign equality of states and multilateral decision-
making." Kjell Goldmann (1994: 2) has defined internationalism as "a set of beliefs to
the effect that if there is more law, organization, exchange, and communication among
states, this will reinforce peace and security." In the post-Cold-War era, liberal internationalist ideas surrounding multilateralism and liberal peace became key norms again,
and these have been supported by the Social Democratic Party (SAP) and its opponents
alike. In this context one might also add that liberal internationalism post-9/11 has frequently been associated with the West's ongoing military and non-military interventionist projects and impositions of liberal democratic principles on non-Western states
(Jahn 2007). Sweden has not been unaffected by this reconstitution of liberal internationalism, having participated in a number of military operations beyond borders in
the post-9/11 era (Kronsell 2012; Bergman Rosamond 2011; Aggestam and Hyde-Price
in this volume) as well as having sought to contribute to the democratization of places
such as Afghanistan.

Social democratic internationalism, as pursued by Sweden, in fact, shares many of the
ideas associated with liberal internationalism, not least an ethical commitment to international cooperation and peaceful settlement of conflict within and beyond borders.
Eduard Bernstein, a nineteenth-century German proponent of reformist socialism,
believed that it was possible to combine Kantian ethics with Marxist economic principles to achieve a moral order built on socialist principles. He argued that "(o)f course we
don't have to slavishly adhere to Kant's form, but we must match his method" (cited in
Steger 1997: 67) to further the reformist socialist project. While being historically rooted
in nineteenth-century Marxist ideology, European social democracy soon surrendered
its revolutionary ambition and moved toward a gradual (and democratic) transformation of international and domestic society. This in turn had constitutive effects on
social democratic internationalism, which historically has favored peaceful coexist-
ence between states and a rule-bound international society, much in line with the liberal
internationalist tradition (Bergman 2002), while being cautious in assuming that free
market policies can alone solve the world's injustices. Key here is the idea "that affluent
societies have moral obligations to assist the populations of the poorer states" (Linklater

1998: 208), an objective that Swedish social democrats have sought to realize through a strong commitment to a more equitably redistributed global income (Bergman 2007; Browning 2007).

Crawford Pratt argued in the 1990s that, although there are many different internationalisms, "there is much in the political values of social democracy and of other socialist movements which is responsive to humane internationalist appeals" (1990: 145). Furthermore, "the most compelling evidence of the strength of the humanitarian component of their internationalism is provided by the substantial development assistance programmes of these countries" (Pratt 1989: 7; also see Bergman 2007). Social democratic internationalism is thus located within redistributive discourses of global income that are broadly in line with a cosmopolitan global ethic, which seeks to aid the least privileged in international society (Bergman Rosamond 2013). Moreover, Alison Brysk's (2009: 62) study of Sweden as a "Global Good Samaritan" identifies a strong link between the country's promotion of global "human rights norms" and its distinct notion of "national democracy" and "national ideology of social democracy." However, there are critical voices that question the distinctiveness of contemporary social democratic policies and their global legitimacy. Luke Martell (n.d.: 5), for example, suggests that contemporary social democracy needs to reconstitute itself in a fashion that is "friendlier to outsiders" at least "if it wants to call itself cosmopolitan" and as such stay faithful to its previously noted Kantian roots. This echoes the point already made that Sweden's self-perception as a "good state" (Lawler 2005) is being challenged by growing intolerance towards newcomers. Below, the domestic and global attributes of Sweden's social democratic internationalism will be discussed with emphasis on redistributive justice and its policy of nonalignment.

Sweden's Social Democratic Self-Identity

Here, a broad social constructivist framework (Bergman 2007, 2002) will be employed to identify the ideational roots of Swedish social democratic internationalism. This involves asking questions about the social origins of the country's self-identity and how these can be traced through to its internationalist tradition (Bergman 2007), and taking account of poststructural assumptions about the construction of national identity (Hansen 2006). Research exploring constructions of selfhood has frequently focused on the manner in which the self discursively emerges through the identification of difference in the other, whether a state, a region, or an individual. Identity then is relational and it is only by positioning the self in relation to the other that the self can be fully understood and constituted. But as Lene Hansen and others have pointed out, the self does not have to come about through radical othering, but can emerge through less hostile forms of identity construction (Campbell 1992; Hansen 2006: 39). This insight allows for an investigation of "Sweden's international self-identity" that "traces its distinctiveness rather than juxtaposing it with" a radically different other (Bergman Rosamond 2011: 60). So what are the distinct markers of Sweden's self-understanding? A central feature is its commitment to a universal welfare model that does not discriminate on the basis of gender, class, and ethnicity. Social democratic notions of solidarism and welfare are "majoritarian" since they encompass the Swedish "people" rather than "class" (Esping-Andersen 1985: 32). Historically, the universal welfare model "crowds out the market, and consequently constructs an essentially universal solidarity in favour of the welfare state" (Esping-Andersen 1985: 28). Solidarity is viewed as a universal value, which has wider appeal than the working class. What is more, the practices and discourses of solidarity domestically have helped to constitute Sweden's self-narrative and sense of ethical obligation to distant others (Palme 1968: 179; Bergman 2002, 2007; Lawler 1997; Aigus 2006). Steinar Stjernö (2005: 182) captures this position well in the following passage:

> From around 1960 until the beginning of the 1980s the concept of solidarity with the Third World became part of the modern social democratic ideology of solidarity in party programs. Electoral considerations were hardly conducive to this development. The inclusion of this aspect of solidarity was not based on ideas about self-interest, but on an altruistic compassion for the plight of people living in the poor world.

Pertti Joenniemi (1997: 212) has noted that "the word solidarity has had a real meaning in Norden, providing leeway for a generative grammar that goes beyond the dictates of states' sovereignty." The Nordic states have "branded" (Browning 2007) themselves as "exceptional" states (Lawler 1997), having pursued a "middle way" between socialism and capitalism and having a preference for "solidarist internationalism and the general peacefulness of the Nordic region" (Schouenborg 2012: 106). Sweden's self-identity then is the embodiment of specific domestic understandings of normative relations between the self and other and the preference for universal justice, at home and abroad. Solidarity is meaningful in the Swedish context, rather than being an unattainable ideal reserved to fellow citizens alone, even if this self-narrative is somewhat mythical and has been challenged in several ways (Bergman 2007; Ryner 2002). Indeed, Olof Palme (1972: 1) argued that "Social Democracy means solidarity" and internationalism and solidarity have meaningfully "acquired a status of national ideology" (Trädgårdh 2002: 152). Olof Palme (1968: 202) furthermore argued that "solidarity has no boundaries," which is suggestive of a mutually co-constitutive relationship between domestic and international appeals to justice. As will be discussed, the recipients of Sweden's borderless solidarism were frequently small states with experiences of colonial repression. In his discussion of *Norden* as a distinct brand, Browning (2007: 34) observes that "solidarity with the Third World was perhaps most important to Sweden, where it became a highly idealistic element of the country's foreign policy." Such idealism has produced generous commitments to ODA over time.[1] Key to Sweden's aid policies, historically and contemporarily, has been its wish to promote gender equality globally, and here the SAP and the Alliance do not differ much in their sense of ethical obligation (Bergman Rosamond 2013).

SOCIAL DEMOCRATIC INTERNATIONALISM, NEUTRALITY, AND NONALIGNMENT

Swedish internationalism is ideationally linked with the country's longstanding neutrality and nonalignment traditions, the latter of which remains the normative basis for Swedish defense policy (Bjereld and Möller in this volume). Aigus (2006: 6), for example, identifies a strong link between neutrality, solidarity, and self-identity. Neutrality is, in part, an identity-building exercise that sits at the core of Sweden's state-building project (Aigus 2006: 6). Aigus's contention is that "the folkhem (People's Home), solidarity and universalism were potent metaphors which were tied to Swedish neutrality as much as they were to Swedish society, economics and politics" (Aigus 2006: 7). Neutrality did not significantly restrict Swedish internationalism during the Cold War, but enabled it to adopt an active role as mediator and bridge builder in conflicts (Bjereld 1992; Jerneck 1990; Viklund 1989) and supporter of developing nations (Aigus 2006: 6; Bergman and Peterson 2006). By projecting itself as a neutral partner of small and medium-sized postcolonial states in need of foreign assistance, Sweden sought to disperse democratic and peaceful ideas, as well as contributing to economic development across the globe (Bergman 2006).

Sweden's entry into the European Union (EU) in 1995 required a departure from its strict neutrality policy in favor of nonalignment, which allowed it to become a full member of the EU, including its Common Foreign and Security Policy (CFSP). In 2002, the main political parties agreed on a new policy direction stating that "Sweden is militarily nonaligned" and should "remain neutral in the event of conflicts within its vicinity" (Bergman and Peterson 2006: 151). In June 2009 the Swedish parliament adopted a "Solidarity Declaration" stating that "Sweden would not stand passive if a neighbor is threatened or attacked. We expect others not to stand passive if Sweden is threatened. We must be able both to provide and receive support, with relevant capabilities, also of a military nature" (Tolgfors 2009: 1). This discursive turn confirms the country's departure from its previous neutrality doctrine in favor of active engagement in EU- and NATO-led operations and crisis management strategies (Bergman Rosamond 2011; Kronsell 2012). Sweden has participated in NATO-led operations in Afghanistan and Libya, although both were sanctioned by the UN. Sweden's participation in such operations has been supported by the SAP and the Alliance alike. Both sides of the party spectrum have sought to reconcile Sweden's "roles as a peaceful former neutral and a war-fighting NATO associate in a fashion consistent with its internationalist tradition" and "the ongoing internationalization of the Swedish Armed Forces is key to the country's self-identification as a good internationalist state" (Bergman Rosamond 2011: 63).

Yet, the SAP maintains its position that there is a strong link between nonalignment and the country's internationalist tradition (Bergman Rosamond 2011: 62).

So far, we have established that solidarism within and across borders as well as neutrality are key components of Swedish social democratic internationalism. However, Swedish practices and discourses of solidarity have been challenged by the broad trends of globalization and neoliberalism (Ryner 2002, 2003; see also Lindvall and Rueda 2013: 1), the liberal reconstruction of social democratic ideology (Aigus 2007), the electoral success of the Alliance, and the liberalization of welfare provisions, as well as growing hostilities towards immigrants in Swedish society. A broad social constructivist approach would, nonetheless, tell us that key historical values might be sufficiently embedded within the fabric of a society to withstand some of the pressures for change (Bergman 2002). The next section focuses on the internationalist discourses of the SAP and those of the Alliance.

INTERNATIONALIST DISCOURSES IN A DEVELOPMENT CONTEXT

A key assumption within most forms of discourse analysis is that discourses are not neutral reflections of reality, but rather help to constitute that reality: for example, the reality/ies of Swedish internationalism. Put another way, the ideational and the material are co-constitutive. The material is always mediated through discourse (Hansen 2006). Discourses then attach "meanings to social and physical realities. It is through discourse that individuals ... and states make sense of themselves, of their ways of living, and of the world around them" (Epstein 2008: 2). In what follows an attempt will be made to understand the meanings that are attached to Swedish internationalism across the party spectrum by closely studying a set of official documents. In 2005, while still in office, the SAP launched an international program which placed the well-being of individuals across borders and their "development, ... freedom, ... will to grow, ... sense of obligation to other generations, ... solidarity with others" at the center of its international agenda. This can be understood as a commitment to human security and development, rather than an orthodox conception of state security. Furthermore, the program emphasizes a "wish to combat economic and social cleavages, expand upon solidarity and contribute to a world in which poverty and powerlessness are in the past" (*Socialdemokraterna* 2005: 2), thus retaining a commitment to typically social democratic internationalist values. Furthermore, the SAP launched an "Agenda for Global Development" in 2013 in which it presented its broad visions of development and globalization in international society:

> Almost a billion people go to bed hungry every evening and many billions of people live in poverty ... People's basic rights are not respected. Social and economic cleavages are growing in parallel with rapid economic growth ... Globalization

is a strong ... force. Trade, migration, technical innovation, meetings and movements bring people and countries closer together ... We human beings are mutually
dependent on each other ... In a globalized world there is more demand for stronger
forms of international co-operation ... Shared international and multilateral forums
need to be strengthened. Our policy for global development is about eradicat-
ing poverty and promoting economic, social and environmental development ...
The Social Democrats believe in the opportunities of globalization but we also note
that many human being and countries cannot make use of these opportunities
(*Socialdemokraterna* 2013: 4, my translation).

The document also contains references to the SAP's historical narrative as an actor deeply
committed to bilateral development assistance. For example, it refers to Proposition 100,
a significant piece of legislation dating back to 1962 that laid out the future platform for
Swedish bilateral assistance (*Socialdemokraterna* 2013: 6, my translation). Furthermore,
the SAP makes discursive use of its legacy as an international movement which "for generations has combatted poverty, exploitation of people and the environment, repression
and injustices." By invoking its historical identity as a long-established development
actor it adds legitimacy to its current policy commitments.

In opposition, the SAP has criticized the governing coalition's aid policy for being
misused (*Socialdemokraterna* 2007) and poorly governed (*Socialdemokraterna* 2014). In
2007 the SAP delivered an alternative foreign policy declaration to parliament in which
it rejected the "undermining of aid carried out by the government" by allocating "1.5
million SEK from the 2007 aid budget to write off debts for Swedish companies' deals
in Liberia and the Congo in the 1970s," reiterating its position that "aid funds ought to
be used only for development cooperation and fighting poverty" (*Socialdemokraterna*
2007: 15). This could be understood as an early criticism of the Alliance's liberalization
of Swedish aid policy. In its 2014 shadow foreign policy declaration, the SAP criticized
the Alliance's aid policy for being ineffectively governed and lacking in vision as well as
being generally insufficient in its operation (*Socialdemokraterna* 2014: 8). Moreover, the
SAP foreign policy spokesperson Urban Ahlin criticized the Alliance for neglecting the
UN as a platform for Swedish internationalism and solidarity more broadly (*Omvärlden*
2013).

The social democratic story about Sweden as recounted throughout this chapter is
an important one. However, it is not the only one. Kjell Goldmann's (2008) criticism of
Christine Agius's (2006) singular reading of Sweden's social democratic identity is telling here. In his view there are multiple articulations of *Swedishness*, and social democracy is but one source of ideational inspiration. The center-right coalition, the Alliance of
Sweden,[2] during its eight years in office challenged the SAP by introducing reforms in the
welfare, health, and education sectors, while introducing large-scale tax cuts, the effects
of which have been felt across weaker parts of national society. Yet the liberalization of
services was initiated by the SAP in the late 1980s and early 1990s (Ryner 2002). As Aigus
(2007: abstract) puts it, "(f)or some decades, a 'battle of ideas' has developed over the
Swedish Model and the welfare state" which enabled the center-right Alliance to "realign
the public towards a greater acceptance of individualism and the free-market economy."

Part of the Alliance's electoral success can be attributed to the Swedish Conservative Party *Moderaterna*'s deliberate effort to reconstitute itself as a new labor party and, as such, adopt some of the SAP's rhetorics, including that of full employment. In this context, Bo Rothstein has argued that *Moderaterna* had to tone down its conservative agenda and adopt certain social democratic features to win the 2006 election (Rothstein cited in *Dagens Nyheter*, 2006). In his view, the election of the coalition was a "Social Democratic triumph" because typically social democratic values had become sufficiently embedded in Swedish political culture to withhold significant shifts to the right.

Yet, the Alliance's election manifesto of 2006 was ideologically situated within broad liberal discourses, by which individual freedom, responsibility, and entrepreneurship were highlighted (*Nya Moderaterna* 2006). The full employment strategy that had helped the Alliance's electoral success in 2006 was repeated in its joint 2010 election manifesto: "we want to take responsibility for our country and create good conditions for work and welfare" (*Alliansen* 2010: 2). Furthermore, there is a strong liberal undertone running through the discourses informing the 2010 manifesto whereby individuals are encouraged to use their own initiative and "realize their ambitions," thus invoking the liberal message of human progress, liberty, and choice. These commitments have been continuously echoed throughout the Alliance's second period in office.

Having briefly identified the broad discursive markers of the Alliance's domestic policy profile, the chapter now turns to the coalition's joint foreign policy vision and internationalist rhetoric, with a focus on development. The alliance's policy discourses on global welfare commitments beyond borders, peace support, and multilateralism are couched within broad liberal language that emphasizes "freedom, peace and reconciliation ... democracy, human rights and sustainable development ... and multilateral cooperation" (*Regeringskansliet* 2014: 1). The Alliance's emergent internationalist tradition is thus liberal, exhibiting a strong commitment to the rights and freedoms of individuals. In a speech to the UN the Swedish Foreign Minister Carl Bildt (2012: 1) stated his government's commitment to "protecting individual human beings—their life, their freedom, their future" by "promoting peace, stability and prosperity across the globe. And critical to these efforts are gender equality and empowerment of women. Because it's right, because it's smart and because it's fundamental to realizing the economic and political potential of societies."

Similarly, the Alliance's (*Regeringen* 2014) development policy is discursively framed within cosmopolitan notions of obligation to distant others, in a fashion similar to the SAP as well as the broad principles of liberal internationalism. In practice, the coalition matches such language with comparably generous budget commitments to ODA, with Sweden now being one of the very few states in the OECD that lives up to the UN-set target of 1 percent in Gross Net Income (GNI) (see Table 34.1). However, the liberal (and social democratic) undertones of the Alliance's development policy are coupled with a good deal of emphasis on neoliberal economic principles, such as entrepreneurship and market-orientated solutions to global poverty. The Alliance's position is clearly outlined in the text "Development Policy Platform" in which it highlights the significance of using Swedish development assistance to improve the private sector in the recipient countries so as to create new and gender-neutral jobs (*Regeringen* 2014: 24–6). Moreover, Swedish ODA should promote entrepreneurship with an emphasis on women's initiatives, innovation,

Table 34.1 Provisions of ODA as a percentage of GNI, 2011

Year	Denmark	France	Luxembourg	Netherlands	Norway	Sweden	USA	UK
2005	0.81	0.47	0.84	0.82	0.94	0.94	0.22	0.47
2011	0.85	0.46	0.97	0.75	1.00	1.02	0.20	0.56

Source: OECD (2011)

and industry, as well as enabling small companies to grow and develop. Such initiatives are promoted against the backdrop of a broader Swedish commitment to corporate social responsibility and sustainable development (see Swedish International Development Agency 2009). Moreover, the significance of "inclusive and effective markets" (*Regeringen* 2014: 25) and property rights are emphasized, as these are believed to facilitate the reduction of poverty and lead to job creation as well as access to financial markets and in the final analysis economic growth. Sweden's former development minister Gunilla Carlsson (2012: 1) has reiterated this position on several occasions by arguing that:

> We need a dynamic approach that focuses on the individual; where entrepreneurs and human rights activists are active drivers of change; where women and girls are in control of their lives; where innovators offer new solutions to old problems. Development will not happen without institutions … Aid alone will not do the trick. In order to combat poverty and increase the rights and freedoms of people, we need to use all the policy tools available to us … Aid needs to go hand-in-hand with policies for trade liberalization, peace and security and climate change.

In sum, it would seem that the Alliance's development discourses are an outflow of a dual commitment to universal justice and such things as entrepreneurship and innovation, the latter of which can be viewed as an outflow of the Alliance's domestic preference for such values at home. The next section will explore the practical expressions of Swedish development policy by taking stock of the co-constitutive relationship between its domestic and international welfare commitments (Bergman 2007).

DEVELOPMENT POLICY: AN OUTFLOW OF CO-CONSTITUTIVE OBLIGATION

A key argument developed throughout this piece has been that there is a connection between Sweden's commitments to universal welfare within and beyond borders. As the present author has proposed elsewhere (Bergman 2006: 76):

> [S]tates that do not practise universal welfare at the domestic level are less likely to do so at the international level, a glaring example being the USA, a state that

only provides a minimal level of social welfare to its own citizens and whose ODA provisions only amounted to 0.15% of GNI in 2003, a figure that is well below the OECD average and barely more than one-fifth of the Nordic states' national contributions.

This argument is illustrated in Tables 34.1 and 34.2. For example, they demonstrate that the three Scandinavians, Denmark, Norway, and Sweden, are amongst the most generous providers of ODA while retaining a strong commitment to domestic welfare. A word of caution should be entered here though, as Sweden has experienced a good number of cutbacks in the welfare sector with unemployed and people on long-term sick leave having seen their benefits being reduced in recent years.

As the figures show, Sweden, however, remains one of the most generous welfare regimes globally and the assumption that there is a co-constitutive relationship between states' provisions of overseas development assistance and their domestic welfare commitments seem to hold water. Because generous provisions of ODA are closely linked with Sweden's self-narrative as a provider of welfare at home and abroad, it would be difficult for any political party, irrespectively of ideological tradition, to reduce such financial commitments. Recent opinion polls show that the great majority of Swedes are in favor of generous provisions of development assistance (Swedish International Development Agency 2012: 12). Indeed, the Swedish public retains a strong commitment to ODA and does not seem to suffer from donor fatigue. In 1982, approximately 70 percent of the Swedish people were reported to hold a positive attitude towards foreign assistance, and this figure has remained approximately the same for the past 30 years (Swedish International Development Agency 2012). Generally speaking, women are more in favor of ODA than their male counterparts, and people living in urban areas are also more positive in their attitudes than rural populations (Liljeström 2012: 12). Moreover, the figures do not significantly fluctuate over time or as result of change of government (Liljeström 2012), thus suggesting that Third World solidarity is a universal Swedish value not necessarily confined to SAP voters. In the next section the recipients of Swedish ODA will be outlined in an effort to identify recent shifts in the selection of such countries.

Table 34.2 Total public social expenditure as a percentage of GNI, 2005 and 2011

YEAR	Denmark	France	Luxembourg	Netherlands	Norway	Sweden	USA	UK
2005	27.7	30.1	22.8	20.7	21.6	29.1	16.0	20.5
2011	30.0	32.1	22.4	23.7	22.6	27.6	19.7	23.9

Source: OECD (2013)

RECIPIENTS OF ODA

During the Cold War period the recipients of Swedish ODA were frequently small and medium-sized states in Africa and elsewhere, whose new postcolonial ruling elites were sympathetic to Sweden's social democratic conceptions of justice and freedom (Bergman 2006). The four Nordic states' individual and collective opposition to the apartheid regime in South Africa is testament to this claim (Sellström 1999, 2002; Morgenstierne 2003).[3] However, as Table 34.3 shows, Sweden has redirected its provisions of ODA in the past ten years so as to target states that not only suffer poverty, but also long-lasting conflict, with Afghanistan being a typical example here. This could also be seen as an effort on the part of the ruling coalition and the SAP to justify Sweden's participation in military operations beyond borders to the general public. The Afghan operation, for example, has frequently been constructed as an effort to bring peace and development to that country as well as liberating Afghani women, which has become a foreign policy strategy in its own right (Bergman Rosamond 2013).

In sum, there is a strong connection between Sweden's current external security and peace commitments and its provisions of aid, with Afghanistan and the Democratic Republic of Congo being among the three most favored recipients of ODA during the period 2010–11. This strategy was also employed by the Social Democrats when they were in power prior to 2006. Military engagements during this period were accompanied by generous provisions of ODA, with Serbia and Bosnia Herzegovina being prioritized recipient countries during the last SAP government (see Table 34.3). Sweden's participation in international operations in the former Yugoslavia, the DRC, Darfur, and Afghanistan indicates that there is a constitutive relationship between the country's provisions of international peace support and participation in military interventions,

Table 34.3 Swedish provisions of ODA, country by country

Country by country 2000–1	Country by country 2010–11
1. Tanzania	1. Democratic Republic of Congo (DRC)
2. Mozambique	2. Tanzania
3. Honduras	3. Afghanistan
4. Vietnam	4. Mozambique
5. Serbia	5. Sudan
6. Bangladesh	6. Kenya
7. South Africa	7. West Bank/Gaza Strip
8. Nicaragua	8. Somalia
9. West Bank Gaza Strip	9. Uganda
10. Bosnia Herzegovina	10. Ethiopia

Source: OECD (2006, 2011)

albeit for humanitarian purposes, and the geographical distribution of Swedish aid across the world.

CONCLUSION

By employing a broad inside-out social constructivist framework and offering a brief discursive analysis of key texts, this chapter has contended that Sweden's self-narrative is that of an internationalist state with a strong sense of obligation to distant others. What is more, this vision seems to be largely shared by the center-right coalition and the SAP, both of which have a strong commitment to old-style liberal internationalist principles such as support for human rights, international institutions, and law. Yet, as has been contended in the last sections of this chapter, there are significant variations between the two political camps, with the Alliance discursively framing its development policy within more pronouncedly market-orientated language. The overarching question informing the discussion throughout this piece is whether there is sufficient room for two competing internationalist traditions in Sweden? It is too early to offer a full assessment of the future of Swedish internationalism at this stage. However, what we can say with some certainty is that Swedish internationalism is situated at the crossroad between a historically constituted, social democratically inspired model and liberal reinterpretations of that model. Both the SAP and the Alliance are engaged in the export and promotion of what they interpret as typically Swedish norms, with Third World solidarity, tolerance, peaceful conflict resolution, gender equality, and sustainable development being amongst the most significant normative goals here. The Alliance is to a greater extent inclined to place entrepreneurship and the human being's liberal freedoms at the heart of its development policies, which can be traced back to its preference for such values domestically. What is perhaps more revealing is that both the Alliance and the SAP have come increasingly to view participation in military operations for humanitarian purposes as a significant aspect of Sweden's internationalist tradition. Such military ventures have been accompanied by redirections in the geographical dispersion of Swedish ODA to conflict societies such as the DRC, Sudan, and Afghanistan, where Swedish troops have been employed for humanitarian purposes. Here it is also worth mentioning the 2010 electoral success of the populist anti-immigrant party *Sverigedemokraterna*, which has seriously challenged Sweden's international reputation as a welcoming and tolerant cosmopolitan nation. Intolerance towards immigrants and the interventionist logic that underpins much of contemporary Swedish foreign and security policy challenge the country's historically constituted self-identity as an exceptional state (Lawler 1997). Moreover, the liberalization of Swedish society more broadly and structural changes to the Swedish welfare sector challenge the ethos of Sweden's co-constitutive welfare obligation within and beyond borders. This, if anything, promises to be an interesting normative research agenda for students of Swedish internationalism and foreign policy more broadly.

Notes

1. See Bergman (2007: 86) for an account of Western states' budget commitments to ODA as well as their social expenditure at home in earlier periods.
2. The Alliance is composed of the Swedish Conservative Party (*Moderaterna*), the Liberal Party (*Folkpartiet*), the Christian Democratic Party (*Kristdemokraterna*), and the Center Party (*Centerpartiet*).
3. The present author has thoroughly explored the Nordic states' post-Cold-War relationship with their three Baltic neighbors, which she argues is closely related to the former's historical pursuit of small-state internationalism in Africa and elsewhere. She has labeled this solidarist arrangement "adjacent internationalism" (Bergman 2002, 2006).

References

Aigus, C. (2006). *The Social Construction of Swedish Neutrality: Challenges to Swedish Identity and Sovereignty*. Manchester: Manchester University Press.

Aigus, C. (2007). "Sweden's 2006 Parliamentary Election and After: Contesting or Consolidating the Swedish Model?" *Parliamentary Affairs* 60/4: 585–600.

Alliansen (2010). *Valmanifest 2010–2014*, <http://www.moderat.se/sites/default/files/attachments/valmanifest_2010.pdf>, last retrieved April 8, 2014.

Bergman, A. (2002). "Adjacent Internationalism: The Concept of Solidarity and Post-Cold War Baltic–Nordic Relations," PhD thesis, Sussex European Institute, University of Sussex.

Bergman, A. (2006). "Adjacent Internationalism: The Concept of Solidarity and Post-Cold War Nordic–Baltic Relations," *Cooperation and Conflict* 41/1: 73–97.

Bergman, A. (2007). "Co-constitution of Domestic and International Welfare Obligations: The Case of Sweden's Social Democratically Inspired Internationalism," *Cooperation and Conflict* 42/4: 73–99.

Bergman, A. and Peterson, J. (2006). "Non-aligned States and the ESDP," in R. Dannreuther, and J. Peterson (eds), *Security and the Transatlantic Alliance*. London: Routledge, 147–64.

Bergman Rosamond, A. (2011). "The Cosmopolitan-Communitarian Divide and the Swedish Military," in A. Bergman Rosamond and M. Phythian (eds), *War, Ethics and Justice: New Perspectives on a Post-9/11 World*. London: Routledge, 55–75.

Bergman Rosamond, A. (2013). "Protection Beyond Borders: Gender Cosmopolitanism and Co-constitutive Obligation," Special Issue, *Global Society* 27/3: 319–36.

Bildt, C. (2012). Statement at the General Debate of the 67th Session of the General Assembly, United Nations, <http://gadebate.un.org/67/sweden>, last retrieved April 14, 2014.

Bjereld, U. (1992). *Kritiker eller medlare? Sveriges utrikespolitiska roller 1945–1990*. Stockholm: Nerenius & Santérus Förlag.

Browning, C. (2007). "Branding Nordicity: Models, Identity and the Decline of Exceptionalism," *Cooperation and Conflict* 42/1: 27–51.

Campbell, D. (1992). *Writing Security: United States Foreign Policy and the Politics of Identity*. Manchester: Manchester University Press.

Carlsson, G. (2012). *Speech at the Nobel Symposium at the Institute for International Economic Studies*, September 5, <http://www.government.se/sb/d/15823/a/198419>.

Clark, I. amd Reus-Smit, C. (2013). "Liberal Internationalism, the Practice of Special Responsibilities and Evolving Politics of the Security Council," *International Politics* 40: 38–56.

Epstein, C. (2008). *The Power of Words in International Relations: Birth of Anti-Whaling Discourse.* London: MIT Press.

Esping-Andersen, G. (1985). *Politics Against Markets: The Social Democratic Road to Power.* Princeton: Princeton University Press.

Goldmann, K. (1994). *The Logic of Internationalism: Coercion and Accommodation.* London: Routledge.

Goldmann, K. (2008). *Identitet och Politik.* Stockholm: SNS.

Halliday, F. (1988). "Three Concepts of Internationalism," *International Affairs* 64: 187–98.

Hansen, L. (2006). *Security as Practice, Discourse Analysis and the Bosnian War.* London: Routledge.

Jahn, B. (2007). "The Tragedy of Liberal Diplomacy: Democratization, Intervention, Statebuilding," *Journal of Intervention and Statebuilding* 1/2: 211–29.

Jerneck, M. (1990). "Olof Palme—En internationell propagandist i Socialdemokratin och den svenska utrikespolitiken," in B. Huldt and K. Misgeld (eds), *Socialdemokratin och svensk utrikespolitik: Från Branting till Palme.* Stockholm: Utrikespolitiska Institutet, 121–42.

Joenniemi, P. (1997). "Norden as a Post-Nationalist Construction Neorealism or Regionality," in P. Joenniemi (ed.), *The Reconstructing of Political Space Around the Baltic Rim.* Copenhagen: NORD REFO, 181–235.

Kant, I. (1991). *Perpetual Peace.* Cambridge: Cambridge University Press.

Kronsell, A. (2012). *Gender, Sex and the Postnational Defense: Militarism and Peacekeeping.* Oxford: Oxford University Press.

Lawler, P. (1997). "Scandinavian Exceptionalism and European Union," *Journal of Common Market Studies* 35/4: 565–94.

Lawler, P. (2005). "The Good State," *Review of International Studies* 31/3: 427–49.

Lawler, P. (2013). "The 'Good State' Debate in International Relations," *International Politics: Special Issue "Purposes beyond Ourselves: The Politics of Liberal Internationalism"* 50/1: 18–37.

Liljeström, M. (2012). "En sammanfattning av resultaten i Sidas SCB-undersökning av svenska folkets kunskap om och intresse för utveckling och bistånd," January 2012, Stockholm: Sida, <http://www.sida.se/Global/Development%20and%20cooperation/Den%20svenska%20opinionen/SCB%202011.pdf>, last retrieved August 12, 2013.

Lindvall, J. and Rueda, D. (2013). "The Insider–Outsider Dilemma," Policy Network Think Tank, <http://www.policy-network.net/pno_detail.aspx?ID=4441&title=The-insider-outsider-dilemma>, last retrieved April 1, 2014.

Linklater, A. (1998). *The Transformation of Political Community: Ethical Foundations of the Post-Westphalian Era.* Cambridge: Polity Press.

Martell, L. (n.d.). "The Future for Cosmopolitan Social Democracy," Draft Discussion Note, <http://www.academia.edu/990707/The_Future_for_Cosmopolitan_Social_Democracy>, last retrieved August 13, 2013.

Morgenstierne, C. M. (2003). *Denmark and National Liberation in Southern Africa.* Uppsala: Nordiska Afrikainstitutet.

Nya Moderaterna (2006). "Valmanifest Allians för Sverige: Nytt Hopp för Sverige från 2006," <http://www.moderat.se/sites/default/files/attachments/valmanifest_2006.pdf>, last retrieved April 14, 2014.

OECD (2006). "Final ODA Data for 2005," <http://www.oecd.org/investment/stats/37790990. pdf>, last retrieved August 16, 2013.

OECD (2011). "Comparison of Flows by Type in 2011," <http://www.oecd.org/statistics/>, last retrieved July 12, 2013.

OECD (2013). "Government Social Spending: Total Public Social Expenditure as Percentage of GDP," <http://www.oecd-ilibrary.org/social-issues-migration-health/ government-social-spending_20743904-table1>, last retrieved August 15, 2013.

Omvärlden (2013). "Kritik av ointresse för FN," February 13, <http://www.omvarlden.se/ Branschnytt/Utrikesdebatt-Kritik-av-ointresse-for-FN>, last retrieved October 12, 2013.

Palme, O. (1968). Politik är att vilja. Stockholm: Prisma.

Palme, O. (1972). Democratic Socialism Means Solidarity: Inaugural Address. Stockholm: Socialdemokraterna.

Pratt, C. (1989). "Human Internationalism: Its Significance and its Variants," in C. Pratt (ed.), Internationalism under Strain: The North–South Policies of Canada, the Netherlands, Norway and Sweden. Toronto: University of Toronto Press, 5–23.

Pratt, C. (1990). "Has Middle Power Internationalism a Future?" in C. Pratt (ed.), Middle Power Internationalism: The North–South Dimension. Kingston: McGill-Queen's University Press, 142–67.

Regeringen (2014). "Biståndspolitisk plattform," Regeringens skrivelse 2013/14:131, <http://www. government.se/content/1/c6/23/64/47/57032a9e.pdf>, last retrieved April 13, 2014.

Regeringskansliet (2014). "Statement of Government Policy in the Parliamentary Debate on Foreign Affairs," <http://www.government.se/content/1/c6/23/44/22/44d32dbc.pdf>, last retrieved April 12, 2014.

Rothstein, B. (2006). "Valet är en triumf för socialdemokraterna," Dagens Nyheter, September 20.

Ryner, M. (2002). Capitalist Restructuring, Globalisation and the Third Way: Lessons from the Swedish Model. London: Routledge.

Ryner, M. (2003). "What Is Living and What Is Dead in Swedish Social Democracy?" Radical Philosophy 117 (January/February): 23–33.

Schouenborg, L. (2012). The Scandinavian International Society—Primary Institutions and Binding Forces, 1815–2010. London: Routledge.

Sellström, T. (1999). Sweden and the National Liberation in Southern Africa, vol. 1. Uppsala: Nordiska Afrikainstitutet.

Sellström, T. (2002). Liberation in Southern Africa Regional and Swedish Voices. Uppsala: Nordiska Afrikainstitutet.

Socialdemokraterna (2014). "Socialdemokraternas utrikesdeklaration 2014: En rättvis värld är möjlig," <http://www.socialdemokraterna.se/upload/Internationellt/2014/utrikesdeklara-tion_2014.pdf>, last retrieved April 10, 2014.

Socialdemokraterna (2013). "Agenda för global utveckling—Fokus på internationellt utvecklingssamarbete." Stockholm: SAP, <http://www.socialdemokraterna.se/upload/ Internationellt/2013/S_Agenda%20för%20global%20utveckling_2013.pdf>, last retrieved April 7, 2014.

Socialdemokraterna (2007). "A Just World is Possible: Foreign Policy Declaration," <http:// www.socialdemokraterna.se/upload/Internationellt/Dokument/ForeignPolicy-DeclarationSocialDemocraticParty2007.pdf>, last retrieved April 8, 2014.

Socialdemokraterna (2005). En rättvis värld är möjlig: Socialdemokraternas internationella program. Stockholm: SAP.

Steger, M. B. (1997). *The Quest for Evolutionary Socialism: Eduard Bernstein and Social Democracy*. Cambridge and New York: Cambridge University Press.

Swedish International Development Agency (2009). "Women's Economic Empowerment: Scope for Sida's Engagement," SIDA Working Paper, December, <http://sidapublications. citat.se/interface/stream/mabstream.asp?filetype=1&orderlistmainid=2906&printfileid=29 06&filex=3959916456908>, last retrieved March 25, 2013.

Swedish International Development Agency (2012). "Attitydundersökning 2012: Svenskarnas syn på global utveckling och bistånd." Stockholm: SIDA 26, December.

Stjernö, S. (2005). *Solidarity: The History of an Idea*. Cambridge: Cambridge University Press.

Tolgfors, S. (2009). "Anförande av försvarsminister Sten Tolgfors i Almedalen om Östersjösamarbetet" [Speech by the Minister for Defense Sten Tolgfors at Almedalen on the Baltic Sea Cooperation], <http://www.regeringen.se/sb/a/129884>, last retrieved January 23, 2014.

Trägårdh, L. (2002). "Sweden and the EU: Welfare State Nationalism and the Spectre of Europe," in L. Hansen and O. Wæver (eds), *European Integration and National Identity*. London: Routledge, 130–81.

Viklund, D. (1989). *Neutralitetsdebatten—Tro, vetande och illusioner*. Stockholm: Norstedts.

CHAPTER 35

"A FORCE FOR GOOD"?

Paradoxes of Swedish Military Activism

LISBETH AGGESTAM AND ADRIAN HYDE-PRICE

INTRODUCTION

ONE of the most striking developments in Swedish foreign and security policy since the end of the Cold War has concerned its military policy and the changing roles and structure of the Swedish Armed Forces (SAF). Over the last two decades, successive Swedish governments have pursued an activist military policy that has resulted in the Swedish army, navy, and airforce being deployed on a broad range of new and very varied operations. Not only has Sweden pursued an activist military agenda, its armed forces have also used coercive and kinetic military force in expeditionary operations that are a long way from traditional Swedish peacekeeping during the Cold War. This military activism is a very distinctive feature of Swedish foreign policy, and distinguishes Sweden not only from other nonaligned or neutral states in Europe, but from many EU and NATO member states. Moreover, Swedish military policy since the end of the Cold War cannot be attributed simply to its membership of the EU or to its partnership with NATO, but reflects something more essential and deep-rooted within Sweden's foreign policy role conceptions and its strategic culture, as well as more profound changes in the nature of the international system since the end of Cold War bipolarity.

This chapter thus addresses a topic of considerable consequence and importance that has been relatively little examined in academic literature on Swedish foreign and security policy. Whilst there has been considerable academic discussion and political debate on issues such as neutrality and nonalignment, membership of the EU, or partnership with NATO (Möller and Bjereld 2010 and in this volume), very little attention has been paid to the actual practice of Swedish military policy in the post-Cold-War era—particularly in terms of the use of force and its links to statecraft, both crucial aspects of strategic culture. This military activism constitutes an interesting—and often overlooked—dimension of Swedish foreign policy, which poses some complex theoretical puzzles for international relations theory and the subfield of foreign policy analysis. Sweden's post-Cold-War military policy is not attributable to its militarily nonaligned status, and is in stark contrast to the more reticent military policy of cognate neutral and nonaligned states like Finland, Austria, Switzerland, or Ireland. Nor is it necessarily a consequence of its membership of the EU or its partnership with NATO, given that there are EU members and even NATO members who are not as active as Sweden in either EU CSDP (Common Security and Defense Policy) or NATO operations. Swedish military "exceptionalism" thus poses an empirical puzzle that requires elucidation and explanation.

The chapter begins by outlining the ways in which Swedish approaches to the use of military force have changed and adapted since the end of the Cold War, and examines the sources, dimensions, and political implications of Sweden's military activism. It considers the impact of the demise of Cold War bipolarity on Swedish conceptions of international security and "military nonalignment," and analyzes the evolution of Swedish foreign policy role conceptions and strategic culture in response to the transformed international environment. It also tracks the shifts and recalibration of Swedish military policy from the early 1990s to the present, highlighting the change from peacekeeping and national territorial defense to more varied and complex military missions, including peace support operations, humanitarian military interventions, conventional deterrence, and counter-insurgency operations.

The Political Instrumentality of "Doing Good"

One significant finding that emerges from this study of post-Cold-War Swedish military policy is the political instrumentalism that is driving it. War, Clausewitz famously argued, "is a continuation of politics by other means." An active military policy, for Swedish governments, has been a continuation of foreign policy by other means. This military activism is broadly supported by public opinion, because it is legitimized in terms of the Swedish internationalist tradition of "doing good" in the world and acting in solidarity with others less fortunate (Aggestam 2007; Bergman 2004; Strömvik 2006). Nonetheless, Sweden's military undertakings are not simply a manifestation of altruism and ethical behavior, but serve to enhance Sweden's diplomatic and foreign policy influence. While participation in multinational military operations is justified in terms of working toward defending peace, security, and development, there are also instrumental reasons accompanying these changes to Swedish security and defense policy; namely, the influence that Sweden seeks to gain by being involved in these international structures of security cooperation. The former Swedish Minister for Defense, Sten Tolgfors (2007), explicitly stated this ambition for Sweden to "punch above its weight": "We also gain influence in international organizations and conflict resolution. Our participation strengthens Sweden's voice abroad."

What is also quite striking is that this changing approach toward the use of force as an instrument of Swedish foreign and security policy has taken place largely below the public political radar. Moreover, the practice of Swedish military policy is much more diverse and kinetic than many Swedes realize, leading to a disconnect between military practice and the public political discourse (Rieker 2003: 124; Cottey 2013: 468). Nevertheless, there is broad public and cross-party support for Sweden's policy of military engagement in overseas operations, which are legitimized in terms of its foreign policy role conceptions of internationalism, "saving strangers" (Wheeler 2000), and acting as a "force for good" in the world.

In particular, the idea of "solidarity" has taken central place in Sweden's foreign policy role conceptions, "providing another justification [for military activism] which even the most neutralist of Swedes will find it hard to argue" (Huldt 2005: 43). Sweden's engagement with a wide range of multilateral military operations in the post-Cold-War era—in the framework of the UN, EU, and NATO—are seen as a continuation of a longstanding tradition of "first-generation" Swedish peacekeeping missions. At the same time, however, the full implications of the new type of military operations the Swedish Armed Forces now undertake—which are considerably beyond traditional UN peacekeeping—have perhaps not been fully registered by the Swedish public. As Joakim Berndtsson et al. note (2014: 14), "the transition to an AVF [all-volunteer force] and the strategic shift to more combat-like missions appear to have low levels of support among the Swedes," reflecting "poor information on the part of the political leadership," as well as a "general lack of debate on the Swedish Armed Forces and their activities."

The Paradoxes of Swedish Military Policy

Sweden's military activism therefore exposes a number of central paradoxes in its security and defense policy that we explore in this chapter. The first paradox is that the end of Cold War bipolarity has led to unprecedented levels of military activity by all European democracies, despite the promise of a "peace dividend" following the lifting of the shadow of nuclear Armageddon from the continent. "Europe," the *European Security Strategy* of 2003 noted, "has never been so prosperous, so secure nor so free. The violence of the first half of the 20th Century has given way to a period of peace and stability unprecedented in European history" (EU 2003: 3). Yet paradoxically, Europe's armed forces have never been so actively engaged on military operations—Sweden's military activity being a prime example.

Second, Sweden's membership of the EU has led to a significant "Europeanization" of its security and defense policy, as the country has adapted to being part of European multilateral structures. Yet as a despite being a small state, Sweden has also been effective in projecting its interests and approaches to security into the EU, shaping the

Union's approaches to both comprehensive security and civilian and military crisis management. Paradoxically, therefore, the "Europeanization" of Swedish foreign and security policy has gone hand in hand with a strengthening of the instrumental use of the Swedish military for political influence.

Finally, there is what can be termed the "realist paradox"—namely that at the same time as its armed forces have been heavily engaged in expeditionary operations as part of multilateral coalitions abroad, the ability of the Swedish Armed Forces to provide credible and effective national territorial defense has been degraded. This is a theme to which we shall return in the conclusion.

From the Cold War to the "New World Order"

To understand the roots and the significance of Swedish military activism, one needs to look back to Swedish security and foreign policy in the postwar period. Prior to the onset of the Cold War, Sweden was able to act as a small power on the periphery of the European security system, able to "hide" from the machinations of great power politics—a policy it pursued with some success after the end of the Great Northern War. However, the onset of the East–West conflict changed the geostrategic environment within which Sweden operated: having kept a relatively low profile on the margins of Europe, the country now found itself occupying neutral territory between NATO and the Warsaw Pact within the context of a delicate "Nordic balance" (Jervas 1987).

Given its location in the strategically important northern flank of the East–West conflict, Sweden responded by developing significant military capabilities with which to deter aggressors and preserve its territorial integrity. The credibility of its neutral and nonaligned status was to be maintained by the creation of a strong and self-reliant territorial army (based on conscription) and an independent arms industry—therefore giving it greater weight in the European security architecture than many other small states. In peacetime, Sweden's "armed neutrality" was viewed as contributing to stability and confidence-building between the blocs in the strategically sensitive northern flank. European security cooperation was promoted through the pan-European Conference on Security and Cooperation in Europe (CSCE).

Sweden's "armed neutrality" and its sensitive geostrategic location gave rise to a distinctive foreign policy tradition—small-state realism. This was expressed through a preoccupation with "national survival" and national sovereignty. At the same time, however, successive Swedish governments—most notably those led by Olof Palme—pursued an activist foreign policy with an outward-looking global perspective, giving rise to a second key foreign policy role conception: that of liberal internationalism. During the Cold War, liberal internationalism was pursued primarily through the UN system. Swedish nonalignment within the context of the UN was seen to provide Sweden with a unique opportunity to pursue a progressive foreign policy that built on ideas of "common security" and a more extended concept of duties beyond national borders. This entailed a commitment to international development, confidence-building, disarmament, and peacekeeping operations. To this day, the United Nations enjoys wide-ranging support from Swedish political parties and the domestic population alike, which helps explain why the transference of peacekeeping and support operations to the European Union and NATO have been relatively uncontroversial (Aggestam 2007: 207). Moreover, the Swedish armed forces were well suited to peacekeeping because it was a military mission "quite compatible with their own military ethos" (Dandeker and Gow 2000: 60).

These two traditions—or "role conceptions"—defined the parameters of Swedish security and foreign policy during the Cold War. It should be noted, however, that they were based on two distinct logics. Small-state realism, with its focus on sovereignty and survival, was linked to military power, statecraft, and national interests. Liberal internationalism, with its concern for duties beyond borders, was grounded on a broad conception of security and a normative commitment to cooperation, mediation, and the peaceful resolution of disputes. These two traditions overlapped in Sweden's role in UN peacekeeping, "thus marrying Mars with Pax," in Bo Huldt's striking phrase (Huldt 2005: 42).

With the fall of the Berlin Wall and the demise of the Cold War, the geopolitical foundations of Swedish security and foreign policy have shifted dramatically. With the breakup of the Soviet Union and the dissolution of the Warsaw Pact, Sweden no longer faced an existential threat. Sweden and its Scandinavian neighbors no longer had to base their security policies on explicit or implicit security guarantees from the USA: in this sense, they were no longer security consumers. This transformed and largely benign regional security milieu has been formally recognized by the Swedish government on a number of occasions. In its Defense Policy Bill (for the period 2005–7), the government argued that an act of armed aggression by another state against Sweden is unlikely for the foreseeable future (i.e. at least ten years). More recently, the Swedish Defense Committee stated in its report in 2013 that a direct military attack against Sweden was "not probable in the foreseeable future." Former Prime Minister Reinfeldt has argued that the most pressing threats are not military and that "[s]ince the end of the Cold War, we have experienced the most secure and peaceful situation on our continent—ever" (Reinfeldt 2014). Moreover, he added, the "cooperation in the EU and NATO makes it difficult to envisage that any significant military threat against any country in Europe" will emerge (although he did voice some concerns about the emergence of a more assertive Russia).

MILITARY NONALIGNMENT, SECURITY COOPERATION, AND SOLIDARITY

In the context of a transformed and much more benign geostrategic environment, Swedish security policy underwent significant changes. Most significantly, the focus on national defense associated with small-state realism has been gradually superseded by a broader conception of security that seeks to address a more diffuse and multifaceted range of threats, risks, and challenges, many of which are non-military in nature (Aggestam 2001: 191). This has led to a significant conflation of Swedish security interests with broader questions of international peace and security, given the perception that the fate of Sweden is now inextricably entangled with what happens in a world being reshaped by globalization and interdependence. "We cannot have Armed Forces," former Prime Minister Reinfeldt has noted, "focusing on territorial invasion at a time when the threats are borderless and complex" (Reinfeld 2014). The perceived blurring of the boundary between national and international security is also evident from the 2007 *National Strategy for Swedish Participation in International Peace-Support and Security-Building Operations* (Government Communication 2007/8: 5):

> International operations are an integral part of Swedish security, foreign and defense policy. By contributing to international operations, Sweden does not just contribute to the security and development of others, we also increase our own security while gaining experience beneficial to the development of our national crisis management capability.

At the same time as it has developed a broader and more inclusive concept of security, Sweden has also redefined its basic foreign policy orientation. In part, this is a function of Sweden's membership of the EU and its "partnership for peace" with NATO. Sweden now defines its approach to foreign and security policy in terms of a policy of "military nonalignment" (rather than "neutrality"). But this has been accompanied by a strong commitment to both *cooperation* and *solidarity*. In other words, Sweden does not formally exclude any form of security cooperation other than binding agreements on mutual security guarantees and formal membership of military alliances (most importantly, NATO). As the 2004 Swedish Defense Bill notes:

> Sweden is militarily nonaligned and does not enter into agreements on defense guarantees of a binding character. There is no contradiction between military nonalignment, as stated here, and the strong solidarity that exists between the members of the Union. It is hard to imagine that Sweden would remain neutral in case of an armed attack against another Union country. It is just as difficult to imagine that the other EU countries would not act in the same way. (Quoted in Huldt 2005: 43)

Given the importance attached to the conceptions of cooperation and solidarity, therefore, Sweden has in effect both given—and expects to receive—what might be termed "soft security guarantees." The commitment to the principles of broad-ranging security cooperation and solidarity with European neighbors and partners has led the government to say formally that it is difficult to imagine that Sweden would remain neutral in the case of armed aggression against another EU member state (Bjurner 2005: 36). This is a position that enjoys broad cross-party consensus, and which was made explicit in the 2009 security and defense doctrine: "Sweden will not remain passive in a catastrophe or if an attack happens against another [EU] member state or Nordic country. We expect in return that these countries will act in the same way if Sweden is attacked. Sweden should have a capacity to give and receive military support."

"An Era of New and Savage Wars"

The recalibration of Swedish security and defense doctrine was driven essentially by the transformation of the wider international system in the wake of the demise of Cold War bipolarity. Although initially there were widely shared hopes that a "new world order" was dawning, it soon became apparent that the dreams of a cooperative and peaceful international order were unfounded. For most Europeans, the first major indication of the new security challenges they faced was the violent breakup of Yugoslavia. Writing with the experience of having served as EU Special Envoy to the Balkans, Carl Bildt noted that the wars that broke out in the Balkans in the first half of the 1990s "shattered Europe's belief in eternal peace and a bright future" and marked "the end of the post-war European period." "Suddenly," he argued, "we realized that we were no longer living in the post-war world, but in an era of new and savage wars" (Bildt 1998: 12, 369).

With the breakup of the USSR and the unravelling of the territorial status quo in eastern Europe and the Balkans, new patterns of conflict and instability emerged in and around Europe's periphery. Many of these conflicts were perceived as "new" in character because they were intra-state; involved irregular forces and militias; were driven by identity politics based on ethnicity and/or religion; and much of the violence was directed against civilians and noncombatants (Duyvesteyn and Angstrom 2005). None of these conflicts directly impinged on Sweden and the Nordic countries, whose security environment was the most benign in their history. But the indirect effects of "new wars" were evident from a wave of asylum seekers and immigrants, along with other concerns about the potential risks of "spillover" into EU member states situated closer to these conflict regions.

In this changed geostrategic environment, all European democracies found themselves no longer security consumers—as they had been in the Cold War, when they were dependent on US military guarantees—but potential security providers. Given their relative wealth, military capabilities, political stability, and benign security environment, Europeans were in a position where they could begin to focus on what Arnold Wolfers (1962) termed "milieu shaping," i.e., projecting power, influence, and resources into neighboring regions in order to manage crises, resolve conflicts, and shape a more peaceful external milieu (see Hyde-Price 2007).

Given the outward-looking liberal internationalism which characterized its foreign policy during the Cold War, and the emphasis on cooperation and solidarity that was so marked from the 1990s onwards, Sweden was keen to play a role within multinational European milieu-shaping. The government pioneered civil crisis management within the EU's CFSP, and also developed a broad understanding of "comprehensive security" that focused on the security of individuals and communities within state borders. Former Prime Minister Reinfeldt has argued that Sweden, as a member of the international society of states, has a responsibility to protect vulnerable people, particularly given that Sweden "has a long tradition of standing up for democracy and human rights in other countries" (Reinfeldt 2014). This emphasis on the human dimension of comprehensive security has also led to a focus on the security–development nexus: "Security and development go hand in hand," Carl Bildt has argued (Bildt 2014). This idea was more fully developed in the *National Strategy for Swedish Participation in International Peace-Support and Security-Building Operations* (2007: 51):

> A stable security situation is a fundamental requirement if a country is to achieve democracy with a functioning machinery of state and economic and social development. Similarly, democracy and development are a prerequisite if newly won, fragile peace is to endure. In deciding whether to participate in military operations, Sweden must therefore be convinced that the engagement is long-term and comprehensive.

Beyond Traditional Peacekeeping

As Sweden took up the tasks of milieu-shaping and projecting security into conflict regions, it soon found itself facing a new set of military missions with complex operational requirements. In the context of the "new wars" that proliferated in the post-Cold-War world, the old dichotomy between peacekeeping and combat operations broke down. Many of the new military operations took place in a "gray zone" between war and peace, and involved neither traditional peacekeeping (based on the principle of consent and the use of kinetic force only in very exceptional circumstances) nor high-intensity warfighting (Cottey 2008). Rather, they fell in an ambiguous legal category between Chapter VI of the UN Charter (peacekeeping) and Chapter VII (enforcement operations), and were thus variously categorized as "chapter 6 1/2 operations," "second-" and then "third-generation peacekeeping," "extended peacekeeping," or "wider peacekeeping." What was evident, however, was that this "new and prolific breed of operation" raised some very difficult questions for Europe's postmodern militaries (Moskos et al.).

> Only one thing was certain. Whereas soldiers and scholars in Europe and the United States had been writing volumes about war for 200 years, there was no manual for this vast new area, which had suddenly opened up. There was no doctrine, no instruction book. (Bellamy 1996: 151)

As Erwin Schmidl has noted, the peace-enforcement operations that proliferated in the post-Cold-War international system often "involve combat and in many respects resemble the traditional counter-guerrilla or counter-insurgency operations, especially regarding the physical and—most of all—psychological stress for the soldiers and personnel" (Schmidl 2000: 6). The new intra-state asymmetrical conflicts that Swedish soldiers have had to deal with over the last two decades thus "have more in common with insurgency than they do with any other type of warfare," involving as they do "belligerents who do not accept the legitimacy of the established state" (Mockaitis 2000: 43). Having honed their skills in nonkinetic peacekeeping operations based on the principle of consent and impartiality, the Swedish armed forces have found themselves participating in multinational expeditionary operations, which have frequently involved the coercive use of military power. "Sweden," Joakim Berndtsson has noted,

> … has only recently become familiar with significant combat operations, something that has not occurred since Sweden's engagement in the Congo in the early 1960s. … The operations undertaken during the past two decades have in some cases turned out to be substantially more combat-intensive than most "Blue Helmet" operations of the past—a strategic shift to more combat-intensive missions such as Afghanistan and Libya. (Berndtsson et al. 2014: 6, 9)

The demands of more combat-orientated expeditionary operations on the Swedish armed forces have provided an important stimulus to military transformation. As the military security of Sweden itself has improved and the operational requirements of expeditionary missions have become clearer and more pressing, the armed forces have been restructured away from a focus on national territorial defense to one that is more flexible and suited to international crisis management and stabilization operations (Wyss 2011). The steady "globalization" of Swedish military policy (Reinfeldt 2014) has resulted in the phasing out of conscription (by 2010); the creation of more flexible structures suitable for expeditionary operations; and an increase in rapid response capabilities for international crisis management. The 2004 Defense Plan led to major cuts in the armed forces, transforming a conscript army into a semi-professional division-sized force (Huldt 2005: 42). At the same time, the capabilities for international stabilization and peace-support operations—including rapid-response forces— were improved (Bjurner 2005: 37). A more radical military reform process—enjoying cross-party support—was launched in 2008, and it is expected that by 2018 Sweden will have a professional all-volunteer army with considerably enhanced flexibility and deployability. Moreover, all Swedish soldiers are now obliged to serve in international operations.

UN Operations: Bosnia and the Forging of "New Military Traditions"

One distinctive feature of Swedish military activism is that although it embodies a mix of high-minded normative values ("doing good" and "saving strangers") and Realpolitik interests ("arms for influence"), there is no ideological preference for any particular multilateral institution. In this sense, Sweden is institutionally promiscuous, utilizing whatever multinational framework is of greatest practical utility. Different institutions for security cooperation tend to be seen as mutually reinforcing and overlapping, rather than as rivals. This is reflected in the approach taken to the transformation of the Swedish armed forces which is aimed at enhancing their flexibility and ability to work within different institutional frameworks—the UN, EU, and NATO. Sweden's institutional flexibility is apparent from the government statement in February 2014 announcing Swedish contributions to two missions—one UN-led, the other an EU mission;

> Sweden is ready to contribute military capabilities to peace support operations led by the UN, the EU or NATO. In the next few months the Government will seek the support of the Riksdag for a substantial contribution to the United Nations Multidimensional Integrated Stabilization Mission in Mali (MINUSMA). The Government also supports the decision to establish an EU operation in the Central African Republic, which is now being planned.

Nonetheless, the UN continues to hold a central symbolic and political place in Swedish foreign policy, given the platform it provided neutral and nonaligned Sweden in the Cold War to develop its liberal internationalism. Sweden sent its first battalion of peacekeepers abroad to serve with the UN in 1956, and since then, Sweden has been active in a wide range of UN peacekeeping missions. In the Cold War, these peacekeeping operations were primarily consensual; they were based on the consent of the government and/or parties to the conflict, and usually involved some form of monitoring of a negotiated ceasefire or peace agreement, i.e. post-conflict situations. Above all, they were nonkinetic operations that did not involve the use of force; peacekeepers were deployed after the fighting had ceased in order to reinforce, monitor, or support the ceasefire or peace settlement: at best, their military role was deterrence.

In the post-Cold-War world, the UN has been called on to provide peacekeepers for even more conflict situations—particularly in the 1990s. Yet, as noted above, these peacekeeping missions have significantly changed in character, as the principles of consent, impartiality, and the minimum use of force have come under increasing strain. The changing demands of peacekeeping—where no peace exists—were first experienced by the Swedish military in Bosnia, in the context of the UNPROFOR (United Nations Protection Force) mission. The Bosnia operation was of considerable geostrategic and military significance for Sweden for two reasons: first, it was the first major UN operation on the European continent and involved a challenge to a Europe now "whole and free"; previously, Swedish internationalism was focused on issues far from Europe (such as Vietnam or the Middle East), and peacekeeping operations had been carried out in distant lands where they would not prejudice the status quo in Cold War Europe. With Bosnia, this changed, and Swedish peacekeepers were directly involved in managing the regional security order in Europe. The violent disintegration of Yugoslavia also affected Sweden profoundly in terms of the large number of refugees that came to Sweden due to its liberal refugee policy.

Second, UNPROFOR witnessed a major transformation in the nature of peacekeeping, with a transition from impartial peacekeeping based on consent and the minimum use of force, to a more robust model of "peace support operations" involving kinetic force and a more ambiguous approach to impartiality and consent (Hillen 2000: 142). By 1994, it was evident that a more robust approach to the use of force—and a more flexible interpretation of the principles of consent and impartiality—were essential if UNPROFOR was to be more effective in addressing the humanitarian problems in Bosnia.

Eventually a new campaign plan was drawn up by the UNPROFOR commander, General Rose. This campaign plan was a pragmatic attempt to square the circle of the UN's focus on containment and amelioration, and NATO's shift to a more proactive and muscular use of force. The more forceful approach to peacekeeping was welcomed by the Swedes, along with the French and some of the other Scandinavian countries, and led to actions that pushed the envelope on peacekeeping. Thus for example the Swedish commander, Colonel Hendrikson, overcame the obstruction of a Serb soldier who insisted he had no orders to allow the aid convoy through by putting his pistol to the Serb's head and informing him he now had "new orders" (Rose 1998: 36).

The development of new and more robust approaches to the use of force in the context of peace support operations was further facilitated by cooperation in the framework of IFOR, the "Implementation Force" deployed to Bosnia after the Dayton peace accords were signed. As Carl Bildt notes, there were "considerable differences between the attitudes of the various national forces taking part in the operation. This reflected not different national policies primarily, but far more the difference in military cultures coming out of the experiences of the various armies." The Scandinavians and Canadians, on the one hand, had a long experience of participation in "first-generation" UN peacekeeping missions and "excelled in civil–military relations." The British and French, who had been key contributors to UNPROFOR, had considerable experience in counter-insurgency and low-level military confrontations around the world, and were "the most forward-leaning when it came to using force in order to achieve political ends." The US military, on the other hand, was equipped and trained for high-intensity warfare, and for them, "there was little between doing nothing and a massive use of military force." They were also "very much concerned with their own security." However, Bildt (1998: 302–3) notes that:

> Over time, I saw the differences between these diverse military traditions becoming somewhat less important. The Scandinavians started to be tougher, and the Americans started to use force in ways resembling the British and the French. Bosnia started to forge a new military tradition impacting on them all.

EU Missions

Since joining the EU in 1995 (in tandem with Austria and Finland), Sweden has engaged with considerable commitment and enthusiasm in the ESDP/CSDP (Bailes et al. 2006; Lee-Ohlsson 2009). As is well known, it has played an important role in trying to shape the character of the EU as a security actor, pushing for a formal link between the EU and the WEU (Western European Union) during the intergovernmental conference of 1996–7, and advocating the development of a civilian crisis management capability during the Swedish EU Presidency in 2001. This serves both to strengthen the EU as a security actor and to enhance Sweden's position in the international security system:

> EU cooperation occupies a special position in Swedish foreign and security policy. Common Foreign and Security Policy (CFSP) and European Security and Defense Policy (ESDP) are a key platform for security-policy interests. The role of the EU as a player in security policy has changed and been reinforced. The opportunities for the Union to influence the security situation in the wider world also entail greater opportunities to safeguard Swedish interests. Sweden has established itself as a credible and influential player through its great conceptual involvement and extensive participation in ESDP operations. (Government Communication 2007/8: 4)

Along with its advocacy of conflict prevention and a civilian crisis management capability within the EU, Sweden has also recognized the importance of the development of credible and effective capabilities for military crisis management (Tolgfors 2007). Indeed, Sweden has contributed to all ESDP/CSDP military and civil missions to date—including contributing naval and air surveillance assets to the EU's counter-piracy Operation Atalanta since 2010. While most of the military missions have been small-scale and involved "first-generation peacekeeping" activities, some—most notably Operation Artemis in the DRC (Democratic Republic of Congo), during which Swedish special forces were deployed alongside their French counterparts—have involved significant kinetic force and intense combat.

The Swedish military have also assumed the lead nation role in the Nordic Battlegroup, to which it contributes the largest share with over 2,300 troops (out of a total of 2,800). Consisting of Swedish, Finnish, Estonian, Latvian, Lithuanian, Norwegian, and Irish troops, the Nordic Battlegroup's insignia is a lion holding an olive branch in one paw and a sword in the other—symbolizing its potential for both humanitarian aid and combat operations. Much to the frustration of the Swedish government, the EU battle groups have never been used, despite Swedish efforts to change the rules for their deployment during the 2009 Swedish EU Presidency (Herolf 2013: 5).

PARTNERSHIP WITH NATO

Sweden's involvement in UN peacekeeping and EU CSDP missions is well known; what is more surprising is the enthusiasm with which Sweden has embraced its "partnership for peace" with NATO. Tellingly, Sweden has committed more troops to NATO-led operations than to EU ones (Aggestam 2007: 213), participating in IFOR/KFOR, the ISAF mission in Afghanistan, and Operation Unified Protector in Libya. "NATO," former Prime Minister Reinfeldt has argued, "is central to security and stability in Europe" (Reinfeldt 2014), and the current center-right coalition government contains two parties that favor full NATO membership.

In light of Swedish public opinion, NATO membership is not likely in the foreseeable future—even if the issue has been raised again in the wake of the Ukraine crisis. What is evident, however, is that even without formal membership, Sweden has taken full advantage of the Partnership for Peace (PfP) scheme and the Euro-Atlantic Partnership Council (EAPC) to forge very close cooperation with the alliance—to an extent unthinkable in the Cold War. PfP involves no security guarantees or military commitments, although in the event of aggression a mechanism for political consultation does exist. What it does offer is an invaluable forum for extensive cooperation and integration, which has facilitated the growing interoperability and standardization of the Swedish armed forces with their NATO counterparts. Swedish units and officers participate extensively in NATO training exercises, which have had a critical impact on Swedish military doctrine and strategic culture (Huldt 2005: 43). By 2012 for example, Sweden had participated in 42 NATO exercises, 13 of them taking place in Sweden (Herolf 2013: 6). In November 2013, Sweden participated in NATO's Article V military exercise in Poland and the Baltic states (Operation Steadfast Jazz), signaling a "soft" commitment to the defense of its EU allies and NATO partners. In addition, Sweden contributes to the NATO Response Force, which has familiarized the Swedish military to some very advanced and "high-end" operational doctrines and procedures.

Sweden's consistent participation in major NATO operations in the Balkans, Afghanistan, and Libya marks it out as one of the most active and engaged of NATO's partners. Indeed, Sweden is more active in NATO operations than some NATO members (Cottey 2013), underlying once again the extent to which Sweden's military nonalignment has been accompanied by a policy of military activism. The commitment to Afghanistan has been one of the most significant in terms of the difficulty and complexity of the military mission.

Originally deployed as part of the UN-sanctioned ISAF, the mission was initially defined in terms of peace support and post-conflict stabilization, building on ideas of comprehensive security which emphasized the close link between security and development. However, as the insurgency grew in intensity, the Swedish military found themselves engaged in challenging forms of counter-insurgency, rather than simply peace support. In 2006, Sweden took over command of the Provincial Reconstruction Team (PRT) in Mazar-e-Sharif, with responsibilities for four provinces in northern Afghanistan (Allen 2010).

If Afghanistan has been important for the Swedish army—underlining the doctrinal and operational link between peace enforcement operations and counter-insurgency— Libya has been equally important for the Swedish airforce. Following a formal request from NATO in March, the Swedish government sent eight JAS 39C Gripen to Libya as part of Operation Unified Protector (OUP), with the caveat that they must not take part in combat strikes against ground targets. The Gripens were deployed in Sicily from April–October 2011, their mission being to provide tactical air reconnaissance across the full spectrum of UN-mandated tasks, including enforcing the no-fly zone (NFZ) and the arms embargo as well as protecting civilians (Hellenius 2014).

OUP was the first international operation for the Swedish air force in more than 50 years, and provided invaluable lessons—on how to operate within the NATO alliance and on the capabilities and potential of the Gripen as well. There were initially some teething problems (such as fuel incompatibility and the lack of access to NATO's Secret Mission Network), but these were soon resolved, and the Swedish airforce went on to provide high-quality photoreconnaissance and accurate image analyses.

CONCLUSIONS

As this chapter has demonstrated, Sweden provides an interesting case of a militarily nonaligned European democracy that has pursued a policy of military activism. This policy of military activism serves a number of important instrumental functions: first and foremost, it is a means by which the Swedish government seeks to gain political leverage and diplomatic influence in multilateral organizations, allowing it to "punch above its weight"; second, it facilitates collective milieu-shaping through power projection into conflict regions in and around Europe's neighborhood; and last but not least, it provides a vital way for enhancing the military effectiveness and interoperability of Sweden's armed forces.

Sweden's military activism is legitimized by reference to the foreign policy tradition of liberal internationalism and the concepts of "cooperation" and "solidarity," and enjoys broad public and cross-party support. Nonetheless, there has been relatively little public or political discussion of the extent to which the Swedish armed forces have engaged in a range of new military missions, many of them involving kinetic force and more combat-orientated tasks. These include peace enforcement in the Balkans and Africa; counter-insurgency in Afghanistan; humanitarian military intervention and coercive crisis management in Libya; and contributions to deterrence by the NATO alliance in the Baltic Sea region. Despite its formal military nonalignment, Sweden has also given "soft" security guarantees to its EU and Baltic neighbors, and clearly expects these to be reciprocated in the event of armed aggression.

Nonetheless, whatever its perceived advantages, this policy of expeditionary military activism is starting to be questioned. The concern is that the Swedish armed forces are now no longer able to provide effective defense of the Swedish homeland—not least, in terms of protecting its own airspace. With heightened security competition over Ukraine and the Russian annexation of Crimea, these worries have intensified. Anders Borg, the Finance Minister, indicated in March 2014 that the defense budget—which for decades has been shrinking—may now be increased. Looking to the future, it now seems that the debate on Swedish security and defense policy may soon be resumed. One issue that is due for more informed debate is the paradox identified at the start of this chapter; namely, the appropriate balance to be struck between a commitment to expeditionary operations on the one hand, and national territorial defense on the other. Given the harsher winds now blowing from the East, and the continuing turbulence to Europe's South, this is a debate that is long overdue.

References

Aggestam, L. (2001). "An End to Neutrality? Continuity and Change in Swedish Foreign Policy," in R. Niblett and W. Wallace (eds), *Rethinking European Order: West European Responses 1989–97*. Basingstoke: Palgrave, 182–206.

Aggestam, L. (2007). "The European Internationalist: Sweden and European Security Cooperation," *Nação & Defesa* 118/3: 203–18.

Allen, N. (2010). *Embed: With the World's Armies in Afghanistan*. Stroud: Spellmount.

Bailes, A., Herolf, G., and Sundelius, B. (eds) (2006). *The Nordic Countries and the European Security and Defence Policy*. Oxford: Oxford University Press.

Bellamy, C. (1996). *Knights in White Armour: The New Art of War and Peace*, updated edition. London: Pimlico.

Bergman, A. (2004). "The Nordic Militaries—Forces for Good?" in L. Elliot and G. Cheeseman (eds), *Forces for Good? Cosmpolitan Militaries in the 21st Century*. Manchester: Manchester University Press.

Berndtsson, J., Dandeker, C., and Ydén, K. (2014). "Swedish and British Public Opinion of the Armed Forces after a Decade of War," *Armed Forces & Society* 40/1: 1–22.

Bildt, C. (1998). *Peace Journey: The Struggle for Peace in Bosnia*. London: Weidenfeld & Nicolson.

Bildt, C. (2014). Speech at the Swedish Institute for International Affairs, Stockholm, September 29.

Bjurner, A. (2005). "Sweden," in E. Munro (ed.), *Challenges to Neutral and Non-Aligned Countries in Europe and Beyond*. Geneva: Geneva Centre for Security Policy, 35–40.

Cottey, A. (2008). "Beyond Humanitarian Intervention: The New Politics of Peacekeeping and Intervention," *Contemporary Politics* 14/4: 429–46.

Cottey, A. (2013). "The European Neutrals and NATO: Ambiguous Partnership," *Contemporary Security Policy* 34/3: 446–72.

Dandeker, C. and Gow, J. (2000). "Military Culture and Strategic Peacekeeping," in E. Schmidl (ed.), *Peace Operations between War and Peace*. London: Cass, 58–79.

Duyvesteyn, I. and Angstrom, J. (eds) (2005). *Rethinking the Nature of War*. Abingdon: Frank Cass.

EU (2003). *A Secure Europe in a Better World: European Security Strategy*. Paris: EU Institute for Security Studies.

Government Communication (2007/8). "National Strategy for Swedish Participation in International Peace-Support and Security-Building Operations," <http://www.government.se/contentassets/f1eeedbd51784b4db60c2a2d3fea4738/national-strategy-for-swedish-participation-in-international-peace-support-and-security-building-operations>, accessed November 7, 2014.

Hellenius, B. (2014). "Griffin Takes Wing: SAAB JAS 39 Gripen," *Air Forces Monthly* 312: 50–73.

Herolf, G. (2013). "European Security Policy: Nordic and Northern Strategies," International Policy Analysis. Berlin: Friedrich-Ebert-Stiftung.

Hillen, J. (2000). *Blue Helmets: The Strategy of UN Military Operations*, 2nd edn. Washington, DC: Brassey's.

Huldt, B. (2005). "Swedish Commentator," in E. Munro (ed.), *Challenges to Neutral and Non-Aligned Countries in Europe and Beyond*. Geneva: Geneva Centre for Security Policy, 41–6.

Hyde-Price, A. (2007). *The Challenge of Multipolarity: European Security in the Twenty-First Century*. London: Routledge.

Jervas, G. (1987). "Sweden in a Less Benign Environment," in B. Sundelius (ed.), *The Neutral Democracies and the New Cold War*. Boulder: Westview Press, 57–74.

Lee-Ohlsson, F. (2009). "Sweden and Development of the European Security and Defence Policy: A Bi-Directional Process of Europeanization," *Cooperation and Conflict* 44/2: 123–42.

Mockaitis, T. (2000). "From Counterinsurgency to Peace Enforcement: New Names for Old Games?" in E. Schmidl (ed.), *Peace Operations Between War and Peace*. London: Cass, 40–57.

Möller, U. and Bjereld, U. (2010). "From Nordic Neutrals to Post-Neutral Europeans: Differences in Finnish and Swedish Policy Transformation," *Cooperation and Conflict* 45/4: 363–86.

Moskos, C., Williams, J., and Segal, D. (eds) (2000). *The Postmodern Military: Armed Forces after the Cold War*. Oxford: Oxford University Press.

Reinfeldt, F. (2014). "Sverige i en globaliserad värld." Speech at Folk och Försvars rikskonferens, Sälen, January 12.

Rieker, P. (2003). "Europeanisation of Nordic Security: The EU and Changing Security Identities of the Nordic States," dissertation, Department of Political Science, University of Oslo.

Rose, M. (1998). *Fighting for Peace: Bosnia 1994*. London: Harvill Press.

Schmidl, E. (ed.) (2000). *Peace Operations between War and Peace*. London: Cass.

Strömvik, M. (2006). "Starting to 'Think Big': The Nordic Countries and EU Peace-building," in A. J. Bailes, G. Herolf, and B. Sundelius (eds), *The Nordic Countries and the European Security and Defence Policy*. Oxford: Oxford University Press, 199–214.

Tolgfors, S. (2007). "Enhanced Nordic Cooperation in a Euro-Atlantic Context." Speech at the Swedish Atlantic Council conference, Stockholm, November 9.

Wheeler, N. (2000). *Saving Strangers: Humanitarian Intervention in International Society*. Oxford: Oxford University Press.

Wolfers, A. (1962). *Discord and Collaboration: Essays in International Politics*. Baltimore: Johns Hopkins University Press.

Wyss, M. (2011). "Military Transformation in Europe's Neutral and Non-Allied States," *RUSI Journal* 56/2: 44–51.

SECTION 8

SWEDEN AND THE EU

SECTION EDITOR
ULRIKA MÖRTH

CHAPTER 36

INTRODUCTION

Sweden and the EU

ULRIKA MÖRTH

In July 1991 the Swedish Prime Minister, Ingvar Carlsson, submitted Sweden's application for membership in the European Community. The negotiations lasted just over a year and at the Corfu Summit in the summer of 1994 the agreement of accession was signed. On November 13 the same year, a total of 52.3 percent of Swedes voted in favor of membership in a referendum, 46.8 percent voted against, and 0.9 percent registered blank votes. The turnout was high: 83 percent. On December 16, 1994, the Riksdag (Swedish parliament) formally approved the decision to join what now had become the European Union at Maastricht in 1993. Sweden had been part of the EEA (European Economic Agency) agreement since 1992, which regulated most of the terms of entry for Sweden's participation in the EU's internal market. However, with the formal membership in the EU, policy areas such as agriculture and regional policies were now formally embodied in the EU agreement.

This section takes the formal membership as a starting point in the political analysis of Sweden and the EU. Three major empirical and theoretical aspects of Sweden and the European Union are analyzed in these chapters: What kind of polity is the EU? In what ways has Sweden been transformed due to the EU, and what role does a relatively small member state play in the European political arena?

In her chapter, Ulrika Mörth argues that when Sweden entered the EU it became a member of a multigovernance polity, characterized by multiple actors, governance structures, and political levels. Mörth analyzes three interpretations of the governance turn in the EU—the soft turn, the market turn, and the societal turn—and discusses how these turns relate to Swedish politics. It is argued that there is a fit between the soft turn in the EU and the Swedish intergovernmental position towards the Union. However, the strong presence and the power of law in the EU have also revealed differences and tensions between Sweden and the EU. The early privatizations and deregulations of parts of the public infrastructure have made Sweden one of forerunners in the market turn, but they have also created tensions between core Swedish national issues and the EU.

Interestingly, the societal turn in the EU follows Swedish traditions on corporativism and other components of participatory democracy. However, the societal turn shows that the search for new types of democratic legitimation strategies in the EU can also be interpreted as business as usual.

Mörth's analysis, an outside-in approach to understanding Swedish politics and the EU, is followed by Bengt Jacobsson and Göran Sundström's chapter, an inside-out approach on how the Swedish state has changed due to membership. An overall argument in the chapter is that states are scripted—they follow rules invented by others. These rules and ideas are then translated in order to make them fit with local practice. For Sweden, this was obvious in the case of agricultural policy. The Swedish parliament decided to deregulate agriculture policy only one year before the Swedish government applied for membership, and this reform had to be abandoned as soon as Sweden became a full EU member. States also follow more soft rules. One empirical example mentioned in the chapter is educational policy, namely the Bologna Process, and how Sweden has adapted voluntarily to these guidelines. The authors argue that the Swedish administrative state is embedded in the EU. Government units within all policy areas, at all levels, are affected by the EU. European networks have become an important part of government officials' everyday work. The Swedish state is fragmented: a conclusion that goes against the traditional image of coherent and coordinated states in international organizations.

The next chapter, by Douglas Brommesson, continues the analysis of how Swedish policy is Europeanized by studying the role conceptions of Swedish foreign policy and how this role has changed since Sweden joined the European Union. He argues that the role conception has changed rather rapidly since the end of the Cold War and the EU membership. Sweden's historical traditions of nonalignment and independent support for the Third World have changed toward a more European-oriented foreign policy. The Swedish people have not only expressed a strong desire to integrate Swedish foreign policy with other European countries, but also to support decision-making capacity in foreign policy at the European level. This Europeanized role is likely to remain in Swedish foreign policy in parallel with an emerging complementary Nordic role conception. This finding shows that multiple roles of different salience are possible in foreign policy, and that states develop new role conceptions and even rediscover old familiar ones.

Finally in this section, Malena Rosén Sundström analyzes how the Swedish government managed the challenges and opportunities presented while holding the Presidency of the Council in 2001 and in 2009, and what results and consequences this has had. The analysis shows that a small state can have influence in the EU by upholding the Presidency, but that the scope and conditions of the influence are very much determined by factors beyond the country holding the Presidency. The first Presidency provided the Swedish Government with an opportunity to demonstrate its dedication to the EU and encourage EU-skeptical citizens in Sweden to become more interested in the Union, although the so-called "Presidency effect" did not have a noticeable impact on public opinion. Sweden was considered to have been a successful mediator in the areas of enlargement of the EU and adoption of the EU regulation on transparency. The political context was radically different when Sweden took over the chair the second time, with the pending ratification of the Lisbon Treaty, the issue of the EU's leadership on security and foreign policy, and the ongoing worst economic and financial crisis since the 1930s.

....

CHAPTER 37

SWEDEN IN A MULTIGOVERNANCE POLITY

....

ULRIKA MÖRTH

INTRODUCTION

....

WHEN Sweden joined the European Union in 1995 it joined an organization that is very much characterized as a multigovernance polity or as a "multiperspectival polity" (Ruggie 1993). By this I simply mean that the EU is a complex organization characterized by multiple actors, governance structures, and political levels. In this chapter I analyze the governance turns in the EU, or to be more accurate, the turns that Sweden has encountered since it became a member of the EU.

The concept of governance "signifies a change in the meaning of government, referring to a *new* process of governing; or a *changed* condition of ordered rule, or the *new* method by which society is governed" (Rhodes 2003: 65, emphasis added). Thus, governance is an umbrella concept that can be used for many types of political reform that are not necessarily consistent. Indeed, there is a hybrid character to EU governance consisting of a focus on output legitimacy—performance and efficiency—*and* on input legitimacy—a more deliberative and inclusive policy-making process (Scharpf 1999).

The analysis of governance in the EU is fairly new. The use of legal instruments has historically been one of the most important features of the European Union. In parallel, there has always been a more informal side of EU policy and decision-making, but this has seldom been discussed in the literature (Christiansen and Piattoni 2003; Kleine 2013). Instead, analysis of the EU has for a long time been dominated by legal scholars and textbooks on EU formal decision-making with regard to both primary and secondary legislation. Political analysis of the EU has been dominated by theories of the integration process which either explained decisions in the EU as the result of intergovernmental negotiations or as the result of an omnipotent European Commission (for an overview of European integration theories, see Rosamund 2000). In the mid-1990s the description of the EU as a multilevel governance was presented as a middle way between these two ideal types (Marks et al. 1996). In parallel to this system-oriented analysis there was also a breakthrough in thick empirical analysis of why decisions happen inside the EU (Cram 1997; Mazey and Richardson 1995; Héritier 1999; e.g. March 1994). The question that was asked was: how can we explain policy-making in a political system that is characterized by diversity and deadlocks (Héritier 1999)? One answer to this question was that the EU is, like many other political systems, multifaceted and that there are different ways of making decisions happen. Indeed, the EU is a multigovernance polity.

There are essentially three interpretations of what the governance turn in the EU entails (Mörth 2008, 2009). I analyze these three interpretations as three parallel reforms which are sometimes interlinked and together create a multigovernance polity. In addition, they are also to some extent contradictory.

The first is the soft turn which means new decision-making and policy instruments. The second is the market turn which has to do with better regulation and other manifestations of New Public Management in the EU. The third, the societal turn, entails reforms in the EU that are focused on democratic legitimacy, especially on input legitimacy. I discuss these three turns in this very order—from decision-making and policy instruments to market reforms and finally to the question of the overall steering system of the EU. The reason for this is that it reflects the way the EU functions as a political system. The mechanisms for change in the EU do not start with a grand constitutional design. They start with everyday politics and how decisions can be reached in a multigovernance polity. There are empirical illustrations in Swedish politics that are relevant to each turn.

The chapter argues that there is a fit between the soft turn in the EU and the Swedish intergovernmental position towards the Union. However, the strong presence and power of law in the EU have also revealed differences and tensions between Sweden and the EU.

The early privatizations and deregulations of parts of the public infrastructure have made Sweden one of forerunners in the market turn, but they have also created tensions between core Swedish national issues and the EU. Interestingly, the societal turn in the EU follows Swedish traditions on corporativism and other components of participatory democracy. However, the societal turn shows that the search for new types of democratic legitimation strategies in the EU can also be interpreted as business as usual.

THE GOVERNANCE TURN—WHICH TURN?

The Soft Turn

In the late 1990s and the early 2000s it was alleged that a new mode of governance emerged in the EU (Héritier 2001; NEWGOV 2004; Kohler-Koch and Rittberger 2006). This new mode of governance was often described in terms of less coercive regulations, frequently as soft law (Mörth 2004).

The "discovery" of soft law is interesting because of the fact that informal legislative instruments have been part of the EU for a very long time. Guidelines and codes of conduct have been important regulative instruments, especially in policy areas in which the EU lacks or has a weak legal competence. Even within perceived hard law policy areas, for instance state aid policy, there are soft law instruments (Aldestam 2004).

The concept of soft law is an anomaly because law, defined as legal rules, is soft rather than hard. This means that the legal rules are not binding and that legal sanctions cannot be used in cases of noncompliance. The rules are voluntary and not coercive. These rules can be guidelines, codes of conduct, standards, and other voluntary rules.

I argue that there are two explanations of why soft law became politically important in the EU. The first explanation has to do with the integration process and how it had reached a stage where the internal market was in place, even though it had not been completed. It was now time to decide on more politically and nationally salient issues on welfare state policies, and for those type of issues the EU had to turn to soft law in order to reach decisions. The other explanation that is linked to this functional need for softer regulations is how the EU works as a system.

Retaining Sovereignty

The first explanation for why soft law was "discovered" in the late 1990s and early 2000s is that it was more explicitly and frequently used by the EU, particularly within policy areas that were politically controversial. Soft law was regarded as an important way forward in the EU when member states wanted to retain national sovereignty over certain issues (Scharpf 1999, 2002). These controversial questions often went beyond issues to do with the internal market and concerned areas of the welfare state, such as taxes, pensions, economic policy, and other welfare topics that are exclusively decided within the member states. Hard law is not, in practice, seen as an alternative to soft law because of the unwillingness of EU member states to delegate supranational decision-making powers to the EU when it comes to politically controversial welfare state issues. Soft law regulations are often seen as a way of retaining political power over policy-making in the EU instead of being subject to rulings by the European Court of Justice. However, soft law may precede hard law, which means that using soft law is not a guarantee for retaining national sovereignty. Guidelines can be incorporated into EU directives, and the European Court of Justice can rule that a soft law regulation should be turned into hard law (Aldestam 2004; Österdahl 2004).

This fact has not prevented national governments from arguing to their EU-skeptical citizens that soft law rules are voluntary and that they have not delegated national sovereignty to the EU (Mörth 2004).

This is exactly how the then Swedish Prime Minister, Göran Persson, reacted when the Open Method of Coordination (OMC) was discussed at the European Council meeting in Lisbon in 2000. "The process is political, not judicial. If some country fails it does not wind up in front of the EU Court ... The road chosen in Lisbon surely means more cooperation, but it does not mean more supranationality"[1] (Swedish Parliament, Protocol 1999/2000:92).

The OMC is a mix of soft and hard law and entails cooperation among the member states based on continual reporting, measuring, and ranking of the member states' policies (Jacobsson and Sundström, this volume). Through peer pressure among the member states it is argued that this would achieve more effective convergence in policy areas that are controversial and in which the EU lacks or has limited competence to legislate. The method is attractive for member states that are more skeptical towards a supranationally oriented EU and Sweden is one of those members that traditionally advocate a more intergovernmental approach to European integration (Mörth 1996). Indeed, Swedish governments, irrespective of political ideology, have all been in favor of an intergovernmental integration process (Mörth 2003a) and have had a very skeptical attitude toward what is perceived by some as a supranational state at the European level. One example of this skepticism is that the Swedish electorate rejected Swedish participation in the final stage of the EMU process in a referendum in 2003.

An empirical illustration of this Swedish reluctance to embrace the supranational components of the EU is the role of the law in EU politics. When Sweden entered the Union there was hardly any Swedish discussion of the role of EU law and how the rules of the internal market could have any impact on policy areas that were defined as national policy issues. To the political establishment it therefore came as a shock when the European Court of Justice pronounced on the compatibility of the Swedish retail monopoly on alcohol beverages with the free-market principles in the Franzén case (Cisneros Örnberg 2009; Case-1989/95). Although the court concluded that the sales monopoly was not in opposition to the EC Treaty, it was an eye-opener for the Swedish Government that a core national issue on public health could be questioned by the court based on the rules of the internal market. Ten years later the court stated that Sweden could no longer ban private imports of alcohol because the "monopoly has a discretionary power to refuse to import alcohol beverages requested by clients ..." (Cisneros Örnberg 2009: 52; Case-170/04). The Swedish law changed in order to comply with the ruling of the court that retail monopoly is not the same thing as import monopoly.

The case of alcohol illustrates that the traditional relationship between law and politics in the Swedish political system has been that of the supremacy of politics over law. Sweden has no constitutional court which has constrained the legal system to be political like the German Constitutional Court in Karlsruhe or the European Court of Justice. The strong presence of law in the EU has put pressure on the Swedish political system regarding the balance between law and politics—in particular the process by which Swedish citizens can claim that EU law is applicable in Swedish courts. This is one important causal factor leading to skepticism among politicians regarding supranationalism. Another factor that has changed the balance between law and politics is the reform of New Public Management which has turned many political issues into legal contracting (more on this in the section on the market turn; see also Jacobsson and Sundström, this volume). The soft turn is therefore in line with the Swedish intergovernmental approach towards the EU and the European integration process. Swedish governments want cooperation in many policy areas at the European level, but they want to keep discretionary political powers at the national level.

The Ambiguous Organization

The second explanation for why soft law is more frequently and explicitly used in the EU has to do with how the EU works as a system. The EU has multiple cores which makes it a fluid system and generates a porous policy-making process with many channels for influence. The Treaties of the EU codify political and social practice in the EU rather than the other way around. The history of the EU is full of examples of how political deadlocks have been handled using different strategies (Héritier 1999). These strategies are often codified in the Treaties, which creates demand for new creative strategies to escape deadlocks if the treaties are too specific on how to handle a complex political issue. The very use of soft law is a case in point for how political stalemates result in the use of voluntary rules that in addition are often open to multiple interpretations.

To be unclear in the EU—which goes for both soft law and EU directives— is one important problem-solving mechanism. The trick is to be sufficiently clear for decision-makers to be able to agree on a decision, but it is also necessary to be unclear and open to multiple interpretations in order to reach agreement on sensitive political issues. Indeed, the absence of a common goal or objective does not stop the EU from acting. On the contrary, the development of the OMC "appealed as a policy instrument to start a process when there was no agreement on the policy goals" (Kassim and Le Galès 2010: 8; see also Dehousse 2004). "Policy instruments thus offer a means of structuring space for short time exchanges, for negotiations and agreements, setting aside the most problematic issues, and thereby allow for ambiguous consensus (Kassim and Le Galès 2010: 8; see also Palier 2005). Furthermore, it can be argued that the OMC mobilized social partners in the labor market field and that it was designed to support learning by encouraging exchanges of knowledge in iterative processes between different types of actors from the national and the European level (Jacobsson 2004). In the literature on Europeanization it is often argued that EU decisions need to have national resonance in order to be implemented (Mörth 2003a). In the OMC processes the national resonances were created along these iterated dialogues that to some extent followed a Swedish corporatist tradition. In policy terms the OMC has meant little new when it has been used in the policy field of social inclusion in Sweden (Jacobsson and Johansson 2007). The very method has, however, empowered social NGOs in relation to the government in the sense that the production of so-called NAPs (National Action Plans) has created arenas for dialogue between NGOs and government officials (Jacobsson and Johansson 2007).

This dialogue on complex political matters illustrates how organizations "do not have simple, consistent preference functions. They exhibit internal conflict over preferences" (March 1981: 215). Indeed, policy-making in the EU is typified more by ambiguity and inconsistency than by clarity and consistency (March 1994, 1997).

To sum up, Swedish governments are positive toward the soft turn in the EU because it gives an ("illusory"?) impression of retaining sovereignty while at the same time Swedish politicians can be "good" Europeans in Brussels. Soft law is an important component in a complex political system that needs to negotiate a balance between political clarity and national interests.

THE MARKET TURN

The New Public Management reform is a " 'shopping basket' of management ideas and techniques. It includes managerial devolution and discretion, explicit performance standards focused on outputs, 'hands-off' strategic control and accountability mechanisms based on clear objectives and measurable outputs and outcomes (for example, the contract), and performance incentive based on greater autonomy and self-regulation (for example through competition)" (Painter 2001: 211). In the EU there has been an increased focus on impact assessment and other measures aimed at increased efficiency and output legitimacy. This has created a new regulatory and normative European landscape (Renda 2006). The toolkit for better regulation varies but often consists of market-friendly alternatives to command and control (Radaelli 2007a). Thus, the governance turn in the EU is not only about new ways of reaching decisions, but is also part of an "ideological shift from politics towards the market" (Pierre and Peters 2000: 55).

The background to the market turn in the EU goes back to the mid-1990s when there were political concerns about both the contents and the numbers of the legislative acts. The European Council Meeting resulted in the formation of groups of member states and of business groups working on how to simplify and improve the legislation (EC 1995; Unice 1995). The emphasis on consultation with various stakeholders in the White Paper on Governance (EC 2001) is an example of how the Commission wanted to improve the traditional legislative process. The role of civil society and various interest organizations was considered crucial in the establishment of various collaborations between the Commission and the societal actors (ibid.). These types of collaboration were not supposed to have any formal legislative power but were considered to be an essential part of the Commission's consultation phase within the community method. The Commission emphasized the need for "a reinforced culture of consultation and dialogue" (ibid.: 16). By involving business, civil society, and other actors in the legislative process, the legislation can, according to the White Paper, be better and more easily implemented.

The frequent use of soft law is often linked to the market turn in the EU. Under the heading of "Better Lawmaking" and "Better Regulation," which was instituted in 1992 at the European Council Meeting in Edinburgh, concerns were expressed about the quality of the legislation and "the tide of rules coming from Brussels" (Radaelli 2007b: 192). The real concern among politicians and other decision-makers behind the reform of better regulation seemed to be the fact that there were disappointing years for those who wanted a more performance-oriented EU. As Andrea Renda puts it, "In the frantic environment surrounding the European Union after the French and Dutch 'no' on the Constitutional Treaty, EU policy-makers are striving to identify the key drivers that will lead Europe back on track. 'Competitiveness' is the keyword in Brussels now, and one of the recognized drivers of competitiveness is 'better regulation'. As a matter of fact, the EU Better Regulation Action Plan is perceived as one of the most crucial milestones for achieving the ambitious Lisbon Goals" (Renda 2006: 1). The reform of Better Regulation did not only tackle the perceived performance problems in the Union, but also seems to have functioned as a way of mobilizing support for the European project itself. The reform became more in line with the reform of New Public Management. The model of impact assessment was introduced in 2002 (EC 2002; EC 2004).

In the mid-2000s the focus on economic competitiveness and the reduction of administrative burdens seemed to be more important than the socially inclusive decision-making process. The UK Presidency in the spring of 2005 had an emphasis on simplifying the existing regulatory environment and reducing administrative burdens which were largely pursued under the motto "more value with less money" (Renda 2006). This motto lay at the core of New Public Management reform in the UK and very much overshadowed the deliberative and inclusive ideas in the earlier texts on better regulation. However, already in the Mandelkern Report in 2001, followed by the Commission's White Paper on the governance of the European Union the very same year, the improvement of the regulatory environment with the overall aim of becoming the most efficient economy of the world was placed high on the political agenda. The argument was that improving the quality of legislation was "a public good in itself, enhancing the credibility of the governance process and contributing to the welfare of the citizens" (Radaelli 2007b: 194). The term governance was less linked to inclusive decision-making processes and more directed to growth and jobs in the Union and to impact assessment. Originally the impact assessment model should give fair treatment to the three cornerstones of the Lisbon process—economic competitiveness, sustainable development, and social cohesion (EC 2002). "Since then, the redefinition of the Lisbon agenda has emphasized the economic dimension. And a new Commission is operating in Brussels, arguably with more business-friendly attitudes than the previous one" (Radaelli 2007b: 194). An interinstitutional agreement on better regulation in 2003, the "Doorn motion" within the Legal Affairs Committee of the European Parliament, the joint letter of the Irish, and the three incoming presidents of Ecofin in 2004 followed by the Irish, Dutch, Luxemburg, UK, Austrian, and Finnish Presidencies on "Advancing Regulatory Reform" showed that there was rather strong political support in the EU for linking impact assessment to economic competitiveness (Renda 2006).

The political leaders in 2007 agreed to sign up to a target of reducing the burden of EU legislation by 25 percent by 2012 (*European Voice*, March 8–14, 2007). The political opposition against parts of the reform package for better regulation came primarily from the European Parliament. The Parliament feared that a simplified regulatory framework would exclude the Parliament and thus diminish the influence of the only directly elected European institution in European politics (Frykman and Mörth 2004). There was also some political criticism from national parliamentarians who argued that a simplified legislative process, in particular an increasing use of soft law, would increase the EU's competence without prior changes in the treaties (ibid.). However, there seemed to be consensus on the overall goal of improving Europe's economic competitiveness. The disagreement did not concern the general development towards a more performance-oriented Union and the goal of becoming the strongest economy in the world. Given this political background it is logical that there was an increasing interest in getting more private financing in various public sectors. The search for private financing of the transport infrastructure had already been emphasized in the mid-1990s by the Christopherson Report presented to the European Council in Essen, Germany, in December 1994. The importance of TENs was also given high priority in the European Commission White Paper on "Growth" (EC 1993). An important driving force behind the single market was to be accelerated by trans-European infrastructure networks. The main argument for private financing in the Christopherson Report was that it would reduce pressure on public budgets and on public debt levels (Teisman and Klijn 2002).

There was also an ideological shift in the EU, as in many EU member states, the main idea being that market reforms in the public sector were more efficient in providing citizens with public goods and services (Mörth 2008, 2009). Neoliberal economic ideas have been resilient in European politics since the 1980s (Schmidt and Thatcher 2013). Interestingly, these ideas did not only emanate from the EU and the OECD (the famous PUMA—Public Management Committee), at least not the market turn that was oriented towards privatizations of the welfare sector. There were member states that preceded the EU on deregulations and privatizations of former state-owned companies.

The Forerunner

Sweden has been at the forefront among the EU member states in embracing the market turn in the public sector. The Swedish deregulations of the telephone market were formally decided in 1992 and the electricity market was decided in 1996 (Blomgren et al. 2003; Forssell 1999). In conversations with officials in the European Commission the Swedish decisions to deregulate parts of the public sector have been used as a role model for the European Commission in their effort to persuade other member states to follow (Mörth 2003b). One case in point is the Swedish railway system. In 1988 there was a division between the Swedish Railway Company and what is now called the Swedish Transport Administration (Blomgren et al. 2003) that opened up the opportunity to commercialize the railway system.

The Swedish market-oriented policy toward the public sector also encompassed highly sensitive political policy areas, such as defense and security policy. The Swedish defense industry was privatized in the 1990s and early 2000s, a move which coincided with increased "civilianizing" and commercialization of this sector (Britz 2004). At the European level the Swedish government argued that a European defense industry market must be able to bear its own costs (Mörth 2003b; Britz 2004; Britz and Mörth 2004).

Thus, Swedish governments have advocated a market frame in many policy areas in the EU. They have in general been critical of any alleged instances of state protectionism and barriers to free trade. After the end of the Cold War that emphasis on market economy and free trade became even more pronounced (Brommesson, this volume). However, the market framing of the Swedish governments is not without exceptions.

One important exception from the Swedish market framing of policy areas in the EU is the policy on alcohol. Basically, the policy of how to regulate issues on alcohol encompasses two conflicting frames—a market frame and a public health frame. These two frames activate different types of rules and actors in the EU. The market frame belongs to the rules on the internal market (hard law) whereas the public health frame is less regulated by the EU, and then often formulated in terms of soft law. Swedish governments have "battled" for a public health frame on alcohol since the country became a member of the Union. Restrictive alcohol policies have a long history in Sweden, and since Sweden joined the EU the national policies have been eroded (Cisneros Örnberg 2009). The setbacks are several. I have already mentioned the ban on import. Another major setback was when Sweden had to abandon low traveler's allowances and gradually had to adopt the higher European levels for importation of alcohol by January 1, 2004. Although the EU, the Court, the European Commission, and some of the member states have during recent years increased their awareness of the public health frame regarding the issue of alcohol policy, it is quite clear that the market frame dominates how the issue is regulated.

To sum up, the market turn consists of reforms that are mainly performance-oriented and therefore emphasize efficiency and output legitimacy. In the case of Sweden there has been a fit, although not without tensions, between this policy at the EU level and Swedish decisions to deregulate infrastructure and other parts of the public sector. Overall, Sweden could be characterized as a "marketizer" interested in the introduction of more competition within the public sector (Pollitt and Bouckaert 2004).

The Societal Turn

The third and last governance turn is the societal turn. This turn is often interpreted as a societally inclusive decision-making and policy-making process. Soft law and other soft forms of regulations are alleged to aim at a more participatory style of governance (European Commission 2001; Caporaso and Wittenbrink 2006). The societal turn is thus interpreted as a break from the traditional government tradition of the EU. This turn is, as are the other two turns, double-edged. They entail a mix of components of input legitimacy and output legitimacy.

In general, the societal turn entails that governance rests upon multiple authorities that are not necessarily public. The rules are decided by both public and private actors. This means that the traditional distinction between the private and the public spheres that are so fundamental in the liberal thinking of democracy can be questioned (Hirst

1997). The public sphere is not necessarily state-based but can consist of private actors, non-profit organizations, and profit organizations. "The public sphere is based on representative government and the rule of law ... The private sphere is that of individual action, contract, and market exchange, protected by and yet independent of the state" (Hirst 1997: 116). Hirst argues that "In fact both state and civil society are made up of large complex organizations, and the boundary between the two is not at all clear" (Hirst 1997: 117). It is argued that the public domain cannot be analyzed in terms of states and interstate relations but as a domain in which states are embedded in a broader "institutionalized arena concerned with the production of global public goods" (Ruggie 2004: 500). Thus, various private actors take part in authoritative regulatory processes (cf. Cutler et al. 1999; Hall and Biersteker 2002). The regulatory processes in systems of governance often result in soft law. The latter can be of several types but the main characteristic is that it lacks the possibility of legal sanctions.

The democratic base of the authority system of governance is very little developed in the EU. The democratic model behind the authority system of governance is deliberative and societally based. People's opinions are formed in ongoing public dialogues and discussions. Indeed, one important rationale for questioning liberal and representative democracy is the fact that the political issues change (Barnett 1996). Drawing on Beck's argument of the risk society, the party politics of representative democracy were constructed to deal with non-reflexive issues and not with the new modernity of how the risk society is reflexive: "Humans have left the cycle of fate and entered a world whose parameters are now man-made" (Barnett 1996: 172; Dryzek 1999). "The idea that individuals and societies are increasingly able to reflect upon and chart their own course into the future, rather than adapt to fate or the flow of events, is encapsulated in recent work by theorists such as Ulrich Beck, Anthony Giddens, and Scott Lash on the concept of reflexive modernization" (Dryzek 1999: 37). In a society in which complex issues must be balanced against each other—economic concerns (growth, wealth, etc.), social concerns (for instance, inclusion), ecological sustainability, and political democratic concerns (for instance, accountability, participation)—"it is less obvious who are the experts and how to adjudicate the necessary trade-offs involved" (Olsen 2003: 6). Thus, the fact that issues change and require more participation from ordinary people challenges the traditional democratic system of hierarchy and parliamentarization.

Democratic reforms in systems of governance are focused on open structures and network building (ibid.). This means that regulations are not necessarily viewed as weak because of their lack of legal sanctions. Instead, social sanctions and processes of socialization are viewed as powerful compliance mechanisms. The use of soft law can therefore be argued to be more effective in terms of national implementation than traditional law (Jacobsson and Sundström, this volume). Governments can, as we saw in the section on the soft turn, argue that they are "masters" of the political process and independently translate the voluntary European agreements into national politics. One case in point is the already mentioned Open Method of Coordination, the OMC. The reform was legitimized by deliberative democracy and not as a reform that focused on hierarchy and parliamentarization (de la Porte and Nanz 2004). Interestingly, it has also been legitimized in terms of improved efficiency and performance—that is, output legitimacy, as we saw in the section on the market turn.

From a Swedish perspective, the societal turn in the form of a broadening of societal actors in the policy-making process follows a Swedish tradition of corporativism whereby organized interests are invited to take part in deliberation with the government. However, the societal turn also challenges this tradition. Societal actors are no longer limited to organized interests in the labor market. NGOs and other actors in the civil society are part of global society and put pressure on state actors (Bexell and Mörth 2010). As we saw in the section on the soft turn, the social NGOs have to some extent empowered social NGOs in relation to the Swedish government. However, the societal turn is also a turn to for-profit actors—a turn in which Sweden has been a forerunner in the EU. The combination in Swedish politics between a strong welfare sector and a strong civil society, funded by public funding, with market reforms in the public sector has been somewhat of a puzzle. One explanation given is how the Social Democrats (the party that was in government for almost 40 years) have seen market capitalism as a means to an end, which was to build a strong welfare sector (Berggren and Trädgårdh 2009).

In sum, paradoxically, the societal turn can be interpreted as change from government to governance in the sense that the emphasis falls more on steering through networks than through hierarchies. It is also a change from a more procedure-oriented administration to more market-friendly alternatives to command and control. My interpretation of the societal turn is that it entails a broadening of actors and regulative mechanisms, but that the democratic legitimization of these decisions has not changed. They are still dependent on democratic accountability mechanisms according to the hierarchical system of command and control. The deliberative traits of the EU are still weak.

CONCLUDING REMARKS

Political labels for reforms are open to multiple interpretations and can play a role both in performance and in a more deliberative policy-making process. The soft turn suggests both a more societally inclusive process and a more performance-oriented process. The market turn suggests that a general political malaise in the European project triggered reform activities that had social ambitions. Indeed, reforms designed to improve regulation seem to have functioned as a way of mobilizing actors and making things happen. Whether politics by reform and labeling or as turns has entailed profound changes in how the EU works is another question. The use of soft law goes back to the very start of the Community. Market capitalism, albeit politically regulated, is at the very core of the Community. The societal turn suggests a more inclusive decision-making and policy-making process that breaks with the traditional government tradition in the EU. However, the EU is formally to a large extent based on the authority system of government in which hard law and public actors (parliaments and governments) are the authoritative rule-makers and legislators. The governance turns are interlinked with this legal system, and they can be said to constitute each other. So, multigovernance polity is perhaps not telling us something new about how the EU works. The turns are ways of making decisions happen in a political project which recurrently faces political deadlocks and legitimacy crises.

The Swedish political position in the soft turn reflects a member that is in favor of European cooperation but is very reluctant to accept supranational cooperation at the European level. The section on the market turn shows that the supranational parts of the EU are also embraced by Sweden as long as they do not challenge core national issues, such as the issue of alcohol.

NOTE

1. "The process is political, not judicial. If one country fails it does not end up in front of the EU Court … The road selected at Lisbon means more cooperation but it does not mean more supranationality" ("Processen är politisk, inte juridisk. Om något land misslyckas hamnar det inte inför EG-domstolen. … Den väg som valts i Lissabon innebär förvisso mer av samarbete men den innebär inte mer av överstatlighet"). Translation from Swedish by the author.

REFERENCES

Aldestam, M. (2004). "Soft Law and State Aid Policy Area," in U. Mörth (ed.), *Soft Law in Governance and Regulation: An Interdisciplinary Analysis.* Cheltenham: Edward Elgar, 11–36.

Barnett, A. (1996). "The Creation of Democracy?" in P. Hirst and S. Khilnani (eds), *Reinventing Democracy.* London: Blackwell Publishers, 157–75.

Berggren, H. and Trädgårdh, L. (2009) *Är svensken människa? Gemenskap och oberoende i det moderna Sverige.* Stockholm: Norstedt.

Bexell, M. and Mörth, U. (eds) (2010). *Democracy and Public–Private Partnerships in Global Governance.* London: Palgrave.

Blomgren, H., Thorngren, B., Haegermark, H., Hulten, S., Eriksson, A., and Lindgren, F. (2003). "För en långsiktig positiv teknikutveckling på avreglerade marknader. Vad vi kan lära av telekom-, energi-, järnvägs- respektive försvarssektorn," IVA-report.

Britz, M. (2004). "The Europeanization of Defence Industry Policy," PhD dissertation, Department of Political Science, Stockholm University.

Britz, M. and Mörth, U. (2004). "European Integration as Organizing: The Case of Armaments," *Journal of Common Market Studies* 42: 957–73.

Caporaso, J. and Wittenbrinck, J. (2006). "The New Modes of Governance and Political Authority in Europe," *Journal of European Public Policy* 13: 471–80.

Case-1989/95 and Case-170/04. Opinions by the Court of Justice of the European Union.

Christiansen, T. and Piattoni, S. (eds) (2003). *Informal Governance in the European Union.* Cheltenham: Edward Elgar.

Cram, L. (1997). *Policy-making in the EU.* London: Routledge.

Cutler, C., Haufler, V., and Porter, T. (eds) (1999). *Private Authority and International Affairs.* New York: State University of New York Press.

Dehousse, R. (2004). "La méthod ouverte de coordination, quand l'instrument tient lieu de politique," in P. Lascoumes and P. Le Galès (eds), *Gouverner par les instruments.* Paris: Presses de Sciences Po, 331–56.

Dryzek, J. S. (1999). "Transnational Democracy," *Journal of Political Philosophy* 7: 30–51.

European Commission (1993). "Growth, Competitiveness, Employment: The Challenges and Ways Forward into the 21st Century," COM (700), Final. Luxembourg: Office for Official Publications of the European Communities.

European Commission (1995). "Report of the Group of Independent Experts on Legislative and Administrative Simplification," COM (288), Final.

European Commission (2001). "European Governance: A White Paper," COM (428), Final.

European Commission (2002). "Communication from the Commission on Impact Assessment," COM (276), Final.

European Commission (2004). "Who Is Doing What on Better Regulation at the EU Level—Organization Charts," Commission Working Document compiled by the Secretariat General, Brussels.

European Voice (2007). March 8–14.

Forssell, A. (1999). "Offentlig reformation i marknadsmodellernas spar?" *SCORE Rapportserie* 1999:5.

Frykman, H. and Mörth, U. (2004). "Soft Law and Three Notions of Democracy: The Case of the EU," in U. Mörth (ed.), *Soft Law in Governance and Regulation: An Interdisciplinary Analysis.* Cheltenham: Edward Elgar, 155–70.

Hall, R. B. and Biersteker, T. (eds) (2002). *The Emergence of Private Authority in Global Governance.* Cambridge: Cambridge University Press.

Héritier, A. (1999). *Policy-Making and Diversity in Europe: Escape from Deadlock.* Cambridge: Cambridge University Press.

Héritier, A. (2001). "New Modes of Governance in Europe: Policy-making without Legislating?" in A. Héritier (ed.), *Common Goods: Reinventing European and International Governance.* Lanham, MD: Rowman & Littlefield, 185–206.

Hirst, P. (1997). *From Statism to Pluralism.* London: UCL Press.

Jacobsson, K. (2004). "Between the Deliberation and Discipline: Soft Governance in EU Employment Policy," in U. Mörth (ed.), *Soft Law in Governance and Regulation: An Interdisciplinary Analysis.* Cheltenham: Edward Elgar, 81–102.

Jacobsson, K. and Johansson, H. (2007). "The Micro-Politics of the OMC: NGOs and the Social Inclusion Process in Sweden." Paper for presentation at the International Meetings on Law and Society in the 21st Century, Humboldt University, Berlin, July 25–28.

Kassim, H. and Le Galès, P. (2010). "Exploring Governance in Multi-Level Polity: A Policy Instruments Approach," *West European Politics* 33: 1–21.

Kleine, M. (2013). *Informal Governance in the European Union: How Governments Make International Organizations Work.* Ithaca, NY: Cornell University Press.

Kohler-Koch, B. and Rittberger, B. (2006). "Review Article: The 'Governance Turn in EU Studies," in U. Sedelmeier and A. Young (eds), *The JCMS Annual Review of the European Union 2005.* London: Blackwell, 27–49.

March, J. (1981). "Decision-Making Perspective," in A. Van de Ven, and W. Joyce (eds), *Perspectives on Organization Design and Behavior.* New York: John Wiley & Sons, 205–44.

March, J. (1994). *A Primer of Decision Making: How Decisions Happen.* New York: Free Press.

March, J. (1997). "Understanding How Decisions Happen in Organizations," in Z. Shapira (ed.), *Organizational Decision Making*. Cambridge: Cambridge University Press, 9–34.

Marks, G., Hooghe, L., and Blank, K. (1996). "European Integration from the 1980s: State Centric v. Multi-Level Governance," *Journal of Common Market Studies* 34: 341–78.

Mazey, S. and Richardson, J. (1995). "Promiscuous Policymaking: The European Policy Style," in C. Rhodes and S. Mazey (eds), *The State of the European Union*, vol. 3: *Building a European Polity?* Boulder, CO: Lynne Rienner.

Mörth, U. (1996). "Vardagsintegration—La vie quotidienne—i Europa: Sverige i EUREKA och EUREKA i Sverige," PhD dissertation, Department of Political Science, Stockholm University.

Mörth, U. (2003a). "Europeanisation as Interpretation, Translation and Editing of Public Policies," in K. Featherstone and C. Radaelli (eds), *The Politics of Europeanisation: Theory and Analysis*. Oxford: Oxford University Press, 159–78.

Mörth, U. (2003b). *Organizing European Cooperation: The Case of Armaments*. Lanham, MD: Rowman & Littlefield.

Mörth, U. (ed.) (2004). *Soft Law in Governance and Regulation: An Interdisciplinary Analysis*. Cheltenham: Edward Elgar.

Mörth, U. (2008). *European Public–Private Collaboration: A Choice between Efficiency and Democratic Accountability?* Cheltenham: Edward Elgar.

Mörth, U. (2009). "The Market Turn in EU Governance: The Emergence of Public–Private Collaboration," *Governance* 22: 99–120.

NEWGOV (2004). *Integrated Project New Modes of Governance: Description of Work*. Florence: European University Institute.

Olsen, J. (2003). "What Is the Legitimate Role for Euro-Citizens?" *Comparative European Politics* 1/1: 91–110.

Örnberg Cisneros, J (2009). "The Europeanization of Swedish Alcohol Policy," PhD dissertation, Department of Political Science, Stockholm University.

Österdahl, I. (2004). "The ECJ and Soft Law: Who's Afraid of the EU Fundamental Rights Charter?" in U. Mörth (ed.), *Soft Law in Governance and Regulation: An Interdisciplinary Analysis*. Cheltenham: Edward Elgar, 37–60.

Painter, M. (2001). "Policy Capacity and the Effects of New Public Mangement," in T. Christensen and P. Laegreid (eds), *New Public Management: The Transformation of Ideas and Practice*. Aldershot: Ashgate, 209–30.

Palier, B. (2005). "Ambiguous Argument, Cumulative Changes: Social Policies in France in the 1990s," in K. Thelen and W. Streek (eds), *Beyond Continuity*. Oxford: Oxford University Press, 127–44.

Pierre, J. and Peters, G. (2000). *Governance, Politics and the State*. Basingstoke: Macmillan.

Pollitt, C. and Bouckaert, G. (2004). *Public Management Reform*. Oxford: Oxford University Press.

Porte, C. de la and Nanz, P. (2004). "The OMC—A Deliberative Democratic Mode of Governance? The Cases of Employment and Pensions," *Journal of European Public Policy* 11: 267–88.

Radaelli, C. (2007a). "Towards Better Research on Better Regulation." Paper delivered to the Advanced Colloquium on Better Regulation, Centre for Regulatory Governance, University of Exeter, January 25–26.

Radaelli, C. (2007b). "Whither Better Regulation for the Lisbon Agenda?" *Journal of European Public Policy* 14: 190–207.

Renda, A. (2006). *Impact Assessment in the EU: The State of the Art and the Art of the State*. Brussels: CEPS.

Rhodes, R. (2003). "What Is New about Governance and Why Does It Matter?" in J. Hayward and A. Menon (eds), *Governing Europe*. Oxford: Oxford University Press, 61–73.

Rosamund, B. (2000). *Theories of the European Integration*. London: Palgrave Macmillan.

Ruggie, J. G. (1993). "Territoriality and Beyond: Problematizing Modernity in International Relations," *International Organization* 47: 139–73.

Ruggie, J. G. (2004). "Reconstituting the Global Public Domain: Issues, Actors and Practices," *European Journal of International Relations* 10: 499–531.

Scharpf, F. (1999). *Governing in Europe: Effective and Democratic?* Oxford: Oxford University Press.

Scharpf, F. (2002). "Legitimate Diversity: The New Challenge of European Integration," *Cahiers Europeens de Sciences Po*, No. 1. Paris: Centre d'études européennes at Sciences Po.

Schmidt, V. and Thatcher, M. (eds) (2013). *Resilient Liberalism in Europe's Political Economy*. Cambridge: Cambridge University Press.

Swedish Parliament (1999/2000:92). Protocol (Riksdagen, snabbprotokoll).

Teisman, G. and Klijn, E.-H. (2002). "Partnership Arrangements: Governmental Rhetoric or Governance Scheme?" *Public Administration Review* 62: 197–205.

Unice (1995). *Releasing Europe's Potential through Targeted Regulatory Reform: The Unice Regulatory Report*. Brussels: Unice.

CHAPTER 38

THE EUROPEANIZATION OF THE SWEDISH STATE

BENGT JACOBSSON AND GÖRAN SUNDSTRÖM

Introduction

STATES are highly integrated in and influenced by their broader environments. The importance of European and global information flows as well as European and global regulation (either in soft or hard forms) is conspicuous. The European Union is an obvious example of an increasing governance directed toward European states. Interests, strategies, and identities of politicians and administrators in all the states of Europe are increasingly influenced by EU activities. Sweden is no exception to this.

In this chapter we will show how the Swedish state has been transformed as a consequence of its integration in the broader European and global environment. We will distinguish three typical processes that shape state activities: regulative, inquisitive, and meditative. We argue that the Swedish state, more than before, can be described as highly fragmented and typically as a rule-following entity. We will also reflect on the implications of Europeanization for the capacity and the legitimacy of the Swedish state.

Environments of States

Governance activities directed toward states have expanded. The European Union has developed into a powerful governing body, but there are also many other organizations involved in issuing rules for states, in monitoring these rules, and in all kinds of consultations, rankings, peer reviews, and other discussions of states. In every field, there is a plethora of cultural and organizational material in the form of policies, programs, rules, guidelines, etc. that have to be consulted and deliberated by states. Some are produced by the European Union, some by other organizations (the UN, OECD, Freedom House, IMF, Amnesty, IASB, ISO, etc.).

To be able to understand recent developments in states, it is reasonable to start by looking at these environments. However, most theoretical perspectives do otherwise. It is often assumed that states have stable and rather precise interests, i.e. it is understood that they know what they want. Organizations like the European Union are in this account basically perceived as arenas where states meet and battle with one another, each seeking to realize its own strategies. In our view, this depiction of states is disturbingly undersocialized. We will show that states often learn what they want by being associated with wider environmental processes: by relating to standards and other rules, by being scrutinized by others, and by participating in discussions with others about their own activities.

States are governed in three ways. Governing may, first, come as rules. Among such *regulative mechanisms* we include mandatory rules. For example, the EU members are required to implement the full acquis communautaire; that is, the whole body of EU law and practice. Often, however, rule-making tends to be based on at least some elements of voluntary compliance. It is then often shaped as standards or other kinds of "soft rules" (Brunsson and Jacobsson 2000; Jacobsson and Sahlin-Andersson 2006). One example of softness in EU regulation is the use of an "open method of coordination," where member states have to work towards agreed goals, follow specified procedures, and open themselves to critical examination by the Commission and other member states, but still retain the right to determine the content of their activities (Borrás and Jacobsson 2004).

Second, there are *inquisitive mechanisms*. Member states are not obliged to follow certain specific policies, but they are required to "open up" and let others examine and critically judge what they are doing (as in the abovementioned open method of coordination). Generally, we see a great deal of auditing, comparison, and ranking of diverse state practices and of entire states. Sometimes the inquisitors conduct their audits according to rules that they themselves have devised, thereby connecting inquisition with rule-making. Sometimes they apply rules produced by other organizations. Such audits can be very influential. Those evaluated may even change their behavior in order to look good in the eyes of their inquisitors. As has been pointed out, audits frequently not only represent activities but also shape the activities of the state (Power 1997).

Third, there are *meditative mechanisms*. There are plenty of organizations and arenas where state policies and programs are discussed. These organizations and arenas generate and share ideas about what to do and how to do it, and function as spaces where experiences are transmitted and compared, and ideas are generated and shared. Meditation can be seen as one distinct mechanism, but also as one that conditions and envelops others. Rankings or audits are often starting points for discussions, seminars, conferences, etc. Processes of imitation, learning, and innovation require activities that yield best practices. All these processes are embedded in discourses about the kinds of structures, policies, and activities appropriate to modern states.

Obviously, states are not isolated entities that have to find out everything for themselves. Not only are they influenced by what is going on in their broader environment, but they are by and large constructed by this environment. Through the mechanisms sketched above, the activities of the state as well as the states as actors are fashioned. If for instance a territory like Sápmi (the region in the European North traditionally inhabited by the Sami people) wants to become a proper state, it does not have to start from scratch and try to find out what it needs. Instead, it just has to "open up" to all the experts and specialists in the EU and in other organizations that know exactly what the would-be state needs in terms of organizations, rules, policies, etc.

The Sápmi example is an extreme one, since Sweden as a state is often already usually perceived as highly modern and enlightened. However, in Sweden, too, the strength of these environmental forces in constituting both state preferences and state policies is obvious. In the following sections we shall show how the state has developed from the point in time when Sweden became a member of the European Union, or rather when it became part of the internal market (European Economic Area). We will show (with empirical examples) how both Swedish politics and Swedish administration have been embedded in its European and global environment, and that this has resulted in a situation where the Swedish state could be seen, first, as more fragmented than ever, and second, as an entity that typically follows rules produced by others.

THE EMBEDDED STATE

This and the following sections draw on several different kinds of empirical studies of Europeanization processes. We have ourselves conducted case studies of the Europeanization of specific policy fields (Jacobsson and Sundström 2006). An important study that will be referred to below is a questionnaire to all units in the central state (both ministries and agencies) put by ourselves in 1998 and 2003 (see Jacobsson and Sundström 2006; Jacobsson et al. 2004). The questionnaire was part of a Nordic project, and the same questionnaire was sent out in Denmark, Norway, Finland, and Iceland.

Practically all units in the Swedish state saw themselves as affected by activities in the European Union. Half of them reported that the consequences of EU membership had been significant. Four out of ten units claimed that they spent a large proportion of their time on EU-related work. Many were forced to recruit specialized staff in order cope with their EU-oriented work. EU-related work was highly decentralized. Transnational contacts were by no means reserved for the Ministry of Foreign Affairs. Instead, they existed within virtually all policy fields and at all administrative levels. Separate units within both ministries and agencies participated frequently in transnational, EU-related networks. These networks also included organizations other than the European Union; they were transnational and/or global.

A distinct pattern was discernible: the more embedded in the EU (in terms of contacts with different EU organizations, time spent on EU issues, traveling days etc.), the more contacts with other Swedish actors (other governmental units, companies, interest organizations etc.). Talking with the EU meant talking with others, possibly about what was talked about with the EU. Contacts in EU matters were often informal. Only a few units (16 percent in our survey) pointed to "formal written contacts" as the most common form of contact with the European Commission/Directorates General. Regarding preparatory or expert committees of the Commission, the figure was even lower. As expected, "formal meetings" were more common in these relations, but it was obvious that informal contacts were of great importance in relations between Swedish government units and EU organizations.

Informality was even more salient in the different units' relations with other Swedish actors. Especially interesting was the high degree of informality both within and between ministries and agencies. Apparently, the long Swedish tradition of semi-autonomous agencies, and the formal control system which prescribes that instructions in EU matters should be in writing, did not prevent informal exchanges between politicians and officials. The informality of the Swedish state administration was apparent. Interestingly enough, the other Nordic countries showed much lower figures for informal contacts in these kind of relations, and this in spite of the fact that Denmark and Norway have a system of ministerial rule.

Frequent contacts between Swedish politicians and government units indicated that politicians tried to keep a close eye on their civil servants. However, our survey showed that 25 percent of the units did not get any guidance at all from their political superiors concerning their participation in different EU committees or working groups. When signals were given, they were typically general and informal. However, the lack of detailed instructions did not seem to bother Swedish officials. Seven out of ten units maintained that it was easy to know what their political superiors wanted. Few conflicts arose between officials and politicians. However, and seemingly contradictorily, as many as 40 percent of the units agreed with the statement that short time limits made it difficult to discuss EU matters with their own politicians.

We suggest that this observation—officials on the one hand claiming their relations with the politicians to be extensive and basically working fine, and on the other hand claiming a need for clearer instructions and more time to discuss EU issues with politicians—should be seen as an expression of Swedish officials' eagerness to anchor their behavior at the political level. The frequent contacts between the two groups were not about politicians taking initiatives and trying to exercise detailed control over officials. Rather, officials tried to keep politicians informed, to have their "blessing," or to get them to clarify their wishes and opinions on various matters. The demand for steering signals from civil servants exceeded the supply of such signals from politicians.

Government units within all policy fields, and at all levels, were affected by the EU. They spent a considerable proportion of their working hours on EU matters. They participated in different "arenas" within the EU and they had lots of contacts—often informal ones—in their handling of EU issues. European networks had become an important part of government officials' everyday work. In later stages of a process, especially, national officials attended meetings with fairly well-defined national "points of view." However, more often and especially in the early stages of a process, ideas about what was desirable and what was possible were created in these European networks as processes evolved. Often, it was in exchanges with other European actors that Swedish officials learnt who they were, what they wanted, and what it was possible to expect.

THE FRAGMENTED STATE

With these observations in mind, the view of states as primarily purposeful and strategic is difficult to adhere to wholeheartedly. Purposes and strategies are to a large extent learned and picked up in wider European and global environments. Another belief about states that is difficult to reconcile with empirical observations is that they are coherent and meticulously coordinated, and that—in interaction with other states—they are able to "speak with one voice." The coherence of states can be seriously contested as they become increasingly integrated in European and transnational networks.

States are fragmented. In our studies, this fragmentation manifested itself in a number of different ways. For one thing, even though units that were deeply embedded in the European Union had a lot of contacts with many different kinds of actors, the networks were quite narrow. Membership of the EU resulted in increased exchanges between different actors within the same policy field, while contacts between government units from different policy fields became rarer (Vifell 2009).

As an example of this fragmentation, the National Board of Trade (*Kommerskollegium*) found after interviewing Swedish officials within twenty-five agencies about their EU-related work that:

> ...few are satisfied with the coordination of broader EU issues, which involves several ministries or agencies. In these situations insufficient coordination, lack of understanding, and poor communication can result in issues falling between the chairs. [...] The Europeanization has strengthened the boundaries between different sectors. Within each sector, exchanges and cooperation with actors in other countries—and in the private sector—are deepened. (National Board of Trade 2005: 9, 16)

The National Board of Trade stated that separate units and experts sometimes lived a life of their own *inside* ministries and agencies, and that superior officials often did not see—let alone approve—the Swedish proposals brought to EU meetings by officials at lower levels.

Similar observations were made in a study of the internationalization of three different policy fields. Vifell (2009) noticed that the fragmentation of the state was not about whole sectors drifting apart but instead about "enclaves," i.e. constellations which included different kinds of actors, sometimes from different sectors, and which were defined by the point at issue. What characterized "enclaves" was that people who participated in them worked closely together over longer periods of time, in ways that resulted in mutual learning, common understanding, and trust and respect for each other's competence. These people were to some extent dissociated from their "home organiza-tions." Organizations like the EU and the UN often acted "hosts" for these "enclaves" (Slaughter 2005; Boström 2006).

In these "enclaves," Swedish ministries and agencies worked closely together, and offi-cials could develop very strong feelings of togetherness. Similar observations have been found in case studies covering such different policy areas as statistics (Mannfeldt 2000), customs (Heinegård 2000), employment (Etzler 2004), environment (Savelli 2000), competition (Sundström 2000), and medical products (Nilsson 2000). To what extent politicians were involved in the "enclaves" differed. However, officials both within min-istries and agencies had quite a good knowledge of what their political superiors wanted.

The National Board of Trade claimed that certain agencies had gained extreme independence vis-à-vis politicians. These agencies were formulating their EU instruc-tions themselves, and if politicians tried to change these instructions the agencies got annoyed. The Medical Products Agency (*Läkemedelsverket*) maintained that the gov-ernment neither could, nor should, try to control the agency, because the majority of the issues handled with European cooperation were purely scientific. Similar observations were made in a study of competition policies. Here the credibility of the agency was imagined to be greater if the politicians were kept at a distance, and increased credibil-ity also meant a better opportunity to influence issues handled by the EU's competition committees (Sundström 2000).

All in all, important decisions were being taken within limited and network-like constellations in which national officials, EU officials, and private and public experts participated. There were many such "enclaves" built around different kinds of issues, working in parallel, often far away from national politicians. This—in combination with the detailed character of many EU issues, the rapid pace of the processes, and the impor-tance attributed to expertise—made it difficult for national politicians to supervise and influence EU-related decision-making processes. One interpretation of the observa-tions is that national politicians (more than before) were in a process of losing control over issues for which they were held accountable.

The Scripted State

What we observed was a situation where states followed rules invented by others. After becoming an EU member, the state had to comply with EU regulations. For Sweden, this was obvious in the case of agricultural policy. Here, the Swedish Parliament had decided to deregulate agricultural policy just one year before the Swedish government submitted an application for EU membership. The deregulated Swedish policy diverged strongly from the EU's Common Agricultural Policy (CAP), and, consequently, it had to be abandoned as soon as Sweden became a full EU member.

States do not follow only formal or "hard" rules. As has been pointed out, many rules directed towards states are "soft," and come in the shape of advice, recommendations, standards, goals, strategies, guidelines, etc. Such rules are based on voluntary compliance, and they often contain a high degree of reciprocity in that states also take part in their creation. Sometimes, this voluntariness and reciprocity can be illusory. It can be difficult for states not to follow the rules. Educational policy, with the Bologna process, is one example. This process dates back to 1999, when the twenty-nine European ministers in charge of higher education met in Bologna to lay the basis for establishing a European Higher Education Area by 2010, and promoting the European system of higher education worldwide. In what has become known as the Bologna Declaration, the ministers affirmed their intention to adopt a system of easily readable and comparable degrees, which had two main cycles (undergraduate/graduate): establish a system of credits (such as ECTS), promote mobility, and support European cooperation in quality assurance. Legally, the declaration contains no binding rules. Rather it is a kind of framework, to which countries can adapt voluntarily.

Employment policy is another area characterized by soft rules. Here, the EU is working with the so-called "Open Method of Coordination" (OMC). This method was introduced at the Lisbon Summit in March 2000 as a tool for strengthening the "Community dimension." The idea was that all EU states should take part in efforts to improve people's employability, spirit of enterprise, adaptability, and equality regarding opportunities on the European labor market. The OMC rests on several soft law mechanisms, such as guidelines, indicators, benchmarking, and sharing of best practices. There are no official sanctions for laggards. Rather, convergence is attained through a form of peer pressure and "naming and shaming" (Jacobsson and Vifell 2005). The OMC has also been applied within other policy areas.

Public Management Policy (PMP) is another policy field highly influenced by global ideas and activities. Here, the World Bank and the OECD have been important rule-makers for many years (Pollitt and Bouckaert 2004). They have been spreading different ideas and practices aimed at governments. These ideas and practices have been summarized in concepts like *New Public Management* and *Good Governance* (Hood 1991), and the rules associated with these standards have been extremely soft. The OECD has gathered information from different states about achievements and setbacks and used it to make comparisons, lists, and rankings. The information has then been spread not only through publications, but also through conferences and seminars hosted by the OECD (meditative mechanisms). Sweden has been an industrious participant in these activities (Premfors 1998). Convergence in this case has been attained through peer pressure and naming and shaming.

These examples could be multiplied, but our point is to illustrate the dependence of states on a wider European and global environment (Jacobsson 2006). Many of these rules originate from the EU, but many also stem from a wider, global context. The examples also show that there is a mix of mechanisms involved as states open up to environmental forces. One is, of course, the rules as such. The rules may be "hard" or "soft," and rules intended for states often seem to be of the latter kind. Soft rules are also often accompanied by different kinds of scrutinizing and monitoring, i.e. inquisitive activities. There is no shortage of large and influential international organizations that scrutinize the activities of states. In recent decades we have also seen an increase in state agencies that specialize in auditing, evaluating, and supervising other state agencies (Hood et al. 1999; Premfors et al. 2003). And, as we noted in the examples above, many of these agencies follow international rules or national rules which originate from international rules.

The examples also showed that rules—especially soft ones—aimed at states are often surrounded by discourse. Convergence is to a considerable extent achieved by opinions and notions being formed through conversations and discussions. International organizations are important actors in the making of these discourses. They act as "hosts," making sure that representatives of states not only read the same documents, but also meet repeatedly to discuss the various issues; they have a kind of meditative function. The OECD has acted as "host" within the PMP area. Yet, the OECD has neither worked out rules, nor conducted formal evaluations. Instead it has put together knowledge and experience about how different PMP methods have worked in different states, then pointed out which states have been successful (and worth emulating) and which states have failed (and need to pull themselves together and speed up the adaptation).

Transformations of the Swedish State

If we summarize our arguments so far, states are often presented as organizational units that decide for themselves and form their own preferences, strategies, and positions. They are thought of as actors that are coordinated and coherent, and they are described as organizational units that with the help of rules and rule enforcement procedures are able to make decisions affecting the lives of individuals that live within a particular geographical area. This "command-and-control" model of states is popular, and it surely dominates the reform agenda in states.

However, a more complex picture has emerged in our analysis of the Europeanization of the Swedish state. Swedish state organizations do produce strategies and national positions. However, these strategies and positions are not created in isolation, but rather in exchanges with others (other EU organizations, agencies in other states, interest organizations, corporations, etc.), and they are embedded in wider systems of discourse, examinations, and rule-making.

States are sometimes extraordinarily fragmented, and this in spite of the fact that relentless efforts have been put into the creation of coordination and control. In practice, policies are frequently formed in segments that transcend national borders. Policies emerge and are fashioned within European and global networks. We get more fragmentation, and the gap widens between what state politicians are held responsible for, on the one hand, and what they are actually able to influence, on the other.

States are to a large extent scripted. The Swedish state still produces rules. However, more than ever, their work seems to be to make sure that rules issued by other organizations (European Union, United Nations, World Trade Organization, International

Accounting Standards Board, etc.) are followed inside Swedish territory. This does not mean a withdrawal or hollowing out of states. In many fields, it is through states that European and global rules are implemented and legitimized.

If we do not know how states are connected to their wider European and global environment, we will not understand the transformations going on. We have argued that states should be seen as organizations deeply embedded in their environments, severely fragmented, and scripted by systems of rules and ideas that are produced in that environment. Despite all the talk about globalization, the retreat of states, and the importance of regions, etc., what we see in Europe and in the world is not that states are becoming less attractive than before. Rather, the role of state is in flux. In order to understand what this means, we have argued that it is necessary to consider governing forces in the environment of states and investigate different kinds of regulative, inquisitive, and meditative activities that influence states.

LEGITIMATION STRATEGIES

Sweden has become deeply embedded in the European Union and in the global environment. What has been the reaction to this from Swedish governments? How has this increased dependence on the European Union been legitimated? This is an intriguing question, since the legitimacy of the Swedish state compared to many other countries has traditionally been (and still is) quite high. During the negotiation period with the EU as well as during the first years of membership, it was often asked whether it was possible to keep the traditional Swedish way of handling issues while still being perceived as good Europeans.

A first legitimation strategy has been to maintain that Sweden has only been affected to a limited extent by the EU, to talk about the EU as something remote, and to portray ongoing European processes as something quite inconsequential for Sweden. This has been an obvious strategy within many different fields. Our empirical observations contradict the substance of such arguments. As mentioned earlier, large portions of the central state have become deeply embedded in the EU and many changes have been made within several policy areas as a result of this embeddedness. Contact patterns, steering signals, modes of organizing, competences, values, etc. have all changed.

A second strategy has been to maintain that Sweden can "pick and choose" what to adopt from the EU. The basic argument is that Sweden benefits from membership within certain restricted fields of activities. In cases where problems are transnational—as they are in the cases of organized crime and environmental protection—European cooperation is needed, but as for the rest, Swedish rules and organizations should be maintained and protected. In line with this, it has been important to argue that Swedish national politicians are in control of whichever policy fields are "handed over" to the EU and those which are kept on the national level. Such arguments do have some support (not leaving the krona for the euro is one example), but basically it has been more and more difficult to find and uphold exceptions.

A third legitimation strategy has been based on the argument that Sweden has been influential in the European Union. The Government has tried to convince citizens that politicians and civil servants in the Swedish state together with other Swedish actors (NGOs, private industries, local authorities, and regions, etc.) have been able to act jointly and successfully when working on EU matters and participating in different EU organizations (Sundström 1999). Judging from our studies, it is hard to claim that Swedish politicians and officials in general have been particularly influential and been able to market themselves as models for others, even if there have been a handful of such accomplishments.

A fourth strategy has been to assert that the changes Sweden has been undergoing in recent years would have taken place whether we were EU members or not, and that the EU's ideas and ambitions to a large extent correspond with Swedish ideas and ambitions. It has been important to point out that the Swedish state can easily integrate changes coming from the EU with established Swedish ways of doing things. One way of doing that has been simply to maintain that new (and old) EU ideas and rules correspond reasonably well with what Sweden is already doing—or has long planned to do.

Thus, several different strategies have been used in an effort to legitimate Swedish EU work. The strategies have been based on several distinct arguments, but they all emphasize the boundary between the Swedish and the European, and that the Swedish way of doing things is usually preferable to whatever Europe has to offer. The Swedish state can be described as a reluctant European, and this hesitant position can largely be explained by the Swedes being reluctant Europeans. It is important to recall that when the Swedish people voted for an EU membership in 1994 the victory for the Yes side was a narrow one, and when they voted on the Euro in 2003 a clear majority took the No side (56 against 42 percent). We will now leave the specific Swedish adaptation and instead discuss some theoretical implications of our studies of Europeanization processes.

Making Sense of Europeanization

Most interpretations of Europeanization processes share some common features. They all regard states as purposive and rational actors that know what they want. States "have" interests and use their power to pursue or safeguard them. States are also regarded as unitary actors. Loose couplings between talk and action, as well as between different administrative levels, are seen as temporary and pathological, something to be remedied by reform. Much of this view of states is also reinforced by what those in charge (i.e. politicians and bureaucrats) actually say and do. In recent decades, due to planning ideals of the 1960s and 1970s as well as New Public Management ideals of the 1980s and 1990s, states have worked hard to become exactly the purposive, goal-directed rational actors that the models assume.

This has not resulted in a situation, however, where states have become more controlled and coordinated than before. We have argued that the conventional model fails to appreciate important aspects of the transformation of states. We advocate a model that emphasizes environmental pressures and the offering of ideas, models, solutions, and reforms that accompanies these pressures. Instead of a top-down model that starts with the goals, purposes, and interests of states, and then discusses how to organize to reach the goals, we start with the acknowledgment that states (like most organizations) are open and responsive to their environments. This goes for states as collective actors and for state organizations in specific fields (e.g. the environment, education, and labor market policy).

As soon as states open up, they are immediately flooded with advice about what to do. The problem for states (as for most other organizations) is not one of accepting and applying the ideas and models offered concerning how to work, but of being able to resist such ideas if they so wish. It is easy to follow the advice; what is difficult is to reject it. In particular, if certain ideas have become institutionalized—for example, that states should have aspirations and programs for democracy, education, research, and the environment—it becomes extremely difficult for any state *not* to espouse these ideas (Meyer et al. 1997). There are pressures to conform to this agenda at all levels in the organization, and if someone (especially in a leading position) wants something else, he or she may be in big trouble.

The basic logic is one of rule-following; the wish to become something else (e.g. normal, modern, Western, or European) that triggers the reform process (March and Olsen 1989; Powell and DiMaggio 1991). Imagined identities change, as do the situations facing the states. Rules do not have to be sought; instead they are offered in abundance by other states, the EU itself, other international organizations, standards organizations, experts and scientists, consultants, NGOs, and many other actors that know how to do things. All these pundits are in a position to offer advice to the state in question, to help it achieve the desired identity. Such processes are mainly solution-driven, and have sometimes been orchestrated by the European Union, especially in the pre-membership stage. Even without that boost, however, reform processes will be launched, since they are in the interest of these organizations.

The logic is also one of preference formation. The consequence of opening up is that a state becomes involved in processes by which it learns what other states do, as well as what various authorities in the field advise it to do. It may well be that the initial attitude of the leadership of state organizations is to stick to established ways of doing things. However, as they engage in various processes (e.g. meetings, conferences, rankings, high-level consultations, low-level consultations, and other kinds of meditations), preferences change and state representatives may start to want something different from what they wanted at the outset. They come to learn what they want as a state, and they do this via the processes by which they interact with others (Weick 1995).

Processes that follow this logic will probably result in a certain amount of decoupling in state organizations (Weick 1976; Meyer and Rowan 1977), though not necessarily in the Goffman sense that there are rationalized, front-stage presentations, on the one hand, versus inert back-stage practices, on the other (although this could be the case). Everyday practices may change, since the candidate states interact with their colleague states and other advisors at all levels. This may lead to changes in practices "at the bottom," without any change in presentations "at the top." Since most interaction and meditation takes place in specific field networks involving experts and bureaucrats who have common interests and worldviews (e.g. about food inspection, work safety, and competition policies), we may also have changes in one policy field, without this necessarily influencing any other field.

Symbolically, it may be extremely important to point out that changes are underway, especially in states that want to turn their backs on the past. In those cases, rationalized presentations are important, and we may experience many ceremonies, rituals, etc., celebrating the transformations. However, in situations where the historic legacies are more legitimate than the pressures from the European Union, we may witness something different. In those cases, we may instead see attempts to claim that very little really has changed or needs to be changed because of the opening up to Europe. Sweden is an interesting case here, as the pretense has been that very little did have to change in Swedish politics and administration. As we saw in the previous section, this grossly underestimates actual transformations.

Theoretically we find the development described interesting. According to institutional theories, organizations exposed to new external demands will answer by creating structures and procedures that give the impression that the demands are being met, at the same time as practices continue as before (Meyer and Rowan 1977). Following this, we should expect to find a decoupling between stable practices and changing presentations of these practices. However, here it is the other way around: the presentations are stable, while practices are changing. Our explanation of this "inverted decoupling" is that the legitimacy of the political and administrative system, as well as of welfare state arrangements in general, is high in Sweden. Even if most things are changing as a consequence of reforms and regulative initiatives emanating from the EU, the impression most politicians want to give is that existing arrangements are both stable and resilient.

Conclusion

As we have pointed out, the Swedish state is subject to various forms of governance. State identities, structures, and behavior are more than before shaped via processes of European and global rule-making, inquisition, and meditation. No doubt, the Swedish state still has ambitions to govern, and sometimes it can do this successfully (more about this in Jacobsson and Sundström's chapter about the governing function of states in this volume). However, the Swedish state has also increasingly developed into being more of a fragmented rule-follower, than a coordinated rule-maker. This does not mean that the Swedish state (or states in general in Europe) has become less significant. On the contrary, it is still important in many ways. The state guarantees that rules are implemented (not always perfectly but at least to some extent). And the state is crucial when it comes to legitimizing contemporary forms of governance. Even if its shapes and strengths are transformed by the forces of Europeanization, the Swedish state is still both significant and solid.

REFERENCES

Borrás, S. and Jacobsson, K. (2004). "The Open Method of Co-ordination and New Governance Patterns in the EU," *Journal of European Public Policy* 11/2: 185–208.

Boström, M. (2006). "Regulatory Credibility and Authority through Inclusiveness: Standardization Organizations in Cases of Eco-Labelling," *Organizations* 12/3: 345–67.

Brunsson, N. and Jacobsson, B. (2000). *A World of Standards*. Oxford: Oxford University Press.

Djelic, M.-L. and Sahlin-Andersson, K. (eds) (2006). *Transnational Governance. Institutional Dynamics of Regulation*. Cambridge: Cambridge University Press.

Etzler, N. (2004). "Implementeringen av Växtkraft mål 3 i Sverige: Om styrningen av ett arbets-marknadspolitiskt strukturfondprogram och dess förvaltningsmyndighet," Masters graduating paper, Department for Political Science, Stockholm University.

Heinegård, C. (2000). "Fallstudie av det svenska EU-arbetet på tullområdet," in *Fallstudier av tre EU-intensiva politikområden*. Statskontoret 2000:20B.

Hood, C. (1991). "A Public Management for all Seasons," *Public Administration* 69/1: 3–19.

Hood, C., James, O., Jones, G., Scott, C., and Travers, T. (1999). *Regulation inside Government: Waste-Watchers, Quality Police, and Sleazebusters*. Oxford: Oxford University Press.

Jacobsson, B. (2006). "Regulated Regulators: Global Trends of State Transformation," in M.-L. Djelic and K. Sahlin-Andersson (eds), *Transnational Governance: Institutional Dynamics of Regulation*. Cambridge: Cambridge University Press, 205–24.

Jacobsson, B., Lægreid, P., and Pedersen, O. K. (2004). *Europeanization and Transnational States: Comparing Central Nordic Governments*. London: Routledge.

Jacobsson, B. and Sahlin-Andersson, K. (2006). "Dynamics of Soft Regulations," in M.-L. Djelic and K. Sahlin-Andersson (eds), *Transnational Governance: Institutional Dynamics of Regulation*. Cambridge: Cambridge University Press, 247–65.

Jacobsson B. and Sundström, G. (2006). *Från hemvävd till invävd: Europeiseringen av svensk förvaltning och politik*. Malmö: Liber.

Jacobsson, K. and Vifell, Å. (2005). "Soft Governance, Employment Policy and Committee Deliberation," in E. O. Eriksen (ed.), *Making the European Polity: Reflexive Integration in the EU*. London: Routledge.

Mannfeldt, B. (2000). "EU och statistiken: Styrningen av SCB:s EU-arbete," Masters graduating paper, Department for Political Science, Stockholm University.

March, J. G. and Olsen, J. P. (1989). *Rediscovering Institutions: The Organizational Basis of Politics*. New York: Free Press.

Meyer, J. W., Boli, J., Thomas, G. M., and Ramirez, F. O. (1997). "World Society and the Nation-State," *American Journal of Sociology* 103: 144–81.

Meyer, J. W. and Rowan, B. (1977). "Institutionalized Organizations: Formal Structure as Myth and Ceremony," *American Journal of Sociology* 83: 340–63.

National Board of Trade (2005). "Europa—ja men hur? Svenska myndigheters uppfattning om EU:s inre marknad," Memo 2005-01-04, diary no. 100-172-2004.

Nilsson, P. (2000). "EU—ett nätverk av exporter: En studie av Europasamarbetet inom läke-medelsområdet," Masters graduating paper, Department for Political Science, Stockholm University.

Pollitt, C. and Bouckaert, G. (2004). *Public Management Reform: A Comparative Approach.* Oxford: Oxford University Press.

Powell, W. W. and DiMaggio, P. J. (eds) (1991). *The New Institutionalism in Organizational Analysis.* Chicago: University of Chicago Press.

Power, M. (1997). *The Audit Society: Rituals of Verification.* Oxford: Oxford University Press.

Premfors, R. (1998). "Reshaping the Democratic State: Swedish Experiences in a Comparative Perspective," *Public Administration* 76/1: 141–59.

Premfors, R., Ehn, P., Haldén, E., and Sundström, G. (2003). *Demokrati och byråkrati.* Lund: Studentlitteratur.

Savelli, A. (2000). "Fallstudie av det svenska miljöarbetet i EU," in *Fallstudier av tre EU-intensiva politikområden.* Statskontoret 2000:20B.

Slaughter, A.-M. (2005). *A New World Order.* Princeton: Princeton University Press.

Sundström, G. (1999). "Att tala med en röst: En studie av hur EU-medlemskapet påverkar samordningen inom Regeringskansliet." Score Rapportserie 1999:8.

Sundström, G. (2000). "Förvaltningsmodellen och EU: Om relationerna mellan Näringsdepartementet och Konkurrensverket i EU-arbetet," in *Fallstudier av tre EU-intensiva politikområden.* Statskontoret 2000:20B.

Vifell, Å. (2009). "Enclaves inside the State: The Internationalisation of the Swedish Public Administration," Score Research Report 2009:7.

Weick, K. (1976). "Educational Organizations as Loosely Coupled Systems," *Administrative Science Quarterly* 21: 1–19.

Weick, K. (1995). *Sensemaking in Organizations.* Thousand Oaks: Sage Publications.

CHAPTER 39

THE EUROPEANIZATION OF SWEDISH FOREIGN POLICY AND BEYOND

On Multiple Roles in Swedish Post-Cold-War Foreign Policy

DOUGLAS BROMMESSON

INTRODUCTION

ACCORDING[1] to the standard narrative of research on Swedish foreign policy,[2] three different role conceptions characterized Sweden's foreign policy after World War II: the passive (from the end of World War II through the 1950s), the active (1960s, 1970s, and 1980s) and the European (1989 to the present) (cf. Bjereld et al. 2008). According to this narrative, Sweden, a traditionally reluctant European (Jerneck 1993), embarked on a journey of Europeanization from the fall of the Berlin Wall, a process that was formally finalized with membership in the EU in 1995. Research on the Europeanization of Swedish foreign policy presents evidence of a Europeanization process, both on an institutional level and as regards the more fundamental subjective understanding of Sweden's role in foreign policy—role conception—at both the elite and mass level. Since Sweden often emphasized an international rather than European identity during the latter half of the Cold War, the Europeanization of Swedish foreign policy has been understood as a radical change (Brommesson 2010).

However, after some ten years as a member of the EU, a stronger Nordic engagement reappeared in Swedish foreign policy. Signs of this engagement include cooperation on foreign policy, defense, and armaments, as well as ongoing discussions about an even more ambitious common security and defense policy for the Nordic countries (Doeser et al. 2012). Hence, we may be facing a situation in which there are competing or at least multiple roles in Swedish foreign policy.

Given this, the aim of the present chapter is to analyze the role conceptions of Swedish foreign policy since the end of the Cold War. This is largely done by examining the results of influential research that has been conducted about Sweden's foreign policy during this period. The chapter thus aims to provide the reader with an understanding of the current state of affairs in research on modern Swedish foreign policy. Another aim of the chapter is to contribute to our theoretical understanding of role conceptions in foreign policy analysis and especially of conceptions of multiple roles.

The chapter begins with a discussion of role theory and the issue of multiple roles. After that, the possibility of a process of Europeanization of foreign policy roles is discussed. Using this theoretical framework as a point of departure, the chapter then turns to an empirical analysis of the Europeanization of Swedish foreign policy since the beginning of the 1990s. In a second empirical section, the chapter counters the dominant narrative of Europeanization, arguing instead that we see increasing heterogeneity and multiple roles in Swedish foreign policy. In the concluding section of the chapter, both empirical and theoretical conclusions are discussed.

ROLE CHANGE AND MULTIPLE FOREIGN POLICY ROLES

When foreign policy analysts try to capture the subjective understanding of the place and mission of a state in international politics, they traditionally use the concept of foreign policy roles. The first wave of research on foreign policy roles was published in the 1970s, and it generated great optimism, especially about the notion of the self-conceptualizing of the purpose of states (Neack et al. 1995). Despite this, role theory research subsequently lost momentum. Twenty years later, from the 1990s, the constructivist turn in foreign policy analysis (FPA) refocused researchers' attention to the origins of role theory in other disciplines such as sociology, social psychology, and anthropology (Harnisch 2011: 7). By doing so, the re-emergence of role theory in FPA has led to the abandonment of the dominant individualistic research agenda of the 1970s in favor of an approach that encompasses the social dynamic behind role change (ibid.).

Before proceeding to a discussion of the dynamics behind such role change and the development of multiple roles according to role theory, some key concepts must be defined. To do so, I draw on work by Sebastian Harnisch (2011). First, according to Harnisch, following the "social turn of role theory," roles should be understood as "social positions that are constituted by ego and alter expectations regarding the purpose of an actor in an organized group." Hence, the role is formed in a social dynamic between different actors. Secondly, based on understandings of particular roles, actors adopt role expectations, an understanding of "what the appropriate role is and what it implies." These expectations can concern the role of oneself or others. Thirdly, role conceptions have to do with what is expected, i.e. how something is supposed to be, and deal with "an actor's perception of his or her position vis-à-vis others (the ego part of a role) and the perception of the role expectations of others (the alter part of a role) as signaled through language and action" (Harnisch 2011: 8).

The renaissance of role theory in FPA, with a new focus on the social nature of roles, has led to the emergence of new theoretical challenges. One of these is a core concern of this chapter. Can states adopt multiple role conceptions, and, if so, how do states balance between/among them (Breuning 2011: 32–3)? Based on previous research, Marijke Breuning argues that there seem to be a number of studies that implicitly or explicitly imply the existence of multiple roles in foreign policy. Despite this, Breuning argues that the issue of multiple roles is one of several blind spots within role theory, especially when it comes to the dynamics between different roles. More specifically, Breuning identifies three core issues for future research on role theory. First, do multiple roles with different saliences exist? Secondly, can changes in role conception be explained by "decision makers gradually [reducing] emphasis on certain role conceptions and, presumably, simultaneously [increasing the] relative prominence of other role conceptions"? Finally, "under what circumstances [are] such gradual role conception shifts ... most likely" (ibid.)? The last question relates to the issue of the scope conditions of foreign policy change. Rachel Folz has narrowed this discussion down to three specific scope conditions that she argues are likely to facilitate change in both foreign policy and role conceptions: uncertainty, identification, and resonance (Folz 2011: 150). I will return to these scope conditions in the empirical sections of the chapter.

The three questions posed by Marijke Breuning provide the work presented here with theoretical tools that can be used to study changes in Swedish role conception since the end of the Cold War. These tools will be employed in two different sections. The first one examines the Europeanization of Sweden's foreign policy role conception. I use previous studies, official statements and public opinion data in order to present the dominant argument that an empirical case can be made for the Europeanization of the Swedish foreign policy role conception. In the second empirical section I introduce a counter-argument. Based on the same kinds of sources, I discuss the possible enactment of multiple role conceptions in Swedish foreign policy. In the final section of the chapter, I present conclusions regarding both our empirical understanding of Swedish foreign policy after Sweden joined the EU and our theoretical understanding of multiple roles in the foreign policy of states.

THE EUROPEANIZATION OF SWEDEN'S FOREIGN POLICY ROLE CONCEPTION

According to the dominant narrative, Swedish foreign policy underwent a sweeping process of Europeanization starting in the beginning of the 1990s, when Sweden began reorienting its relationship with the EC (later the EU) toward membership. The process accelerated when Sweden formally became a candidate for membership and later with membership from 1995 (see Doeser 2008: 221–50; Hallenberg 2000; Miles 2000; Strömvik 1999). Previous studies have pointed out that the process of Europeanization of Swedish foreign policy involved both formal structures and more deep-reaching norms and identities expressed through the country's foreign policy. This finding is in keeping with the development of the academic literature on Europeanization itself.

Early research characterized Europeanization as a top-down process in which the EU affects both member states and non-members to varying degrees (cf. Lenshow 2006: 57). This understanding remains very much alive in the current debate and serves as a somewhat common ground for discussion. Over time, however, the debate has become more nuanced, and Europeanization research has also begun to include a constructivist-influenced understanding of how the EU affects what both member states and others perceive as appropriate, i.e. logics of appropriateness (Börzel and Risse 2003, 2006; Mörth 2003; Rieker 2004). This understanding of Europeanization includes changes in states' fundamental normative points of departure (Brommesson 2010).

Turning to developments in Swedish foreign policy during the 1990s, trends in the academic debate on Europeanization are reflected in the foreign policy role conceptions articulated by various governments, as well as in the role conception held by the public. The institutional setting of Swedish foreign policy decision-making changed when the government declared its intention to apply for membership in the EC, and the change was even more pronounced when Sweden became a candidate state and later a member. At first Sweden voluntarily coordinated its foreign policy with other European states. When it joined the EU, coordination became mandatory. During this process the Swedish government created new formal structures for coordination, including a new EU minister, additional resources for EU coordination at the Foreign Ministry, and a parliamentary committee on EU affairs that created a new power structure within Swedish parliamentarianism (Hegeland 2006). In addition, in keeping with treaty provisions, an ambassador's post to the Committee on Foreign and Security Policy of the Council of Ministers in Brussels was established. As Ulrika Mörth illustrates in her chapter in this volume, not only were Swedish domestic structures Europeanized, but Swedish decision-making was also incorporated into a wider European multigovernance system, a development likely to exert an even stronger Europeanization effect on national policies due to processes of socialization and the diffusion of norms (Checkel 2001, 2005).

Taken together, it is likely that these new structures have had an impact on the substance of Swedish foreign policy. In a study on the Europeanization of Swedish defense and security policy, Arita Eriksson has shown that the Europeanization of Swedish decision-making procedures was followed by a Europeanization of both the definition of security policy problems and, somewhat later, solutions to these problems. At the end of the 1990s and the beginning of the 2000s, both problems and solutions were defined from a European point of view (Eriksson 2006). Moreover, Sweden not only coordinated and incorporated its positions on various day-to-day issues into the European context; the country's more fundamental conception of its foreign policy role changed.

In particular, it was Europeanized in accordance with constructivist understandings of the process of Europeanization.

Turning to the role conceptions held by Swedish governments during the post-Cold-War era, previous studies of Sweden's publicly stated foreign policy provide a foundation for further analysis. In research focused on the annual foreign policy declaration of the Swedish government, I have previously shown how Sweden turned away from the activist, third-way foreign policy often associated with Olof Palme, towards more liberal moral beliefs at the beginning of the 1990s (Brommesson 2007; cf. Bergman Rosamund, this volume). This development was manifested both when social democratic and center-right governments held office. Foreign policy was still characterized by a high degree of activity, and governments with different ideological underpinnings continued to emphasize the need for a clear Swedish voice in the world. However, the values of that voice had changed. Whereas Sweden had previously promoted the economic and social liberation of the Third World, it now began to emphasize the universal human rights of individuals, a market economy, and free trade. More importantly for the argument of this chapter, Europe was identified as the territorial home of these values. According to Swedish foreign policy, to be European meant that one had a responsibility to promote and defend these values (Brommesson 2007: 184–5). In his thorough analysis of Swedish foreign policy during the events that took place a couple of years before and after the end of the Cold War, Fredrik Doeser shows how leading Swedish politicians of various political parties embarked on a road that gradually moved them closer to an explicit Europeanized role conception (Doeser 2008: ch. 7). Expressed differently, the Europeanized role brought along with it a European responsibility. After four years of EU membership, Anna Lindh, Sweden's foreign minister at the time, illustrated this when addressing humanitarian concerns in the Balkans. According to Lindh, "Sweden has a European identity and a European responsibility" (Lindh 1999). During the 2000s this identity began to be expressed even more clearly in characterizations of Swedish foreign policy. In older articulations of foreign policy, spokespeople argued that Sweden ought to act in particular ways. From the 2000s, however, Swedish governments started referring to the EU as the actor that conducts the foreign policy of which Sweden is a part (e.g. Bildt 2012, 2013).

Another important example is Swedish security political doctrine. During the Cold War, Sweden always emphasized that the country was "nonaligned in peacetime, with the intention (later 'the possibility') of remaining neutral in the event of war." During the new millennium the Swedish government began to say instead that Sweden would not remain passive if a member of the EU or a Nordic country were attacked or faced a catastrophe (see Regeringen.se 2011 for an overview).

In another study, it is argued that changes in moral beliefs reflect a normative Europeanization, i.e. "a top-down process based on the logic of appropriateness, where states with a close relationship to the EU, i.e. candidate and member states, develop a commitment to a European center (cf. Olsen 2001), and their normative point of departure is changed" (Brommesson 2010: 228). According to this definition, it is not only roles that change due to an understanding of what is appropriate; role-playing in accordance with what is seen as appropriate also has an impact on deeper convictions about what is normatively right and wrong, true and false.

It is worth emphasizing that the Europeanization of formal structures, understandings of what is appropriate, and the normative convictions reflected in Swedish foreign policy are consistent over time and across governments with different ideological profiles. As showed by Brommesson and Ekengren, Swedish foreign policy after the end of the Cold War has been characterized by stability and continuity despite elections that have brought new governments to power (Brommesson and Ekengren 2013).

Turning to public opinion data, Swedish election studies reveal strong signs of the Europeanization of role conception at the mass level as well. In an exit poll conducted during the 2009 election to the European Parliament, Swedish voters were asked which policies they thought should be decided at the European level. Foreign policy came out as the second most "integration friendly" policy area (Berg 2010: 171). On a scale from 1 (only national level) to 7 (only European level), foreign policy got a score of 4.4, which was an increase from the 2004 European elections, when foreign policy got a 4.0. These results can be compared with agriculture (3.2 in 2009 and 2.9 in 2004) and financial politics (3.5 in 2009, 2.9 in 2004). Only environmental policy scored higher (5.0 in 2009 and 4.5 in 2004). It is also worth noting the rather strong support for decision-making at the European level within defense policy (3.9 in 2009, 3.5 in 2004) (ibid.). This is particularly interesting, given strong Swedish opinion against membership in NATO (Bjereld 2013). In short, despite the fact that Sweden has a strong historical tradition of nonalignment and an identity as an independent supporter of the Third World and a "hesitant European," the population now expresses a strong will to integrate its foreign policy with other European countries, and even to transfer decision-making authority over foreign policy to the European level. Hence, we can conclude that the strong Europeanization that is observable at the elite level corresponds to support for a European foreign policy role at the mass level.[3]

The discussion thus far has focused on what, in this chapter, is considered to be the output of the Europeanization process; that is, a Europeanized role conception. And based on the research presented here, it must be said that the output is clear. The role conception of Swedish foreign policy has been Europeanized since the early 1990s. The question that remains is what explains this shift away from the role conception of the "exceptional third way" in international politics (Lawler 1997; cf. Bergman Rosamund, this volume) in favor of the Europeanized role conception? In order to answer this question, I turn to an examination of the scope conditions presented above to provide a theoretical response to Marijke Breuning's query about the "circumstances [under which] such gradual role conception shifts are most likely" (Breuning 2011).

Three scope conditions have been presented as a potential answer: uncertainty, identification, and resonance. Based on studies analyzing the Swedish decision to join the EC and other work focused on the situation that decision-makers found themselves in at the time, it can be concluded that the latter comes close to being an ideal type of these scope conditions. In his study on the decision to join, Jakob Gustavsson shows how it was possible due to three conditions: the changing international structure with the end of the Cold War, Sweden's problematic economic situation combined with the poor prospects of the ongoing EEA negotiations, and, finally, the end of the Swedish third way in international politics (Gustavsson 1998: 191). To this Gustavsson adds the learning process of the Prime Minister, Ingvar Carlsson, as an intervening variable. At the end of the learning process, Carlsson and Minister of Finance Allan Larsson realized that membership in the EC was the appropriate road for Sweden, and then they provided important leadership toward the goal of submitting an application (ibid.). Although Gustavsson's study deals with the more general issue of membership, it can still be said to illustrate the dynamic of foreign policy change, because foreign policy change was an integral part of Sweden's decision to join an EC committed to the Maastricht Treaty, which included a common foreign and security policy (CFSP).

Two of the variables highlighted by Gustavsson—the end of the Cold War and Sweden's problematic economic situation—point in the direction of uncertainty. After about 40 years of relative geopolitical stability, during which Sweden stood between two super-powers (at least officially) and enjoyed strong growth and welfare state expansion (with the exception of a period of crisis during the 1970s), Sweden now faced a new situation in international politics. First, this included developments in the world economy that had consequences for the Swedish economy. The second variable points in the direction of an unclear Swedish identity. Sweden had a very strong foreign policy identity during the Cold War, as an independent voice representing a third way between capitalism and communism. When the Cold War ended, it became more or less impossible to uphold this identity because one of the two roads had disappeared. The third variable, resonance, is not covered by Gustavsson's study, because he deals only with decision-making at the government level. However, even though there was only a small majority for EC membership in the 1994 referendum, the public opinion data discussed earlier illustrates an increase in resonance of a reorientation of foreign policy during the years following membership.

Based on the discussion already presented, we can draw three conclusions. First, Sweden's foreign policy role conception began to change from the beginning of the 1990s. Second, this change was initiated during a period when scope conditions were favorable. Finally, the scope conditions suggest a possible answer to Breunings' question about when a gradual change in role conception is most likely.

To this point, the analysis has centered on what can be described as the dominant narrative about Swedish foreign policy from the early 1990s. While it is fair to say that this Europeanized role conception is still the dominant one, there is reason to discuss the possibility of complementary role conceptions, and thus to try to answer Breunings' first question about whether "multiple roles of different salience exist" in Swedish foreign policy.

A COMPLEMENTARY NORDIC ROLE CONCEPTION IN SWEDISH FOREIGN POLICY?

When the international security climate became colder during the "second wave" of the Cold War, from the late 1970s until at least the mid-1980s, the focus of Sweden's foreign and security policies changed. The Soviet Union's violation of Swedish territorial airspace and territorial waters, the uprising in Poland, and increased tension between the two superpowers changed Sweden's image of its immediate geographic neighborhood. In both public debate and governmental rhetoric, it was characterized as considerably more insecure. Sweden responded to the challenge with a stronger focus on national defense, the rights of small states, and international law (Brommesson 2007; cf. Bjereld et al. 2008). In other words, the role of internationalist supporter of the liberation of the Third World was complemented by the role of responsible defender of national integrity and independence. Nordic[4] cooperation, most often in less sensitive policy areas (e.g. education, culture policy, etc.), was part of the formula and included a focus on the country's own geographic neighborhood.[5] Since this focus was motivated with the same language that was used to support the rights of the Third World (e.g. the rights of small states, international law, etc.), these roles were possible to combine.

While the focus on the immediate Nordic neighborhood vanished with the emergence of greater optimism after the end of the Cold War (Andersson 2001: 269), signs of a return to a Nordic focus reappeared some years into the new millennia. Sweden's role conception started to show signs of change in the direction of a situation in which the country might assume multiple roles, with the European role being complemented by a Nordic one, according to which Sweden has a special responsibility and also a special relationship with the Nordic states. A number of what can be seen as interrelated developments occurred. The European integration process stagnated, as did the European economy, which suffered a series of economic crises. In addition, EU-friendly Swedish politicians began to argue for a smaller but sharper EU, and politicians arguing in favor of stronger defense and closer attention to the neighborhood around Sweden reappeared. In 2008 the Swedish parliamentary commission on defense policy argued that the litmus test of which future path Russia would choose was how the country behaved toward former members of the Soviet Union over the coming years (Försvarsberedningen 2007: 36). Two months later, Russia invaded Georgia, thereby fueling renewed Swedish debate about defense and security policy. In 2014 the debate gained new momentum after the Russian annexation of Crimea and the events that followed in Ukraine.

After the first signs of more uncertain circumstances, cooperation among the Nordic states started to gain momentum (Doeser et al. 2012). In the official doctrine of Swedish security policy, the Nordic states outside the EU were given the same status as EU members and Sweden guaranteed its solidarity with them (Regeringen.se 2011). Alongside existing cooperation among their overseas embassies and the joint Nordic Battlegroup within the EU, the Nordic states began to develop cooperation in additional areas of foreign, defense, and security policy, including increased cooperation in military training and military armament (Säkerhetspolitik.se 2012; Britz 2012). Even before the war in Georgia, in January 2008, Swedish Foreign Minister Carl Bildt stated that Sweden regarded Nordic cooperation "with a completely new openness" (Regeringen.se 2008). Later that same year, Defense Minister Sten Tolgfors declared that Sweden was "ready to defend its Nordic neighbors" (Tolgfors 2008). The openness Bildt expressed was manifested in November 2009, when the Nordic states formed NORDEFCO (Nordic

Defense Cooperation), an umbrella organization for previously established cooperation initiatives within the field of defense and security policy.

Another important input into the process of closer Nordic cooperation was the so-called Stoltenberg Report (formally "Nordic Cooperation on Foreign and Security Policy"), authored independently by Thorvald Stoltenberg, former foreign minister of Norway. The report called for closer Nordic cooperation within foreign and security policy and even for a clause of Nordic solidarity (Stoltenberg 2009). The Nordic governments adopted the idea of a solidarity clause, and when the foreign ministers met in Helsinki in April 2011 they agreed on the following Nordic declaration on solidarity:

> On the basis of common interest and geographical proximity it is natural for the Nordic countries to cooperate in meeting challenges in the area of foreign and security policy in a spirit of solidarity. In this context Ministers discussed potential risks, *inter alia* natural and man-made disasters, cyber and terrorist attacks. Should a Nordic country be affected, others will, upon request from that country, assist with relevant means. ("The Nordic Declaration on Solidarity," 2011, cited in Britz 2012: 224)[6]

As we already have seen, in 2008 and 2009 Swedish ministers expressed support for the idea of closer Nordic cooperation. In the annual Declaration of Government at the Riksdag in 2012, this support was expressed in a formal setting and placed in a wider context. The government stated that "Nordic cooperation, as well as cooperation within EU and UN, constitute important arenas for our foreign policy cooperation" (Regeringen.se 2012).

As already discussed, it is possible to detect resonance at the Swedish mass level for closer foreign policy cooperation within the EU. However, the resonance for Nordic cooperation is likely to be even greater. Sweden has a long tradition of Nordic cooperation and even alliances. During the nineteenth century, Sweden and Norway, inspired by "Scandinavianism," supported Denmark in several conflicts concerning Danish control over Schleswig and Holstein (Bjereld et al. 2008; Doeser et al. 2012). After World War II the same three Scandinavian states engaged in serious discussions about a Scandinavian defense union. Although Nordic cooperation during the Cold War excluded security issues (Joenniemi 2007), there were examples of cooperation between Sweden and other Nordic countries on various defense-related issues, albeit in secret (Holmström 2011). In other words, there is a long tradition of Nordic cooperation in foreign and security policy. In other political areas, including education, passport union, and cultural exchange, cooperation within the Nordic Council and the Nordic Council of Ministers has been ongoing since the 1950s. The Nordic states also have much in common, including similar languages in Sweden, Norway, Denmark, and the Swedish-speaking parts of Finland, a common history, and even a shared identity (on Nordic identity, see Andersson 2001: 263). The long tradition of cooperation and similar background has left its mark at the mass level, with many Swedes expressing a sense of shared identity with the other Nordic states (Berg 2007).

To conclude this discussion of Nordic cooperation, it has been argued that we are witnessing a renaissance of a Nordic role conception in Swedish foreign policy. Furthermore, it can also be argued that this role conception has gained momentum after the two important events in 2009—the Stoltenberg Report and the establishment of NORDEFCO (Doeser et al. 2012). This has been happening during a period in Swedish security policy in which, according to many commentators, the environment is once again becoming more insecure. It is also a form of cooperation that is supported by a strong sense of shared identity, both at the elite level—where there is a long tradition of various forms of cooperation—and at the mass level, where there is strong support for Nordic cooperation.

Should this development of closer Nordic cooperation and the renaissance of the Nordic role in Swedish foreign policy be seen as a competing role with the Europeanized one described above? Not necessarily. First and foremost we still lack sufficiently convincing reasons to conclude that European and Nordic roles are incompatible. On the contrary, previous research has argued that under certain circumstances a stronger European role can also mean a stronger Nordic one (Rieker 2004). Pernille Rieker argues that cooperation within the EU in the direction of more international conflict management and European battlegroups has pushed the Nordic countries (interestingly, also non-member Norway) toward stronger coordination of their conflict management capacity. This includes the development of the Nordic Battlegroup, one of the battlegroups established within the context of the EU in order to enable the Nordic states to more efficiently contribute to the EU's conflict management capacity. Hence, it is possible to see the Europeanization of security policy as a Trojan Horse bringing along with it a stronger Nordic cooperation and fostering a stronger Nordic role conception that has encouraged even deeper cooperation in the future. Secondly, although we have seen a rapid increase in Nordic cooperation in foreign and security policy, it must be said that it is still considerably more limited, both in number of issues and intensity of cooperation, than cooperation, coordination, and even common decision-making in the EU. Thirdly, studies of Swedish foreign policy rhetoric illustrate how the European role is still Sweden's default role (Brommesson 2007, 2010). In Swedish foreign policy declarations, Swedish governments are no longer the sole actor of Swedish foreign policy; instead, the EU acts in various ways, and Sweden tries to shape these actions.

Nonetheless, the possibility of a symbiosis of the European and Nordic roles does not contradict the argument that a stronger Nordic role conception exists. This role has emerged during a time in which the future of the European integration process is uncertain and when possible security challenges from the East have re-emerged on the Swedish horizon. In times marked by such circumstances, Sweden seems to return to a well-known role: that of a small Nordic state cooperating with equals in close geographic proximity. This role can thus far be seen as one that is complementary to the Europeanized role. Thus, what we see is a multi-role conception in Swedish foreign policy.

Conclusions

This chapter started out with the aim of analyzing the role conceptions of Swedish foreign policy since the end of the Cold War. It has been empirically demonstrated that the Europeanized role conception evolved rather rapidly in Swedish foreign policy during the first half of the 1990s. Soon after Sweden joined the EU in 1995, the Europeanized role had become Sweden's default role in foreign policy. This was a dramatic step for a country that had been labeled as "exceptional" in its strong support for internationalist values only a short time before (Lawler 1997; cf. Bergman Rosamond 2007). The devotion of the newly converted to its new role seems to have lasted for somewhat more than a decade. It is probably fair to say that the Europeanized role was the only role in Swedish foreign policy during this time.

The Europeanized role still characterizes Swedish foreign policy, and is certainly likely to remain the dominant role for the foreseeable future. However, it has been complemented by the re-emergence of the Nordic role, at least since 2009. The empirical analysis does not provide evidence to suggest that this role is challenging the dominant Europeanized one. Nonetheless, the mere fact that another role is (re-)emerging in Swedish foreign policy says something interesting about the decreased dominance of that role. It is especially interesting to note that the Nordic role, well-known to Sweden from the past, re-emerged in insecure times, when the EU turned out to be a less secure haven, and when new potential geopolitical challenges in northern Europe appeared on the horizon.

Based on these findings it is also possible to contribute to role theory, especially the discussion about multiple roles in foreign policy. The analysis of this issue has been structured around the three questions raised by Marijke Breuning (2011). First, do multiple roles of different salience exist? The empirical analysis in this chapter indicates that they do. It is still too early to draw any clear conclusions on the exact weight of the two Swedish role conceptions, but there is firm ground to conclude that multiple roles of different salience exist. Secondly, can changes in role conception be explained by "decision makers gradually [reducing] emphasis on certain role conceptions and, presumably, simultaneously [increasing the] relative prominence of other role conceptions"? As discussed above, it is hard to see this gradual shift in focus as an explanation in itself, but the analysis does support the expectation that states gradually develop a new role conception—or rather rediscover old familiar roles—at the same time as the dominant role is losing some of its dominance. To answer Breuning's third question, "under what circumstances such gradual role conception shifts are most likely," the analysis of the Swedish case indicates that when the dominant role conception lacks the potential to guide the actor under new uncertain circumstances, then the actor will develop a parallel role conception. This is more likely to happen when a role conception based in a firm identity is "available," thereby providing "shortcuts, cues and buffets" to make "the socially easier" action possible (Checkel 2005: 810).

Notes

1. The author wants to thank Jon Pierre, Ulrika Mörth, Ole Elgström, Lee Miles, and fellow contributors to this volume for valuable comments on previous drafts of this chapter.
2. Swedish foreign policy should be understood here in a traditional and fairly delimited manner, including the responsibilities of the Swedish Foreign Ministry and parts of the security policy in the intersection between defence policy and foreign policy, but leaving out other kinds of external relations.
3. Unfortunately, the data provided does not allow us to compare it with public opinion during the 1990s. However, support for European level decision-making in foreign policy in 2004 and 2009 can still be seen as illustrative snapshots of an increasingly integration-friendly electorate within this specific policy field. Given Sweden's tradition of an independent foreign policy profile during the Cold War, it is also likely that these figures illustrate the result of a process of role change among the voters.
4. The Nordic includes Denmark, Finland, Iceland, Norway, and Sweden.
5. Joenniemi (2007) argues that Nordic cooperation during the Cold War and even into the new millennia was desecuritized, meaning that security policy was not on the table and thus not an issue that could affect the relations between the countries (see also Britz 2012: 224). As will be shown, this has changed radically.
6. Malena Britz shows that this declaration was preceded by other declarations in the years before 2011. In 2009 the Nordic government adopted the Reykjavik declaration, which underlined a common will to and interest in contributing to Nordic security and support for broader Nordic cooperation within foreign and security policy in a spirit of solidarity to meet future challenges. That same year, the Nordic governments also signed the Haga agreement on cooperation within the field of civil contingencies (Britz 2012: 223–4).

References

Andersson, H. E. (2001). *Homo Nordicus?* Gothenburg: Gothenburg University, Department of Political Science.

Berg, L. (2007). *Multi-level Europeans: The Influence of Territorial Attachments on Political Trust and Welfare Attitudes.* Gothenburg: Gothenburg University, Department of Political Science.

Berg, L. (2010). "Solidaritetens och identitetens gränser" [The Boundaries of Solidarity and Identity], in H. Oscarsson and S. Holmberg (eds), *Väljarbeteende i Europaval* [Voter Behavior in European Elections]. Gothenburg: Gothenburg University, Department of Political Science, 163–78.

Bergman Rosamond, A. (2007). "Co-Constitution of Domestic and International Welfare Obligation: The Case of Sweden's Social Democratically Inspired Internationalism," *Cooperation and Conflict* 42: 73–99.

Bildt, C. (2008). "Nu måste vi göra EU till en military fredsmakt" [Now We Must Turn the EU into a Military Force for Peace], available at <http://www.dn.se/debatt/nu-maste-vi-gora-eu-till-en-militar-fredsmakt/>, accessed June 9, 2015.

Bildt, C. (2012). Regeringens deklaration vid 2012 års utrikespolitiska debatt i Riksdagen, onsdagen den 15 februari 2012 [Statement of Government Policy in the Parliamentary Debate on Foreign Affairs, Wednesday, February 15, 2012], available at <http://www.regeringen.

se/contentassets/72a070ae4357403bb6e19ce1dbb623c3/regeringens-deklaration-vid-2 012-ars-utrikespolitiska-debatt-i-riksdagen-onsdagen-den-15-februari-2012>, accessed June 9,2015.

Bildt, C. (2013). "Regeringens deklaration vid 2013 års utrikespolitiska debatt i Riksdagen, onsdagen 13 februari 2013" [Statement of Government Policy in the Parliamentary Debate on Foreign Affairs Wednesday, February 13, 2013], available at <http://www.regeringen. se/contentassets/3f435e49030a4954a799aa5d8e044c9a/regeringens-deklaration-vid-2 013-ars-utrikespolitiska-debatt-i-riksdagen-onsdagen-den-13-februari-2013>, accessed June 9, 2015.

Bjereld, U. (2013) "Fortsatt starkt Nato-motstånd i svensk opinion," in L. Weibull, H. Oscarsson, and A. Bergström (eds), *Vägskäl* [Crossroads]. Gothenburg: Gothenburg University, SOM-institute, 611–15.

Bjereld, U., Johansson, A. W., and Molin, K. (2008). *Sveriges säkerhet och väldens fred: Svensk utrikespolitik under kalla kriget* [The Security of Sweden and the Peace of the World: Swedish Foreign Policy During the Cold War]. Stockholm: Santérus Academic Press.

Breuning, M. (2011). "Role Research: Genesis and Blind Spots," in S. Harnisch, C. Frank, and H. W. Maull (eds), *Role Theory in International Relations: Approaches and Analyses*. Abingdon: Routledge, 16–35.

Britz, M. (2012). "Ett oväntat uppsving för nordiskt säkerhetspolitiskt samarbete" [An Unexpected Rise in Nordic Security Policy Cooperation], in F. Doeser, M. Petersson, and J. Westberg (eds), *Norden mellan stormakter och fredsförbund* [The Nordic between Great Powers and Peace Unions]. Stockholm: Santérus Academic Press, 223–60.

Brommesson, D. (2007). *Från Hanoi till Bryssel: Moralsyn i svensk deklarerad utrikespolitik 1969–1996* [From Hanoi to Brussels: Moral Beliefs in Declared Swedish Foreign Policy 1969–1996]. Stockholm: Santérus Academic Press.

Brommesson, D. (2010). "Normative Europeanization: The Case of Swedish Foreign Policy Reorientation," *Cooperation and Conflict* 45/2: 224–44.

Brommesson, D. and Ekengren, A.-M. (2013). "What Happens when a New Government Enters Office? A Comparison of Ideological Change in British and Swedish Foreign Policy 1991–2011," *Cooperation and Conflict* 48/1: 3–27.

Börzel, T. and Risse, T. (2003). "Conceptualizing the Domestic Impact of Europe," in K. Featherstone and C. Radaelli (eds), *The Politics of Europeanization*. Oxford: Oxford University Press, 55–78.

Börzel, T. and Risse, T. (2006). "Europeanization: The Domestic Impact of European Union Politics," in K. E. Jørgensen et al. (eds), *Handbook of European Union Politics*. London: Sage Publications, 483–504.

Checkel, J. (2001). "The Europeanization of Citizenship?" in M. G. Cowles, J. Caparaso, and T. Risse (eds), *Transforming Europe: Europeanization and Domestic Change*. Ithaca, NY: Cornell University Press, 180–97.

Checkel, J. (2005). "International Institutions and Socialization in Europe: Introduction and Framework," *International Organization* 59/4: 801–26.

Doeser, F. (2008). *In Search of Security after the Collapse of the Soviet Union: Foreign Policy Change in Denmark, Finland and Sweden, 1988–1993*. Stockholm: Stockholm University.

Doeser, F., Petersson, M., and Westberg, J. (eds) (2012). *Norden mellan stormakter och fredsförbund: Nordiskt säkerhetspolitiskt samarbete i det gamla och nya Europa* [The Nordic between Great Powers and Peace Unions: Nordic Security Policy Cooperation in the Old and New Europe]. Stockholm: Santérus Academic Press.

Eriksson, A. (2006). *Europeanization and Governance in Defence Policy: The Example of Sweden*. Stockholm: Statsvetenskapliga institutionen.

Folz, R. (2011). "Does Membership Matters? Convergence of Sweden's and Norway's Role Conceptions by Interaction with the European Union," in S. Harnisch, C. Frank, and H. W. Maull (eds), *Role Theory in International Relations: Approaches and Analyses*. Abingdon: Routledge, 147–64.

Försvarsberedningen (2007). *Säkerhet i samverkan: Försvarsberedningens omvärldsanalys* [*Security in Collaboration: Defense Intelligence*]. Ds 2007:46. Stockholm: Regeringskansliet.

Gustavsson, J. (1998). *The Politics of Foreign Policy Change: Explaining the Swedish Reorientation on EC Membership*. Lund: Lund University Press.

Hallenberg, J. (2000). "Swedish Foreign and Security Policy," in L. Miles (ed.), *Sweden and the European Union Evaluated*. London: Continuum, 19–32.

Harnisch, S. (2011). "Role Theory: Key Concepts," in S. Harnisch, C. Frank, and H. W. Maull (eds), *Role Theory in International Relations: Approaches and Analyses*. Abingdon: Routledge, 7–15.

Hegeland, H. (2006). *Nationell EU-parlamentarism: Riksdagens arbete med EU-frågorna* [*National EU Parliamentarism: The Work of the Riksdag on EU Affairs*]. Stockholm: Santérus Academic Press.

Holmström, M. (2011). *Den dolda alliansen: Sveriges hemliga NATO-förbindelser* [*The Hidden Alliance: Sweden's Secret NATO Relations*]. Stockholm: Atlantis bokförlag.

Jerneck, M. (1993). "Sweden—the Reluctant European?" in T. Tiilikainen and P. Damgaard (eds), *The Nordic Countries and the EC*. Copenhagen: Copenhagen Political Studies Press, 23–42.

Joenniemi, P. (2007). "Towards a European Union of Post-Security?" *Cooperation and Conflict* 42/1: 127–48.

Lawler, P. (1997). "Scandinavian Exceptionalism and European Union," *Journal of Common Market Studies* 35: 565–94.

Lenshow, A. (2006). "Europeanization of Public Policy," in J. Richardson (ed.), *European Union—Power and Policymaking*, 3rd edn. London: Routledge, 55–72.

Lindh, A. (1999). "Statement of Government Policy in the Parliamentary Debate on Foreign Affairs, February 10, 1999," *Tidigare utrikesdeklarationer och översättningar*. Available at <http://www.regeringen.se/sb/d/10229/a/18985>, accessed September 1, 2009.

Miles, L. (ed.) (2000). *Sweden and the European Union Evaluated*. London: Continuum.

Mörth, U. (2003). "Europeanization as Interpretation, Translation, and Editing of Public Policies," in K. Featherstone and C. Radaelli (eds), *The Politics of Europeanization*. Oxford: Oxford University Press, 159–80.

Neack, L., Hey, J., and Haney, P. J. (1995). *Foreign Policy Analysis Continuity and Change in its Second Generation*. New Jersey: Prentice Hall.

Olsen, J. P. (2001). "The Many Faces of Europeanization," *Journal of Common Market Studies* 40: 921–52.

Regeringen.se (2011). "Sveriges säkerhetspolitik" [Swedish Security Policy], <www.regeringen.se/sb/d/10660>, last accessed June 20, 2013.

Regeringen.se (2012). "Regeringsförklaringen 18 september 2012" [Declaration of Government September 18, 2012], <http://www.regeringen.se/sb/d/108/a/199469>, last accessed June 9, 2015.

Rieker, P. (2004). "Europeanization of Nordic Security: The European Union and the Changing Security Identities of the Nordic States," *Cooperation and Conflict* 39/4: 369–92.

Säkerhetspolitik.se (2012). "Nordiskt försvarssamarbete" [Nordic Defense Cooperation], <www.sakerhetspolitik.se/Forsvar/Internationellt/Nordiskt-forsvarssamarbete/>, last accessed June 20, 2013.

Stoltenberg, T. (2009). "Nordisk samarbeid om utenrikes- och sikkerhetspolitikk" [Nordic Cooperation on Foreign and Security Policy]. Oslo.

Strömvik, M. (1999). "Sverige och EU:s utrikes- och säkerhetspolitik: Ett intensivt men hemligt förhållande?" [Sweden and the Foreign and Security Policy of the EU: An Intense but Secret Relationship?], in K.-M. Johansson (ed.), Sverige i EU [Sweden in the EU]. Stockholm: SNS Förlag, 248–65.

Tolgfors, S. (2008). "Vi är redo att försvara våra nordiska grannländer" [We Are Ready to Defend our Nordic Neighbors], Dagens Nyheter, November 20.

CHAPTER 40

....

LEADING THE EUROPEAN UNION

Sweden's EU Presidencies 2001 and 2009

....

MALENA ROSÉN SUNDSTRÖM

INTRODUCTION

THE Presidency of the Council rotates among the European Union (EU) member states for a period of six months at a time. Sweden has held the EU Presidency twice. The first, in 2001, was described as by far the most important European political event since Sweden joined the EU in 1995 (Tallberg 2001: 9). The Presidency provided "the reluctant European" Sweden (Jerneck 1993; Brommesson, in this volume) with an opportunity to demonstrate its dedication to the EU and to get its EU-skeptical citizens to become more interested in, and hopefully also more positive toward, European integration (Broman and Rosén 2001: 205). Another of the government's aims was to make its own imprint on the political agenda of the EU, important not least for small member states (Tallberg 2001: 17; Bunse 2009).

The context was radically different when Sweden took over the Chair the second time, in 2009. At the time, the EU was holding its breath over the pending ratification of the Lisbon Treaty. When it was achieved, a few months into the Presidency period, the delicate questions of whom to appoint as Permanent Chair of the European Council as well as High Representative of Security and Foreign Policy according to the new treaty, rose to the top of the agenda. In addition, the worst economic and financial crisis since the 1930s had started to unfold the year before, which also called for attention and actions. Sweden was caught up in these events, and the room for political priorities of its own was therefore limited.

The aim of this chapter is to analyze how Sweden has acted upon the challenges and opportunities provided when holding the Presidency of the Council, by applying role theory. The Presidency is associated with different roles, which makes role theory a suitable theoretical framework. The different Presidency roles will be applied to the Swedish cases in order to shed light on, firstly, the expectations prior to the Presidency periods on how Sweden would enact these roles, and, secondly, how it actually performed them. Previous research has found different approaches to the Presidency and its roles by small and big member states, respectively. In line with this, the chapter will analyze to what extent Sweden acted in accordance with a "small-state strategy" when holding the Presidency.

In the next two sections, the theoretical framework is introduced, along with previous research on the Council Presidency. In the following analysis, in addition to the Presidency roles, the chapter will home in on the prioritized issues of the two Presidencies. It will also analyze how other member states as well as national and European media perceived the Presidency periods. The chapter concludes by comparing the two cases and summarizing the view of Sweden as Council Presidency.

The Roles of the Presidency

Researchers and practitioners alike disagree on the extent of the political influence of the Council Presidency. Even before the implementation of the Lisbon Treaty in December 2009, some argued that the Chair was about "responsibility without power" while others claimed it provided the member states with actual and important opportunities to affect decision-making in the EU (Thomson 2008: 593). With the Lisbon Treaty, the rotating six-month Presidency of the European Council was replaced with a permanent President, but it remained in place for the Council (Thomson 2008: 594).

Irrespective of the stance taken on what actual power the Presidency might exert, a useful way to analyze its different functions is to use role theory and hence the concept of *roles*. As stated by Ole Elgström, it refers to "patterns of expected or appropriate behaviour" (2006: 172). Roles are embedded in social structures, with rather firm expectations on what activities an actor in that position should perform and how a particular role should be enacted. The Presidency position is surrounded by certain *norms* regarding how to take on the different functions, which means there is a strong "logic of appropriateness" at work: "Action involves evoking an identity or role and matching the obligations of that identity or role to a specific situation" (March and Olsen 1998: 951).

The external expectations on how Sweden would perform as a Presidency can be described at three levels, focusing: (1) on the Presidency role as such; (2) on small-state Presidencies; and (3) on Sweden specifically as a Presidency. *Role performance* refers to "how and in what ways a role is actually played" (Elgström 2006: 172), and it is the result of an interactive process between the expectations surrounding the role and the actor's self-image and role conception. The latter will decide how the actor chooses to take on the role, i.e. what aspects of the role it will emphasize and what it considers to be an appropriate behavior in that position. In addition, the institutional structures in which the Presidency is situated will also enable or constrain the role performance of any actor holding the Chair (Elgström 2006: 174).

The specific Presidency roles are those of administrator, agenda-setter, mediator, and representative[1] (cf. Tallberg 2001; Elgström 2006; Bengtsson 2010a). Leader is sometimes described as a fifth role (e.g. by Elgström 2006). In this chapter, leadership will be analyzed as part of the mediator role, as these two roles can be argued to constitute two sides of the same coin, both with the aim of advancing the decision-making process (cf. Broman 2010: 204–5).

As an administrator, the Presidency prepares and coordinates the work of the Council, distributes documents, and convenes and chairs meetings. As an agenda-setter, the Presidency sets the political priorities for its six-month period. More specifically, a Presidency might introduce new issues to the agenda (agenda-setting), emphasize or downplay already existing issues (agenda-structuring), or exclude issues (agenda exclusion) (Tallberg 2003). Here, the term "agenda-setting" refers to all these options. As a mediator or leader, the Presidency guides the Council negotiations in order to get results. This role will be referred to as that of mediator, unless otherwise stated. Hence, leader will only be referred to in cases where there is a clear point in distinguishing between the two.[2]

Regarding the roles the Council Presidency is enacting, the main difference between the pre- and post-Lisbon Treaty concerns the one as *external representative* of the EU, which is now played by the elected President of the European Council in cooperation with the High Representative (Dinan 2013). At the time of the Swedish Presidencies, the Presidency was still acting as the external representative of the Council, by chairing meetings in the European Council as well as between the EU and third parties. In addition, the Presidency acted as an *internal representative* of the Council toward other EU institutions, such as the European Parliament (EP) and the Commission.

Based on the theoretical foundations presented above, the chapter asks how the two Swedish Presidencies approached the different roles of the Presidency, i.e. their own role conceptions, as well as the expectations of other member states and the media. It also asks how the two Swedish Presidencies enacted the Presidency roles, i.e. their role performances, and how these were perceived.

NATIONAL OR EUROPEAN INTERESTS?

A member state can use its Presidency in, simply put, two different ways: as an *amplifier*, i.e. as an enhancer of national interests, or as a *silencer*, i.e. by downplaying its own interests in order to promote what is best for Europe (Bengtsson et al. 2004). According to international relations theories of realism and liberalism, states are rational actors, who act so as to promote the national interest. States only cooperate when they cannot reach their goals unilaterally. Therefore, states will use a power position such as the Presidency to enhance their national interests, and hence make it serve as an amplifier.

Constructivist theory has a broader view of national interest by linking it to national identities and arguing that ideational frameworks may constitute perceived interests. Still, constructivism also argues that states are likely to use a formal power platform such as the Chair to promote these interests (ibid.).

There are many examples in empirical research on the Presidency when this has been the case. With regard to constitutional matters, the French Presidency in 2000, preceding the first Swedish Presidency, is a case in point. The French insisted on equality with Germany, despite the latter's considerably larger population, and openly defended great power interests. It is also common for Presidencies to prioritize the own geographical area (e.g. Finland with the Nordic dimension in 1999; Spain and Portugal promoting cooperation with states around the Mediterranean and Latin America), or relations with former colonies (Bengtsson et al. 2004: 314; cf. Bunse 2009: 52).

Even though all states, according to realist thinking, are assumed to make use of a power position to their own advantage, small and less powerful states are nonetheless expected to act more carefully. Small states are not assumed to confront more powerful ones, and are thus expected to use the "silencer strategy" to a larger extent (Bengtsson et al. 2004). Empirical research has demonstrated that this is often the case. Small member states tend to be consensus-seeking, to cooperate closely with different EU institutions, and to promote European interests to a larger extent than big member states (Tallberg 2001: 11).

As stated above, a member state holding the Presidency is also expected to act according to certain norms, one of the strongest being that of an "honest broker," which means to act impartially and to put European interests before national ones. Accordingly, this norm is in line with the "silencer strategy." Although there are examples of small states deviating from this norm and pushing for national interests, they tend to do so in a more discrete way (Bengtsson et al. 2004: 330; Bunse 2009: 43).

Drawing on these two different approaches to holding the Presidency, the chapter asks to what extent the two Swedish Presidencies acted in accordance with a "small-state strategy."

THE 2001 PRESIDENCY

Priorities and Expectations

The Swedish government chose to put three "E"s at the top of its first Presidency agenda: enlargement, employment, and environment. Transparency was another very important issue to the government, even though it was not included among the formal top issues. Employment and environment, as well as transparency, are issue areas at the heart of Swedish politics. Enlargement to East and Central Europe, the absolute top priority, had more recently become a Swedish interest. However, the issue was well in line with Swedish foreign policy interests after the end of the Cold War, where northern Europe and the Baltic Sea states had especially been in focus. In addition, to contribute to the reunion of Europe would be a historical event and the fact that the EU-skeptical Swedes were quite positive toward this priority made it even better in the eyes of the government (Bengtsson 2001: 72–3).

The prospects for success—to make progress in or even conclude negotiations—looked promising in all four issue areas. Regarding transparency, the Amsterdam Treaty had stated that the new openness regulation had to be decided upon no later than May 2001. The previous Presidency, France, had not been able to move the issue forward. Employment was also already on the EU agenda. In 2000, the European Council had decided that the informal summit in Stockholm in March 2001 would provide a first opportunity to follow up on the Lisbon Strategy.[3] As for the environment, a milestone control was scheduled during the Swedish Presidency period regarding sustainability and integration of environmental concerns into other issue areas, a decision taken by the European Council in 1999. Finally, in November 2000 the Commission had presented a plan for negotiations with the candidate countries in East and Central Europe, a plan Sweden had criticized, arguing that the pace was too slow (Bengtsson 2001: 72).

Hence, the four issue areas were already on the EU agenda, but Sweden was eager to push them forward, actively making use of its role as an *agenda-setter*. However, the government was careful when stating its ambitions prior to the period, downplaying rather than raising expectations. Prime Minister Göran Persson emphasized the need to be on the alert for unforeseen events, which might impact on the prioritized issues and Sweden's room for maneuver (Elgström and Tallberg 2001: 39). Enlargement was the exception to the Swedish government's low profile, with the clearly stated aim of a political breakthrough during its Presidency. This called for a strong *leadership*, in addition to acting as a *mediator*, in order to reach an agreement. The candidate countries, several member states, and to some extent European media also expressed high expectations on achievement in this issue area (Bengtsson 2001: 71–2; Broman and Rosén 2001: 215).

Openness-oriented actors, e.g. European journalists and members of the European Parliament, viewed the Swedish Presidency as a window of opportunity for increasing transparency in the EU, due to Sweden's longstanding and far-reaching laws in this area, not least the Freedom of Information Act from 1766. Sweden was expected to act as a *mediator* in order to secure an agreement. Swedish journalists, however, expressed concern that the outcome would compromise the country's high standard on openness (Bjurulf 2001: 127; Broman and Rosén 2001: 215–16). The expectations on achievement were rather low regarding the other two prioritized issue areas, employment and environment, in the media as well as by other member states (Broman and Rosén 2001).

A general picture of the Swedish performances in the different Presidency roles demonstrated highest expectations on the role of *administrator*. There are different aspects that might explain this. On a general level, small states often work hard to demonstrate efficiency in planning and carrying out their term of Presidency. More specifically, the administration of the Finnish Presidency in 1999 was very successful, and there were certainly parallels between these two states, which contributed to the expectations: both are small states in the northern periphery of the EU, and perhaps more importantly, it was their first Presidency, respectively, and they had put great effort into preparing the national administration for meeting this challenge in a successful way (Broman and Rosén 2001; Tallberg 2001).

There were also high hopes among other member states that Sweden would act as a consensus-driven *mediator*, an honest broker, not least in the light of the preceding French Presidency, which was perceived to have acted against this norm. In addition, Swedish foreign policy has a tradition of neutrality and of actively pursuing a mediating role in international politics (Elgström and Tallberg 2001: 44–5; cf. Brommesson, this volume). Sweden was expected to perform well as an *internal representative*. As stated earlier, small states tend to work more closely with other EU institutions, which probably explain this. In contrast, the media and other member states did not expect Sweden to fulfill the role of *external representative* to the same extent.

Overall, the external expectations were quite well in line with the Swedish government's own (stated) role conceptions, with an emphasis on the roles of administrator, mediator, and internal representative, which also fits with the "silencer" strategy of small states.

The Presidency Period: Issues and Roles

Employment was the main topic of the informal summit in Stockholm in March, with the follow-up on the Lisbon Strategy. There were questions as to what Sweden could possibly add to this rather encompassing strategy. The main task was to make sure the process was on track: that the member states kept up with the reforms agreed upon. As a consequence, there were few concrete outcomes at the meeting. In the employment area, Sweden did manage to persuade the other member states about the need to pay attention to the demographic challenge and to actively work with pension issues. Other policies successfully raised by the Presidency in this issue area were the importance of increasing incentives for women to work and extending child care (Jacobsson 2001: 93–6). These small achievements could be said to demonstrate some *agenda-setting* power.

There were several environmental issues on the agenda, but climate change issues came to dominate the Presidency period to a large extent, due to the fact that the new Bush administration decided to withdraw the US from the Kyoto Protocol. At an informal meeting in March–April, the Environmental Ministers spent much time discussing strategies for the EU to pursue in relation to the US. After the meeting, an EU delegation with the Swedish Minister for the Environment, acting as an *external representative* for the EU, went to the US. The delegation tried to persuade the US government to fulfill its commitments, but to no avail. This demonstrated how the Presidency's room for maneuver is restricted by external events. However, the actions of the US had a uniting effect on the EU member states, which quickly developed a common position (Kronsell 2001: 106–7). The achievements regarding sustainable development and integration of environmental concerns into other issue areas were not very far-reaching. These issues are of an overarching character and more diffuse, which might explain the lack of progress.

The negotiations on transparency were the most challenging to the Swedish Presidency, with regard to the impartiality norm. Since the negotiation outcome might affect the Freedom of Information Act, it was a constitutional matter to Sweden and thus of high importance. The government knew it would meet fierce opposition in the domestic arena if the result negatively affected the national rules (Bjurulf and Elgström 2005: 54–5). Despite its strong national interests, it could not pursue these too openly or too hard. At the same time, the openness-oriented member states only made up a minority in the Council. Sweden chose to make use of the institutional opportunities provided by the Presidency position, by initiating informal negotiations and presenting compromise proposals, as well as by using the co-decision procedure to its advantage. With a radically more openness-oriented Parliament, Sweden could use the gap between the Council majority and the Parliament to its own benefit, acting as a "biased mediator" to broker a compromise (ibid.). In this way, it managed to move the Council position towards that of the minority, and its own preferences, and to have an agreement.

There were substantial achievements with regard to enlargement during the Presidency period, both by closing "chapters" as well as opening new ones in the negotiations with individual candidate countries. Sweden also dealt with several difficult or sensitive issues, one of them being the free movement of persons. Some member states expressed worries about an influx of people from the candidate countries and therefore wanted to restrict the free movement of workers. The candidate countries, on the other hand, argued that this would create a segregated EU. The negotiations ended in a compromise, which left it up to each member state to decide its own policy on the matter during a limited time period of two years (Bengtsson 2001: 76–8).

In addition, the Swedish Presidency left its imprint on how enlargement was *framed*: Sweden regarded the issue ultimately as one of security and of safeguarding peace and welfare in Europe, a perception of enlargement in stark contrast to e.g. a threatening invasion of workers or economic strains (ibid.: 80). The aim of a timetable for the enlargement was met at the summit in Gothenburg at the end of the Presidency, and the process of enlargement stated as definite. All in all, Sweden was perceived as a successful *mediator* in this area, by member states, candidate countries, and the Commission alike. The Swedish Presidency also acted as a *leader* in the enlargement negotiations, actively driving the negotiations forward, with initiatives of its own in order to advance the process.

Evaluations

Overall, there was a positive view of Sweden's performance as a Chair. The most obvious substantial achievements were made in the areas of transparency and enlargement. In contrast, the results in the environment and employment areas were weak. Concerning the different roles associated with the Presidency, the high expectations on the *administrative* role were met. It is more difficult to evaluate how Sweden performed as an *agenda-setter*. The fact that the Swedish government chose to prioritize issues that were already on the EU agenda meant that Swedish and European interests seemed to be entangled (Tallberg and Elgström 2001: 227). At the same time, Sweden managed to move certain issues of great national concern in its preferred direction, which was most apparent in the cases of transparency and enlargement. However, not least the former was clearly also a result of actions as a "biased mediator," even if Sweden in general was regarded as a consensus-seeking Presidency.

European media described the Swedish Presidency as particularly successful in the transparency issue, while Swedish journalists were much more skeptical about the transparency agreement and its consequences (Broman and Rosén 2001). Swedish media instead valued the progress in the enlargement process as being the most important. Compared to the overall picture described above, the media expressed a slightly different opinion on how Sweden performed in the different Presidency roles. In European media the role as *internal representative* was ranked as number one, followed by *mediator* and *administrator* (Broman and Rosén 2001: 212). Swedish media, on the other hand, viewed *external representation* as the most successfully performed role, followed by *mediation* (ibid.: 211).

Sweden clearly demonstrated that it was no longer a reluctant European, but committed to the EU and to advancing European interests. However, it did not hesitate to defend vital national interests, mainly in the transparency area, when these were at stake. Sweden's overall approach to the Presidency could be described as in line with the expectations on small states, and hence the "silencer strategy"—but as a "biased mediator" when strong national interests were handled.

THE 2009 PRESIDENCY

Priorities and Expectations

"The Swedish Presidency is ready to take on the challenge," Prime Minister Fredrik Reinfeldt stated in the Work Program for Sweden's second Presidency (Regeringen 2009), starting in July 2009. There were indeed several challenges facing the Presidency: one was the global financial crisis, another a high degree of institutional uncertainty within the EU. The latter consisted of several aspects. Firstly, the European Parliament elections took place in May, but the new Parliament did not convene until September, which meant that the Presidency did not have a "Parliament partner" to cooperate with until then. Secondly, a new Commission was appointed in September. Even though the Commission President José Manuel Barroso was re-elected, the ensuing process of nominating Commissioners, distributing the portfolios, and finally securing the

Parliament's approval proved time-consuming, and there was a gap of several months before the new Commission was fully and formally installed (Broman 2010: 212).

Thirdly, there was the question of the ratification of the Lisbon Treaty. When Sweden took over the Chair, some member states had not yet ratified the treaty. Among these, Ireland and the Czech Republic were the most uncertain ones. Ireland, who had rejected the treaty in a referendum in 2008, was to hold another referendum in October 2009. The Czech President refused for a long time to sign the treaty, despite the fact that the Czech parliament had approved it. The pending ratification was the most difficult of the three institutional challenges, since the other two were known beforehand. Regarding the treaty, Sweden had to prepare for different scenarios (Bengtsson 2010a: 19–23).

In a speech in the Swedish Parliament on June 23, 2009, Prime Minister Fredrik Reinfeldt stated that Sweden aimed at carrying out an efficient and goal-oriented Presidency, which focused primarily on the financial crisis and environmental issues, and especially on reaching a legally binding agreement at the UN climate conference in December. These two priorities were closely followed by the launch of the Lisbon Treaty. The context did of course affect the priorities and the *agenda-setting* of the Presidency. The priorities could be argued to be of two different kinds: "mandatory" and voluntary ones (Bengtsson 2010a: 20). The financial crisis and the Lisbon Treaty clearly belonged to the former: it was impossible for the Presidency not to handle these issues. The environment was also a given priority due to the UN climate conference, but in addition it is a "traditional" Swedish policy area. The other voluntary priorities were asylum and migration policies, an EU strategy for the Baltic Sea region, and enhancing the EU's position in foreign policy. Part of the foreign policy priority consisted of establishing an Eastern Partnership, with six countries in eastern Europe and Southern Caucasus[4] (Bengtsson 2010b).

The Presidency is always dependent upon other actors for results or agreements in the prioritized (as well as other) issue areas. For the Swedish Presidency in 2009, the situation was exceptional as demonstrated by the discussion above. The financial crisis, the Lisbon Treaty, and the climate summit were, if not out of its hands, definitely dependent on many factors it could not influence. The other three priorities, however, were of a more "regular" character, meaning there was more room of maneuver for the Presidency trying to influence the outcomes.

In 2009, as well as in 2001, the government downplayed expectations on the possibilities of enhancing Swedish interests during the Presidency period. The uncertain institutional situation and the financial crisis made the European mission even more pressing this time, which also explains why the *agenda-setting* role was perceived as more limited (Bengtsson and Tallberg 2010: 326). In addition, the EU had institutionalized 18-month programs for rotating Presidencies in 2007, which meant that three following Presidencies ("trios") presented a common program for the period. Sweden made up a trio with France and the Czech Republic and thus had to coordinate its *agenda-setting* with those of these two member states—a fact that also contributed to lower expectations on the *agenda-setting* power (Broman 2010).

Expectations were, on the other hand, relatively high on an efficient and well-run Presidency, i.e. on the role as *administrator*, by other member states as well as by media (Rosén Sundström 2010). This was in line with the government's own role conception, e.g. as stated in the previously mentioned speech by the Prime Minister. There were certain expectations on *leadership*, especially with regard to the climate summit in Copenhagen. In this respect, Sweden would also have an important role to play as the *external representative* of the EU. Here, the EU's self-imposed image as world leader of climate-related issues and that of Sweden as one of the most environmentally concerned member states in the EU overlapped, which can explain these expectations. In most other issue areas, Sweden was expected to guide the EU toward results as a *mediator*, rather than as a leader.

The Presidency Period: Issues and Roles

Preparations for the Lisbon Treaty meant close contacts with other EU institutions (e.g. the Commission, EP, and Council Secretariat) for the Swedish Presidency, acting as an *internal representative* of the Council, as well as with the other member states. The Presidency also played an important role in persuading the Czech President to sign the treaty, by the use of quiet diplomacy, pushing the process forward at critical junctures (Miles 2010: 88).

When the Irish referendum had approved the treaty in October, and the Czech President signed it in early November, the Presidency became involved in the delicate task of finding candidates for the new EU posts that all member states could agree upon. Sweden acted as a *mediator* in the process, but received criticism from other member states as well as in the media for being too concerned about reaching a consensus, and hence demonstrating a lack of *leadership* (Rosén Sundström 2010: 305; Broman 2010: 195–6, 220). At an extra, informal summit on November 19, 2009, Herman Van Rompuy was appointed as the Permanent President of the European Council, and Catherine Ashton as the High Representative of Foreign and Security Policy.

During the autumn, in preparation for the UN climate summit, Prime Minister Reinfeldt and Commission President Barroso visited several developing and newly developed countries, discussing the issues on the agenda (Broman 2010: 215). The internal EU mandate, negotiated prior to the summit, ended in a decision that the EU's actions would be dependent on that of other states (mainly the US and China), and the member states disagreed on how much to spend (ibid.: 219). Further, they could not agree on raising the EU's unilateral ambitions regarding emission reductions in the long term. The Swedish Presidency failed in its *mediating* role, and the outcome negatively affected the EU's perceived integrity in the climate negotiations, and hence the conditions for *external representation* of the Swedish Presidency in the same (Bäckstrand 2010: 49).

At the climate summit, neither Sweden nor the EU could live up to the *leadership* role. The aim of the Presidency to create a legally binding agreement, replacing the

Kyoto Protocol, was not achieved. The EU also failed to act as a *mediator* at the summit. At the end, the deal was settled by the US and China. The failures in Copenhagen was mainly due to the EU's and ultimately the member states' actions, rather than those of the Presidency. The EU had fundamentally misperceived the new power structure in climate issues, with recently developed countries such as the BASIC[5] alliance exercising considerable influence, and had not foreseen the lack of political will among the participating states (Bäckstrand 2010: 32).

In addition to the UN climate summit, climate change was in focus at the G20 meeting in September, along with the global financial crisis, where Reinfeldt and the Minister for Finance Anders Borg acted as *external representatives* of the EU (Bäckstrand 2010: 39). Borg received much appreciation for his work in Ecofin during the Presidency, not least from the EP and the Commission (Broman 2010: 205). There was some general progress during the Presidency period with regard to financial issues, e.g. a new structure for financial oversight, with the aim of creating three new authorities for supervision of financial services in the EU (Miles 2010: 89).

The Baltic Sea strategy is an example of how issues of national priority can be framed as, and actually made into, European interests. The strategy had been a work in progress since 2006, when the European Parliament asked the Commission to launch a proposal for such a strategy, and was on Swedish initiative stated as a priority in the 18-month program of the trio (Broman 2010: 206). The strategy included plans for creating a sustainable environment and bridging social and economic differences in the region. Its adoption by the European Council in October was definitely a success for the Presidency (Bengtsson 2010b: 131).

One of the other priorities concerned the adoption of a new strategic work program for the area of justice and home affairs, and more specifically, specifying EU measures for e.g. border and customs issues, migration, visa policy, and asylum for the period 2010–14. The Presidency managed to guide the negotiations toward an adoption of the program; however, whether or not the actual agreement could be seen as a success was left for the future to decide, depending on whether and how the goals of the Stockholm program, as it was named, translated into practical measures (Miles 2010: 85–6). The last priority, the EU's position in foreign policy, involved rather diverse issues: the European Neighborhood Policy, the transatlantic partnership, the Eastern Partnership, and the enlargement process (Miles 2010: 86). The goals within the area, as stated in the Work Program, were also vague. The most obvious achievements were made on enlargement, with progress in the accession negotiations with Croatia and Turkey (Bengtsson 2010b: 146).

Evaluations

Sweden's second EU Presidency was well-managed. Sweden successfully performed its role as *administrator*, and was also seen as a good *mediator* and *internal representative* by other member states and EU institutions (Broman 2010: 196). In the media, *mediation* was ranked as Sweden's best-performed role, which was mainly due to its workings behind the scenes with preparations for the Lisbon Treaty. The main exception to this was the drawn-out process of selecting candidates for the new EU posts. Sweden also guided the negotiations, as a *mediator*, towards the adoption of the Baltic Sea strategy and the Stockholm program, respectively.

The Presidency received its most negative evaluations, in the media as well as by other member states, with regard to climate issues, even though, as stated above, most of the explanations for the failure in Copenhagen were attributed to external factors (Rosén Sundström 2010: 306, 313). As the very last rotating Presidency with the task to act as an *external representative* of the EU, Sweden participated in G8 and G20 meetings and the UN climate summit, as well as in bilateral summits with the US, Russia, and China. However, it was clear that the EU is not as much of a central actor in global politics, as its own role conception would suggest, which was most explicitly demonstrated at the climate summit. Also, it was sometimes apparent that a small state like Sweden, despite being the external representative of the EU, is not in the same league as the large member states. This was evident when France, Germany, and the UK presented a post-financial-crisis plan, without including the Presidency—or even informing Sweden in advance (Rosén Sundström 2010: 307).

As stated by Lee Miles in an evaluation of the 2009 Presidency, "there was always a risk that there would be a mismatch with the low-key diplomatic style of the Swedes" and the broad Work Program, but in order to succeed "in a diplomatically complex EU-27," a Presidency has to be quite low key in order to find agreements (Miles 2010: 92). Sweden acted as a *mediator*, promoting European interests at a time when this was highly needed. Its overall approach is in accordance with that of silencer, i.e. as the "small-state strategy" to the Chair.

Comparing and Summarizing: Swedish EU Presidencies

The first Swedish Presidency was summarized as "dull but successful" in *Financial Times* (Broman and Rosén 2001: 213), the second as "effective, but not exciting" by a Swedish journalist (Mats Engström in Miles 2010: 87). These quotations are rather representative of how the two Presidencies were evaluated, in the media as well as by other member states. In both cases, Sweden was a well-prepared and efficient Presidency, living up to its own role conception as well as others' expectations on a well-*administrated* and efficient Presidency. This is in line with expectations especially on small member states, which usually put considerable effort into the preparation and administration of their Presidencies.

Overall, both Presidencies performed well as *mediator*, with Sweden living up to its historical self-image in this aspect (Brommesson, this volume) as well as to the other two levels of expectations in this regard: the Presidency norm of "honest broker" and of small states in particular paying attention to this norm. In addition, for the most part of the two Presidencies, Sweden was perceived as a "good team-player" in its role as *internal representative*, not least by the EU institutions it interacted with.

The Presidency offers small states an opportunity to influence the decision-making process in the EU, not least through the possibility to affect the agenda. Even though many of the issues on the respective agendas were pre-determined, the possibility of exercising *agenda-setting* power was greater during the first Presidency. Also, among the issues that had to be handled by the first Presidency, many were of genuine "Swedish" interest, while the second Presidency had to deal with the Lisbon Treaty and the financial crisis. Still, there were opportunities even for the second Presidency to work with issues of Swedish concern, such as the Baltic Sea strategy.

In both Presidencies, Sweden kept a low profile prior to its six months in the spot-light, downplaying the expectations on what could be achieved and, especially, to what extent Swedish interests could benefit from the Presidency. The main exceptions to this were the stated aim of a breakthrough in the enlargement process during the first Presidency, and the aim of achieving a legally binding agreement at the UN climate summit during the second. The former was successfully achieved, while the latter failed. The failure at the UN climate summit in 2009 was mainly due to factors external to the Presidency. Nonetheless, it was a blow to Sweden's self-image of mediator, but perhaps even more so, to the EU's own role conception as a global leader in climate and environment issues.

Irrespective of the very different contexts in which the Swedish Presidencies took place, the "handling" of the Chair was relatively similar in both cases. In 2001 as well as in 2009, the overall approaches were in accordance with the "small state"—or "silencer"—strategy. In 2001, Sweden was eager to demonstrate that it was no longer a "reluctant" European, which affected its approach. In 2009, Sweden was considerably more embedded in the EU (cf. Jacobsson and Sundström, this volume). This time, how-ever, the European interests were of an even more pressing kind, as was the need for a committed European as Presidency. In addition, the diplomatic situation was more complex, with twenty-seven member states compared to fifteen in 2001 (Miles 2010: 92).

Relating the two Swedish Presidencies to the research on Council Presidencies, they add to the picture of small member-state Presidencies as often being well-managed and efficient. Also, it is clear that the Presidency does provide important opportunities for small member states to influence the decision-making process, and perhaps even more important, to be on parity with the big member states for a while. Simone Bunse has described the rotating Presidency, prior to the Lisbon Treaty, as "a mechanism to equalise power differences between the EU's small and big Member States" (2009: 5), and hence as "a guardian of equality" (2009: 28). As stated in the introduction, there are different opinions on how much the reforms of the Lisbon Treaty have impacted upon this, but the fact is that the role of external representative no longer exists and there are indications of less room for agenda-setting.

NOTES

1. Since the two Swedish Presidency periods took place pre-Lisbon, the roles and tasks are here analyzed according to that context.
2. A leader can be defined as "an actor actively driving the negotiations forward, concerned primarily with collective goals rather than pure self-interest," while a mediator is "an actor who intervenes when a conflict has occurred, in order to secure the reaching of an agreement" (Rosén and Jerneck 2005: 65).
3. The Lisbon Strategy was intended to make Europe a more attractive place for investments and to create more and better jobs, turning the EU into the most competitive knowledge-based society in the world in 2010.
4. These were Armenia, Azerbaijan, Georgia, Moldavia, Ukraine, and Belarus.
5. The BASIC countries are Brazil, South Africa, India, and China.

REFERENCES

Bäckstrand, K. (2010). "Klimatförhandlingarna: EU:s roll som global klimatledare," in R. Bengtsson (ed.), *I Europas tjänst: Det svenska ordförandeskapet i EU 2009*. Stockholm: SNS Förlag, 31–63.

Bengtsson, R. (2001). "Utvidgningen—höga förväntningar infriade," in J. Tallberg (ed.), *När Europa kom till Sverige: Ordförandeskapet i EU 2001*. Stockholm: SNS Förlag, 71–86.

Bengtsson, R. (2010a). "Introduktion: Det svenska ordförandeskapet i EU 2009," in R. Bengtsson (ed.), *I Europas tjänst: Det svenska ordförandeskapet i EU 2009*. Stockholm: SNS Förlag, 9–28.

Bengtsson, R. (2010b). "Närområdet: Regional prioritering som alleuropeiskt intresse," R. Bengtsson (ed.), *I Europas tjänst: Det svenska ordförandeskapet i EU 2009*. Stockholm: SNS Förlag, 127–53.

Bengtsson, R., Elgström, O., and Tallberg, J. (2004). "Silencer or Amplifier? The European Union Presidency and the Nordic Countries," in *Scandinavian Political Studies* 27/3: 311–34.

Bengtsson, R. and Tallberg, J. (2010). "Avslutning: Lärdomar från två svenska EU-ordförandeskap," in R. Bengtsson (ed.), *I Europas tjänst: Det svenska ordförandeskapet i EU 2009*. Stockholm: SNS Förlag, 315–33.

Bjurulf, B. (2001). "Öppenheten—framgång bakom lyckta dörrar," in J. Tallberg (ed.), *När Europa kom till Sverige: Ordförandeskapet i EU 2001*. Stockholm: SNS Förlag, 119–34.

Bjurulf, B. and Elgström, O. (2005). "Negotiating Transparency: The Role of Institutions," in O. Elgström and C. Jönsson (eds), *European Union Negotiations: Processes, Networks and Institutions*. London: Routledge, 45–62.

Broman, M. (2010). "Ordförandeskapet i EU:s institutionella dynamik: Sverige som lagspelare," in R. Bengtsson (ed.), *I Europas tjänst: Det svenska ordförandeskapet i EU 2009*. Stockholm: SNS Förlag, 195–223.

Broman, M. and Rosén, M. (2001). "Ordförandeskapet och pressen—en mediabild blir till," in J. Tallberg (ed.), *När Europa kom till Sverige: Ordförandeskapet i EU 2001*. Stockholm: SNS Förlag, 205–24.

Bunse, S. (2009). *Small States and EU Governance: Leadership through the Council Presidency*. Basingstoke: Palgrave Macmillan.

Dinan, D. (2013). "The Post-Lisbon European Council Presidency: An Interim Assessment," in *West European Politics* 36/6: 1256–73.

Elgström, O. (2006). "The Presidency: The Role(s) of the Chair in European Union Negotiations," *The Hague Journal of Diplomacy* 1: 171–95.

Elgström, O. and Tallberg, J. (2001). "Den politiska utmaningen—nationella och europeiska intressen i konflikt?" in J. Tallberg (ed.), *När Europa kom till Sverige: Ordförandeskapet i EU 2001*. Stockholm: SNS Förlag, 35–50.

Jacobsson, K. (2001). "Sysselsättningspolitiken—att förvalta ett arv," in J. Tallberg (ed.), *När Europa kom till Sverige: Ordförandeskapet i EU 2001*. Stockholm: SNS Förlag, 87–104.

Jerneck, M. (1993). "Sweden—The Reluctant European?" in T. Tiilikainen and I. Damgaard Petersen (eds), *The Nordic Countries and the EC*. Copenhagen: Copenhagen Political Studies Press.

Kronsell, A. (2001). "Miljöpolitiken—föregångslandets dilemma," in J. Tallberg (ed.), *När Europa kom till Sverige: Ordförandeskapet i EU 2001*. Stockholm: SNS Förlag, 105–18.

March, J. G. and Olsen, J. P. (1998). "The Institutional Dynamics of International Political Orders," *International Organization* 52/4: 943–69.

Miles, L. (2010). "The Swedish Presidency," *Journal of Common Market Studies* (Annual Review) 48: 81–93.

Regeringen (2009). *Work Programme for the Swedish Presidency of the EU*.

Rosén, M. and Jerneck, M. (2005). "Reform Negotiations: The Case of the CAP," in O. Elgström and C. Jönsson (eds), *European Union Negotiations: Processes, Networks and Institutions*. London: Routledge, 53–78.

Rosén Sundström, M. (2010). "Förväntningar och utfall: Mediebilder av ordförandeskapet," in R. Bengtsson (ed.), *I Europas tjänst: Det svenska ordförandeskapet i EU 2009*. Stockholm: SNS Förlag, 298–314.

Tallberg, J. (2001). "Inledning—Sveriges ordförandeskap i EU 2001," in J. Tallberg (ed.), *När Europa kom till Sverige: Ordförandeskapet i EU 2001*. Stockholm: SNS Förlag, 9–32.

Tallberg, J. (2003). "The Agenda-Shaping Powers of the EU Council Presidency," *Journal of European Public Policy* 10/1: 1–19.

Tallberg, J. and Elgström, O. (2001). "Avslutning—ordförandeskapet och den svenska Europapolitiken," in J. Tallberg (ed.), *När Europa kom till Sverige: Ordförandeskapet i EU 2001*. Stockholm: SNS Förlag, 225–37.

Thomson, R. (2008). "The Council Presidency in the European Union: Responsibility with Power," *Journal of Common Market Studies* 46/3: 593–617.

SECTION 9

THE POLITICAL ECONOMY OF SWEDISH GOVERNANCE

SECTION EDITOR
JOHANNES LINDVALL

CHAPTER 41

....

INTRODUCTION

Sweden's Political Economy

....

JOHANNES LINDVALL

SWEDEN'S economic policies, labor market institutions, and welfare programs have long fascinated scholars at home and abroad. Andrew Shonfield's *Modern Capitalism* (1965)—one of the very first contributions to comparative political economy—observed half a century ago that Sweden was "more firmly committed than other nations to the triple objective of full employment, rapid growth, and a very high level of social welfare," and from the 1930s to the final years of the twentieth century, Sweden's attempts to combine a growing capitalist economy with egalitarian politics and a high level of social protection were associated with the idea of a "Swedish model"—a "middle way" between capitalism and socialism.

The Swedish model was often idealized, perhaps even idolized (especially by left-of-center academics and political commentators, who regarded Sweden as an example to be followed), but there is no doubt that Sweden's approach to economic and social policy *was* distinctive, and in some respects it still is.

The contributors to this section of the *Handbook* address questions of economic policy and political economy that should be particularly interesting to foreign students and scholars who wish to learn more about the Swedish experience. The chapters are not only concerned with the institutions and policies that are typically seen as emblematic of the twentieth-century Swedish model; they also describe some of the important changes that these institutions and policies have undergone since the 1980s.

The first chapter, by Jenny Andersson, explains how the idea of the Swedish model emerged and developed. Andersson's chapter also accounts for the role of the Swedish model as an ideological construct: she shows that the main objective of social democratic policies in the middle of the twentieth century was to achieve a mutually reinforcing dynamic of increasing economic efficiency and increasing equality. She then goes on to show how this model broke down in the 1970s and 1980s, in the wake of attacks from both left and right, and she ends with a discussion of how the idea of a Swedish model continues to inform current Swedish policy-making.

In the following chapter, Leif Lewin and Johannes Lindvall take a historical approach to Swedish economic policy-making. The chapter has three aims. The first is to describe how Swedish economic policy-making has evolved over time. The second is to show if and when Swedish governments have pursued economic policies that set Sweden apart from other rich democracies. The third is to introduce and examine a number of scholarly debates on how to explain some of the economic policy shifts that have occurred in Sweden since the country's transition to democracy in the 1910s.

Lars Calmfors' chapter is concerned with Sweden's current economic policy model—with how it emerged after the deep economic crisis of the 1990s, and how it has functioned since then. Calmfors describes a series of reforms in the 1990s and 2000s that introduced central bank independence, flexible inflation targeting, a highly structured budgetary process, and an independent fiscal policy council (of which Calmfors himself was the first chair). Calmfors' chapter also accounts for some important contemporary economic policy controversies.

In the final chapter of this section, Torsten Svensson examines another aspect of the Swedish political economy that has interested foreign observers since long before World War II: Sweden's vast landscape of interest organizations and their relationships to each other and to the state. Svensson pays particular attention to labor market organizations and labor market institutions, showing what is distinctive about Sweden's current labor market model, and how it differs from the highly centralized model of the past.

Reference

Shonfield, A. (1965). *Modern Capitalism*. Oxford: Oxford University Press.

....

CHAPTER 42

A MODEL OF WELFARE CAPITALISM?

*Perspectives on the Swedish Model,
Then and Now*

....

JENNY ANDERSSON

INTRODUCTION

THE so-called "Swedish model" has attracted a lot of attention from the international social sciences. Understood as the quintessential welfare state and the primary example of European social democracy, Sweden became a given reference point for comparative research (see, for instance, Stephens 1979). A series of successive arguments constructed the Swedish case as something of an ideal type of postwar social science, and over time the idea of a Swedish model developed into a kind of tropism which seems to have played a role also in steering interpretations of change within Sweden. For a long time, social science research described the Swedish welfare state as essentially stable. Meanwhile, however, there was significant institutional change in Sweden, the content of economic and social policies evolved, and political interpretations of the Swedish model changed significantly. Fundamental struggles in Swedish politics in recent decades have focused on reforming the Swedish model and adapting it to internal and external challenges.

This chapter examines central shifts in ideas of the Swedish model—both in the social sciences and in political usage—and places these ideas in the context of institutional change within the Swedish welfare state. The first section lays out a history of the concept of the Swedish model in social science, and its relationship to interpretations of the Swedish welfare state. The second section focuses on the question of neoliberalism in Sweden and how we may understand its impact in an institutional environment that for a long time was seen as offering particular forms of resistance to it—a "social democracy par excellence" (Blyth 2002: 14). The final section argues that processes of marketization and financialization in the Swedish welfare model necessitate a fundamental rethinking of our understanding of the Swedish case as a model of welfare capitalism.

The Swedish Model between History
and Social Science

The concept of the Swedish model does not denote any fixed relationship between economic and social policy-making. The Varieties of Capitalism school—falling back on functionalist notions of change in different policy fits—treated Sweden as a prime example of a coordinated market economy due to overlaps between economic and social policy-making and a highly coordinated labor market (Hall and Soskice 2001). However, the hierarchy between economic and social policy objectives has changed over time, as resources have diminished, and so have the policy objectives. In the postwar period, economic and social policy-making had important coordination effects, resulting from the ambition to marry objectives of growth and security in a full employment society (Andersson 2006). In later periods, growth policies have taken precedence, social objectives have had to fall back, and ideas of the welfare state as a productive investment in the Swedish economy have given way to forms of retrenchment, flexicurity, and so-called social investment strategies (Andersson 2010; Palier, Morel, and Palme 2012). This shift is in line with Jessop's notion of the transformation of the contemporary welfare state from Keynesian Fordism to a Schumpetarian model of postindustrial capitalism (Jessop 2002).

Interpretations of what the concept of the Swedish model actually connotes are, I propose, historically specific and vary with conceptions of the rational organization of a capitalist society over the twentieth century (Andersson 2009). The notion of a "model" has itself functioned as an ideational carrier of such reinterpretations over time, in social science and politics alike. The idea of the Swedish model is also a discursive battlefield. The term was hardly used in domestic politics before the end of the 1960s. It emerged as part of a social democratic reaction to the rise of contestation from the Swedish left, and as a way of lending coherence to economic and social policies that had emerged as a result of a series of cumulative reforms since the interwar period (Stråth 2004). Recent decades have seen other attempts at politicization, and depoliticization, of the idea of the Swedish model. In the early 2000s, the notion of the Swedish model, dismissed by international observers following the 1990s recession (see Lindert 2004), was redeployed by Swedish policy-makers as part of a branding exercise aimed at restoring market confidence in a high-tax, high-public-expenditure economy. Encompassing today a series of neoliberal reforms, the concept has become a common denominator for both left- and right-wing politics. Apparently, even the British premier David Cameron is a fan of the Swedish model.

In other words, the concept of the Swedish model does not denote a specific set of policy solutions that is stable over time, but rather shifting and historically specific interpretations of the nature of welfare capitalism. If we understand it as such, we can revisit some of the key debates about Sweden, the model, and the welfare state. The concept of the Swedish model (the *middle way*) is usually traced back to the American diplomat Marquis Childs, who on his return from a European journey in the mid-1930s described Sweden as a model society in which the best aspects of capitalism seemed joined together with the best possible aspects of the planned economy. In Sweden, the products of economic growth were redistributed to common, social objectives (Childs 1936; Marklund 2009). Marquis Childs set words on a relationship that would then remain the common theme of many interpretations of Swedish success in the twentieth century; namely, the idea of Sweden as occupying a space in-between capitalism and communism (Andersson 2009).

A second strand in this line of observations of the Swedish model came with comparative studies of welfare states in the 1950s and 1960s, and in particular Richard Titmuss's argument that Sweden was an example of the institutionally redistributive welfare state. Contrasted, by Titmuss, to the liberal and means-tested Beveridge model, the Swedish welfare state stood out as one in which social problems were handled through the systematic redistribution of wealth between social classes (Titmuss 1974). Originally a conservative and liberal concept, the idea of the "welfare state" was thus reattributed to Sweden and associated with social democracy.

A range of studies in the 1980s confirmed this analysis of the role of the Swedish welfare state as an institutional intervention into the capitalist economy, and developed it by linking the welfare state to the agency of organized labor. The so-called "power resources school" argued that the welfare state could be understood as a strategic social democratic invention, designed to redistribute economic and political resources to the working class. By building institutional arrangements that allowed for the redistribution of resources between classes, organized labor could shape the preferences of the population towards a general acceptance for redistribution and use the welfare state to entrench its political power (Esping-Andersen and Korpi 1986; Esping-Andersen 1985). Walter Korpi thus adapted his previous Marxist study on the labor movement as the ruling class into an argument about the institutional strength of social democracy. Esping-Andersen's book *Politics Against Markets* (1985) argued that welfare state arrangements can be understood as serving the chief purpose of a strategic decommodification of the working class, hence its emancipation within the limits of capitalist society (Esping-Andersen 1985). His book *The Three Worlds of Welfare Capitalism* (1990) confirmed this picture, driving home the idea of an inseparable historical link between social democracy and the social model, and turning Sweden into an ideal type of the decommodifying welfare state (Esping-Andersen 1990).

From this point on, we can see an awakening of interest in the institutional architecture of the welfare state and the particular institutional mechanisms that seemed to create public support for it. Korpi's argument was taken further by the Swedish political scientist Bo Rothstein, who saw the social democratic state as the effective replacement of the bourgeois state through the building of a welfare bureaucracy which could control capitalist society and free individuals from repressive state action (Rothstein 1996). Rothstein emphasized the idea of *universalism* as a particular political theory designed to autonomize individuals through an impartial state bureaucracy (Rothstein 1998). By the 1980s and early 1990s, a series of studies had also pinpointed the political strategy of Swedish social democracy, emphasizing again its profound links to the welfare state but also its rationalist and pragmatic political theory (Heclo 1974; Lewin 1988; Tilton 1990). By the 1990s the Swedish model thus appeared to be the expression of a rationalist culture of continuous reform, and of a rationally ordered hierarchy between the policy process and the social sciences.

A MODEL FOR OR AGAINST THE MARKET?

Throughout the twentieth century, objections were raised to the ideas described in the previous section, in politics as well as in the social sciences, but the first fundamental reinterpretation of the Swedish model appeared in the 1990s, as feminist scholars pointed out that the analysis of the way that the welfare state intervened into gender relations was lacking. In this literature, positive notions of Sweden as a dual breadwinner model enabling female labor participation—built on observations of key reforms such as the introduction of separate taxation in 1974 and the expansion of public child care services in 1975—clashed with notions of Sweden as a fundamentally gender-segregated labor market. The state, it was argued, had freed women from the household but kept them in care work only in public employment (Sainsbury 1994).

This literature took up some of the strands from a previous Marxist critique of the working-class state, and it also pointed, albeit unwittingly, toward a radical critique of the paternalist state that emerged in the early 1990s from Swedish liberal feminists, who saw the state as a worse oppressor than the family or the market (see Ulmanen 1998). Importantly, this debate pinpointed the question of the relationship between the welfare state and the market, and the role of the Swedish model in challenging or accommodating market relationships, which has been a recurring debate. A second strand of studies, influenced by the economic crisis that shook Sweden and the other Nordic countries in the early to mid-1990s, focused on the role played by conditionality in the allegedly universal welfare model. A series of studies written mainly by Swedish scholars affiliated with the Stockholm Institute for Social Research showed that universal structures for those inside of the labor market were matched by much more conditional practices for those on the margins. A series of studies from the Balance Sheet for Welfare commission, investigating the social effects of the 1990s crisis, showed how harsher forms of conditionality in the aftermath of crisis reinforced historically anchored patterns of dualization. A series of historical studies also exposed the fundamentally workfarist orientation of the Swedish model and saw links between the idea of a "People's home" on the one hand and a disciplinary work ethic on the other, and even associated this idea with important forms of illiberalism against groups on the margins of society. It was not until the 1990s, for instance, that historians systematically addressed the question of eugenics in the Swedish welfare state (Tydén 1996). Several studies also nuanced the role of social democracy as an enlightened class actor and brought out a more callous and rationalist culture, deeply influenced by economism and productivism (Andersson 2006; Karlsson 2001). These studies thus added up to a questioning of the nature of the Swedish model. What comparative research had understood as institutionally redistributive and decommodifying structures were now increasingly described—in Swedish debates deeply influenced by the economic crisis and the changing political climate of the 1990s—as a Janus-faced social contract where universalist practices were coupled with important forms of conditionality. In short, the Swedish model was reinterpreted as incorporating a profound market orientation and important practices of social segregation.

Throughout the 1990s and 2000s, international social science continued to portray the Swedish welfare state as a resilient social democratic model in a world of aggressive neoliberalism (see, for instance, Schmidt 2000). Comparative studies of change in Western welfare states tended to underline changes in Sweden as essentially incremental, undertaken without significantly changing the institutional setup of the model (for a discussion of the conservative bias in the institutionalist literature, see Thelen and Streeck 2005). Detailed studies of particular policy areas, meanwhile, did show significant change, particularly in labor market policy and social policy. In labor market policy, workfarist arrangements that emphasized individual obligation, activation, and entrepreneurship were introduced from the mid-1990s on (Clasen and Clegg 2005). The highly individualized content of these policies was arguably very different from the collective, rights-based, and structurally oriented active labor market policies that were associated with the postwar "Rehn Meidner model" (Johansson 2006; Garsten and Jacobsson 2004). Such policy changes have been further entrenched under both social democratic and right-wing governments in the late 1990s and 2000s, leading to dualization (Lindvall and Rueda 2012).

Recent OECD studies have singled out Swedish labor market policies as dramatically losing in quality and efficiency, and have also pinpointed the increasing levels of inequality in the Swedish model (OECD 2011). Swedish statistics show that unemployment has become a poverty trap, following the restructuring of unemployment insurance in recent years—shaking, one would have to argue, one of the fundaments of the postwar model. Political debates on labor market policy and social policy have focused on strengthening *arbetslinjen*, the work ethic that is presumed to be the hallmark of the Swedish model, essentially by increasing conditionality. In other words, reforms that can very well be interpreted as introducing fundamental forms of change in the model were marketed politically as policies defending the historical gains of the Swedish welfare state and its active labor market policies, and not as a question of model change (Andersson 2010). As the cumulative effects of these and other changes (for instance, changes in taxation and the effects of deregulation of credit markets) are increasingly visible in Swedish society, social scientists have begun to describe Sweden as a case of fundamental change and "winner-takes-all politics" (Svallfors 2015).

Neoliberalism in the Swedish Model

The economic crisis that shook the Swedish economy between 1992 and, roughly speaking, 1996 paved the way for neoliberal reform. However, the economic crisis should not be seen as a simple exogenous factor explaining policy change. Rather, the economic crisis was a catalyst, accelerating changes that were in fact political and had been in preparation since the late 1970s. The recession had multiple causes, including the growing volatility in price movements following massive deregulations of the financial markets in Sweden and internationally, and the ensuing vulnerability of the Swedish krona. The dominant interpretation of the 1990s crisis, however, was that it was generated by structural problems emerging from within the institutional setup of the Swedish model itself. This interpretation was codified, after the fall of the krona, by the Lindbeck Commission, which argued that corporatism and trade union pressure corrupted political action and drove inflationary wage demands (SOU 1993:16). Through this prevailing crisis narrative, emphasizing the incompatibility of the Swedish model with global capitalism, arguments which had their origins in public choice theory, monetarism, and New Public Management became legitimate in Sweden.

But the origins of neoliberalism in Sweden are more complex. A number of recent studies have shown that neoliberal ideas are often introduced in national contexts through actors with a footing in transnational debates who are also influential nationally (Mirowski and Plehwe 2009). The success of what was simply called, in the late 1970s, "new economic ideas" was that they allowed for a strategic marriage between neoliberal ideas and social democracy (compare Mudge 2011). This marriage is an essential part of the explanation of the profound political and institutional changes within the Swedish model since the 1980s and also explains why these changes were seen as publicly legitimate for such a long time. The alliance was possible because neoliberalism seemed to play into historical legacies of productivism and discipline within social democracy itself, and because the new policy tools that new economic ideas and ideas about New Public Management introduced in the 1990s were understood as neutral instruments of steering, befitting a political culture of pragmatic problem-solving, affecting only the means, not the ends, of political action (Andersson 2010).

Moreover, the remarkable success of neoliberalism in Sweden was a result of the growing political uncertainty and increasing contestation around the idea of a Swedish model from the late 1960s onward. International research has tended to overestimate the stability and hegemony of the Swedish Social Democratic Party, which has suffered from the same trend of eroding support for organized labor as have social democratic parties in the rest of Europe. The party's best election was the election of 1968. The period thereafter has been one of increasing electoral competition and political uncertainty, characterized not only by social democracy's increasing dependence on alliances, but also by increasing tensions within the labor movement itself. To this we need to add important frictions within social democracy's "natural environment"—in particular its link to and control of the welfare state bureaucracy and its relationship to the social sciences (Andersson 2006; Lindvall 2004).

A number of studies have explained change in the Swedish Model with reference to the influence of economic ideas in the 1980s and 1990s and the importance of economic expertise in shifting social democratic positions away from Keynesianism (Lindvall 2004; Blyth 2002). A slightly longer political history perspective brings out that social democracy's relationship to forms of expertise in the social sciences had been deeply fraught since the late 1960s. The increasing influence of economists was a result of the fact that they replaced other experts that lost influence—not necessarily because of policy learning, but for political reasons. The first dent in the social democratic edifice actually resulted from left-wing critique, coming from groups situated within the bureaucracy and planning apparatus of the welfare state. The Swedish version of 1968 was not just about rebellious university students; more importantly, the late 1960s saw a fundamental split between the social democratic party and its historical allies in the building of the welfare state apparatus, as sociologists, social workers, and teachers, influenced by Marxism, began to attack the welfare state, which they saw as a social democratic reenactment of the capitalist state. Several important studies in the early 1970s brought out the existence of new forms of poverty and marginalization in the Swedish model, introducing themes of postindustrialism and alienation that would also shape New Left thinking elsewhere (Andersson 2006). The SAP eventually integrated this critique in a fundamental turn to the left in party strategy in the late 1960s and in the 1970s. This shift in orientation culminated eventually in the economic democracy agenda and wage earner funds, which produced a major clash with Swedish employers around 1980 (Pontusson 1992).

It is hard to understand the shift to neoliberal ideas in the 1980s without this thicker account of the increasing contestation around the Swedish model already in the period from the 1960s onward, and it is significant that the first accounts of the failures of the universal welfare state did not come from liberal economists but from professional groups on whom the reformist project had in fact depended throughout the postwar period. It was arguably the breakup between social democracy and its "organic intellectuals" in the sociological elite that paved the way for the rise of economists within the planning and policy apparatus from the 1970s on. The radicalized political agenda of the SAP in the 1970s set in motion a series of complex causalities. On the institutional level, welfare policy ambitions increased, particularly toward previously marginalized groups such as the disabled, immigrants, social welfare recipients, and children. This was a significant change in what used to be a highly labor-market-oriented model. Paradoxically, this recalibration of social policy toward groups that were essentially outside of the sphere of production went against the party's historic insistence on the economic rationale of the welfare state as a productive investment in the economy. This discursive rupture would have significant effects since it reframed welfare spending as a form of cost to the productive economy.

New forms of expertise also brought new forms of steering. Throughout the 1970s there was a traceable continuity in how new tools from the social sciences—such as the social indicators that reached Western planning systems in the early 1970s to monitor new aspects of poverty—became carriers of political change, especially as they were, in turn, recalibrated as performance indicators monitoring not social but economic performance. The Planning, Programming, and Budgeting System (PPBS), which became a core element in New Public Management policies in the 1980s, was first used in Sweden in the early 1970s as part of an overhaul of the budget process in the context of rising social ambitions. It was a direct import from the US Ministry of Defense and the War on Poverty. Following the first oil crisis, however, PPBS and related policy instruments such as cost–benefit analysis were used, rather, in order to evaluate the rising costs of public services per output—in other words, to assess the lack of efficiency of the public sector (Andersson 2006). Such changes in instruments carried ideational change well before the battle of ideas erupted in the political arena.

A good illustration of these shifts in the forms of expertise underpinning the model is *Expertgruppen för studier i offentlig ekonomi* (ESO), which started doing evaluations of public sector performance in the late 1970s. ESO was a novelty in the Swedish knowledge-producing apparatus when it was created by the liberal government in 1979. It was not a planning agency as such but something rather like a think-tank of institutionalized economic expertise. ESO played a crucial role in breaking with the Keynesian thinking behind the Swedish model and in reframing the discussion about the welfare state. It is telling that the Social Democrats took over ESO from the liberal government on its return to power in 1982. This permitted social democratic policy-makers to sidestep alternative forms of economic thinking such as those prevailing within its own ranks.

The 1980s did not only see a break between the party and the sociologists, but also a break with the influence of the economic thinking of Myrdal, Wigforss, Rehn, and Meidner within the party, and to some extent also within the the Trade Union Confederation (LO). The importance of Keynesianism for the development of Swedish economic and social policy-making cannot be overstated. From the interwar period onward, Keynesianism was tied to a rationalist argument that defended the welfare state as a form of ordered, efficient capitalism, investing in the nation's human capital (see Jonung 1991). Keynesian ideas thus allowed for important forms of policy coordination, but they also enabled larger political alliances around the Swedish model.

From this perspective, the crisis of Keynesian ideas in Sweden and the rise of monetarism from the late 1970s onward had larger stakes than a change of epistemic community (Alder and Haas 1992) or even paradigm (Hall 1993). Lindvall's important study of shifts in economic policy-making argued that the gradual changes from the late 1970s to the eventual abandonment of the flagship goal of full employment in 1991 were a question of policy learning and matching demand and supply between politics and existing epistemic communities (Lindvall 2004). But the question of a shift in economic expertise was a much larger question that did not only involve economists and their ideas, but also the fundamental redrawing of the limits of the state vis-à-vis the market in Swedish society. Mark Blyth, in his 2002 book, argued that the period from the 1970s onward could be seen as part of a great unraveling, a Polanyian double movement in which market forces—legitimitized through economic ideas—regained territory that had been lost through the rise of the welfare state (Blyth 2002).

RETRENCHMENT OR REFORM? A NEW HISTORIC COMPROMISE AROUND THE WELFARE STATE FROM THE 1990S ONWARD

Fundamental transformations in the sociopolitical composition of the Swedish model—and in the power constellations in Swedish politics—were already well under way when the center-right Bildt government was formed in 1991. From a historical perspective, the early 1990s stand out as exceptional. It was the only period in recent history for which there is evidence that public opinion turned against the welfare state, fueled by economic crisis and the emergence of a populist party with an aggressively neoliberal platform. The electoral mood changed quickly, however. Social democracy's return in 1994 was preceded by a swing back to massive support for a publicly funded welfare state, and, as Stefan Svallfors has repeatedly shown, the welfare state continues to enjoy high levels of support (Svallfors 2004).

It is difficult to explain the far-reaching privatizations in education, health care, and welfare services as a simple question of political adaptation to changing electoral preferences. Political actors constantly interpret and anticipate electoral preferences (compare Hay 1998). Moreover, policies have effects on preferences, and welfare reform can be used by policy-makers as a means of shifting the electoral ground on contested issues (Soss and Schram 2007). It is worthwhile, from this perspective, to consider the profound *ideologization* of welfare politics in the 1990s and 2000s and the increased emphasis on middle-class values in political discourse. Even if a series of institutional changes in the 1990s and 2000s seemed to depoliticize the welfare state by handing over a large part of it to the market, such a shift is deeply ideological, shifting the boundaries of politics.

The reforms that were introduced under the Bildt government in 1991–4 in areas such as housing, education, media, and business regulation had a central cultural element. They were aimed to break, in a lasting manner, the grasp of social democracy on Swedish political culture, and to unleash forms of individualism that were understood as having been repressed (see Moderaterna och Folkpartiet 1991). The market was thus not understood as merely an organizational form or a provider of service, but as a vehicle of preference shaping. For example, the introduction of vouchers in the school system introduced mechanisms of choice that would unleash consumerist pressures from parents and pupils and pave the way for a market in education. Another reform with important consequences for political culture was membership in the European Union, embraced in the early 1990s by Swedish policy-makers not only as a structural but as a *structuring* reform, or, in other words, as a way of shifting macroeconomic policy from the political sphere to a nonpolitical legal and economic one (see Blyth and Katz 2005). Within the European Union, the Swedish model would have to embrace the economic truths of competitive globalization and reinvent itself in ways that were compatible with market pressures. In retrospect, therefore, the ambitions of the Bildt government can be quite clearly discerned: to deregulate parts of the welfare state, thereby creating a welfare market which would in turn have the role of unlearning fundamental values of social solidarity and learning values of entrepreneurship, creativity, and choice.

"Thatcherism," in the shape of Carl Bildt, did not last very long, as the Bildt government was ejected in 1994 by an electorate attached to the welfare state and disenchanted with crisis management. The bulk of neoliberal reform was implemented, therefore, by the Social Democrats as a part of their Third Way platform, beginning with the tax reform in 1990 and culminating, in a sense, with the pension reform in 1994 (which introduced a highly individualized and financialized system, as described by Belfrage and Ryner 2009). Social democracy's full-scale acceptance of the structural reforms of the early 1990s marks the emergence of a new political compromise around the welfare state as a fundamentally market-oriented entity.

This is a bit of a puzzle. The Social Democrats seemed to have a popular mandate, in 1994, to go against and even undo elements of the neoliberal reform agenda, and they also faced significant internal pressure to do so. We therefore have to consider why the party chose instead to pursue unpopular reforms that not only seemed to run against its ideological principles but also came at the cost of internal fracture and loss of popular support. Early explanations of Third Way policies referred to ideological change as an outcome of organized labor's need to adapt to the economic constraints of globalization (see Giddens 1998; Pontusson 1995). A second strand of literature has pointed instead to social democracy's own agency and to ideological change as an internal process driven by party elites (Lundberg 2005; Moschonas 2002; Blyth and Katz 2005). In other words, social democratic elites adopted neoliberal politics either because they thought they were ideologically correct (arguably this was the case in the UK) or because they understood them as being essentially in tune with the historic legacies of social democracy, and as essentially nonideological changes in a long continuity of "puzzling" and problem-solving—which appears to be an important part of the explanation in the Swedish case (Andersson 2010).

As Sweden embarked on a massive scaling-down of the public deficit in the mid-1990s, policy-makers defended changes to the Swedish model as a matter of successful modernization that did not alter its fundamental composition. The alternative reading is that retrenchment added up to fundamental change. The policy changes were framed, politically, as active *reforms* of the Swedish model, moving toward market values. It was not a process dictated a priori by economic constraints, but a politically driven one. As argued, it had begun before the 1990s recession, prepared by important changes in the expertise underpinning the Swedish model. After the crisis, the process was consolidated through a political realignment which depended on the decisive resettlement of social democracy as a center force. As part of this settlement, changes in the model were normalized through an emerging political consensus between social democracy and the political right. This process was confirmed, arguably, by the successful reinvention of the Swedish Conservative Party, the Moderates, as the "new labour party" (*nya arbetarpartiet*) in the run-up to the 2006 election.

From this perspective, we can revisit Bo Rothstein's 2006 observation on the electoral victory of the Swedish right, which he interpreted as a historic victory of the Swedish model. Only by showing that it embraced the welfare state could the Swedish right win popular support, Rothstein argued. It is possible to draw the opposite conclusion. Only due to a fundamental reinterpretation of the meaning of the Swedish model and due to profound changes in its policy content was the model appropriable for right-wing policy-makers that were smart enough to play up, in rhetoric, a continuity with postwar values.

Nevertheless, the policy changes of the 1990s and 2000s would not have been possible without the active agency of social democracy and its role in the stabilization of a political alliance around a limited and fundamentally market-oriented welfare state. This alliance has come at significant cost of electoral support for social democracy in Sweden as elsewhere (Arndt 2014; compare Przeworski and Sprague 1986).

A Model of Welfare Capitalism?
Political and Financial Capital
in the Welfare Market

This alliance between social democracy and neoliberalism around the welfare state has been coupled, arguably, with the rise of new strategic alliances between political and financial capital. Since the 1990s, a fundamental process of marketization has taken place in the domain of the welfare state. Today, at least 20 percent of welfare services are produced by private providers, and Sweden has some of the most lax regulations in the world concerning this de facto welfare market. The providers are increasingly revealing themselves to be directly connected not only to Swedish political elites but also to global financial capital (Vlachos 2011; Werne et al. 2014). In a play on Eisenhower's famous phrase "the military-industrial complex," the journalist Fredrik Jansson recently deployed the term the "welfare-industrial complex" to denote the apparent fact that global hedge funds have identified the Swedish welfare market as a suitable object of speculation (Jansson, quoted by Svallfors 2015).

As the social sciences, both domestically and internationally, appear to have been stuck in a historically anchored reading of the Swedish case as a model of welfare capitalism, this process of privatization, marketization, and financialization remains fundamentally understudied. There is a remarkable lack of social science research on the effects of 20 years of privatization in Swedish society, and there is even less research on the economic, social, and political transformations that made this process possible

(Svallfors 2015). A recent contribution comes from a collective of Swedish journalists, who have shown that what began as relatively small-scale attempts to introduce principles of freedom of choice and experiments with private or semi-public providers in the welfare sector snowballed when the financial markets realized that they could make important profits on a market with almost perfectly foreseeable consumer demand, state-guaranteed public funding, and wonderful opportunities for cost-cutting (Werne et al. 2014). In the last years such investigative journalism has triggered a number of public scandals. In the summer of 2012, the private care provider Carema was the subject of a series of investigations that showed how service providers owned by entities registered in international tax havens systematically squeezed quality. Such scandals are now common.

The existence of a "welfare-industrial complex" seems to call for a fundamental reinterpretation of the idea of "welfare capitalism," and it also pushes us to consider the future orientation of the Swedish model and the emerging power constellations in Swedish politics. First of all, as argued most notably by Colin Crouch and Wolfgang Streeck, the interwoven links between the state and financial capital in a post- or privatized Keynesian world can be understood as a new Polanyian double movement (Crouch 2009, Streeck 2011). While welfare states, short of funding in the deregulated era, seek to embed the markets in their institutional arrangements, thereby domesticating them as vehicles of social change, deregulated markets in search of financial returns seek to use welfare states as potential markets for new speculative commodities. This double movement seemed to work relatively smoothly up until the financial crisis—but the result post-crisis is, as shown by Streeck, possible dramatic lock-ins of state action due to their fundamental indebtedness (Streeck 2011).

Let us add to this that while Sweden has not suffered from financial crisis to the same extent as other countries and is not in a similar situation of deficit, Sweden has—through the far-going privatizations and lack of regulation of market actors in the welfare state—integrated markets to the point that the effects of market action may well become sudden and dramatic. Moreover, "welfare capitalism" is not merely driven by market actors; it is a socially embedded phenomenon in which the structures of the welfare state interact with processes of marketization. From that perspective, we may have to consider the possibility that neoliberalism had a profound impact on the Swedish model not despite but *because* of the legacies of a strong state, serving as the institutional platform for the embedding of neoliberal practices. The state was directly involved in reorganizing welfare as a series of quasi-markets regulated through public subsidies and agencies and rendered publicly legitimate through politics. Finally, a notable feature of the "welfare-industrial complex" is that strategic alliances are formed between political and market-based elites, and it has led to new forms of exchange of financial and political capital in contemporary Swedish politics. This raises crucial questions about how to interpret the nature of the historic "politics against the market" model, about the role of social democracy in the creation of modern welfare capitalism, and about its future capacity to reform or contain such a system.

References

Adler, E. and Haas, P. M. (1992). "Conclusion: Epistemic Communities, World Order, and the Creation of a Reflective Research Program," *International Organization* 46/1: 367–90.

Andersson, J. (2006). *Between Growth and Security: Swedish Social Democracy from a Strong Society to a Third Way*. Manchester: Manchester University Press.

Andersson, J. (2009)."Nordic Nostalgia and Nordic Light: The Swedish Model as Utopia 1930–2007," *Scandinavian Journal of History* 34/3: 229–45.

Andersson, J. (2010). *The Library and the Workshop: Social Democracy and Capitalism in an Age of Knowledge*. Palo Alto: Stanford University Press.

Arndt, C. (2014). *The Electoral Consequences of Third Way Reforms: Social Democracy's Transformations and its Political Costs*. Amsterdam: Amsterdam University Press.

Blyth, M. (2002). *Great Transformations: Economic Ideas and Institutional Change in the Twentieth Century*. New York: Cambridge University Press.

Blyth, M. and Katz, R. (2005). "From Catch-All Politics to Cartelisation: The Political Economy of the Cartel Party," *West European Politics* 29/1: 33–60.

Belfrage, C. and Ryner, M. (2009). "Renegotiating the Swedish Social Democratic Settlement: From Pension Fund Socialism to Neoliberalization," *Politics and Society* 37/2: 257–87.

Childs, M. (1936). *The Middle Way*. New Haven: Yale University Press.

Clasen, J. and Clegg, D. (2005). "New Labour Market Risks and the Revision of Unemployment Protection Systems in Europe," in K. Armingeon and G. Bonoli (eds), *The Politics of Postindustrial Welfare States*. London: Routledge, 192–211.

Crouch, C. (2009). "Privatized Keynesianism, an Unacknowledged Policy Regime," *British Journal of Politics and International Relations* 11: 382–99.

Esping-Andersen, G. (1985). *Politics Against Markets*. Princeton: Princeton University Press.

Esping-Andersen, G. (1990). *The Three Worlds of Welfare Capitalism*. Cambridge: Polity Press.

Esping-Andersen, G. and Korpi, W. (1986). "From Poor Relief to Institutional Welfare States: The Development of Scandinavian Social Policy," *International Journal of Sociology* 16/3–4: 39–74.

Garsten, C. and Jacobsson, K. (2004). *Learning to be Employable: New Agendas on Work, Responsibility, and Learning in a Globalizing World*. Basingstoke: Macmillan.

Giddens, A. (1998). *The Third Way: The Renewal of Social Democracy*. Cambridge: Polity Press.

Hall, P. A. (1993). "Policy Paradigms, Social Learning, and the State: The Case of Economic Policymaking in Britain," *Comparative Politics* 25/3: 275–96.

Hall, P. A. and Soskice, D. (eds) (2001). *Varieties of Capitalism: The Institutional Foundations of Comparative Advantage*. Oxford: Oxford University Press.

Hay, C. (1998). *The Political Economy of New Labour*. Manchester: Manchester University Press.

Heclo, H. (1974). *Modern Social Policy in Britain and Sweden: From Relief to Income Maintenance*. New Haven: Princeton University Press.

Jessop, B. (2002). *The Future of the Capitalist State*. London: Polity.

Johansson, H. (2006). *Svensk aktiveringspolitik i nordisk belysning*. Stockholm: ESS 2006:3.

Jonung. L. (1991). *The Stockholm School of Economics Revisited*. Cambridge: Cambridge University Press.

Karlsson, S. (2001). *Det intelligenta samhället: En omtolkning av socialdemokratins historia*. Stockholm: Atlas.

Lewin, L. (1988). *Ideology and Strategy: A Century of Swedish Politics.* Cambridge: Cambridge University Press.

Lindbeckkommissionen (1993). *Nya villkor för politik och ekonomi.* Stockholm: SOU 1993: 16.

Lindert, P. (2004). *Growing Public: Social Spending and Economic Growth since the 18th Century.* Cambridge: Cambridge University Press.

Lindvall, J. (2004). *The Politics of Purpose: Swedish Macroeconomic Policy after the Golden Age.* Göteborg: Göteborg University, Department of Political Science.

Lindvall, J. and Rueda, D. (2012). "Insider-Outsider Politics: Party Strategies and Political Behavior in Sweden," in P. Emenegger et al., *The Age of Dualization: The Changing Face of Inequality in Deindustrializing Societies.* Oxford: Oxford University Press, 277–300.

Lundberg, U. (2005). *Social Democracy Lost: The Pension Reform in Sweden.* Stockholm: Institute for Future Studies.

Marklund, C. (2009). "The Social Laboratory, the Middle Way and the Swedish Model: Three Frames for the Image of Sweden," *Journal of Scandinavian History* 34/3: 264–85.

Mirowski, P. and Plehwe, D. (eds) (2009). *The Road from Mt Pelerin: The Making of the Neoliberal Thought Collective.* Cambridge, MA: Harvard University Press.

Moderaterna and Folkpartiet (1991). *Ny start för Sverige.* Stockholm.

Moschonas, G. (2002). *In the Name of Social Democracy.* London: Verso.

Mudge, S. L. (2011). "What's Left of Leftism? Neoliberal Politics in Western Party Systems, 1945–2004," *Social Science History* 35/3: 337–80.

OECD (2011). *Divided We Stand: Why Inequalities Keep Rising.* Paris: OECD.

Palier, B. Morel, N., and Palme, J. (eds) (2012). *Towards a Social Investment State: Ideas, Policies and Challenges.* Bristol: Policy Press.

Pontusson, J. (1992). *The Limits of Social Democracy: Investment Politics in Sweden.* Ithaca: Cornell University Press.

Pontusson, J. (1995). "Explaining the Decline of European Social Democracy: The Role of Structural Economic Change," *World Politics* 47: 495–533.

Przeworski, A. and Sprague, J. (1986). *Paper Stones: A History of Electoral Socialism.* Chicago: University of Chicaco Press.

Rothstein, B. (1996). *The Social Democratic State: The Swedish Model and the Bureaucratic Problem of Social Reforms.* Pittsburgh: University of Pittsburgh Press.

Rothstein, B. (1998). *Just Institutions Matter: The Moral and Political Logic of the Universal Welfare State.* Cambridge: Cambridge University Press.

Sainsbury, D. (1994). *Gendering Welfare States.* London: Sage Publications.

Schmidt, V. A. (2000). "Values and Discourse in the Politics of Adjustment," in V. A. Schmidt and F. Scharpf (eds), *Work and Welfare in the Open Economy.* New York: Oxford University Press, 228–309.

Soss, J. and Schram, S. (2007). "A Public Transformed? Welfare Reform as Policy Feedback," in J. Soss, J. S. Hacker, and S. Mettler (eds), *Remaking America: Democracy and Public Policy in an Age of Inequality.* New York: Russell Sage, 99–118.

Stephens, J. D. (1979). *The Transition from Capitalism to Socialism.* London: Macmillan.

Streeck, W. (2011). "The Crisis of Democratic Capitalism," *New Left Review* 71: 5–29.

Streeck, W. and Thelen, K. (2005). *Beyond Continuity: Institutional Change in Advanced Political Economies.* Oxford: Oxford University Press.

Stråth, B. (2004). *Mellan två fonder.* Stockholm: Atlas.

Svallfors, S. (2004). "Class, Attitudes and the Welfare State: Sweden in Comparative Perspective," *Social Policy & Administration* 38/2: 119–38.

Svallfors, S. (2015). "Politics as Organized Combat: New Players and New Rules of the Game in Sweden," MPIfG Discussion Paper 15/2, <http://www.mpifg.de/pu/mpifg_dp/dp15-2.pdf>.

Tilton, T. (1990). *The Political Theory of Swedish Social Democracy: Through the Welfare State to Revolution*. New York: Clarendon Press.

Titmuss, R. (1974). *Social Policy: An Introduction*. London: Pantheon Books.

Tydén, M. (1996). "Eugenics in Sweden: Efficient Care," in G. Broberg and N. Roll-Hansen (eds), *Eugenics and the Welfare State*. East Lansing: Michigan State University Press, 77–149.

Ulmanen, P. (1998). *Sveket mot kvinnorna och hur högern stal feminismen*. Stockholm: Atlas.

Vlachos, J. (2011). "Friskolor i förändring," in L. Hartman (ed.), *Konkurrensens konsekvenser*. Stockholm: SNS, 66–111.

Werne, K. et al. (2014). *Den stora omvandlingen*. Stockholm: Ordfront.

....

CHAPTER 43

ONE HUNDRED YEARS OF SWEDISH ECONOMIC POLICY

....

LEIF LEWIN AND JOHANNES LINDVALL

THIS chapter is concerned with the development of Swedish economic policy from the early 1920s to the present. We begin in the aftermath of the World War I, when Sweden became fully democratic. We end with Sweden's response to the Great Recession almost one hundred years later.

The chapter has three objectives. The first is, quite simply, to describe how Swedish economic policy-making has evolved over time, concentrating on a few especially important periods: the adoption of expansionary fiscal policies in the 1930s, the development of Sweden's postwar economic model in the 1950s, the struggle to maintain full employment in the 1970s and 1980s, the deep financial crisis of the early 1990s, and Sweden's response to the worldwide Great Recession of 2008–9.

The second objective is to show if and when Swedish governments have pursued economic policies that set Sweden apart from other rich democracies. Many scholars of comparative politics—including, in the last three decades, Weir and Skocpol (1985), Gourevitch (1986), Scharpf (1991), Iversen (1999), Notermans (2000), Blyth (2002), and Lindvall (2010)—have used the Swedish example to support general claims about economic policy-making in the advanced industrialized states. To evaluate such claims, it is important to establish if, when, and how Sweden has differed from other countries.

Finally, we wish to examine a number of scholarly debates on how to explain some of the economic policy shifts that have occurred in Sweden since its transition to democracy in the 1910s. We cannot do justice to all of the important arguments that scholars of Swedish economic policy have made about these events, but we do address some of them.

IN THE GREAT DEPRESSION

We begin by considering the economic policy debates of the 1920s and early 1930s, and how these debates informed the fiscal policies that Per Albin Hansson's new Social Democratic government introduced in the spring of 1933.

The Swedish economy recovered quickly after the World War I and the economic downturn of the early 1920s. After a late start in the second half of the nineteenth century, industrialization had transformed Sweden from one of the poorest and least-developed countries in northern Europe to a fast-growing modern society whose high level of economic growth was driven by industrial innovations. Safety matches, ball bearings, telephones, and separators had brought Sweden into a "second period as a great power," a leading industrialist noted at the time (De Geer 1928).

Sweden's center-right parties, who were in government for most of the 1920s, emphasized three explanations for this increasing prosperity. The first was the basically harmonious interplay of market forces. Adam Smith's invisible hand was ever-present in center-right political speeches and newspaper articles from this period: so wonderful were the mechanisms of the market that general welfare was promoted even if it was not part of the calculations of individual actors; what was good for individuals was good for society.

Second, economic freedom was the breath of life for economic growth. Precisely because of the prevailing harmony of market forces, politicians should acknowledge that by intervening in the economy, they often did more harm than good. Moreover, economic freedom was closely related to political and intellectual freedom. The right for everyone to speak out without asking politicians for permission, to introduce new ideas, and to be the architects of their own fortune—these were the basic principles of a prosperous society. Laissez-faire liberalism had little support; by the 1920s, all political parties agreed that the state was responsible for social security for all, and to this end, some redistribution of income was necessary. But there were limits. The state must ensure that it did not interfere with society's wealth-creating forces.

Third, and finally, there was a need for so-called "positive economic policies." Some state support, for some economic activities, was inevitable; but as an exception, not as a rule. This was especially true for agriculture. Here, the center-right parties offered slightly different remedies: the Conservative Party and the Agrarian Party recommended tariffs, whereas the Liberals suggested other arrangements.

Within the Social Democratic Party, which formed its first three short-lived governments in the first half of the 1920s, Marxist ideas were still predominant. According to Marx, capitalism was characterized by an ever-increasing exploitation of industrial workers. Whereas wealth was concentrated in the hands of fewer and fewer and richer and richer capitalists, the workers were paid less and less. Consequently, the workers were unable to buy all the products that the capitalists tried to sell, and society was affected by repeated underconsumption crises. These crises were expected to become worse and worse until capitalism would finally meet with a great catastrophe, the workers would seize power, industries would be nationalized, and socialism would triumph.

It was increasingly clear, however, that Swedish society diverged in many ways from this Marxist scenario. The workers saw their wages rise in tandem with the upswing of national income—the wage share increased sharply in the 1920s—and there was no sign of a catastrophe for capitalism. Nevertheless, Marxism remained the official ideology of the Social Democrats. This placed the party in a bind. Social Democratic voters expected the party to act for a more generous social welfare system. Such reforms would of course improve the purchasing power of the workers, counteract exploitation, and thus reduce the likelihood of economic catastrophe. In other words, the more successful the Social Democrats were in the short term, the less likely it was that their long-term grand theory of catastrophe would be realized.

As a result of this dilemma, the Social Democrats were ideologically paralyzed—as were their sister parties elsewhere, as Adam Przeworski (1985) and others have shown. When they were in power they had their hands full with everyday politics, yet their short-term economic thinking was decidedly liberal, and the fiscal policies that they pursued in the 1920s were conservative, with balanced budgets and falling government spending. The Social Democrats could not align their economic ideas with their ideological aims. "Our party's contributions to economic policy have thus far not been positive," the party leader Per Albin Hansson admitted at the 1928 party congress. "What we need is a practical program that translates our economic policy demands into concrete proposals."

The chronically high unemployment of the 1920s was a challenge to liberals and Marxists alike. The center-right parties could not explain how to reconcile their belief in the harmonious interplay of market forces with the fact that so many people were willing to work but could not find jobs. The Social Democrats, who claimed to represent the interests of the working class better than any other party, ran the risk of appearing morally irresponsible when they assured their supporters that the development toward socialism was predetermined and that there was not much they could do to hasten it. The center-right parties blamed unemployment on high wages, which made it too expensive for companies to hire; if wages were lowered, everyone could be offered a job. The Social Democrats had no distinct answer to the unemployment problem. When in government, they pursued the same unemployment policy as the center-right parties; in opposition, they criticized those policies, but without suggesting a clear alternative.

By the end the the 1920s, however, some leading Social Democrats began to oppose the hegemony of liberal economic ideas. Ernst Wigforss, an academic linguist and amateur economist, saw no connection between low wages and high employment. According to Wigforss, in recessions, "the amiable spendthrift who gives people jobs by throwing around his money" was "socially useful," whereas the miser who put his money under the mattress instead of investing it stood in the way of economic recovery. In a series of pamphlets, newspaper articles, and parliamentary speeches in the late 1920s, Wigforss anticipated John Maynard Keynes's economic theories about the role of fiscal policy; Wigforss also followed the British economic debate closely. But the inspiration from Marx was even more important. For both Marx and Wigforss, under-consumption was the cause of unemployment. Consequently, the remedy was to spend more money, not to save money.

The beauty of this program was that it was easy to reconcile with the Social Democratic instinctive belief that the living standards of the working class should be raised. Marx should not be abandoned. Quite the opposite: where liberal economics had failed, Marx showed a way out of the unemployment problem. Wigforss argued that Sweden's labor market policies must change. At this time, in accordance with liberal economic ideas, social benefits were kept low, to avoid interfering with market forces. Wigforss instead suggested that social benefits—in particular, compensation for relief workers—should be raised to the same level as the wages in the open market, to increase purchasing power and bring about economic recovery.

Wigforss's reasoning had far-reaching consequences for the economic strategy of the Social Democrats, and—since the 1930s proved to be the beginning of a long period of Social Democratic dominance in Swedish politics—for government policy. The nation-alization of industries was not what socialism was all about, Wigforss argued. The essen-tial idea was that the state (and it was understood that the state should be controlled by the Social Democrats) ought to have a more dominant role in the economy; this was the best way to implement the Social Democratic vision of a good society.

The party followed Wigforss, and the Social Democrats first presented their new labor market program in a bill that was introduced in parliament while the party was still in opposition, in 1930.

In other words, the Social Democrats had a carefully developed economic program *before* Sweden was affected by the Great Depression (cf. Lundberg 1985: 6). When the Social Democrats won the election in 1932 and formed a government with Hansson as Prime Minister and Wigforss as minister of finance, the economy was in worse shape, however: real GDP per capita was approximately 5 percent lower in 1932 than it had been in 1930. The new government was a minority government, and it was only by log-rolling with the Agrarian Party that the new government was able to make its position more secure. Through the so-called "Cow Trade" in the spring of 1933, the Social Democrats agreed to tariffs for agriculture in exchange for Agrarian support for their new economic policies. This was how Sweden became a pioneer of Keynesian economic strategies. The government's policy was neither nationalization nor liberal nonintervention; instead, Sweden opted for "the middle way" between the two (to cite Marquis Child's famous book on Sweden from the late 1930s).

Since the macroeconomic policy changes that we have just described coincided with the Social Democratic rise to power (with the exception of a few months in the summer of 1936, the party ruled Sweden from 1932 to 1976) the question of how to explain the events in the early 1930s has been debated by generations of scholars, in Sweden and abroad. We would like to discuss two aspects of this problem.

First of all, there is the matter of how significant the policy changes in 1933 really were. Many economists have suggested that the new programs were rather small, consid-ering the depth of the recession (see, for example, Jonung 1977: 55–7), and economic historians have long argued that since the government loans were paid back quickly and the funds were not fully utilized, the macroeconomic impact of the "Cow Trade" was limited (Helmersson 1972). There are strong reasons to believe that the economic recovery in the mid-1930s was mainly due to other factors—especially the abolishment of the gold standard in 1931 (Lundberg 1985: 9).

The spending on public works that parliament approved in the spring of 1933 amounted to approximately 2 percent of GDP, although only 98 million kronor, or 1.2 percent of GDP, were actually utilized. In comparison with Sweden's discretionary stimulus programs in postwar recessions, including the one adopted in the Great Recession of 2008–9, fiscal policies in the 1930s were relatively cautious (Lindvall 2012). But it is also important to compare Swedish economic policies with the policies pursued in other democracies in the early 1930s, and such a comparison suggests that Sweden's economic policies were less conservative and more oriented toward objectives such as growth and employment. In that sense, the "Cow Trade" was an important *political* event. In the political and intellectual climate of the early 1930s, even modest expansionary programs represented a significant break with the past.

The second question is what *explained* the policy shift in the early 1930s. In the 1960s, Swedish scholars such as Landgren (1960) and Lewin (1967), as well as foreign observers such as Winch (1966) and, later, Berman (1998), emphasized the early adoption of Keynesian or proto-Keynesian economic ideas by Social Democratic politicians, and especially by Wigforss himself (although Lewin's analysis was mainly concerned with the importance of ideological and party-political conflict). Scholars such as Unga (1976) and Rothstein (1992), by contrast, downplay the role of economic ideas, arguing that the Social Democrats and their trade union allies were motivated less by the expected macroeconomic effects of the new policies than by their implications for the balance of power in the labor market. But it may be possible to reconcile these views: although it is likely that underlying conflicts over labor market regulation and the role of the state in the economy were the main causes of the economic policy disagreements between the Social Democrats and the center-right parties in the early 1930s, new economic ideas helped the Social Democrats in their efforts to get out of the ideological impasse they found themselves in in the 1920s.

THE POSTWAR BOOM AND
THE REHN–MEIDNER MODEL

We turn next to the development of Sweden's postwar economic model, and especially to the so-called Rehn–Meidner model (named after the two trade union economists who developed it around 1950, Gösta Rehn and Rudolf Meidner).

By the end of World War II, Sweden's center-right parties had come to accept many of the new economic policies that the Social Democrats had introduced in the

1930s. Indeed, the new leader of the Liberal Party, Bertil Ohlin, was an internationally renowned Keynesian economist who had supported the Cow Trade. It was generally agreed, after the war, that the state was both responsible for and capable of bringing about full employment.

Because of this consensus on macroeconomic policy, one might have expected a *rapprochement* between the political parties. Instead, the late 1940s witnessed the hardest ideological fight in modern Swedish history. The reason was that the Social Democrats wished to go further than they had before the war: not content with merely returning to full employment, the Social Democrats now sought to *prevent* unemployment crises from recurring by increasing the role of the state in the economy even more. In the Swedish Labor Movement's "Postwar Program," which was prepared by a committee headed by Wigforss, a detailed analysis of Swedish economy was made: the state should have overall responsibility for the efficient allocation of resources and the preservation of full employment. If the private sector achieved these goals on its own, it could be left alone, but if not, the state should intervene using various methods, including nationalization.

The center-right parties read the Postwar Program as a call for nationalization and mobilized an ideological offensive. Free-market doctrines became popular once more, as the liberal concept of freedom from the state clashed with the socialist concept of freedom from the insecurities of the market. Friedrich Hayek's book *The Road to Serfdom* played a major role in this discussion, especially as interpreted by Herbert Tingsten, a professor of political science and the editor-in-chief of Sweden's leading newspaper, *Dagens Nyheter*. The consequence of the postwar economic program, Tingsten argued, would be the suppression of democratic liberty. For state investments to become successful, criticism would not be tolerated; the public debate would be censored, and in the long run, democracy would be undermined. State intervention in the economy would indeed lead to "serfdom."

A full-scale, business-funded propaganda war against the Social Democrats ensued, and the public debate in 1944–8 can be characterized as one long election campaign. To the surprise of many—and to the bitter disappointment of the center-right parties—the Social Democrats managed to hold on to power in the election of 1948. But the postwar program was nevertheless not implemented. Swedish politics has always oscillated between consensus and conflict. Cooperation between different parliamentary groups was already regarded as natural and desirable in the late nineteenth century. But in some periods, tensions have been strong—especially during the fight over democratization in the 1910s, the fight over postwar economic policy in the 1940s, and—as we will see—the fight over "wage earner funds" in the 1970s and 1980s. By 1948 there was a general feeling that it was time to end the confrontation. The Social Democrats seemed impossible to beat, and it was necessary to reach some *modus vivendi*.

To this end, the Social Democrats simply abandoned their postwar program. Private business had managed quite well, it was argued, so perhaps there was no need for state intervention after all. The center-right parties suspended their propaganda campaign and began to work with the government on a number of policy committees. Via the so-called "Thursday Club," leading representatives of the Social Democrats met regularly with private business (later, these meetings took place at Harpsund, a manor donated to the Prime Minister by a leading industrialist, and the term "Harpsund Democracy" was coined). The business community's well-funded propaganda apparatus was transformed into a think tank for social science research. Meanwhile, relations between employer organizations and unions were pacified: strikes almost vanished, wages increased steadily by a few percent every year, and centralized wage negotiations for the whole labor market began in the early 1950s. This was the period when the consensual labor market model that Sweden has long been known for was consolidated.

The center-right parties adopted a strategy of wait and see. The Social Democrats were still in government (in the early 1950s, a coalition government between the Social Democrats and the Agrarians was formed). But for each election, it seemed, the Social Democrats lost a few percent of the electorate to the center-right parties. Socialism, the center-right believed, was for the poor; the more and more prosperous Swedish citizens would develop liberal preferences. Sooner or later the center-right parties would start to win elections.

But Tage Erlander, Per Albin Hansson's successor as Prime Minister and leader of the Social Democrats, had other ideas. He believed that more state intervention was required in an affluent society, not less. If people bought cars, it was necessary to build roads. If people got more income security, they would demand better schools for their children. If they were accustomed to full employment, they would start to expect higher pensions and a high standard of living in their old age.

In the 1930s the main objective of the government's economic policy was to reduce unemployment. In the prosperous 1950s and 1960s, by contrast, more or less full employment could be taken for granted. The challenge that the government faced was therefore how to manage a high-growth economy, where the main threat was inflation, not unemployment—and particularly the possibility that conflicts between Sweden's powerful trade unions and employer organizations would result in rising prices and industrial strife.

Fiscal policies were therefore kept fairly tight, to contain inflationary pressures. Meanwhile, a new "active" labor market policy was developed to support workers who wished to move from less productive regions and firms to more productive ones, and a "solidaristic" wage policy ensured that wage increases were high across the labor market—if certain industries could not pay high wages, it was a sign that they were not good enough and should be shut down, so that labor and capital could be used in a more productive way. The economic goal of social democracy was, in other words, to realize "what the free market according to its pretentions should but could not accomplish by itself" (LO 1961). As Rudolf Meidner, one of the inventors of this three-pronged strategy, observed many years later, the Rehn–Meidner model was a highly market-oriented economic model. It was far removed from the ideas of nationalization and socialism. (On the ideas behind the Rehn–Meidner model, see, for example, Lindbeck 1974: ch. 3; for a famous critique, see Lundberg 1957 [1953].)

But these policies did plant the seeds of the last major ideological confrontation between liberal and socialist economic ideas in Sweden so far: the struggle over "wage earner funds" in the 1970s and 1980s. One of the main ideas of the Rehn–Meidner model, as we have seen, was that everybody should have wages on the same high level, in prosperous as well as in less successful industries. This "solidaristic wage policy" meant that workers in the least profitable industries might force firms to go bankrupt, whereas workers in the most successful industries refrained from fighting for higher wage increases. What happened, then, with the profits of the most productive firms? Critics maintained that the money went into the pockets of the capitalists. In terms of wages, Sweden had grown into a more equal society than most; but as far as wealth was concerned, the gap between rich and poor was still vast.

According to Meidner and like-minded economists on the left, there was only one way to handle this problem: to attack the private ownership of business, the fundamental principle of capitalism. By means of "wage earner funds," Meidner proposed, a share of company profits would be put into funds managed by the trade unions. "This is how we will deprive the capitalists of their power," Meidner explained. The proposal caused an outcry from the center-right parties, dominated the election campaign in 1976, led to an ideological mobilization that was comparable to the one in the 1940s, and contributed, in 1976, to the first Social Democratic election defeat since the 1920s.

When it comes to explaining the development of Sweden's postwar economic strategy, most scholars have emphasized how the Rehn–Meidner model reconciled the interests of Sweden's trade unions and employer organizations, and how it simultaneously depended on and helped to support the highly centralized wage-bargaining model that emerged in this period (see Pontusson 1992 and Swenson 2002 for contributions by political scientists). A comparison of Sweden and other countries in this period—none of which introduced active labor market policies as early on as Sweden—also suggests that political institutions played an important role. The premise of the Rehn–Meidner model was that it was possible for politicians, bureaucrats, trade unions, and employer organizations to *coordinate* wage bargaining, macroeconomic policy, and new active labor market policy programs. This ambitious idea required a highly integrated, corporatist political system, and would probably not have occurred to politicians and trade unionists in many other countries in this particular period.

FROM THE OIL CRISIS TO THE FINANCIAL CRISIS

A series of economic and political changes in the late 1960s and early 1970s presented Swedish governments with new and difficult economic policy challenges. The rate of productivity increases fell. The Bretton Woods system of international economic cooperation broke down in 1971–3, and the sharp increase in oil prices in 1973 led to a deterioration in terms of trade for rich Western states, including Sweden. Meanwhile, Swedish party politics became more competitive. The Social Democrats, in power since the 1930s, now faced a united center-right opposition that questioned the government's economic record. In the early 1970s a younger generation of Social Democratic ministers—including the future finance minister Kjell-Olof Feldt—also questioned the cautious economic policies of Gunnar Sträng, who had been finance minister since the 1950s, calling for more expansionary measures in order to reduce unemployment, which, at 3 percent of the labor force, was seen as very high (today, of course, 3 percent would be regarded as a very low unemployment rate).

After the oil price increases in 1973, the Social Democratic government at first hesitated about how to respond. In the spring of 1974, however, the government and the center-right parties (in what was then a hung parliament) agreed on a program of expansionary fiscal policies. These "bridging policies"—designed to support domestic demand and "bridge" the international downturn—were pursued until the late 1970s, first by the Social Democrats and later by the center-right parties (who won power in 1976).

There was nothing unique about Sweden's pursuit of expansionary fiscal policies in the immediate aftermath of the first oil crisis; other small West European democracies did the same. But Sweden was unusually persistent. Whereas many other governments had already changed course by 1975–6, opting for lower inflation and lower current account deficits, Swedish governments did not phase out their expansionary policies until 1980, in the aftermath of the second oil crisis (Lindvall 2010: ch. 2).

Swedish governments were well aware, in the mid- to late 1970s, that most other rich countries gave priority to low inflation and external balance, but they were prepared to accept temporary inflation and current account deficits in order to maintain full employment. This applied to the center-right parties, who won power in 1976, as well as to the Social Democrats.

In the 1950s and 1960s, as we have seen, governments sought to use microeconomic means, especially active labor market policy, to maintain full employment, but as soon as mass unemployment became a threat once more in the 1970s, economists and politicians, on the left as well as on the right, remembered the old lesson from the 1930s: in a deep economic downturn, the government could and should increase economic activity by means of expansionary economic policies. It is interesting to note that this all happened at a time when the Social Democrats and the Center Party (the old Agrarian Party)—the same constellation that voted for the fiscal programs of the 1930s—dominated Swedish politics, effectively sharing power (after the election of 1973, the three center-right parties controlled exactly half of the Riksdag's then 350 seats).

In the early 1980s, however, Swedish governments (consisting first of the center-right parties, then of the Social Democrats, who returned to power in 1982) stopped using fiscal policy as a macroeconomic instrument. Following the international trend at this time, neither side believed that fiscal policy could be used to steer the economy. But unwilling to give up on full employment, governments resorted to exchange rate adjustments. The center-right government that was formed in 1976 devalued twice in 1977, and in September 1981 and October 1982 there were two larger devaluations—first by 10 percent and then by 16 percent (the second devaluation was implemented by the Social Democrats). The 1981 and 1982 devaluations were more "offensive," in the sense that they were combined with new, austere fiscal policies (on the macroeconomic policy shift in the 1970s and 1980s, see, for instance, Lindbeck 1997: 1302–3).

The incoming Social Democratic government later referred to their economic policies in the 1980s as a "Third Way"—between the austerity and monetarism of Thatcher and the expansionary fiscal programs associated with the "Mitterrand Experiment." The idea was to make a final, big devaluation that would be followed by austere fiscal policies that were expected to transfer resources from sheltered economic sectors—including the public sector—to the export-oriented sector.

An explanation of the decisions that Swedish governments took in the 1970s and 1980s must account for three facts. First of all, Swedish governments pursued expansionary fiscal policies for a long time after the first oil crisis. Second, both the center-right and the Social Democrats switched to devaluations around 1980, but still did not give up on full employment. Third, Sweden's center-right parties were just as eager as the Social Democrats, if not more, to preserve full employment (and they used a combination of fiscal policy measures and direct support to ailing industries to achieve this goal). A number of explanations have been suggested. One is that Sweden's low public debt and flexible wage-bargaining institutions allowed Sweden to do things that other countries could not do. Another is that governments were guided by Keynesian economic ideas. A third is political: pursuing a policy that risked high unemployment would have had knock-on effects in other policy domains, necessitating reform of Sweden's welfare model—something that most political parties were unwilling to consider at the time.

Only in the late 1980s and early 1990s, some ten to fifteen years later than in comparable countries, low inflation became the main objective of Swedish economic policy. To make their commitment to price stability credible, Swedish governments—the Social Democrats that were in power until 1991 and the center-right coalition that took over in 1991–4—declared that they would stick to the fixed exchange rate. Rising unemployment was not to be met with an expansion of the domestic economy, as in the 1970s, or with devaluations, as in the 1980s.

Instead, a commitment to a fixed exchange rate (the Swedish krona was pegged to a currency basket until 1991, then the *ecu*) was supposed to function as a nominal anchor, bringing down inflation expectations. A declaration by the Social Democratic government on October 26, 1990, when the government announced that the fight against inflation "must take priority over all other ambitions and demands" (the same phrase appeared, famously, in the 1991 budget bill), is often seen as the decisive turning-point— the moment when Sweden joined the European mainstream in the domain of economic policy (Lindbeck 1997: 1303). In one sense, the strategy did not work, for under the new center-right government that was formed in 1991, the central bank was forced to adopt a floating exchange rate (in November 1992). But the switch to a low-inflation-oriented regime was permanent, as we explain in the next section.

Why did Swedish governments make these crucial decisions, and why did they only make them in the early 1990s, much later than governments in most other European countries? Again, several explanations have been suggested. One is that Swedish governments wished to adopt "normal" European economic policies out of a desire to join the European Union. But there is also strong evidence that it was the other way around—that a desire to change economic policies led to a change of policies on Europe. A second explanation is concerned with economic ideas. One difficulty with this explanation, however, is that the policies that Swedish governments had pursued in the 1980s were not obviously "Keynesian" in origin. A third explanation is that the economic policy changes that occurred in the early 1990s were associated with deeper political changes at this time. As many other contributions to this *Handbook* show, the late 1980s and early 1990s was a period characterized by a rapid and wide-ranging reform across the Swedish welfare model. For decades, one of the guiding ideas of Swedish politics had been that there was a special "Swedish model" that must be maintained at all costs, even if this meant pursuing economic policies that went much further in the defense of full employment than the policies of governments in other rich democracies. When this idea was no longer controlling—when the "Swedish model" was crumbling or changing—economic policies changed too.

THE CURRENT SWEDISH ECONOMIC POLICY MODEL AND THE GREAT RECESSION

The economic crisis in Sweden in the early 1990s was exceptionally deep. Open unemployment increased from less than 2 to 8–10 percent of the labor force, and GDP growth was negative for three consecutive years (1991–3). This was an unprecedented macroeconomic disaster. Between 1960 and the Great Recession of 2008–9, there are only two other examples of negative growth three years in a row in the twenty OECD countries that have been democracies since World War II: in Finland (also in the early 1990s) and in New Zealand (in the late 1970s).

It is impossible to understand the development of Swedish economic policy since the early 1990s, including Sweden's reluctance to join the EMU, without considering the effects of the crisis of the 1990s. The crisis was a fundamental break with Sweden's postwar economic model in at least two ways. First of all, it was the defining event for a generation of economic policy-makers, for whom avoiding a repetition of the macroeconomic disaster and perceived policy failures of the 1980s and 1990s became a paramount goal (see, for example, Jonung 1999). In the course of the 1990s, Swedish economic policy changed radically, as we will explain, and as Lars Calmfors discusses in more detail in a separate chapter. Second, the transition from the full-employment economy of the first half-century after the war to an economy with mass unemployment, widespread economic insecurity, and increasing inequality had a number of indirect political effects that are explored in other chapters of this *Handbook*.

The first element of the new macroeconomic regime that was established in the 1990s was a new monetary policy strategy. Ever since the floating exchange rate was introduced in November 1992, monetary policy has been Sweden's most important macroeconomic policy instrument, and in January 1993, just a few months after the fixed exchange rate was given up, the central bank introduced an inflation target of 2±1 percent (defined as a yearly increase in the Consumer Price Index) to replace the earlier exchange rate target. This target has guided monetary policy ever since, even if there have been subtle but important changes in the methods that the Riksbank uses to measure and evaluate inflation expectations.

The second element of Sweden's new macroeconomic regime was central bank independence. Sweden's Riksbank has traditionally been relatively dependent on the executive, although formally it reports to Parliament, not the government. In practice, it became much more independent from the government in the course of the 1980s and 1990s. However, in legal terms the central bank only gained full independence in 1999. An amendment to the constitution provides that no external authority is allowed to instruct the central bank in matters of monetary policy. This is an integral part of the new regime, but also a result of Europeanization: after Sweden became a member of the EU, the Social Democrats, who had previously opposed constitutional reform, supported an increase in central bank independence since it was required by the Maastricht Treaty.

The third element of the new macroeconomic regime was a set of budgeting procedures that were gradually introduced between 1992 (when this issue was first raised inside the Ministry of Finance) and 1997 (when the new Budget Act came into force). This important piece of legislation was introduced to improve the government's control of national-level budgeting, and to avoid excessive spending.

Over time, this institutional framework won a great deal of support among Sweden's political parties and interest organizations, and at least prior to the Great Recession, it was widely regarded as successful. This has also been a period when Sweden has been a part of the mainstream in European economic policy, implementing policies that were based on the idea that the role of macroeconomic management was largely to use monetary policy to stabilize inflation expectations, as the only viable method of keeping the output gap as small as possible. That Sweden, like Britain and Sweden's Scandinavian neighbor Denmark, has chosen not to participate in the Third Stage of Europe's Economic and Monetary Union does not alter this basic fact.

What was interesting about the response to the Great Recession of 2008–9, the last period that we will consider here, is that for a brief time it represented a return to active, discretionary macroeconomic policies, although, as a consequence of the fiscal framework that was introduced in the 1990s, the expansionary programs that were introduced during the crisis were modest, compared to earlier crises. Again, Sweden was not alone in this. In comparison with the conservative fiscal policies that most European states had pursued in the 1980s, 1990s, and 2000s (and the orthodox ideas that were predominant in this period), the coordinated stimulus program that the EU member states agreed on in the 2008–9 downturn was a significant event, for European macroeconomic thinking before the crisis was based on the premise that fiscal policy should be oriented toward medium- and long-term objectives, not short-term macroeconomic management.

Conclusions

For most of the period that we consider here, foreign observers have regarded Sweden as a country where governments place full employment, income equality, and social security higher on their lists of priorities than governments elsewhere. In the mid-1960s, for example, Andrew Shonfield observed in his famous book *Modern Capitalism* (1965) that the Swedish government "has taken the policy of full employment more seriously than other Western countries," and he suggested that Sweden was "more firmly committed than other nations to the triple objective of full employment, rapid growth, and a very high level of social welfare." This was true for a long time. It is less true today.

Swedish governments put more emphasis on the need to maintain full employment than other governments did throughout the 60-year period from the Great Depression to the early 1990s. One may question the scale and scope of the expansionary fiscal policies of the 1930s, but the fact remains that Swedish governments did more than the governments of other countries to reduce unemployment in the 1930s. After the war, the Social Democratic Postwar Program emphasized the goal of full employment, and the Rehn–Meidner model of the 1950s introduced new policy instruments—active labor market policy—in order to secure this goal, making Sweden a world leader in active labor market policy until the 1990s. In the crisis-ridden 1970s and 1980s, finally, Sweden went much further than most comparable countries in the pursuit of full employment, using both fiscal and exchange rate policy to achieve this goal.

This period—from the early 1930s to the early 1990s—coincides with the heyday of Swedish social democracy, and there is no doubt that the power of the Social Democratic Party is an important part of the explanation for the priorities that we have just described. When the center-right parties were in power in 1976–82, however, they went *even further* than the Social Democrats in the pursuit of full employment, having criticized the Social Democrats for their passive economic policies already in the first half of the 1970s, and in the 1930s and 1940s, as we have seen, it did not take long for the center-right parties to accept the new economic policies that the Social Democrats introduced in 1930–3: the center-right parties thus adjusted to the policies that the dominant Social Democrats introduced, with the exception of the radical socialist policies that the Social Democrats pursued in the 1940s and the 1970s. In the last two decades, however, Sweden no longer stands out as a country that prioritizes full employment over other goals. Although Sweden has chosen to hold on to its own currency rather than seeking full membership in Europe's Economic and Monetary Union, Sweden's economic policies are hard to distinguish from those of its partners in the European Union.

REFERENCES

Berman, S. (1998). *The Social Democratic Moment*. Cambridge, MA: Harvard University Press.

Blyth, M. (2002). *Great Transformations*. Cambridge: Cambridge University Press.

De Geer, G. (1928). *Sveriges andra stormaktstid*. Stockholm: Bonniers.

Gourevitch, P. A. (1986). *Politics in Hard Times*. Ithaca: Cornell University Press.

Hayek, F. (1944). *The Road to Serfdom*. Chicago: University of Chicago Press.

Helmersson, E. (1972). "Svensk krispolitik under 1930-talet," unpublished manuscript, Department of Economic History, Uppsala University.

Iversen, T. (1999). *Contested Economic Institutions*. Cambridge: Cambridge University Press.

Jonung, L. (1977). "Knut Wicksells prisstabiliseringsnorm och penningpolitiken på 1930-talet," in J. Herin and L. Werin (eds), *Ekonomisk debatt och ekonomisk politik*. Stockholm: Norstedts, 35–83.

Jonung, L. (1999). *Med backspegeln som kompass*. Stockholm: Fakta Info Direkt.

Landgren, K.-G. (1960). *Den "nya" ekonomien i Sverige*. Stockholm: Almqvist & Wiksell.

Lewin, L. (1967). *Planhushållningsdebatten*. Stockholm: Almqvist & Wiksell.

Lindbeck, A. (1974). *Swedish Economic Policy*. Berkeley: University of California Press.

Lindbeck, A. (1997). "The Swedish Experiment," *Journal of Economic Literature* 35/3: 1273–1319.

Lindvall, J. (2010). *Mass Unemployment and the State*. Oxford: Oxford University Press.

Lindvall, J. (2012). "Politics and Policies in Two Economic Crises: The Nordic Countries," in N. Bermeo and J. Pontusson (eds), *Coping with Crisis*. New York: Russell Sage Foundation, 233–60.

LO (1961). *Samordnad näringspolitik*. Stockholm: Landsorganisationen.

Lundberg, E. (1957 [1953]). *Business Cycles and Economic Policy*. London: Allen & Unwin.

Lundberg, E. (1985). "The Rise and Fall of the Swedish Model," *Journal of Economic Literature* 23/1: 1–36.

Notermans, T. (2000). *Money, Markets, and the State*. Cambridge: Cambridge University Press.

Pontusson, J. (1992). *The Limits of Social Democracy*. Ithaca: Cornell University Press.

Przeworski, A. (1985). *Capitalism and Social Democracy*. Cambridge: Cambridge University Press.

Rothstein, B. (1992). *Den korporativa staten*. Stockholm: Norstedts.

Scharpf, F. (1991). *Crisis and Choice in European Social Democracy*. Ithaca: Cornell University Press.

Shonfield, A. (1965). *Modern Capitalism*. Oxford: Oxford University Press.

Swenson, P. (2002). *Capitalists Against Markets*. Oxford: Oxford University Press.

Unga, N. (1976). *Socialdemokratin och arbetslöshetsfrågan 1912–34*. Lund: Arkiv.

Weir, M, and Skocpol, T. (1985). "State Structures and the Possibilities for 'Keynesian' Responses to the Great Depression in Sweden, Britain, and the United States," in T. Skocpol, P. B. Evans, and D. Rueschemeyer (eds), *Bringing the State Back In*. Cambridge: Cambridge University Press, 107–63.

Winch, D. (1966). "The Keynesian Revolution in Sweden," *Journal of Political Economy* 74/2: 168–76.

....

CHAPTER 44

THE SWEDISH MACROECONOMIC POLICY FRAMEWORK

....

LARS CALMFORS

SWEDEN'S macroeconomic policy framework has recently come to be seen as a role model for other countries.[1] The decade before the international economic crisis erupted in 2007/8 was characterized by low and stable inflation (Figure 44.1), as well as small fluctuations in economic activity. There were fiscal surpluses (Figure 44.2), and government debt (Figure 44.3) was reduced substantially to levels far below the Maastricht benchmark of 60 percent of GDP. Sweden also weathered the international crisis well. Public finances remained in good shape. The rise in unemployment (Figure 44.4) was limited.

The recent Swedish performance stands in stark contrast to earlier developments. In the 1970s and 1980s, Sweden was trapped in a devaluation cycle, which culminated in a deep financial crisis when a real estate price bubble burst in the early 1990s. The crisis involved large fiscal deficits (Figure 44.2) and huge rises in unemployment (Figure 44.4).

In the aftermath of the 1990s crisis, a new macroeconomic policy framework was established. In the monetary policy area it involved the adoption of *inflation targeting* and the granting of more *independence* to the central bank. In the fiscal policy area it meant a *stricter framework*, imposing more discipline, and *pension reform*.

The first section discusses the monetary policy framework and the second section the fiscal policy framework. Both sections consist of three parts: (a) a review of the current framework; (b) an analysis of how the framework was established; and (c) a discussion of future challenges. The third section draws some general conclusions on how crisis experiences can trigger reforms and the roles played by academic research and international influences.

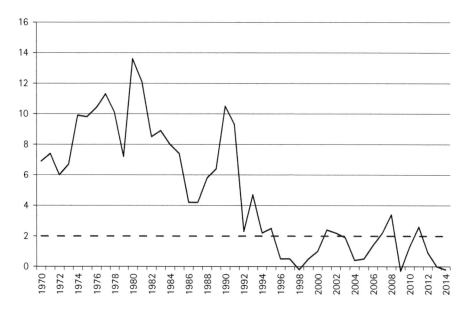

FIGURE 44.1 CPI inflation, percent

Note: The broken line indicates the 2 percent inflation target.

Source: SCB, Sweden

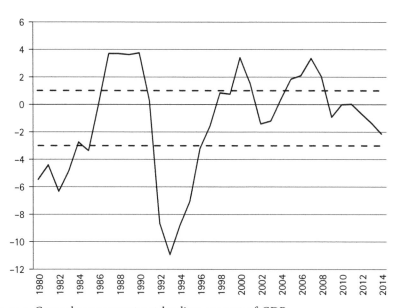

FIGURE 44.2 General government net lending, percent of GDP

Note: General government net lending is the difference between the sector's revenues and expenditure as defined in the national accounts. The broken lines indicate the surplus target of 1 percent of GDP and the EU deficit ceiling of 3 percent of GDP respectively.

Source: IMF World Economic Outlook

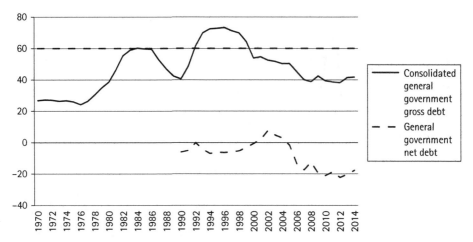

FIGURE 44.3 Government debt, percent of GDP

Note: Consolidated general government gross debt is general government total debt after all internal claims and liabilities in the sector have been netted out. General government net debt is the sector's gross financial debt minus its financial assets (including claims on the private sector). The horizontal broken line indicates the EU debt ceiling of 60 percent of GDP.

Source: IMF World Economic Outlook

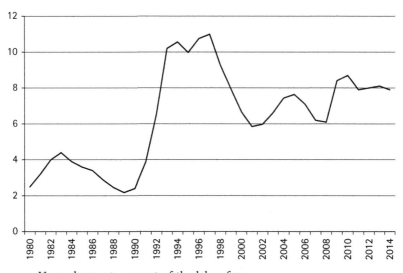

FIGURE 44.4 Unemployment, percent of the labor force

Source: SCB, Sweden

THE MONETARY POLICY FRAMEWORK

The Current Framework

According to the Constitution, the central bank (the *Riksbank*) is in charge of monetary policy. The bank's activities are regulated in the Riksbank Act. It stipulates that the Riksbank's objective is "to maintain price stability," but does not define this concept explicitly. The bank itself has adopted an *inflation target* of an annual 2 percent increase in the CPI. The Act does not specify any output or employment objectives. However, the Government Bill proposing the currently existing monetary policy framework pointed out that the Riksbank, as a member of the European Central Bank System (ECBS), is, without prejudice to the price stability objective, obliged to support the EU's general economic policies which seek among other things to achieve "balanced economic growth" and "full employment" (*Proposition 1997/98:40*). The minutes from the meetings of the bank's Executive Board (see next part) also show that the bank sees it as an objective to stabilize output and employment around their equilibrium (sustainable) levels. This policy is often referred to as *flexible inflation targeting*. According to established theory, such a policy does not involve any conflict in the long term between the price stability and output (employment) targets, as the equilibrium output and employment levels are defined as the ones consistent with stable inflation.

The Riksbank has a high degree of independence from the political system. First, the bank has *institutional* independence. The government is prohibited from giving instructions to the bank, and the bank is not allowed to take instructions from the government.[2] Second, the Riksbank's *Executive Board*, which takes all policy decisions, has *personal* independence from the political system, i.e. the government and Parliament. The six members are appointed by the bank's *General Council*, which is elected by Parliament. The Council's members are affiliated to political parties, but only some are MPs (currently both the Chair and the Vice Chair are not) and some are politicians who are no longer active. The idea is to have the appointment procedure to the Executive Board at arm's length from day-to-day politics. Board members are appointed for five or six years. They cannot be MPs, ministers, or employees in the government offices or at the national level of the political parties. They should be persons with a broad experience of society and economics. The General Council can retire a member of the Executive Board if the member "no longer fulfills the conditions required for the performance of his duties or if he has been guilty of serious misconduct," but the decision can be appealed.[3] Third, the Riksbank has considerable *economic autonomy*. Parliament decides—on a proposal from the bank's General Council—how much of the annual profit should be paid to the government budget.

It is a challenge how to hold an independent central bank accountable for its policy without interfering with its independence. The Riksbank Act does not require the Executive Board to publish minutes from its meetings, but the Board itself has chosen to do so. The law, however, requires the bank to deliver an account of its policy to Parliament twice a year. There are also regularly open hearings with the Governor and other members of the Executive Board in Parliament's Committee on Finance. It publishes an annual evaluation of the bank's performance. The committee also commissions evaluations of the bank's performance by leading foreign monetary policy experts.

The Establishment of the Monetary Framework

The current monetary policy framework is very different from the one in the 1970s and 1980s. Sweden then tried to maintain a fixed exchange rate, first vis-à-vis the D-mark and later vis-à-vis a trade-weighted basket of currencies. The exchange rate peg was supposed to anchor domestic inflation to that abroad. This did not happen, however, as the fixed exchange rate policy had low credibility. High inflation expectations repeatedly triggered high wage increases, eroding Sweden's international competitiveness and causing unemployment in mainly the tradables (manufacturing) sector. The wage increases were from time to time (1976, 1977, 1981, and 1982) accommodated through currency devaluations, which fed inflation expectations further, thus triggering new rounds of high wage increases and keeping the inflation–devaluation cycle alive.[4]

An important role in the economic policy debate in the 1980s was played by the Economic Policy Group at the Center for Business and Policy Studies (*SNS Konjunkturråd*), a group of independent academic economists. The Group argued that the government should declare the fixed exchange rate the overriding objective of macroeconomic policy with full employment being only a subordinate goal.[5] The intention was to make it clear to the parties in the labor market that high wage increases would cause unemployment rises and profit falls that would not be accommodated through new devaluations. An explicit commitment to such an *exchange rate norm* would impose a high reputation cost on the government for abandoning it. This would make the commitment credible and induce the labor market organizations to negotiate wage increases compatible with the fixed exchange rate. Hence the threat of high unemployment would never have to be realized.

In the 1980s, the Riksbank was still very dependent on the government. Policy decisions were taken by the bank's General Council comprised of politicians. Monetary policy objectives were not explicitly defined. The strong incentives for politicians to maintain low unemployment under all circumstances therefore undermined the credibility of the fixed exchange rate. For this reason, the SNS Economic Policy Group advocated more independence for the Riksbank. The Group was strongly influenced by the then recent research on the *time inconsistency problem* of monetary policy, which emphasized how politicians interested in both low unemployment and low inflation had *ex post* incentives to renege on *ex ante* announcements of low inflation policy in order to improve employment outcomes. Such policies would, however, in the long term only result in high inflation without any long-run impact on unemployment, as the public would learn about the behavior of policy-makers and thus anticipate it.[6]

The SNS Group's recommendations first met with strong political resistance. However, during the second half of the 1980s it became increasingly evident that fundamental changes were needed to bring down inflation. The economy was strongly overheated, the boom being fueled by fast credit growth in the wake of credit market deregulations. In this situation, the ideas of the SNS Group gained increased acceptance. After a failed government attempt in 1990 to legislate against high wage and price increases, the Social Democratic government in 1991 announced that the main economic policy objective "over the coming years must be to permanently reduce inflation" and that "this task is superior to other ambitions and requirements."[7] The exchange rate peg was then also shifted from a trade-weighted currency basket to the ecu (a weighted average of EU currencies). The SNS Group had an even greater influence on the thinking of the Liberal–Conservative government which came to power in the autumn of 1991. In the spring of 1992 it declared that "the fixed exchange rate is a crucial and definitive norm for economic policy."[8]

The attempt to establish an exchange rate norm was not backed by any major institutional changes. When the norm was introduced, the inflation that it was designed to prevent had already occurred and eroded Sweden's competitiveness. The boom came to an abrupt end in 1990/1 when the property price bubble burst—in much the same way as occurred in, for example, the US, the UK, Ireland, and Spain during the recent economic crisis which started in 2007/8—and Sweden entered a deep recession. This triggered expectations of a new devaluation, so the Riksbank had to defend the krona through big interest rate hikes which deepened the downturn. This created an impossible situation and in November 1992 the fixed exchange rate was abandoned. This was amidst a period of general European exchange rate turbulence. Pegging the exchange rate again did not seem a credible option in this situation.

At the same time, there was widespread agreement that an anchor was needed to keep inflation under control. There was a strong case for trying to capitalize on the investment in reputation for inflation fighting that had been made during the defence of the fixed exchange rate. Therefore, in January 1993 the Riksbank decided to adopt an annual *inflation target* of 2 percent. The decision was inspired by the monetary policy regimes that had earlier been introduced in Canada and New Zealand.

The Riksbank's formal status was analyzed by a Government Commission, initially appointed by the Social Democratic government in 1990, but which received new terms of reference and a new composition in 1991 by the Liberal–Conservative government that had just taken office. The Commission proposed more independence for the bank in its final report in early 1993 (Riksbanksutredningen 1993). The importance of more autonomy for the Riksbank was also underlined by the *Lindbeck Commission*, another Government Commission, appointed by the Liberal–Conservative government, consisting of academics and given the remit to propose both policies and institutional reforms to take Sweden out of the economic crisis (Lindbeck Commission 1994).[9]

The proposals on a more independent Riksbank were not adopted when they were made. The idea was opposed by the Social Democrats, who came to power again in 1994. The main reasons were a worry that monetary policy would be decided by experts not sharing the political objectives of the government and a fear of insufficient coordination with fiscal policy (Bergkvist and Gradin 1993).

However, in 1997 the Social Democratic government changed its position and initiated a five-party agreement on more independence for the Riksbank, which in some respects went even further than the proposals by the earlier Government Commission. There were two main reasons for why this happened. The first has to do with Sweden's entry into the EU in 1995 (which interestingly cannot just be seen as an exogenous political event changing preconditions for both economic institutions and policies, since the then Social Democratic government's decision to apply for EU membership in 1990 was partly motivated by expectations that this would contribute to macroeconomic stability; Carlsson 2003). As a member of the EU, Sweden was obliged to strengthen the independence of its central bank. The second reason is related to the Swedish decision in 1997 to stay outside the EU's monetary union. This course of action was recommended in 1996 by the *Calmfors Commission*, another Government Commission, consisting of academics, which had been given the remit to analyze the pros and cons of Swedish membership in the monetary union.[10] The Commission regarded central bank reform, strengthening the Riksbank's independence, as "a necessary prerequisite for stable macroeconomic developments if Sweden does not participate in the monetary union."[11]

To sum up, the current monetary policy framework in Sweden is the outcome of a long process. Its establishment was a response to an earlier malfunctioning system, which motivated a number of academic proposals on reforms, to a large extent inspired by international resarch developments in the monetary policy area. The ideas gained increased acceptance in Sweden around 1990 when the failure of the earlier monetary regime became even more apparent than before. The final transition to the current regime was triggered by two developments: Swedish EU membership, which imposed requirements to do central bank reform, and the Swedish decision to stay outside the monetary union, which made it clear that credibility for low-inflation policy had to be built at home.

Challenges for the Monetary Policy Framework

The current monetary policy framework has been successful in achieving low inflation—in fact too successful, as average CPI inflation 1997–2014 was only 1.0 percent, i.e. 0.8 percentage points below the 2 percent target (see Figure 44.1). This has led to a debate on the Riksbank's policy. It has been claimed that undershooting the inflation target has caused unnecessary unemployment (Svensson 2015). Critics have also argued that the bank has acted asymmetrically in the case of deviations from the inflation target, reacting more to upward than to downward deviations (e.g. Assarsson 2011).

An issue raised by these experiences is whether a *price level target* over a defined period would be superior to the current annual *inflation target*, since the former target would require periods of inflation below the target to be compensated by periods of inflation above it. Another issue is whether the objective of stabilizing unemployment around its equilibrium level should be stated explicitly in the Riksbank Act. It has also been claimed that a somewhat higher inflation target might be desirable, as this would likely imply higher inflation, and hence a lower real interest rate that would stimulate the economy in a deep recession when the repo rate approaches zero.[12] However, both the politicians and the Riksbank have been reluctant to contemplate such changes because of a worry that they could undermine the credibility of low-inflation policies.

In 2009–13, during the economic crisis, there was considerable disagreement within the Riksbank's Excecutive Board. A minority consistently argued for lower interest rates than the ones decided by the majority. The conflict reflected divergent views on how *financial stability* should be promoted. To contain household debt and house prices, the majority set the repo rate higher than the level that would be desirable for reaching the inflation target and stabilizing unemployment around its equilibrium level. The minority in the Board questioned the idea that financial stability was in danger and that the repo rate was an effective instrument to achieve it.[13] The Riksbank Act stipulates that the bank is "to promote an effective and secure payments system." This was interpreted by the Executive Board's majority as a go-ahead for using interest rate policy to promote financial stability. It is a contentious issue whether this interpretation was consistent with the Riksbank Act.[14] It is a problem that the use of interest rate policy to achieve financial stability is problematic for the accountability of the Riksbank, as almost any (downward) deviation from the inflation target could be motivated by concerns about future financial crises.

The conflict in the Riksbank's Executive Board reflected the increased awareness of the risks of financial instability in the wake of the international financial crisis that erupted in 2007/8 and the lack of knowledge of how to best avoid such crises. However, in 2013 it was decided that the Financial Supervisory Authority (FSA) should be given control over a number of new financial stability tools (Finansdepartementet 2013). The tools include loan-to-value regulations and risk weights for different types of bank loans as well as liquidity and capital requirements for banks. The establishment of these tools under the FSA's control seems to have mitigated the conflicts in monetary policy between traditional stabilization objectives and financial stability objectives. From 2013 the Riksbank began to put more emphasis on the inflation target and initiated a series of interest rate cuts which resulted in negative repo rates in 2015. However, coordination problems between monetary and financial stability policies could still arise. The idea is that they should be resolved in the newly established Financial Stability Council, which is composed of the Minister for Financial Markets and the heads of the FSA, the Riksbank, and the National Debt Office.

THE FISCAL FRAMEWORK

The Current Fiscal Framework

The fiscal framework consists of several parts:

1. A *top-down* approach when Parliament decides the annual budget. Decisons are taken in two steps. In the first step, Parliament determines total government expenditure and its allocation among twenty-seven expenditure areas. In the same step, changes in tax rates and various fees are decided. These decisions are taken on the basis of a proposal from Parliament's Committee on Finance. In a second step, individual expenditure items within each expenditure area are determined. These decisions, which are based on proposals from other committees in Parliament, cannot change the overall expenditure level in an expenditure area. This decision process ensures that there is an overall decision on total government expenditure so that it (and the budget balance) is not just the outcome of a large number of uncoordinated individual decisions. Fiscal transparency is promoted by rules on completeness of the budget, which do not allow the use of any extrabudgetary funds, and on gross budgeting, prohibiting the netting out of expenditures against revenues.

2. According to the Budget Act, the government is obliged to propose an annual *ceiling* for *central government expenditure* three years ahead. If there is a risk that the ceiling will be broken, the government has to take action or propose actions to Parliament such that this is avoided. The ceiling puts a limit to budget slippages on the expenditure side of the budget.

3. The Budget Act also stipulates that the government is to propose a target for general government net lending (a *surplus target*) to Parliament. The numerical target is not specified in the Act and can thus be changed by Parliament without any change in the Act itself. But since its inception in 1997 the target has—in effect—been held unchanged at 1 percent of GDP.[15] The target does not apply to an individual year but "over a business cycle." However, no attempts are made to measure the length of the cycle. Instead, adherence to the target is evaluated by a number of indicators: a ten-year backward-looking average of actual net lending, a partly forward-looking average of net lending (actual figures three years back and forecasts for the current and three future years), and the current structural net lending (which is adjusted for both the cycle and one-off measures). There is no requirement that past violations of the target must be compensated for. On the contrary, the government has made it clear that earlier developments are just a guide to judge the likelihood of meeting the target in the future.[16] This is in line with the idea of *tax smoothing*, i.e. that it is optimal—in order to minimize tax distortions—at each point of time to set tax rates so that if they are held constant at current levels also in the future, they can be expected to finance all future government

expenditure. Then temporary budget shocks are allowed to result in permanent changes in government debt.

4. There is a *balanced budget requirement for local governments* (municipalities and regions). They must budget for an excess of revenues over expenditures. If this requirement is not met, it must be compensated for within three years. Unlike the surplus target for the entire public sector, the balanced budget requirement for local governments does not apply to net lending, which is calculated without accruing investment expenditure, but to the economic result after such accrual. Also, in contrast to the surplus target, the balanced budget requirement for local governments applies annually. Possibilities have, however, been introduced for local governments with strong finances to build up balancing accounts (rainy-day funds) in good times that can be activated in cyclical downturns.

5. The state *pension system* is one with *defined contributions*, which means that benefits are adjusted to fixed contributions. Pensions are indexed to per capita wage growth, but there is a balancing mechanism that limits the degree of indexation if the long-run financial stability of the system is threatened: this occurs if the capitalized value of contributions plus the assets in existing buffer funds fall below the value of pension liabilities. The balancing mechanism is automatic according to a predetermined formula. Hence, no political decisions are required to ensure the long-run sustainability of the pension system (but new political decisions that endanger sustainability can, of course, be taken).[17]

6. Central government budget decisions are based on a procedure where an annual *scope for reforms* is calculated by the Ministry of Finance.[18] The scope for reforms is defined as the total sum of permanent tax reductions and government expenditure increases that can be actively decided by Parliament and that are compatible with the surplus target. The scope for reforms arises because tax revenues grow automatically more or less in line with GDP, whereas government expenditure does not. The reason is that only some expenditures are tied to wages (which grow at about the same rate as nominal GDP), whereas others are linked to wages only after deductions for productivity increases, are indexed to prices (which grow more slowly than wages), or are fixed in nominal terms. Absent discretionary decisions, government net lending thus tends to improve automatically. The Finance Ministry's calculation of the scope for reform forms the basis for the budget discussions within the government. The calculation has usually also been accepted by the main opposition parties.

7. A *Fiscal Policy Council* evaluates the government's fiscal policy.[19] The Council is to assess whether public finances are sustainable in the long run and whether they are consistent with the surplus target and the expenditure ceiling as well as with the cyclical situation of the economy. The Council consists of six members with either "high scientific competence in economics" or "practical experience of economic policy work." An annual report is published in May each year, about one month after the government has presented its Spring Fiscal Policy Bill. The report is formally addressed to the government, but is also the subject of a public hearing

in Parliament's Committee on Finance. In addition, the public finances are regularly monitored also by the National Institute for Economic Research, the Office for Budget Management, and the National Audit Office.

The Establishment of the Fiscal Framework

The major part of the fiscal framework was established as a consequence of the economic crisis of the early 1990s, when very large fiscal deficits emerged (Figure 44.2).[20] In 1993, the deficit was 12 percent of GDP. Government debt was increasing fast (Figure 44.3) and government bond yields were high. The then Liberal–Conservative government made it one of its top political priorities to stop the accumulation of debt in 1993. This objective received an even higher priority when the Social Democrats came to power in 1994 and formulated a fiscal consolidation program. It contained clearly stated objectives: in November 1994 that government debt should be stabilized as a share of GDP by 1998 at the latest, in April 1995 that a balanced budget (zero general government net lending) should be achieved in 1998, and that government debt as a share of GDP should be stabilized by 1996. In June 1995 the government set the objective that government net lending was not to exceed 3 percent of GDP (a convergence criterion for joining the monetary union) in 1997.

In its first Budget Bill in 1995 (*Proposition 1994:95:100*), the Social Democratic government also announced that the fiscal consolidation program was to be complemented by institutional changes of the budget process. The first changes to be imposed were the central government expenditure ceiling and the top-down budget process, which were used for the first time in 1996.

The consolidation program was very successful and the set objectives were achieved (see Figures 44.2 and 44.3). The success was to a considerable degree attributed to the formulation of clear and well-publicized objectives. This served as an important inspiration for the formulation of the surplus target, which was decided in 1997. The numerical level chosen—1 percent of GDP—was based on the insight that the strains on future public finances arising from an ageing population could be eased through pre-funding (saving in advance) and that fiscal surpluses would increase the scope for counter-cyclical fiscal policy in downturns.[21] In 2000, the described reforms of the fiscal framework were complemented by the balanced budget requirement on local governments, which was motivated by a desire to avoid fiscal discipline in the public sector being jeopardized by a lack of discipline in local governments.

As with the reforms to the monetary framework, academic input was important for the reform of the budget process, but the impact was more indirect. The direct influence came from work in Parliament on reforming the process already initiated before the crisis and from experts in the Ministry of Finance, based on their earlier experiences of budget work. A key role was played by a study, made by a civil servant, which found that the Swedish budget process was very weak in an international comparison and recommended a stricter framework including a top-down budget approach and a government expenditure ceiling (Molander 1992).[22] A main conclusion in the study was that earlier economic crises in Sweden depended to large extent on an inability to contain expenditures in good times (Molander and Holmquist 2013). The study was inspired by an academic analysis of budget processes in EU countries, which found that they had an important effect on fiscal outcomes (von Hagen 1992). The conclusions in the Molander study were endorsed by the Lindbeck Commission (1993), which was important for gaining acceptance for these ideas in the political system. They were first adopted by Parliament in its work on the budget and subsequently by the government in its internal preparation of the budget.[23]

European influences were also important for the introduction of the stricter fiscal framework. The fiscal crisis and the consolidation process in the 1990s coincided in time with the formulation of the EU fiscal rules in the Maastricht Treaty and the stability pact.[24] Paradoxically, it appears that Sweden took these rules much more seriously than the member states joining the monetary union. The government stated that Sweden had to demonstrate its ability to establish a fiscal surplus "at least as clearly" outside as inside the monetary union (*Proposition 1997/98:25*). Establishing a sufficient margin to the EU 3-percent-of-GDP deficit ceiling in normal times, in order to avoid violations in downturns, was also an explicit deliberation behind the formulation of the surplus target.[25]

After the fiscal reforms in the 1990s, no further changes were implemented for some time. There were fiscal surpluses, and government debt was gradually reduced (see Figures 44.2 and 44.3). However, the Liberal–Conservative government coming to power in 2006 implemented additional reforms. They were not motivated by any acute fiscal problems. Instead, they were responses either to academically based proposals or to a general political desire to further improve the fiscal framework. The latter motive reflected a strong political will in the Liberal–Conservative government to show that it could handle the public finances well (the earlier Liberal–Conservative coalition governments in 1976–82 and 1991–4 presided over large deteriorations in the fiscal balance).[26]

The first reform was the establishment of the Fiscal Policy Council (FPC) in 2007.[27] In recent years there has been a strong international trend to set up such national fiscal watchdogs. Here, Sweden was quite early and the Swedish Council has to some extent served as a role model for similar institutions elsewhere. The idea of such independent fiscal monitoring institutions first appeared in the international academic debate in the 1990s as an attempt to find ways of transferring the benefits of independent policy-making in the area of monetary policy to that of fiscal policy. In Sweden, the idea was picked up by a Government Commission with the remit of analyzing fiscal policy in the event of membership in the monetary union (*Stabilisation Policy in the Monetary Union* 2002). Based on a background report by Wyplosz (2002), the Commission proposed the establishment of an independent fiscal watchdog.[28]

The proposal was rejected by the Social Democratic government at the time, but was more popular with the Liberal–Conservative opposition. It was endorsed by the then chief economist of the Moderates (the Swedish Tory Party), Anders Borg (Borg 2003). In 2006 he became Minister for Finance in the Liberal–Conservative government and then pushed through the establishment of the FPC. This was done, although the parties of the left (Social Democrats, the Greens, and the Left Party) opposed it on the grounds that unelected experts would get too much power and that the FPC's analyses were bound to have a Liberal–Conservative bias. However, these parties changed their views gradually and in 2011 entered an agreement with the government regarding the FPC, extending its remit also to analysis of income distribution issues.

Other later changes in the fiscal framework were made on the government's own initiative, largely without any major input from more academic thinking. They seem to have reflected a genuine interest by the Finance Minister in 2006–14 (Anders Borg) in fiscal framework issues—an interest which was further stimulated by the sovereign debt crises in the euro area. The Spring Fiscal Policy Bill in 2008 set out clear principles for calculating the annual scope for reforms (see previous section), based on the surplus target and the cyclical situation, as a means of imposing more discipline on the budget process (*Proposition 2007/08:150*). Before 2011 it was not obligatory for the government to propose an expenditure ceiling (although it had always been done after the possibility was introduced in the Budget Act of 1996) and the surplus target had no formal legal backing. From 2011 the Budget Act makes it obligatory for the government to propose both an expenditure ceiling and a surplus target to Parliament.

To sum up, the establishment of a stricter fiscal framework took place in two steps. The most important reforms were done in the second half of the 1990s as a reaction to the fiscal crisis that was triggered in the first half of the 1990s. The proposals on reforms came mainly from experts inside the Ministry of Finance. The formulation of fiscal rules at the EU level provided an important source of inspiration, not least because there was a wide consensus that Sweden should live up to these rules and hence be able to decide for itself from "a position of strength" whether or not to join the monetary union. There was a second round of reforms, though less pervasive, from 2007. It was not triggered by any acute fiscal problems in Sweden, but was instead motivated by arguments of principle on how to strengthen the framework further. In this phase, academic reasoning played a direct role for the establishment of a fiscal watchdog.

Challenges for the Fiscal Framework

On the whole, the fiscal framework has worked well and delivered fiscal discipline. Figure 44.2 shows that the surplus target of 1 percent of GDP has sometimes been exceeded, and Figure 44.3 that government debt has fallen strongly. It is noteworthy that this has occurred without any formal sanction procedures being in place: instead, the respect for the fiscal framework seems to have been based on a political consensus never again to get into a fiscal crisis situation requiring harsh consolidation measures as in the 1990s (EEAG 2012; Calmfors 2012, 2013a). However, recently fiscal deficits have arisen (1.4 and 1.9 percent of GDP in 2013 and 2014, respectively; see *Proposition 2014/15:100*) and the Fiscal Policy Council (2015) has concluded that the surplus target had not been met. This reflects a conflict of goals between the objective of fiscal discipline and the objective of counter-cyclical fiscal policy. It is unclear how the violation of the fiscal target will be dealt with.

A related issue concerns the numerical value of the surplus target. If government net lending is 1 percent of GDP on average, government net financial wealth will, under plausible assumptions, continue to increase from the current level of around 20 percent of GDP and ultimately converge to a level somewhere around 65 percent (Fiscal Policy Council 2014).[29] It is not obvious that such a large precautionary buffer is needed in the event of future fiscal crises. The government, consisting of Social Democrats and the Green Party, which took office in 2014, has announced that it wants to change the fiscal target to a balanced budget target (*Proposition* 2014/15: 100). A Government Commission with the remit to analyze such a change has been appointed.

Yet another issue concerns the Fiscal Policy Council. Although set up earlier and acting as a role model for many of its counterparts in other countries, the Council has a rather weak formal position compared to arrangements elsewhere. This likely reflects reluctance among politicians to expose themselves to "too much monitoring"; it is obvious that the Minister for Finance in the Liberal–Conservative government 2006–14 (Anders Borg) was very uncomfortable with the Council's critique of some government policies in the first years of its existence, which led to a stressed relationship, as described in Calmfors and Wren-Lewis (2011) and Calmfors (2013b). An interesting proposal is that the Council's remit could be extended also to monetary policy (Socialdemokraternas forskningskommission 2014). One aim is to strengthen the monitoring of monetary policy. Another motive is a worry that there may not be sufficient coordination between the monetary policy decided by the central bank and the government's fiscal policy. Common monitoring of the two policies might help ensure an appropriate policy mix.

In the autumn of 2013 the earlier political consensus on the budget process was challenged by a conflict between the government and the opposition parties on the top-down approach. After the initial overall decision on the budget had been taken in Parliament, including a tax cut for high-income earners, Parliament reversed the tax cut in a new decision. This was possible since the government was a minority one. The government argued that this was a violation of the "spirit" of the top-down approach, whereas the opposition parties instead claimed that the decision was consistent with both the formal and informal rules, as it strengthened the budget (Mattson 2014). The earlier consensus was re-established in an agreement between the government (Social Democrats and the Greens) that took office in 2014 and the Liberal–Conservative parties (the so-called December Agreement that year). According to the agreement, Parliament should not later reverse tax or expenditure decisions included in the overall budget decision once that has been taken.[30]

Conclusions

Major changes in the monetary and fiscal frameworks in Sweden were undertaken in the 1990s. They were direct responses to severe macroeconomic problems of inflation and large fiscal deficits. The granting of more independence to the Riksbank in the late 1990s was to a large extent motivated by the inflation–devaluation cycle characterizing the Swedish economy in the 1970s and 1980s, when low credibility for politicians' commitment to a fixed exchange rate in the case of short-run conflicts with the objective of full employment was a key factor in keeping the cycle alive. The adoption of inflation targeting in 1993 was a response to the forced move to a flexible exchange rate. The aim was to capitalize on the earlier, but failed, investment in the defence of the fixed exchange rate as a means to achieve low inflation. The top-down budget process, the central government expenditure ceiling, the surplus target, and the balanced budget requirement on local governments were all reforms seeking to lock in the gains from the fiscal consolidation process in the second half of the 1990s.

EU membership played an important role in establishing the new monetary and fiscal frameworks. EU Treaty obligations required greater central bank independence. The EU fiscal rules did not directly require any changes in the domestic fiscal framework, but served as an important source of inspiration. At the same time, EU membership cannot be seen as a purely exogenous factor, as the decision to seek entry into the EU partly came about as a measure to enhance macroeconomic stability. EU membership was used as a vehicle for change in the economic policy frameworks. The question of EMU entry toward the end of the 1990s played a particular role. When Sweden decided not to join, the desire to preserve credibility for policies outside the monetary union became rather more a motive for more stringent monetary and fiscal frameworks than would have been the case inside.

Academic thinking played a greater direct role in the reforms in monetary policy than in the fiscal policy area. Explicit commitment to a price stability target and central bank independence in order to increase credibility for a low-inflation policy had consistently been advocated by academic policy groups throughout the 1980s. This created a fertile soil for the adoption of the inflation target and the move to central bank independence in the 1990s. The fiscal reforms in the 1990s were instead more directly driven by technocrats inside the Ministry of Finance (who were, however, influenced by the academic thinking in the field) and by a desire in Parliament to have a better functioning budget process. But a decade later, the establishment of a fiscal watchdog, the Fiscal Policy Council, was the result of direct academic proposals and not any response to existing fiscal problems. Other measures after 2007 to further strengthen the fiscal framework, such as guidelines for computing an annual scope for reforms and a stronger legal status for the government expenditure ceiling and the surplus target, seem to have been taken mainly on the initiative of a Minister for Finance with an unusually great interest in fiscal framework issues. This interest was probably further enhanced by the sovereign debt crises in several EU countries.

The inflation target has been instrumental in anchoring inflation expectations at a low level, and the budget surplus target has become generally accepted as a norm for fiscal policy. Both targets were, however, formulated without any underpinning in-depth analysis. It is not clear that they were set optimally. A somewhat higher inflation target would make it easier to achieve negative real interest rates, and thus to stimulate the economy, in recessions. The surplus target has been motivated as a measure to reduce government debt radically, but once this has been achieved it is not obvious that precautionary considerations motivate such a favorable long-run financial position for the government as is implied by the surplus target. A key issue is whether the political system has the capability to reformulate these targets and still maintain credibility for low inflation and fiscal discipline. This likely requires a broad political consensus, transparent explanations, and a clear message that any changes are one-off measures and not the start of a number of successive revisions. The fact that inflation has been held consistently below the inflation target and that fiscal outcomes have been much stronger than in most other countries ought, however, to give policy-makers considerable leeway to reformulate the targets without loss of credibility. In the fiscal field, a reformulation of the surplus target, for example, to a balanced budget requirement, could be combined with a strengthening of the role of the fiscal watchdog, the Fiscal Policy Council, such that it comes to match the best international practice, which is not now the case.

To conclude, Sweden provides a good example of how deep economic crisis, in interaction with independent thinking by experts and policy influences from other countries, can lead to fundamental reforms of policy frameworks. Academic thinking is a crucial input that must be there as an intellectual basis when the need for reform arises. International considerations are an important vehicle that can be used to push through changes. Although reforms in fundamental economic policy frameworks are often crude, the design of new institutions tends to be regarded as dogmas that are not to be questioned. It remains to be seen whether it will be possible in Sweden to adapt the monetary and fiscal frameworks to changed circumstances, while still preserving the benefits they have delivered. This requires a continued political consensus which may be more difficult to maintain as the memory of the fiscal crisis in the 1990s fades away. A key issue will be how to secure an appropriate policy mix between the central bank's monetary policy and the government's fiscal policy.

NOTES

1. I am grateful for comments from Karolina Ekholm, Niklas Frank, Johannes Lindvall, Ingvar Mattsson, Jon Pierre, and Joakim Sonnegård.
2. As it is the government that decides on the exchange rate system, it could in principle peg the Swedish krona to the currency of another country (or set of countries) with high inflation, which could make it impossible for the central bank to achieve its inflation target. This may seem as an inconsistency. It has, however, been argued that since the Riksbank is responsible for the implementation of the exchange rate regime, it can always adjust the exchange rate parity in a way that is consistent with its price stability target (*Proposition 1997/98:40*).
3. The Governor can appeal to the European Court of Justice and the other Board members to the Swedish Supreme Court.
4. See, for example, Jonung (1999) and *Finans- och penningpolitiskt bokslut för 1990-talet* (2001).

5. The thinking of the SNS group was developed in SNS (1985, 1986, 1987). Similar thoughts had earlier been advanced by e.g. Calmfors et al. (1976), Myhrman (1977), Jonung (1978), Lindbeck (1978), and Calmfors (1979). See also Calmfors (1996) for a survey of the debate.

6. The seminal contribution was Kydland and Prescott (1977). See also Barro and Gordon (1983a,b).

7. *Proposition* 1990:91:100, bil.1, p. 4.

8. *Proposition* 1991/92:150, bil.1, p. 1.

9. The Commission was named after its chair, Professor Assar Lindbeck. The Swedish version of the report was published in 1993.

10. The Commission was named after its chair, Professor Lars Calmfors, the author of this chapter. An English version of the Commission's report was published in 1997 (Calmfors Commisssion 1997).

11. According to the Government Bill on a new Riksbank Act, the government shared the view of the five-party working group on the status of the Riksbank that "it is of particular importance with high credibility for monetary policy in a situation when Sweden remains outside the monetary union when it starts" (*Proposition 1997/98:40*). According to the Government Bill proposing that Sweden should stay outside the monetary union, Sweden must *at least* demonstrate its willingness to achieve price stability (and fiscal surpluses) as clearly outside as inside the monetary union (*Proposition 1997/98:25*).

12. See, for example, Calmfors (2013c).

13. See, for example, Svensson (2015).

14. In the view of the Executive Board's majority, financial stability was seen as a prerequisite for the achievement of the inflation target in the long term, since a financial crisis could lead to very low inflation or deflation in the future.

15. The target was decided in 1997 and fully applied in 2000 after a phasing-in period.

16. See, for example, *Proposition 2009/10:150* and Fiscal Policy Council (2010).

17. See, for example, EEAG (2007) for a brief description of the Swedish pension system.

18. See Fiscal Policy Council (2011).

19. See Calmfors (2013b).

20. See, for example, *Finans- och penningpolitiskt bokslut för 1990-talet* (2001) and Fiscal Policy Council (2008).

21. Ibid. See also *Stabilisation Policy in the Monetary Union* (2002).

22. The study was commissioned by the Expert Group for Public Economics (ESO), an independent committee attached to the Ministry of Finance, with the remit "to make an independent contribution to expanding and deepening the knowledge data available to future socio-economic and fiscal policy decisions."

23. The main ideas were set out in Talmanskonferensen (1994) and Molander et al. (1995).

24. The Maastricht Treaty was agreed in 1992 and adopted in 1993. The discussions on the stability pact started in 1995 and the pact was finalized in 1997.

25. See, for example, *Stabilisation Policy in the Monetary Union* (2002), *Utvärdering av överskottsmålet* (2010), and *Proposition 2009/10:150*.

26. See Calmfors (2013a,b).

27. The author of this chapter was the FPC's first chair in 2007–11.

28. See, for example, Calmfors (2003) and Debrun et al. (2009) for surveys of proposals on independent fiscal monitoring institutions. Existing such institutions have been surveyed by the European Commission (2006), Hagemann (2010), and Calmfors and Wren-Lewis

(2011). See also OECD (2013) for a list of OECD notes on such institutions in various countries.

29. The exact level will depend on how the value of the stock held by the government sector develops.

30. The December agreement also stipulated that Parliament should pass the budget of a minority goverment if it has support from "the largest party constellation" even if there is not a majority in favor (Fiscal Policy Council 2015). The motivation was to make it easier for a minority government to govern and avoid a situation like the one that occurred in 2014 when the red–green government could not get its budget through Parliament. The government had instead to govern with the budget proposed by the Liberal–Conservative parties. That budget was approved by Parliament because it was supported also by the populist and anti-immigration Sweden Democrats with which the Liberal–Conservative parties did not want to cooperate. In October 2015, the December agreement was abandoned by the Liberal-Conservative parties. At the time of writing the implications for future budget decisions are not clear.

References

Assarsson, B. (2011). "Penningpolitiken i Sverige," *Ekonomisk Debatt* 39/3: 46–59.

Barro, R. J. and Gordon, D. B. (1983a). "A Positive Theory of Monetary Policy in a Natural-Rate Model," *Journal of Political Economy* 91/4: 589–610.

Barro, R. J. and Gordon, D. B. (1983b). "Rules, Discretion and Reputation in a Model of Monetary Policy," *Journal of Monetary Economics* 12: 101–21.

Bergkvist, J. and Gradin, A. (1993). *Reservation till Riksbanksutredningen: Riksbanken och prisstabiliteten*, SOU 1993:20.

Borg, A. (2003). "Modern finanspolitik—en syntes mellan Keines och Friedman," *Ekonomisk Debatt* 31/7: 17–28.

Calmfors Commission (1997). *EMU—A Swedish Perspective*. Dordrecht: Kluwer Academic Publishers.

Calmfors, L. (1979). "Lärdomar av kostnadskrisen," *Ekonomisk Debatt* 79/8: 541–53.

Calmfors, L. (1996). "Nationalekonomernas roll under det senaste decenniet—vilka är lärdomarna?" in L. Jonung (ed.), *Ekonomernas roll i debatten—gör de någon nytta?* Stockholm: IVA and Ekerlids Förlag.

Calmfors, L. (2003). "Fiscal Policy to Stabilise the Domestic Economy in the EMU: What Can We Learn from Monetary Policy?" *CESifo Economic Studies* 49/3: 319–53.

Calmfors, L. (2012). "What Can Europe Learn from Sweden? Four Lessons for Fiscal Discipline," March 12, <http://www.voxeu.org/article/what-can-europe-learn-sweden-four-lessons-fiscal-discipline>.

Calmfors, L. (2013a). "Sweden—From Macroeconomic Failure to Macroeconomic Success," in M. Maguire and G. Wilson (eds), *Business and Government*, vol. IV: *Challenges and Prospects*. London: Routledge.

Calmfors, L. (2013b). "Watchdog with a Broad Remit," in G. Kopits (ed.), *Restoring Public Debt Sustainability: The Role of Independent Fiscal Institutions*. Oxford: Oxford University Press.

Calmfors, L. (2013c), "Våga ompröva Riksbankens mål", *Dagens Nyheter*, 3 April.

Calmfors, L., Lundgren, N., Matthiessen, L., and Nordin, A. (1976). *Den onödiga inflationen*. Stockholm: Trygg-Hansa.

Calmfors, L. and Wren-Lewis, S. (2011). "What Should Fiscal Councils Do?" *Economic Policy* 26/68: 649–95.

Carlsson, I. (2003). *Så tänkte jag*. Stockholm: Hjalmarson & Högberg.

Debrun, X., Hauner, D., and Kumar, M. S. (2009). "Independent Fiscal Agencies," *Journal of Economic Surveys* 23/1: 44–81.

EEAG (2007). "Report on the European Economy." Munich: CESifo.

EEAG (2012). "Report on the European Economy." Munich: CESifo.

European Commission (2006). "Public Finances in EMU 2006—The First Year of the Revised Stability and Growth Pact," European Economy 3, Brussels.

Finans- och penningpolitiskt bokslut för 1990-talet (2001), *Proposition 2000/01:100*, bilaga 5. Stockholm: Riksdagen.

Finansdepartementet (2013). "Ett förstärkt ramverk för finansiell stabilitet," Stockholm.

Fiscal Policy Council (2008). *Swedish Fiscal Policy 2009*, Stockholm.

Fiscal Policy Council (2010). *Swedish Fiscal Policy 2010*, Stockholm.

Fiscal Policy Council (2011). *Swedish Fiscal Policy 2011*, Stockholm.

Fiscal Policy Council (2012). *Swedish Fiscal Policy 2012*, Stockholm.

Fiscal Policy Council (2014). *Swedish Fiscal Policy 2014*, Stockholm.

Fiscal Policy Council (2015). *Swedish Fiscal Policy 2015*, Stockholm

Hagemann, R. (2010). "Improving Fiscal Performance Through Fiscal Councils." Paris: OECD ECO/WKP(2010/85).

Hagen, J. von (1992). "Budgeting Procedures and Fiscal Performance in the European Communities," Commission of the European Communities (DG-II), Economic Papers no. 96.

Jonung, L. (1978). "En stabil stabiliseringspolitik," *Ekonomisk Debatt* 5/1: 7–18.

Jonung, L. (1999). "Med backspegeln som kompass—om stabiliseringspolitiken som läroprocess," Ds 1999:9. Stockholm: Finansdepartementet.

Kydland, F. and Prescott, E. (1977). "Rules rather than Discretion: The Inconsistency of Optimal Plans," *Journal of Political Economy* 85/3: 473–92.

Lindbeck, A. (1978). "McCracken-rapporten—en kommentar," *Ekonomisk Debatt* 2/78: 109–19.

Lindbeck Commission (1994). *Turning Sweden Around*. Cambridge, MA: MIT Press.

Mattson, I. (2014). "Formal vs. Informal Fiscal Rules: Lessons from Sweden," IMF Public Financial Management Blog, April 11, <http://blog-pfm.imf.org/pfmblog/2014/04/formal-vs-informal-fiscal-rules-lessons-from-sweden.html>.

Molander, P. (1992). "Statsskulden och budgetprocessen," Ds 1992:126, Finansdepartementet, Stockholm.

Molander, P., Bengtsson, U., and Karlstam, C. (1995). "Fortsatt reformering av budgetprocessen," Ds 1995:73, Finansdepartementet, Stockholm.

Molander, P. and Holmquist, J. (2013). "Reforming Swedens Budgetary Institutions—Background, Design and Experiences," Rapport till Finanspolitiska rådet 2013/1.

Myhrman, J. (1977). "Nya perspektiv på konjunkturpolitikens villkor," *Ekonomisk Debatt* 5/1: 29–40.

OECD (2013). "OECD Principles for Independent Fiscal Institutions," GOV/PGC(2013)9REV1. Paris: OECD.

Proposition 1990:91:100. Stockholm: Riksdagen.

Proposition 1991/92:150. Stockholm: Riksdagen.

Proposition 1994/95:100. Stockholm: Riksdagen.

Proposition 1997/98:25. Stockholm: Riksdagen.

Proposition 1997/98:40. Stockholm: Riksdagen.

Proposition 2009/10:150. Stockholm: Riksdagen.

Proposition 2010/11:150. Stockholm: Riksdagen.

Proposition 2014/15:100. Stockholm: Riksdagen.

Riksbanksutredningen (1993). *Riksbanken och prisstabiliteten*, SOU 1993:20. Stockholm.

SNS (1985). *Konjunkturrådets rapport*. Stockholm.

SNS (1986). *Konjunkturrådets rapport*. Stockholm.

SNS (1987). *Konjunkturrådets rapport*. Stockholm.

Socialdemokraternas forskningskommission (2014). "Arbetsmarknadsreformer för jobb och välfärd." Stockholm.

Stabilisation Policy in the Monetary Union (2002). Summary of SOU 2002:16, Stockholm.

Svensson, L. (2015). "The Possible Unemployment Cost of Average Inflation below a Credible Target," *American Economic Journal: Macroeconomics* 7/1: 258–96.

Talmanskonferensen (1994). "Reformera riksdagsarbetet 2, Budgetprocessen." Stockholm: Riksdagen.

Utvärdering av överskottsmålet (2010). Ds 2010:4. Stockholm: Finansdepartementet.

Wyplosz, C. (2002). "Fiscal Policy: Institutions vs Rules." Appendix to *Stabiliseringspolitik i valutaunionen*, Swedish Government Commission on Stabilisation Policy in the EMU, SOU 2002:16, Stockholm.

CHAPTER 45

....

THE SWEDISH MODEL OF
INDUSTRIAL RELATIONS

....

TORSTEN SVENSSON

UNIONS and employer organizations have played a very important role in modern Swedish political history. Membership has been widespread and labor market organizations have been strongly involved and integrated in political life, turning Sweden into one of the clearest examples of a corporatist country (Öberg and Svensson 2012; see also Öberg as well as Lewin and Lindvall in this volume). This chapter focuses on labor market actors and their relationship with the state. The first section deals with the classical "Swedish model," the challenges to this model in the 1980s and 1990s, and the manner in which it has been reformed. It is followed by two sections describing the employer organizations and the unions. The fourth section analyzes the current model of industrial relations. The fifth section concludes.

Industrial relations in Sweden confronted fundamental challenges in the last decades of the twentieth century. To what extent this led to extensive institutional changes is debated. Some researchers, particularly those who study Sweden in comparative perspective, interpret the changes as extensive and important (Fulcher 1991; Visser 1996: 179; Törnqvist 1999; Iversen 1998; Swenson and Pontusson 2000; Wallerstein and Golden 2000; Baccaro and Howell 2011; Howell and Kolins Givan 2011). There are a number of arguments for this interpretation. First and foremost, the centralized bargaining system, a central part of the Swedish model, was replaced with more decentralized forms of bargaining, as peak organizations lost ground to individual unions and many important aspects of wage agreements were settled in local bargaining. Unionization has declined. Within the political sphere, the strong ties between the unions and the Social Democratic Party have become looser. Industrial organizations have partly withdrawn and partly been excluded from administrative agency boards responsible for implementing welfare and labor market policies. Labor laws and welfare policies have been put under pressure, implying less support for union demands.

Nevertheless, some researchers argue that compared to changes in other countries, the changes to Sweden's labor market regime should not be exaggerated (Thelen 2001;

Elvander 2002a; Svensson and Öberg 2002, 2005). Industrial relations in Sweden have involved important coordinating mechanisms during the whole period. In the wake of the economic crisis of the 1990s—in response to the perceived threats of wage infla-tion and rising unemployment—a new regime for collective bargaining, the Industrial Agreement, saw the light of day. In comparative perspective, unionization is still extraordinarily high, and the universal welfare state persists.

In the following, the characteristics of Swedish labor market organizations and the development of the Swedish model of industrial relations are described and evaluated.

THE BASIC MODEL OF INDUSTRIAL RELATIONS

From the 1930s onward, industrial relations in Sweden can be characterized as a tripar-tite corporatist system based on bipartite collective bargaining with the state remaining in the background but ready for action within the institutionalized dialogue between unions and employer organizations, concerning the basic conditions and main policy goals. The real breakthrough for the corporatist model came in the late 1930s in a "his-toric compromise" between labor and capital. This breakthrough implied both a politi-cal compromise and a new industrial relations regime.

At the time, Sweden suffered hard from unemployment and labor market conflicts, the level of strike activity being among the highest in Europe. The state therefore threat-ened to intervene in the labor market. Faced with the prospect of a fundamental blow against their power and independence, unions and employers concluded the so-called Basic Agreement—also called the Saltsjöbaden Agreement—in 1938 (Swenson 1991a; Kjellberg 1998, 2000). Employer prerogative and labor peace were exchanged for social reforms and full employment. Eventually, this compromise brought about centralized collective agreements at the peak level, built on strong centralization of organizations (Kjellberg 2000: 609–10). The first central agreement was signed in 1952. From 1956 onward, all unions took part, and centralized wage bargaining lasted for more than 30 years. It was above all endorsed by the Employers' Federation, SAF, who wanted to keep down inflationary wage increases and secure labor supply by curbing internal competition. Unions in the high-productive export industry accepted, though more hesitantly (Alexopoulos and Cohen 2003; Öberg and Hallberg Adu 2009).

During the 1950s, the central agreements were complemented with an active labor market policy aiming for full employment and economic growth. It implied supply-side measures in the form of employment assistance, labor market training, and employ-ment subsidies, as well as direct job creation. The Keynesian-like toolbox got some new instruments, which were combined into the so-called "Rehn–Meidner solidaristic wage policy" (Lindvall and Sebring 2005; Bonoli 2010). Wage bargaining had to follow pro-ductivity in sectors exposed to the world market, and the unions insisted on the rule "equal pay for the same kind of work." The policy actually implied wage compression from below and wage moderation on behalf of skilled workers in the export industry. This policy was a response to labor shortages in the high-productivity industries, stimulated technical change, and led to the closing of unproductive plants and worker mobility. Active labor market policy facilitated the transition back to work for those who suffered from the policies. Welfare policies encompassing all citizens and combining universal coverage with generous benefits compensated for restrained wage demands (Meidner 1986; Alexopoulos and Cohen 2003; Magnusson 2006).

Beside union–employer relations and universal welfare policies, the Swedish model involved regularly and institutionalized talks and cooperation between the state and the leaders of the peak organizations on overall policy aims. Unions and employer organizations were involved in the whole policy-making process as they took part in pre-legislative government commissions of inquiry, as well as in the implementation of policies within the boards of various administrative agencies in a system of administrative corporatism, most importantly in the National Labor Market Board (Lindvall and Rothstein 2006; Svensson and Öberg 2005; Öberg, this volume). In short, the corporatist system can be described as a system of exchange: "The purpose was to make organizations capable of moderating members' demands and to secure industrial peace. In exchange, unions obtained comprehensive welfare policies, protective measures and the right to collective bargaining and strike" (Öberg et al. 2011: 370–1).

Industrial relations and the strength of the labor movement in Sweden were based on historically strong relations and close cooperation between the unions (LO) and the Social Democratic Party. Collective bargaining and labor and welfare legislation became two different but still complementary means of safeguarding the interests of workers (Åmark 1988; Svensson 1994; Kjellberg 2000). Local collective affiliation to the party, complemented with the possibility of individual exit, preserved strong relations between the two organizations on equal footing. Mutual dependence worked as an important vehicle for massive unionization as well, and increased the strength of the Social Democrats.

The agreement in the 1930s contributed to a distinctive feature of Swedish unions: the combination of centralization and decentralization, strong local presence and organization. These particular characteristics, together with the strong relations between the unions and the Social Democratic Party—especially as the party turned into a hegemonic political force—had great impact on unionization. In comparative perspective, Swedish union density stands out as remarkably high (Åmark 1988; Svensson 1994; Kjellberg 1998, 2000). Another unique feature of Swedish unions is the pronounced divide between workers' unions and unions representing other employees. This divide is clearer in Sweden than anywhere else. There are separate confederations for blue-collar workers (LO), white-collar employees (TCO), and academics (SACO), including unions within both private and public sectors, all with a high degree of unionization.

The introduction of a public unemployment insurance scheme in 1934 was crucial for the development of union strength. It was a voluntary unemployment insurance-system—a so-called Ghent system, "owned," administered, and run by the unions, albeit financially supported and controlled by the state. The unions were given an instrument with which they could counteract wages below settlements. An insured union member did not have to accept a job on a salary below wage levels set in collective agreements. In addition, union membership was perceived as a condition for being insured. In practice, together with other selective incentives, the unemployment insurance system became a powerful system for "recruiting and keeping members" supported by the state (Rothstein 1990: 329–30; cf. Oskarsson 1997; Scruggs 2002; Kjellberg 2011; Holmlund and Lundborg 1998).

Swedish employers organized early, at least partly as a consequence of the development of strong unions. The export-oriented and internationally exposed Swedish industry had to find ways to curb wage demands and counteract strike activity (Swenson 1991a). The class compromise in the 1930s implied equilibrium between two strong actors, both strongly dependent on the export industry, and political institutions that supported the compromise (as well as the interests of both sides). A social democratic corporatist system emerged where strongly organized employers, dominated by the export-oriented industry, and strong unions found common ground with the government when it came to adjusting to the global market (Katzenstein 1985). Firms became embedded in a web of relations and a political and institutional setup supporting such relations as a financial system, welfare policies, educational institutions, and systems for vocational training and wage bargaining. According to theories focusing on production regimes, Sweden developed into one of the coordinated market economies in which national-level bargaining institutions have been "shored up" by employers that have oriented their competitive strategies around "high value-added production that depends on a high degree of stability and cooperation with labour" (Thelen 2001: 73; see also Hall 1999; Hall and Soskice 2001).

CHALLENGES AND POLITICAL REFORMS

Corporatist exchanges presuppose that actors can deliver what they promise. In the wake of the oil crises in 1973 and 1979 and as a consequence of a weakened world market, declining growth, rising inflation, and unemployment and globalization, the state's ability to distribute wealth and uphold full employment was undermined (cf. Calmfors, this volume). Deindustrialization changed the configuration of the labor force, leading to a heterogeneous cluster of labor unions. White-collar unions grew stronger and union centralization was weakened. There was a growing discontent with wage moderation among high-skilled workers. Individualization grew, and the electorate, not least union members, experienced political radicalization. Some of the protests were directed against union leaders, who were seen as responsible for the effects of the structural transformation of society that they had agreed to. Moderation became hard to achieve (cf. Öberg et al. 2011; Alexopoulos and Cohen 2003).

Another challenge to the Swedish system of industrial relations during the last decades has been the implications of the Swedish EU membership in 1994, especially in the 2000s, when EU legislation threatened to interfere in domestic labor legislation and make collective agreements obsolete (Andersen 2006: 35; on the Laval conflict, see Woolfson and Sommers 2006).

As the possibility of bargaining for wages became restricted in the 1970s, unions turned to the Social Democratic government for political reforms. Several laws on employment protection such as rules for codetermination, employment security, and improved working environments and safety were introduced. In the view of the employers, some of these measures were perceived as attacks on management prerogative and a clear break with the historical compromise from the 1930s. The politically controversial proposal for wage-earner funds especially agitated the employers, and it was looked upon as a fierce and hostile socialist attack on the core of capitalism. When the final watered-down version was approved in 1982, the relations between the labor market parties had turned from cooperative to hostile (Elvander 2002b: 128; cf. Lewin and Lindvall in this volume).

Economic growth came to a halt in 1990. Sweden experienced a deep economic downturn; indeed, a crisis comparable to the depression in the 1930s (cf. Svensson 2002; Svensson et al. 2006; Calmfors, this volume). Unemployment rose dramatically and employment declined rapidly. The crisis partly coincided with and partly opened up to institutional and structural changes in the labor market. Consequently, the crisis of the 1990s paved the way for market-liberal ideas, huge public deficits, and a neoliberal center-right government (Lindgren 2011: 49)

This coincided with growing discontent within important parts of the electorate with high taxes, excessive bureaucracy, lack of individual freedom and self-determination, and nonresponsive public arrangements and welfare solutions (Petersson 1991). These new sentiments, especially among important swing voters, were closely connected to the open political opposition and mobilization from the employers' organizations towards the wage-earner funds, and to discontent with codetermination laws and demands for decentralization and decorporatization (Pontusson 1993).

Political reforms that were adopted in response to the crisis challenged the labor market organizations and the Swedish model of industrial relations. During the second half of the 1980s, the Social Democrats introduced several welfare state reforms in order to meet the challenge from economic stress, globalization, and technological change, while adjusting to the interests of swing voters. Marketization in the form of far-reaching deregulation and privatization of product markets and infrastructure followed. Subsequent center-right governments have continued and reinforced these reforms. Product market deregulation has been extensive, and Sweden is today among the most liberal countries in this respect (Svensson 2002; Lindgren 2011; cf. Andersson, this volume).

The wave of reforms that started in the 1980s also included changes in core labor market programs. A period of qualifying time has been reintroduced into health insurance, individual contributions to the pension scheme have been increased, and the qualifying years have been lengthened. The strictness in employment protection shows the same pattern of liberalization. Some former restrictions on vacancies and time-limited jobs have been repealed and some exceptions have been made in the rules of priority in case of redundancies. These changes have increased the dependence on the market, making it more costly to remain outside the workforce even for a short time.

Unemployment benefits were formally untouched for a long time, although as rising wages hit income ceilings in the insurance system, actual contributions have decreased. More recently, the right-wing governments intervened in the insurance system by raising the membership fees dramatically and at the same time abolishing tax deductions for individual contributions and for union dues. In the following year, the reform was complemented with a differentiation of the fees between insurance funds with low and high unemployment rates. The idea was to finance the unemployment insurance system through membership contributions and thereby put pressure on the unions in wage negotiations: unions would get an incentive to keep their demands low, as they and their members would be punished with higher fees if unemployment rose as a result of wage demands. The effects on union density and fund membership were dramatic (Kjellberg 2011).

Labor Market Actors and Changing Industrial Relations

Employers and Employer Organizations

The introduction of laws on employment protection and codetermination in the 1970s and the introduction of wage-earner funds in 1982 were perceived by the employers as attacks on managerial prerogative and as a clear break with the historical compromise from the 1930s. The employers reacted with demands for the deregulation of the labor market and for a decentralized wage-bargaining system (Kjellberg 2000: 610; Elvander 2002b: 128). One important step was the decision, in 1990, to unilaterally withdraw from several corporatist institutions. The main target was the Labor Market Board, one of the pillars of corporatist labor market policy-making (Rothstein and Bergström 1999; Johansson 2003).

A few years earlier, the dominant proponent for centralized bargaining in the past, the employers' association for the metalworking industry, had broken with earlier settlements and bargaining traditions. It turned to a radical new strategy and struck a deal at the industry level with the metalworkers' union in 1983. This was an attack on solidaristic wage setting as well as an attack on the whole system of centralized bargaining. In parts of the "employers' family" it was seen as a first step toward decentralization down to the firm-level (Thelen 2001: 86–8).

The transformation of the employers' own peak organization in 2001, merging the Swedish Employers' Confederation (SAF) with the Federation of Swedish Industries into the

Confederation of Swedish Enterprise (SN), was an essential part of the changed strategy and implied a development of employer organizations from negotiating organizations to lobby organizations. In the future, the central organization should not take part in negotiations and make decisions in the name of Swedish business. Bargaining had already been decentralized, and now the organization seemed to close the door to recentralization. Furthermore, political participation should be carried out in the open public debate, not within state agencies and board meetings (Rothstein and Bergström 1999; Svensson and Öberg 2002).

These changes in the policies of employer organizations were expressed in ideological terms, but the change in strategy was based on an analysis of whether existing solutions served their interests or not. Participation within state agency boards carried the risk that employer representatives became victims of "capture" instead of serving the interests of industry. Centralized bargaining, meanwhile, implied low pay-differentials and worked against the interest of the export industry (Lewin 1994; Rothstein and Bergström 1999; Johansson 2003). However, the idea of fully decentralized wage bargaining failed in the mid-1990s. As they confronted strong national and local unions, the strategy also became controversial within employer organizations (Thelen 2001). Likewise, participation within state agencies and governmental committees continued, but in other forms and more focused to certain areas.

Meanwhile, employer organizations have developed their public relations and political contacts in a much more profound and professional way than their counterparts. Just like the unions, employers' associations almost doubled their direct political contacts between 1999 and 2005. However, employers' associations also almost doubled their use of professional consultants and beat unions to almost the same degree (Öberg et al. 2011; Öberg and Svensson 2012). Employers' organizations are highly integrated in the political system and put a lot of effort into participating in the political game.

The ambition among employers to fight labor laws and wage-earner funds and to dismantle the classical corporatist model, as well as central bargaining, did not mean that they also dismantled their own organizations. Even as union density has declined, employers remain highly organized, as Table 45.1 shows.

Organizational density among employers has remained well above 80 percent since the 1990s, measured on the basis of the number of employees in the firms involved (cf.

Table 45.1 Union density and employer density in Sweden, 1970–2010

	1970–4	1975–9	1980–4	1985–9	1990–4	1995–9	2000–4	2005–10
Union density	71.0	75.7	79.1	83.3	84.8	83.5	78.3	72.6
Employer density						86	83	83

Note: Union density: Net union density in percent: Visser (2011); Medlingsinstitutet (2012); Employer density: Kjellberg (2011), based on Statistics Sweden

Kjellberg 2011: 85–6). Most employers, covering well over 80 percent of the workforce, are members in nationwide employers' organizations, which are coordinated by the Confederation of Swedish Enterprise.

In sum, employers and employers' organizations seem to have strengthened their relative positions vis-à-vis the unions. More general political developments may also speak in favor of business interests, opening the window for further reforms of industrial relations.

Trade Unions

The historical figures on unionization are impressive. Union density was around 60 percent in 1945 and reached its peak, 88 percent, during the economic crisis in 1994. However, unions have experienced a consistent and gradual decline during the last fifteen years, reaching less than 73 percent in the most recent data. Table 45.1 shows how the figures have developed on average for five-year periods during the time frame between 1970 and 2010. On the one hand there is a clear decline from the middle of the 1990s onward. The drop seems consistent and quite dramatic. On the other hand, the present figures are still higher than in the beginning of the 1970s, and way above the international average.

True, widespread unionization among different categories of employees has mitigated the effects of structural changes. The extraordinarily high unionization among employees has implied that density figures have remained quite resistant to structural changes. As unionization became widely spread among all groups, recent developments within the labor force following deindustrialization do not seem to have had the huge negative influence on union membership that these trends have had in other countries (Kjellberg 1998, 2000). However, changes in workforce composition linked to deindustrialization, as well as political decisions aiming for a reduced public sector through tax cuts, privatization, and outsourcing, have still led to a gradual decline. As Kjellberg puts it: "[J]obs are transferred from the sector with the highest unionization to that with the lowest" (Kjellberg 2011: 71). These changes have interacted with the marked decline in unionization among young people and foreign-born workers. Young people show the most critical attitudes towards unions, while at the same constituting a large part of the temporary workers who are weakly linked to the labor market (Kjellberg 2011: 68–72; Medlingsinstitutet 2012: 31–4). This tendency is considered to be one of the most urgent problems for the unions (LO-rapport 2007).

The latest dramatic fall in unionization after 2007 was a result of the abovementioned changes to the rules in the unemployment insurance system that were implemented by the right-wing government. These political reforms also reflect changing political conditions for the unions due to changes on the political arena as well as value changes in the electorate. As the Social Democrats slowly lost their hegemonic political position, the unions had to reconsider the strong links and be open to cooperation with other parties. Discontent also grew within the party. As the working-class share of the electorate decreased, the strong links between the party and the blue-collar unions, and with LO, the blue-collar union confederation, were increasingly perceived as an impediment to the party's chances of regaining political power and reforming the public sector in order to appeal to new groups of voters. This coincided with a growing urge for individual freedom and with discontent with the social democratic "strong society," with bureaucracy, and with statist policies within important parts of the electorate, outside the organized working class, and with strong opposition from industry toward socialist reforms initiated by the unions. A mutual need for a looser party–union relationship emerged in the 1980s (Gidlund 1988; Swenson 1991b: 385–7; Taylor 1993; Allern et.al. 2007). A clear sign was the decision at the party congress in 1987 to abolish the collective affiliation of individual union members (Gidlund 1988: 299–303; Svensson 1994: 51–8; Kjellberg 2000: 607–8).

In sum, unions have been weakened during the last few decades. Several factors work in the same direction: falling union density, less public support, a weaker link to the Social Democratic Party, a weaker central confederation, and the emergence of a European labor market based on individual legal rights rather than national collective agreements. Cooperation among unions at the Nordic or European levels cannot compensate for the lost ground.

Industrial Relations

In the 1930s, employers first initiated and then strongly adhered to centralized wage bargaining in order to make the export-sector wage-leading and keep wages down within the sheltered sector. The "solidaristic wage policy" narrowed wage differentials between skilled and unskilled workers. In the short term, it made it possible to transfer workers to the highly productive sectors. However, in the long run it resulted in growing problems related to the recruitment of skilled workers to manufacturing and especially the export industries, as improvements in skills did not result in high wages. Over time, representatives of the export industry, especially the Metal Industry (VI), in alliance with the metalworkers' union, reconsidered their support for central wage bargaining, and in 1983 they defected from central agreements (Hall and Thelen 2009: 15–16; Traxler et al. 2008).

Wage settlements shifted between the central level and the industry level during the 1980s. The ultimate break with centralized bargaining came in 1990, when the peak-level organization of the employers, the Swedish Employers' Confederation (SAF), settled the matter by turning the organization into a lobby organization (Kjellberg 2011: 85–6; Öberg et al. 2011; Lindgren 2011). The decision signaled a clear movement toward decentralized wage bargaining. The movement was temporarily delayed and moderated by the economic crisis, and an agreement was reached under the guidance of a mediation commission initiated by the government (Rehnberg-kommisionen) after a spectacular governmental intervention proposing a wage and strike freeze. The following bargaining round in 1993 was more decentralized and carried out in a pattern-bargaining mode, however accomplished in the same spirit as the preceding round, guided by a mediating negotiation group. In the following round, in 1995–6, the Metal Industry employers (VI) once again took the initiative. This bargaining round was the most uncoordinated and decentralized since the end of World War II (Elvander 2002a and 2002b; Lindgren 2011).

Thus, wage bargaining was decentralized in the 1980s and 1990s and peak organizations lost their dominant position. These changes signified a development from the three-tier to a two-tier bargaining system where the collective agreements at the national level between national unions and the employer representatives in different sectors of the economy were mostly concerned with basic aims, the detailed and concrete parts of the agreements being transferred to workplace negotiations between employers and local unions (Kjellberg 1998). Statistics clearly show this downward trend in wage coordination from the 1970s to the end of the 1990s. However, in a comparative perspective coordination remained quite high, and due to strong national unions and high union density, bargaining never became fragmented or placed on the firm level (Kenworthy 2001; Visser 2011; Lindgren 2011); see Table 45.2.

The bargaining round in 1995–6 led to great tensions in the labor market, resulting in a lack of wage moderation, uncoordinated wage demands, and wage drift. In the words of one researcher, it "was the most conflict ridden in Sweden since that of the 'great conflict' in 1980, caused great discord within the employer collective and increased awareness of

Table 45.2 Collective agreements[a] in the Swedish wage-bargaining system in the 1950s, 1980s, 1990s, and 2000–10—a simplified overview

	1950s	1980s[b]	1990s	2000–10
Central level: peak-level org.	LO-SAF-agreements	LO-TCO-Saco negotiate with employer organisations[c]	–	(Coordination within LO)
Industry level: National unions & trade associations	Implementation	Bilateral agreements	Bilateral agreements	Co-ordinated Agreements[d] & pattern-setting
Local level	Implementation	Agreements & implementation	Agreements & implementation	Agreements & implementation

Note: (a) Basic agreements and agreements on insurance schemes, codetermination and other non-wage issues excluded. (b) Alternating between central level and industry level. (c) Private employees coordinate in a cartel (PTK) from the 1970s. Separate negotiations with public employer organization. (d) Coordination through industrial agreements creating the norm for the whole labor market. Actual wage levels negotiated at local level.

the risks associated with uncoordinated wage bargaining" (Lindgren 2011: 55; Elvander 2002b).

As in the 1930s, the Social Democratic government threatened to intervene in the wage-bargaining process unless the social partners began to cooperate. The demand resulted in two important events: the Industrial Agreement in 1997 and the creation of a new mediation institute, "Medlingsinstitutet," introduced by Parliament in 2000. The first agreement in 1997 was initiated by unions within the industrial sector, led by the metalworkers, and covered almost the whole competitive sector and included both blue-collar and white-collar unions. The first round of negotiations based on this agreement was carried out in 1998 under the guidance of a private mediator, appointed by a joint committee, and with a successful outcome, establishing a wage norm in line with the EU average and without any industrial disputes. The settlement set the pattern for other sectors, which quickly concluded settlements without any threats or actions (Elvander 2002a and 2002b).

The first Industrial Agreement has been followed by several bargaining rounds and the pattern-setting by the manufacturing sector has been more or less respected from other sectors since then, in spite of growing discontent among non-manufacturing unions (Lindgren 2011). And even if LO no longer bargains, it is important to note the importance of peak organizations for the far-reaching internal coordination in recent years. The LO representative assembly has worked successfully as the nexus of this coordination (Öberg and Hallberg Adu 2009: 129–31). A new Industrial Agreement was concluded in 2011 and the subsequent figures for lost work hours owing to conflicts were almost zero (Industriavtalet 2011). Central bargaining has not been re-established, but we have witnessed the revival of coordinated capitalism.

Consequently, the decentralization and movement toward an uncoordinated labor market in the 1990s became an interregnum between two different means of wage coordination. There has been a transition from central wage bargaining to coordination through pattern bargaining. The proportion of employees covered by collective agreements is still as high as 90 percent for the whole labor market (Medlingsinstitutet 2011; Kjellberg 2011: 86).

The formerly neoliberal Conservative Party (Moderaterna), which strongly supported the movement for decentralization and liberal reforms of the labor market at the beginning of the 1990s, has shifted its policy dramatically during the last twenty years. The latest sign is that in 2012, informal talks were held with the main labor market organizations, reaching an agreement on shorter working hours in times of crisis and on aims for formal institutionalized tripartite talks and settlements in the future regarding several crucial issues affecting the labor market (LO-tidningen 2012; on political motives and implications for welfare policies, see Svensson 2013: 235–8). The employers' peak organization also seems to have stepped back from its self-chosen abdication as a representative of employers' interests. In other words, neocorporatism seems to have returned, albeit in a slightly new dress.

DISCUSSION AND CONCLUSIONS

After remarkable economic progress following World War II, the Swedish economy slowed down during the 1970s and 1980s. The economic crisis that ensued seems to have paved the way for market-liberal ideas, huge public deficits, and unstable and shifting political majorities. The crisis also opened the way for changes in the labor market regime.

The unions had less public support and their links to the Social Democratic Party were weakened. Since the 1990s, union density has declined to the levels of the 1970s. Peak organizations have lost their dominant positions and the development of a European labor market based on individual legal rights rather than national collective agreements has further weakened union organizations. Employers are still highly organized. The former peak organization was transformed into a political lobby organization. As a consequence of stronger political influence due to professionalized political lobbying, the occurrence of non-socialist governments, and the end of centralized wage bargaining, employers and employers' organizations seem to have strengthened their relative positions vis-à-vis the unions.

Industrial relations clearly changed during the period considered in this chapter. Wage settlements varied between centralized and industry level during the 1980s. The ultimate break came in 1990 when the employers' peak-level organization openly abdicated as a corporatist negotiating partner, actively aiming for decentralized wage bargaining. The bargaining round in 1995 was the most uncoordinated and decentralized since the end of World War II. It also led to great tensions in the labor market, as well as a lack of wage moderation, as uncoordinated wage demands were combined with wage drift. Exposed to a threat of governmental intervention, organizations representing the manufacturing sector took the lead and struck a new deal, the Industrial Agreement, in 1997, which set the pattern for all following bargains. A couple of years later, the government introduced a new mediation institute, "Medlingsinstitutet," to support these agreements. The first Industrial Agreement has been followed by several bargaining rounds. Pattern-setting by the manufacturing sector has been more or less respected by other sectors since then. The period of decentralization and movement toward an uncoordinated labor market in the 1990s became an interregnum between two different means of wage coordination.

One interpretation of the events during the last decades focuses on the revival of coordination and emphasizes continuity resulting from institutional complementarities. As wages increased way above acceptable levels and new conflicts developed, it became apparent that the liberal experiment was simply not compatible with existing institutions (Lindgren 2011: 56). According to proponents of this school of thought, market forces (as well as ideological swings) make a difference, but differently in different "systems." Globalization has an impact, but the direction and size of its effects are determined in the interplay between actors and institutions, creating divergent trajectories under different institutional setups (Svensson 2002; Oskarsson 2003; Hall and Thelen 2009). The cross-class alliance between organized labor and capital that emerged in the 1930s, formerly characterized as social corporatism, organized capitalism, or negotiated solidarism, has reemerged in a new, modernized version where Sweden still seems to be a typical coordinated market economy. The Industrial Agreement can be seen as a new cross-class coalition between the partners within the manufacturing sector, leading to the revival of coordination through new pattern-setting mechanisms.

This interpretation is disputed, however. Some researchers find the focus on the formal institutions misleading. Coordination in Sweden today is minimalist and concerned only with basic procedures and principles. Actual wages are set locally or even individually, and the national agreements permit "wide discretion at the firm" (Baccaro and Howell 2011: 544). Strong unions have so far been influential in wage determination, and they have mitigated the effects of the decentralization. However, the unions are becoming weaker both with regard to local activity and coverage. Moreover, union density is declining and the changes to the unemployment insurance rules have reinforced this downward spiral. According to this interpretation, "recent developments in both institutional functioning and organizational capacity constitute a neoliberal turn for Swedish industrial relations" (Baccaro and Howell 2011: 545; cf. Howell and Kolins Givan 2011).

References

Alexopoulos, M. and Cohen, J. (2003). "Centralised Wage Bargaining and Structural Change in Sweden," *European Review of Economic History* 7: 331–66.

Allern, E. H, Aylott, N., and Christiansen, H. J. (2007). "Social Democrats and Trade Unions in Scandinavia," *European Journal of Political Research* 46: 607–35.

Åmark, K. (1988). "Sammanhållning och intressepolitik," in K. Misgeld, K. Molin, and K. Åmark (eds), *Socialdemokratins samhälle: SAP och Sverige under 100 år*. Stockholm: Tiden, 57–82.

Andersen, S. K. (2006). "Nordic Metal Trade Unions on the Move: Responses to Globalization and Europeanization," *European Journal of Industrial Relations* 12/1: 29–47.

Baccaro, L. and Howell, C. (2011). "A Common Neoliberal Trajectory: The Transformation of Industrial Relations in Advanced Capitalism," *Politics & Society* 39/4: 521–63.

Bonoli, G. (2010). "The Political Economy of Active Labor-Market Policy," *Politics & Society* 38/4: 435–57.

Elvander, N. (2002a). "The New Swedish Regime for Collective Bargaining and Conflict Resolution," *European Journal of Industrial Relations* 8/2: 197–216.

Elvander, N. (2002b). "The Labour Market Regimes in the Nordic Countries," *Scandinavian Political Studies* 25/2: 117–37.

Fulcher, J. (1991). *Labour Movements, Employers, and the State: Conflict and Co-operation in Britain and Sweden*. Oxford: Clarendon Press.

Gidlund, G. (1988). "Folkrörelsepartiet och den politiska styrelsen: SAP:s organisationsutveckling," in K. Misgeld, K. Molin, and K. Åmark (eds), *Socialdemokratins samhälle: SAP och Sverige under 100 år*. Stockholm: Tiden, 282–310.

Hall, P. A. (1999). "The Political Economy of Europe in an Era of Interdependence," in H. P. Kitchelt, G. Lange, D. Marks, and J. Stephens (eds), *Continuity and Change in Contemporary Capitalism*. Cambridge: Cambridge University Press, 135–63.

Hall, P. A. and Soskice, D. (2001). "An Introduction to Varieties of Capitalism," in P. A. Hall and D. Soskice (eds), *Varieties of Capitalism: The Institutional Foundations of Comparative Advantage*. Oxford: Oxford University Press, 1–68.

Hall, P. A. and Thelen, K. (2009). "Institutional Change in Varieties of Capitalism," *Socio-Economic Review* 7: 7–34.

Holmlund, B. and Lundborg, P. (1998). "Wage Bargaining, Union Membership, and the Organization of Unemployment Insurance," *Labour Economics* 6: 397–415.

Howell, C. and Kolins Givan, R. (2011). "Rethinking Institutions and Institutional Change in European Industrial Relations", *British Journal of Industrial Relations* 49/2: 231–55.

Industriavtalet (2011). Industrins samarbetsavtal och förhandlingsavtal.

Iversen, T. (1998). "Wage Bargaining, Hard Money and Economic Performance: Theory and Evidence for Organized Market Economies," *British Journal of Political Science* 28: 31–61.

Johansson, J. (2003). "Mid-Level Officials as Policy Makers: Anti-Corporatist Policy Change in the Swedish Employers' Confederation, 1982–1985," *Scandinavian Political Studies* 26/4: 307–25.

Katzenstein, P. (1985). *Small States in World Markets: Industrial Policy in Europe*. Ithaca and London: Cornell University Press.

Kenworthy, L. (2001). "Wage-Setting Measures," *World Politics* 54 (October): 57–98.

Kjellberg, A. (1998). "Sweden: Restoring the Model?" in A. Ferner and R. Hyman (eds), *Changing Industrial Relations in Europe*. Oxford: Blackwell.

Kjellberg, A. (2000). "Sweden," in B. Ebbinghaus and J. Visser (eds), *The Societies of Europe: Trade Unions in Western Europe Since 1945*. London: Macmillan.

Kjellberg, A. (2011). "The Decline in Swedish Union Density Since 2007," *Nordic Journal of Working life Studies* 1/1: 67–93.

Lewin, L. (1994). "The Rise and Decline of Corporatism: The Case of Sweden," *European Journal of Political Research* 26/1: 59–79.

Lindgren, K. O. (2011). "The Variety of Capitalism in Sweden and Finland," in U. Becker (ed.), *The Changing Political Economies of Small West European Countries*. Amsterdam: Amsterdam University Press, 45–72.

Lindvall, J. and Rothstein, B. (2006). "Sweden: The Fall of the Strong State," *Scandinavian Political Studies* 29/1: 47–63.

Lindvall, J. and Sebring, J. (2005). "Policy Reform and the Decline of Corporatism in Sweden," *West European Politics* 28/5: 1057–74.

LO-rapport (2007). "Röster om facket och jobbet: Ungdomar och facket." Stockholm: Landsorganisationen i Sverige.

LO-tidningen (2012). "Hemliga samtal med parterna," May 27.

Magnusson, L. (2006). "The Swedish Model in Historical Context," *Kobe University Economic Review* 52: 1–8.

Medlingsinstitutet. "Avtalsrörelsen och lönebildningen 2011", Medlingsinstitutet 2012; "Avtalsrörelsen och lönebildningen 2012", Medlingsinstitutet 2013.

Meidner, R. (1986). "Swedish Union Strategies towards Structural Change," *Economic and Industrial Democracy* 7: 85–97.

Öberg, P. O. and Hallberg Adu, K. (2009). "The Deceptive Juncture: The Temptation of Attractive Explanations and the Reality of Political Life," in L. Magnusson and J. Ottosson (eds), *The Evolution of Path Dependence*. Cheltenham, Edward Elgar, 108–38.

Öberg, P. O. and Svensson, T. (2012). "Civil Society and Deliberative Democracy: Have Voluntary Organisations Faded from National Public Politics?" *Scandinavian Political Studies* 35/3: 246–71.

Öberg, P. O., Svensson, T., Munk Christiansen, P., Sonne Nørgaard, A., Rommetvedt, H., and Thesen, G. (2011). "Disrupted Exchange and Declining Corporatism," *Government and Opposition* 46/3: 365–91.

Oskarsson, S. (1997). *Påverka och påverkas: 1994 års reformering av arbetslöshetsförsäkringen*. Uppsala universitet: PISA-projektets rapporter.

Oskarsson, S. (2003). *The Fate of Organized Labor*. Uppsala: Acta Upsaliensis Universitatis.

Petersson, O. (1991). "Democracy and Power in Sweden," *Scandinavian Political Studies* 14/2: 173–91.

Pontusson, J. (1993). "The Comparative Politics of Labor-Initiated Reforms: Swedish Cases of Success and Failure," *Comparative Political Studies* 25/4: 548–78.

Rothstein, B. (1990). "Marxism, Institutional Analysis, and Working Class Power: The Swedish Case," *Politics & Society* 18/3: 317–45.

Rothstein, B. and Bergström, J. (1999). *Korporatismens fall och den svenska modellens kris*. Stockholm: SNS Förlag.

Scruggs, L. (2002). "The Ghent System and Union Membership in Europe," *Political Research Quarterly* 55/2: 275–97.

Svensson, T. (1994). *Socialdemokratins dominans*. Uppsala: Acta Universitatis Upsaliensis.

Svensson, T. (2002). "Globalisation, Marketization and Power: The Swedish Case of Institutional Change," *Scandinavian Political Studies* 25/3: 197–229.

Svensson, T. (2013). "Sweden," in J. Kelly and C. Frege (eds), *Comparative Employment Relations*. Basingstoke: Palgrave Macmillan, 227–44.

Svensson, T. and Öberg, P. O. (2002). "Labour Market Organisations' Participation in Swedish Public Policy-Making," *Scandinavian Political Studies* 25/4: 295–315.

Svensson, T. and Öberg, P. O. (2005). "How Are Coordinated Market Economies Coordinated?" *West European Politics* 28/5: 1075–1100.

Svensson, T., Mabuchi, M., and Kamikawa, R. (2006). "Managing the Bank-System Crisis in Coordinated Market Economies," *Governance* 19/1: 43–74.

Swenson, P. (1991a). "Bringing Capital Back In, or Social Democracy Reconsidered," *World Politics* 43 (July): 513–44.

Swenson, P. (1991b). "Labor and the Limits of the Welfare State: The Politics of Intraclass Conflict and Cross-Class Alliances in Sweden and West Germany," *Comparative Politics* 23/4: 379–99.

Swenson, P. and Pontusson, J. (2000). "The Swedish Employer Offensive against Centralized Wage Bargaining," in T. Iversen, J. Pontusson, and D. Soskice (eds), *Unions, Employers, and Central Banks*. Cambridge: Cambridge University Press, 77–106.

Taylor, A. J. (1993). "Trade Unions and the Politics of Social Democratic Renewal," *West European Politics* 16/1: 133–55.

Thelen, K. (2001). "Varieties of Labor Politics in the Developed Democracies," in P. A. Hall and D. Soskice (eds), *Varieties of Capitalism: The Institutional Foundations of Comparative Advantage*. Oxford: Oxford University Press, 71–103.

Traxler, F., Brandl, B., and Glassner, V. (2008). "Pattern Bargaining: An Investigation into its Agency, Context and Evidence," *British Journal of Industrial Relations* 46/1: 33–58.

Törnqvist, C. (1999). "The Decentralization of Industrial Relations: The Swedish Case in Comparative Perspective," *European Journal of Industrial Relations* 5/1: 71–87.

Wallerstein, M. and Golden, M. (2000). "Postwar Wage Setting in the Nordic Countries," in T. Iversen, J. Pontusson, and D. Soskice (eds), *Unions, Employers and Central Banks*. Cambridge: Cambridge University Press, 107–37.

Visser, J. (1996). "Corporatism beyond Repair? Industrial Relations in Sweden," in J. Van Ruysseveldt and J. Visser (eds), *Industrial Relations in Europe*. London: Sage, 175–204.

Visser, J. (2011). "ICTWSS: Database on Institutional Characteristics of Trade Unions, Wage Setting, State Intervention and Social Pacts in 34 Countries between 1960 and 2007," Version 3. Amsterdam: University of Amsterdam Institute for Advanced Labour Studies. Available at <http://www.uva-aias.net/208>.

Woolfson, C. and Sommers, J. (2006). "Labour Mobility in Construction: European Implications of the Laval un Partneri Dispute with Swedish Labour," *European Journal of Industrial Relations* 12/1: 49–68.

SECTION 10

POLICY-MAKING IN SWEDEN

SECTION EDITOR
CARL DAHLSTRÖM

CHAPTER 46

···

INTRODUCTION

Policy-Making in Sweden

···

CARL DAHLSTRÖM

In his book *Modern Social Politics in Britain and Sweden*, Hugh Heclo (1974: 14) writes that since the 1930s Sweden has "stood out as an oasis of good sense." Although Heclo is specifically discussing social policy-making, his comment probably captures a view more generally held by scholars of comparative politics. For example, Olof Petersson notes in his chapter that Sweden's policy process often is portrayed as both rational and consensual by outside observers.

Two features of Swedish policy-making have been particularly important for the emerging of the idea of a consensual and rational process. The first, and most well known, is the corporatist policy-making style, which, at least up to the 1990s, guaranteed policy influence from interest organizations generally, and labor market organizations particularly. The second feature is the commissions of inquiry and referral systems. Both Öberg's and Petersson's chapters discuss the strong emphasis on the preparation of policy proposals in Sweden. Almost all complicated policy proposals are first investigated by a commission of inquiry and then sent to agencies and organizations, both private and public, for referral, before the government bill is sent to Parliament. These systems help to gear the policy process towards problem-solving, and are important for building broad support among specialists as well as parties and organizations.

Two other important characteristics of the Swedish policy process concern coordination and the creation of party-political support. The cabinet always prepares policy proposals. Under the Social Democratic minority governments, coordination was, for natural reasons, not an issue within the Government Offices. Instead, the role of Parliament and especially Parliament's standing committees were important arenas for building support for policy proposals. This has, however, changed over time, and different coordination mechanisms have developed within the Government Offices, which from time to time de facto have decreased Parliament's influence.

The chapters in this section describe these four features of the Swedish policy-making process and pay special attention to changes over time.

In the first chapter, Thomas Persson describes policy-making processes and coordination under minority and majority rule in the Government Offices. He shows how the pressure for policy coordination within the government has increased over time, for both single-party and coalition governments. Social Democratic single-party governments in the past could get policy proposals through Parliament through ad hoc agreements, because of the marginalization of the Communists (today the Left Party) and conflicts between the center-right parties. During the 1990s, both of these conditions changed and thus the Social Democrats had to develop a more formalized system for policy coordination with parties outside the government, especially after they returned to government in 1994. Persson also describes the internal coordination mechanisms used by the center-right coalition governments, and the learning process among the center-right parties toward a more centralized, and probably more well-functioning, coordination of policy proposals.

Olof Petersson's chapter "Rational Politics: Commissions of Inquiry and the Referral System in Sweden" studies the unique system of commissions of inquiry and the referral system associated with these commissions and with government bills. He describes the historical roots of these systems, their functions, and current trends. He concludes that, although the formal rules indicate stability, there are also signs of change. Perhaps most importantly, Petersson shows that broad commissions of inquiry, that also involve politicians from opposition parties and interest organizations, have almost disappeared. As a consequence, commissions of inquiry are today much less of an arena for negotiation and consensus-seeking than they used to be.

This observation is confirmed by Per-Ola Öberg in the following chapter. Öberg studies the close connections between interest groups and the state in Sweden, even before democracy was introduced, but he also notes the declining influence of interest organizations, both formally and informally. The historically very strong institutionalized involvement of interest representation at almost all stages of the policy process has indeed weakened over the last 20 years. He warns, however, against drawing the conclusion that interest groups do not influence policy-making in Sweden anymore. In comparative terms, the organized interests are still strong, but the channels through which they operate are increasingly directed toward lobbying and media.

In the final chapter in this section, Ingvar Mattson analyzes the policy-making process in the Swedish parliament, the Riksdag, and he pays special attention to the parliament's standing committees. He shows that although Parliament and its standing committees are strong in comparative terms, inferences from this should not be made too far. There are relatively small amendments to the government budget bill, especially after the reformation of the budget process in 1997, and most government bills are approved by the Riksdag. He notes that Parliament and its standing committees have had special significance during the Social Democratic minority governments before 1995, and during the center-right minority coalition governments before 2006. There are, however, also periods when the Riksdag has played a less important role, and most policy deals have already been made before the government bill is sent to Parliament. Mattson points out that because of the stable division between the political left (including the greens) and the political right, the importance of the committees as grounds for working out com-promises has decreased after the center-right coalition came to power in 2006.

REFERENCE

Heclo, H. (1974). *Modern Social Politics in Britain and Sweden*. New Haven: Yale University Press.

....

CHAPTER 47

POLICY COORDINATION UNDER MINORITY AND MAJORITY RULE

....

THOMAS PERSSON

INTRODUCTION

....

CURRENT scholarship suggests that policy coordination varies more between different countries than between different types of government within a given country (Blondel and Müller-Rommel 1993). However, as this chapter will show, policy coordination may also vary significantly within a stable political system such as Sweden's. In Sweden, different mechanisms for policy coordination have been utilized by minority and majority governments, and by single-party and coalition governments, respectively. This chapter analyzes patterns of policy coordination at the national level in Sweden over recent decades. While policy coordination is often analyzed as a strictly administrative problem (see, e.g., Gulick 1937), this chapter also highlights the strong *political* dimension inherent in policy coordination.

If we are to understand how political parties coordinate policy in Sweden, we must bear several features of contemporary Swedish politics in mind. First, the Social Democrats played a dominant role in Swedish politics for long periods, and were able to form single-party governments despite having only minority support in parliament. Since the 1990s, however, policy coordination with parties outside the government (referred to here as *external policy coordination*) has become increasingly important for the Social Democrats to secure parliamentary support (Bergman and Bolin 2011; see also the chapters by Bäck and Bergman, and Aylott in this volume). Since the 1970s, moreover, the country has experienced recurrent periods of coalition government, where center-right parties have been able to form both minority and majority coalitions. This development has created strong pressure for policy coordination inside the government (referred to here as *internal policy coordination*).

Second, governments in the Swedish administrative model work in a dualistic environment. The Government Offices—consisting of the Prime Minister's Office and the ministries—are separated organizationally from the central government's administrative agencies. Thus, only a small percentage of civil servants work in the ministries; the vast majority are employed by semi-autonomous government agencies (Larsson and Bäck 2008; see also the chapters by Hall and Ehn in this volume). Additionally, there is a general ban on ministerial rule—meaning that individual ministers are not allowed to determine how agencies decide in particular cases (Wockelberg 2003). This administrative model implies a strong need for policy coordination between the Government Offices and the semi-autonomous government agencies (*vertical policy coordination*)—a need that has been accentuated by Sweden's accession to the European Union.

Third, there are few formal rules regarding policy coordination among government ministries (referred to here as *horizontal coordination*). The Instrument of Government (*Regeringsformen*) provides little information on how government policies are to be prepared, stating only that Government Offices shall exist in order to prepare decisions and assist government ministers in their other duties. In fact, what has evolved over the years are Government Offices composed of a small group of political appointees, complemented by a permanent and merit-based civil-service staff (see also the chapter by Jacobsson and Sundström in this volume). While the civil-service staff work according to procedures and administrative practices that are often difficult to change, political appointees vary with changes in the government, and may develop different solutions for internal policy coordination (Larsson 1986; Persson 2003; Premfors and Sundström 2007).

This chapter analyzes mechanisms for *political* rather than administrative policy coordination, both inside and outside the Government Offices. It looks at how governments of different types have coordinated their policies, and focuses on the mechanisms used by single-party minority governments and by coalition minority and majority governments—the most common types of government in Sweden. For example, it examines the internal coordination mechanisms used by center-right coalition governments in the 1970s and early 1980s, and compares them with those used by the Bildt government in the 1990s and the Reinfeldt governments in the 2000s and 2010s. It then looks at external coordination mechanisms among different governments, comparing the less formalized policy deals of Social Democratic minority governments in the 1980s with their more formalized deals during the 1990s and 2000s.

The chapter is structured as follows. In the first section I define and discuss the concept of policy coordination in relation to prior research, and with regard to Sweden specifically. In the second I look at experiences of policy coordination in Sweden under minority and majority rule, and both single-party and coalition governments. The third and final section of the chapter offers some general observations on current trends and challenges for policy coordination in Sweden.

CENTRAL POLICY COORDINATION—THE CASE OF SWEDEN

Many regard coordination as a necessary part of modern government. Public-sector expansion and greater specialization have increased the demand for coordination among public administrative offices and agencies. New Public Management (NPM) reforms—adopted primarily to promote efficiency in public organizations—have led to greater administrative fragmentation and autonomy from central government control (Verhoest et al. 2007; Bouckaert et al. 2010). In the face of diminished political control, governments have resorted to a variety of measures aimed at restoring their prior authority over subordinate administrative bodies. They have also sought to enhance horizontal coordination and administrative coherence (Pollitt 2003; Christensen and Lægreid 2007; Peters 2013).

Notwithstanding the great importance attached to the coordination of government policy, the concept of policy coordination—while "used with almost universal approbation"—is "less often defined" (Peters 1998: 296). While policy coordination is a commonly discussed topic in political science and public administration literature (see, e.g., Six 2004), there is no commonly agreed definition of policy coordination that can be easily applied in an analytical study of central government administration. Before proceeding further, therefore, we must define what the term "coordination" means, and in the context of governmental operations specifically.

In a general sense, coordination refers to a cooperative effort that enables the different parts of a complex body, such as the central government, to work together effectively. Coordination may refer both to a process through which decisions in an organization are brought together to an end-state, and to an outcome of that process. For purposes of this analysis, it would seem better to focus on the process or organization of coordination, rather than to try to evaluate its effectiveness or extent (see, e.g., Hustedt and Tiessen 2006). Hence, coordination refers to *the instruments and mechanisms used by political and administrative actors to enact and to carry out coherent and jointly approved government policies.* The extent to which polices are in fact coherent and jointly approved is not analyzed here, but rather the way in which cooperative efforts inside and outside the central administration are organized to achieve these goals. Furthermore, the focus is mainly on policy coordination after a government has been formed (although the way parties work together before an election affects the nature of their post-election cooperation).

Another thing to keep in mind is that coordination in the public sector is both an administrative and a political process. Given the political nature of policy coordination, this chapter devotes more attention to political coordination than to administrative coordination. To quote Döhler et al. (2007: 9), "ministers and their departments not only represent different sectoral and increasingly crosscutting interests but are also linked either to different parties or party factions with policy preferences of their own."

Hence, *internal* policy coordination—inside the government—is especially important in coalition governments, as the different parties that make it up have to agree on policy. Single-party governments, on the other hand, only need to coordinate policy within their own party. A minority government may also need to engage in external coordination—outside the government—when seeking support from other parties in Parliament for its policies; by contrast, a majority government can rule more or less on its own. Governments of different types, then, often have different needs for coordination.

Furthermore, we must distinguish between short-term daily coordination and more long-term policy commitments. The mechanisms for dealing with everyday coordination are highly formalized, even though they are not spelled out in the Constitution. The Swedish administrative model implies a strong need for coordination, both horizontally (among ministries within the Government Offices) and vertically (between the Government Offices and the semi-autonomous government agencies). Sweden thus has a unique division between fairly small ministries on the one hand, and semi-autonomous agencies under these ministries on the other. As mentioned above, individual ministers are not allowed to determine how agencies decide in particular cases (Wockelberg 2003; see also the chapter by Hall in this volume).

The Government Offices in Sweden form a single integrated public authority, comprising the Prime Minister's Office, ten line ministries, and the Office for Administrative Affairs. These ministries and offices are divided in turn into approximately 100 units, each with its own special tasks to perform. In addition, Sweden's Permanent Representation to the European Union in Brussels is an extended arm of the Swedish Government, and functions as a miniature version of the Government Offices. The number of ministers or ministries is not subject to regulation. It is up to the government to decide how the various duties are to be divided up. The Government Offices employ about 4600 employees, of whom only some 200 are political appointees (Premfors and Sundström 2007; see also the chapter by Jacobsson and Sundström in this volume). However, there is a long-term trend toward a greater number of political appointees in the Government Offices, which has helped to reinforce central political control (Dahlström and Pierre 2011).

Swedish ministers make very few decisions on their own, beyond those concerning the internal organization and administration of their own ministries. Almost all government decisions are made collectively—a marked contrast to the situation in most other countries, where ministers make most decisions independently. The strong commitment of the Swedish government to collective decision-making is institutionalized through a *joint preparation procedure* (*gemensam beredning*) whenever a decision involves more than one ministry. Moreover, it is common practice to circulate all government bills among ministries, as well as responses to questions raised in Parliament and instructions to government commissions of inquiry through a *joint drafting procedure* (*delning*) (Larsson and Bäck 2008: 179–80). These procedures ensure that all government decisions are prepared jointly and that all relevant ministries are involved. Many decisions can be settled through coordination between different administrative levels in the Government Offices, although more contentious issues need to be settled through political coordination, and ultimately by the entire cabinet in an informal session (*allmän beredning*). Formal government decisions are made at weekly cabinet meetings (*regeringssammanträden*) and on the basis of ministerial unanimity (Larsson 1986; Persson 2003).

The requirement of collective decision-making in all government matters creates a need for an effective coordination process in the Government Offices. In practice, the Ministry of Finance has a special position in this process. Any reform that involves spending public funds gives the Finance Minister leverage in negotiations. In addition, however, the Ministry of Finance often intervenes in the affairs of other ministries even when purely budgetary matters are not at issue. Ultimately, however, it is the Prime Minister who settles conflicts and decides on contentious issues. The Prime Minister's Office has grown stronger over time. In part, this has been the result of an organizational strengthening of said office. The Prime Minister did not have his own office initially. In the early 1950s, however, Prime Minister Tage Erlander hired a small number of employees to staff his office. The Prime Minister's Office was then formed in the 1960s, and its staff has increased in the years since (Larsson 1986; Persson 2003).

A number of measures have been taken over the years to improve the government's coordination capability. Several commissions of inquiry have highlighted problems, such as strong ministerial cultures, a lack of coordination among ministries, and weak political guidance in the Government Offices. Many reforms have been implemented to remedy or ameliorate these problems. One of the most significant was carried out in 1997. It transformed the Government Offices into a single authority under the leadership of the Prime Minister. Before that, all ministries had been separate authorities under the leadership of their own minister (Elder and Page 2000; Persson 2003; Erlandsson 2007; Premfors and Sundström 2007). Furthermore, the Government Offices are currently undertaking a reform—the so-called RK-Styr reform—in an effort to improve their internal coordination. The aim of this reform is to facilitate coordination among line ministries, thereby enhancing the ability of the government to direct its subordinate agencies (Dahlström and Pierre 2011).

The task of coordination has furthermore grown in complexity, due to Sweden's accession to the European Union. The central administration, which only needed to coordinate its domestic policy-making previously, must now defend its policy proposals in Brussels. It must also ensure that coherent policies are presented at both national and European levels. EU membership seems to impose demands for better policy coordination on all member states. Since Sweden's entry into the Union in 1995, EU-related policy-making and coordination have come increasingly under the direct control of the Government Offices. Initially, EU affairs were coordinated by the Ministry for Foreign Affairs. Over the years, however, there has been a steady transfer of responsibilities in this area to the Prime Minister's Office. Indeed, EU affairs have increasingly become domestic affairs (Persson 2007; Johansson 2008; Johansson and Raunio 2010). The strengthening of the Prime Minister's Office in this area accords with international trends, as does the corresponding weakening of the Ministry for Foreign Affairs (Kassim, Peters, and Wright 2000). The ongoing internationalization of political and economic life—not least through European integration—has also contributed to a more prominent position for the Prime Minister (Persson 2007; Johansson and Tallberg 2010).

To meet rising demands for policy coordination, Sweden has established special administrative bodies with responsibility for cross-departmental EU coordination, along with several ad hoc constellations and informal networks of civil servants. Despite these reforms, however, EU-related matters are generally handled in the same manner as other policy issues in the Government Offices—i.e., all ministers are responsible for their own policy area, while overall responsibility lies with the government as a whole. The Prime Minister's Office concentrates on issues of particular political weight, and on resolving inter-ministerial disputes (Larue 2006). It has been argued, however, that EU affairs have involved significant departures from the Swedish administrative model. EU issues are not generally considered government affairs, which means that decisions on such questions are not made collectively. This gives individual ministers far more influence within their own subfields than is normally the case (*Förvaltningskommittén* 2008).

The weak regulation of coordination processes by the Swedish constitution gives wide leeway to each government to develop different coordination mechanisms. Therefore, each government utilizes a variety of such mechanisms. The particular ones it uses tend to reflect what type of government it is: minority or majority, single-party or coalition. That is the subject of the next section.

COORDINATION UNDER MINORITY AND MAJORITY RULE

In Swedish politics, the parties have typically banded together into two blocs, with the Social Democrats, the Left Party, and (since the late 1990s) the Green Party making up the "socialist bloc"; and the Center Party, the Liberal Party, the Christian Democrats, and the Conservatives making up the "bourgeois bloc" (see also the chapters by Bäck and Bergman and by Möller in this volume). However, the Social Democratic Party has long dominated the scene, having held power for nearly seven decades of the nearly century-long era of parliamentary government in Sweden. Social Democratic dominance was due in part to the Left Party's passive support in Parliament, and in part to serious divisions among the center-right parties. It was considered impossible for the Left Party to unite with the bourgeois parties in order to force the resignation of a Social Democratic government. The typical Swedish government, accordingly, has been a single-party minority government.

Since the end of World War II, the center-right parties have only been able to form coalition governments on three occasions: 1976–82, 1991–4, and from 2006 –14. Thus, a strong correlation exists between government type and government party composition. The "rule" is that the bourgeois bloc forms a coalition government (sometimes with majority support in Parliament, but usually with just a minority), while the Social

Democrats form a single-party minority government. During the decades since World War II, the Social Democrats have had a majority for only two years: 1968–70. Other rare exceptions to the typical pattern include a short-lived single-party government consisting only of the small Liberal Party in 1978, a majority coalition between the Social Democrats and the Center Party in the 1950s, and a minority coalition between the Social Democrats and the Green Party in 2014 (Hermansson and Persson 2010a).

SINGLE-PARTY MINORITY (AND MAJORITY) GOVERNMENTS

During the long period of Social Democratic rule, policy agreements with other parties were usually made on an ad hoc basis in parliamentary committees. Social Democratic governments coordinated their policies from within the Government Offices and within the party. They could then find support in parliament for their policies from either the Left Party or any of the center-right parties (which found it hard to unite among themselves). In this way, Social Democratic governments could orchestrate major policy reforms—e.g. the pension reform of the 1950s, the wage-earners' funds in the 1980s, the tax reform of the early 1990s—despite their minority status.

Beginning in the 1980s, however, the Left Party started to act less as a loyal supporter of the Social Democrats. As a result, it became increasingly important for the government to seek support for its policies in advance. This became especially evident in 1990, when the government was in trouble due to an overheated economy and a lack of parliamentary support for structural economic reforms. The government proposed a crisis programme consisting of a freeze on wages, rents, and municipal income taxes, as well as restrictions on the right to strike. The Left Party rejected this program, however, and showed that it was now prepared to bring down a Social Democratic government. In February 1990, Ingvar Carlsson's government resigned (although some weeks later he was appointed Prime Minister once again). This event had an important consequence for subsequent Social Democratic minority governments: increasingly, they would need to resort to external policy coordination in order to secure parliamentary support for their policies.

When the Social Democrats regained power in 1994, after three years of bourgeois rule, the government was able to rely briefly on the Left Party to furnish parliamentary support for its fiscal policies. In 1995, however, following a deep economic recession, the Social Democrats sought support from the Center Party in order to carry out comprehensive fiscal consolidation. The two parties launched an emergency program, and agreed on far-reaching budget cuts. However, "the arrangement, or any of the specific policy agreements the parties made, was not based on any formal contract, but on personal trust and the specifics of each separate negotiation" (Bale and Bergman 2006a: 432). Cooperation between the Social Democrats and the Center Party lasted until 1997, embracing not just economic and fiscal policy but defence policy as well. This cooperation meant that, for a short time, far-reaching political agreements were reached across the line separating the two blocs (which does not often happen in Sweden).

However, the Social Democrats and the Center Party did not form a coalition government. Instead, in order to minimize problems of coordination, members of the Center Party elite were hired as political advisors at the Ministry of Finance and the Ministry of Defense, alongside other politically appointed civil servants (Bergman 2000; Lagercrantz 2005). This practice—giving positions within the Government Offices to a support party—was an innovation in Swedish politics. Its purpose was to improve policy coordination. Placing high officials from a party outside the government within the Government Offices set an important precedent in the development of Swedish "contract parliamentarism" (Bale and Bergman 2006a; Dahlström and Pierre 2011; see also the chapter by Aylott in this volume).

In the election of 1998, both the Social Democrats and the Center Party suffered from this cooperation. Yet the Social Democrats managed to stay in power, by turning to the Left Party and the Greens for support. In this case too, there was no formal coalition at the level of the cabinet. In one respect, however, the arrangement differed from that made with the Center Party earlier: this time, the cooperating parties did not reach any agreement to place officials from the support parties within the Government Offices. Instead, the three parties agreed to cooperate in five specific areas: economic and fiscal policy; employment policy; income distribution; gender equality; and environmental policy. They also stated their intention to work together for the full electoral period. The agreement was announced in a media release in October 1998, but it was never formalized in any explicit contract.

Agreements were reached in all of these areas through negotiation. This was particularly evident in the case of the budget, where the negotiating position of the support parties was relatively strong. However, the government and the support parties were not on an equal footing during these negotiations. It was not just that the government had greater resources than the support parties; the latter also had no political advisors in any of the government ministries. This meant they entered the policy-making process at a late stage. Hence, a "coordination group"—consisting of the Greens' party secretary, the Left Party's chief budget negotiator, and an advisor to the Prime Minister from the ruling Social Democratic Party—was created in order to facilitate political cooperation (Bale and Bergman 2006b).

The support parties were not happy with this arrangement. As the election of 2002 approached, the support parties made it clear that they wanted a change. The Left Party sought influence in a wider range of policy areas, and the Greens wanted to be part of the government. The Social Democrats rejected the latter's demands for ministerial posts, however. Hence, the 2002 election resulted in a post-election agreement between the Social Democratic minority government, the Left Party, and the Green Party. The three parties agreed to cooperate, but without establishing a formal coalition. The agreement featured a 121-point political program, as well as a contract to create a coordination office (*samarbetskansli*) in the Ministry of Finance composed of six appointed officials—two from each party. (These concessions were even more far-reaching than those made to the Center Party in 1995–7.) In addition, the support parties were each allowed to appoint up to six political advisors to other ministries. Thus, each political party was allowed a total of eight full-time political advisors (Ullström 2005; Olsen 2007).

This new form of "contract parliamentarism" gave the support parties greater access to information and a greater ability to set the agenda within the Government Offices. Nevertheless, they still lacked the formal power to make government decisions. The arrangement fell somewhere between a legislative coalition and an executive coalition (Bale and Bergman 2006a and 2006b). From a democratic point of view, this is a problematic form of parliamentarism. The support parties in such a case are not formally part of the government; thus, they cannot be held accountable for government decisions. At the same time, they *do* have considerable influence over the political agenda and government policy.

This form of cooperation between a minority government and its support parties has enabled the Social Democrats to secure government power without having to share ministerial posts. The support parties, for their part, have gained influence over policy without formally being in power. Since the 1990s, accordingly, minority governments have found external policy coordination more and more necessary for securing the requisite support in parliament. As the years have passed, moreover, the structures embodying such external coordination have become increasingly formalized and institutionalized (Bale and Bergman 2006a, 2006b).

Where internal coordination in single-party governments is concerned, Sweden differs from most other countries with similar systems, in that it has no formal *government committees* or *inner cabinets* (Andeweg and Timmermans 2008). There have been a few exceptions to this, as in the 1970s, when Social Democratic governments set up something similar to a government committee—consisting of the Minister of Finance, the Minister of Labor, and the Minister of Industry (thus known as the *troika*)—to discuss issues relating to economic growth and employment. However, these earlier bodies also included ministerial state secretaries, as well as the Director-General of the National Labor Market Board; thus, they were not true government committees (Persson 2003: 239).

The Carlsson government (1988–91) took further steps toward establishing government committees. It created an informal preparatory structure spanning three policy areas: welfare, growth, and foreign affairs. These government committees (*regeringskommittér*) consisted of a couple of ministers each, and there was a management team under the Prime Minister's own supervision, which can be likened to an *inner cabinet* (*inre kabinett*). This experiment with government committees and an inner cabinet disappeared after the center-right coalition won the election of 1991, and it did not reappear when Carlsson regained power in 1994. Later, the Social Democratic government of Göran Persson (1996–2006) used ad hoc groups for internal government coordination and for dealing with specific problems, such as labor supply, demographic issues, and sustainable growth. Prime Minister Persson wanted to avoid creating an inner cabinet similar to the one formed under Carlsson (Persson 2003: 238–42). An inner cabinet would be re-established, however, when a new center-right government was formed following the 2006 election, as described in the next section.

Single-party *majority* governments, finally, are extremely rare in Sweden. A government of this kind has been formed only once, after the election of 1968. It lasted only two years, and involved no new forms of policy coordination.

COALITION MINORITY AND MAJORITY GOVERNMENTS

In 1976, after 44 years of Social Democratic rule, the center-right parties managed to form a majority coalition government. In a coalition government, all of the participating parties must agree on all decisions made; accordingly, internal policy coordination is essential in cases of this kind. Since the 1970s, such coordination has become more and more institutionalized.

When the center-right government was formed in 1976, the leaders of the parties within it were each given a group of staff within the Government Offices, known as coordination offices (*samordningskanslier*). The task of these political advisors was to coordinate cabinet business. However, this innovation did not in fact facilitate effective coordination. Instead, it created an environment of distrust and excessive surveillance. It also tended to worsen political conflict among the parties in the coalition (Larsson 1986; Bergman 2000). It is clear from prior research that the center-right parties were never well coordinated—neither during their term in power nor before the election of 1976 (Bergström 1987). A bourgeois coalition government was forced to resign in 1978, due to interparty disputes (over nuclear power), and again in 1981 (over tax policy). The center-right finally lost power in the election of 1982 (see also the chapter by Möller in this volume).

To prevent a repeat of these past experiences, the four center-right parties determined to manage their joint affairs more effectively. Prior to the election of 1991, the Conservative Party and the Liberals agreed on a joint manifesto; and they managed to convince the other two parties—the Center Party and the Christian Democrats—to support it subsequently. The bourgeois parties then won the election and proceeded to form a minority government. Once the government was formed, a more integrated coordination system was set up within the Prime Minister's Office, consisting of political advisors and a state secretary from each of the four parties. It is important to note, however, that each coalition party had its own coordination office (*samordningskansli*). This system seems to have worked reasonably well at managing policy coordination, especially as compared with the previous system, in which different ministries each had a separate coordination organ (Bergman 2000).

But bourgeois rule was turbulent in this period too, mainly because of the deep economic crisis at the time. Despite reaching agreements with the Social Democratic opposition on how to manage the crisis, the center-right government only lasted a single term. It was succeeded by a Social Democratic minority government in 1994. In the election of 2006, however, the bourgeois parties regained power. They did so after having formed a pre-electoral coalition—the *Alliance for Sweden*—based on extensive preparations and a joint election manifesto (Haugsgjerd and Aylott 2009; see also the chapter by Aylott in this volume).

Under the new majority coalition government, the previous coordination model of a secretariat within the Prime Minister's Office was reintroduced. This time, however, only one joint coordination office was set up. It included state secretaries and coordinators from each of the four parties, according to ministerial or substantive area. All government matters had to be cleared by the coordination office before they could be approved by the cabinet. Questions that could not be resolved in the coordination office were transferred to the inner cabinet (*inre kabinettet*), consisting of all four party leaders and the state secretary to the Prime Minister. The inner cabinet has no basis in the Constitution; rather, it represents an institutionalized form of negotiation among coalition partners. No voting takes place within it; decisions are made by consensus (*Dagens Nyheter* 2008a and 2008b).

This organizational model for resolving disputes reappeared in 2010, when the center-right parties formed a minority government after the election of that year. Over the last decade, then, these parties have formalized their cooperation by forming pre-election coalitions with joint manifestoes. In their capacity as parties of government, moreover, they have coordinated their common affairs through the coordination organ in the Prime Minister's Office. Further research is required to evaluate the efficacy of these forms of collaboration, particularly within the Government Offices. Similar coordination models have been adopted in Norway, where the so-called "cabinet subcommittee"—consisting of the Prime Minister and coalition party leaders—has developed into a multi-party cabinet core (Kolltveit 2013).

After the elections in 2014, the Social Democrats regained power, this time in the form of a minority coalition government with the Green Party. But this excluded the Left Party from the coalition, once again leading to an asymmetry between the red–green parties. The Greens now received ministerial posts in government while the Left Party sought to influence policies from outside. However, the three parties did not hold a majority in parliament and would need support from at least one more party in order to pass the budget and legislation. The problem of coordinating policy and gaining support for it in Parliament became apparent when the government's first budget was voted down. It was the far-right Sweden Democrats that sank the government's budget by using their pivotal position to swing their votes behind the center-right Alliance. Following the defeat, the government struck a deal with the center-right Alliance—"the December Agreeement"—to ensure that minority governments could pass a budget, thus limiting the influence of the far-right Sweden Democrats.

The final section of this chapter considers the implications of these models for achieving a better coordination of government policy, and notes some problems that remain unresolved.

CHALLENGES FOR POLICY
COORDINATION IN SWEDEN

This chapter has reviewed some notable trends in policy coordination in Sweden. Over time, Swedish political parties have developed methods for achieving stable, long-term cooperation, and these methods have become increasingly formalized and institutionalized. Coordination takes place both before and after elections, and tends to blur the boundary between majority and minority governments.

Social Democratic governments, to begin with, have concluded post-election agreements with the Left Party and the Greens, according to a pattern known as "contract parliamentarism" (Bale and Bergman 2006a and 2006b). Initially, the cooperation among the three parties was based on ad hoc agreements and negotiations over single issues. Over time, however, it has become more and more formalized, with joint manifestoes and negotiated contracts. The arrangement works much as a coalition, but without ministerial portfolios being given to the support parties. It thus embodies an asymmetrical relationship, where power and responsibility are concerned. It also creates a great need for external coordination, as with the placement of political advisors from the support parties within the Government Offices, which contributes to a further blurring of responsibility for government policies.

The bourgeois parties, on the other hand, have formed pre-election coalitions with joint manifestoes. Then, once in power, they have devised institutionalized forms of internal policy coordination. From a democratic point of view, the kind of coordination found in an outright coalition government is less problematic than is contract parliamentarism. It should be emphasized, however, that the institution of inner cabinets—which gives more weight to some ministers than to others—represents a major departure from the collective decision-making otherwise characteristic of the Swedish form of parliamentary government.

These practices seem to be consolidating the grouping of Swedish parties into two blocs. More than ever before, a coherent center-right bloc—the *Alliance for Sweden*—confronts a somewhat less coherent left bloc, consisting of the Social Democrats, the Left Party, and the Greens. The Sweden Democrats, a right-wing populist party, are the only party that does not fit into either bloc. This system of two opposing blocs was reinforced in the "December Agreement" of 2014, which ensured that minority governments could pass a budget. Taken together, these developments are gradually turning the Swedish system into a modified two-party system, notwithstanding the continuing dominance of minority governments. What long-term consequences this may have for the Swedish parliamentary model is still unclear. Throughout Sweden's democratic era, its political parties have been able to adapt to prevailing political circumstances in a flexible and responsible manner. They have not shrunk from assuming responsibility for the country's governance, even in times of national crisis or when faced with powerful opposition (Hermansson and Persson

2010b). This suggests that a consolidation of bloc politics will impart a greater rigidity to Swedish parliamentary democracy.

Furthermore, these new patterns of cooperation pose new challenges to the government's ability to coordinate policy. The relative silence of the Swedish Constitution on the issue of the government's internal organization affords ample opportunity for the parties to negotiate such forms of cooperation as they see fit. This review has demonstrated that, over time, the center-right parties have become better coordinated—both before and after elections. The Left Party and the Greens, for their part, cooperate increasingly with the Social Democrats on policy issues, and Social Democratic minority governments in turn have opened up the Government Offices to officials from these parties. The future challenge for the Left Party and the Greens will be to try to nudge this cooperation in the same direction as that observed among the center-right parties. The election of 2014 was a first step in that direction when the Green Party formed a coalition government with the Social Democrats. But the Left Party was not allowed to join the government; instead it has sought to influence policies from outside. For the bourgeois parties, the main issue is whether their alliance can be sustained over the long run, given that participating in it appears to be costly.

Notwithstanding these attempts to institute better policy coordination, many of the problems typical of central administrations remain. For example, while the Government Offices form a single integrated public authority, major differences among the various line ministries persist. Borders between the ministries are sharply drawn, and civil servants often have strong opinions—and are prepared to fight for them. It may therefore be difficult for political leaders to overcome divisions or to get ministries to work in the intended direction. Not everyone, for instance, appreciates the central role given to the Ministry of Finance for policy coordination. Some contend that said ministry has too much power; others argue it still has too little. However that is, the Finance Ministry has a prominent role in policy coordination. It acts as a super-ministry vis-à-vis the others. This is true both for Social Democratic single-party governments and for center-right coalition governments (Larsson and Bäck 2008: 186).

In addition to coping with potential disagreements among different ministries and administrative levels, the Government Offices have to deal with such challenges as the internationalization of Swedish political and economic life, as well as with the increasingly powerful role of the media. These factors put significant internal and external pressure on the government and reduce its room for maneuver. Swedish leaders have tried to offset these pressures by increasing the number of political appointees in the Government Offices (Dahlström and Pierre 2011). However, while this may mitigate some problems of coordination and enhance political control of the coordinating process, the Government Offices still suffer from a leadership deficit. For instance, while the Prime Minister's Office has been expanded, it is but little involved in daily coordination issues, being restricted to settling disputes when needed and supervising policy coordination at a general level.

Regardless, however, of how the parties handle the task of central policy coordination, major challenges will remain. Recent decades have seen a strong trend toward more formalized and institutionalized solutions for coordination among parties. Policy coordination is taking place to an increasing extent within the government, and to a diminishing degree within Parliament. This has reduced governmental transparency. To that extent, this trend represents a major challenge to democratic governance. Policy coordination will continue to be a major task, requiring new instruments and mechanisms in order to achieve coherent and jointly approved policies. The question is not just how the government can coordinate its policies most effectively. The solutions adopted must also be in harmony with the principles of Swedish parliamentary democracy.

REFERENCES

Andeweg, R. B. and Timmermans, A. (2008). "Conflict Management in Coalition Government," in K. Strøm, W. C. Müller, and T. Bergman (eds), *Cabinets and Coalition Bargaining: The Democratic Life Cycle in Western Europe*. Oxford: Oxford University Press, 269–300.

Bale, T. and Bergman, T. (2006a). "Captives No Longer, But Servants Still? Contract Parliamentarism and the New Minority Governance in Sweden and New Zealand," *Government and Opposition* 41: 422–49.

Bale, T. and Bergman, T. (2006b). "A Taste of Honey Is Worse Than None at All? Coping with the Generic Challenges of Support Party Status in Sweden and New Zealand," *Party Politics* 12: 189–202.

Bergman, T. (2000). "Sweden: When Minority Cabinets are the Rule and Majority Coalitions the Exception," in W. C. Müller and K. Strøm (eds), *Coalition Governments in Western Europe*. Oxford: Oxford University Press, 192–230.

Bergman, T. and Bolin, N. (2011). "Crumbling Political Parties, a Feeble Riksdag, and Technocratic Power Holders?" in T. Bergman and K. Strom (eds), *The Madisonian Turn: Political Parties and Parliamentary Democracy in Nordic Europe*. Ann Arbor: The University of Michigan Press, 251–93.

Bergström, H. (1987). *Rivstart? Om övergången från opposition till regering*. Stockholm: Tidens förlag.

Blondel, Jean and Müller-Rommel, Ferdinand (1993). *Governing Together: Extent and Limits of Joint Decision-making in Western European Cabinets*. Basingstoke: Palgrave Macmillan.

Bouckaert, G., Peters, B. G., and Verhoest, K. (2010). *The Coordination of Public Sector Organizations*. Basingstoke: Palgrave Macmillan.

Christensen, T. and Lægreid, P. (2007). *Transcending New Public Management: The Transformation of Public Sector Reforms*. Aldershot: Ashgate.

Dagens Nyheter (2008a). "Makten pratar ihop sig på torsdagar," May 4 (Stockholm).

Dagens Nyheter (2008b). "Ett inre kabinett gynnar småpartierna," May 4 (Stockholm).

Dahlström, C. and Pierre, J. (2011). "Steering the Swedish State: Politicization as a Coordination Strategy," in C. Dahlström, B. G. Peters, and J. Pierre (eds), *Steering from the Centre: Strengthening Political Control in Western Democracies*. Toronto: University of Toronto Press, 193–211.

Döhler M., Fleischer, J., and Hustedt, T. (2007). *Government Reform as Institutional Politics: Varieties and Policy Patterns from a Comparative Perspective*, Forschungspapiere "Regierungsorganisation in Westeuropa", Heft 03. Potsdam: Universitätsverlag Potsdam.

Elder, N. C. M. and Page, E. C. (2000). "Sweden: The Quest for Co-ordination," in B. G. Peters, R. A. W. Rhodes, and V. Wright (eds), *Administering the Summit: Administration of the Core Executive in Developed Countries*. London: Macmillan, 134–52.

Erlandsson, M. (2007). *Striderna i Rosenbad: Om trettio års försök att förändra Regeringskansliet*, Stockholm Studies in Politics. Stockholm: Stockholm University, Department of Political Science.

Förvaltningskommittén (2008). "Styra och ställa—förslag till en effektivare statsförvaltning," Statens Offentliga Utredningar 2008:118. Stockholm: Fritzes.

Gulick, L. (1937). "Notes on the Theory of Organizations," in L. Gulick and L. Urwin (eds), *Papers on the Science of Administration*. New York: Institute of Public Administration.

Haugsgjerd Allern, E. and Aylott, N. (2009). "Overcoming the Fear of Commitment: Pre-electoral Coalitions in Norway and Sweden," *Acta Politica* 44: 259–85.

Hermansson, J. and Persson, T. (2010a). "Att regera under parlamentarism," in J. Hermansson (ed.), *Regeringsmakten i Sverige: Ett experiment i parlamentarism 1917–2009*. Stockholm: SNS Förlag, 9–32.

Hermansson, J. and Persson, T. (2010b). "En ifrågasatt regeringsform," in J. Hermansson (ed.), *Regeringsmakten i Sverige: Ett experiment i parlamentarism 1917–2009*. Stockholm: SNS Förlag, 199–206.

Hustedt, T. and Tiessen, J. (2006). *Central Government Coordination in Denmark, Germany and Sweden—An Institutional Policy Perspective*, in Forschungspapiere "Regierungsorganisation in Westeuropa," Heft 02. Potsdam: Universitätsverlag Potsdam.

Johansson, K. M. (2008). "Chief Executive Organization and Advisory Arrangements for Foreign Affairs: The Case of Sweden," *Cooperation and Conflict* 43: 267–87.

Johansson, K. M. and Raunio, T. (2010). "Organizing the Core Executive for European Union Affairs: Comparing Finland and Sweden," *Public Administration* 88: 649–64.

Johansson, K. M. and Tallberg, J. (2010), "Explaining Chief Executive Empowerment: EU Summitry and Domestic Institutional Change," *West European Politics* 33: 208–36.

Kassim, H., Peters, B. G., and Wright, V. (2000). *The National Co-ordination of EU Policy: The Domestic Level*. Oxford: Oxford University Press.

Kolltveit, K. (2013). *Cabinet Decision-Making and Concentration of Power: A Study of the Norwegian Executive Centre*. Oslo: University of Oslo, Department of Political Science.

Lagercrantz, A. (2005). *Över blockgränsen: Samarbetet mellan Centerpartiet och Socialdemokraterna 1995–1998*. Hedemora: Gidlunds Förlag.

Larsson, T. (1986). *Regeringen och dess kansli: Samordning och byråkrati i maktens centrum*. Lund: Studentlitteratur.

Larsson, T. and Bäck, H. (2008). *Governing and Governance in Sweden*. Lund: Studentlitteratur.

Larue, T. (2006). *Agents in Brussels: Delegation and Democracy in the European Union*. Umeå: Umeå University, Department of Political Science.

Olsen, L. (2007). *Rödgrön reda. Regeringssamverkan 1998–2006*. Stockholm: Hjalmarsson & Högberg Förlag.

Persson, T. (2003), *Normer eller nytta? Om de politiska drivkrafterna bakom regeringskansliets departementsindelning*. Uppsala: Acta Universitatis Upsaliensis.

Persson, T. (2007). "Explaining European Union Adjustments in Sweden's Central Administration," *Scandinavian Political Studies* 30: 204–28.

Peters, B. G. (1998). "Managing Horizontal Government: The Politics of Coordination," *Public Administration* 76: 295–311.

Peters, B. G. (2013). "Toward Policy Coordination: Alternatives to Hierarchy," *Policy & Politics* 41: 569–84.

Pollitt, C. (2003). "Joined-Up Government: A Survey," *Political Studies Review* 1: 34–49.

Premfors, R. and Sundström, G. (2007). *Regeringskansliet*. Malmö: Liber.

Six, P. (2004). "Joined-Up Government in the Western World in Comparative Perspective: A Preliminary Literature Review and Exploration," *Journal of Public Administration Research and Theory* 14: 103–38.

Ullström, A. (2005). "Samarbetskanslierna—vårtor på, länkar till eller delar av Regeringskansliet?" Score report no. 2005:3. Stockholm: Score.

Verhoest, K., Bouckaert, G., and Peters, B. G. (2007). "Janus-Faced Reorganization: Specialization and Coordination in Four OECD Countries in the Period 1980–2005," *International Review of Administrative Sciences* 73: 325–48.

Wockelberg, H. (2003). *Den svenska förvaltningsmodellen: Parlamentarisk debatt om förvaltningens roll i styrelseskicket*. Uppsala: Acta Universitatis Upsaliensis.

CHAPTER 48

RATIONAL POLITICS

*Commissions of Inquiry
and the Referral System in Sweden*

OLOF PETERSSON

SWEDISH policy-making style is often regarded as distinctive when compared to other countries. Policy-making in Sweden is said to be *deliberative* to the extent that problem-solving is left to well-trained specialists. Moreover, Swedish politics is considered as *rationalistic* in that great efforts are made to develop the fullest possible information about political issues. It is also *open* in the sense that all interested parties are consulted before the final decision. Furthermore, it is seen as *consensual* in that broad agreements are highly valued. For the outside observer Swedish politics is marked by a decision-making style which never seems rash, abrupt, irrational, or indeed, exciting (Anton 1969).

Similar steps in the decision-making process can certainly be found in several countries but the Swedish system stands out because of its strong emphasis on the preparatory stages. Considerable time and effort is spent on investigations and discussions before a policy proposal becomes a government bill. This can partly be explained by a political culture based on the sounding out and "anchoring" of policy proposals in different segments of Swedish society. Another explanation has to do with particular features of the Swedish justice system and legal culture. According to the dominating view, the courts are supposed to base their judgments on the will of the legislator, hence the need for elaborate texts explaining the intent behind laws. When adjudicating a case, a Swedish judge does not primarily refer to legal precedents set by the courts of law. More important are the "travaux préparatoires" of the policy process, which consist of a chain of legal sources such as legislative acts, parliamentary committee proposals, government bills, and, importantly, reports from the commissions of inquiry and results from the referral process.

The characterization of Swedish politics as deliberative, rationalistic, open, and consensual stems from the 1960s. The question is whether it still holds today, several decades later. Commissions of inquiry and the referral system, being central to the political decision-making process throughout this entire period, can serve as an important indicator of stability and change in Swedish politics.

FORMAL REGULATION

Policy investigations can be carried out by Parliament, government ministries, public agencies, county councils, municipal governments, or other public bodies. However, some commissions of inquiry have special legal status. The concept of "kommitté" is defined in a government ordinance on this particular subject ("Kommittéförordningen," SFS 1998:1474). Commissions of inquiry have two distinguishing traits. Firstly, they are appointed by the Cabinet and have a legal status similar to other government agencies. Secondly, commissions of inquiry are set up with a mandate to investigate a special subject (the official Swedish term is "utredningsuppdrag"). In colloquial political language the word "utredning" (meaning investigation) is not only used for a commission of inquiry itself but also for the report published by the commission. Centralized political control is exercised in the design of each commission of inquiry, being given a uniform identification number (for example, "Ju 2010:09" where "Ju" stands for the Ministry of Justice). Parliamentary approval is not required, which means that the Cabinet can initiate and abolish commissions at its own discretion.

The legal framework of the commissions of inquiry is regulated by the government ordinance mentioned above. The specific instructions for each commission are decided collectively by the Cabinet, not by an individual minister (see also the chapters by Bäck and Bergman in Section 3 and by Persson in this section of the book). These instructions are numbered chronologically and published in a separate series ("Kommittédirektiv"). Commissions can be given additional tasks by the Cabinet issuing a new directive. The official name of the commission is decided by the commission itself.

A commission of inquiry consists of a chairperson and one or more members. The power to appoint the chairperson and the members resides with the Cabinet but in most cases the decision is delegated to the responsible minister. Neither Parliament nor any other public body is involved in the formal selection of commission members. The Cabinet may also select one individual to be responsible for the inquiry. Since "commission" refers to a plurality of people, the official term for single-member inquiries is "special investigator" ("särskild utredare"). Commissions of inquiry, including special investigators, may be assisted by subject specialists ("sakkunniga") and experts ("experter"). These two terms might sound synonymous but there is a difference in formal powers. Subject specialists are entitled to be briefed to the same extent as commission members and permitted to participate in the meetings and deliberations of the committee. Subject specialists are allowed to write dissenting opinions to the commission report. The role of "experts", on the other hand, is entirely defined by the commission or its chairperson.

The ordinance on commissions contains some general guidelines for the commission reports. If the proposals can be expected to have financial consequences, the commission must present an estimate of the costs and benefits for the state, regional and local governments, private business, and individual citizens. If proposals concern regions and municipalities, the commission must assess how local self-government is affected. Other consequences to be taken into account include law enforcement, employment, public services, small business, gender equality, and integration. In actual practice many commission reports neglect to present this type of impact analysis (Riksrevisionen 2012). Sweden is often wrongly viewed as a leading country when it comes to better regulation through impact assessments. In fact, Sweden barely fulfills the more stringent criteria of Regulatory Impact Analysis (RIA) and is lagging behind many other European countries (Erlandsson 2010).

This brief overview shows that the formal regulation of commissions of inquiry could be described as detailed but weak. Administrative procedures are elaborated in length but commissions of inquiry are not part of the constitutionally defined institutions of Sweden. In fact, the Cabinet could appoint any number of commissions or abolish all sitting commissions overnight.

Compared to commissions of inquiry the referral system represents a different type of regulation. In this area the rules are not very specific but they are constitutionally binding. The Instrument of Government contains a clause which makes it mandatory to seek advice from outside sources: "In preparing Government business the necessary information and opinions shall be obtained from the public authorities concerned. Information and opinions shall be obtained from local authorities as necessary. Organizations and individuals shall also be given an opportunity to express an opinion as necessary" (Chapter 7, Article 2, official translation) (see also the chapter by Ahlbäck Öberg and Wockelberg in Section 2). This constitutional article defines three types of sources. The Cabinet has an obligation to seek advice from "public authorities concerned." Municipal and regional government is given slightly lower priority since the Cabinet itself could decide when it is "necessary" to obtain information and opinions from regional and local authorities. The third category consists of private bodies such as organizations and individuals, which should be "given the opportunity" to express opinions when it is judged necessary to do so.

The obligation to seek advice pertains to all types of "Government business," not only legislation but decisions in individual cases as well. However, the constitution remains silent about the specifics of the referral procedure. The responsible minister can decide which authorities and other bodies to hear. In actual practice the selection of referral partners is decided by a civil servant in the ministry concerned. There is a close link between commissions of inquiry and the referral system. The vast majority of commission reports are sent out for comments to a broad range of public and private bodies, which are normally given a few months to react. The written referral responses are sent to the ministry in charge. These responses are covered by the general principle of open government and hence available for anyone to consult. In some important cases the referral responses are summarized and published in a separate volume. If a commission report leads to legislation, the Government bill normally contains an overview of the most important arguments given in the referral responses.

Historical Development

Precursors of the present system of commissions of inquiry can be found in the seventeenth century. During the ascent of royal power and the territorial expansion of the realm, temporary commissions were used in order to collect information and prepare decisions. The dominance of the legislature during the Age of Liberty in the eighteenth century meant that the Riksdag took the initiative for most of the special commissions, which often had a strong representation of Members of Parliament. Although political power shifted back to the King in the nineteenth century, there was still a significant element of parliamentary involvement in the temporary commissions. During the nineteenth century around eight temporary commissions were set up yearly. About 60 percent of these commissions were appointed by the executive and 40 percent by the Riksdag (Hesslén 1927; Zetterberg 1990).

With the introduction of parliamentary democracy around 1920 and the subsequent expansion of the public sector, commissions of inquiry became a frequently used instrument to prepare legislation. In the first half of the twentieth century more than fifty new commissions were set up every year. After a while, the system of temporary commissions almost seemed to have become too popular. The commissions were criticized for being costly, slow, bureaucratic, and even prone to corruption. In 1922 the Social Democratic Minister of Finance F. V. Thorsson initiated a cut in the public sector budget, a decision which became known as a "commission slaughter." This led to a decline in the number of commissions, but after a few years the number of commissions started to rise again (Meijer 1956; Zetterberg 1990).

The commissions of inquiry had become an integral part of the Swedish policy-making process. Commissions of inquiry were initiated by the Cabinet, which was also given the power to write the instructions and appoint the members. However, Parliament still kept its influence since Members of Parliament, including the opposition parties, were regularly invited to participate in the commissions. By the 1970s more than half of the commissions had some kind of parliamentary representation. At this time many commissions could be described as policy planning commissions. By working out the basis for formal legislation, these commissions of inquiry became important centers of political power in areas such as research, housing, energy, defense, labor conditions, regional policy, and constitutional reform. The plans for many of the political reforms during the construction of the Swedish welfare state were drawn up by commissions of inquiry. Sometimes these commissions became semi-permanent institutions and even in some cases developed into permanent public agencies (Zetterberg 1990).

This type of policy-making machinery worked very efficiently. It has been estimated that more than 40 percent of all legislation in Sweden during the late 1960s and early

1970s was based on commission proposals (Brantgärde 1979; Premfors 1983). A study of all commissions of inquiry which delivered their final reports between 1968 and 1973 showed that 90 percent presented specific policy proposals. In this particular period of time, almost half of the commissions argued for increased government spending. A vast majority of these proposals led to government bills that were sent to Parliament. The commissions were not only able to develop policy proposals but also to build political consensus. Unanimous proposals had a high likelihood of passing the subsequent stages of the policy process without modifications. However, commissions with dissenting opinions were often criticized in the hearing process, changed by the ministries, amended by Parliament, or simply abandoned (F. Johansson 1979).

Most commissions of inquiry had a mixed composition. In the first half of the twentieth century around a quarter of the members were politicians, primarily Members of Parliament. Around half of the commission members were recruited from the public sector, including the courts. That meant that senior civil servants from national agencies and ministries as well as high judges took an active part in the preparation of legislation in different policy areas. The remaining quarter were members from civil society and other areas external to the administrative, governmental, and parliamentary sphere. Trade union federations and business associations were frequent participants in the commissions of inquiry. This was a central ingredient in the Swedish variety of neo-corporatist cooperation between politics, bureaucracy, and interest groups (Meijer 1956; Johansson 1992).

Experts were a prominent feature in the commissions of inquiry. While experts rarely exceeded 10 percent of the total number of commission members, they formed an important link to academic research in different fields. Furthermore, experts were recruited as secretaries, staff, and consultants. Around one fourth of the commission reports published between 1959 and 1973 contained social science contributions from disciplines such as political science, public law, economics, business administration, public administration, geography, sociology, social medicine, criminology, and pedagogy (Foyer 1969). However, one should not draw the conclusion that the commissions were primarily instruments of objective inquiry. Rather, they could best be described as an integral part of an often highly politicized process of policy-making (Premfors 1983).

By the early 1980s it became obvious that some basic conditions for the Swedish policy-making model had changed. The economic crisis of the 1970s demonstrated that the public sector could no longer expand at the same rate as in the previous decades of continuous economic growth. As in many other European countries, Sweden experienced new problems of policy-making, including ungovernability and overload. When the Social Democrats returned to power in 1982, Prime Minister Olof Palme announced that the number of commissions of inquiry would be decreased and that many of the remaining commissions would have their mandate reduced. The established system was criticized for being cumbersome and generating fiscally unrealistic proposals. From now on, policy proposals would be prepared in a more tightly controlled manner; for instance, by relying on internal resources of the ministries and public agencies (Premfors 1983).

Olof Palme's "commission slaughter" led to a temporary reduction in the number of commissions, but the number soon started to rise again, thus following the pattern of the 1920s. In the 1990s commissions of inquiry were just as frequent as in the past. However, the character of the commissions was profoundly changed. The political conflict level started to rise, as measured by the proportion of commissions unable to find unanimous support among their members. At the same time, parliamentary representation began to decline and the Cabinet increasingly came to rely on expert commissions or even an individual "special investigator" (J. Johansson 1992; Gunnarsson and Lemne 1998). Political planning commissions with the broad participation of Members of Parliament, representatives of large interest organizations, civil servants, and experts, reflecting the type of commission that epitomized the Swedish policy-making process, became less and less frequent. A study of remiss referrals between 1964 and 2009 shows that the participation of voluntary organizations has declined. Furthermore, the proportion of conflict-oriented and member-benefit-oriented organizations has decreased, while consensus-oriented and public-benefit-oriented organizations have increased their relative share of participation (Lundberg 2012; see also the chapter by Öberg in this section).

VARIETIES OF COMMISSIONS

Looking back at the political history of Sweden, it is obvious that there has been considerable variation among the many thousands of commissions of inquiry. One can distinguish at least eight main categories (Meijer 1956, 1969; F. Johansson 1979; J. Johansson 1992; Hirschfeldt 1999; Ruin 2008, 2012).

Policy sector planning. The classical commission of inquiry has been set up with the purpose of proposing legislation in a specific policy area. This type of commission often had members representing different political parties, large interest organizations, and civil servants from ministries and agencies, as well as academics and other experts. Such policy planning commissions were often able to "anchor" decisions in different segments of Swedish society, channel research results into the political decision-making process, and ease the future implementation of political reforms.

Long-term policy-making. Commissions of inquiry have been used to formulate overarching and long-term policy goals but not necessarily propose specific legislation. Long-term surveys of the Swedish economy ("Långtidsutredningar") have been carried out on a triannual basis since the late 1940s. Nowadays these long-term surveys are coordinated by the Ministry of Finance and are often devoted to specific problems, such as demographic trends or the labor market.

Public administration. Some commissions of inquiry have purely administrative tasks, such as setting up or dismantling a permanent public agency. After a new policy has been decided, often on the basis of the proposals from a policy planning commission, the Cabinet might appoint a special investigator to prepare the organizational changes necessary for the implementation of the policy decision.

Consultation. When the Cabinet wants to consult with experts and representatives of organized interests it might use the formal framework of a commission of inquiry. This is particularly the case if the consultation process is supposed to last for a longer period of time. Some of these consultation committees have acquired a semi-permanent status. Often distinguished by names ending in "delegation" or "beredning," these commissions are found in areas such as environment, research policy, social issues, migration, and gender issues.

Special inquiries. Commissions of inquiry are sometimes appointed after disasters, scandals, and other events when public trust is at stake. Members might include representatives of different political parties, outside experts, and well-respected citizens. For example, such commissions of inquiry were set up to investigate the events in Ådalen in 1931 when the military killed demonstrating workers on strike, the use of secret intelligence during World War II, the assassination of Prime Minister Olof Palme in 1986, the Estonia ferry catastrophe in 1994, and the political and bureaucratic responses to the tsunami disaster in Southeast Asia in 2004.

Expert teams. Sometimes the Cabinet appoints a team of scholars to investigate a certain problem, without necessarily giving them the task of proposing specific policy proposals. One example is the Study of Power and Democracy in Sweden ("Maktutredningen") which was set up in order to answer questions about the distribution of power resources in Swedish society and the quality of Swedish democracy (SOU 1990:44). During the final years of the state church system, one commission of inquiry consisted of theological and linguistic experts who were given the task of translating the Bible into modern Swedish ("Bibelkommissionen" 1973–2000, SOU 2000:100).

Symbolic action. In the 1920s the Social Democrats initiated one commission on the nationalization of Swedish industry and another on industrial democracy. Neither led to any practical results, but the government could refer to these commissions in order to demonstrate its ideological fervor.

Political burial. By appointing a commission of inquiry the Cabinet can win political time. Hot and sensitive political problems might be defused or cooled down if they are referred to commissions which keep them at arms-length distance from the political decision-making process.

CURRENT TRENDS

The standard type of decision-making procedure in Sweden can be rather cumbersome. The different phases of the policy-making process involve several types of participant. Normally a commission of inquiry is appointed by the Cabinet in order to investigate the problem and make recommendations. These proposals are published in a special series ("Statens offentliga utredningar," SOU) and in most cases submitted to public agencies and relevant interest groups for comments. The Swedish term for this referral system is "remiss," from the French word "remise." The commission report and the referral replies serve as the basis for the bill submitted by Cabinet to Parliament. Every government bill is scrutinized by a parliamentary committee. The committee submits its written argument and proposals to the whole Parliament for deliberation and vote. Finally, the Cabinet and the administrative agencies can supplement the parliamentary decision with detailed regulations and instructions (Ruin 1982).

One might get the impression that not much has changed during the last decades. The formal rules are basically the same. The annual output volume from the commissions of inquiry is still quite high. Around 100 titles in the SOU series are published yearly. This is certainly lower than the peak years of the 1990s, when the average was around 150 titles, but significantly higher than the 50–60 volumes published yearly during the 1950s and the 1960s (Figure 48.1). Judging from the average number of pages, there is no decline in the total text volume produced by the commissions of inquiry. However, behind this impression of stability are some important indicators of change (J. Johansson 1992; Gunnarsson and Lemne 1998; Riksrevisionen 2004; Ruin 2008; Amnå 2010; Lemne 2015).

First, the composition of commissions has changed dramatically. The most obvious transformation is the shifting gender balance among commission members. In pre-democratic times, the world of commissions, like the rest of politics, was exclusively male. After the democratic breakthrough the proportion of women started to rise, but at a slow pace. As late as 1988, only 8 percent of the commissions had women

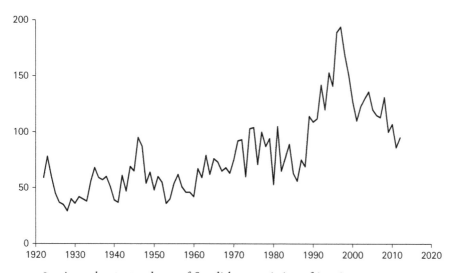

FIGURE 48.1 Annual output volume of Swedish commission of inquiry reports, 1922–2012.

Note: The graph shows the number of reports published yearly in the series of Statens Offentliga Utredningar (SOU). The data has been collected and analyzed by the author. In order to assess the total text volume, two more pieces of information have to be taken into account. Firstly, the number of pages per report has varied over the years but there is no universal trend toward shorter reports. The annual mean number of pages for selected years: 1940 = 137, 1960 = 245, 2010 = 298 pages. Secondly, changing typesetting practices have led to a slight decrease in the number of characters per page. The overall conclusion is that the total written output volume from the commissions peaked in the late 1990s and has declined during the last 20 years.

Source: Swedish National Bibliography; Swedish Union Catalogue Libris, <http://libris.kb.se>

as chairpersons. In 2012 this figure had risen to 32 percent. In 2012 the proportion of women commission members was 43 percent (Zetterberg 1990; Riksdagsskrivelse 2012/13:103).

Second, the type of broad commission of inquiry with politicians, interest organizations, experts, and bureaucrats, which was so characteristic until a few decades ago, has now become a rare exception. Today only around 10 percent of the commission members are Members of Parliament. Politicians are primarily found in consultation panels in areas such as security policy, international law, defense policy, environmental issues, and media violence. Instead, the typical commission of inquiry has become a special investigator. Today around 75 percent of the commissions consists of one single person and in most cases a judge or a senior civil servant. The special investigator is often supported by a specialist staff and can, in some cases, rely on an advisory board of politicians and representatives from business and civil society.

This means, thirdly, that the commissions of inquiry have more or less ceased to be an arena for negotiation and consensus-seeking. The opposition parties are rarely invited to participate in the preparation of new legislation. As a general rule, commissions of inquiry have become less independent, thus giving the Cabinet tighter control of the entire decision-making system. New commissions are given less time than before to complete their work. In 2010 the average life span of Swedish commissions of inquiry had declined to slightly less than one-and-a-half years. For single-member specialist commissions the average length was even less (Riksrevisionen 2012). This change from formal and long-term to informal and short-term procedures means, together, that the Swedish commissions of inquiry have lost their unique function in the production of a qualified knowledge base for political decision-making.

Several explanations can be offered for the changing character of the commission system. The pace of political decision-making has increased, giving less time for the old type of broad consensus-seeking commissions. At the same time, the political conflict level has risen. Neocorporatist arrangements, such as interest organizations being represented in the board of state agencies, had already been dismantled in the 1990s (see also the chapter by Öberg in this section).

When Sweden became a member of the European Union in 1995, the preparation of new legislation in areas such as agriculture and trade moved from Stockholm to Brussels. Even though the basic structure of the Swedish decision-making process remains intact, European Union membership has had consequences for the commissions of inquiry. In EU matters the Cabinet normally seeks advice and collects information through other channels and primarily from the permanent public agencies. Commissions of inquiry are, therefore, rarely used to prepare Swedish positions in the European decision-making arena.

The system of "remiss" referrals might also look well established. The vast majority of commission reports are still sent out to public agencies, interest organizations, and other interested actors in order to collect opinions and advice. But there are signs of change and weaknesses in this Swedish type of hearing process. Written replies continue to dominate, while procedures such as public hearings and oral arguments are used rarely. Well-prepared and thoroughly argued responses to commission reports could certainly still be found, but there are several examples of superficial responses with low information value (Eriksson, Lemne, and Pålsson 1999).

RATIONAL POLITICS REDEFINED

The general conclusion is that Swedish politics can still be portrayed as deliberative, rationalistic, open, and consensual, but only if these four concepts are reinterpreted.

When Sweden was described as *deliberative* in the 1960s this concept was given a quite narrow meaning. Deliberation at that time signified that formal political decision-making was preceded by "long periods of time during which more or less attention is given to some problem by well-trained specialists" (Anton 1969). Today the situation has changed in at least three different respects. Firstly, the time span of the policy-making process has become much shorter. Only in exceptional cases are commissions of inquiry allowed to devote several years to investigating political problems. Secondly, "well-trained specialists" certainly still play a role in the elaboration of public policy but the authority of experts and scientists has declined. The philosophy of social engineering and expert rule has been challenged by technological failures, environmental problems, and increasingly critical media and citizens. Thirdly, if Swedish policy-making is still to be characterized as deliberative, the preparation of legislation can no longer be confined to the closed elite arenas of the 1960s. Rather it must include new arenas for public discourse opened up by increased pluralism and innovations in communication technology. In short, the stakeholders of Swedish politics have changed from elite to mass. It has also changed from a long-term "sounding-out" style of policy-making to a short-term and iterative trial-and-error method.

Sweden in the 1960s was characterized as *rationalistic* in a very special sense. The commissions of inquiry were used as evidence for the conclusion that "great efforts are made to develop the fullest possible information about any given issue, including a thorough review of historical experiences as well as the range of alternatives suggested by scholars in and out of Sweden" (Anton 1969). In fact, many commissions reports at that time contained long historical background chapters as well as international comparisons. Different policy alternatives were probed in detail and possible consequences were methodically investigated. This situation changed in the 1980s when commissions were ordered to finish their assignments in less time and deliver shorter reports. Although the quest for factual correctness and disdain for emotional arguments, captured by the Swedish word "saklighet," is still central to the political culture of Sweden, political decisions today are taken on a much less solid factual ground. This transformation is captured by the well-known distinction between, on the one hand, full or perfect rationality and, on the other hand, bounded or satisficing rationality (Simon 1957). If contemporary Sweden should still be described as rational it is certainly not in the utopian and perfect sense but rather bears an unexceptional, possibly satisficing meaning.

The depiction of Swedish politics in the 1960s as *open* carried a particular connotation. Sweden was open "in the sense that all interested parties are consulted before a decision is finally made" (Anton 1969). This situation has changed. It is no longer the case that "all interested parties" are consulted beforehand. The most obvious example is the decline in the number of commissions with parliamentary representation. Only on rare occasions are the opposition parties invited to participate in the preparation of new legislation. The involvement of interest organizations has declined in a similar fashion. Today the commissions of inquiry are more tightly controlled by the Cabinet and the government ministries. When interest groups are no longer invited to participate in the commissions of inquiry, they are forced to use other ways of influencing political decision-making. This is one explanation of the increase in lobbying, opinion-making activities, and communication consultants (Micheletti 1984). Thus, the political process has moved from a system based on selected access for a few major interests to an open-ended system characterized by competition and unpredictability.

Lastly, Swedish politics was once characterized as *consensual*. Political decisions were "seldom made without the agreement of virtually all parties to them." This conclusion is not supported by contemporary evidence. One can no longer say "virtually all parties" agree to the political decisions taken by the Cabinet and Parliament. In many cases the affected groups are not even invited to participate in the preparatory stages. In certain respects Swedish politics can no longer be characterized as consensual. The conflict level has risen and parliamentary politics has become more polarized. The old type of broad agreements based on elite compromise belongs to Swedish political history. However, certain elements of the old consensual culture are still intact. Open conflicts are often avoided and the political rhetoric of the major political actors is still comparatively low-keyed and open-minded. A frequent gesture used in political discourse by politicians from the government as well as the opposition is to stretch out a hand as invitation to the opponent to negotiate a broad agreement on a specific issue. In contrast to the old closed-room arenas of yesteryear, present-day consensus-seeking is played out in the openness of the public sphere and should be seen as an element of influencing public opinion.

It is safe to conclude that the transformation of the commissions of inquiry and the system of referrals indicates a more general change in Swedish politics. For political decision-makers, the system has become more unpredictable and more difficult to govern. For individual citizens and civil society organizations, it has become more open, and the difference between insiders and outsiders has become less pronounced. For political scientists in the field of comparative government Sweden has become more similar to other European polities, thus slightly less interesting.

Acknowledgment

The author wishes to acknowledge the helpful comments and suggestions made by Carl Dahlström, Marja Lemne, Michele Micheletti, and Fredrik Sterzel.

REFERENCES

Amnå, E. (2010). "Speaking Truth to Power: Statsvetarna och Kommittéväsendet," in M. Jerneck and B. Badersten (eds), *Kontraster och nyanser: Svensk statsvetenskap i en brytnings-tid*. Lund: Statsvetenskaplig Tidskrift, 552–67.

Anton, T. J. (1969). "Policy-Making and Political Culture in Sweden," *Scandinavian Political Studies* 4: 88–102.

Brantgärde, L. (1979). *Utredningsväsendet och svensk efterkrigslagstiftning*. Göteborg: Institute of Political Science, University of Göteborg.

Eklöf, J. (2007). *Gene Technology at Stake: Swedish Governmental Commissions on the Border of Science and Politics*. Umeå: Department of Historical Studies, Umeå University.

Eriksson, L.-E., Lemne, H., and Pålsson, I. (1999). "Demokrati på remiss," Demokratiutredningen skrift nr 30. Statens offentliga utredningar, SOU 1999:144.

Erlandsson, M. (2010). "Regelförenkling genom konsekvensutredningar," Sieps Report 2010:1. Stockholm: Swedish Institute for European Policy Studies.

Foyer, L. (1969). "The Social Sciences in Royal Commission Studies in Sweden," *Scandinavian Political Studies* 4: 183–203.

Gunnarsson, V. and Lemne, M. (1998). "Kommittéerna och bofinken: Kan en kommitté se ut hur som helst?" Expertgruppen för studier i offfentlig ekonomi, Ds 1998:57. Stockholm: Finansdepartementet.

Hesslén, G. (1927). *Det svenska kommittéväsendet intill år 1905: Dess uppkomst, ställning och betydelse*. Uppsala: Berlings.

Hirschfeldt, J. (1999). "Kommissioner och andra undersökande utredningar: En utflykt i gräns-markerna mellan politik och juridik," in Lena Marucsson (ed.), *Festskrift till Fredrik Sterzel*. Uppsala: Iustus Förlag, 143–67.

Johansson, F. (1979). "Offentliga utredningars genomslag i politiska beslut," Report 1979:2. Göteborg: Institute of Political Science, University of Göteborg.

Johansson, J. (1992). *Det statliga kommittéväsendet: Kunskap, kontroll, konsensus*. Stockholm: Statsvetenskapliga institutionen, Stockholms universitet.

Lemne, M. (2015). "Det svenska kommittéväsendet utveckling under de senaste decennierna," *Statsvetenskaplig Tidskrift*, forthcoming.

Lundberg, E. (2012). "Changing Balance: The Participation and Role of Voluntary Organisations in the Swedish Policy Process," *Scandinavian Political Studies* 35: 347–71.

Meijer, H. (1956). *Kommittépolitik och kommittéarbete: Det statliga kommittéväsendets utveck-lingslinjer 1905–1954 samt nuvarande funktion och arbetsformer*. Lund: Gleerup.

Meijer, H. (1969). "Bureacracy and Policy Formulation in Sweden," *Scandinavian Political Studies* 4: 103–16.

Micheletti, M. (1984). "Arbetsmarknadsorganisationer och politik," in Tore Frängsmyr (ed.), *Kan Sverige styras? Att förstå och styra samhället*. Stockholm: SNS Förlag, 94–127.

Premfors, R. (1983). "Governmental Commissions in Sweden," *American Behavioral Scientist* 26: 623–42.

Riksrevisionen (2004). "Förändringar inom kommittéväsendet," Report RiR 4002:2. Stockholm: Riksrevisionen.

Riksrevisionen (2012). "Att tänka efter före: En promemoria om kraven på kommittéers ana-lyser," Report, December 12. Stockholm: Riksrevisionen.

Ruin, O. (1982). "Sweden in the 1970s: Policy-Making Becomes More Difficult," in J. Richardson (ed.), *Policy Styles in Western Europe*. London: Allen & Unwin, 141–67.

Ruin, O. (2008). "Det statliga kommittéväsendet," in S. Heckscher and A. Eka (eds), *Festskrift till Johan Hirschfeldt*. Uppsala: Iustus Förlag, 445–53.

Ruin, O. (2012). "Utredningsväsendet," in *Maktens former: Tretton essäer om politik*. Stockholm: Hjalmarson & Högberg, 179–90.

Simon, H. A. (1957). *Models of Man: Social and Rational*. New York: Wiley.

SOU 1990:44. *Demokrati och makt i Sverige: Maktutredningens huvudrapport*. Stockholm: Statens offentliga utredningar.

SOU 2000:100. *Bibeln. Bibelkommissionen*. Stockholm: Statens offentliga utredningar.

Zetterberg, K. (1990). "Det statliga kommittéväsendet," in U. Larsson (ed.), *Att styra riket: Regeringskansliet 1840–1990*. Stockholm: Allmänna Förlaget, 284–309.

....

CHAPTER 49

INTEREST ORGANIZATIONS IN THE POLICY PROCESS

Interest Advocacy and Policy Advice

....

PEROLA ÖBERG

INSTITUTIONALIZED PARTICIPATION AND AUTONOMY

SWEDISH interest groups have played a major role in policy processes over the last hundred and fifty years. The most important large interest organizations in Sweden grew out of opposition toward powerful institutions in pre-democratic society and were important forces in the democratization process itself. After democracy was established, organized interest groups participated in and influenced every stage of the policy process, from agenda setting to implementation of public policy. Some organizations were even formally integrated into the policy process by the beginning of the last century. Soon, a tacit norm was established which prescribed that concerned organized interests should be integrated into the policy formulation stage (in government commissions of inquiries) as well as into the implementation stage (e.g. as members of government agency boards). This norm has characterized Swedish politics for more than a century.

The institutionalization of civic participation has created a dynamic and complex relationship between interest organizations and the state. Lobbying by hired professionals from outside government has been a less important channel for influence than formal participation in public policy. In effect, conflicts of interest have been managed by negotiation or even deliberation among the contenders. Basic conflicts have not been solved, but regulated. The organizations have moderated their claims as well as disciplined loyal members to accept compromises.

At the same time, this has produced a system where the balance between policy advice and policy advocacy has been more delicate than in many other political systems. Hence, it would be a mistake to conclude that interest organizations in Sweden have been subdued and powerless. Autonomy from the state has always been a cornerstone of Swedish civil society. Even before government was democratized, interest organizations had ample opportunities and lawful rights to express their views in public. The "inner life" of organizations has never been controlled by state laws, even if discussions about this have occurred from time to time. Most Swedish interest groups have an internally democratic structure where elected members establish aims and strategies in local, regional, and national conferences. It is true that a large part of organizational life has been, and still is, dependent on government funding, but this funding has been allocated by universalistic principles primarily based on member activity without any strings attached (Wijkström and Lundström 2002; SOU 2007:66). This has made it possible for the organizations to maintain independence not only from the state but also from other donors, such as businesses and influential (rich) individuals. In spite of, or maybe due to, the close connection to the state, interest groups in Sweden have been able to influence public policy in many important ways and still preserve their autonomy to a considerable degree.

Obviously, the balance between autonomy and institutional participation, between advocacy and advice, has been evasive. At times, it has been argued that the system has tipped over and captured organizations into powerlessness; at other times, it has instead been emphasized that interest groups control policy processes and override the democratic system. But for most of the 1900s, a stable equilibrium based on interest group autonomy and influence, combined with institutionalized, organized participation in the policy process, characterized Swedish politics. The state was able to implement public policy more easily because it had been legitimized by concerned interests; at the same time, interest group leaders thought they were able to influence politics to the advantage of their members.

Over the last couple of decades, the situation has changed. Institutional participation has not vanished but has decreased significantly. This means that interest group participation in the public policy process in Sweden, as well as in the other Scandinavian countries, can no longer claim to be unique. In this chapter we take a closer look at the development of institutional participation of interest groups in public policy processes: that is, corporatism—its establishment, function, and dismantlement. First, we examine the ideological and strategic foundations for corporatism, then explain the development of corporatism within different phases of the policy process. We discuss the effects and functions of corporatism and conclude with a focus on explanations for the decrease in corporatism.

IDEOLOGICAL AND STRATEGIC FOUNDATIONS OF SWEDISH CORPORATISM

Given that Swedish organizations have been guaranteed (at least formal) autonomy, and that comparably high membership rates have given them tremendous resources to influence politics, it may be presumed that the state has tried to resist their involvement in public policy processes as far as possible. A state confronted with such strong, organized interests may become especially eager to keep organizations out of democratic decision-making bodies. However, this has not been the case in Sweden. Instead, as we have emphasized, interest organizations have been invited to participate in all stages of the policy process. There are many reasons for this. Interestingly, different ideological positions and strategic considerations of the Social Democrats *as well as* those of the important parties on the political right have been combined in a consensus to accept the participation of organized interests in the public policy process.

The ideologies of the dominant political parties before democratization were characterized by traditional conservative ideas of harmony among different interests in society. During the first decades of the twentieth century, several propositions of a constitution based on corporatist principles (that is, representation of interests and not individuals) as an alternative to liberal democracy were discussed within the Conservative Party. Although this never came close to gaining majority support in the Swedish parliament, these ideas were instead implemented in different parts of the administration: for example, in the Public Employment Service, established 1903–7 (Rothstein 1996: 81), and in the National Board of Health and Welfare in 1912. According to Bo Rothstein, an important breakthrough of corporatist principles took place under a Liberal government strongly supported by the Conservative Party (Rothstein 1992).

The Social Democrats had similar, but at the same time other reasons to support formal participation of organized interests in the policy process. Swedish Social Democrats embraced ideas of harmonizing interests in society too. In tough conflicts with more radical groups, leaders of the Social Democratic Party defended a reformist transformation of society in collaboration with what they perceived to be progressive Liberals. It was often emphasized that a socialist society would never be possible without the consent of the Swedish population, and hence different groups in society had to be included in the process. When the first Social Democratic government came into power in the early 1920s, its first step toward fundamental changes in the economy was to establish two government investigations that had the task of empirically investigating different options for socialization and worker codetermination. It is significant that both investigations had a corporatist composition with representatives from trade unions *and* from Swedish enterprise. Hence, reconciliation between representatives of different interests was already a basic idea also for Social Democrats in the early 1920s.

Although it was important to legitimize far-reaching political and economic reforms, this was obviously not the Social Democrats' only or even main interest. More important for the inclusion of organized civil society into the policy process was the deep distrust of top managers of the public administration. At the time of democratization in Sweden, public administration was (as in many other countries) dominated by persons with degrees from law school. They were treated with much suspicion by the Social Democratic leadership for being politically conservative and hence unwilling to implement Social Democratic policy. Creating civic transparency—that is, to make it possible for citizens to keep an eye on public administration—was important in order to have

bureaucrats implement reformist political decisions (Rothstein 1985). It was also important in order to create trust in the state apparatus among the working class. Expanding
corporatist representation on government agency boards became an important vehicle
to achieve this.

To harmonize interests, establish implementation efficiency, and create trust in public administration were not the only reasons for Social Democrats to include organized
interests in the policy processes. There were also political power positions at stake. The
basic idea of democratic corporatism is, of course, to involve different interests and balance them against each other: employers against employees, producers against consumers, landlords against tenants. But in most cases this strengthened the position of
organizations close to the Social Democratic Party itself. The Social Democratic leaders
were of course well aware of this. It was obvious, for example, that a corporatist governance of the labor market sector would facilitate the realization of a Social Democratic
labor market policy in the 1940s (Rothstein 1985, 1996).

At the same time, political parties on the right had similar interests. When the labor
movement celebrated its victories in the first half of the 1900s, it seemed almost impossible that a non-Social-Democratic government could be realized in the foreseeable
future. The combination of a growing labor class and a constitution with a proportional
electoral system with two chambers that favored larger parties made it easy to forecast
a Social Democratic dominance for many years to come. This would leave the political right and its allies in Swedish industry without political influence. However, at least
some influence was guaranteed if the Employer's Confederation was involved in government commissions and agency boards. Hence, the political right also had strategic
interests to promote formal participation of interest group representatives in the policy
process. This way, preparatory and administrative corporatism also became part of the
historical compromise between labor and capital in Sweden that was established in the
1930s (see also the chapters by Andersson and by Lewin and Lindvall in this book).

There is one more essential piece required to understand why corporatist governance
was established. Clearly, high membership density and strong internal organization
are power resources that can distort policy processes since they strengthen the possibility of enforcing particular interests. However, while power may drive out trust in
other fields, this is not the case, for example, in Swedish labor market policy (Öberg
and Svensson 2010). One reason is that power (in certain contexts) also makes strong
interest organizations trustworthy parties in negotiations (Öberg et al. 2011). Since
leaders of trade union confederations organizing a vast majority of employed citizens
had the mandate to negotiate in the name of their members, it was extremely important and efficient to strike deals with them. This is a key to understanding an important
part of Swedish politics. Most organizations have been able to discipline their members
to accept agreements with the state and other interest groups. Although accusations
of top-down control have been common, it has been accomplished by formal democratic means. Usually, the national congress of organizations have given their leaders
leeway to maneuver before negotiations and have confirmed agreements in retrospect
(Öberg 1994). Hence, representatives of organized interests have not only contributed

information and expert knowledge to the policy process, but have also been able to legitimize decisions within the organizations afterward. This explains why the Swedish state has encouraged centralization of existing organizations and even created organizations within policy fields where interest organizations had not existed before. Instead of communicating with heterogeneous, disgruntled crowds, state officials wanted to negotiate with a few legitimate leaders of a disciplined organization.

The factors we have described explain why, in spite of the deeply politicized, anti-establishment tradition of the Swedish civil society and its threatening power resources, interest organizations were invited to formally participate in almost every stage of the policy process in Swedish politics. In the next section we look more closely at each stage and how institutionalized participation has developed during the era of democracy.

Development of Interest Group Influence in the Policy Process

Participation in Government Committees of Inquiry

A main characteristic of the policy process in Sweden is its emphasis on the preparatory stage of the process (see also the chapter by Petersson in this section). Before the cabinet presents important bills to Parliament, considerable resources are spent on investigating alternatives and their consequences. Often, in more complex or especially important issues, the task of providing information for policy advice to the politicians is given to government committees of inquiry. As already mentioned, when the first Social Democratic cabinet deliberated over socialization and extensive worker codetermination, its first step was to set up a government committee of inquiry. Rationalization of the agricultural industry, constraints on the selling of alcohol, introduction of social health insurance, and expansion of infrastructure were all prepared in government committees of inquiry. During most of the 1900s it was considered standard to involve concerned interests in the commissions. For many years, more than every fifth committee—especially those that dealt with contested political issues—had interest group representation (Christiansen et al. 2010).

Government committees of inquiry have been powerful because their suggestions have often been considered the main policy alternative that the cabinet has to relate to—especially so, if the composition of the committee has included the most obvious interest groups and political parties, and they have been able to produce a final report in consensus. It has been almost impossible to confront an alliance, for example, of both the trade unions and the employers' confederation. Moreover, it has been a strong norm that the parties adhere to the negotiation results presented as a joint proposal from an investigation.

However, over the last 20 years, the function of commissions of inquiry has changed (Lindvall and Rothstein 2006: 50; see also the chapter by Petersson in this section). The government has reduced the time available for each commission and given them more detailed instructions. Moreover, the formerly standard composition of representatives from both political parties and interest groups has become less common. Instead, a committee often consists of only one person, often an expert in the field (Gunnarsson and Lemne 1998; Johansson 1992; Hermansson et al. 1999; Riksrevisionen 2004; Christiansen et al. 2010).

All this has, of course, affected the opportunities for interest groups to participate in this part of the policy process. Interest group participation is nowadays often reduced to advisory boards, or being only invited to express views without being confronted with other interests in open discussions. Even though the decrease in interest group representation at this stage is not as obvious in Sweden as in other Scandinavian countries, there is clear evidence of a decline in interest group participation in this stage of the policy process (Christiansen et al. 2010).

Participation in Public Consultations (Referrals)

Before the government formulates a legislative proposal based on the final report from commissions, its content is referred for consideration to relevant authorities and the public in what is called the referral process. Authorities and groups that are considered to have a stake in the policy area are invited to comment on the proposal. More than one hundred different actors are invited each time, and approximately a quarter of these are interest groups and voluntary organizations (Lundberg 2012, 2013). This is an open process of consultation; anyone can participate, hence an additional number of organizations participate without being invited. This opens up for a variety of organizations to participate, but the process has always been dominated by the large and established organizations, primarily the labor unions and business organizations. Social movements and other protest-oriented organizations have not been invited to any significant degree, and neither have they themselves decided to participate. Instead, organizations that are already involved in policy networks and informal reference groups are also the ones that get invited to the referral process (Lundberg 2013).

Although this is still an important channel for interest organizations to influence public policy, its importance has diminished in recent decades, and the organizations have increasingly chosen to abstain from the process (Lundberg 2013). The number of interest groups that participate in this stage of the policy process has been stable, and the diversity of organizations has actually increased. However, the relative share of interest organizations decreased during the latter half of the first decade of this century, while other actors, primarily state and market actors, increased (Lundberg 2012, 2013). Taken together, this means that this stage of the policy process is not as important now as it historically has been for interest group participation.

Participation in Parliamentary Decision-Making

Interest organizations do not have formal representatives in the Swedish parliament, of course. But several parliamentarians have close ties to organized interests. One reason is that interest groups have always been an important base for recruitment to political parties, and a significant number of parliamentarians have traditionally also been active in organized civil society groups, especially within parties associated with the labor movement ("Demokrati och makt i Sverige," SOU 1990:44).

Most obvious is the influence that trade unions have through involvement in the Social Democratic Party (see also the chapters by Svensson and Andersson in Section 9 in this book). For a great part of the twentieth century, local trade union associations collectively joined the party by majority decision at their annual meetings. This is no longer the case, but the blue-collar unions especially are still an important force inside the party, and they can, for example, organize support for their own candidates for Parliament in internal party meetings. This close collaboration has ensured that a significant number of active members of the Swedish Trade Union Confederation are also Members of Parliament, and hence, have ensured influence over parliamentary decision-making for that interest group (see also the chapters in Section 3).

Organized farmers have also been well represented in Parliament. During parts of the last century, more than half the members of the parliamentary committee on agriculture also held, at the same time, important positions within the farmers' union (Hermansson et al. 1999: 25). Several other cross-party groups have members active in interest groups. Another particularly interesting example is the association of parliamentarians (*Riksdagens nykterhetsgrupp*), which pursues a restrictive alcohol and drug policy. This group has coordinated parliamentarians in addressing these issues since 1895. Many of them have had close contacts with interest groups within the field, primarily the temperance movement. The influence of the farmers and the temperance movement decreased in the latter part of the century, but for a very long period of time these organized interests were assured direct access to Parliament through extensive overlapping memberships. Hence, even in the decision-making stage of the policy process, interest groups have been able to participate through Members of Parliament who also hold power positions within the interest groups.

Participation in Public Administration

The Swedish Constitution differs from most other countries in one important aspect. The government agencies are independent of the cabinet, and hence not organizationally subordinated to a ministry (see also the chapter by Ahlbäck Öberg and Wockelberg in Section 2). The formal rule that regulates the relationship between the cabinet and the government agencies states that neither the cabinet as a collective actor, nor a single member of the cabinet, can interfere in specific cases. The cabinet can only control its agencies by universal rules, appointing board members and directors-general, and assigning specific tasks in the budget. This means, for example, that the Minister for Employment is not formally the head of the government agency that handles employment (*Arbetsförmedlingen*). Hence, winning the election and holding a ministerial post might not be enough to implement reforms if there is severe resistance from within the public administration. This is one of the reasons why Social Democrats over the years have emphasized the need for transparency and representation of different interests in the public administration (Rothstein 1996).

For a very long period it was more or less a default solution that government agency boards should consist of representatives from concerned interests. Since issues concerning welfare, infrastructure, and enterprise have been considered to concern primarily employers and employees, this meant in fact that the trade unions and the employers' confederation were extensively represented. In the most important agencies, the Labor Market Board being the prime example, these organizations were usually represented by their presidents. In fact, even in 1912, when the National Board of Health and Welfare was established, the blue-collar confederation, LO (the Swedish Trade Union Confederation), as well as SAF (the Swedish Employers' Confederation) were each represented by their presidents. When institutionalization of the corporatist arrangement reached its peak, unions and employers were even represented on agency boards that administered culture—for example, theatre, literature, and art. At least half the agency boards, again especially the most important ones within the welfare sector, had formal interest group representation (Christiansen et al. 2010).

The importance of the agency boards might also have been the explanation why they were the main targets for the employers in their campaign against corporatism in the 1980s. After internal discussions, the employers' confederation (SAF) decided to voluntarily withdraw all its representatives from government agency boards. Externally, they argued that corporatist representation was undemocratic. But the main reason for the withdrawal from corporatism was that the employers felt captured in a system that legitimized policies with which they did not always agree, and even more importantly, which sustained union power (Johansson 2005). The strategy was to pressure the government to dismantle corporatist boards; that is, force the unions to leave. Employers felt sure that they could achieve relatively more by making use of lobbying strategies from the outside, and in the meantime, ruin an important power basis for the unions. The strategy was successful. A center-right government coalition abolished formal interest representation on government agency boards in 1992. Since then, the cabinet has appointed board members only on a personal mandate.

However, this did not immediately end participation of organized interests in this stage of the policy process. For many years, persons "on a personal mandate" were considered representatives of interest organizations anyway. In some boards, even employers kept their representatives on the board (Christiansen et al. 2010; Öberg et al. 2011). Hence, the decision to dismantle corporatism in the early 1990s did not immediately take effect. Traditions were strong and were resistant to change.

Over the last ten years, however, the degree of interest group participation on the government agency boards has decreased to a considerable degree. There are few representatives of interest groups on the government agency boards nowadays. They have been replaced by experts, not the least by professors and specialists from the private sector. To some extent, this has been compensated by participation in consultative or advisory boards but, in this sense also, participation in the formal policy process has diminished.

Participation in Consultations with the Cabinet

The participation of interest groups in the political economy of Sweden is described elsewhere in this book (see Section 9). There is reason, however, to emphasize that this in fact may be considered participation in public policy too, and hence connected to the public policy process.

A main characteristic of the Swedish model has indeed been that organizations in the labor markets have been "left in peace" to decide their own matters. Wage negotiations, discussions over workplace safety, and even gender equality have been considered something for the "parties in the labor market to handle." However, many of these issues have taken place in the shadow of the government and been connected to fiscal and economic policy.

Hence, informal deliberation between the government and actors in the labor market has been common, especially since the government is an employer itself (e.g. Elvander 1990). To this should be added the important consultations over economic policy that were more or less institutionalized during the second half of the 1900s. These consultations between the government, the trade unions, and representatives of Swedish enterprise were very important to fiscal and tax policies. Without any doubt, this was a very substantial participation in public policy for the most powerful interest groups (Compston 1995). Over recent decades, the interest in engaging in these kinds of consultations has diminished significantly; the center-right government and Swedish enterprise have been especially unwilling to re-establish something that was a Social Democratic trademark for the Swedish model for many years.

EFFECTS OF CORPORATISM: INSTITUTIONALIZATION OF INTEREST CONFLICTS

For most of the last century, large organizations in Sweden were seen as schools of democracy, almost ideal types resembling what Tocqueville had imagined in the United States many years earlier. Leaders of the organizations were regarded almost as statesmen, who negotiated honestly and shook hands after having reached agreements that would help the country move even further forward. When they compromised it was seen as taking responsibility for the common good. Interest organizations, perhaps the unions primarily, were seen as the reason for economic and democratic prosperity. Almost everybody accepted formal participation by interest groups in all stages of the policy process. Swedish politics was characterized by conflicts between strong organized interests *and* by a culture of consensus (see also the chapter by Petersson in this section).

The institutionalization of interest conflicts within a corporatist framework (Rothstein 1987) is the main explanation for how two seemingly contradictory pictures of relative consensus and fierce special-interest advocacy could be combined in the same country. Influencing policy proposals formulated by government committees of inquiry, making use of the referral system to pressure the cabinet to formulate bills in advantageous ways, and controlling implementation on government agency boards were the essential channels for interest advocacy during most of the twentieth century—not protests, demonstrations, or other extra-parliamentary activities. Informal participation, i.e. lobbying and media campaigning, was indeed extensively used too, but was not as important as in many other countries. Hence, the main organized interests have been confronting each other within a context of jointly established and accepted—i.e. institutionalized—norms and rules.

This does not mean that conflicts of interests have disappeared or that special interests have not influenced Swedish politics. Notice, for example, that the design of the Swedish welfare state, including the tax system, reflects power positions held by the trade unions and organized employers (Swenson 2002; Korpi 2006; see also the chapter by Rothstein in Section1). It is also correct that cross-class alliances have been important in Swedish politics (Swenson 1991; see also the chapter by Lindbom in Section 1). But the consensus reached has mainly included rules on how to handle disagreements, while there has been less consensus over specific issues (Rothstein 1987). That organizations, for example, in the labor market have different interests has been the natural, necessary, and unavoidable presumption for the system and, consequently, the three large trade union confederations have usually teamed up against the employers' confederation in all stages of the policy process. But there have been strong norms on how the different interests can be argued for, and what mechanisms are needed to mitigate negative effects of conflicting interests.

Hence, the conflicts have not disappeared but have been mitigated. Organizations that originally disagreed with the majority within a government committee of inquiry have often abstained from submitting formal reservations and, instead, accepted consensus decisions often based on compromises. And reservations by participants on government agency boards with corporatist composition have been almost nonexistent (Rothstein 1996: 192). Discussions in these institutions have even, to some extent, taken the form of deliberation and problem-solving rather than negotiation (Öberg 2002). It is fair to say that what has been created is some form of *meta-consensus*, where representatives of organized interests have accepted each other's legitimate right to hold specific positions, as well as a common understanding of the rules that regulate the conflicts (cf. Niemeyer and Dryzek 2007).

It is important to notice that this kind of meta-consensus is not necessarily good from a democratic point of view. On the contrary, it might establish and reinforce a specific power structure in a society. Remember, not all interests are organized, and it is not obvious which group or individuals are the legitimate representatives of an interest. This is clearly illustrated, for instance, by fierce fighting between competing trade unions and indeed *within* some unions (Jansson 2012). A consensus decision, even when it is a result of perfect deliberation between representatives from identified interests, is not necessary in line with a public interest for the whole society.

EXPLAINING THE DECLINE OF CORPORATISM

The consensus on harmony between contesting interests that was established in the 1930s and continued well into the 1970s was dissolved in the late 1980s and 1990s. The change in public discourse came suddenly and was dramatic. Already in the mid-1970s, accusations of top-down control from radical as well as conservative groups started to be difficult to handle for organizations under fire. Supported by an international trend, neoliberal think-tanks launched a campaign that would turn out very successful (Boréus 1997). The main engine in the campaign was the employers' confederation. As described before, employers openly argued that corporatism was undemocratic, but internally they emphasized that they were captured in a system that sustained union power (Johansson 2005). The strategy to change public discourse was incredibly successful. Soon, the former statesmen of organizations were considered bigwigs. Formerly responsible organizations were instead seen as manipulators and defenders of group interest and not at all promoting public interest. The later half of the 1980s and much of the 1990s were in many ways a backlash against interest organizations. The Social Democratic Party, in a situation of declining support among voters, could not defend the system or organizations that in the public eye were no longer the backbone of democracy but the cause of its problems.

Hence, ideological—and possibly more so—strategic reasons are main explanations for the decline of corporatism in Sweden. But there are other, structural explanations to be taken into account too. The perceived harmony between interests manifested in the historical compromise, created an equilibrium where the state and the organizations were in a win–win situation. A prerequisite of such equilibrium is that both the state and the organizations can actually deliver what the other actor has an interest in. The government needs control over policy at national level; it must have solid parliamentary support and sufficient financial resources to control allocation of privileges. The interest groups, on the other hand, need to have the authority to bargain on behalf of the interests they represent; they need enough cohesiveness and high membership support to control votes and protests. All these prerequisites have now changed in Sweden (Öberg et al. 2011).

The government's mandate to engage in corporatist exchange, i.e. its authority to make decisions, has weakened. The independence of the Swedish central bank, liberalization of capital flows, and other decisions that have further opened up the already open economy has left the national government with less control over financial policy. In combination with increased Europeanization, it leaves the government with less control over decisions than its counterparts in a corporative exchange desire. In addition, the dramatic economic downturn in the 1990s decreased control over the assets needed for reforms. The four-party coalition government that after the 2010 election became a minority coalition also weakened the government's unity.

Prerequisites for a corporatist exchange have been weakened too among the interest groups (see also the chapter by Svensson in Section 9). The organizational structure has changed and, in particular, the trade unions and employers are less united. Several trade unions have merged over the last decade, but the decrease in concentration that was most apparent in the 1960s and continued in the 1970s dramatically changed the position of the confederations. Moreover, union density has fallen significantly in recent decades. To this must be added increased electoral volatility among members (see also the chapter by Oskarsson and Holmberg in Section 4). While the trade unions for many years could be trusted to deliver votes for a party that supported a specific reform, this has become much more difficult. For example, the Social Democratic share of LO votes has decreased since the 1980s, and union members are no longer the only core constituency of Social Democratic governments.

In sum, the ideological and strategic reasons to support corporatism have changed. The political center-right and Swedish enterprise no longer have the same reasons to commit to the historical compromise. On the contrary, dismantling corporatism in favor of upgrading the importance of informal contacts and media strategies was aimed at disempowering unions and increasing relative influence. The rather idealistic picture of a democratic "people's movement" has been tainted by a critical discourse that has emphasized top-down controlled organizations that defend special interests. This has made it more difficult and perhaps less attractive for Social Democrats to defend formal influence by interest groups in the policy process. It is no longer obvious that interest group representation in government agencies will be considered to increase transparency and trust. At the same time, structural changes have affected the prerequisites for corporatist exchange. Neither the state nor the main organizations have the same mandate, assets, or unity that made it easy to exchange favorable politics for legitimacy to implement reforms in the heyday of corporatism.

LOOKING AHEAD: WILL THEY STILL TALK TO EACH OTHER?

As we have illustrated, these changes did not immediately have far-reaching effects on interest group participation in public policy. Structure, norms, and habits were resilient to changes, and for many years now it has been reported that the decline of formal participation in public policy has not been as thorough as expected (Christiansen et al. 2010). However, we can now see the long-term effects. Formal influence in commissions and referrals has declined; at least, the relative participation of interest groups is significantly lower. Representatives of interest organizations have been moved from government agency boards to advisory boards. At the same time, arenas that institutionalized political interest conflicts in Sweden have declined in importance. Commissions no longer have the same position as problem-solving institutions and instead deliver expert opinions on specific issues ordered by the government (Lindvall and Rothstein 2006; see also the chapter by Petersson in this section). New Public Management has replaced deliberative government agency boards with more efficient expert-based boards or more hierarchical governance by the directors-general. The causal relationship between these two trends is not clear but, obviously, interest groups are less involved and there are fewer efficient institutionalized arenas to be involved in.

It is a mistake, however, to draw the conclusion that interest groups do not influence public policy anymore. Memberships are still impressive in a comparative perspective and there are several large interest groups with great resources. These resources are now directed toward more traditional lobbying and media campaigning, increasingly directed by professional information consultants permanently working in specialized internal units or contracted for specific issues (Öberg and Svensson 2012).

Although this chapter has focused on participation in formal public policy-making, it does not mean that direct and informal contacts with policy-makers have not existed in Sweden. On the contrary, politicians have been extremely available to the public or to anyone with intentions to influence them. Only recent security concerns have restricted anyone from walking around in Parliament or talking to parliamentarians. In a small country like Sweden, of course, networking and personal connections have been very efficient. Persons in elite positions within interests groups, politics, and administration also meet often in informal situations with plenty of opportunities to influence each other. There are no records of these informal meetings, but there are good reasons to believe that this kind of lobbying has been very common throughout Swedish political history. But there is no doubt that the political landscape has changed, which has increased the importance of informal participation and media attention. At the same time as the institutionalized channels have been closed or rendered obsolete, competition for attention in the public sphere is much harder. This has left behind the traditional amateur activists, such as the union ombudsman, while professional public relation departments have stepped in. Nowadays, interest organizations already include professional information consultants when internal inquiries begin their investigations, just to make sure that their organizations will to be able to communicate the results efficiently through the media noise when it is time to present the report. This trend of more professional lobbying and media campaigns has not been accompanied by increased participation in open debates (Öberg and Svensson 2012). Hence, organizations are still very politically active, promoting their group interests, but there is a risk that face-to-face meetings with other interests with the assignment to solve or at least discuss a common interest, are fading.

To this trend must be added the growth of other arenas, driven by new ideas of governance and organization of the welfare state. As in many other countries, governance networks in Sweden have increased in number (Jacobsson and Sundström 2006). Hence, interest groups as well as private companies increasingly participate in what was formerly considered public policy. These arenas are mostly informal and constitutionally unclear, since borders between what is public and what is private, as well as what does or does not belong to public decision-making, has been blurred (Larsson 2013). An obvious example is the agreement between the center-right government and several organizations within the welfare field (Johansson 2003). The agreement means basically that certain organizations that are mostly involved in welfare services rather than interest advocacy have taken on a greater role as service providers of what was formerly public welfare provided by municipalities. In the meantime, conflict-oriented organizations are less involved in the referral system; instead, service organizations and community-based organizations have strengthened their positions. (Lundberg 2012).

This all fits the pattern. Sweden is clearly changing from a corporatist system where primarily large, member-based, policy-advocating organizations participated in well-regulated public institutions, to a more pluralist system where service organizations with unclear member bases participate in an impenetrable network governance that handles (formerly) public policy. A system that clearly favored certain special interests over others, but was fairly transparent to the extent that it was possible to identify accountable actors, is being replaced by a typically pluralist system, with a variety of participating actors of complicated hybrid structures, where power is dispersed, but political accountability is more difficult to accomplish.

Independent of whether we welcome this development or not, it will change interest group participation in public policy. As the large policy-advocating organizations increasingly turn—or are referred to—less institutionalized channels, there is an apparent risk of losing the meta-consensus that brings the main actors into agreement over how political conflicts should be handled. It is high time for people who believe that such a meta-consensus is an asset to the Swedish economy and democracy to begin a discussion on what future arenas are needed to accomplish this in modern Sweden.

REFERENCES

Boréus, K. (1997). "The Shift to the Right: Neo-liberalism in Argumentation and Language in the Swedish Public Debate since 1969," *European Journal of Political Research* 31/3: 257–86.

Christiansen, P. M., Nørgaard, A. S., Rommetvedt, H., Svensson, T., Thesen, G., and Öberg, P. (2010). "Varieties of Democracy: Interest Groups and Corporatist Committees in Scandinavian Policy Making," *Voluntas: International Journal of Voluntary and Nonprofit Organizations* 21/1: 22–40.

Compston, H. (1995). "Union Participation in Economic Policy Making in Scandinavia, 1970–1993," *West European Politics* 18/1: 98–115.

"Demokrati och makt i Sverige," SOU 1999:44.

Elvander, N. (1990). "Incomes Policies in the Nordic Countries," *International Labour Review* 129/1: 1–21.

Gunnarsson, V. and Lemne, M. (1998). *Kommittéerna och bofinken: Kan en kommitté se ut hur som helst? Rapport till Expertgruppen för studier i offentlig ekonomi-[ESO]*. Stockholm: Fritzes offentliga publikationer.

Hermansson, J., Lund, A., Svensson, T., and Öberg, P. (1999). "Avkorporativisering och lobbyism—konturerna till en ny politisk modell," Demokratiutredningens forskarvolym XIII. SOU 1999:121.

Jacobsson, B. and Sundström, G. (2006). *Från hemvävd till invävd: Europeiseringen av svensk förvaltning och politik*. Malmö: Liber.

Jansson, J. (2012). *Manufacturing Consensus: The Making of the Swedish Reformist Working Class*. Uppsala: Acta Universitatis Upsaliensis.

Johansson, J. (1992). *Det statliga kommittéväsendet: Kunskap, kontroll, konsensus*. Stockholm: Statsvetenskapliga institutionen, Stockholms universitet.

Johansson, J. (2005). "Undermining Corporatism," in P. Öberg and T. Svensson (eds), *Power and Institutions in Industrial Relations Regimes*. Stockholm: Arbetslivsinstitutet, 77–106.

Johansson, S. (2003). "Independent Movement or Government Subcontractor? Strategic Responses of Voluntary Organizations to Institutional Processes," *Financial Accountability & Management* 19/3: 209–24.

Korpi, W. (2006). "Power Resources and Employer-Centered Approaches in Explanations of Welfare States and Varieties of Capitalism: Protagonists, Consenters, and Antagonists," *World Politics* 58/2: 167–206.

Larsson, O. L. (2013). "Sovereign Power beyond the State: A Critical Reappraisal of Governance by Networks," *Critical Policy Studies* 7/2: 99–114.

Lindvall, J. and Rothstein, B. (2006). "Sweden: The Fall of the Strong State," *Scandinavian Political Studies* 29/1: 47–63.

Lundberg, E. (2012). "Changing Balance: The Participation and Role of Voluntary Organisations in the Swedish Policy Process," *Scandinavian Political Studies* 35/4, 347–71.

Lundberg, E. (2013). "Does the Government Selection Process Promote or Hinder Pluralism? Exploring the Characteristics of Voluntary Organizations Invited to Public Consultations," *Journal of Civil Society* 9/1: 58–77.

Niemeyer, S. and Dryzek, J. S. (2007). "The Ends of Deliberation: Meta-consensus and Intersubjective Rationality as Ideal Outcomes," *Swiss Political Science Review* 13/4: 497–526.

Öberg, P. (1994). *Särintresse och allmänintresse: Korporatismens ansikten*. Uppsala: Acta.

Öberg, P. (2002). "Does Administrative Corporatism Promote Trust and Deliberation?" *Governance* 15/4: 455–75.

Öberg, P. and Svensson, T. (2010). "Does Power Drive Out Trust? Relations between Labour Market Actors in Sweden," *Political Studies* 58/1: 143–66.

Öberg, P. and Svensson, T. (2012). "Civil Society and Deliberative Democracy: Have Voluntary Organizations Faded from National Public Policy?" *Scandinavian Political Studies* 35/3: 246–71.

Öberg, P., Svensson, T., Christiansen, P. M., Nørgaard, A. S., Rommetvedt, H., and Thesen, G. (2011). "Disrupted Exchange and Declining Corporatism: Government Authority and Interest Group Capability in Scandinavia," *Government and Opposition* 46/3: 365–91.

Riksrevisionen (2004). *Förändringar inom kommittéväsendet*. Stockholm: Swedish National Audit Agency, Riksdagstryck.

Rothstein, B. (1985). "Managing the Welfare State: Lessons from Gustav Möller," *Scandinavian Political Studies* 8/3: 151–70.

Rothstein, B. (1987). "Corporatism and Reformism: The Social Democratic Institutionalization of Class Conflict," *Acta Sociologica* 30/3–4: 295–311.

Rothstein, B. (1992). "Explaining Swedish Corporatism: The Formative Moment," *Scandinavian Political Studies* 15/3: 173–91.

Rothstein, B. (1996). *The Social Democratic State: The Swedish Model and the Bureaucratic Problem of Social Reforms*. Pittsburgh: University of Pittsburgh Press.

SOU 2007:66. "Rörelser i tiden," Slutbetänkande av Utredningen om den statliga folkrörelse-politiken i framtiden. Stockholm: Fritze.

Swenson, P. (1991). "Bringing Capital Back In, or Social Democracy Reconsidered: Employer Power, Cross-Class Alliances, and Centralization of Industrial Relations in Denmark and Sweden," *World Politics* 43/4: 513–44.

Swenson, P. (2002). *Capitalists Against Markets: The Making of Labor Markets and Welfare States in the United States and Sweden*. Oxford: Oxford University Press.

Wijkström, F. and Lundström, T. (2002). *Den ideella sektorn: Organisationerna i det civila samhället*. Stockholm: Sober.

CHAPTER 50

PARLIAMENTARY COMMITTEES

A Ground for Compromise and Conflict

INGVAR MATTSON

WHAT role does the Swedish parliament, the Riksdag, have in the policy process? From a formal constitutional point of view, the answer is straightforward. The Riksdag legislates and decides the annual central government budget. It also performs oversight on the way in which the government and public agencies execute their duties.

However, as in many other parliamentary democracies, it would be wrong to overemphasize the duality of powers and to overstate the decision-making role of Parliament. In reality, the parliament mainly approves the bills presented to it from the government. Party discipline in voting is very strong which means that it is the parties and party leaderships that control the Members of Parliament (MPs). These observations have prompted some observers to imply that the Riksdag is a pure stamp pad for governmental legislation (e.g. Pålsson 2012).

That is a role that has been depicted for many parliaments around the world. The role of parliaments, especially in the Westminster type of parliaments, has been described in the international literature as being in decline. This thesis has a long history. In his classic work on the English Constitution first published in 1867, Walter Bagehot wrote:

> The dignified aspect of the House of Commons is altogether secondary to its efficient use ... The House of Commons needs to be impressive, and impressive it is: but its use resides not in its appearance, but in its reality. Its office is not to win power by awing mankind, but to use power in governing mankind. (quoted in Norton 1992: 36)

Bagehot's interpretation of the role of House of Commons at that time has been questioned, but it is significant because it illustrated the idea that there was a "golden age" of Parliament when the House of Commons was central to the governing of the country, whereas its present role is much less significant when it comes to shaping policies.

An assumption for this conceptualization of parliaments is that the government has a majority of its own in Parliament. Similar to its Scandinavian neighbors Denmark and Norway, Sweden has, however, a tradition of minority governments (cf. Bäck and Bergman's chapter in this volume). This implies a potentially stronger role for the Riksdag in the policy-making process than in the typical Westminster type of parliamentary democracy. Governments have not always been in a position to anticipate sufficient support for their bills in Parliament. It has thus from time to time been necessary for them to negotiate with opposition parties and to adjust their proposals in order to get their bills through Parliament.

Moreover, Sweden has often been classified as a consensual democracy by international observers (Anton 1969; cf. Ruin 1981). Describing Swedish politics, a foreign scholar applied the term "politics of compromise" in his work of the same title in the 1950s (Rustow 1955). The policy-making process is characterized by a low degree of conflict. When conflicts occur, they are occasionally solved by compromises between the main political parties. Assuming that these compromises are struck in or in connection with parliament, this also implies a comparatively strong role for parliament in the policy process.

On top of being known for a consensual political culture Sweden is also known for a matter-of-fact style of policy process (Ruin 1981). This, too, implies a possible role for Parliament in the policy process. A strong, logical argument and expertise are assumed to be sources of influence in the policy process.

In sum, Sweden has for long periods of time been governed by minority governments or coalition governments, and the literature suggests that consensus and a matter-of-fact style of policy-making characterize the Swedish policy process. This paves the way for a potentially strong role for Parliament in the policy-making process. We could thus expect Parliament to be an arena for

- political *negotiations* between minority governments and opposition parties where opposition parties have influence on policy-making,
- *compromises* between the political parties to settle political conflicts, and
- *objective debates* based on expertise (and thus less politicized).

In this chapter we will describe and analyze the role that the Riksdag and the parliamentary committees in particular play in the policy process. We start with a descriptive exploration of the committee system in Sweden to get an overview of the institutional framework and institutional powers of the committees and Parliament.

THE PARLIAMENTARY COMMITTEES

The unicameral Riksdag consists of 349 Members of Parliament from twenty-nine constituencies. The number of parties in Parliament is eight at present. For many years after

World War II it was five parties, but in 1988 the number started to grow step by step (cf. Aylott's chapter in this volume). In order to scrutinize governmental bills and private member's motions, and thus to prepare the debates and decisions in the Chamber, the Riksdag has fifteen permanent committees.

In line with the classification of committees by Mattson and Ström (2004) the committees in the Riksdag are characterized by being:

- permanent;
- specialized;
- small (seventeen committee members in a parliament of 349 MPs);
- closed;
- chaired by both governmental and opposition party MPs;
- given strong legislative authority and the right to arrange public hearings.

Two permanent committees may form a joint, temporary committee for a special purpose if they want to, which occurs from time to time (the committees for foreign affairs and defense in particular have cooperated on several governmental bills in this form). When necessary, temporary or special committees may also be set up and matters referred to from the Chamber, but this is very unusual. Even though temporary committees may from time to time exist, the permanent committees dominate the Riksdag.

The permanent committees are specialized and organized according to policy areas. And they fulfill several tasks within their remit. They scrutinize proposals for legislation and budget as well as follow up and evaluate earlier Riksdag decisions in their area of responsibility. The committees are also expected to keep an eye on matters that are on the EU agenda and discuss them with representatives from the government.

The committees should consist of at least fifteen members and have for many years consisted of seventeen members. All parties are represented in the committees in proportion to their number of seats in the Chamber, and the committees thus function as microcosms of the Chamber.

Members of the committees are appointed for the election period and many serve the same committee for more than one period (Hagevi 1998). This means that they earn knowledge in their policy field, and since experience and knowledge are potential leverages for influence, that may increase the relevance of the committee in the policy process. Moreover, the parties often choose their spokespersons for certain policies among the committee members of relevant competence. The spokespersons are pivotal within the party groups in their policy fields. That makes these persons relevant for other party spokespersons if a negotiation between the parties might be on track. Typically, the different party spokespersons sit in the same committee.

Committee powers are formally strong. The committees have the right to initiate legislation and budget items themselves, and they have the unlimited right to amend any legislative bill or budget bill from the government. They may arrange public hearings, and they have the right to decide the timetable for the scrutiny of a bill themselves, without taking instructions from the government or the Chamber.

This observation is confirmed in international comparisons. Committee powers have been compared among the West European parliaments in two dimensions relating to legislative powers: drafting authority and agenda control (Mattson and Ström 1996). Sweden scores high on both dimensions of committee power. The two dimensions are created by factor analysis and based on formal powers of legislative committees in the West European parliaments under study.

In addition to the permanent committees, the Riksdag has a Committee on European Union Affairs. The government is obliged to consult the Committee on European Union Affairs prior to meetings of the Council of Ministers on what opinion Sweden should pursue with regard to various EU policies. During the government's consultations with the Committee on EU Affairs, the government discusses with the Riksdag what point of view Sweden should take on various EU matters prior to meetings of the Council of Ministers. The government is expected to observe the Committee's positions. The European Union Affairs Committee has thus an important role to play in the policy-making process regarding matters that are decided by the EU during the negotiations in the union (cf. Hegeland 2006), also when it comes to important economic policy in times of crisis (Auel and Höing 2014). The committee's practice is regarded as consensual and important for the internal EU policy-making process in Sweden. However, we will not consider the role for this committee in the following analysis, due to the fact that its modus vivendi is different from the other committees. The Committee on European Union Affairs is not part of the legislating or budgeting decision-making processes of the Riksdag.

The role of committees varies among parliaments (Shaw 1979; Mattson and Ström 1996). The fact that the Swedish committees are permanent and specialized in policy areas facilitates a potentially strong role for them in the policy process.

Within parliaments in general we have reason to expect the committees to be important arenas for negotiations, bargaining, and compromises (Mattson 1996b; Damgaard and Mattson 2004). Gunnar Hecksher has stressed the point in the following way for Sweden:

> The traditional market for compromise is to be found in the committees of Parliament, where agreement can sometimes be reached over the head of the Cabinet and with considerable amendment of Government proposals. (Heckscher 1984: 207)

This view, however, is not the only one in the literature. David Arter has reached another conclusion. He claims that the committees are not as crucial negotiating sights as might first appear:

> Important compromises and deals ... are only very rarely worked out in standing committee; rather, conflict is resolved within and between the parliamentary groups and the ensuing arrangements are merely given formal ratification in standing committees. (Arter 1984: 206; cf. Arter 2006)

In order to shed light on the role of the Riksdag and its committees in the policy-making process we will look into empirical findings. We will do so by focusing on the decision-making process in parliament. As David M. Olson and Michael L. Mezey (1991) and others have observed, it is not only by making the major decisions that parliaments can influence policies. Their role must be understood in more subtle ways. It is through public debates, the private interactions of their members with the executive, and activities in regard to oversight that parliaments influence policies.

One of those subtle effects is that a minority government may refrain from proposals when it knows that it will not get the bill through Parliament. It will thus not lose any battles in the Riksdag, but will on the other hand not see its intended policies materialized.

This is all true, but this chapter will nevertheless focus on the decision-making function of parliament. We will describe and analyze the actual proposals and decisions taken by Parliament and leave it for others to describe the other dimensions of power (cf. Lukes 1974) as well as other potential functions of the Riksdag (cf. Loewenberg and Pattersson 1979).

If the role of Parliament is to facilitate compromises, being the place where compromises are struck, we could expect that the committees should amend governmental bills and that the committees should issue reports unanimously. We could also expect the committees to be open to private member's bills.

In the following sections we will in turn describe and analyze the following aspects of the decision-making role of Parliament:

- the frequency of amendments to governmental legislative bills;
- the frequency of budget bill amendments;
- the success rate for private member's bills; and
- the frequency of unanimous committee reports.

The purpose is to shed light on the role of Parliament when it comes to influencing the policy process and the extent to which Parliament settles conflicts.

AMENDING LEGISLATIVE BILLS

There are no limits for committees' right to amend governmental legislative bills. The committees may totally rewrite any bill and actually introduce their own bills of legislation if they want. An overwhelming majority of legislation is, however, initiated by the government. Committees have for many decades approved governmental bills and only made few minor amendments, typically in order to correct errors.

There are two obvious reasons for this. The first one is that the committees and the Riksdag lack the resources to make the proper preparation of complicated legislative bills. The second reason is that the government typically has sought and got support from opposition parties during the preparation of the bill, at least for important bills.

Important legislation is traditionally, but to a much lesser extent today, prepared by governmental commissions of inquiry, often comprising party representatives, before introduction to Parliament (cf. Olof Petersson's chapter in this section).

A new third reason can be added; namely, that since Sweden became a member of the EU in 1995 a large share of legislation today is aimed at implementing EU law. Regarding these bills, the process in Sweden becomes more technical and less political since membership of the union obliges us to adopt the legislation put down in directives. Any political objection is belated at this stage.

In some policy areas, compromises have been achieved between the leading political parties across the political blocs. Those compromises typically include the Social Democratic Party and the Moderates, and typically also the Liberals, the Center Party, and the Christian Democrats. Nowadays they also include the Greens and occasionally the Left Party. The Sweden Democrats are however always excluded from actual negotiations and compromises on legislation (although they are invited to participate in governmental commissions).

Important examples of such compromises include the reform of the pension system in the 1990s and the legislation on banking in the aftermath of the Lehman Brothers crash in 2008. The first was negotiated in a governmental commission that worked for many years. The second was achieved in the Committee on Finance during an intensive week when Parliament worked under heavy time pressure.

Yet another example of a compromise in committee between the leading parties concerned a bill on financial support to the political parties in the spring 2014. The Social Democrats wanted stricter rules for anonymous party contributions and their proposal for a stop on state subsidies to any party that accepts anonymous contributions was accepted by the other parties (except the Sweden Democrats) during preparation of the bill in the Committee on the Constitution.

Legislation initiated in Parliament is also rare. Some significant legislation has, however, been initiated in the Riksdag. One example is the legislation on same-sex marriages. The Alliance government, including the Christian Democrats, was unable to introduce a bill on this matter, irrespective of the fact that all parties except the Christian Democrats wanted it. Instead, the legislation was initiated by the Committee on Civil Affairs and only the Christian Democrats voted against it.

Another, and even more controversial, example was a tax law adopted by the Riksdag during the fall of 2013. The Riksdag first decided on a tax reduction for high-income earners within the framework of the budget process (where decision-making is restrained in a top-down process). However, this tax cut was restored by the opposition parties after an initiative by the Finance Committee, in the face of overt resistance from the governmental parties in the committee. This matter triggered a furious debate and indeed profound conflict in Parliament over the proper way to make decisions in the Riksdag.

The various individual examples are significant, but should not blur the main picture. The number of amendments on legislative bills is very small, as is the amount of legislation initiated in the Riksdag, and it has been so for a long time.

Let us now turn to the central government budget and see if this also holds for budgeting. To what extent is the Riksdag amending the budget bill?

AMENDING THE BUDGET BILL

We have already noticed that the committees, and thus the Riksdag, have strong formal powers when it comes to initiating legislation and amending governmental law bills. This is also true for the central government budget (which in Swedish constitutional tradition is not a law but a sui generis constitutional figure of its own). This is decided annually by Parliament in the autumn session before the fiscal year starts on January 1.

There are no restrictions on what MPs and opposition parties may propose regarding expenditures and revenues. Examples of such restrictions in other parliaments include the need for approval from the Minister of Finance to propose and decide new or extended expenditures. Swedish MPs are free to propose any expenditure or tax they want, and Parliament may make any amendments to the government's budget bill that it wants.

The strong formal powers of the committees and the Riksdag are confirmed in international comparisons, notably the findings in a survey among the OECD countries and fourteen additional countries made by Joachim Wehner (2006). Sweden is in this comparison one of the strongest parliaments with regard to formal powers in the budget process. Also Lienert (2005) and Hallerberg, Strauch, and Von Hagen (2009) put Sweden in top position in their similar comparative studies. This is the case from a constitutional point of view also, following the comprehensive budget reform that took place after the economic crisis in Sweden in the 1990s, even if in practice it enhanced a minority government's chances of getting its budget through Parliament (cf. Blöndal 2001; Wehner 2007).

Is, then, the Riksdag using these formal powers to amend the budget bill or is the government getting its budget through the Riksdag without too much ado? Earlier studies have shown that the Riksdag is actually only making minor changes to the budget bill (Mattson 1996a; Wehner 2007). Moreover, the major reform of the budget process in the 1990s had a huge impact on the scope of amendments. The number of changes as well as the effects on the budget amounts decreased significantly after 1997. As a matter of fact, the budget reform of the 1990s also helped to counteract the normal tendency to increase budget imbalances as the date of general elections approaches (Wehner 2013).

Is there, then, a variation on the number of amendments to the budget bill depending on type of government? Yes, there is. Sweden had majority governments during budget preparations in 1977–8, 1980–1, and 2006–9. In 1996–2006 the minority government had established a stable cooperation with some opposition parties (cf. the chapter by Bäck and Bergman in this volume). The cooperation meant that the parties negotiated the budget bill before it was presented to Parliament, thus securing parliamentary support for it in advance. This means that we had "pure" minority governments presenting their budget bills in 1971–6, 1979, and 1982–95.

In sum, we have seen that the Riksdag usually approves the governmental budget bill without any major amendments. We have also seen that it amends less now than before the budget reform in the 1990s and that the number of amendments differs depending on the parliamentary situation. Amendments are more probable during periods of minority governments, especially when they have not established a compact cooperation with any opposition party.

Success Rate for Private Member's Motions

The possibility of presenting a private member's motion is used frequently by MPs in the Swedish parliament. Thousands of motions are presented each year. It is actually, in an international comparison, more popular in Sweden than in other countries to introduce private member's motions (Mattson 1996c).[1] This is partly due to the fact that opposition MPs and parties propose amendments to governmental bills in motions rather than proposing amendments during committee deliberations, which is common in most parliaments. But the main reason is that it has for decades been extremely popular to present motions during the period at the beginning of each year when MPs can propose anything within the competence of parliament.

Presenting private member's motions is popular because the Riksdag must refer all such motions to a committee which must scrutinize it and return it to the chamber for a vote after analysis and deliberation in the committee. That means that motions cannot be killed in committee and thus MPs see that their motions must be taken care of. Moreover, there is a pressure from the media and voters on individual MPs to present private member's motions. MPs need to show the voters their individual policy preferences with relevance to their constituencies. It does happen that the local press hang MPs who do not present individual motions—guilty of laziness!

What are the chances, then, that motions pass through parliament? And do the chances increase when we have minority governments? If motions are passed we could claim a stronger role for the Riksdag in the policy process, and we could expect the decision-making role to be strongest in times of minority governments.

The success rate for motions is very low. We are talking about a single percent at the most. However, taking into account that there are so many motions introduced each year, the actual numbers should not be underestimated. Moreover, when Sweden has minority governments, some of the approved motions may include controversial issues for the government. The government may, for instance, be asked to introduce legislation that it does not really want and which the governmental parties have voted against. They may therefore sometimes be of political significance.

The success rate varies over time. The average success rate for parliaments during minority governments is higher compared with periods with majority governments. Moreover, the success rate has decreased during recent decades. There are significantly fewer resolutions based on private member's motions today than 20 years ago. During the election period 2006–10, when the Alliance parties governed with support of a majority of seats in the Riksdag, the success rate was down to a decimal of a percentage.

In sum, we can note that MPs and opposition parties frequently present motions. We also know that the success rate is low (0.1–1.0 percent) and that it varies depending on type of government. Finally, the success rate has decreased in recent decades. The level was particularly low during the period 2006–10, when Sweden had a majority government, but the level has decreased over time, indicating a decreasing role for backbenchers and much more centralized decision-making within the parliamentary party groups.

FREQUENCY OF MINORITY REPORTS AS A SIGN OF CONFLICT AND CONSENSUS IN COMMITTEES

The committees write reports to the Chamber on all initiatives raised in Parliament. (Killing in committees, i.e. rejection during committee stage, is not possible in Sweden where all matters must be decided on by the Chamber.) Any member of the committee who loses a vote in the committee has the right to enclose a minority report to the committee's report.

The number of minority reports has risen. The share of committee reports with at least one minority report enclosed was as low as 20 percent about 100 years ago and stayed at that level for several decades. However, the level of dissenting opinions on matters dealt with by the committees is about three or four times higher today. However, the level of dissenting opinions on matters dealt with by the committees is about three or four times higher today. Something happened in the 1970s and 1980s (Sannerstedt 1992; cf. Sjölin 1993; Isberg 1984). This indicates an increased level of activity and possibly also an increased level of conflict. It is less common today that members of a committee find compromises; instead they vote and the losing members file dissenting opinions. Partly, this increase can be explained by the fact that the number of parties represented in the Riksdag has increased, but that is not the full explanation.

The share of committee reports with minority reports has been used to indicate the level of conflict in the Riksdag and other parliaments (cf. Damgaard 1990; Sannerstedt 1992; Sjölin 1993; Damgaard and Mattson 2004). The observation implies that the level of activity has risen in the committees and that it is less common to have consensus today than it was in the decades before and after World War II. The increase came in the 1980s according to the data—a result that has been confirmed by others (Hermansson 1993).

CONCLUSION

Many international observers have found that the Riksdag and the Swedish parliamentary committees are powerful in international comparison and fulfill an important role in the policy-making process. In a political system that is characterized by political consensus, Parliament and the committees are indeed possible grounds for negotiating compromises in a rational policy-making process. I am inclined to agree with this overall description from an international perspective, giving Parliament an important role in the policy-making process, but the picture must be painted with more colors and with a thinner brush to be fully true to results from empirical research.

The empirical findings indicate that the Riksdag does indeed amend the government's budget bill to some extent in some years, as well as approving a number of private member's motions every year (even without the consent of the governing party or parties) and sometimes initiating legislation of its own. Research also shows that the Riksdag does so most frequently when a minority government is in power. And since minority governments are actually more common in Sweden than majority governments, this is not a totally uncommon situation. So, the Riksdag does sometimes make decisions that contradict the government's intended policies. Nevertheless, it does in the main approve governmental proposals for both budget and legislation.

We can conclude that the committees are important arenas in the Riksdag. They cannot, however, be said to be key political actors though, since committee members identify themselves primarily as party members and only secondarily or less as members of a certain committee (cf. Jensen 1995). The fact that the spokespersons from the parties often sit in relevant committees increases the importance of the committees. They are from time to time involved in negotiations and bargaining in order to strike deals. The negotiations do not usually take place during committee meetings, but the fact that the negotiating parties often appoint their spokespersons as negotiators makes the committee members the significant players on such occasions. That in turn gives the committees an important indirect role in the policy process—both because minority governments need parliamentary support and because Sweden has a consensual and practical-minded political culture.

However, the fact that Parliament amends the budget bill to a lesser extent than in the past, that the success rate for private member's bills has fallen, and that the share of unanimous committee reports has decreased in recent decades would seem to indicate that Swedish politics is shifting away from its former harmonious, consensus-driven image. The committees are still grounds for working out compromises between the main political parties, but less so now than before.

NOTE

1. It must be noted that most motions are not proposals on new legislation—i.e. they are not private member's bills in that sense. Most motions propose that the Riksdag should request the government to start an investigation (commission of inquiry) or introduce legislation on a certain topic. There are no formal requirements on the form for such motions.

REFERENCES

Anton, T. J. (1969). "Policy-Making and Political Culture in Sweden," *Scandinavian Political Studies* 4: 88–102.

Arter, D. (1984). *The Nordic Parliaments: A Comparative Analysis*. London: Hurst.

Arter, D. (2006). *Democracy in Scandinavia: Consensual, Majoritarian or Mixed?* Manchester: Manchester University Press.

Auel, K. and Höing, O. (2014). *Scrutiny in Challenging Times: National Parliaments in the EuroZone Crisis*. Stockholm: SIEPS.

Blöndal, J. R. (2001). "Budgeting in Sweden", *OECD Journal of Budgeting* 1/1: 27–57.

Damgaard, E. (ed.) (1990). *Parlamentarisk forandring i Norden*. Oslo: Universitetforlaget.

Damgaard, E. and Mattson, I. (2004). "Conflict and Consensus in Committees," in H. Döring and M. Hallerberg (eds), *Patterns of Parliamentary Behavior: Passage of Legislation Across Western Europe*. Aldershot: Ashgate, 113–40.

Hagevi, M. (1998). *Bakom riksdagens fasad*. Göteborg, Akademiförlaget Corona.

Hecksher, G. (1984). *The Welfare State and Beyond: Success and Problems in Scandinavia*. Minneapolis: University of Minnesota Press.

Hallerberg, M., Strauch, R. R., and Von Hagen, J. (2009). *Fiscal Governance in Europe*. Cambridge: Cambridge University Press.

Hegeland, H. (2006). *Nationell EU-parlamentarism: Riksdagens arbete med EU-frågorna*. Göteborg: Santérus Academic Press Sweden.

Hermansson, J. (1993). *Politik son intressekamp: Parlamentariskt beslutsfattande och organiserade intressen i Sverige*. Stockholm: Norstedts Juridik.

Isberg, M. (1984). *Riksdagens roll under 1970-talet*. Stockholm: Akademilitteratur.

Jensen, H. (1995). *Arenaer eller aktörer? En analyse af Folketingets stående udvalg*. Frederiksberg: Samfundslitteratur.

Lienert, I. (2005). "Who Controls the Budget: The Legislature or the Executive?" IMF Working Paper, WP/05/115. Washington DC: IMF.

Loewenberg, G. and Pattersson, S. C. (1979). *Comparing Legislatures*. Lanham: University Press of America.

Lukes, Steven (1974). *Power: A Radical View*. London: Macmillan.

Mattson, I. (1996a). *Förhandlingsparlamentarism: En jämförande studie av riksdagen och folketinget*. Lund: Lund University Press.

Mattson, I. (1996b). "Negotiations in Parliamentary Committees," in L.-G. Stenelo and M. Jerneck (eds), *The Bargaining Democracy*. Lund: Lund University Press, 61–146.

Mattson, I. (1996c). "Private Members' Initiatives and Amendments," in H. Döring (ed.), *Parliaments and Majority Rule in Western Europe*. Frankfurt: Campus Verlag and New York: St. Martin's Press, 448–87.

Mattson, I. and Ström, K. (1996). "Parliamentary Committees," in H. Döring (ed.), *Parliaments and Majority Rule in Western Europe*. Frankfurt: Campus Verlag and New York: St. Martin's Press, 249–307.

Mattson, I. and Ström, K. (2004). "Committee Effects on Legislation," in H. Döring and M. Hallerberg (eds), *Patterns of Parliamentary Behavior: Passage of Legislation across Western Europe*. Aldershot: Ashgate, 91–112.

Norton, P. (ed.) (1992). *Legislatures*. Oxford: Oxford University Press.

Olson, D. M. and Mezey, M. L. (1991). "Parliaments and Public Policy," in D. M. Olson and M. L. Mezey (eds), *Legislatures in the Policy Process: The Dilemmas of Economic Policy*. Cambridge: Cambridge University Press, 1–21.

Pålsson, A.-M. (2012). *Knapptryckarkompaniet: Rapport från Sveriges riksdag*. Stockholm: Atlantis.

Ruin, O. (1981). *Att komma överens och tänka efter före: politisk stil och 1970-talets svenska samhällsutveckling*. Stockholm: Statsvetenskapliga institutionen, Stockholms universitet.

Rustow, D. A. (1955). *The Politics of Compromise: A Study of Party and Cabinet Government in Sweden*. Princeton: Princeton University Press.

Sannerstedt, A. (1992). *Förhandlingar i riksdagen*. Lund: Lund University Press.

Shaw, M. (1979). "Conclusions," in J. D. Lees and M. Shad (eds), *Committees in Legislatures: A Comparative Analysis*. Oxford: Martin Robertsson, 361–434.

Sjölin, M. (1993). *Coalition Politics and Parliamentary Power*. Lund: Lund University Press.

Wehner, J. (2006). "Assessing the Power of the Purse: An Index of Legislative Budget Institutions," *Political Studies* 54: 767–85.

Wehner, J. (2007). "Budget Reform and Legislative Control in Sweden," *Journal of European Public Policy* 14/2 (March): 313–32.

Wehner, J. (2013). "Electoral Budget Cycles in Legislatures," *Legislative Studies Quarterly* 38/4: 545–70.

INDEX

Please note that locators followed by (f) relate to figures, those followed by (n) relate to footnotes, and those followed by (t) relate to tables.